JAZZ

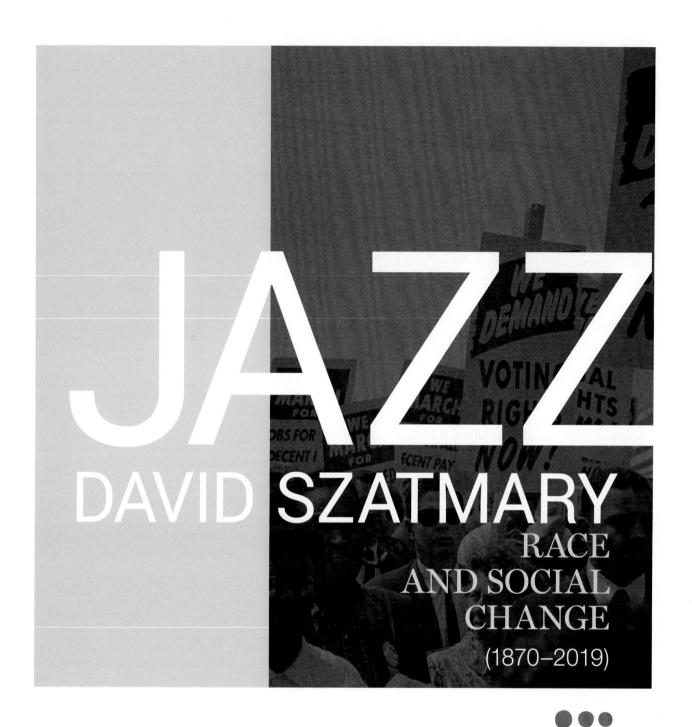

JAZZ

DAVID SZATMARY

RACE AND SOCIAL CHANGE

(1870–2019)

New York   Oxford
Oxford University Press

Photo on title page: Protesters at the March on Washington, 1963.
Photograph by Marion S. Trikosko, 1963.
Library of Congress Prints and Photographs Division.

Oxford University Press is a department of the University of Oxford.
It furthers the University's objective of excellence in research, scholarship,
and education by publishing worldwide. Oxford is a registered trade mark of
Oxford University Press in the UK and certain other countries.

Published in the United States of America by Oxford University Press
198 Madison Avenue, New York, NY 10016, United States of America.

For titles covered by Section 112 of the US Higher Education
Opportunity Act, please visit www.oup.com/us/he for the latest information
about pricing and alternate formats.

Library of Congress Cataloging-in-Publication Data
Names: Szatmary, David P., 1951- author.
Title: Jazz : race and social change (1870-2019) / David Szatmary.
Description: First edition. | New York : Oxford University Press, 2020. |
    Includes bibliographical references and index.
Identifiers: LCCN 2019041313 (print) | LCCN 2019041314 (cbook) | ISBN
    9780190846121 (paperback) | ISBN 9780190846152 (epub)
Subjects: LCSH: Jazz—History and criticism. | Jazz—Social aspects—United
    States—History.
Classification: LCC ML3508 .S95 2020 (print) | LCC ML3508 (ebook) | DDC
    781.6509—dc23
LC record available at https://lccn.loc.gov/2019041313
LC ebook record available at https://lccn.loc.gov/2019041314

Printing number: 9 8 7 6 5 4 3 2 1
Printed in Mexico by Quad/Mexico

To my wife, Mary,
with love

Contents

9 WORLD WAR II AND JAZZ: Sentimental Bands, All-Female Big Bands, and a New Musical Idol 175

10 THE BEBOP REVOLUTION: The Rise of African-American Pride 201

Introduction

"Music reflects the times in which you live."
—DIZZY GILLESPIE (GILLESPIE 1979, 201)

Jazz: Race and Social Change offers a new, balanced approach to jazz as a musical genre that has developed over the past century and a quarter within the context of social, economic, and racial issues, which influenced its development. This book contends that jazz and its many styles resulted from and in part shaped the transformation of American society. Rather than being a compendium of jazz artists or a guide to jazz musical theory, it explains jazz from roughly 1870 to 2019 through the struggles for racial and gender equality, major demographic upheavals, technological advances, economic turmoil, music-business practices, and political struggles and wars. It explains *why* jazz developed by pinpointing the social conditions surrounding it and, in the process, addresses when and how jazz changed and who served as major proponents of its many variations. I hope this approach will engage you and provide an understanding about jazz as both a musical and cultural force.

Jazz arose from the innovations of African Americans and largely evolved around the struggle for African-American civil rights. It has its origins in the African culture of enslaved Americans that persisted through the African-American church and, ironically, minstrel shows. In St. Louis and New Orleans among the free-black Creoles, African-American ragtime pianists and brass bands merged European and African traditions to jump-start jazz, demonstrating the creativity and flexibility of the African-American tradition. During the late twenties and early thirties, Duke Ellington and his orchestra epitomized the flowering of the Harlem Renaissance, which sought equality through success in the arts. The bebop revolution of the forties arose from a renewed and sometimes militant quest for the equal treatment of African Americans who, during World War II, had fought against tyranny to liberate Europe and Asia but had not achieved equal rights at home. During the next two decades, hard bop, soul jazz, and the avant-garde directly reflected and contributed to the accelerating civil-rights movement and a sense of pride among African Americans. More recently, hip-hop jazz and a mashup-type jazz, which sprung from the Black Lives Matter movement, demonstrated the ongoing pursuit of African-American rights and the need for an African-American identity. "You cannot look at African-American music in the context of music in and of itself because it comes out of the social, political and economic phenomena that deal with black people. It's all related," contended jazz multi-instrumentalist Ken McIntyre (Ullman 1980, 180).

White performers helped develop jazz by sometimes borrowing from and adding to its African-American heritage. Paul Whiteman first made jazz a household word by adding jazz elements to an orchestra, and Benny Goodman spearheaded the swing craze by grafting a teen-age-friendly, hyperactive spin onto big band music. Bing Crosby and Frank Sinatra, the first top-selling jazz vocalists, introduced new vocal styles to the music. During the paranoia of the Cold War, Stan Kenton introduced a jittery, jagged variant of jazz, and Gunther Schuller promoted the classical–jazz merger, which he termed the Third Stream. In the fifties, jazz men on the West Coast perfected a cool jazz, which extended the relaxed sound of African-American saxophonist Lester Young.

Though undoubtedly benefiting from ongoing racism against African Americans, many white jazz artists generally worked to curb discrimination and acknowledged the contributions of their African-American colleagues. During the forties, white stars such as Benny Goodman and Artie Shaw courageously integrated their bands in advance of other sectors of society. In the next decade, Dave Brubeck assembled an integrated combo and refused to play in venues that did not welcome the African-American member of his band. Fusion jazz, first ascending the charts during the late sixties, featured mostly racially integrated bands. In many instances, whites and African Americans collaborated with one another and judged each other by their abilities rather than the colors of their skin to help integrate America.

The changing and enhanced role of women as leaders in American society also has been reflected in jazz. In the twenties, when American women earned the right to vote and flapper fashion became a fad, female blues singers such as Bessie Smith were among the most popular performers. During World War II, when male jazz musicians were drafted en masse, women formed big bands to tour the countryside and proved that women could deliver exceptional jazz. By the twenty-first century, female jazz artists such as Diana Krall, Esperanza Spalding, and Norah Jones who excelled at their chosen instruments as well as singing became stars. Most recently, female jazz artists joined the feminist #MeToo movement to secure equal rights for women in jazz.

In addition to equal rights for African Americans and women, seismic demographic shifts in the American population over the past hundred years affected the emergence and styles of jazz. During the 1910s and early twenties, a fundamental reshuffling of the population urbanized America and provided jazz with an audience. As farm work became mechanized and droughts swept parts of the country, unemployed farmers moved in droves to expanding cities such as Chicago and New York. Finding new types of employment that paid much more than farming, urbanites spent newfound disposable income on goods and services generated by a new consumer culture, which included entertainment by jazz bands in clubs that sprouted up in their new hometowns. The new urban masses danced in nightspots that offered syncopated jazz for dance-happy customers. From the final years of the nineteenth century through the big-band era and again with jump blues, urban Americans danced to jazz until bebop and a cool style turned the music into a listening rather than a dancing experience.

The mass migration of African Americans from the South to Northern cities created markets for certain types of jazz. At the dawn of the twentieth century, as African Americans journeyed from their Southern homes to Midwestern cities such as St. Louis and Chicago, they listened to fellow migrants who played ragtime. During World War I, African Americans streamed into Chicago and other Northern cities looking for work and became a ready audience for female blues singers and African-American instrumental jazz groups, which spotlighted such budding stars as Louis Armstrong. Amid the next world war, a second great migration of African Americans flooded the North to fuel interest in the jump blues of artists such as Louis Jordan.

The emergence of teenagers as a demographic force thrust jazz into the national spotlight. During the thirties and forties, more and more teens stayed in high school and, when the economic situation brightened, they became an identifiable market. Teenagers jitterbugged to energetic big bands such as Benny Goodman's, and young girls swooned over Frank Sinatra. Hip teens wore goatees and berets to signify their allegiance to bebop and, later, hard bop. During the seventies, amid economic troubles, young adults from the baby-boom generation abandoned heavy rock for the more cerebral fusion jazz and eventually embraced smooth jazz.

As well as the pursuit of civil rights and major demographic shifts, technology fundamentally altered both America and jazz. New technologies changed the centuries-old practice of listening to live music near one's home. At the beginning of the twentieth century, the invention of the player piano and the piano roll replicated and disseminated the music of ragtime and stride piano players such as Scott Joplin and James P. Johnson.

Even more transformative, the inexpensive record player allowed people to experience the sounds of an ensemble in their living rooms. As part of the consumer culture, phonographs revolutionized the way music could be heard by transforming it into a commodity. For the first time, Americans throughout the country could hear the same music by the same artists such as Louis Armstrong, Bessie Smith, and Paul Whiteman, who assumed star status among millions of listeners.

The evolution of the record likewise led to changes. Replacing wax cylinders, the first, mass-manufactured flat discs consisted of a shellac-based compound with lateral grooves and spun around a turntable at 78 revolutions per minute (rpm). Introduced in 1948, the long-play (LP) record, made of polyvinyl and less fragile than its precursor, accommodated extended solos, which started in earnest with bebop. The 45 rpm record offered café and barroom operators a sturdy alternative to the 78 rpm for their jukeboxes. During the eighties, the compact disc, offering greater fidelity and even more durability than the LP and 45, created a new market for old material and permitted nearly anyone to produce a high-quality recording.

Radio, the first national non-print media, assumed a paramount role in the development of jazz. By the twenties, hundreds of stations were broadcasting records and live performances throughout America to popularize jazz on a national scale. During the Great Depression, relatively affordable radios brought jazz into the homes of Americans at a nominal cost and served as ideal entertainment for families too poor or tired to go to nightclubs. During the forties and early fifties, radio jump-started the careers of nearly every jazz band, which relied on radio wires in clubs and ballrooms to widely broadcast performances. For the next sixty years, radio continued to serve as a prime medium for disseminating jazz.

The condenser microphone transfigured jazz as well by permitting singers to intimately croon to their audiences in person or on the radio, rather than shouting into a megaphone to loudly project their voices over backing ensembles. It enabled singers such as Bing Crosby and Frank Sinatra to develop a calming, smooth style of singing perfect for troubled times. In recording sessions, the enhanced fidelity and quality of the condenser microphone pushed such instruments as the guitar, acoustic bass, and drums from a muffled background to the forefront. It also allowed pianists to move from the more pounding, octave-based approach of Earl Hines to the delicate right-hand runs of Teddy Wilson.

Advances in electronic technology recast jazz. During the late sixties, electrified instruments and devices such as distortion units, the electric guitar, and especially the synthesizer expanded the sound palette of jazz players and resulted in fusion music. By the eighties, samplers permitted jazz artists to easily and digitally capture and interweave bits of music to create new compositions, leading to such genres as acid jazz and hip-hop jazz.

The Internet fundamentally transformed jazz. By altering the way music is distributed and heard, it offered jazz fans a wide array of easily accessible music unimaginable before the web. The Internet encouraged consumers to replace physical discs with digital downloads or simply listen to jazz via streaming media such as Spotify. New technologies also gave jazz artists new do-it-yourself business models to produce music and market themselves.

Jazz styles have changed with shifting economic conditions. Ragtime emerged amid rapid urbanization and the rise of companies such as United States Steel (1901) and Pepsi-Cola (1902). During the Roaring Twenties, jazz became a national phenomenon when consumers first had enough discretionary income to purchase records and frequent jazz clubs. When the economy precipitously declined during the Great Depression, the soothing sounds of Bing Crosby eased Americans. The ebullient dance music of Benny Goodman and jump blues reflected improved economic times. During the early seventies and eighties, when the economy again turned sour, the complex, calming sounds of fusion and smooth jazz climbed the charts. After the Great Recession hit Americans in 2008, consoling vocalists held sway.

Throughout its history, jazz has remained a business. Initially, music publishers such as John Stark hawked sheet music for ragtime composers. After the development of the phonograph amid an emerging consumer society, record companies arose to sell discs to eager customers. When major record labels consolidated and refused to take risks on newer jazz artists, independent companies such as Blue Note, Prestige, Dial, and ESP-Disk' provided forums for musicians to experiment with new types of jazz. During the forties, the business side of jazz became painfully apparent, when the American Federation of Musicians union engineered two recording bans in retaliation against major labels and nearly immobilized the music industry. At times, entrepreneurial jazz collectives such as the Association for the Advancement of Creative Musicians in Chicago and the Black Artists Group in St. Louis asserted financial as well as racial autonomy from the established recording industry by scheduling concerts and recording albums themselves.

Along with record executives, other entrepreneurial businessmen promoted jazz. Venue operators, some of them mobsters, brought jazz to the public in riverboats, bars, clubs, ballrooms, and theaters. Booking agents such as the Theatre Owners Booking Association sold jazz acts to club owners, and managers such as Irving Mills boosted their clients' careers. As the jazz audience multiplied, advocates such as George Wein showcased the music in festivals and concert halls.

The political winds that confronted Americans over the past century-and-a-quarter also influenced jazz. By creating labor shortages that enticed thousands of Southern African Americans to move to the North, two world wars created an urban African-American audience for jazz. During the mid-thirties, President Franklin D. Roosevelt's New Deal engendered a national optimism, which provided the setting for the rise of Benny Goodman and the ebullient swing style. When the United States entered World War II, the hot sounds of Benny Goodman gave way to the sweet strains of Glenn Miller and all-female big bands. At the end of the War, the GI Bill allowed many jazz musicians to attend college, where they learned classical theory and integrated it into jazz. The nerve-racking Cold War between the United States and the Soviet Union generated the tense music of Stan Kenton and persuaded the State Department to use jazz as a cultural weapon to demonstrate the superiority of the American way of life. In the twenty-first century, wars raged on several fronts and pushed Americans toward smooth singers who reworked the easygoing Sinatra style, which had comforted Americans during World War II.

This social history proceeds chronologically. Each chapter begins with a brief, relevant story to engage the reader and then explains a jazz era through the social context that surrounds it. For example, it outlines how the Chicago jazz of Louis Armstrong and the Kansas City sounds of Bennie Moten emerged from gang-controlled venues in an urbanizing America dominated by political machines, a prohibition on alcohol, and the new technology of radio. The book shows how jazz reflected and, at times, influenced the tumultuous changes in society at large.

Though separating jazz into different stylistic eras, this book acknowledges that history does not fit neatly into time-delineated packages and that many types of jazz coexisted and overlapped. The popularity of Paul Whiteman, Louis Armstrong, and Bessie Smith happened nearly at the same time, and Frank Sinatra went solo while big bands still stormed the country. The author understands that big-band jazz did not suddenly and irrevocably disappear when bebop emerged, recognizes that hard bop, soul jazz, and avant-garde music overlaid one another, and that fusion and the traditionalism of Wynton Marsalis coexisted on the charts. This book also recognizes that most forms of jazz still exist and did not disappear when new styles surfaced. As Reggie Workman, a bassist who played with John Coltrane, noted about music during his youth, "when you put a quarter in the jukebox, you might get Billie Holiday and Charlie Parker right next to Wynonie Harris or Buddy Johnson. It was all happening" (Birnbaum 1996, 36). This book separates jazz into categories and time periods only to more clearly explain the social influences that affected it.

As a social history, this book does not judge the merits of different types of jazz. Hopefully, it objectively views the many jazz eras from ragtime to the present without disparaging any of them. The book presents Paul Whiteman alongside Duke Ellington, Dave Brubeck next to Charlie Parker, and Michael Bublé beside Bing Crosby to show their respective places in jazz and American history.

Last, this book takes an expansive view of the music. It includes such somewhat disparate genres as ragtime, the New Orleans style, crooners, big bands, bebop, soul jazz, free jazz, fusion, and hip-hop jazz. During the past 125 years, jazz has evolved tremendously amid the move toward African-American and women's rights, disruptive mass migrations of Americans, startling technological innovations, tumultuous financial booms and busts, different business models for the music industry, and political battles. Most likely, it will continue to change with the times to challenge and entertain us for years to come.

Acknowledgments

I have many people to thank for this book. I want to start with everyone from the Seattle record stores Second Time Around, Roxy Music, Yesterday and Today, and Nanoo's, who introduced me to jazz and served as a source of my coolest records. Thanks go to the guys at Silver Platters in Seattle, especially Mike Batt, who helped me refine my ideas about jazz. A special acknowledgment goes to Bud Young and James Rasmussen at Bud's Jazz Records in Seattle, who shared many insights and stories about jazz with me.

I want to recognize all the record collectors in the Northwest such as the late Bill Shonk, who piqued my interest in jazz and taught me the value and scope of jazz recordings. Venues such as Jazz Alley in Seattle introduced me to the many styles of jazz and made it immediate and real to me. A very special thanks to the late Gene Wentela, who trudged with me in search of the perfect jazz record and who taught me more about jazz than he will ever know. I also want to recognize the late David Green for prodding me to listen to and collect jazz records. The late Bob Campbell edited several early versions of chapters in this book and changed my thinking on various topics.

I want to mention my gratitude to the many jazz writers who diligently uncovered many aspects of the music and did the thorough research without which this book would not have been possible. My visit to the Jazz Institute at Rutgers University many years ago offered me important and still relevant information.

I am grateful for the many well-known and obscure musicians who have labored and continue to work to make jazz a viable, vibrant music. Special thanks to the musicians who took the time to talk with me including Red Rodney, Charlie Rouse, Marc Seales, Frank Morgan, Ahmad Jamal, Benny Golson, and many others. I want to extend my gratitude to George Wein for interrupting his busy schedule for an interview, and to Kenyon and Darlene Chan, who put me in touch with George and others.

Thanks to the group at Oxford University Press, especially Richard Carlin, Olivia Clark, Keith Faivre, and James Fraleigh, who provided wonderful suggestions and edits that greatly improved the book. I am grateful to the following reviewers for their helpful comments on the manuscript: Philippe Baugh, Tarrant County College; Stephen Clickard, Bloomsburg University; Kim Corbet, Southern Methodist University; Robert L. Hughes Jr., Saint Louis University; David Kidger, Oakland University; James T. Lindroth, Northeastern State University; Elizabeth W. McDowell, University of Delaware; Wayne Roberts, Westfield State University; Craig Thomas, University of Delaware; Jerry Tolson, University of Louisville; Yiorgos Vassilandonakis, College of Charleston; Carlos Vega, Florida A&M University; Michael Woods, Hamilton College; and three anonymous reviewers.

I would also like to thank John Francis Bagnato of the University of Pittsburgh and Anthony Marasco, who created the innovative ancillary materials that accompany this work.

Thanks to the jazz photographers who graciously allowed me to use their wonderful work. Special thanks go to Brian McMillen, Mika Vaisannen, Guy

Kopelowicz, and Daniel Berger; Jason Weiss generously provided contact information for the last two of them.

I want to thank my grandson, Alex Fantl, for expanding my musician horizons. Special thanks go to my daughter, Sara, who constantly encouraged me as I wrote the book and lent her considerable editing skills to the final product. Most of all, I want to express my heartfelt gratitude to my wonderful wife, Mary, who edited the manuscript, encouraged me throughout the entire process, and on a daily basis gives me everything that I could ever want. Without her, I would never have written this book, and I love her deeply.

JAZZ

●●●

THE ORIGINS OF JAZZ

African Music, the African-American Church, Brass Bands, and New Orleans Culture

This chapter looks at the origins of jazz through the lens of race. The enslaved peoples brought to the New World carried with them their African musical traditions, including unique ideas about rhythm. These persisted in the African-American church; minstrel shows, which promoted racism but ironically gave African-American musicians new performance opportunities; and the complex racial culture in New Orleans, where Creoles combined European brass band and African-American music to lay the groundwork for jazz.

In 1859, on his way from Branchville, South Carolina, to Charleston on the South Carolina Railroad, a white traveler noticed cotton fields stretching for miles on both sides of the train. He saw gangs of enslaved workers picking bolls of cotton and shoving them into long baskets. As he passed, the train rider heard them singing some rhythmically "wild, simple melody, by way of mutual cheer, which usually ends in a chorus, in which all join in a right hearty good will in a key so loud as to be heard from one plantation to another" (Epstein 2003, 163).

Other travelers noticed similar songs among the enslaved population as they worked. During the Civil War, one white teacher stationed in Beaufort, South

Carolina, watched enslaved workers grind grain into hominy and heard them keep "time by clapping their hands and stomping their feet" in a practice called "pattin' juba." Another contemporaneous visitor to the South commissioned a ride on a rowboat and witnessed the enslaved boatmen trading improvised lyrics with one another in a "call-and-response" pattern. Though they did not realize it, the newcomers to the South had witnessed the beginnings of a distinctive African-inspired American music called jazz, which would incorporate complex and insistent rhythms, improvisation, and call-and-response (Epstein 2003, 163, 170).

The Term "Jazz": Its Meanings, Origins, and Connection to Race

The word "jazz" means different things to different people who all uncover part of the truth. Some fans describe jazz as a specific style. A few equate jazz with New Orleans and the subsequent Dixieland music, others identify it with big-band swing, and still others associate jazz with bebop. More recently, some use the term to denote a fusion of jazz with rock or hip-hop while others utilize the word to describe the experimental sounds of the avant-garde. At times, the jazz label has been applied to vocalists who have incorporated it into their singing. Taken together, all of these styles indicate the richness and multifaceted nature of jazz. "Our music is really based on hybrid music," contended bandleader, composer, and producer Quincy Jones. "One great thing about jazz is that its very essence is like osmosis. It absorbs and eats everything in its path" (Woodard 1990, 19).

Some musicians have defined jazz in racial terms. Jimmy McPartland, a white cornetist from Chicago who gained prominence during the twenties, thought of jazz "as the wedding of the races" (Peretti 1992, 193). On the other hand, in 1924, ragtime pianist Eubie Blake and composer/bandleader Noble Sissle insisted to the African-American *Chicago Defender* that "jazz originated with the American Negro. It was his way of expressing his religious emotions" (Bell 1924, 6). During the eighties, trumpeter Wynton Marsalis contended that "jazz is something Negroes *invented* . . . It is the nobility of the race put into sound" (Marsalis 1986, 131). Bebop trumpeter Dizzy Gillespie found the roots of jazz in "jasi," a word in the Malenke tribal language of Africa that expresses uncommon, uninhibited, and exciting actions (Gillespie 1979, 492).

Other artists thought that a distinctive rhythm distinguished jazz from other types of music. Charles "Pee Wee" Russell—a clarinetist/sax player who, during the twenties and thirties, played in the bands of Jean Goldkette and Red Nichols, among others—believed jazz musicians possess "a rhythm in their systems that you can't budge" (Shapiro and Hentoff 1955, 406). "Jazz has to swing," commented drummer Jo Jones, who played with Count Basie from 1934 to 1948 (p. 406).

Many musicians identified jazz with individual expression. Texas reed player John Carter isolated "the element in jazz that truly separates this music from other kinds of music" as the "whole notion of improvising and composing on the spot" (Smith 1992, 10). Pianist Bill Evans believed that improvisation within a framework distinguished jazz from other music.

Some musicians refused to use the word at all to describe their music. New Orleans saxophone/clarinet player Sidney Bechet sniffed that the term jazz was "a name that white people have given to the music" (Bechet 1960, 3). "I play music," saxophonist John Stubblefield declared. "You might label it African-American Classical Music. You can label it American music. You can label it anything but jazz because I don't know what jazz is" (Schwartz 1993, 5).

A few people have tried to explain the origins of the word "jazz." Clarence Williams, the pianist and music publisher who helped bring blues singer Bessie Smith to prominence, took credit for the word. "I was the first to use the word 'jazz' on a song," he proudly asserted (Shapiro and Hentoff 1955, 57–58). Arnold Loyacano, who played piano and string bass with Tom Brown's band, ostensibly the first white band to play jazz music in Chicago (1915), claimed that "people started calling our music 'jazz'" after hearing the band. "The way the Northern people figured it out, our music was loud, clangy, boisterous, like you'd say 'Where did you get that jazzy suit?' meaning loud and fancy. Some people called it 'jass.' Later, when the name stuck, it was spelled with a 'z,' 'jazz'" (Shapiro and Hentoff 1955, 81). In an 1925 essay called "Jazz at Home," J. A. Rogers attributed the new word to cabaret singer Jasbo Brown, who delighted patrons to such an extent that they "would shout 'more Jasbo, more Jas, more. And so the name originated" (Ogren 1989, 121).

Though no one will ever know the true origins of the word, "jazz" had entered wide public use immediately before World War I. On April 5, 1913, *San Francisco: The Bulletin* used the term in an article titled "In Praise of Jazz, a Futurist Word Which Has Just Joined the Language." Two years later, the *Chicago Daily Tribune* used "jazz" to refer to music, and in 1916 both the *Chicago Defender* and the *New Orleans Times-Picayune* referred to "jas bands." The next year, the *New York Times* wrote about "jazz." In 1926 in his book, *This Is Jazz!,* Henry Osbourne Osgood, the editor of the *Musical Courier*, wrote, "JAZZ! The word is new and different, just like the thing itself" (Ogren 1989, 140). By 1931 in "Echoes of the Jazz Age," writer F. Scott Fitzgerald proclaimed that "the word jazz in its progress toward respectability has first meant sex, then dancing, then music" (Fitzgerald 1931, 3).

The African Musical Heritage of Jazz

Jazz developed from a combination of African-American and European-American cultures in the Southern, Midwestern, and Eastern parts of the United States. It included African musical traits carried to America by enslaved peoples, the tradition of marching bands, and distinct characteristics of the free-Black Creole culture. These elements surfaced in minstrel shows and at performances for funerals, lawn parties, and other venues, which served as precursors to jazz.

The enslaved population brought to America retained African musical qualities, which shaped and helped define the essence of jazz. Torn from their kin, enduring a brutal journey from their homes in West Africa to the American South on overcrowded ships, and forced into a servile way of life, the enslaved peoples preserved their African heritage in a variety of ways, including music. Their voices glided between the lines of the more rigid European musical scale by bending or dropping the pitch of the third, seventh, and sometimes the fifth tones. These distinctive tones became known as "blue notes," which are used so frequently in jazz and the blues. William Francis Allen, one of the white editors of *Slave Songs of the United States* (1996), described how African-American vocalists "strike sounds that cannot be precisely represented by the gamut [scale], and abound in 'slides' from one note to another" (Allen, Ware, and Garrison 1996, v–vi). To plantation

AMERICA

God bless you massa! you feed and clothe us. When we are sick you nurse us, and when too old to work you provide for us!

These poor creatures are a sacred legacy from my ancestors and while a dollar is left me, nothing shall be spared to increase their comfort and happiness.

Enslaved people patting juba, 1841. *Library of Congress Prints and Photographs Division*

owners and overseers, the technique of seemingly sliding notes or glissando appeared to make the music rise and fall, sounding "weird and wild" (Southern 1983, 191).

This music featured a unique form that became known as "call-and-response." Often used to decrease the monotony of work in the fields, the call-and-response pattern involved one singer calling or playing a lead part, and the fellow workers following with the same phrase or an embellishment of it until another took the lead. Sir Charles Lyell, a British geologist traveling in America during 1845, heard this style of singing. While traveling by ship, he noticed one of the black enslaved oarsmen "taking the lead, first improvised a verse, paying compliments to his master's family, and to a celebrated black beauty of the neighborhood who was compared to the 'red bird.' The other five then joined in the chorus, always repeating the same words" (Stearns 1956, 70–71). In 1853, as a young man, Frederick Law Olmsted—later the landscape architect who designed New York's Central Park—traveled through South Carolina. He observed enslaved workers singing in this same style, noting that "suddenly one slave raised such a sound as I have never heard before, a long, loud musical shout, rising and falling, and breaking into falsetto. As he finished," continued Olmsted, "the melody was caught up by another, and then, another, and then, by several in chorus" (Southern 1983, 156).

Some workers, especially those originally from the Bantu tribe, whooped or jumped octaves during the call-and-response. This served as a basis for the swooping field hollers that they sang.

The African peoples brought to America had been accustomed to dancing and singing to the beat of drums. However, in the American South they were barred from using percussion instruments by plantation owners who feared that drums would be used to coordinate insurrections against their masters. To offset anti-drum laws, the enslaved population focused on other ways to create the rhythm—defined as the controlled development of sound over time into patterns—that became a cornerstone of jazz. In a single song, they rapidly clapped, danced, and slapped their bodies in several different rhythms to compensate for the absence of drums. In 1853, Solomon Northup, once enslaved himself, called the practice "patting juba." It was performed by "striking the right shoulder with one hand, the left with the other—all the while keeping time with the feet and singing" (Southern 1983, 179).

The enslaved workers focused on rhythm, the linchpin of African music, to work more effectively as they picked cotton and performed other menial duties. Born into slavery, the tireless abolitionist Frederick Douglass reported in 1855 that "slaves are generally expected to sing as well as to work." Many favored a sprightly rhythm for work in the fields. An ex-enslaved field worker described the songs as

 LISTENING GUIDE 1

John Williams and his fellow inmates at the Virginia State Penitentiary in Richmond, Virginia, 1936

"CAN'T YOU LINE 'EM"

Work songs that enslaved African Americans sang provided the link between African music and spirituals, the blues, and jazz. Generally, they contained flatted notes (a note or tone in which the pitch has been lowered or bent by a semitone or a half step). In the United States, music theorists explained this semitone as a blue note, or the bending of the third, fifth, or seventh notes. The work songs also included lyrical improvisation, call-and-response (a musical element in which an instrument or a voice plays or sings a passage and then

another instrument or voice answers the initial lead voice), and other African attributes.

Here the singers demonstrate many of the attributes of work songs. Though recorded at the Virginia State Penitentiary in May 1936, the song remains little changed from the type of work song sung a century earlier. It starts with leader James Williams, who begins with a refrain, improvises verses, and then restates the refrain repeatedly. The refrain is punctuated by a moaning response from his seven fellow inmates in affirmation.

0:00–0:14	The leader starts with the main refrain of the song.
0:15–0:20	The leader states the first verse with the punchy response from the other men.
0:20–0:26	Restatement of the main refrain
0:27–0:40	Second verse
0:41–0:48	Main refrain
0:49–0:57	Third verse
0:58–1:07	Refrain
1:08–1:20	Fourth verse
1:21–1:51	Refrain

"animated" (Epstein 2003, 162). In March 1851, a plantation owner had "no objection to their whistling or singing some lively tune . . . for their motions are almost certainly to keep time with the music" (Southern 1983, 160). Though varying the rhythm by the type of work that they performed, workers invariably pushed rhythm to the forefront as they toiled in thankless jobs.

Many times, these singers placed rhythm on top of rhythm to create multiple simultaneous rhythms or a "polyrhythm," which West Africans commonly used. The editors of *Slave Songs* noticed the "effect of a marvelous complication and variety [of rhythm], and yet with the most perfect time, and rarely with any discord." They heard "the curious rhythmic effect produced by single voices chiming in at irregular intervals" (Allen, Ware, and Garrison 1996, vi). In contrast, President John

Adams commented that whites "droned out [Protestant hymns] . . . like the braying of asses in one steady beat" (Stearns 1956, 22).

Like their African brethren, African-Americans accented normally weaker beats of the rhythm to create syncopation, another basis of jazz. The authors of *Slave Songs* remarked about the "apparent irregularities in the time" of the songs that they collected. A few years later, Georgia-born poet Sidney Lanier insisted that syncopations "are characteristic of Negro music. I have heard Negroes change a well-known melody by adroitly syncopating it" (Allen, Ware, and Garrison 1996, vi).

Many of these songs featured improvisation, the spontaneous invention of music, which became a core element of jazz. Writing in 1853 about her travels, Swedish feminist and journalist Frederika Bremer commented that "all these songs are peculiarly improvisations. This improvisation goes forward every day," she concluded (Southern 1983, 201). Robert Mallard likewise recalled an "improvised song of endless proportions" among enslaved African Americans during a mid-19th century rice festival (p. 163).

Like African griots or storytellers who communicated and conserved tribal histories through music, African Americans substituted lyrics at will to explain their immediate circumstances. "The blacks themselves leave out old stanzas and introduce new ones at pleasure," noticed J. Kinnard in 1845 (Southern 1983, 93).

The enslaved peoples, though relying on their African past, adopted musical characteristics from their new environment. Their songs became "imbued with the mode and spirit of European music—often, nevertheless, retaining a distinct tinge of their native Africa." They incorporated melody, defined as an arrangement of successive notes to create a musical shape or a tune, which formed the bedrock of European music. Like the plantation owners, they at times musically worked together in harmony, which consists of two or more notes delivered at the same time that work together to produce a chord. As the editors of *Slave Songs* commented, "The chief part of the Negro music is *civilized* in its character—partly composed under the association with whites, partly actually imitated from their music" (Allen, Ware, and Garrison 1996, viii).

The African-American Church Preserves the African Musical Tradition

The enslaved African Americans used an original mix of African and European musical traits in their religious ceremonies. In 1867, one writer in the *Nation* described a "praise-meeting": "At regular intervals one hears the elder 'deaconing' a hymn-book hymn which is sung two lines at a time, and whose wailing cadences, borne on the night air, are indescribably melancholy." The subsequent response from the congregation to the call of the minister created a call-and-response, a rhythmic complexity, and the minor-key, bluesy sound common in African music (Allen, Ware, and Garrison 1996, xiii–xv).

Congregations also engaged in the African-inspired ring shout during religious ceremonies. According to the editors of the *New York Nation* on May 30, 1867, they performed the practice on Sundays or a special praise day in a room where the benches had been pushed against the wall to allow maximum floor space. The participants "begin first walking and by-and-by shuffling round, one after the other, in a ring. The foot is hardly taken from the floor, and the progression is mainly due to a jerking, hitching motion." After the ring shout progressed over four or five hours, some of the congregation fell from the ring and lined the walls of the building, shouted praise, and generated polyrhythms or multiple, simultaneous rhythms by slapping their knees and sides. They encouraged the remaining members of the ring like jazz audiences later exhorted jitterbug dancers (Allen, Ware, and Garrison 1996, xiii–xv).

Church songs introduced European-American elements to African-American religious ceremonies. The hymns sung in the African Methodist Episcopal Church (AME) represented the African-American favorites from the standard Methodist songbook published in 1801 by AME founder and formerly enslaved Reverend Richard Allen as *A Collection of Spiritual Songs and Hymns*. By the 1860s, the songs had circulated widely in the enslaved and free-black communities and became known as spirituals.

African-American church music, a largely African-inspired genre with European components, provided one of the underpinnings for jazz, when musicians applied religious music to secular themes. Cornetist Buddy Bolden adapted "Holy Roller church" music for his incipient jazz. "Each Sunday, Bolden went to church and that's where he got his idea of jazz music," insisted New Orleans guitarist Bud Scott (Shapiro and Hentoff 1955, 37). "All the different forms [of black music] can be traced to Negro church music," asserted stride pianist Willie "The Lion" Smith (Smith 1978, 3).

Minstrel Shows: Perpetuating Racism but Promoting African-American Musicians

Minstrel shows, a form of nineteenth century American entertainment that generally mocked African Americans through songs, comic acts, and dancing, ironically preserved and promoted the music of these enslaved peoples. Initially, whites smeared their faces with burnt cork and reenacted the songs and dances that they had observed on plantations. Though usually poking fun at African Americans by exaggerating their dialects and movements, minstrels exhibited a keen interest in their culture. "Who are our true rulers? The Negro poets to be sure," observed the *Knickerbocker Magazine* in 1845. When an African American composes a new song, the magazine explained, "it no sooner reaches the ear of a white amateur, than it is written down, amended, printed and then put upon a course of rapid dissemination, to cease only with the utmost bounds of Anglo-Saxondom, perhaps with the world" (Southern 1983, 92). "I used to sit with them in front of their cabins, and we would start the banjo twanging, and their voices would ring out in the quiet night air in their weird melodies," explained well-known white minstrel Ben Cotton about the origins of his minstrel material (Toll 1978, 96).

By the nineteenth century, white minstrels regularly disseminated African-American songs and a racist view of their culture. In 1829, Thomas "Daddy" Rice, nicknamed the Father of Minstrelsy, started the trend. In early 1843, a quartet banded together as the Virginia Minstrels and performed in New York and Boston. The next year, the long-lasting Christy Minstrels started to play along the Atlantic Coast and throughout Europe. According to E. P. Christy, the group reproduced "the life of the plantation darky" and mimicked the "Negro peculiarities of song" (Southern 1983, 92). The two-hour evening shows usually consisted of three parts. They began with a series of songs, dances, and jokes; moved to several variety acts collectively called the olio; and ended with a grand finale, when all the performers assembled on stage.

Though the majority of minstrels were white before the Civil War, African-American minstrels appeared after 1865 to become some of the first free black

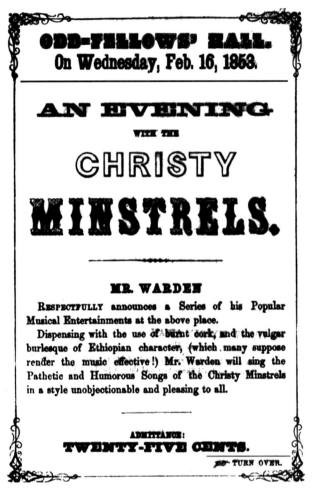

Christy Minstrels poster, 1853. *Library of Congress Rare Book and Special Collections*

performers. Immediately after the Civil War, white businessman W. H. Lee hired fifteen formerly enslaved people from Macon, Georgia, to organize the Georgia Minstrels. The same year, African-American entertainer Charles Hicks established the first black-owned-and-operated minstrel show, which he also called the Georgia Minstrels, and toured with the group constantly for five years. Hicks later collaborated with other African-American showmen to found minstrel troupes such as Hicks-Sawyer Colored Minstrels and the Hicks-McIntosh Minstrels. Other African-American-operated minstrel companies included McCabe and Young's Minstrels, Billy Kersands' Minstrels, Ernest Hogan's Minstrels, and the Henry Hart Minstrels. The groups featured African-American minstrel stars such as James Bland, who played banjo, sang, and composed songs; the singer-guitarist-songwriter Sam Lucas; and Billy Kersands, who performed with most of the major minstrel groups including his own. By the 1870s, "the minstrel show was one of the greatest outlets for talented [African-American] musicians and artists," wrote W. C. Handy, the composer of "St. Louis Blues" and himself a member of the W. A. Mahara minstrel company for twelve years. "The composers, the singers, the musicians, the speakers, the stage performers—the minstrel shows got them all" (Handy 1941, 36). Though suffering the indignities of racism, African-American entertainers looked to minstrel shows as one of the few opportunities to perform their music to broad audiences.

The Brass Band Craze as a Precursor to Jazz

Brass bands were often featured as part of a minstrel show. They became increasingly popular among American blacks and whites and served as a prototype for jazz bands. As early as the 1790s, the military formed bands with drums, flutes, clarinets, horns, and bassoons that were likely patterned after those in French militia units. In the War of 1812, brass bands recruited American troops and entertained soldiers before and after battles.

During and after the Civil War, African Americans became involved in brass bands. While fighting, they had been encouraged to form battalions, which featured brass outfits. Most of the 166 African-American regiments featured a small band with tubas, trumpets, cornets, clarinets, and drums. Some African Americans such as the recruits in the Sixty-eighth United States Colored Infantry, stationed at Fort Pickering in Tennessee, bought their own instruments with army pay. Within a brief time, the African-American soldiers played proficiently. At one event, noted an observer, "the band played well and showed the difference between Negroes as soldiers and as slaves a year ago" (Wilson 1990, 35). "Credit is due the army bands for training early Negro clarinetists as well as Negro bandmasters," asserted W. C. Handy (Handy 1941, 68).

Celebrities such as Patrick Gilmore ignited a brass-band craze, which boosted the use of brass instruments among African Americans. During 1859 in Boston, Gilmore organized a band and, when war erupted, he enlisted in the Union Army with the Twenty-fourth Massachusetts Volunteers. He served as the Bandmaster-General and Chief Musician of the State of Massachusetts until 1862, when he mustered out of the army. Gilmore then assembled musical extravaganzas for the public. In 1864, he traveled to New Orleans with a five-hundred-member brass band for a performance, which showcased his composition, "Johnny Comes Marching Home." During the summer of 1869, he staged the National Peace Jubilee, a five-day celebration in Boston that featured twenty thousand singing school children, ten thousand members of musical clubs, and a thousand-member orchestra. Two years later, the bandleader organized an event to commemorate the end of the Franco-Prussian War that spotlighted a two-thousand-person orchestra, a twenty-thousand-member chorus, a hundred firemen performing on anvils, and the United States Marine Band. After 1872, Gilmore led a smaller brass band and performed at least a concert a day for more than nineteen years to promote brass bands.

John Philip Sousa, head of the Marine Band from 1880 to 1892, further sparked a national interest in marching bands. Prodded by his manager and marketer David Blakely, Sousa wrote and performed brass-band marches, which he hoped "catered to the many rather than the few" (Harris 1983, 5). Like other march composers, Sousa embellished a repeated drum rhythm to mostly 2/4 or 4/4 time in such classic marches as "Semper Fidelis" (1888) and "Stars and Stripes

Black brass band at Claflin University, in Orangeburg, South Carolina, 1900. *Library of Congress Prints and Photographs Division*

Forever" (1897) and by the turn of the century he became a household name. By 1890, due to the efforts of Gilmore and Sousa, more than ten thousand brass bands dotted the country. A decade later, the number doubled.

The number of African-American brass bands multiplied amid the band craze by appealing to African Americans due to the rhythmic, drum-based march style. In Kansas City early in the twentieth century, Oscar Lewis, the father of Kansas City trumpeter Big Ed Lewis, performed in Shelly Bradford's Brass Band. "They played all the parades and funerals," recalled Ed Lewis, who played in such Kansas City outfits as the Bennie Moten band (Driggs 1959a, 16). At the same time in Missouri, near the Illinois border, the father of Bennie Moten band alumnus trumpeter Booker Washington played cornet in a marching band for parades and picnics. "It was a black band," Booker proudly exclaimed. "They made all the parades from home, clean to Forest Hill, all around St. Charles County, which is a pretty big county. The brass band was the main thing in my hometown," he added (Pearson 1987, 16–17). Joseph Hines, the father of future jazz pianist Earl Hines, led the cornet section in Pittsburgh's Eureka Brass Band. In Chicago, African Americans formed the Knights of Pythias Band, headed by Alexander Armant. African Americans in the relatively sparsely populated Sedalia, Missouri, organized several brass bands including the twelve-piece Queen City Concert Band.

New Orleans Brass Bands

African-American brass bands arose in New Orleans in greater numbers than in most towns and epitomized the brass-band mania. After the Spanish-American War ended in 1898, most army bands dispersed in New Orleans, so the pawnshops had a plentiful supply of instruments, reminisced New Orleans guitarist Danny Barker. Anyone with an interest in music could buy inexpensive brass horns.

By the late 1890s, Joe Petit had established several important African-American brass bands. "He founded just about every good band there was in those days—the Eagle, the Imperial, the Superior and the Olympia among them," remarked saxophonist Sidney Bechet, who became friends with Petit's son, cornetist Buddy (Bechet 1960, 77).

Many of the best African-American musicians in town joined brass bands. Trumpeter Mutt Carey played with Frankie Duson's Eagle Band, Baby Ridgley's Tuxedo Band, and the Superior Band fronted by Jimmy Brown. "I played with Joe Oliver in a brass band, too," he added (Shapiro and Hentoff 1955, 41). Manuel Perez headed the Onward Brass Band and, according to Danny Barker, "was a military man, played on a Sousa kick" (p. 49). Louis Armstrong marched in Oscar "Papa" Celestin's Tuxedo Brass Band. Trombonist Kid Ory "had a brass band. I had a sign on my house, 'ORCHESTRA AND BRASS BAND.' You couldn't miss it" (p. 24). Buddy Bolden, sometimes heralded as the first jazz man, directed a brass band in New Orleans from 1897 to 1907. Even children formed their own groups, called spasm bands, which used a variety of makeshift instruments such as musical saws, spoons, washboards, bells, pipes, sandpaper, and bottles as well as more traditional brass instruments. As late as 1917, Danny Barker remembered that "the most exciting form of musical entertainment was not the jazz band but the brass bands. . . . The marching brass bands used more instruments than the dance bands," continued Barker, "and those brass bands could play legitimate marches, the same marches the Army Band of the United States would play for the President if he died" (20–21).

Most New Orleans brass bands consisted of a handful of instrumentalists. According to Nat Towles, a New Orleans–born bassist and eventually a bandleader in the Southwest, "usually there were six musicians in a band: a clarinetist, trombonist, banjo player, drummer, bass man and a trumpeter [or cornetist] who was almost always the leader." The more well-known bands such as Manuel Perez's Onward Band grew to more than twenty members to get a larger, louder sound for parades (Shapiro and Hentoff 1995, 17).

Band members dressed in typical marching-band uniforms. When he first joined a brass band, the young Louis Armstrong marveled at "his long white pants turned up to look like knickers, black easy-walkers, or sneakers as they are now called, thin blue gabardine coats, black stockings and caps with black and white bands" (Armstrong 1955, 40). Sidney Bechet especially liked the "hats with an emblem on them and the name of the band all blazed out" (Bechet 1960, 88).

The uniformed small bands generally played established songs with little improvisation. Edmond Hall, New Orleans clarinetist, reported that early brass bands worked from "music that was mostly written. . . . As time went on there was more improvising" (Shapiro and Hentoff 1955, 22). Though some musicians could not read musical notation, most did and others learned their parts by listening to the music over time.

The majority of the New Orleans musicians performed in bands on a part-time basis. Zutty Singleton, a drummer who played in several of the brass bands, recollected that "most of the musicians had day jobs, you know—trades. They were bricklayers and carpenters and cigar makers and plasterers. Some had little businesses of their own—coal and wood and vegetable stores" (Shapiro and Hentoff 1955, 17). Singleton worked as a drayman, hauling goods in a wagon. Manuel Perez and clarinetists Lorenzo Tio Sr. and his son, Lorenzo, Jr., made cigars; and guitarist Johnny St. Cyr labored as a plasterer. Alphonse Picou worked as a tinsmith. "I joined The Imperial, the finest band in town at the time," he recalled. "I worked at my trade all week, but all day Saturday I would play in a wagon to advertise the dance that night. Play all night" (Lomax 1950, 73). "Being a musician was usually not a full-time job in New Orleans. The musicians had trades and professions," attested Danny Barker. "On weekends, or on some nights, you played music" (Shapiro and Hentoff 1955, 18).

The part-time brass bands sporadically appeared in a variety of venues. Zutty Singleton remembered that "we played for society kids on Saturday afternoons— that was with Papa Celestin and the Tuxedo Band. We also played at the New Orleans Country Club and the Louisiana Restaurant" (Shapiro and Hentoff 1955, 17). Musicians such as Louis Armstrong and Sidney Bechet entertained rowdy spectators at prize fights. Bands performed at private picnics along Lake Pontchartrain and for marriages, birthday parties, christenings, and business openings. Some staged concerts at open-air parks such as Lincoln Park and Johnson Park. Other brass bands played in dance halls such as Economy Hall, Electric Light Hall, and Jeunes Amis, or rougher places such as the Masonic and Odd Fellows Halls on Perdido and Rampart Streets, Globe Hall, Perserverance Hall, and the Union Sons Hall, known popularly as "Funky Butt Hall."

Many bands marched with one another in Sunday parades at the request of social clubs, which hired bands to extol their virtues. "There'd be parades of different [social clubs] and often times it would happen that two or three clubs, they would be parading the same day and they'd have engaged these different brass bands," remembered Sidney Bechet. Clarinetist Alphonse Picou recalled performing at "parades with Manuel Perez and the Onward Brass Band, also with Joe Oliver and [trumpeter] Kid Rena" (Shapiro and Hentoff 1955, 24).

Brass-band-led parades thrilled crowds for hours. "The parades were really tremendous things," raved Jelly Roll Morton (b. Ferdinand LeMothe), a pianist from the Crescent City. The grand marshal, the leader of the club who dressed in a smart uniform topped with a sash from his shoulder to the ground, led "his boys

Jelly Roll Morton, about 1918. *Pictorial Press Ltd/Alamy Stock Photo*

up one side of the street and down the other while the band played on the front steps" of their headquarters. "The drums would start off, the trumpets and trombones rolling into something like the 'Stars and Stripes [Forever]' or the national anthem and everybody would strut down the street," Morton continued, "the bass-drum player twirling his beater in the air, the snare drummer throwing his sticks up and bouncing them off the ground, the kids jumping and hollering, the marshal and his aides in their expensive uniforms moving along dignified, and women on top of women strutting along the back of the [marshal's] aides and out in front of everybody" (Lomax 1950, 11–12). The parade continued throughout town. "When a club paraded it would make several stops called 'punches' during the day at houses of the members, where there were sandwiches, cold beer and, of course, lots of whisky," chuckled Louis Armstrong (Armstrong 1955, 178).

As they pranced around the neighborhood, bands sometimes encountered and competed with one another. "We used to come to work or go on parades in big horse-drawn trucks," laughed clarinetist George Lewis, "and when two trucks met, there would be a 'cutting contest'" between the brass bands (Shapiro and Hentoff 1955, 25). "One band, it would come right up in front of the other and play at it," explained Sidney Bechet about a typical competition. "The first band, it would play right back, until finally one band just had to give in" (Bechet 1960, 63, 67).

African-American brass bands in New Orleans most notably played for funerals at the request of social clubs. Following a practice established by West African social organizations, at least one and sometimes multiple brass bands marched at the funeral of a social-club member to ensure a proper burial. "He was nothing if he didn't have a band," contended Zutty Singleton about the deceased.

Brass bands played a pivotal role in a funeral. According to New Orleans–born trumpeter Joseph "Wingy" Manone, "on the way to the graveyard, the [band] all walked slowly, following the cornet player" (Shapiro and Hentoff 1955, 16). The band attracted neighborhood toughs and aspiring musicians who tagged alongside the funeral cortège to form the second line, which wielded sticks, bottles, and baseball bats and marched at the head of the funeral procession to "protect" the band from opposing social clubs. For several hours, the brass band led the funeral parade of friends and relatives who "just swayed to the music and moaned," asserted Manone. After reaching the cemetery, the band waited outside the graveyard while white-clad family members of the deceased chanted and buried their loved one. "Then, after the body was buried, they'd go back to town and all the way [the band would] swing," smiled Manone. "They played the hottest music in the world" (Shapiro and Hentoff 1955, 16). For their efforts, the band earned three or four dollars, depending on the length of time for the funeral service (Shapiro and Hentoff, 16).

Creole Culture: Distinctions of Color and the European Connection to Jazz

New Orleans nurtured a distinctive Creole culture, which resulted from a mix of African-American enslaved people and French colonialists and fostered musical participation in African-American brass bands. Unlike other Southern cities, New Orleans was ruled by the French, Spanish, and then the French again before the United States bought it in 1803 as part of the Louisiana Purchase to secure access to the mouth of the Mississippi River.

Founded on May 7, 1718, by the French Mississippi Company, the city featured a different set of policies for blacks than cities farther north. In 1724, it established the French Code Noir in Louisiana that allowed any master to free their enslaved "property" at will. Many French slaveholders engaged in sexual relations with their female enslaved people. With the passage of this new law, many freed their mistresses and the children from these liaisons to greatly increase the free black population. In 1729, the French governor freed hundreds of people, who helped the French defeat the Natchez Indians.

By 1737, black freemen and freewomen had developed a distinct culture. Though not having the same status as whites, free blacks enjoyed an elevated position compared to enslaved blacks. The free blacks belonged to special social clubs, spoke in a French-based dialect, attended Catholic churches, danced the French quadrille, and attended social events in the city, including the opera and classical-music concerts. Many free blacks, children of unions between a white man and a black woman, were classified as "mulattos" and had much lighter skin than enslaved African Americans. The Francophile free blacks, steeped in French culture and practices, became known as "Creoles of color."

After France lost New Orleans to Spain in 1763 during the aftermath of the Seven Years' War, the Spanish continued liberal policies toward blacks. Many Spanish settlers in New Orleans took part in the practice of *placage*, which allowed men to maintain two households, one with a black mistress and another with a white wife. Because the Spanish government offered slaveholders the ability to manumit, or free, their enslaved people easily, many freed their black mistresses and mulatto children, who gained the legal and property rights afforded to a white person. In addition, the Spanish allowed their enslaved populations to purchase their freedom. By 1785, the free black population numbered 1,175 compared to 9,766 whites and 15,000 who were still enslaved.

A revolt among the enslaved in Saint-Domingue (present-day Haiti) funneled hundreds more free blacks into New Orleans. Fueled by the example of the French Revolution, many in this French-held colony revolted for their freedom. Led by Toussaint Louverture—himself once enslaved—in August 1791, they allied with the Spanish, who occupied the nearby island of Santo Domingo, and demanded the abolition of slavery. Employing slogans used during the French Revolution, Toussaint wanted "Liberty and Equality to reign in St. Domingue" (Bell 2007, 18). After four years of intense, guerrilla-like fighting, in May 1794 the French buckled to their demands and abolished slavery on the island.

Following this abolition, blacks loyal to Spain fled the country. Many initially journeyed to Cuba and eventually to New Orleans. They brought with them such Caribbean rhythms as the tresillo (with beats of 3+3+2), the son clave [(3+2) +2], and the cinquillo [(2+1) + (2+1) +2], and dances such as the tango and rumba. Over time, these beats filtered into jazz through Creole musicians in New Orleans.

When, in 1799, French leader Napoleon Bonaparte reasserted French dominance in Saint-Domingue by reinstituting slavery to support the lucrative sugar cane industry, more free blacks abandoned their homes for New Orleans. From 1803 to 1806, the refugees doubled the city's free black population. By the dawn of the Civil War, Louisiana had more free blacks than the free-black population of Mississippi, Alabama, Georgia, and South Carolina combined. Eighty percent considered themselves mulattoes or Creoles.

Though annexed by the United States on April 30, 1803, New Orleans retained its nearly unique attitude and policies toward blacks. While other Southern states enforced strict racial division between blacks and whites, Louisiana had three distinct racial classes: whites, free blacks, and enslaved peoples. As late as 1856, the Louisiana Supreme Court confirmed that "in the eyes of Louisiana law there is . . . all the difference between a free man of color and a slave that there is between a white man and a slave" (Foner 1970, 417).

In New Orleans before the Civil War, free blacks enjoyed a privileged position. They had complete legal rights, including the ability to testify against whites. They owned property, and some even started plantations with their own enslaved workers. By 1859, nearly 90 percent of the free-black population worked in trades such as carpentry, shoemaking, barbering, tailoring, and as mechanics in contrast to the menial farm labor and dock work performed by the enslaved. Creoles had accumulated $15 million in property, had organized literary societies and musical performances, and published their own newspapers, including the New Orleans *Tribune*.

From their privileged position, Creoles looked with contempt upon the enslaved blacks. On July 17, 1852, the *New Orleans Daily Delta* found that Creoles "regard the slave with more disdain and antagonism than the white man." They looked lighter and dressed, acted, ate, and spoke differently than the enslaved, from whom they distanced themselves to establish and reinforce a higher social status.

After the Civil War, the division between Creoles and more recently liberated peoples remained unchanged through the early twentieth century. Living in downtown New Orleans rather than the uptown section of the city, which housed most blacks, many Creoles spoke a French-based dialect or even French, attended better schools and Catholic churches, and worked in the trades. They had much lighter skin than most uptown blacks.

Many Creoles banded together in exclusionary social-aid and pleasure clubs for entertainment, relaxation, and status. "You see, New Orleans was very organization-mind," mentioned Jelly Roll Morton, a Creole. "I have never seen such beautiful clubs as they had there—the Broadway Swells, the High Arts, the Orleans Aides, the Bulls and Bears, the Tramps, the Iroquois, the Allegroes—and that was just a few of them" (Lomax 1950, 11). Other social organizations included the Odd Fellows, the Tulane Club, the Zulu Club, the Eagles, the Lions, the Knights of Pythias, and the Vidalia. When performing at a Creole club in 1900, Creole Alphonse Picou noticed that they didn't "allow a dark man to come in. If you were dark you had to stay out" (Shapiro and Hentoff 1955, 24). The Creole social clubs hired only Creole brass bands for their functions such as parades and funerals. One New Orleans musician attested that many Creole bandleaders "wouldn't hire a man whose hair wasn't silky" (Teachout 2009, 25).

Creoles emphasized classically based music lessons for their children to maintain an elevated status. Creole clarinetists and prominent early jazz men Barney Bigard and "Big Eye" Louis Delisle Nelson studied musical theory with Lorenzo Tio Sr. and Luis "Papa" Tio, who graduated from the Conservatory of Music in Mexico City and performed classical music at the New Orleans opera house. Jelly Roll Morton decided on a musical career after a trip to a recital at the French Opera House. Trumpeter Bunk Johnson took lessons from a member of the Tio family. Lorenzo Tio Jr., taught musical notation to several New Orleans Creole jazz men including clarinetist/sax players Sidney Bechet, Johnny Dodds, Louis Cottrell Jr., Jimmie Noone, and Albert Nicholas.

By the turn of the century, Creoles dominated the New Orleans music scene. In a survey of *Soard's New Orleans City Directory* from 1880 to 1915, Creoles represented approximately 75 percent of the 103 musicians listed, most of whom could read music in contrast to "fakers" who learned by listening. As the non-Creole Louis Armstrong quickly learned, "most of the musicians were Creoles. Most of them could pass for white easily . . . Most of these were good sight readers" (Armstrong 1999, 32).

Many Creole musicians expressed a deep-seated prejudice against their darker counterparts. Creole pianist Jelly Roll Morton, as his friend Lovie Austin related, "shunned dark-skinned blacks for their lack of refinement." Morton's wife insisted that "Jelly Roll didn't like Negroes" (Lomax 1950, 208–9). Creole clarinet player Albert Nicholas lectured an interviewer that "I'm from a different culture [than the blacks]. I don't have nothing to do with that [black working class] part of New Orleans" (Fiehrer 1991, 34). "The mulattoes were actually more prejudiced than the white people at that time," remarked Creole Johnny St. Cyr. "They just wouldn't affiliate with dark people. Wouldn't intermarry" (Lomax 1950, 80, 103). "The worst Jim Crow around New Orleans was what the colored did to themselves," remarked bass player George "Pops" Foster. "The lighter you were the better they thought you were" (Teachout 2009, 25). "They had a caste system in New Orleans," affirmed Danny Barker about New Orleans at the turn of the century (Shapiro and Hentoff 1955, 50).

The foundation of jazz arose from a combination of European-based music, exemplified by brass bands, and musical carryovers from the African heritage such as the ring shout, improvisation, call-and-response patterns, and complex rhythms, which black churches and minstrel shows preserved and promulgated. It also owed a debt to the distinctive African-American Creole culture in New Orleans that combined European influences and African-American traditions, which formed the bedrock of a music later called jazz.

For Discussion and Further Study

Chapter Quiz

1. Reflect on the different meanings that have been given to the word "jazz." How do these meanings reflect cultural attitudes toward race, particularly white attitudes toward black creative culture?

2. What elements of African musical culture were preserved in the work songs sung by enslaved African Americans?

3. What was the role of the African-American church and its music in the development of jazz?

4. How were white attitudes toward African-American music shaped by the minstrel tradition?

5. Why did performers like W. C. Handy join minstrel troupes? What kinds of sacrifices did they have to make to fit into the minstrel mold?

6. Why did the brass-band tradition appeal to African-American musicians? How did this tradition blossom in New Orleans?

7. How did distinctions of skin color play a role in social divisions within the African-American community in New Orleans during the eighteenth and nineteenth centuries?

RAGTIME AND THE EMERGENCE OF JAZZ

Race, Urbanization, and New Technology

This chapter examines the popularity of ragtime through the perspectives of race, urbanization, and technological innovations. It focuses on the African-based syncopation of African-American piano players who incorporated these new rhythms into their compositions. Many used the European march form, following Booker T. Washington's philosophy of "uplifting the race" by incorporating white musical models into their work. Growing urban centers provided a ready audience for this new music that expressed the speed, optimism, and innovation of the new century. The chapter also shows ragtime's rapid spread through such new technologies and products as piano rolls, the phonograph, records, and sheet music.

On a sultry morning in 1894, Scott Joplin reached Sedalia, Missouri, with his friend and fellow pianist Otis Saunders. Born in Texarkana, Texas, on November 24, 1868, Joplin had been in Sedalia before. In 1885, the gifted teenage pianist had landed in St. Louis, where he stayed for eight years, periodically traveling to nearby Missouri cities such as Sedalia. In 1893, Joplin and dozens of other talented pianists from the American heartland converged on Chicago to entertain twenty-seven million people who attended the World Columbian Exposition. The next year, Joplin returned to St. Louis and adjoining towns, where he played piano and organized a vocal harmonizing group, the Texas Medley Quartette, which performed minstrel songs.

By the time of the World Columbian Exposition, Joplin had composed his own music. Inspired by the popular marches of the day, his first published works were "The Great Crush Collision March" and the "Combination March." He embellished traditional marches with elements of his African-American heritage to syncopate or change the rhythm of the songs by emphasizing the weak beats, and sometimes played marches in double-time (twice the notated rhythm). When he returned to Sedalia in 1894, the pianist brought a new style that would revolutionize American popular music. According to an eyewitness, some initially called it "jig piano." Eventually, the music became known as ragtime.

Ragtime: Merging African-American and European Music

Developed primarily by African Americans, ragtime combined African-based and European music to jump-start a long line of creative styles that comprise the jazz legacy. It fused the marching-band sound of innovators such as John Philip Sousa with the syncopation and improvisation of African music for a hybrid that swept the nation from the late 1890s to the end of World War I. Promoted on steamboats and railroads and at national exhibitions, ragtime flourished amid dance crazes, financial prosperity, and a technological revolution that changed music forever.

The syncopated sound of the banjo served as the foundation of ragtime. The American banjo, based on the five-stringed halam or cambreh of the Wolof tribe in Senegal and Gambia, was regularly played in the American South on plantations and at minstrel shows. When strummed and picked by African Americans and their white imitators in a rhythm with sudden stops and starts, the instrument produced a syncopated sound reminiscent of its African forerunner.

By the 1880s, African-American musicians were applying syncopated banjo rhythms to the piano. In 1881, traveler Lafcadio Hearn asked a friend, "Did you ever hear Negroes play piano by ear? . . . They use the piano exactly like a banjo" (Schreyer 1985, 58). When using syncopation on the piano, African Americans played a steady march-based "om pah" with the left hand. With the right hand, the pianists produced single-note runs with a syncopated rhythm, which accentuated the measures of the second and fourth beats. Musically, white writers referred to syncopation as *alla zoppa*, translated to "lame" or "limping," to describe the ragged flow of the music. "Syncopation intensifies the anticipated beat into an imperative bodily motion," explained the *American Mercury* in August 1924. "The shorter the anticipation, the stronger the effect" (Thompson 1924, 466).

Many understood the connection between ragtime and the uneven rhythm of the banjo. "Real ragtime on the piano," explained rag pioneer Ben Harney, "is the contribution of the graduated Negro banjo-player" (Blesh and Janis 1959, 226).

Ragtime pianist Henry "Plunk" Johnson, also a banjo player, earned his nickname from his banjo-derived piano adaptations of popular tunes.

Building on their African heritage, many ragtime pianists improvised on basic European song structures. "None of the original pianists played ragtime the way it was written," contended S. Brun Campbell, the white ragtime pianist who migrated to Sedalia and learned his craft from Scott Joplin. "They played their own style" (Campbell 1985, 151). The application of sometimes improvised, syncopated, banjo-based rhythms on the piano to European-styled melodies became known as ragtime.

Early Rags

In 1895, Kentuckian Ben Harney, a young white piano player, published the first ragtime, or at least proto-ragtime, composition, "You've Been a Good Old Wagon but You've Done Broke Down." His publisher, Bruner Greenup, billed Harney as the "Original Introducer to the Stage of the Now Popular 'Rag Time' in Ethiopian Song." The next year, Harney scored a ragtime hit with "Mister Johnson (Turn Me Loose)," which the *New York Clipper* characterized as "a genuinely clever plantation imitation and excellent piano playing" (Blesh & Janis 1959, 94). In 1897, Harney published the book *Ben Harney's Rag Time Instructor*, which informed readers how to syncopate popular tunes.

The so-called coon song tradition inspired many early ragtime compositions. Based upon a derisive term for blacks, coon songs started in minstrel shows. Before the Civil War, groups such as the Christy Minstrels sang such racist tunes as "Oh! Mr. Coon," "Zip Coon," and "The Jolly Darkey," all of which reinforced stereotypes of blacks as strutting but compliant, ignorant fools. By the 1890s, coon songs peaked in popularity and climaxed with the song "All Coons Look Alike to Me," ironically composed by the African-American comedian Ernest Hogan (b. Ernest Crowdus). Supposedly based on "All Pimps Look Alike," which Hogan heard in a Chicago saloon, the tune featured pulsating syncopation that promoted the new ragtime style.

In 1897, some composers specifically identified their songs as rags. In January, William Krell released the first tune with an explicit reference to ragtime, "Mississippi Rag." That December, Tom Turpin—who owned the Rosebud Café in St. Louis that became a hangout for ragtime pianists—became the first African American to publish a rag with "Harlem Rag." Though composing the rag five years earlier, he snagged a publisher for it, when the ragtime wave started to crest. That same year, Warren Beebe published "Ragtime March," R. J. Hamilton released "Ragtime Patrol," D. A. Lewis produced "Rent Rag Ball," and Theo Northrup issued "Louisiana Rag." With the flurry of rags in 1897, one reporter in Chicago coined the term "ragtime" for the new musical genre.

Young, Upwardly Mobile, African-American Ragtime Innovators

In 1899, African-American Scott Joplin catapulted ragtime into the national limelight with the publication of the sheet music for "Maple Leaf Rag," which within several months sold steadily. Two years later, Joplin followed with "Peacherine Rag," and "The Easy Winners—A Ragtime Two-Step" and the next year composed "The Entertainer." The pianist received the title of "The King of Ragtime Writers" from his publisher, John Stark. "We have advertised these as classic rags, and we mean just what we say. They are the perfection of type," contended Stark. "They have lifted ragtime from its low estate and lined it up with Beethoven and Bach" (Blesh and Janis 1959, 253). In all, the number of rags published in 1899 tripled from the previous year.

African Americans dominated the ragtime ranks. African-American raggers included Joplin, James Scott, Tony Jackson, Tom Turpin, Scott Hayden, and Louis Chauvin. The innovating and central role of African Americans in ragtime was clearly stated in publicity for the song "Syncopated Sandy" (1897), which maintained that "the now famous" ragtime, "the musical rage of the century . . . originated with the Negroes and is characteristic of their people" (Blesh and Janis 1959, 89).

Early sheet music for "Maple Leaf Rag," published by John Stark. *Popular Instrumental Sheet Music, Music Division, The New York Public Library*

 LISTENING GUIDE 2

Scott Joplin

"MAPLE LEAF RAG"

Scott Joplin helped create and popularize the ragtime genre, which served as a foundation for jazz. During the fall of 1899, Joplin published "Maple Leaf Rag," likely named after the Maple Leaf Club in Sedalia, Missouri, at which he played. Most probably, he composed the song a year earlier. He signed a contract with John Stillwell Stark who in September 1899 published sheet music for the song and promoted Joplin and ragtime into the twentieth century. The composer hoped that "'Maple Leaf Rag' will make me the king of ragtime" (Blesh and Janis 1959, 33) and received a royalty of one cent on sales of the sheet music. In 1903, Stark published a version of the song with lyrics by Sydney Brown. Throughout the years, dozens of jazz artists such as Sidney Bechet and the New Orleans Rhythm Kings recorded the song.

The song, a ragtime march that served as a model for a rag, features four parts with blue notes throughout, syncopated, insistent bass lines, and a melody on the left hand and a second, syncopated rhythm on the right hand. The double rhythms or cross-rhythms are derived from African practice and are called polyrhythms. Innovatively, Joplin uses polyrhythms to combine the African tradition with the march form.

The ragged rhythm of syncopation can be illustrated with a story told by pianist Herbie Hancock about trumpeter Miles Davis. When walking down the street, Miles and Herbie noticed a woman stumbling hesitantly toward a building. Miles pointed at the woman and said, "Play that." Rather than a steady walk or beat, syncopation can be likened to the stumbling person.

Joplin recorded this version of the song for the Aeolian Company, which made a piano roll of the music in June 1916, less than a year before Joplin's death.

0:00–0:08	An introduction to the theme with the non-syncopated rhythm on the left hand and a syncopated rhythm played with the right hand. The use of syncopation gives the rag a propulsive, toe-tapping feel.
0:09–0:32	After a bass-line piano flourish in a different rhythm and syncopation, he jumps half an octave and then at 0:17 repeats the entire passage including the half-octave jump (from A flat to D flat) and syncopation. Please note that an entire octave consists of two notes with the same letter on the scale (e.g., A), one of which has double the frequency (also called pitch or vibrations per second) as the other.
0:33–0:47	He begins a second, slightly different melody. At 0:33 you can clearly hear the syncopation or seemingly quick-second pause in the music. However, syncopation occurs throughout the majority of the song.
0:48–1:03	He repeats the previous passage.
1:04–1:19	Restates the introductory passage.
1:04–1:19	Restates the initial melody again. Note the pause or syncopation in the music.
1:20–1:35	Changes the tempo or time to a slower-paced section and uses a syncopated stop-start right-hand melody throughout. Jumps a half octave at 1:29 and then returns to original key of A flat.
1:36–2:09	Plays a different melody, which he repeats at 1:52. Note the repetition of the melodies twice. Also, be aware of the minor notes, which give the section a bluesy feeling. He ends the song after the statement of the melody for the second time.

Booker T. Washington, proselytizing an ideology of upward mobility for African Americans within the current social structure, arose at the same time as ragtime. Formerly enslaved and founder of the black college, the Tuskegee Institute, Washington preached a gospel of success through assimilation. He felt that African Americans should show their worth by succeeding within the context of white culture rather than challenging the prevailing Jim Crow laws. Washington believed that education, hard work, and entrepreneurship led to equality among the races. On September 18, 1895, an address at the Atlanta Cotton States and International Exposition vaulted him into national prominence, when he urged African Americans to contribute to "the business and industrial prosperity of the South." Washington condemned African Americans who were dedicated to the "agitation of questions of social equality," which he called "the extremist folly," and insisted that African Americans needed to demonstrate their economic value. Through this conciliatory strategy, he felt that African Americans would eventually gain full participation in society by showing themselves to be responsible, reliable Americans and dispelling the notion that they were lazy and incompetent. He labeled his talk the "Atlanta Compromise." In 1900, Washington solidified his approach by founding the National Negro Business League, which he created as a network of African-American financial and economic leaders in 320 chapters that mirrored the predominantly white Chamber of Commerce structure. The next year, he codified his philosophy in the book, *Up from Slavery*.

Many early African-American ragtime pioneers adopted Washington's philosophy, which became popular around the time of the ragtime craze. In Sedalia, Missouri, the birthplace of ragtime, many African Americans attended the newly established George R. Smith College for Negroes, which included a music department with instruction in piano, violin, organ, banjo, voice, and guitar. The classically trained Scott Joplin took advanced courses in harmony and composition at the college, as did ragtime pianist Arthur Marshall. According to Brun Campbell, "many Negroes came to Smith College to take courses in music." They hoped that a classically based, compositional training would afford them respect and success in a white society, which then viewed African-American musicians as minstrel-show buffoons (Campbell 1985, 150). Reflecting Booker T. Washington's philosophy, in 1911 Joplin published the opera *Tremonisha*, which in twenty-seven musical numbers urged African Americans to rise above superstition through education.

Though not developing ragtime, whites pianists/composers helped popularize the music. Notable white ragtimers included George Botsford, Charles L. Johnson, Percy Wenrich, and Joplin protégé Joseph Lamb. They embraced the African-American-inspired music, performed it in their locales, and became nationally known. Botsford published a dozen rags, and Wenrich more than twenty of them. Charles L. Johnson composed 14 rags including the hot-selling "Dill Pickles Rag." In somewhat of an overstatement, white pianist Brun Campbell asserted that "ragtime was the Negro's music, but it was the white man who made it popular" (Campbell 1985, 151).

Most ragtime pioneers were relatively young. In a study about the age of thirty prominent ragtime composers when they penned their first rag, 33 percent were teenagers and another 50 percent were between the ages of 20 and 25. Thirty-one years old when he composed "Maple Leaf Rag," Scott Joplin was one of the oldest ragtimers.

Ragtime in Red-Light Districts on the Urban Frontier

The ongoing urbanization of America and the accompanying growth of red-light districts generated an audience and venues for ragtime pianists. In 1860, only 20 percent of the American people lived in cities. By 1900, when ragtime swept the nation, almost 40 percent of Americans were urbanites.

Many of the ragtime pioneers started their careers by working in a vice district, sometimes called the Sporting Belt, the Red-Light District, or the Tenderloin, which sprouted up in most burgeoning cities. In Sedalia's Tenderloin, Scott Joplin and his Missouri colleagues played the Black 400 Club and the Maple Leaf Club, both owned by ragtime pianist Tony Williams. "Sedalia was a wide-open town in those days with saloons, gambling houses, dance halls, and a red-light district," observed Brun Campbell, "and it was in these places the pianists could be found selling their musical wares" (Campbell 1985, 150–51). Joplin also played at Tom Turpin's Rosebud saloon and brothel in St. Louis. Percy Wenrich lived in the gambling town of Joplin, Missouri, where he performed at the House of Lords Saloon that featured a bar on the first floor, gambling on the second, and a sporting house (brothel) on the third.

Ragtime pianists took advantage of opportunities in vice districts outside Missouri. The successful Jake Schaefer plied his trade as the "piano king of the New York bordellos." In Atlantic City, remembered Willie "The Lion" Smith, "the busiest center of activity for the piano ragtimers took place in the tenderloin section known as the Line." Eubie Blake, later the co-composer with Noble Sissle of the first African-American Broadway musical, *Shuffle Along*, began his career by playing ragtime in Aggie Shelton's bordello in Baltimore. "Then I went down on what they call the line: sporting houses on this side, sporting houses on that side," he related. "Ragtime," remembered the pianist, "was out of the houses of ill repute, or bordellos" (Rosenweig n.d., 2).

Storyville in New Orleans, one of the most well-known and notorious vice areas in the country, catered to ragtime pianists. It had been established in 1857 and, forty years later, had been further regulated and segregated under a bill sponsored by Alderman Sidney Story. Tom Anderson, the political boss of the Fourth Ward and a leading legislator in Louisiana for sixteen years, oversaw the Tenderloin District and owned several of its establishments. According to New Orleans pianist Jelly Roll Morton, "the Tenderloin District in New Orleans was considered second to France, meaning the second greatest in the world, with extensions for blocks and blocks on the North side of Canal Street. . . . They had everything in The District from the highest class to the lowest [of brothels]," continued Morton, "creep joints where they'd put the feelers on a guy's clothes, cribs [tiny rooms with a bed] that rented for about five dollars a day. . . . Then, of course, we had the mansions where everything was the highest class" (Lomax 1950, 49–50). The District, reported an observer, featured "lights of all colors glittering and glaring. Music was pouring into the streets from every house. Women were standing by in the doorways" (25). In 1902, more than eight hundred saloons and two hundred brothels operated in the District, many of which were owned by Sicilian immigrants with connections to organized crime.

The District hosted many ragtime pianists, referred to as "professors." "The houses [of ill repute] hired nothing but the best, but only piano players," remembered Clarence Williams, who performed in the District (Shapiro and

Hentoff 1955, 12). "It was mostly pianos you heard there," agreed New Orleans soprano sax player Sidney Bechet. "They didn't have orchestras" (Bechet 1960, 53). Tony Jackson, one of the premier ragtimers in New Orleans and composer of "Pretty Baby," played regularly at the high-class Mahogany, Countess Willie Piazza's whorehouse, and Miss Antonia Gonzales's brothel in Storyville. Kid Ross entertained at Lula White's establishment. Jelly Roll Morton regaled patrons at the top-flight brothels of Storyville, where "the best of the piano players worked" (Shapiro and Hentoff 1955, 7). "He was one of the best in 1902," contended New Orleans trumpeter Willie "Bunk" Johnson, "because he played the music the whores liked" (55). The pianists many times doubled as pimps, according to Clarence Williams, and Jelly Roll Morton readily confessed to his pimping past.

Many ragtime pianists adopted flamboyant fashion, appropriate to the venues in which they played and the lives that they lived. In his own account, Brun Campbell arrived in a town "decked out in a loud checkered suit. Cloth-top, colored patent leather shoes with pearl buttons, a light-colored hat with a loud hat band, and that ever-lovin' brilliant silk shirt, together with a loud patterned necktie, about made my ragtime dress complete" (Blesh & Janis 1959, 30).

Critics eagerly noted the connection between ragtime and vice districts, a criminal association that has plagued the reputation of jazz for more than a century. In 1900, a writer in the *Musician* characterized ragtime as "essentially obvious, vulgar, yet strong. Like a criminal novel, it is full of bangs and explosions" (Blesh & Janis 1959, 132).

The Ragtime Craze Begins: Steamboats, Railroads, and the Exposition of 1904

New modes of transportation and communication helped spread ragtime around the country. The Streckfus Steamboat Line helped take ragtime from criminal-run brothels to national prominence. Originally a fleet of freighters, the Streckfus Line shifted to a passenger-only service in 1901, when railroads clearly emerged as the main source for freight transportation. According to one of the captains, the steamboat line of "excursion boats exclusively made short trips, a day, an afternoon, or a moonlight trip. The excursion vessel had no passenger staterooms, and the normal cabin space was devoted to a large dance floor." The boats usually traveled up and down the Mississippi and Ohio Rivers, many times starting in St. Louis and ending in New Orleans (Chevan 1989, 154).

To entertain passengers and make use of the dance floors, the Streckfus Line enlisted bands and increasingly used ragtime pianists. Initially, musical acts played current pop tunes and music for one-step Fox Trots and two-step dances and occasionally included a ragtime pianist such as S. Brun Campbell, nicknamed the "Ragtime Kid." When ragtime became more prevalent, the steamboats showcased bands, which performed rags. By the mid-1910s, observed New Orleans musician Jack Weber, "the riverboats on the Mississippi played ragtime numbers almost exclusively" (Shapiro and Hentoff 1955, 60).

Pianists sometimes used railroads to popularize ragtime. Near the turn of the century, ragtime pianist Tony Williams booked railroad excursions. He rented a train for a short trip and sold tickets to eager listeners at the beginning and ending destinations of the ride. Between the two towns, Williams and several other ragtime musicians entertained the passengers.

Major world's fairs also helped put a spotlight on the new musical style. The Columbian Exposition of 1893 spread ragtime music among musicians and the general public. Held in Chicago to commemorate the 400th anniversary of Columbus' arrival to the New World, the Exposition consisted of two hundred exhibit halls with material from forty-six countries, a giant Ferris wheel, the first moving sidewalk, the first commercial movie house, and such new food brands as Cracker Jack, Quaker Oats, Hershey's chocolate, and Pabst Blue Ribbon beer. The fair attracted more than twenty-seven million visitors during its six-month existence.

At least indirectly, ragtime pianists attracted attention through the Exposition. Though not featured acts, Scott Joplin and Otis Saunders traveled to Chicago to serenade Chicago's red-light-district clients who were visiting the Windy City for the Columbian Exposition. They performed alongside other ragtime men such as Johnny Seymour and Henry "Plunk" Johnson. African-American composer Will Marion Cook contended that "at the World's Fair in Chicago, 'ragtime' got a running start" (Gushee 1994, 14).

The St. Louis Exposition of 1904 brought ragtime more directly to the attention of the nation. Located near the heart of ragtime activity, the fair commemorated the 100th anniversary of the Louisiana Purchase. On 1,200 acres, the exposition constructed fifteen hundred temporary exhibit buildings to feature sixty-four countries; hosted the 1904 Summer Olympics; and drew nearly twenty million visitors despite being delayed for a year.

On February 22 during the festivities, dozens of piano-playing hopefuls competed in an Exposition-sponsored piano contest. Scott Joplin composed the rag "The Cascades" to commemorate a waterfall at the fair, and ragtime pianist James Scott wrote "On the Pike—March and Two-Step" for the event. Tom Turpin produced "St. Louis Rag" for the Exposition. At the end of the day, ragtimer Louis Chauvin won the contest.

Native Chicagoan Axel Christensen promoted the ragtime craze through his schools of ragtime. In 1903, he offered lessons in his hometown. Axel advertised the service in the *Chicago Daily News* as "ragtime taught in ten lessons." By the end of the year, Christensen had instructed more than a hundred students and by December of the next year had given lessons to four hundred pupils. In 1904, he published *Christensen's Instruction Book No. 1 for Rag-time Piano Playing*, which by 1909 had expanded to thirty-six pages and sold for a dollar. By 1915, the music entrepreneur had built an empire of thirty-five well-staffed schools throughout the country and had become known as the "Czar of Ragtime."

Around the turn of the century, ragtime had expanded beyond the confines of its birthplace in Sedalia, Missouri. Joplin traveled to St. Louis and then New York City. The prolific pianists Charles Johnson and Charles Daniels took the lead in Kansas City; the nearly blind Charles Hunter (who published his first rag in 1899) introduced the music to Nashville; and George Botsford presented ragtime to Iowa with "Katy Flyer—Cake Walk, Two Step." In Louisville, "Piano Price" Davis ruled the ragtime roost; and in Mobile, Alabama, Porter King, immortalized in the song "King Porter Stomp," entertained crowds with ragtime. In 1903, ragtime pioneer Scott Hayden moved permanently to Chicago. Pianists Joe Jordan and Louis Chauvin soon joined him and competed there with Ed Hardin, Henry "Plunk" Johnson, and Johnny Seymour.

Memphis boasted its own ragtime stars. During May 1901, the Rialto Theater opened its "summer season in ragtime opera," the African-American *Freeman* newspaper reported on May 25. Its lineup included Nettie Lewis, "the soubrette of ragtime"; Ed Hill, who played "nothing but ragtime"; Bessie Gilliam, "inimitable in ragtime"; and Ora Criswell, billed as "Memphis' own ragtime." The Rag Time Opera Company traveled to Birmingham, Alabama, and then back to Memphis at the end of the year.

Jelly Roll Morton pioneered his version of ragtime in New Orleans. When asked to play a few songs in the early 1900s, Morton performed "all of Scott Joplin's tunes—he was the great St. Louis ragtime composer—I knew them by heart and played them right off. They brought me James Scott's tunes and Louis Chauvin's and I knew them all" (Lomax 1950, 148). "Scott Joplin was his God; and, really, things like 'Maple Leaf Rag' and 'Grace and Beauty' were his models," contended Walter Melrose, the Chicago music entrepreneur who, with his brother Lester, published "Wolverine Blues" and dozens of other hits for Morton (190).

Tony Jackson contributed to the ragtime scene in New Orleans. Jackson, a child prodigy who Morton called "the greatest single-handed entertainer in the world," for a time became the leading exponent of ragtime in the Crescent City. "When Tony came in," confessed Jelly Roll, "the guys would tell me, 'Get off that piano stool. You're hurting the piano's feelings'" (Lomax 1950, 129, 143).

Challenged by the popularity of ragtime, the musical establishment lashed out against the new music. The *Musical Courier* observed that its "vicious influences are highly detrimental to the cause of good music" (Berlin 1980, 46–47). In January 1900, the music monthly *The Etude* lamented that "the counters of the music stores are loaded with this virulent poison which in the form of a malarious epidemic, is finding its way into the homes and brains of the youth to such an extent as to arouse one's suspicions of their sanity" (Berlin 1980, 44). In 1900, when he tried to introduce ragtime at the Agricultural and Mechanical College in Normal, Alabama, the then-teacher W. C. Handy found that "ragtime was not respectable. In some quarters it was condemned because of its Negro origin. In others it was damned because it cut down the sales of more sedate music" (Handy 1941, 64). The next year, at the convention of the American Federation of Musicians in Denver, "resolutions were adopted characterizing 'ragtime' as 'unmusical rot.' Members were encouraged to make every effort to suppress and [to] discourage the playing and the publishing of such musical trash," informed the *Brooklyn Daily Eagle* on May 14. "Back in those early days, churchgoing Negro people would not stand for ragtime playing; they considered it sinful," added stride pianist Willie "The Lion" Smith (Smith 1978, 25–26).

Some musicians disagreed with the critics. "Abolish rag-time?" questioned Goddie Rosenbaum, a bandleader from Kalamazoo, Michigan, in 1901. "You can't do it. It has a grip on the people's hearts that all the band masters in the world can't loosen. . . . Who wants rag-time abolished? None but a few polished musicians. Instead of rag-time being abolished, you'll see it increase and grow," he insisted (Kalamazoo Public Library 2010, 9). At the height of ragtime, classical composers Antonín Dvořák and Claude Debussy took a serious interest in the syncopated music and incorporated it into their work.

By the turn of the century, ragtime had captured America. Ragtime flooded the sheet-music market and in 1900 even the marching-band king, John Philip Sousa, performed rags such as his "Trombone Sneeze" at the Paris Exhibition. On May 23, 1900, the *Musical Courier* reported that "ragtime—a rag-weed of music— has grown up everywhere in the Union."

Dancing to Rags: The Cakewalk and the Castles

New dances fueled the ragtime craze just as dance innovations inspired and accompanied other styles of jazz. During the 1890s, the cakewalk partially replaced more traditional dances such as the quadrille, the cotillion, and polkas, which had been imported from France. Shephard Edmonds, an African-American entertainer and the son of freed people, described the cakewalk as "originally a plantation dance, just a happy movement that they did to banjo music." On Sundays, when enslaved African Americans had free time, "both young and old would dress in hand-me-down finery to do a high kicking, prancing walk-around" to mock the "high manners" of their masters. Missing the irony, white masters watched the dance and awarded a cake to "the couple that did the proudest movement" (Blesh and Janis 1959, 96). The cakewalk tradition continued in minstrel shows with such dance teams as Ned Harrigan and Tony Hart who presented "Walking for Da Cake."

By the 1890s, a cakewalk mania swept the nation. In April 1892, seventy-five thousand fans attended a Jubilee and Cake-Walk at Madison Square Garden, where soprano Black Patti (b. Sissieretta Jones) sang. Four years later, the African-American comedy/dance team of Bert Williams and George Walker, labeling themselves "world-renowned cake-walkers," appeared in the *Gold Bug* on Broadway and introduced the dance. After their performances, mentioned Harlem Renaissance writer James Weldon Johnson, "the execution of the cake-walk steps was taken up by society." Upper-class families concluded their social gatherings with a cakewalk, and charity organizations staged cakewalk competitions as a fundraising strategy. By 1897, remembered one contemporary, "every hamlet in the country had cakewalk contests. White people that did it would often make up in black face" (Blesh and Janis 1959, 98–99).

Ragtime pianists played for dancers who two-stepped and cakewalked. Scott Joplin, one fan at the time recalled, arrived in Sedalia at "about the time the cake walk came out" and "really made music [for dancers]" (Curtis 1994, 78). "Joplin and I and many of the others played for numerous dances in the parks, all piano only," confirmed Arthur Marshall, a protégé of Joplin. "We played rags of note, and they did dances to the ragtime" (Blesh and Janis 1959, 28). Scott Joplin collaborated with Marshall in composing a dance to accompany the cakewalk, the "Swipesy Cakewalk" (1900), and the sheet music of many Joplin rags was publicized as "two-step" numbers.

Ragtime orchestras arose to service the dance crowd. Ragtime bands probably started in Sedalia, inspired by the pianists in the city. When he first arrived in town, Joplin played cornet in the African-American, twelve-piece brass band, the Queen City Concert Band, which had been organized in 1891. Joplin "thought the music was so good that he took his trumpet, went over and joined in," remembered friend and band mate G. T. Ireland (Curtis 1994, 73). Within a few years, the group adopted Joplin's ragtime syncopation and performed his compositions. Brun Campbell identified the band as the "first 'Street and Parade Band' in America to play Joplin's 'Maple Leaf Rag.'" Joplin subsequently took five members of the band to found the "first ragtime orchestra in America," according to Campbell (Campbell 1985, 151).

Near the turn of the century, many New Orleans brass bands drifted away from performing marches toward rags. After 1895, recalled cornetist Manuel Perez, New Orleans band masters Lorenzo Tio Sr. and Charles Doublet "usually played polkas and schottisches but they let themselves be tempted by the infatuation of the audiences and went along with the new music. . . . They constituted the link," he asserted, "between popular music and ragtime" (Gushee 1994, 17). Buddy Bolden played his cornet in a ragtime style on some numbers. Besides describing Bolden as an extremely loud, wild, and flashy player, contemporaries tagged him as "a ragtime cornet player" (Shapiro and Hentoff 1955, 37, 38). His "Buddy Bolden's Blues," otherwise known as "Funky Butt," originated from the 1904 rag, "St. Louis Tickle," which in turn came from the older 1899 rag,

"The Cake Walk in the Sky" by Ben Harney. Edward "Kid" Ory, the trombonist discovered by Buddy Bolden, advertised his group on a horse-drawn wagon as "Kid Ory and His Ragtime Band." His group played "Maple Leaf Rag," "Climax Rag," and other syncopated rags in addition to more traditional marching-band standards. "With bands like Happy Galloway's, Manuel Perez's and Buddy Bolden's we had the best ragtime music in the world," asserted Jelly Roll Morton (Lomax 1950, 13).

When bands burst into ragtime numbers, audiences created more new dances for the music. They gyrated to the Turkey Trot, which consisted of a marching one-step with arms periodically flapping on the sides like turkey wings. Imported from San Francisco in 1910, the dance hit New York City in the show *Over the River*. Others lurched like bears at one another in the Grizzly Bear, another dance from the West Coast that had been introduced in 1911. Still others pranced to the Monkey Glide, the Chicken Scratch, the Bunny Dip, and the Texas Tommy, the last involving three hop-skips and a slide, sometimes followed by acrobatic moves. Between 1912 and 1914, more than one hundred new dances appeared in American ballrooms and cabarets.

The dances transformed social interactions between men and women on the dance floor. Previously, dances involved groups of people who fashionably moved around in set patterns. The new steps focused on two individuals who demonstrated their athletic abilities. Pushing couples to closer physical contact than before, the dances challenged the prevailing Victorian morality.

Two dancers, Vernon and Irene Castle, brought the ragtime-inspired dances to the white mainstream by reworking them for greater social acceptability. In 1911, the English-born Vernon Castle married Irene Foote, the eighteen-year-old daughter of a New Rochelle doctor. After forming a dance team and returning from Paris to New York in late 1912, the couple took New York by storm. They appeared on Broadway, produced dance instruction films, and provided advice to a growing fan base in newspapers and magazines. The duo moved to the beat of ragtime dance bands. "When a good orchestra plays a 'rag' one has simply *got* to move," insisted Vernon (Erenberg 1975, 156).

The Castles toned down many of the dances, which had originated in saloons and red-light districts. They added European elements to African-American-inspired ragtime steps to make the dances respectable for most sectors of white society. The high-society theatrical and literary agent Elisabeth Marbury who championed the Castles during their heyday described the contribution of the Castles succinctly: "The dance craze sweeping America needed regulation, an uplifting influence to bring dignity to it," she explained. "Castle House," established in 1913 as the team's headquarters and training facility, will "be that uplift, a place where their children could go to learn the dance without being exposed to the discredited elements" (Erenberg 1975, 161). Irene Castle clearly outlined her motivation in *Dancing Times*: "We get our new dances from the Barbary Coast [the red-light district in San Francisco]. Of course, they reach New York in a very primitive condition, and have to be considerably toned down before they can be used in the drawing room" (163).

The Castles successfully refashioned ragtime dance through the Fox Trot. In 1913, the dance duo performed the Turkey Trot in the Broadway show, *The Sunshine Girl*. A few months later in their book, *Modern Dance*, they instructed their readers not to "wiggle the shoulders. Do not shake the hips. Do not twist the body. Do not flounce the elbows. Do not pump the arms. Do not hop—glide. Avoid low, fantastic acrobatic dips." The Castles specifically urged dancers to "drop the Turkey Trot, the Grizzly Bear, the Bunny Hug, etc. These dances are ugly, ungraceful and out of fashion" (Castle 1914, 177).

To replace dances that seemed vulgar to them, the dance team wedded the one-step and 4/4 time of the "ugly" Turkey Trot with the smooth, slower movement of the waltz to create the somewhat sedate Fox Trot, which became the most popular dance in America. One day during a break, the dance team heard a slow version of the blues played by James Reese Europe, the classically trained African-American bandleader and musical director for the Castles. "He did this so often that the Castles became intrigued by its rhythm, and Jim asked why they didn't originate a slow dance adaptable to it," remembered W. C. Handy, a friend of Europe's (Handy 1941, 233). The Castles took their musical director's advice and created the Fox Trot, which sanitized the Turkey Trot and swept the nation. "The Turkey Trot," reported the *New York Times* on January 4, 1914, "smacked strongly of the Dahomey-Bowery-Barbary Coast form of revelry, but since then it has been trimmed, expurgated and spruced up until now it is a quite different thing." "The fox-trot, which appeared about 1914," echoed the *American Mercury*, "is the culmination of a tendency in American dancing that has been active ever since ragtime was invented in the early years of the century" (Thompson 1924, 465).

The Piano, Pianolas, and the Sheet-Music Boom

Amid the turn-of-the-century ragtime boom, a rage over pianos and sheet music catalyzed its development. The inexpensive upright piano became extremely popular during the era. In 1870, Americans bought approximately twenty-five thousand pianos a year. During the next few years, salesmen traveled door to door in all types of neighborhoods and sold instruments on installment plans for only a few pennies a month. Meanwhile, music-store outlets such as the Jesse French Company offered pianos and organs to customers for less than $100.

Within twenty years, the market for pianos exploded. The prices for pianos plummeted to as low as $25, and sales in the United States more than doubled to seventy thousand annually. By 1903 at the height of ragtime, Americans bought nearly three hundred fifty thousand pianos a year. *The Etude* magazine called the phenomenal increase "a quiet revolution" and observed that "pianos are becoming so cheap that literally everybody can afford to own one" (Curtis 1994, 108). By 1915, 250 companies manufactured pianos and several firms such as Starr, Wurlitzer, Continental, and Baldwin dominated the market.

Amid the ragtime craze, African-American families as well as white households bought pianos. As early as August 1894, the *Leavenworth Herald* proclaimed that "it's a mighty poor colored family that hasn't got some kind of tin pan called piano nowadays" (Seroff and Abbott 1999, 123). According to William "Count" Basie, his childhood home had a "piano, like most big houses used to have in those days—it was almost like a regular part of the furniture" (Basie 1985, 44). "In the years before World War I," related ragtime and stride pianist James P. Johnson, "there was a piano in every home, colored or white. The piano makers had a slogan: 'What Is a Home Without a Piano?'" (Davin 1985, 171).

Many of the people in homes with newly purchased pianos played ragtime tunes. In December 1894, the *Leavenworth Herald* reported that "Kansas City girls can't play anything on piano except 'rags'" (Seroff and Abbott 1999, 123). "Pass along the streets of any large city on a summer evening when the windows are open and take note of what music you hear being played," echoed *The Etude* in early 1899. "It is no longer the great masters or the lesser classicists," it lamented. "Not a bit of it! It is rag-time" (Curtis 1994, 109).

To fuel the American passion for ragtime piano, entrepreneurs published sheet music for amateur pianists; as the number of pianos soared, the sheet-music business expanded. In 1885, John Stillwell Stark, a Kentuckian who had fought in the Civil War, traveled to Sedalia, Missouri, to start a music store on Ohio Street with his son Will. By 1899, he had begun a music-publishing business, when Scott Joplin approached him to publish "Maple Leaf Rag." Through his ceaseless and very successful promotion of the piece, Stark became a national leader in ragtime sheet music, and by the next year moved with Joplin to expand his business in the more populated St. Louis. Stark continued to publish a plethora of ragtime hits and provided a generous royalty rate to his largely African-American composers on the sales of sheet music. In 1905, he migrated to New York City to better market his songs. Though never becoming a major player in the sheet-music business, Stark published more than 115 ragtime works. In addition to works by Scott Joplin, he printed and promoted rags by the other two composers who formed the "Big Three" ragtime composers: the Missouri-born, African-American James Scott who hit with "Frog Legs Rag" after Joplin introduced him to Stark; and the white New Jerseyan Joseph Lamb, who in 1907 signed with Stark after a chance meeting with Joplin at the publisher's office.

Jerome Remick challenged Stark as the preeminent ragtime sheet-music publisher. Originally from Detroit, in 1902 he established the New York City–based Shapiro-Remick & Company, which produced the massive sentimental hit song, "Under the Old Apple Tree." In 1905, when ragtime had become popular, he hired ragtime composer Charles Daniels as a manager and began publishing rags. By the end of the era, he had surpassed Stark by marketing more than three hundred ragtime compositions.

Like piano salesmen, sheet-music publishers and composers used a variety of strategies to sell their products. Some canvassed neighborhoods with sheet music. African-American pianist, cabaret manager, music publisher, and talent scout Clarence Williams initially went "from door to door with my music. I'd knock on a door and say, 'I've got a new song. It's only ten cents.' And they'd say, 'Come on in.' I'd sit down at the piano and play and sing and pretty soon the neighbors would be in and I'd be sellin' plenty of copies" (Shapiro and Hentoff 1955, 58). Specialty music stores carried sheet music along with their musical instruments and employed piano players and singers who performed well-known songs for their clientele.

Some larger publishing houses opened stands for sheet music in department stores, most notably the F. W. Woolworth Company, which pioneered set-price items for sale initially at five and ten cents. Jerome Remick first stocked Woolworth stores with sheet music. Other publishers such as Leo Feist soon followed suit. W. C. Handy—the composer of "St. Louis Blues" who in 1913 joined forces with Harry Pace to found the African-American-owned publishing firm of Pace and Handy—also sought out retailers. Writing in the African-American newspaper *Freeman*, Handy contended that "it is not always the publisher who has the finest list who succeeds most, but the one who finds the best market for his product. One of the best markets for music is the Woolworth Stores, which number more than 1,000 in America, besides many in Europe and Canada" ("Call" 1920, 5). With such competition at Woolworth, the standard cost of sheet music for a popular song sank and made ragtime tunes even more accessible to budding piano players. By 1910, the different outlets for sheet music sold more than two billion copies annually worth $5.5 million.

The mechanical player piano allowed Americans to hear ragtime piano in their homes without ever mastering the somewhat intricate ragtime on sheet music. In

1876 at the Centennial International Exhibition in Philadelphia to commemorate the Declaration of Independence, the first mechanical piano was unveiled to more than ten million people. It used punched rolls that activated individual keys to play a piece. Initially, the machines featured only fifty-eight or sixty-five keys, but by 1901 a full eighty-eight-key model, the Apollo, became standard fare.

In 1897, the New York–based Aeolian Company commercially launched its own version of the player piano, perfected by Edwin Votey. With a nearly unprecedented marketing campaign, the company offered it for $250 amid great hoopla. By 1903, the Aeolian Company boasted nine thousand rolls of music for player pianos. Within a year, more than forty player-piano manufacturers had opened their doors for business and within a decade had sold nearly a quarter million of the machines. Their owners could choose from hundreds of rolls for purchase at newly established department stores such as Sears, Roebuck and Montgomery Ward.

Though spanning all types of music, piano rolls featured more than a thousand different ragtime compositions on rolls for player pianos. Scott Joplin cut nearly thirty-five rolls for a variety of companies; James Scott offered the public a dozen rags; Joseph Lamb and Percy Wenrich each delivered more than twenty; and Charles L. Johnson produced fourteen, including the hot-selling "Dill Pickle Rag."

The Cylinder-Playing Phonograph and the Expansion of Ragtime

Nascent recording technology further popularized ragtime. In 1853, a thirty-six-year-old French printer and bookseller, Edouard-Leon Scott de Martinville, began to experiment with sound recordings. In March 1857, he received a patent for the first machine to capture sound. He called his device the phonoautograph, which consisted of lampblackened (charcoal-coated) paper or glass wrapped around a hand-cranked cylinder. Scott spoke into a diaphragm and simultaneously cranked the cylinder to record his voice, which was traced on the lampblack by a stylus. In 1860, he used the machine to immortalize the first song on record, a French folk tune, "Au Clair de la Lune." The inventor created the machine to visually record the voice but never explored a method to play back the sound.

In 1877, a young telegraph operator, Thomas Edison, developed an invention to play sound back as well as record it. Using the same methodology as Scott de Martinville, he wrapped tin foil around a hand-cranked metal cylinder to embed the vibrations of sound from a diaphragm and play them back for the first time. Edison initially used "the talking machine," which was eventually called a phonograph, to help the Metropolitan Elevated

A music cylinder (in man's hand) and player, 1885. *Library of Congress Prints and Photographs Division*

Railroad trace excessive noise on trains. Edison intended the machines to be used for dictation and other commercial purposes. Soon after, Alexander Graham Bell, flush with money from his success with the telephone, experimented with recording on wax rather than tin foil to produce better sound reproduction and allow reuse by shaving a layer of wax off the cylinder and then engraving new impressions. Bell's invention was dubbed the "graphophone." By 1887, Edison had developed his own version of a wax cylinder.

The Columbia Phonograph Company was founded in early 1889 to commercialize the cylinder music machines. Rather than using the devices for dictation as originally intended, Columbia recorded music on the cylinders. In 1890, Columbia produced the first music-cylinder catalog, which grew within three years to a thirty-two-page list of songs. Columbia aggressively marketed the Graphophone Type G Baby Grand players for $75 in popular magazines. Despite the depression of 1893, the company experienced a sales spurt and moved its headquarters from Washington, DC to New York City and opened five regional offices elsewhere. In 1896, Edison and Columbia engaged in a price war over the phonograph that led to a drop to around $7.50 to $10.00 for a machine. Within only a few years, the talking machine had become affordable to the general public.

By the turn of the century, cylinder manufacturers employed a time-intensive process to manufacture three hundred to five hundred cylinders a day in such broad categories as sentimental, topical, Negro, comic, and Irish songs to meet growing demand. Generally, a company hired a musician, singer, or spoken-word artist and positioned the person in the middle of a room with three recording diaphragms pointed toward them. The person then sang, played, spoke, or whistled as the machines recorded the performance, which only yielded three finished cylinders. To produce more, the performer needed to repeat the act, which made each cylinder almost unique. For each performance, the company paid the artist twenty cents. For example, in 1895, George Johnson, the first African-American recording artist, popularized a vaudeville tune, ironically the racist "Whistling Coon." To produce the twenty-five thousand cylinders that sold, Johnson had to repeat his performance more than eight thousand times by singing the song fifty times a day for several years.

Companies included popular ragtime tunes in their record catalogs. In 1898, Columbia hired pianist Len Spencer, who churned out such rags as "You've Got To Play Rag Time," "The Wench with the Rag Time Walk," and "Everything is Rag-Time Now." Around the turn of the century, the Edison Company recorded dozens of rags such as "Ragtime Medley," "Rastus Thompson's Rag-Time Cake Walk," and "Ragtime Liz." During the 1890s, the Talking Machine Company of Chicago signed pianists and bands for such songs as "That's One Thing Rag Time Will Do," "The Lady with a Rag Time Walk," and "Ma Rag Time Baby."

Records and the Gramophone

In 1887, Emile Berliner, a former employee of the National Bell Telephone Company, invented the flat disc to replace the cylinder. He replaced the up-and-down movement of a stylus on vertical grooves of a wax cylinder with the side-to-side motion of a stylus on lateral grooves of a flat disc. At first Berliner used celluloid as the disc material, but a few years later settled on a mix of shellac, cotton fibers, and pulverized rock such as slate and limestone for maximum durability, with a small amount of carbon to give the seven-inch discs a distinctive black color. To ensure a steady speed of approximately 70 revolutions per minute (rpm),

Berliner bought a wind-up, spring-driven motor from Eldridge Johnson, a machine-shop owner in Camden, New Jersey. He called his spring-powered, flat-disc machine the gramophone.

Unlike cylinders, discs could be duplicated en masse. In his process to produce multiple copies of a single recording, Berliner manufactured the flat discs from wax-coated glass, which captured the sound vibrations as a stylus moved through the wax. He then coated the completed wax disc with graphite and placed it in a copper sulfate or zinc solution. In a process called electroplating, developed in 1895, the copper adhered to the wax and created a metallic version of the wax platter. This "metal master" could be used to stamp multiple copies of a record rather than forcing an artist to repeat a performance over and over.

Berliner also produced multiple masters. He immersed the original master in a vat of copper sulfate, which created a mirror image in copper of the metal master with ridges instead of grooves. The inventor separated the metal master from the newly minted "mother master," which he used to churn out multiple metal masters that in turn could press hundreds of copies of one recorded performance. Through his efficient process, Berliner transformed the nature of recording and made discs cheaper. To prescient engineer Eldridge Johnson, the multiple metal-master process "changed the Gramophone or disc Talking Machine from a scientific toy to a commercial article of great value. It was the first and most important step in the evolution of the disc talking machine" (Schoenherr 1999, p. 5).

In 1896, Berliner received a US patent for his invention and began to wholesale his gramophones through Frank Seaman's National Gramophone

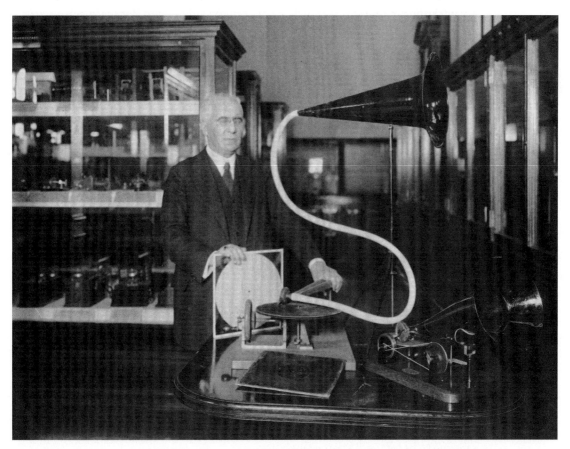

Emile Berliner with his flat disc and phonograph inventions. *National Photo Company Collection, Library of Congress Prints and Photographs Division*

Company. He charged $3 a machine and $1.50 for a dozen flat discs. In a typical music-business fiasco, Seaman stole Berliner's ideas, and by 1900 had driven the inventor out of business. Yet in an odd twist of fate, the next year Eldridge Johnson outmaneuvered Seaman through a series of legal battles and took over the manufacture of gramophones. The engineer called his business the Victor Talking Machine Company. Johnson quickly signed exclusive contracts with internationally known classical stars such as singer Enrico Caruso, violinist Jascha Heifetz, bandleader and composer Victor Herbert, and pianist Sergei Rachmaninoff to release their work.

In 1906, Victor introduced and promoted a new disc player, the Victrola. Victor employee Leon Douglass personally engineered the prototype of the machine because "ladies did not like mechanical looking things in their parlors" (Murphy 2014, 23). He placed the gramophone, a turntable base with an attached horn, in a stylish piece of furniture with the sound-producing horn in a box fronted by doors and underneath the turntable. To market the Victrola and Victor discs, Douglass designed a long-lasting, recognizable logo: he paid 100 British pounds for the use of a painting by Francis Barraud, titled *His Master's Voice*, which pictured a fox terrier intently listening to the horn of a gramophone. The image was placed on the label of each record and on the cover of every issue of a new industry magazine, *Talking Machine World*.

The public responded to Douglass's marketing campaign. By 1910, customers bought more than a hundred thousand Victor phonographs at $200 each. The next year, Americans eagerly purchased Victrolas, when the company marketed more affordable models that started at $15 for a table-top version. By 1914, buyers were snapping up more than two hundred fifty thousand Victrolas annually. To stock the record players, music lovers bought millions of flat discs, which virtually put an end to wax cylinders.

Though recording all musical genres, Columbia and Victor sold dozens of ragtime songs on flat discs. Columbia recorded "A Ragtime Skedaddle," Tom Turpin's "Buffalo Rag," a version of Scott Joplin's "Maple Leaf Rag," and "Florida Rag." Victor released two renditions of "Maple Leaf Rag," multiple rags by the Arthur Pryor band, "The Grand Old Rag," and Irving Berlin's hit "Alexander's Ragtime Band."

Ragtime pianists, now featured on new technologies, promoted the discs. For an in-store appearance in late spring 1916, composer Clarence Williams held a day-long demonstration of the song "Brown Skin, Who You For?" at Maison Blanche Department Store in New Orleans. Williams sang and played the piano with violinist and co-publisher/co-composer A. J. Piron to store customers, who could buy a copy of the song if they liked it. At the end of the day, the duo sold 976 records and more than four hundred player-piano rolls.

Ragtime had been fundamentally and irrevocably transformed through engineering breakthroughs such as piano rolls, cylinders, discs, and the phonograph. Before record technologies, all music existed as a live performance for a group of listeners in a specific time, never to be exactly replicated. With the advent of the cylinder and especially the mass-produced flat disc and the inexpensive phonograph, the performance was ripped from the moment and frozen in time. Music became a commodity that could be bought, shared, treasured, distributed, and heard at will by thousands of people who no longer had direct contact with the performer. Coupled with dance mania and visibility on steamboats and at national exhibitions, technological innovations helped African-American-created ragtime to become a national sensation.

For Discussion and Further Study

Chapter Quiz

1. What elements of European and African-American music are combined in the ragtime style?

2. How did ragtime composers like Scott Joplin reflect the philosophy of Booker T. Washington in their musical works?

3. What role did the growing urban centers and new modes of transportation play in the development of ragtime?

4. How did the new interest in rhythmic dancing foster the demand for ragtime piano players?

5. How did new means of recording and printing music help spread ragtime throughout the country?

THE JAZZ AGE AND THE TRANSFORMATION OF AMERICAN LIFE

White Bands, Urbanization, and a New Consumer Society

This chapter emphasizes the concepts of race and mass urbanization as they relate to jazz. In burgeoning urban cities like Chicago and New York City, white musicians from New Orleans such as the Original Dixieland Jazz Band took their hometown, African-American-inspired music and speeded it up to entertain masses of newly urbanized, largely white Americans who had recently moved from rural America. They inspired other white urban youth to form their own bands and launched a jazz craze among urban whites, who danced to the music and for the first time bought records by the millions along with other consumer goods. By incorporating aspects of African-American jazz into European orchestral music, white bandleader Paul Whiteman developed "symphonic jazz," which was embraced by millions of newly urbanized white Americans and made him the first musical "star" as jazz became a commodity in a new consumer-based society.

On May 13, 1915, trombonist Tom Brown and his New Orleans band arrived in Chicago. Each of the five young white men, ranging in age from twenty-two to twenty-seven, had paid twenty-five dollars for the train ride aboard the Illinois Central Railroad from their hometown to the Windy City, following the promise of lucrative work. The band consisted of Ray Lopez on cornet, pianist and string bass player Arnold Loyacano, Bill Lambert on drums, and eventually clarinetist Larry Shields. Many of them had started playing together in a New Orleans youth group organized by drummer George "Papa Jack" Laine who led the Reliance Brass Band and first popularized the turn-of-the-century ragtime and blues-infused New Orleans brass-band music among whites. The five-piece band left their hometown secretively because, according to Loyacano, "if we didn't make good and had to come back, that'd look pretty bad" (Shapiro and Hentoff 1955, 82).

The five young men found their new environment daunting. "We felt scared, sober and alone," confessed Lopez. They had landed in one of the largest and fastest-growing cities in the country with a population of more than two million. Coming from the balmy and more relaxed New Orleans with a population of less than three hundred fifty thousand, the band immediately felt the difference. "Lordy, it was cold," complained the cornetist. "The damn Yankee air cut through our thin suits, [and] everything was rush, rush, rush" (Sudhalter 1999, 6).

Four days later, "Brown's Band from Dixieland" opened at Lamb's Café in the basement of the Olympic Theater. Loyacano remembered Lamb's Café as a "beautiful place, with tile floors and marble all around the sides; every note you hit would reverberate back about six times" (Sudhalter 1999, 8). The group earned twenty-five dollars a week, a large sum compared to their dollar-a-night salary in New Orleans.

Replacing a string group that had previously performed at the café, the band initially sounded foreign and too boisterous to the patrons. "Remember that there had been a string ensemble playing there, and WE had been playing on the back of a wagon," chuckled Loyacano. "We couldn't play soft. Didn't know what soft was! Here we come with a trombone, clarinet and cornet. People held their ears and yelled, '*Too Loud*'" (Shapiro and Hentoff 1955, 81).

After a slow start during the first week, the roaring Tom Brown band settled into Lamb's. The group played at the swank Lamb's Café until late August, when it closed for renovation. By the time they left, the five musicians had caused a stir in Chicago.

Enthusiastic Chicagoans attached a new name to the music of the New Orleans group, which presented themselves as the "Ragtime Rubes" and "ragtime lugs." Patrons at Lamb's Café called the music "jass" or "jazz," one of the first times listeners had explicitly used the term for a musical group. "That's when people started calling our music 'jazz,'" explained Loyacano. "The way the Northern people figured it out, our music was loud, clangy, boisterous, like you'd say, 'Where did you get that jazzy suit?' meaning loud or fancy. Some people called it 'jass.' Later, when the name stuck, it was spelled with a 'z,' "jazz" (Shapiro and Hentoff 1955, 81). From the summer of 1915 onward, fans in Chicago referred to ragtime brass bands as jazz groups.

The Original Dixieland Jazz Band Starts a Jazz Boom

The Original Dixieland Jazz Band (ODJB), a five-piece ensemble, landed in Chicago nine months after Tom Brown and, through a series of fortuitous events, captured national attention. In late February 1916, drummer Johnny Stein organized a trip for his band aboard the Illinois Central Railroad, which originated in New Orleans and ended at Twelfth Street east of Michigan Avenue in Chicago. Besides their leader, the group included Alcide "Yellow" Nunez on clarinet; trombonist Eddie "Daddy" Edwards; pianist Henry Ragas; and the mercurial Dominic "Nick" LaRocca on cornet. Like the members of Tom Brown's outfit, many of the members had met in a New Orleans youth band organized by "Papa Jack" Laine. They called themselves Stein's Original Dixieland Band after their leader.

Several fateful circumstances brought the band to Chicago. According to Stein, "an actor named Gus Chandler asked me if I would like to go to Chicago with a hot band." When the drummer agreed, Chandler contacted Sam Hare, the manager of Schiller's Café in Chicago. Hare liked the idea, and the five New Orleans youths "left for Chicago to start our engagement at the Schiller" (Shapiro and Hentoff 1955, 82), which began on March 3.

Schiller's Café likely hired the group based upon the success of the Tom Brown band at Lamb's. Unlike the opulent Lamb's Café, Schiller's looked like a beaten-down relic reminiscent of many lower-class dives in Storyville. Rather than beauty graced with marble, it "was strictly a sawdust joint catering to a lot of pimps and whores," according to Ray Lopez (Shapiro and Hentoff 1955, 62).

Ironically, the seedy café helped promote Johnny Stein and his Original Dixieland Band. When women from the Anti-Saloon League protested in front of Schiller's a month after the band's debut, the *Chicago Herald* carried a story about the café and the band under the headline, "Sixty Women Rip Mask from Vice." "It was impossible for anyone to be heard," reported the newspaper. "The shriek of women's drunken laughter rivaled the blatant scream of the imported New Orleans Jass band." The outcry created "a sensation," Nick LaRocca recalled, and established the band's reputation in the Windy City (Sudhalter 1999, 11).

Only a week after achieving notoriety, Stein's band disintegrated and reformed, when the outspoken LaRocca and Stein clashed. "Without warning," complained Stein, "the four men left me holding the bag" (Shapiro and Hentoff 1955, 83). LaRocca joined forces with the remaining band members and eventually replaced Nunez with Larry Shields from the Tom Brown band and added drummer Anthony Sbarbaro, who had just arrived from New Orleans. As with most New Orleans bands, the group included a variety of musical styles in their show. It "played soft and ratty [ragtime]," disclosed trombonist Eddie Edwards. The outfit found work at the Del' Abe in the Hotel Normandy and the Casino Gardens in Chicago.

In mid-January 1917, the Original Dixieland Band moved from Chicago to New York City and national stardom. Helped by New York promoter Max Hart, the five musicians landed a job at Reisenweber's Café in Manhattan. The group delivered New Orleans brass-band ragtime augmented by clowning and stage antics common in vaudeville acts. Within a few weeks, the band packed customers into Reisenweber's. Patrons danced with abandon to the music. "There is one thing that is certain, and that is that the melodies as played by the Jazz organization . . . are quite conducive to making the dancers on the floor loosen up and go to the limit of their steppings," reported *Variety* (Stearns 1956, 155).

An enterprising Nick LaRocca, eager to enhance the band's reputation, wooed the fledgling New York–based recording industry. Then twenty-seven, LaRocca approached Columbia Records and secured a deal for the band. On January 31, 1917, the outfit entered the studio for Columbia, which promptly shelved the project and never issued the material. Not discouraged, LaRocca turned to Victor Records, the largest recording company at the time. On February 26, the band recorded two songs for Victor: the novelty tune "Livery Stable Blues," which featured standard ragtime fare interspersed with noises of cows, roosters, and horses that were simulated by the band's instruments; and "Dixie Jass Band One Step," which copied the introduction from ragtime composer Joe Jordan's "That Teasin' Rag."

The band capitalized on the newly minted term "jass," which a month earlier had been used on a ragtime Victor recording by the million-selling baritones Arthur Collins and Byron Harlan. To promote themselves as part of a new trend, the group used "jass" in the title of the second song and changed their name to the Original Dixieland Jass Band. When Victor released their two-sided disc on March 7, 1917, the ragtime-sounding brass band became the first group to record jazz music.

Original Dixieland Jazz Band. *Pictorial Press Ltd/Alamy Stock Photo*

LISTENING GUIDE 3

Original Dixieland Jazz Band

"LIVERY STABLE BLUES" (SOMETIMES CALLED "BARNYARD BLUES")

The Original Dixieland Jazz Band kicked off the jazz craze with this song. Ray Lopez and Alcide Nunez copyrighted the song, which may have been derived from an old rag called "Meat Ball," but likely most band members contributed to it. On February 26, 1917, the band recorded the tune for the Victor Talking Machine Company in New York City on the top floor of the Victor studio at 46 West Thirty-eighth Street. On the flip side of the disc, the band released "Dixieland Jass Band One-Step" for the first commercially released jazz record.

The twelve-bar-blues song begins with a four-bar introduction, followed by three sections that are each repeated twice. In the distinctive third "barnyard" theme, the clarinet of Larry Shields imitates a crowing rooster, the cornet of Nick LaRocca sounds like a whining horse, and Eddie Edwards's trombone approximates a braying donkey.

The song, though considered by some a novelty hit, has been widely recorded by such jazz luminaries as Benny Goodman, Fletcher Henderson, Bunny Berigan, Glen Gray and the Casa Loma Orchestra, and Jelly Roll Morton.

0:00–0:07	Four-bar introduction.
0:08–0:25	First section starts with LaRocca weaving his trumpet lines above and around the rest of the band. They all play different melodies, which intersect. The playing of multiple melodies simultaneously, present in most ragtime, is referred to as polyphony.
0:26–0:41	Restatement of the first section.
0:42–1:01	The thump of the bass drum establishes the heavy rhythm and starts the second section.
1:02–1:19	Restatement of second section.
1:20–1:35	A third section with band members imitating animals with their horns. This practice originated from an African tradition, and many New Orleans jazz men such as Joe "King" Oliver played such sound effects, which many called "freak music."
1:36–1:54	Restatement of third section.
1:55–2:11	First section repeated.
2:12–2:30	Second section repeated.
2:31–3:04	Animal-imitating section restated twice.
3:05–3:06	The brief ending.

Although the white ODJB was first to record, the Original Creole Band—an African-American outfit of New Orleans musicians headed by bassist Bill Johnson and featuring the cornet of Freddie Keppard—had been offered the opportunity to record before them. Around 1914, the ragtime-oriented brass band formed in Los Angeles and joined the Pantages vaudeville circuit. On August 7, 1914, the Los Angeles *Tribune* referred to the group as a "colored ragtime band." A few days later, the Los Angeles *Record* reported from ringside during a prize fight that "the New Orleans Creole band enlivened the proceedings by rendering a number of ripping good ragtime selections" (Gushee and Carr 1988, 98). In February 1915, the Original Creole Band opened in Chicago at the Grand Theater and the next year landed a spot in the *Town Topics* revue, which started in New York and then toured the country. By 1917, after another vaudeville tour, the New Orleans group ended in a New York City cabaret.

During their stint in a New York City nightclub, the band rejected an offer by the Victor Company to record. Keppard, contended New Orleans trumpeter Mutt Carey, "didn't want to do it because he was afraid that other musicians would steal his stuff" (Shapiro and Hentoff 1955, p. 45). On the other hand, Sidney Bechet dismissed the notion that Keppard feared losing his material. He said that the band members thought a record contract would turn their music "into a regular business, and after that it wouldn't be pleasure music." Facing the prospect of commercialization, he concluded, Freddie Keppard "just didn't care to [record], that was all" (Bechet 1960, 117). The Creole Band "would have been the first to record," insisted Jelly Roll Morton, who offered yet another hypothesis, "but the boys didn't want a percentage deal and held out for a flat fee" (Lomax 1950, 155).

Regardless of the reason that the Original Creole Band refused to record, the Original Dixieland Jazz Band released the first jazz record, which quite accidently reflected the hustle-bustle of the city. "When they went into the studio, they were given a choice: cut one chorus or play the whole thing faster" declared historian Rudi Blesh, who saw the band at their initial gigs in New York City. "They didn't play as fast at Reisenweber's as they did on those first recordings" (Sudhalter 1999, 17). The resulting hyperactive music defined the Dixieland genre.

The Original Dixieland Jazz Band ignited a "jass" mania with their peppy record. By the end of 1917, the kinetic two-sided disc became a bestseller, and the band appeared in the film *The Good for Nothing*. After an eighteen-month stint at Reisenweber's, the group embarked on a tour of Great Britain, where it performed at the London Hippodrome and at Buckingham Palace for King George V, who applauded wildly. Even in New Orleans, the group caught the interest of a young Louis Armstrong, who intently listened to the record with his wife on his upright Victrola. "The Jass band is the very latest thing in the development of music," boasted Victor Records (Ward and Burns 2000, 64).

The band continued to deliver hits. In October 1917, the band scored with "Darktown Strutter's Ball" and "Indiana," the two tunes originally recorded for Columbia and not initially released. The next year, the group released the successful "Tiger Rag" and "At the Jazz Band Ball," which reinforced their status as a "jazz" band. In 1921, the Original Dixieland Jazz Band released six more hits.

The White Dixieland Jazz Explosion

The frenetic, upbeat music of the Original Dixieland Jazz Band spawned other white jazz bands. Nick LaRocca sarcastically noted that groups of white musicians congregated in Chicago and New York City to "cash in on this jazz craze started by the Original Dixieland Jazz Band" (Sudhalter 1999, 16).

A US Army band in World War I at Camp Upton, Yaphank, Long Island, New York State, an example of the explosion of "jass" bands. *Bain Collection, Library of Congress Prints and Photographs Division*

The Original Memphis Five was one of the groups formed to ride the Dixieland wave. Irving Milfred "Miff" Mole, a trombonist from Long Island, New York, had studied with Charlie Randall, who had played in the John Philip Sousa Orchestra. In 1917, he and other budding musicians flocked to Reisenweber's restaurant to hear the Original Dixieland Jazz Band. At one performance, Mole met and forged a friendship with Filippo Napoli from Brooklyn who became professionally known as Phil Napoleon. Napoleon had left Brooklyn at the age of twelve and headed to New Orleans, where he became entranced with the local music and started to play cornet. Mole and Napoleon enlisted Napoleon's childhood friend, pianist Frank Signorelli, and various clarinetists and drummers to establish the Memphis Five, a name chosen to honor W. C. Handy and his Memphis-based band. During the winter of 1917 and into the next year, the fledging group toured the United States on an Orpheum Theater tour and visited Chicago and Los Angeles.

The band stood in awe of the Original Dixieland Jazz Band. "In those lean days," Napoleon wrote to LaRocca, "we, the Memphis Five, had only the Dixieland band to copy from and try to play the many things you all gave to the world. For without your band how would we have been able to make the little success we were able to get?" (Sudhalter 1999, 108). Considering the ODJB their mentors, the Memphis Five agreed not to directly compete with them. "Those guys would play their own stuff, their originals and jazzier novelties, and we'd concentrate on pop tunes," explained Napoleon. "That way, we'd never be in direct competition" (106).

After four years of live performances, the group released its first of many discs, "Shake It and Break It" backed by W. C. Handy's composition "Aunt Hagar's Children Blues." The band continued to record prolifically throughout the decade. "The Original Memphis Five," reported *Variety* on February 22, 1924, "have had the distinction of being the only orchestra to record for every phonograph company in existence."

The Georgians followed in the footsteps of the Original Dixieland Jazz Band. Orchestra leader Paul Specht, a violinist who had attended the Coombs Conservatory in Philadelphia, recognized the growing popularity of New Orleans–style jazz. In mid-1921, he asked trumpeter Frank Guarente, an Italian immigrant who had played in New Orleans before World War I, to pick four other musicians from his band and form a five-piece outfit similar to the ODJB. Guarente selected drummer Chancey Morehouse, clarinetist Johnny O'Donnell, Russell Deppe on banjo, and trombonist Ray Stillwell. The small band played the Dixieland style originally during the breaks of Specht's full orchestra and eventually as a stand-alone ensemble.

The New Orleans Rhythm Kings, NORK for short, coalesced around the same time. In 1919, trumpet player Paul Mares made the long journey from his New Orleans home to Chicago to work with drummer Mike "Ragbaby" Stevens in a New Orleans–style brass band. He subsequently left the city for a stint on a riverboat and in 1921 returned to Chicago.

Looking for a jazz band to play at his bar, the Friar's Inn, Mike Fritzel offered Mares a steady job for ninety dollars a week per person. Mares eagerly contacted a number of his friends. "I had gotten [clarinetist] Leon Roppolo up here and I sent for George Brunies to take the trombone chair," recollected Mares. The trumpeter also recruited pianist Elmer Schoebel, sax player Jack Pettis, Lou Black on banjo, Arnold Loyacano from the original Tom Brown band, and eventually drummer and arranger Ben Pollack. The band called themselves the New Orleans Rhythm Kings and played from eight o'clock in the evening to eight o'clock in the morning at the Friar's Inn (Shapiro and Hentoff 1955, p. 122).

The shabby Friar's Inn looked similar to the lowdown Schiller's Café that had served as the springboard for the Original Dixieland Jazz Band. Composer Hoagy Carmichael, then a law student at Indiana University, reported that "the place smelled just right—funky, run-down, sinister and dusty" (Sudhalter 1999, 32). "There was a post on one side of the bandstand," chuckled Mares, "and Roppolo used to play with his clarinet against it for tone" (Shapiro and Hentoff 1955, 122).

Friar's Inn helped shape the relaxed sound of the band. "You could almost reach up and touch the ceiling," related Loyacano. "If you played loud, you'd drive everyone out of the place" (Sudhalter 1999, p. 34). The low ceiling of the nightclub forced Mares to drape an old felt hat with a hole in it over his trumpet to dampen the volume. The venue seemed appropriate, when the band performed restrained ragtime versions of classical works such as Russian composer Nikolai Rimsky-Korsakov's "Song of India."

Though more sedate than fellow Dixielanders, NORK followed the basic style with a "good old Dixieland beat," according to Brunies (Sudhalter 1999, 37). In August 1922, during their first recording session at Gennett Studios, the band cut two songs previously released by the Original Dixieland Jazz Band as well as some originals by Schoebel.

The band also adopted the comedic vaudeville clowning of the ODJB. "Novelty was still the thing. So I thought up some stunts that I thought were nuts," confessed drummer Pollack. "First I palmed an iron drum key under the cymbal and got a ciss [sizzle effect] . . . Then I tried a fly swatter on a bass drum to get a bass-fiddle buzz" (Sudhalter 1999, 36). Musicians termed the effects "freak" and called musicians who used them "freak" players.

A group of young, future jazz stalwarts, nicknamed the Austin High Gang, idolized the New Orleans Rhythm Kings. Many of them attended Austin High School

LISTENING GUIDE 4

New Orleans Rhythm Kings

"FAREWELL BLUES"

The New Orleans Rhythm Kings played music similar to the ODJB. On August 29, 1922, they recorded this song at the Gennett Studios under the name Friars Society Orchestra. Composed by Elmer Schoebel, Leon Roppolo, and Paul Mares, the song is a sixteen-bar blues tune, which delivers many of the same musical elements as the ODJB. Subsequently, dozens of bands recorded the song, including King Oliver.

0:00–0:01	The song begins with a rousing cymbal blast to set the tone.
0:02–0:09	The band delivers multiple melodies on the clarinet, trombone, trumpet, and saxophone with the banjo strumming the rhythm.
0:10–0:28	The band plays the main melody together backed by the syncopated banjo rhythm.
0:29–0:51	The band restates the melody.
0:52–1:11	Clarinetist Loyacano first states the melody with the rhythmic banjo and then at 1:01 improvises an interesting solo, including a blue note at 1:08, that many musicians subsequently tried to copy.
1:12–1:32	Mares enters with a freak-like trumpet, which sounds like a wah-wah effect, and plays the melody in a solo. Note the cymbal crash at 1:28.
1:33–1:52	Mares repeats his statement of the melody with his trumpet. Note the cymbal crash again at 1:48.
1:53–2:13	After a loud, shrill exclamation by Mares, the band again weaves several melodies together in polyphony.
2:14–2:15	Two brief wah-wah bursts from Mares.
2:16–2:35	The band continues with multi-melodies, which at least partly defines early New Orleans jazz.
2:36–2:38	The band ends the song.

and, after classes, frequented the Spoon and the Straw, where they drank milk, sodas, and shakes. "They had a Victrola there, and we used to sit around listening to a bunch of records laid on the table," cornetist Jimmy McPartland reminisced. One day, the youths spun a disc by the New Orleans Rhythm Kings, "Farewell Blues." "When we heard that—I'll tell you we went out of our minds. Everybody flipped. It was wonderful," raved McPartland. The Austin High School chums played more records by the band and "stayed there from about three in the afternoon until eight at night, just listening to those records, one after another, over and over again," McPartland confessed. "Right then and there we decided we would get a band and try to play like these guys."

The boys found instruments and started to learn songs by their newfound heroes. Frank Teschemacher bought a clarinet, and Jim Lannigan picked the tuba. The McPartland brothers received instruments from their father, who taught music: Dick chose a bass and Jimmy selected a cornet. Bud Freeman purchased a saxophone from the elder McPartland. The band practiced ceaselessly from the moment school ended until midnight by listening to NORK records and learning them measure by measure (Shapiro and Hentoff 1955, 119). Within three weeks, the teenagers had mastered "Farewell Blues" and within a few months had memorized ten songs. The young musicians, after adding the bookish drummer Davey Tough, called themselves the Blue Friars and found work at their high school, weddings, fraternity parties, and even a Chinese restaurant. By 1923, Benny Goodman had joined practice sessions of the Austin High gang. Though never succeeding as a group, the young men individually helped chart the future of jazz.

A few of the early white jazz pioneers took credit for the creation of jazz despite its African-American origins. Tom Brown contended that "the colored are not responsible [for jazz]; the colored only played plantation [music]." Nick LaRocca became progressively more outspoken about his central role in the creation of jazz. He incorrectly asserted that jazz came from the white bands tutored by "Papa Jack" Laine. If African Americans had played "jazz in New Orleans I'm certain whites would have known about it," he proclaimed. LaRocca even alleged that the W. C. Handy song, "St. Louis Blues," had been written by a white because "that chord progression is not from Africa" (Peretti 1992, 80).

In reality, both white and African-American musicians who traveled from New Orleans to Northern cities intermingled with one another and mixed brass-band music, ragtime, and vaudeville elements into a new style. Larry Shields, tutored by "Papa Jack" Laine and an alumnus of both Tom Brown's band and the Original Dixieland Jazz Band, had been raised on the same block in New Orleans as African-American jazz legend Buddy Bolden. Leon Roppolo lived on the second floor of his father's saloon, where "every now and then a colored band would drop by to play a chorus as ballyhoo for a colored dance coming up or a prize fight" (Shapiro and Hentoff 1955, 58). As early as 1918, Miff Mole took the stage with African-American bandleader and cornetist King Oliver. Trumpeter Frank Guarente of the Georgians also played and became friends with Oliver, who performed at his twenty-first birthday party. Paul Mares, admiring King Oliver, proclaimed that "we did our best to copy the colored music we'd heard at home" (123). Living together, New Orleans African Americans and whites, especially whites from the lower rungs of the social ladder, transplanted their hometown music to the North, where it became known as jazz.

The Urbanization of America

Urbanization provided the context for the emergence of jazz. By packing millions of people into urban areas, the cataclysmic demographic shift to the cities led to the need for mass entertainment in urban nightspots and through recorded music. It created a market for jazz among consumers who shared a common urban culture. Increasingly crowded cities also resulted in a frenetic pace, which led to a predilection for fast-moving jazz.

At the turn of the twentieth century, a rural America gave way to an urban nation. Farming became less work intensive and needed fewer laborers per acre with the introduction of equipment such as tractors, trucks, harvesters, and threshers. Coupled with blights such as the boll weevil, the wide use of farm machinery pushed people from farms to burgeoning cities. By 1910, only 33 percent of working Americans remained in rural areas.

During World War I, urbanization progressed rapidly. As the demand rose for workers to manufacture goods for the war effort, the United States government constricted the labor supply by barring immigration into the country. As early as 1916, President Woodrow Wilson warned against immigrants who "poured the poison of disloyalty into the very arteries of our national life. . . . Such creatures of passion, disloyalty and anarchy," Wilson argued, "must be crushed out" (Kennedy 1980, 24). Lawmakers backed Wilson with legislation. In 1917, Congress passed the Immigration Act, which banned Asian newcomers. The next year, the anti-immigrant Sedition Act targeted recent Eastern European migrants, who espoused politically radical beliefs, and organizations such as the International Workers of the World labor union. In 1921, Congress passed the Immigration Enactment Act, which limited immigration of a nationality to 3 percent of its population in 1890.

By the early 1920s, immigration into the United States had nearly ground to a halt. In 1907, 706,000 people annually migrated to the United States, mostly from Eastern Europe. Ten years later, newcomers to America slowed to 116,000 and the next year reached a low point at 85,000.

The ban on immigration amid the war resulted in a profound labor shortage in urban areas. On September 14, 1918, the *New York Times* reported about the "serious shortage of unskilled labor in industries in New York State engaged in the production of war materials." It estimated an immediate need for 350,000 workers and a "constantly increasing" demand ("Labor Shortage Here" 1918). By 1920, many desperate manufacturers had hiked hourly wages paid to unskilled laborers by 17 percent over the previous six years.

Faced with far more limited opportunities on farms due to mechanization and more lucrative jobs in the cities, white and African-American rural families migrated to the urban North in great numbers. From 1910 to 1920, rural white migrants to Chicago numbered 456,000; more than 492,000 flocked to Detroit; 790,000 arrived in New York City; Philadelphia saw a population increase of more than 221,000; and 218,000 migrants made Cleveland their home. The same population spike occurred in every major city of the country. By 1920, more than 75 percent of American workers lived in urban areas.

Many observers at the time equated jazz with the hustle and bustle caused by urbanization. As early as March 29, 1913, *Musical America* condemned jazz as the pillager of "the idyllic village atmosphere" and contended that it "exalts noise, rush and street vulgarity." Ten years later on November 10, the same magazine alleged that "jazz expresses merely the easy joy, insouciance, vulgarity and love of motion characteristic of America's big cities."

The hustle-bustle of State Street in Chicago at noon, 1908. *Photograph by Underwood & Underwood. Library of Congress Prints and Photographs Division*

The Consumer Culture

A consumer culture arose due to urbanization. In tightly packed urban areas, food, clothes, and other essentials needed to be purchased from stores rather than grown or made at home. Ease of consumption, familiarity of certain brands, and uniformity of prepackaged products came to define the lives of residents in a bustling metropolis. Even entertainment, including jazz, moved from being a local, neighborhood activity to a nationally recognized commodity, which record companies and nightclubs sold to the public.

Woolworth's catered to masses of urbanites who purchased goods off the shelf rather than handing a clerk a list of needed items. Successfully launched by Frank Woolworth in 1879, the store stocked goods on racks in a self-service model and undercut local merchants by charging just five or ten cents for their products.

Besides pioneering the self-serve discount store, Woolworth masterminded the franchising and chain-store concepts. Expanding from a single store, Frank Woolworth established a series of Woolworth stores in other towns. He selected a uniform set of merchandise to maximize volume buying, and through franchising— licensing the store's name and controlling the merchandise offered—spread to more locations. In 1912, six franchises owning 596 stores merged to form the F. W. Woolworth Company. Stores in the nationwide chain featured the same bright lighting, glass dividers, sparkling wood floors, and merchandise displays to reassure consumers with a standard look and feel. For urban dwellers, the chain-store strategy offered a comforting, recognizable, and dependable way to shop.

During the war, the grocery business adopted the customer-focused, centralized retail model Woolworth had developed. Started in 1916 at Piggly Wiggly by owner and entrepreneur Clarence Saunders, the self-service grocery store streamlined food shopping by allowing consumers to pick out their own food. By the end of the 1920s, nearly all urban grocery stores had embraced the Piggly Wiggly model. Some established chains to create a uniformity of items and allow volume buying. Ralphs' Grocery Company in California, founded by George Ralphs in 1909, spread throughout the Los Angeles area and, by 1928, included the first supermarket in the country.

Sears, Roebuck & Company sold urban dwellers clothes and needed household items. Founded by Richard Sears and Alvah Roebuck as a mail-order business in 1893, the company first served Americans in rural areas who could not easily find desired items in their local general stores and used the Sears catalog religiously to purchase unique items such as sewing machines, heavy overcoats, and musical instruments. Sears eventually created a highly efficient system for scheduling and delivering orders to serve a widely dispersed rural customer base ("Sears History—1925" 2012).

Amid urbanization, Sears shifted its business strategy. On February 2, 1925, with the influx of rural families into Chicago, the company opened its first retail store. By the end of 1927, Sears, Roebuck & Company had opened twenty-seven stores, and two years later it offered goods to urban consumers at 319 retail outlets. By 1931, retail sales at Sears outpaced its catalog sales and reflected the shift from rural to urban America.

Consumers acquired a broad array of electric home appliances at Sears and other chains as the price of electricity plummeted. In 1913, Fred W. Wolf invented the electric refrigerator for domestic use, and by 1925 thousands of consumers had bought them. By 1928, nearly a million Americans proudly owned an electric washing machine. Others purchased "motor-driven brush and suction cleaners," soon called vacuum cleaners, such as the Hoover Electric. Some city dwellers obtained electric popcorn makers, two-slice bread toasters, and electric waffle makers.

Driven by an urge to buy, from 1912 to 1921 Americans purchased approximately $11 billion in consumer goods.

Companies stoked the interest in consumer goods through advertising. Touting their prepackaged products through ads in newspapers and such magazines as *The Ladies' Home Journal*, businesses tried to harness human instincts by "sublimating" or redirecting the desires of people to purchase their wares. Modern advertising, as pioneered by Edward Bernays for the tobacco industry, created a craving for specific products among targeted consumers. After 1917, when they received a federal tax deduction for advertising, firms expanded their ad campaigns to further a consumer culture.

Urban Americans used credit to buy goods that they wanted but did not necessarily need. As predicted by Thorstein Veblen in *The Theory of the Leisure Class* (1899), they consumed "conspicuously" for status. Urbanites purchased the latest fashions and gadgets and compared their material possessions to those of their relatives, friends, and work mates. One young woman captured the status-driven mindset of many twenties shoppers, when she bragged about her "flowered dress with kind of a lace trim" that made her feel "like a millionaire in it." She commented that "I don't care what you say: a homemade dress is a homemade dress, and a boughten dress is a boughten dress" (Murphy 1996, 55).

The automobile, first manufactured in the United States in 1893 by the Duryea Brothers of Springfield, Massachusetts, emerged as the ultimate symbol of mass production and consumer status. Introduced in 1902 by Ransom Olds at his Oldsmobile factory in Lansing, Michigan, the mass production of automobiles allowed many consumers to purchase a car at a reasonable price. In 1909, a year after he inaugurated the easy-to-operate Model T, Henry Ford promised to "build a motor car for the great multitude. It will be large enough for the family, but small enough for the individual to run and care for. It will be so low in price that no man making a good salary will be unable to own one," he vowed (Jackson 1985, 160). When Ford perfected the moving auto assembly line by 1914, cars rolled out of the factory at a rate of four per hour. By 1927, more than 20 million cars rode the roads in the United States, and 55 percent of all American families owned a car. "America is turning out her merchandise at an unprecedented speed and motor cars are racing along the roads," wrote one commentator in 1926. "Amid this seething, bubbling turmoil jazz harried along its course riding exultingly on the eddying stream" (Ward and Burns 2000, 102).

Jazz in a Consumer Society

Consumer interest in entertainment led to the growth of the music industry and a heightened interest in jazz. In 1914, Americans spent $27 million on phonographs; five years later, they purchased 2.2 million of the machines for $158 million. By 1921, one out of every seventy-two Americans owned a phonograph.

Two major labels built a national production and distribution system to stock record players. Despite the growth of small, independent labels to service niche audiences, Victor and Columbia dominated the marketplace with a national reach. In 1921, the largest company, Victor, posted sales of $51 million or 32 percent of the $159 million in total record purchases. Together, Victor and Columbia earned more than half of industry gross revenues.

Records distributed nationally helped to create an American popular culture. Rather than focus on local musicians, top-selling discs featured musicians and singers who consumers had never met or seen. Musical entertainment, especially in the cities, fundamentally shifted from a local, live experience to participation in a national phenomenon mediated by technology. By the end of the 1920s, one sociologist observed that the music people "listen to comes essentially from the outside, its character is cosmopolitan and national" (Cohen 1989, 9).

The Education of Paul Whiteman

Although not the first to record a jazz disc, Paul Whiteman recast jazz as a national music amid the consumer culture in urban America. Selling millions of records and revered by the public, he surfaced as the first jazz "star" and arguably one of the original icons of popular culture. By the middle of the twenties, Paul Whiteman became the "King of Jazz" by offering a melodic, orchestrated version of the Dixieland sound to the urban masses.

Whiteman adopted a jazz style gradually. Born in Denver, Colorado, to a father who was the supervisor of music for the Denver Public Schools, he played the viola as a youth. In 1907 at the age of seventeen, he joined the Denver Symphony Orchestra, in which he amused his fellow musicians by "ragging" the classics. In 1914, Whiteman moved to San Francisco, where he performed with the prestigious San Francisco Symphony Orchestra, and served as the chair of the Minetti String Quartet. While in the city, he visited the seedy, red-light district of the Barbary Coast, where he heard and became enamored with jazz. Whiteman saw that "men and women were whirling and twirling feverishly there." The music sounded "raucous? Yes. Crude—undoubtedly, unmusical—sure as you live. But rhythmic, catching as the small-pox and spirit–lifting. That was jazz," he gushed (Whiteman and McBride 1926, 35).

Bandleader Art Hickman likely introduced Whiteman to jazz. As a messenger boy for Western Union, Hickman longed "to deliver a message to some hop joint, or honky-tonk in the Barbary Coast," he reminisced to the *San Francisco Examiner* on April 11, 1928. "There was music. Negroes playing it. Eye shades, sleeves up. Cigars in mouth. Gin and liquor and smoke and filth. But music! This is where all jazz originated." Excited by jazz in the red-light district, Hickman snagged a job as a drummer and pianist, worked as a journalist for several music publications, and managed three vaudeville theaters in Sacramento and his hometown of San Francisco. By January 1915, Hickman established his own band and grabbed a long-term residency at the Rose Room of the St. Francis Hotel in San Francisco.

The bandleader made several groundbreaking changes to the music that he had heard in dives at the Barbary Coast. Rather than front the standard five-piece group, Hickman organized a ten-piece band for a fuller sound. He added two saxophones, an instrument that had been patented by Adolphe Sax in 1846 and had first become popular only a few years before the Hickman band with the Six Brown Brothers, who used it in their vaudeville and circus acts. Hickman used the saxophones as lead instruments to replace the trumpet/cornet, which had been dominant in almost all smaller nascent jazz groups. The bandleader separated the instruments into sections for a call-and-response between them to enhance the surging, pulsating rhythm of jazz. In addition, Hickman shed the novelty shrieks and animal sounds of bands such as the Original Dixieland Jazz Band for a more smooth-sounding and professional version of jazz. "Jazz is merely noise, a product of the honky-tonks, and has no place in a refined atmosphere," sniffed Hickman to a reporter for *Talking Machine World* on July 7, 1920. "I have tried to develop an orchestra that charges every pulse with energy without stooping to the skillet beating, sleigh bell ringing contraptions and physical gyrations of a padded cell." By the end of World War I, Hickman had developed a new style of jazz. "Everybody—I mean players, arrangers and leaders of bands," remembered arranger Robert Haring Sr., "was talking about Hickman. What he was doing was utterly unprecedented" (Sudhalter 1999, 160).

By 1918, news of Hickman reached New York City, the recording capital of the world, where he caused a stir. A year later, the Hickman group contracted with Columbia, which brought the band to New York City in a private Pullman car, and in September they cut twenty-one titles. While in New York, the Hickman orchestra played on the roof of the New Amsterdam Hotel for Broadway king Florenz Ziegfeld and at a homecoming event for famed World War I General John "Black Jack" Pershing. The next year, the group returned to New York City for the *Ziegfeld Follies of 1920*, in which it shared the stage with comedian and singer Fannie Brice, singer-dancer-comedian Eddie Cantor, and comedian W. C. Fields. The band's recordings produced two top hits, "Hold Me" and "The Love Nest." Though wildly successful in New York, by the end of 1920 Hickman inexplicably returned to San Francisco and largely faded from public view.

The Whiteman Band

After hearing Hickman in San Francisco, Whiteman formed his own band, moved to New York City, and became the most prominent purveyor of a smooth, orchestral jazz. He slowly expanded the number of orchestra members from nine to thirty and, drawing from his own background, added violins and cellos. Rather than ask players to start with a theme and embellish it, the bandleader hired arranger and pianist Ferde Grofe to compose music for the orchestra. He unabashedly blended jazz rhythms with a classical approach that the *Talking Machine Journal* referred to as "jazz classique" in November 1920. "What we have played is 'syncopated rhythm,'" Whiteman explained in 1923, "and our orchestrations have always been worked out with all the color and beauty of symphonies." He called his concoction "symphonic syncopation" (Kenney 1993, 79) and hoped to combine the power of a large ensemble with the energy of a small jazz band. To achieve his artistic goals, Whiteman employed musicians steeped in the classics. He favored classical artists because "men taken from symphonies are the easiest to train." In contrast, he contended that "the real blues player is more hidebound in his way than the symphony man" (Whiteman and McBride 1926, 241–42).

The bandleader snagged some musicians who became future jazz leaders. In the mid-1920s, he hired cornetist Ernest "Red" Nichols, one of the most prolifically recorded and commercially successful jazz men of the decade who gained fame as the leader of the Five Pennies. Whiteman added trombonist and future swing star Tommy Dorsey. In 1929, he enlisted Eddie Lang (b. Salvatore Massaro) who became a pioneer of jazz guitar. The same year, jazz violinist Joe Venuti joined his friend Lang in the Whiteman orchestra.

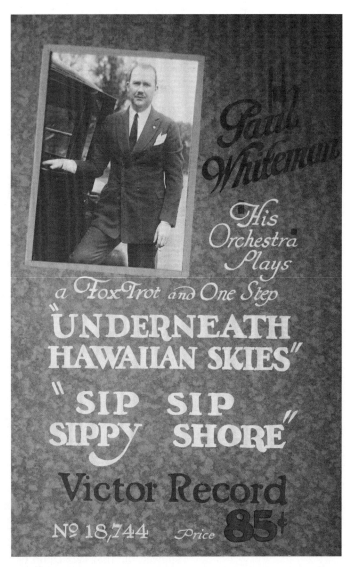

Paul Whiteman sheet music, 1921. *Bain Collection, Library of Congress Prints and Photographs Division*

Two of the most revered white soloists of the era, Frank Trumbauer and Leon "Bix" Beiderbecke, joined the Whiteman fold. Trumbauer grew up in St. Louis and learned the difficult C-melody saxophone, which tended to produce a "mooing" sound unless played extremely well. In 1923, he recorded with Edgar Benson and wove a groundbreaking, lilting solo on "I Never Miss the Sunshine." The next year, the saxophonist connected with the then-popular Mound City Blue Blowers, a St. Louis novelty group featuring kazoo and banjo. In 1926, he joined the Jean Goldkette Orchestra as musical director.

By the mid-1920s, Trumbauer, or Tram as his friends called him, had become well known in the jazz community. "After hearing those old Trumbauer records," remarked saxophonist Benny Carter, who played with several notable African-American bands, "I got very excited about the saxophone. Very early on, it became my goal to play like him" (Kennedy 1994, 115). "There was only one guy to follow, to play like, and that was Frankie," he added (Tynan 1958, 15). "At that time, Frankie Trumbauer was the baddest cat around," agreed African-American sax player Albert "Budd" Johnson, who performed with Louis Armstrong and pianist Earl Hines. "Everybody dug Frankie Trumbauer. He had recorded a solo on a tune called 'Singin' the Blues,' and everybody memorized that solo" (Zwerin 1968, 19). African-American saxophonist Lester Young, who later played with Count Basie, said, "Trumbauer was my idol. When I had just started to play, I used to buy all his records" (Hentoff 1956b, 9).

Bix Beiderbecke followed his friend and band mate Frankie Trumbauer to the Jean Goldkette Orchestra. Bix, a self-taught piano prodigy in his home of Davenport, Iowa, became excited about jazz when he heard records by the Original Dixieland Jazz Band, which inspired him to learn the cornet and pursue the new music. The fifteen-year-old jazz fanatic also heard cornetists Louis Armstrong and Emmett Hardy when they docked in town during riverboat tours. "He'd come to hear the bands, and then go home to practice what he heard," recalled Armstrong (Sudhalter and Evans 1974, 39). In 1921, after a rebellious Bix refused to concentrate on his high-school studies, his middle-class parents shipped him to Lake Forest Academy, a prep school about an hour from Chicago.

In the Windy City, Bix concentrated on music. He heard the New Orleans Rhythm Kings during frequent visits to the Friars Inn, where he met pianist Hoagy Carmichael. When Lake Forest Academy expelled Beiderbecke in May 1922, he packed his bags for Chicago, where he listened to the King Oliver band with its new cornet player, Louis Armstrong. When Armstrong sped through a high-octane solo on "Bugle Call Rag," remembered Carmichael, Bix "was on his feet, his eyes popping" (Shapiro and Hentoff 1955, p. 141).

In late 1923, Bix banded together with six other Chicago jazz players. They found work at the Stockton Club in Hamilton, Ohio, where they named themselves the Wolverine Orchestra in honor of the Jelly Roll Morton song, "Wolverine Blues," which that year had been recorded by the ODJB. When the Stockton Club burned to the ground amidst a fight on New Year's Eve, the band moved to Doyle's Dance Academy in downtown Cincinnati, where they delivered a jazz patterned after the New Orleans Rhythm Kings.

The Wolverines traveled to Richmond, Indiana, to record for Gennett Records. On February 18, 1924, they cut four songs from the repertoire of the Original Dixieland Jazz Band, two of which Gennett released: "Jazz Me Blues" and "Fidgety Feet." The two sides showcased the melodic, smooth, rounded tone of the cornetist. "He selected each note with musical care," explained Hoagy Carmichael. "He showed me that jazz could be musical and beautiful as well as hot. He showed me that tempo doesn't mean fast" (Carmichael 1969, 54). In May, the band returned

Bix Beiderbecke and the Wolverines in Ohio, 1924. Bix is the fourth from the left in the first row.

to Gennett to wax four more songs, which included "Riverboat Shuffle," the first Carmichael composition. Hoagy later gained fame with compositions such as "Stardust" and "Georgia on My Mind."

For the next several months, Beiderbecke drifted between bands. In late 1924, he joined the Jean Goldkette Orchestra, which promised him more money than the neophyte Wolverines could muster. Within only a few weeks, the cornetist left the band at the insistence of Goldkette, when it became apparent that he could not read music. Bix then received a call from Trumbauer who asked him to join his orchestra in St. Louis. For eight months, he stayed with the nine-piece outfit and learned to read music. In May 1926, Bix rejoined the Goldkette ensemble under Trumbauer's lead.

On October 27, 1927, after Goldkette dissolved his band, Bix and Trumbauer quickly signed with the Whiteman Orchestra. "When Bix and I played the Graystone Ballroom in Detroit, and Whiteman was in the balcony, I was leading the band," remembered Trumbauer. "Backstage after a set, Bix said to me, 'That is our next move'" (Shapiro and Hentoff 1955, p. 152).

Both Trumbauer and Beiderbecke perfectly suited the lush Whiteman style. When relaxing, remarked Trumbauer, the two friends generally "listened to symphonies that we liked" (Shapiro and Hentoff 1955, p. 150). Bix especially found the classics compelling. According to bandleader Paul Whiteman, Beiderbecke "was crazy about the modern composers—Schoenberg, Stravinsky and Ravel" (155). "Bix liked little things like some of those compositions of MacDowell and Debussy—very light things. Delius, for example," remembered clarinetist Pee Wee Russell, who played with Bix. "Then he made a big jump from that sort of thing to Stravinsky and stuff like that" (155). Late in his career, the cornetist spoke to Jimmy McPartland "about writing a jazz symphony" (157).

By the end of the decade, Beiderbecke's peers lavishly praised the ballad-like smoothness and polished tone of Bix, who defined a "lovely jazz." Jimmy McPartland felt that "almost any jazz musician—besides all the brass men—have one way or another been influenced by Bix" (Shapiro and Hentoff 1955, pp. 140, 157). Even Louis Armstrong, one of Bix's idols, paid homage to his fellow cornet player, when he called Bix "a great cornet genius. Every musician in the world knew and admired Bix," he explained. "We all respected him as though he had been a god" (Armstrong 1955, 164).

Whiteman ensured a steady stable of virtuoso talent such as Beiderbecke by compensating his men very well. In 1924, he paid saxophonist Ross Gorman nearly fifty thousand dollars a year, and generally gave band members at least three times the amount earned by jazz musicians in other dance bands. In January 1928, he paid Beiderbecke and Trumbauer $200 a week and more experienced men such as trumpeter Henry Busse $300 weekly. "When we joined 'Pops' Whiteman at Indianapolis," Frankie Trumbauer recalled, Whiteman "said, 'Boys, I hope you will be happy. I pay more than any other leader because I want the best, and I have to keep the best happy'" (Shapiro and Hentoff 1955, p. 153). "Don't ever make fun of Paul Whiteman," scolded Joe Venuti. "He did great things for American music. He took pride in having the finest musicians in the world as sidemen, and he paid the highest salaries ever paid" (277).

Paul Whiteman—The King of Jazz

Armed with an orchestra of classically trained, well-paid musicians, Whiteman went into the studio and achieved international fame. One night in 1920, when the band performed at the Palais Royal in New York City, the bandleader attracted attention from a Victor Records talent scout and signed with the label. In November, the band released "Whispering" backed by "The Japanese Sandman," which sold more than a million copies. The next year, the group scored with "My Mammy," "Cherie," "Say It with Music," and "Song of India," the last of which had been adapted by Whiteman from Nikolai Rimsky-Korsakov's *Chanson Indoue*. In 1922, Whiteman's Orchestra recorded four more top-selling discs and earned more than a million dollars annually from record sales and concert dates. The next year, Whiteman connected with two more bestsellers.

On August 13, 1923, Whiteman returned from a triumphal tour of Europe to great fanfare. The bandleader stepped off a steamboat to an applauding crowd, which included the mayor of New York City, the police commissioner, the head of the musicians' union, and Victor executives. Representatives of the Buescher Band Instrument Company, which Whiteman endorsed, waited with a crown in hand. According to the September issue of *Talking Machine World*, "Paul Whiteman was crowned 'King of Jazz.'" The smiling Whiteman proudly wore the crown, which bore replicas of various instruments and included the inscription: "To Paul Whiteman in appreciation of his art and artistry and his aid to self-determination in the music of the nation."

Whiteman solidified his reputation when he conducted "An Experiment in Modern Music" at Aeolian Hall in New York City. Planning the event for a year, he had conceived an idea for a program to showcase the progress of American music, especially jazz. He commissioned composer George Gershwin to write a capstone jazz concerto for the evening that would epitomize the dramatic social changes of the past decade. At the concert held on February 12, 1924, Whiteman

 LISTENING GUIDE 5

Paul Whiteman Orchestra

"JAPANESE SANDMAN"

During the twenties, Paul Whiteman became the most popular jazz figure and was crowned "King of Jazz." Though his music may sound like it has few similarities with modern jazz, Whiteman popularized call-and-response section work in an orchestra that Art Hickman introduced and paved the way for the big-band era. He offered a lush-sounding jazz, which swept America and firmly established jazz as a musical genre.

Written in 1920 by Richard Whiting and Ray Egan, "Japanese Sandman" tells the tale of a Japanese sandman who barters yesterdays for tomorrows for his sleeping subjects. Besides the definitive Whiteman version, it has been recorded by Benny Goodman, Artie Shaw, Earl Hines, and the Andrews Sisters. This version was recorded by Whiteman and his nine-member Ambassador Orchestra for Victor on August 19, 1920.

0:00–0:03	Brief introduction.
0:04–0:31	On soprano saxophone, Hale Byers states the first section of the song, which gives the song an East Asian feel, while the tuba establishes a strong, syncopated, almost oom-pah march beat.
0:32–0:34	Plucks by the violins (including Whiteman on violin) reinforce the exotic atmosphere and separate the first section with the upcoming melody.
0:35–1:14	New Orleans–born Gus Mueller on alto saxophone states the melody with a light background accompaniment from violins, which establish a secondary but complementary melody that gives the tune a bluesy feel.
1:15–2:09	German-born Harry Busse on trumpet, a long-standing star of the Whiteman bands, restates the melody with a string background.
2:10–2:44	Led by Busse, the band launches into the main melody with the syncopated tuba prominently in the background playing a secondary melody.
2:45–2:50	The band ends with an East Asian-sounding flourish.

started with "Livery Stable Blues" by the Original Dixieland Jazz Band, which he considered the "crude jazz of the past" (Whiteman and McBride 1926, 104). The orchestra traced the developments in jazz during the next few years, including songs by composer Irving Berlin and Zez Confrey, the novelty and ragtime pianist. Whiteman ended by conducting the inaugural version of the Gershwin composition, "Rhapsody in Blue," which the composer felt represented "a sort of musical kaleidoscope of America—of our vast melting pot, of our unduplicated national pep, of our blues, our metropolitan madness" (Pollack 2006, 297). *Variety* proclaimed that Whiteman "had proved conclusively that the dance orchestra or the band or the jazz craze, or any other names it has been identified with, will never die. It is part of American culture and an absolute necessity" (Ward and Burns 2000, 100).

After the performance, the audience and the press showered Whiteman with praise. Conductor and classical pianist Sergei Rachmaninoff declared that "Whiteman had the finest orchestra of its size I have ever heard," and composer Arnold Schoenberg immediately bought all of Whiteman's records for further study (Wald 2009, 79). The day after the concert, on February 13, 1924, Olin Downes of the *New York Times* wrote about the "realization of the irresistible vitality and genuineness of much of the music heard on this occasion, as opposed to the pitiful sterility of the average production of the 'serious' American composer. The audience packed a house that could have been sold twice over."

Some African-American jazz men lauded Whiteman. Duke Ellington, who would soon become famous himself, named Whiteman as one of his favorite bandleaders. "He dressed her in woodwinds and strings and made a lady out of jazz," raved Duke (Nicholson 1999, 50). As early as 1921 on a riverboat job, Louis Armstrong and Baby Dodds regularly played the Whiteman tune "Whispering." Louis Armstrong called the bandleader the "great Mr. P.W." (Shapiro and Hentoff 1955, p. 158).

Paul Whiteman transformed jazz by making it respectable and palatable to a general audience. In late 1926, a columnist for the *New Yorker* asserted that "there is no disputing the fact that modern dance music owes to him [Whiteman] much of its sophistication; he is directly responsible for the artistic recognition of jazz and for many of its instrumental methods" (Busch 1926, 26). "The inevitable movement to modify the hideous noisiness of early jazz," echoed another observer three years later, sprung from the Whiteman "reaction against cacophony" (Niles n.d., 982–84).

The public bought millions of Whiteman's classically based jazz records. After the concert in Aeolian Hall, New Yorkers inundated one department store with more than a thousand standing orders for any Whiteman record released. In an amazing string of successes, during the twenties, Whiteman saw music lovers purchase twenty-five bestselling hits and another hundred major records by his orchestra. Fans religiously attended his concerts and felt that he embodied the essence of jazz.

The rotund bandleader became one of the bestselling musicians of all time by smoothing the rough edges of jazz to appeal to millions of new urban consumers. Just as American industry had done with uniform products for new migrants to the city, the bandleader discovered a standardized formula of classically based jazz that appealed to recently arrived urbanites. He shaped a rhythmic, peppy, innovative jazz into a palatable form to conquer the emerging national music scene and assume near iconic status.

Symphonic Jazz Sweeps the Nation

During the twenties, Whiteman's style paved the way for other similar-sounding bands, including the Isham Jones Orchestra. Jones had been raised in Michigan and, at the age of seventeen, published his first song, "On the Alamo." In 1915, he moved to Chicago and assembled a group of mostly classically trained musicians to play his version of symphonic jazz. Renouncing the "'down South Negro type' of blues," he merged jazz with a classical sensibility on titles such as "Aunt Hagar's Children's Blues," "Henpecked Blues," and "Forgetful Blues." During the early twenties, the band received accolades from Chicago drama critic Ashton Stevens, who promoted the group through his newspaper columns. By 1921, in the wake of Paul Whiteman's success, the Jones Orchestra scored with "Wabash Blues" and followed with "Swingin' Down the Lane" (1923). By 1925, when it again connected with the symphonic-sounding "Remember," the orchestra had become a premier Chicago dance band with thirty-three top hits, which featured such jazz virtuosi as cornet player Louis Panico.

Jean Goldkette, advertised as the "Paul Whiteman of the West," joined the symphonic jazz ranks. Born in France and spending his childhood in Europe, in 1911 the pianist immigrated to the United States in hopes of a career as a concert pianist. Four years later, he became obsessed with jazz after witnessing a performance by Tom Brown's band at Lamb's Café. "For the first time in my life I heard jazz music played," he intimated. "It made such a profound impression on me, [and] also gave me ideas as to its unlimited possibilities" (Sudhalter 1999, 306–7). By the early 1920s, Goldkette affiliated with the syncopated syndicate of Edgar Benson, an orchestra leader who controlled bookings at major Midwest hotels.

In 1924, Goldkette established his own band to offer his version of orchestral jazz. He lured such stellar white jazz men as Bix Beiderbecke, Frankie Trumbauer, Joe Venuti, and Eddie Lang to his fold and added arranger Bill Challis and reed player Jimmy Dorsey. Typically, he offered a few "hot" numbers such as "Tiger Rag" paired with more orchestral tunes such as "Fox Trot Classique." At the insistence of Victor's producer, the group waxed commercially oriented songs. "Geez, I think they picked out the *stinking-est* tunes for us," complained arranger Bill Challis about a 1926 session. "They didn't want any improvising," added the arranger. "They were trying to make a hit, and in doing that they made us play the melody" (Deffaa 1990, 73). Though not satisfied with its recording sessions, the Goldkette band hit with "Sorry and Blue" (1926). In September 1927, when it dissolved, the orchestra provided Paul Whiteman with many top-flight musicians as well as arranger Challis.

James Fletcher Henderson, dubbed the "Colored King of Jazz," combined jazz with the classics and led the preeminent African-American orchestra in New York City during the early twenties. Born into a middle-class family, Henderson graduated from Atlanta University and, in 1920, moved to New York City to earn a master's degree in chemistry from Columbia University. After working with Black Swan Records and reluctantly backing blues singers, in January 1924 Fletcher established a ten-piece jazz band, which was influenced by Paul Whiteman and, in his words, consisted "of serious musicians" (Shapiro and Hentoff 1955, 203). By 1926, Henderson and Whiteman traded arrangements or written compositions for each member of an orchestra.

Henderson merged jazz with his classical background out of necessity. Steeped in classical music and described by blues singer Ethel Waters as leaning "more to the classical side" (Waters 1951, 147), Fletcher turned to jazz to support himself. "Before I met Fletcher, I could only play the classics or else what I saw on paper," recalled his wife Leora, who played trumpet, "and Fletcher said, 'You better learn jazz or you won't make no money'" (Shapiro and Hentoff 1955, p. 219).

The bandleader initially found work in the theater district of New York City at the Club Alabam, a dance hall on the lower level of the Norah Bayes Theater. There, the Henderson unit backed African-American Broadway singer Edith Wilson. Later in 1924, the band headlined at the Roseland Ballroom, a white-only downtown dancehall on Broadway that accommodated up to twenty-five hundred dancers, who nicknamed it "the home of refined dancing." Off and on, the Henderson Orchestra stayed at the Roseland for more than seventeen years.

Gaining acclaim at the Roseland, which wired the ballroom for radio broadcasts, the Henderson Orchestra scored with "Charleston Crazy" (1924). The next year, the band hit with "Sugar Foot Stomp" and in 1926 recorded the successful "Carolina Stomp." During the remainder of the twenties, the orchestra released five additional bestsellers.

The bluesy, "stomp-type" hits of the band reflected the dictates of the record business rather than their chosen style. "Although the Henderson band played a variety of music on the tours," mentioned trumpet player Rex Stewart who succeeded Louis Armstrong in the outfit, "the record executives characterized [Henderson's] band as a stomp band. They didn't accept the fact that a Negro band could play sweet, though as a matter of fact, we used to get tremendous applause at Roseland and other places for playing waltzes beautifully" (Sudhalter 1999, 305).

From 1923 to 1927, clarinetist/saxophonist Don Redman arranged bluesy versions of songs for the Henderson band to record. He viewed the band as a four-part group: trumpets, trombones, a rhythm section, and reeds (saxophones and clarinets), and applied the multiple melodies of New Orleans brass bands to a larger outfit. He incorporated blues and ragtime elements to his arrangements as well as solos and breaks. Paving the way for big bands during the swing era, he pitted reed, trombone, and trumpet sections against one another in sectional calls-and-responses.

Though never as commercially successful as the Whiteman orchestra, the Henderson band left its stamp indelibly on jazz. "Fletcher was like the first big band to gain recognition. . . . Particularly, the first Negro group to gain recognition," remarked saxophonist Benny Waters, who played in a rival New York orchestra led by Charlie Johnson (Deffaa 1990, 39). Over time, it included such future jazz leaders as saxophonists Coleman Hawkins, Benny Carter, Buster Bailey, and Chu Berry and trumpet masters Louis Armstrong, Roy Eldridge, Rex Stewart, Henry "Red" Allen, and Joe Smith.

During the twenties, two other African-American bandleaders, Sam Wooding and Fess Williams, contributed to symphonic jazz. After a brief fling with ragtime and the blues, in 1923 Sam Wooding expanded his band to eight members, including bassist Garvin Bushell, who doubled on oboe for a larger, more classically based sound. The next year, Wooding added three more instruments, and, for a year, succeeded Fletcher Henderson at the Club Alabam.

The revamped Sam Wooding group became the first African-American jazz band to tour Europe and spread the word about Harlem abroad. In 1925, it landed a job as the orchestra for the Broadway revue *Chocolate Kiddies*, which had been organized to visit Europe, featured thirty dancers and singers, and told the story of Harlem nightlife. The first act of the program revolved around life in a Harlem café, and the second act highlighted a "Symphonic Jazz Concert at the Club Alabam in New York: Sam Wooding and Orchestra." The band earned rave reviews from critics and toured Europe with the revue for three years. When returning to the United States, the orchestra received an offer from the Cotton Club to serve as the house band to replace the Andy Preer Orchestra. Instead, Wooding and his band mates decided to tour Europe again and left the job open for Duke Ellington, who became a household name through the recognition he gained at the Cotton Club.

Kentuckian Stanley "Fess" Williams, a graduate of Tuskegee University, offered lush, orchestrated jazz. In 1925, he founded the Royal Flush Orchestra and held court at New York's Savoy Ballroom for more than three years. An ebullient Williams, donning a top hat and a white suit for his performances, recorded for a variety of labels including Victor, which pressed his biggest hit, "Hot Town." After moving to Chicago briefly to front the symphonic jazz outfit of Dave Peyton, he returned to New York City to lead the Royal Flush Orchestra until it disbanded in 1930.

Paul Whiteman and other symphonic jazz bands brought jazz to a general audience. They capitalized on an emergent consumer culture in an increasingly urbanized America, where people listened to musical heroes who they did not know and likely would never meet. In a rapidly changing America, Whiteman transformed jazz into a national music. "Jazz is upon us, everywhere," reported the *Atlantic*

Monthly in August 1922. "To deny the fact is to assume the classic ostrich pose, head buried in the sand, tail-feathers to the sun" (Engel 1922, 182). By 1923, one advertising survey found that 75 percent of the American public favored jazz over any other type of music. The next year, consumers spent $480 million on jazz records or 80 percent of the entire amount expended on discs. But as Whiteman captured the imagination of the dominant culture, African-American migrants to the city embraced their own version of jazz delivered by female blues singers.

For Discussion and Further Study

Chapter Quiz

1. How did the Original Dixieland Jazz Band's (ODJB) "Livery Stable Blues" launch the jazz craze? What musical elements did it borrow from African-American music?

2. Why did the popular Original Creole Band turn down an offer to record after the ODJB's success? What does this indicate about the different attitudes of African-American and white musicians at the time?

3. How did the growth of urbanization and consumer culture bring a new audience to jazz? Was the impact of these changes the same on African Americans and white Americans? What elements of the new urban lifestyle were cited as being reflected in this musical style?

4. How did Paul Whiteman develop his "symphonic jazz" style? What instrumentalists played a role in its development? How did it differ from the music played by the smaller white ensembles?

5. How did Whiteman's belief that jazz needed to be "refined" to appeal to a white audience reflect racial stereotypes and prejudices of the day?

JAZZ, THE GREAT MIGRATION, AND THE BLUES

The Rise of the Urban Blues in the Era of the "New Woman"

This chapter deals with race, the role of women, and a seismic population shift during and immediately after World War I. It shows how the blues originated among rural, Southern, male African Americans, but only gained mass acclaim with female African-American singers, such as Bessie Smith, during a time when the role of urban women shifted from the home to the workplace. The chapter also describes the Great Migration of rural Southern African Americans to the industrialized North that brought a new audience for African-American, urban music.

In 1903, vaudeville performer and bandleader W. C. Handy assembled a nine-man group to perform in the Mississippi Delta. The band traveled by train on the Yazoo Delta R. & R., christened the "Yellow Dog," to search for work in large and small towns from Lambert to Clarksdale.

One evening in Tutwiler, music wakened Handy, who had fallen asleep on a bench as he waited at the train station. In his words, a raggedy "lean, loose-jointed Negro had commenced plunking his guitar beside me while I slept. His face had on it some of the sadness of the ages," he continued. "As he played, he pressed a knife on the strings of the guitar" and sang a song about the Yellow Dog. He repeated the first line three times in a twelve-bar blues. "The effect," Handy concluded "was unforgettable" (Handy 1941, 78).

Handy soon understood the power of the blues. Initially, Handy thought the blues was "the weirdest music I had ever heard" that "attained a disturbing monotony." His opinion changed forever after witnessing an audience reaction in Cleveland, Mississippi. After playing ragtime and march standards to an African-American crowd, Handy heard someone shout for "our native music." The band responded with an "old-time Southern melody, more sophisticated than native." After a few more requests from the audience, the bandleader allowed an African-American three-piece band consisting of a guitar, mandolin, and bass to play a few numbers and wondered "if anybody besides small town rounders and their running mates would go for it." Handy was astonished by the reaction to the blues. "A rain of silver dollars began to fall around the outlandish, stomping feet. Dancers went wild. Dollars, quarters, halves—the shower grew heavier. My idea of what constitutes music," remembered Handy, "was changed by the sight of the silver money cascading around the splay feet of a Mississippi string band. That night a composer was born," confessed the bandleader (Handy 1941, 81).

To bolster his income, the bandleader immediately orchestrated versions of local blues songs such as "Make Me a Pallet on Your Floor," and the reputation of his band "increased by leaps and bounds." Though feeling somewhat guilty about performing such "primitive music" and "low folk forms," Handy believed that he needed to incorporate the blues into his repertoire for commercial success in such locales as the red-light district in Clarksdale, Mississippi. "There was money to be made, and who were we to turn up our noses," he reasoned (Handy 1941, 80–82).

By 1909, Handy had secured a regular stint at Pee Wee's saloon on Beale Street in Memphis. When mayoral candidate Edward H. Crump hired the band to campaign for him, the bandleader wrote a tune for the occasion. He integrated blues structures that he heard six years earlier into "Mister Crump," which employed flat thirds and flat sevenths in the melody, three-line stanzas, and twelve instead of sixteen measures. By 1912, the composer published the song under the title "Memphis Blues," which represented one of the first blues songs that had been printed as sheet music. "My part," explained Handy, "was to introduce this, the 'blues' form, to the general public" (Handy 1941, 103).

The Birth of the Rural Blues: Cheap Guitars and the African-American Church

W. C. Handy correctly characterized his mediating role in the development of the blues. Though Handy helped commit the style to written form, he had not created it. The blues came from the work songs, field hollers, and spirituals sung by enslaved people who had carried musical characteristics from Africa and adapted them to their new environment.

During the early 1890s, the secular blues surfaced in the Mississippi Delta, Texas, and Louisiana due to the proliferation of inexpensive guitars. African Americans converted work songs from the fields and spirituals from the Baptist Church into the blues. They accompanied themselves on low-cost Stella guitars manufactured by the Oscar Schmidt Company, which were introduced in 1899. Itinerant bluesman Ishmon Bracey bought one for eleven dollars in Memphis, and Huddie Ledbetter, popularly known as Leadbelly, performed on a Stella. Charlie Patton, a Delta blues guitar innovator who launched his career around 1906, favored a Stella as his "favorite box" (Calt 1988b, 182), as did Blind Lemon Jefferson, a guitarist from Coutchman, Texas.

Montgomery Ward and Sears, Roebuck & Company mass-marketed even lower-priced guitars through mail-order catalogs. First selling mail-order goods in 1875 to farmers in rural areas, by 1894 Montgomery Ward had introduced American-made guitars in their catalogs. A year before, Sears had initiated a mail-order business, advertised as "The Cheapest Supply House on Earth," which included Harmony and Stella guitars. In 1899, when Sears overtook Montgomery Ward in total mail-order sales, it offered relatively inexpensive guitars to its national customer base. Sears sold the Troubadour for $2.95; the Encore for $3.60; the Oakwood for $4.95; the Columbian, designed to coincide with the Columbian Exposition, for $7.95; and the Magnolia, "the handsomest guitar made," for $8.95. By the turn of the century, manufacturers were selling 78,500 guitars annually.

African-American men playing guitars and kazoos, 1909. *National Photo Company Collection, Library of Congress Prints and Photographs Division*

With instruments available at affordable prices, guitarists appeared in rural areas of the South. Booker Miller, born in 1910, asserted that his grandfather, Jim Brown, "was a guitar player" (Calt 1988b, 57). Charleston resident and guitarist Stanford Bennett entertained at local joints before the dawn of the twentieth century (Calt 1988b, 58). By 1905, Mississippian Rich Dickson had become an accomplished guitar player, when he taught Henry Stuckey the instrument. Leadbelly, born in 1888, remembered his uncles Bob and Terrell strumming guitars to him as a young child. Before 1900, Leadbelly himself played guitar at local dances. Together with his cousin Edmond Ledbetter, they "used to make music. Sometimes I played a mandolin and I'd second him [by chording] with a guitar and sometimes we played the guitar together. I used to play all 'round here, up to Mooringsport, [Louisiana] over to Leigh, [Texas] and back to the Jeter Plantation" (Wolfe and Lornell 1992, 18).

Once the guitar gained popularity as an instrument, enterprising youth built guitars from materials found around the house. In 1903, ten-year-old Bill Broonzy, who later composed such blues standards as "Keys to the Highway" and "Looking Up at Down," constructed "a fiddle out of a cigar box, a guitar out of goods boxes" (Bruynoghe 1992, 34). Others simply unraveled the baling wire that held the bristles of a broom together and attached both ends with screws to the outside of a barn or house, which acted as a fretboard or neck. They then placed a bottle underneath it as a bridge. To get a sound, youth plucked the instrument or ran a knife or bottleneck across the wire. They called the primitive instrument, West African in origin, a diddley bow.

Guitarists who performed publicly offered a variety of musical styles for their audiences. Initially, they favored versions of sixteen-bar rags, popular songs such as "My Bucket's Got a Hole in It," and four-bar, up-tempo breakdowns that consisted of chord changes at the beginning of each measure. "We'd play whatever the people request," noted Booker Miller, a protégé of Charlie Patton who worked with his mentor in the Mississippi Delta (Calt 1988b, 118). "Lemon could play anything he had to play," recalled a Wortham, Texas, resident about Blind Lemon Jefferson (Govenar 2000, p. 8). Texas bluesman Mance Lipscomb likewise performed a variety of material for his listeners, calling himself a "songster" (Lipscomb and Allyn 1993, 52).

Near the turn of the century, a few guitarists transformed a sixteen-bar rag into a twelve-bar blues by repeating the four-bar phrases of spirituals three times and substituting secular themes for religious topics. "The first blues he ever heard," remarked interviewer Studs Terkel about Big Bill Broonzy, "concerned the big flood of 1893. It was called 'Cryin' Joe Turner'" (Bruynoghe 1992, 23). Booker Miller dated the first blues to "a little before 1900" (Calt 1988b, 57). Speaking about his early boyhood, Sam Chatmon, born in 1899, "never heard nobody pick no blues till my brother Bud and Charlie Patton, they'se about the first." Nehemiah "Skip" James, born in 1902 and raised in Bentonia, Mississippi, "hadn't heard of blues" as a child, "but after a little period of time, I heard my mother and them speak about 'singin' the blues'" (Calt 1988b, 63). The "Reverend" Robert Wilkins, born six years before James, heard the twelve-bar blues version of such rags as "Spoonful" in his hometown about the same time. Whatever the exact date of the birth of the secular blues, by 1910 Charlie Patton had written a series of now-classic blues such as "Pony Blues," "Banty Rooster Blues," and "Mississippi Bo Weevil Blues" to add to his repertoire.

The blues came from the fields and the church. As many African-American sharecroppers toiled in the fields, they sang updated blues versions of field hollers and work songs that had first been introduced during slavery. "Hard working in the hot sun, I'd make me up a song," explained early bluesman and Mississippi farmer Jack Owens who played guitar and operated a juke joint on the weekends. "I'd start singing in the fields, then come home, and get my guitar and start playing it and singing it; when I'd go back to the same fields, the songs would come back to me"(Olson 1992, 38).

Bluesmen such as Owens merged secular topics found in work songs with four-bar spirituals to create the blues. "Some of the church songs, you can't hardly tell them from the blues," insisted Owens. "Some of us sang the church songs, some of us sang the blues, some of us sang both" (Olson 1992, 36). Skip James always opened his blues concerts with a spiritual. In one instance during a recording session, James began to sing spirituals and refused to record any blues. Charlie Patton included church songs in his performances. "Right in the middle of a dance, it didn't make him no difference," his protégé Booker Miller recalled. "If it hit him, he'd just go to playing church songs right there. They'd [the audience] just back up in a corner and listen." "He could have preached if he a-wanted to," added Son House about Patton. A teenage Blind Lemon Jefferson performed at a picnic sponsored by the General Assembly of Churches in Buffalo, Texas, and won fame by singing to local Baptist congregations such as the members of the Shiloh Primitive Baptist Church. His first record consisted of religious songs. "That was one thing about Lemon," observed a resident of Worham, Texas, who saw Jefferson as a young man. "He'd be singing in a church one day, singing in a house of ill repute the next."

Some bluesmen comingled the secular and sacred by both playing guitar and serving as ministers. Skip James ministered and performed the blues. "I didn't like the way he was doing it, preaching a while, then playing the blues a while," groused his friend Jack Owens. "I'd play the blues with him Saturday night, and the next morning he'd be preaching church" (Olson 1992, 36). Big Bill Broonzy began playing music, then "started to preaching and I preached for four years, and then I went back to playing again," when he realized that music could be more lucrative (Bruynoghe 1992, 35). Bluesman Son House adopted a similar split career by acting as a minister in Northern Mississippi. "If Son House couldn't make enough playing the guitar, he gonna pick up a [church] collection," sniffed blues guitar player Willie Brown. "He'd preach a year, somethin' like that six months again. He could *preach*, you know." Admitted House, "I was trying to hold the blues in one hand and God in the other" (Waterman 1989, 49).

When not preaching, blues guitarists entertained rural audiences in a variety of places. Like the bluesman who W. C. Handy encountered, they traveled by rail to play their songs. Others amused passersby on street corners in small rural towns, and many performed at frolics, which a sharecropper organized at his house for his neighbors. Amid gambling and prostitution, some delighted patrons at juke joints or barrelhouses located near a train station, sawmill, or turpentine camp. Generally, the itinerant bluesmen traveled from place to place in the rural South until the fall, when they stopped to farm to earn extra money.

Sometimes, pianists pumped out the blues for rural audiences. They performed for workers at dangerous saw mills and turpentine camps, located near juke joints, which had invested in cheap upright pianos. Charles "Cow Cow" Davenport, the son of a Baptist minister, who was born in Anniston, Alabama, started on the piano at age 12 and was expelled from a theological school for playing ragtime. After a stint in Banhoof's Traveling Carnival, he incorporated blues songs into his act, including his signature tune, "Cow Cow Blues," and moved from camp to camp with his music. Clarence "Pine Top" Smith, also heralding from Alabama, hammered out such blues as "Pine Top's Boogie Woogie" for camp laborers. Tennessean "Cripple" Clarence Lofton enraptured rural sawmill workers throughout the South with his piano blues.

The Urban Piano Blues

Bands and pianists delivered the blues to urban areas. In New Orleans, string bands played the blues to complement their ragtime tunes. Usually consisting of a guitar, mandolin, and bass, the groups performed for a variety of functions.

In 1897, a young Jelly Roll Morton took the guitar spot in such a band and, according to his account, offered old-time tunes, "different little blues and ragtime numbers" (Lomax 1950, 6).

Some New Orleans brass bands, mostly groups of non-Creoles, blended the blues with marches and rags. Streaming from sugar cane and cotton plantations into the Uptown section of New Orleans from 1880 to 1910, non-Creoles had been exposed to the blues in the rural Southern areas and brought the sound to their new home. Uptown in New Orleans, where most non-Creoles lived, explained Creole violinist Paul Dominguez, musicians "played more rougher, more *hard* music, more blues" (Lomax 1950, 89).

Non-Creole cornet players Buddy Bolden and Mutt Carey blasted forth the blues. Bolden "was playing the blues of all kinds," asserted Bunk Johnson, "so when I got with Bolden [in 1905], we helped to make more blues" such as "Make Me a Pallet on the Floor" (Shapiro and Hentoff 1955, 36). Mutt Carey, the cornetist who played with Kid Ory starting in 1914, held the title of "the blues king of New Orleans" due to his use of a small bucket as a mute that gave his playing a bluesy feel (46).

Non-Creole bandleaders heard elements of the blues at African-American church services. Chris Kelly, "dark of color, low on finance, Baptist from birth, and cultured in canebrakes" who led a brass band in New Orleans and Alabama, performed "church music," remembered guitarist Danny Barker. "He really moved the people. He preached so melodiously with his horn that it was like someone singing a song, and he would go into the blues from there," concluded Barker (Shapiro and Hentoff 1955, 50–51). Buddy Bolden's fascination with the blues arose at least partly from his regular church attendance.

Like guitarists in the rural South, New Orleans blues-playing brass bands usually catered to an unsavory element. Chris Kelly, who spoke "a real broken patois, African almost" played for "those blues, cotton-picking Negroes, what they called in the old days, 'yard and field' Negroes," grimaced New Orleans guitarist Danny Barker. Buddy Bolden became the "absolute favorite" of people in the downtrodden Garden District in New Orleans. According to Jelly Roll Morton, "he played at most of the rough places like the Masonic [and Odd Fellows] Hall on Perdido and Rampart, at the Globe Hall in the downtown section on St. Peter and St. Claude" (Lomax 1950, 57).

Outnumbering bluesy brass bands, blues pianists thrived in cities, where they had easier access to upright pianos than in remote rural areas. "You couldn't fool with no piano too much, not for the country gang," explained Son House. "'Cause [pianos] be too much to move all the time" (Titon 1977, 18). "They only used [guitars] in the country—where there was no pianos," echoed "Georgia" Tom Dorsey, who backed and wrote songs for female blues singers such as Ma Rainey and later became a major promoter and composer of gospel music. In town, he noted, "they used pianos" (O'Neal and Van Singel 2002, 9).

In Shreveport, Louisiana, Leadbelly found pianists who pumped out the blues. "Boogie woogie was called barrelhouse in those days," he explained. "One of the best players was named Chee-Dee. He would go from one gin mill to the next on Fannin Street. He was coal black and one of the old-time players, and he boogied the blues" (Wolfe and Lornell 1992, 35, 37).

At the turn of the century, blues pianists congregated in the many brothels and saloons of New Orleans. In 1901 or 1902, a New Orleans pianist named Game Kid became the favorite of the Garden District. "He was a howler," related Jelly Roll Morton. "The best there was in the section when it came to playing blues." Morton also mentioned Buddy Carter, "a man that could really play those blues and those things we call stomps today" (Lomax 1950, 51).

Blues Compositions

Ragtime pianists and composers such as Jelly Roll Morton included blues elements in their published songs to offer a more refined, slightly more respectable version of the blues. Even before W. C. Handy wrote "Mr. Crump," Morton integrated the blues into his repertoire of rags and popular songs. As early as 1902, he collaborated with ragtime pianist Frank Richard to compose a Spanish-tinged "New Orleans Blues." Three years later, the Creole pianist wrote the well-traveled blues, "Alabama Bound." Though he performed "waltzes and rags for the white people" at upscale hotels, in the brothels "Jelly would sit there and play that barrelhouse music all night—blues and such as that," recalled trumpeter Bunk Johnson who joined Morton in 1903 (Lomax 1950, 104, 113).

Other ragtime composers offered blues compositions. In 1908, white Crescent City pianist Antonio Maggio published "I Got the Blues." Though billed as an "an up-to-date rag," the song featured a twelve-bar blues introduction. The same year, Robert Joplin, the brother of ragtime pioneer Scott Joplin, sang a blues-like "I'll Be a Low-Down Dog" on a vaudeville stage in Knoxville, Tennessee. The next year, Alabama-born, New Orleans-based white pianist Robert Hoffman released the music to "I'm Alabama Bound" (an entirely different song than the one played by Jelly Roll Morton). Tagged as a "ragtime two-step," the song adopted a blues structure and became known as "The Alabama Blues." In 1910, Houston pianist H. "Kid" Love thrilled audiences with his "Easton Blues."

In 1912, when W. C. Handy published "Memphis Blues," other ragtime pianists composed several other seminal blues songs. Hart Wand produced "Dallas Blues," which he heard from a whistling African-American porter and by 1914 had become a staple for the Rabbit Foot Minstrel Gold Band. White minstrel performer Le Roy White released "Negro Blues," a twelve-bar blues collected from various conversations that he had overheard on the streets. The same year, African-American H. Franklin "Baby" Seals, a ragtime pianist and comedian who two years earlier hit with the rag, "Shake, Rattle and Roll," wrote "Baby Seals Blues." He collaborated with the first African-American illustrated newspaper, *The Indianapolis Freeman*, to successfully advertise and distribute the sheet music for fifteen cents a copy. Within a few months, other performers such as Jelly Roll Morton played the song on stage, and on September 13, 1913, the *Freeman* described the tune as "Baby Seals' well-known song."

In 1914, W. C. Handy composed his most commercially successful blues number, "St. Louis Blues." "My aim," he reasoned, was "to combine ragtime syncopation with a real melody in the spiritual tradition" for a secular blues. "Using the humorous spirit of bygone coon songs," he applied "Negro phraseology and dialect." Handy employed a "three-line stanza" for a twelve-bar blues [defined as a three-chord progression that starts with a chord for the first four bars or measures, progresses to the fourth sequential chord for the second four bars, and ends with the fifth sequential chord for the final four bars of the three-line stanza]. He bore "down on the third and seventh tones of the scale, slurring between major and minor" for blue notes and added a new tempo to ragtime that he termed "temp di blues," or very slow. For the first time, the composer added lyrics to a published blues song, which was sung initially by Charles Anderson who called "the blues a phase of ragtime" (Handy 1941, 125). Based upon the success of the song, Handy organized several bands, which employed more than sixty people to play for dances around Memphis and other major cities. "The fortunes of our bands and particularly of the main unit rose with the success of the blues," he boasted (131).

Handy reflected and embraced the bootstraps philosophy of Booker T. Washington that Scott Joplin had espoused. In 1899, Handy asserted that he

W. C. Handy Orchestra

"ST. LOUIS BLUES"

In September 1914, W. C. Handy, noted music publisher, composer, and bandleader, published "St. Louis Blues." He offered a syncopated, slow twelve-bar blues with three stanzas that popularized the blues structure. Unlike most standard blues, it also features a tango-like rhythm, the "Spanish Tinge," in the introduction and sixteen-bar bridge or transitional part of the song that connects two sections. In his autobiography, Handy maintained that "when St. Louis Blues was written the tango [a 2/4, syncopated pattern of beats] was in vogue. I tricked the dancers by arranging a tango introduction, breaking abruptly into a low-down blues. My eyes swept the floor anxiously, then suddenly I saw lightning strike. The dancers seemed electrified. Something within them came suddenly to life" (Handy 1941, 99–100).

The Handy band plays the song in an AABC structure with sections A and C in a twelve-bar blues and section B in a sixteen-bar tango rhythm. The AABC form of a musical piece refers to the way the song has been structured overall. In this case, after an introduction, Handy starts the statement of the song in 12 bars (A) and then repeats it. He then states the B section in sixteen bars. He completes the song with another twelve-bar-blues section (C).

All types of structures exist, including the pop song form of AABA, which begins with introductory verses, which are repeated and followed by a thirty-two-bar refrain or chorus that provides a snappy melody. The pop song ends with a return to the verses (A).

0:00–0:10	An introduction led by Handy's trumpet in a tango-rhythm.
0:11–0:28	In section A, Handy's trumpet, backed by a New Orleans–style Memphis Blues band, states the blues melody. The other instruments weave secondary melodies to the main melody played by Handy, much like the typical New Orleans brass band.
0:29–0:42	Handy and his band mates restate section A with the melody and secondary melodies.
0:43–1:03	The second sixteen-bar section (B) begins and involves a call-and-response between Handy's trumpet and first the clarinet, then the tuba and again the clarinet. The band plays the passage in a tango rhythm as they did in the introduction.
1:04–1:20	A twelve-bar blues with a very brief clarinet solo at the end that restates the first section (0:11–0:28).
1:21–1:36	After a five-second introduction to the section, the entire band slows the tempo and then establishes a tango rhythm with the clarinet in the background that states the main melody.
1:37–1:55	A section led by the clarinet and tuba in a tango rhythm.
1:56–2:11	A twelve-bar blues section (C) played by the clarinet in the lead with the band establishing a secondary melody in the background.
2:12–2:51	The section above restated with a saxophone in the lead.
2:34–2:52	The full band plays the main blues theme in multiple melodies simultaneously in a New Orleans–brass band style.
2:52–2:56	Conclusion, which features Handy's trumpet.

was "a lover of his race and wished to do something for it besides adding to the harmony of its characteristic songs," according to the African-American newspaper the *Freeman* on February 4, 1899. Near the turn of the century, the bandleader brought his group at his own expense to the opening of the African-American-owned Bank of Mound Bayou that featured Booker T. Washington as the speaker "to help them do the thing up in brown" (Handy 1941, 91).

Following Washington's advice to establish African-American-owned companies and thereby uplift the lot of African Americans, in 1912 Handy launched a publishing firm with African-American entrepreneur Harry Pace. The firm, related Handy in the *Freeman* on September 7, 1918, hoped to preserve "the characteristic melodies of the spirituals and add to our wonderful store of Negro music a modern orchestration and scoring, which gives us a secular style of music all our own and known to the world as BLUES." "Mr. Handy wants his work looked into more seriously by those of his race who have had the advantages of a musical education," commented the *Freeman* on December 22, 1917.

Stride Piano

African Americans in Harlem gave birth to a blend of ragtime and the blues known as the stride piano style. Originally, African Americans in New York City lived around the Greenwich Village area surrounded by Irish and Italians. In 1901, they migrated uptown toward Harlem, when noted architect Stanford White—who had built Madison Square Garden—constructed a row of elegant brownstone houses on 139th Street and Seventh and Eighth Avenues that remained vacant due to inadequate transportation. African-American real estate agent Philip Payton convinced white residents to allow middle-class African Americans to move into the area, and the African-American Harlem population mushroomed. By 1910, more than twenty-five thousand African Americans lived in the greater Harlem area with a majority located in the central part of the district.

A red-light district called "Hell's Kitchen" near Harlem catered to the large influx of migrants. In 1913, when Willie "The Lion" Smith relocated to New York City from Newark, "most of the action took place in Hell's Kitchen west of Eighth Avenue from Twenty-Third all the way up to San Juan Hill in the West Sixties" (Smith 1978, 45).

Saloons dotted the streets between Thirty-fourth to Forty-second Streets and between Seventh and Eighth Avenues. Willie "The Lion" Smith recalled that each tavern, usually located in the basement of a building, "had a long bar, sawdust on the floor, and the familiar round-top beer tables with pretzel-backed chairs." Opposite the bar "would be an old upright piano," and pictures of notable boxers hung on the wall. Usually an African-American pianist performed with a drummer, banjoist, or harmonica player who collectively "received hardly any salary and lived entirely on tips, which were sometimes very high," maintained Smith. Each bar also set aside a backroom for gamblers "regardless of race, color or creed" (Smith 1978, 45–46).

Many ragtime pianists found steady employment at the saloons. Willie Smith performed at places such as the Green Gates with a "repertoire that included all the rags that I had managed to learn by ear" (Smith 1978, 50). Ragger Paul Seminole played at Small's cellar. Willie "Egghead" Sewell, "an old-time ragtimer," played at Banks' saloon (54). In 1913, James P. Johnson, a ragtime tickler and soon a stride pianist, "got started up in the Jungles [Casino]. This was the Negro section of Hell's Kitchen and ran from 60th to 63rd Street, west of 9th Avenue. It was the toughest part of New York" (Davin 1985, 173). He entertained at such cellar saloons as Allan's and Lee's. "Before World War I," noted the Lion, "the profession of playing ragtime piano in saloons was very active and growing all the time" (Smith 1978, 54–55).

Each ragtime pianist cultivated a distinctive approach. "Wherever they were from, the old-time piano men tried to develop their own individual style of playing," explained Smith. "Because, you see, if one player had a way of performing that made him stand out from the others it would make him a big hit with the ladies" (Smith 1978, 52). "One-Leg" Willie Joseph "was one of the best of the old-time ragtime players," asserted the Lion. "He had original ideas and never played the same number the same way twice" (55). Florida-born ragtime pianist Paul Seminole improvised on rags. "If he played a song twenty thousand times," recalled Eubie Blake, "it was twenty thousand times different." According to the Lion, each New York City ragtimer at least chose a "signature chord" or "a special chord with which you started off all your performances" (53).

Scuffling to make ends meet in the roughest part of New York City, many ragtime pianists became pimps. "Most of these fellows were big-time pimps or at least did a little hustling on their own," recalled James P. Johnson about the pianists (Davin 1985, 169). "The big-time ticklers walked into these places [saloons] and played for kicks because they made their real money hustling the gals for whom they pimped," agreed Willie Smith (Smith 1978, 50).

Associated with prostitution, many ragtime pianists dressed flamboyantly. Willie Smith "worked in dress suits, tuxedoes or dark suits" and wore a "blue melton overcoat to match," which cost one hundred fifty dollars. "The style was full or box-back cut, square shoulders and a padded lining. My pants were tight with long, peg-topped, fourteen-inch cuffs. I liked to have my suit jacket single breasted so I could show off my gold watch fob and chain," reminisced Smith. He sported custom-made shoes, a "real fancy silk shirt," and a cane. The pianist also wore a derby hat, cocked at an angle, and smoked a cigar, both of which became trademarks for many stride piano players (Smith 1978, 47–48).

As with other ragtimers, the dapper New York pianists leaned toward the classics. At a young age, James P. Johnson attended concerts by the New York Symphony, when his brother received tickets from a friend of the conductor. Johnson subsequently enrolled in formal lessons, learned to compose from a fellow pianist, and devised ragtime versions of such classical pieces as Gioachino Rossini's *William Tell* Overture. "We bordered more on the classical theory of music," explained Johnson about his music and that of his fellow striders (Lomax 1950, 144). Donald Lambert and Paul Seminole similarly ragged classical works of several composers. "In those days," explained Willie Smith, "we always had to have a couple of classical selections in our repertoires. I worked up my own arrangement of [Frédéric Chopin's] 'Polonaise Militaire' and a special ragtime version of a chorus or two of 'Miserere' from [Giuseppe Verdi's four-act opera] *Il Trovatore*" (Smith 1978, 68).

Though relying on many of the same musical conventions as Scott Joplin and his colleagues, New York ragtimers added other elements to produce the "stride" style. They developed "the orchestral piano," which strider James P. Johnson

Willie "The Lion" Smith in his apartment, on his upright piano, with his trademark cigar. *Photograph by William P. Gottlieb. William P. Gottlieb/Ira and Leonore S. Gershwin Fund Collection, Music Division, Library of Congress*

LISTENING GUIDE 7

James P. Johnson

"THE CHARLESTON"

Johnson represented the prototypical stride pianist. He combined his classical training with the blues to develop the stride piano style. Using a strong, insistent left-hand as a rhythmic base, Johnson created a propulsive but orchestral style, which he showcased on piano rolls. Born in New Brunswick, New Jersey, the pianist formed fast friendships with other leading stride pianists such as Willie "The Lion" Smith. Johnson composed dozens of songs including "The Charleston," which debuted on October 29, 1923, in the Broadway musical comedy *Runnin' Wild*. The pianist wrote the song several years before the Broadway production, and Cecil Mack composed the lyrics for the all-African-American-acted show. He based the song on a five-chord ragtime progression and used the first bar of a 3/2 clave for the driving rhythmic beat, which became a basis of accompanying or comping behind instruments and singers.

This song ignited a dance craze in the United States. The dance steps likely originated in Africa with the Ashanti tribe and had been popular in the South for a number of years. "It's a real old Southern dance," explained composer and bandleader Noble Sissle. "I remember dancing it in Savannah around 1905" (Stearns and Stearns 1968, 112). By 1913, the Charleston "had many variations—all danced to the rhythm that everybody knows now," contended Johnson.

The Charleston became a fad. "The first contest I ever won was a Charleston contest," remembered dancer/singer Henry "Rubberlegs" Williams. "It was in Atlanta in 1920" (Stearns and Stearns 1968, 112). Three years later, the Charleston surfaced in such stage shows as *How Come* and the Ziegfeld *Follies of 1923*. That same year, when Johnson wrote "The Charleston" for *Runnin' Wild*, it swept the nation.

By the mid-twenties, the energetic, athletic Charleston was dominating dance floors across America. The *New Republic* described it as a dance that "added the movements of the hips, thighs, buttocks [to the Fox Trot]" to create a "frenetic and voluptuous" series of steps (Spring 1997, 186).

0:00–0:10	Johnson provides an introduction with left-handed rhythm against the right hand, which plays in a syncopated, ragged rhythm.
0:11–0:25	He states the main melody and rhythm of the song in sixteen bars, the last four being a ragtime duel between the left and right hands. In essence, Johnson has combined a twelve-bar blues with ragtime. He uses what is now known as the Charleston beat—two highly accented beats followed by a rest.
0:26–0:49	The pianist restates the first section.
0:50–1:19	Melody stated again, though in the middle of this section he moves to a higher octave before dropping down to the original key.
1:19–1:29	An interesting part of the song, Johnson dives into a second section with ragtime tinkling and a secondary melody on the left hand.
1:30–1:49	He seems to pause or break the section almost entirely before continuing.
1:50–1:56	Back to the first section mostly with his right hand.
2:09–2:28	The first section again stated with the rhythmic left hand added to the melodic right hand.

described as "full, round, big, widespread chords and tenths—a heavy bass moving against the right hand." Though "even Scott Joplin had octaves and chords," contended Johnson, "he never attempted the big hand stretches." Johnson attributed the technique to Richard "Abba Labba" McLean and Charles Luckey Roberts and at least partly copied them to stomp out insistent, propulsive, left-hand chords that rocked the music back and forth in a steady beat (Davin 1985, 170).

The striders added the twelve-bar blues to their rags. By 1916, insisted the Lion, stride masters such as James P. Johnson, Luckey Roberts, Abba Labba, and Stephen "The Beetle" Henderson "had learned to play the twelve-bar blues that had evolved from the spirituals" and incorporated it into their style. "We all knew W. C. Handy's 'St. Louis Blues,' 'Memphis Blues,' 'Beale Street Blues,' and 'Yellow Dog Blues,'" he conceded.

The rocking stride beat coupled with the twelve-bar blues simulated a ring shout in a church gathering. "[Ring] shouts are stride," Willie "The Lion" Smith declared. "When James P. [Johnson], Fats [Waller], and I would get a romp-down about going, that was playing rocky, just like the Baptist people sing" (Smith 1978, 83). The Lion compared Abba Labba to "an old-time Baptist preacher shouting at his congregation" (63).

James P. Johnson helped popularize the sanctified-sounding stride through piano rolls. In 1916, he started to produce piano rolls for the Aeolian Company. "I cut one or two rolls a month of my own pieces," he remembered. Johnson "saw them become famous and studied all over the country by ticklers who couldn't read much music." He then cut rolls for the New York–based QRS company, "which had a bigger circulation." By the end of the decade, James P. Johnson and stride had become nationally known (Davin 1985, 177).

A Mania over Female African-American Blues Singers

During an eight-hour session on August 10, 1920, on a sweltering day in New York City, African-American singer Mamie Smith recorded "Harlem Blues," renamed "Crazy Blues," which had been written by vaudeville trooper/pianist Perry Bradford and been featured in Bradford's all-African-American revue *Made in Harlem*. She cut the song for OKeh Records, a fledgling company established by Otto K. E. Heinemann that had waxed its first record only two years earlier. Smith, called a "flapper" or a young, independent twenties woman by onlookers, sang in front of the Jazz Hounds, which included pianist Willie "The Lion" Smith, a trombonist, a violinist, a cornet player, and a clarinetist but not a drummer or bassist, neither of whom would have been heard distinctly on such an early studio recording (Bradford 1965, 125).

Perry Bradford had struggled to land the pioneering session for two years. Beginning in 1918, he had trudged between record companies to snag the first recording date for an African-American "blues and jazz" female vocalist (Bradford 1965, 119). "I tramped the pavements of Broadway with the belief that the country was waiting for the sound of a voice of a Negro singing the blues with a Negro jazz combination playing," he recounted. "I felt strongly that it should be a girl and that was what I was trying to sell" (13). He approached Victor and then Columbia but was met with rejections. Prodded by his friends at the Colored Vaudeville and Benevolent Association, the composer finally approached Fred Hager, manager of the recording department at OKeh, who ignored prejudicial threats of a boycott of his label if he signed an African-American vocalist. On February 11, 1920, Bradford took Mamie Smith, who had been a member of his *Made in Harlem* cast, to the OKeh Studio near

Times Square and recorded the blues "You Can't Keep a Good Man Down" and "That Thing Called Love." After solid sales prompted Hager to ask for more material, Bradford assembled the Jazz Hounds to back Smith on "Crazy Blues."

In November, when OKeh released the record, "Crazy Blues" met a wild response. In a week, observed Willie Smith "it was selling like hot cakes in Harlem," where seventy-five thousand customers bought it (Smith 1978, 104). Within a few months, the disc was selling by the thousands throughout the rest of the country. In less than a year, "Crazy Blues" racked up sales of more than three million copies. Purchased by many African Americans, the record sparked a craze for African-American female blues vocalists throughout the country.

Mamie Smith, born Mamie Robinson in Cincinnati, built her career upon the success of "Crazy Blues." In 1921, she scored with "Fare Thee Honey Blues" and "Dangerous Blues." Late the next year, she released the successful record, "Lonesome Mama Blues." In all, the singer recorded more than a hundred blues-based songs.

Other African-American female blues singers followed in the path Mamie Smith blazed. Fellow blues vocalists Alberta Hunter remarked that Smith "made it possible for all of us, with her recording of 'Crazy Blues,' the *first* blues record" (Oliver 1969, 95–96). "After 'Crazy Blues' became a big hit," explained Willie "The Lion" Smith, "every record company and every colored singer got on the old bandwagon. They began to turn out blues records by the ton" (Smith 1978, 106). African-American female blues artists included the Georgia-born Lucille Hegamin, who had toured with the Leonard Harper Minstrel Stock Company, and Katie Crippen, who performed with a young William "Count" Basie. In 1922, blues diva Sara Martin signed with OKeh, and Bertha "Chippie" Hill recorded the blues with Louis Armstrong. Others shouting the blues included New Orleans–born Esther Bigeou, billed as the "Girl with the Million-Dollar Smile," and the Chicago-based songwriter Alberta Hunter, who began as a singer in a brothel before connecting with manager Perry Bradford. The tough-talking Smiths—Trixie, Clara, and Laura—belted out the blues as well.

Columbia Records executive Frank Walker signed Bessie Smith, who reached the pinnacle of the blues singers. He had heard about Bessie from pianist and talent scout Clarence Williams. Amid the blues explosion, Walker asked Williams to travel down South to find Smith. When she arrived in New York City, remembered Walker, "she looked about seventeen—tall and fat and scared to death." But "blues were her life. . . . Almost all of the blues she sang told sort of a story" (Shapiro and Hentoff 1955, 240).

The blues of Bessie Smith had elements found in the African-American church. "She had a church deal mixed up in it," remarked New Orleans guitarist Danny Barker. "The South had fabulous preachers and evangelists. Some would stand on corners and move the crowds from there. Bessie did the same thing on stage" (Shapiro and Hentoff 1955, 243). "Bessie's shouting brought worship wherever she worked," echoed Ethel Waters, the sweet-voiced blues singer who had a series of hits starting with 1921's "Down Home Blues" (Shapiro and Hentoff 1955, 242). During many of Bessie's performances, wrote one contemporary, "Amens rent the air" (Albertson 2003, 119).

Bessie took her sanctified blues to the homes of Americans across the country. In 1923, she recorded "Down Hearted Blues," a song written by fellow blues siren Alberta Hunter and pianist/bandleader Lovie Austin (b. Cora Taylor). Releasing it on February 16 as her first record, Smith sold more than two million copies of the disc. The same year, she scored with two more hits: "Baby Won't You Please Come Home" and "Tain't Nobody's Biz-Ness if I Do." During the next four years, Bessie delivered six more blues classics, including a version of W. C. Handy's "St. Louis Blues" and "Careless Love Blues," to become the most commercially successful female blues singer. In all, she recorded more than 160 songs, most of them for Columbia.

▷

Watch Bessie Smith
perform "St. Louis Blues"

LISTENING GUIDE 8

Bessie Smith

🔊 "BACK-WATER BLUES"

Bessie Smith was the archetypical female blues singer of the twenties. Crass, opinionated, courageous, and strong voiced, Smith led the pantheon of female blues singers into the hearts of black and white America.

Initially, many listeners attributed Smith's lyrics in "Back-Water Blues" to the great Mississippi River flood from April to June 1927 that decimated 16.5 million acres of land in seven states, killed nearly a thousand people, and left six hundred thousand African-American Southerners homeless. On June 18, 1927, the Baltimore *Afro-American* contended that "some owners of the record shops attribute the present popularity of [the song] to the publicity given to the Mississippi River floods, which are laying waste to many former haunts of record buyers" (Evans 2007, 101).

Despite popular perception, Smith likely wrote the song about the flood in Nashville, Tennessee, which started on Christmas morning 1926, and continued to rise through New Year's Day. During late December, Bessie performed at the Bijou Theater in Nashville by taking a boat from the Louisville and Nashville railroad depot to the venue, which was located above the flood waters. During ten days in the town, she witnessed downtown buildings collapse and more than ten thousand homeless African Americans and whites search for shelter. Possibly recounting this experience, Smith recorded "Back-Water Blues" in New York City on February 17, 1927, and released it on March 20, 1927, before the disastrous Mississippi River flood occurred.

In 1927, other blues singers such as Lonnie Johnson and Viola McCoy recorded "Back-Water Blues." During the next two decades, dozens of blues men and women including Big Bill Broonzy, John Lee Hooker, Lavern Baker, and Jimmy Witherspoon released versions of the song.

Unlike some of her other tunes, which used small jazz groups as accompaniment, Smith was backed only by stride piano pioneer James P. Johnson for this twelve-bar blues. Significantly, Smith almost never used drums on her songs. "I don't want nobody settin' time for me," she insisted (Hammond 1977, 121).

0:00–0:03	James P. Johnson begins the song with a rolling stride piano that captures the rising flood waters.
0:04–0:10	Smith starts the first verse about the five days of rain, which matches events in Nashville.
0:11–0:13	Johnson separates the verses with rapid-fire notes on the piano that indicate rain falling.
0:14–0:18	Smith lowers the pitch as she repeats the first verse. Like the first verse and throughout the song, she flattens and extends the notes on a word for a bluesy feel.
0:19–0:22	Johnson again tickles the piano keys to indicate rain continuing to fall. Note how the piano answers the lyrics in a call-and-response.
0:23–0:28	Bessie completes the twelve-bar blues with the third stanza.
0:29–0:32	Johnson provides a stride figure before the next twelve bars of the song.
0:33–0:37	Smith begins the next twelve bars with another verse.
0:38–0:41	Johnson again separates the two identical verses with a stride passage.
0:42–0:46	Smith repeats the previous verse at a lower pitch.
0:47–0:51	Johnson provides a highly syncopated, high-register passage between verses.

0:52–0:56	Smith completes the twelve-bar section with another verse.
0:57–0:59	Johnson plays a highly syncopated passage in a lower register than his previous figure.
1:00–1:05	Smith begins another twelve-bar section.
1:06–1:08	Johnson provides a rolling stride passage to indicate the boat rowing across the flood waters.
1:09–1:14	Smith repeats the verse about rowing the boat again, but at a lower pitch.
1:15–1:18	Johnson offers a stride connection between verses.
1:19–1:24	Smith completes the twelve-bar section about packing her clothes in the boat, taking the perspective of one of the homeless African Americans amid the flood.
1:25–1:28	A stride interlude by Johnson to mimic the rolling sensation of the lyric.
1:29–1:33	Smith begins another twelve bars with a new verse.
1:34–1:37	Johnson hits a low-register stride figure to match the lightning and howling wind of the lyrics.
1:38–1:41	Smith repeats the verse in a lower pitch.
1:42–1:44	Johnson by and large repeats his last phrase.
1:45–1:50	Smith completes the twelve bars with another verse.
1:51–1:53	Johnson plays a transitional figure between measures (defined as the smallest metrical division of a song).
1:54–1:59	Smith begins yet another twelve-bar section.
1:59–2:01	Johnson enters with a high-registered stride flourish as Smith finishes the verse.
2:02–2:09	Smith repeats the previous verse in a lower register.
2:09–2:11	Johnson repeats a variant of his previous stride response to Smith.
2:12–2:17	Smith completes the twelve-bar section. As an example of the flatted, blues-based vocals, note the rising and falling of Smith's voice at 2:13 on the word "house."
2:18–2:20	Johnson provides some strong, insistent chords in a stride pattern to signal the desperation of the flood victims.
2:21–2:26	Smith begins another twelve bars with a new verse. Again, note the rise and fall of her voice at 2:22 on the word "blues" to accentuate the bluesy sound.
2:27–2:30	Johnson provides a passage with rapid-fire notes to create a sense of movement to mesh with the lyrics about leaving the town.
2:31–2:35	Smith repeats the last lyric at a lower register.
2:36–2:39	Johnson raises the pitch of his previous passage and again gives the sensation of movement.
2:40–2:44	Smith completes the twelve-bar section with another verse. She again accentuates the importance of the word "house" by flattening and sustaining the note.

2:45–2:48	A stride interlude by Johnson.
2:49–2:53	Rather than provide another set of lyrics, Bessie hums a flattened version of the melody for a few notes and then establishes a phrase, which captures the utter dejection of the homeless African Americans as the words rise and fall, when Smith moves between notes.
2:54–2:57	Johnson pushes the song forward by a flurry of notes, which again signifies movement to match the lyrics.
2:58–3:02	Smith repeats the previous hum/verse.
3:03–3:05	Johnson offers a stride connection between verses.
3:06–3:10	Smith completes the twelve-bar section with another verse.
3:11–3:15	Johnson dynamically increases the volume in a stride pattern to illustrate the magnitude of the homeless plight and ends the song.

The vivacious Bessie Smith, 1936. Photograph by Carl Van Vechten. *Van Vechten Collection, Library of Congress Prints and Photographs Division*

Bessie Smith recorded with stride pianists and jazz musicians. On her breakthrough hit, she had backing from pianist Clarence Williams, who also managed her for a while. Her subsequent singles included pianist Fletcher Henderson and New Orleans musicians such as clarinetist Buster Bailey. Smith also fronted bands, which included a young Louis Armstrong and stride master James P. Johnson.

Other blues singers worked with jazz and stride musicians. Ethel Waters recorded with James P. Johnson, who she felt "could make you sing until your tonsils fell out" (Waters 1951, 145). Gertrude "Ma" Rainey hired Louis Armstrong on her top-selling "See See Rider." Sara Martin sang in front of pianist Clarence Williams and soprano-sax player Sidney Bechet. She also employed young pianist/organist Thomas "Fats" Waller, a protégé of James P. Johnson, who during the late twenties and thirties became the most commercially successful stride pianist with his signature "Ain't Misbehavin'" (1929) and such hits as "It's a Sin to Tell a Lie." Esther Bigeou recorded with Clarence Williams, and Alberta Hunter sang with ragtime pianist Eubie Blake.

Trumpeter/cornetist Joe Smith backed many of the female blues vocalists. Born in Ohio, Smith came to New York in 1923 and joined Mamie Smith's Jazz Hounds. Recruited by Fletcher Henderson, he joined the Black

Swan Troubadours, which backed Ethel Waters. He subsequently supported other blues vocalists. "He had many records with the Smiths, which is our late Bessie Smith, Clara Smith, and Mamie Smith," remembered drummer and Henderson alumnus Joseph "Kaiser" Marshall. "Bessie always wanted Joe and [trombonist] Big [Charlie] Green for her record dates" (Shapiro and Hentoff 1955, 210–11).

The New American Woman

A new view of American women at least partly precipitated the twenties mania over female blues singers. Before the turn of the century, the "Gibson Girl" represented the ideal of womanhood. Created by illustrator Charles Dana Gibson through a series of drawings in newspapers and magazines, the paragon of female beauty featured a full, hourglass figure achieved by tightly cinching a swan-bill corset around the waist to accentuate a voluptuous bust and large hips. The Gibson Girl wore her long hair on top of her head in a bouffant style that exposed a full, round face, and tended to favor long dresses that covered her legs from view. Socially, she tended to upper-class home duties, deferred to her husband, provided stability to her family, and interacted with other women to discuss local events.

A boom economy in urban America helped to drastically change the perception of American women. During the war years, the American economy experienced tremendous growth. In 1918 and 1919, unemployment stood at less than 2 percent due to the demand for war goods and the rebuilding of Europe. With the advent of mechanization and urbanization, the economic bonanza continued throughout the twenties with low unemployment and inexpensive consumer goods. Only a 1921 recession marred the stellar economic picture of the decade.

In this rosy financial context, many women gained greater economic power. During the war, they had been accepted into the workplace due to labor shortages. Starting in the twenties, when urbanization and an accompanying consumer culture flourished, women found work as stenographers, clerks, and typists.

Rather than cinched waists and long gowns, working women needed practical clothing that would be comfortable during a hectic day at the office. They chose loose-fitting dresses, short enough to allow for quick walking. Women abandoned tight corsets for brassieres that hid their bosoms and traded the curved figure for a flat appearance to avoid sexual overtures in the workplace. Most chose to wear beige and black as dominant colors. "With the entrance of women into the business world," suggested a 1926 observer, "the demand came for comfortable dress which did not hamper the wearer in any way" (Yellis 1969, 52). To permit all sorts of work including

A flapper girl, New York City, 1922. *Photograph by C. W. Turner. Library of Congress Prints and Photographs Division*

factory jobs, female laborers wore their hair short in a boyish "Ponjola" bob, a style initiated by dancer Irene Castle. Sometimes they wore hats and used makeup to create the illusion of small, puckered mouths to emulate their hero, actress Clara Bow. Overall, the women, called flappers, projected the image of motion and youth.

The flappers exuded a fierce independence. Entrenched in the workplace, they did not idly accept the passiveness of the home-bound Gibson Girls but instead sought economic power and self-sufficiency. During the twenties, one observer reported, a young woman "is determined to have more of a grip on the bank account than her mother, to help swell it with her own earnings, married or single" (Modell 1989, 107).

The Nineteenth Amendment, which gave women the right to vote, politically recognized the growing power of American women. The movement for women's suffrage had started during the 1870s through the efforts of Susan B. Anthony and Elizabeth Cady Stanton. In 1878, the two women's rights advocates collaborated with Senator Aaron Sargent of California to introduce an amendment to allow women to vote. After 1887, when the Senate defeated the bill, the National American Women's Suffrage Association championed voting rights on a state basis, and in 1910 and 1911 scored unexpected victories in Washington and California. In 1917, Carrie Chapman Catt led a successful campaign to gain women's suffrage in New York and convinced President Woodrow Wilson to support the issue. On August 18, 1920, Tennessee's ratification of the Nineteenth Amendment solidified a new role for women in the political process that continued into the twenty-first century.

Although not typical of African-American urban women who mostly worked as domestics, female blues singers epitomized the independent, self-sufficient, straightforward woman of the twenties. They were young, operated independently, and exhibited a bold demeanor. Many like Bessie Smith exuded self-confidence rather than exhibiting the demure behavior of the Gibson Girl. "Nobody messed with Bessie," related her niece Ruby Walker, "black or white, it didn't make no difference" (Albertson 2003, 66).

As with the flappers, blues singers enjoyed some level of financial independence. Bessie Smith shrewdly managed her considerable finances and carefully doled out money to her husband, Jack Gee, and her sisters. As she rode the crest of the blues wave and became financially successful, Alberta Hunter let her husband "hang around and accept the nickels and dimes from the people where I'm singing," she remembered. Eventually, she moved to Paris and left him in Chicago so he could "make a man of himself. . . . I've always been liberated," she smiled (Peretti 1992, 123).

Vaudeville and TOBA

Female urban blues singers perfected their craft in minstrel troupes, vaudeville shows, and through the Theatre Owners Booking Association (TOBA). Originally popularized in the 1840s with a set repertoire of songs and skits performed by white actors in blackface, post–Civil War minstrel shows sometimes showcased African-American performers including female blues singers who had a rare chance to appear on stage. In 1906, Ma Rainey began her professional career by touring with her husband in the popular Rabbit's Foot Minstrel Company. The troupe was named the "leading Negro show in America" by the *Afro American* newspaper on April 23, 1904, and was originally owned and managed by African-American entrepreneur Pat Chappelle. The company later featured other blues performers, including Bessie Smith, Chippie Hill, and Ida Cox. Once the Raineys became popular enough, in 1914 they formed their own traveling show called Rainey and Rainey, Assassinators of the Blues. After busking with her brother in front of saloons in her hometown of Chattanooga, Tennessee, in 1912 Bessie Smith joined the traveling troupe of Moses Stokes as a dancer and shared the stage with singer Ma Rainey. In 1918, the twenty-four year-old Smith headed her own review. At age 14, blues singer Ida Cox (b. Ida Prather), who recorded seventy-eight blues gems and earned the nickname "Uncrowned Queen of the Blues," left home to tour with White and Clark's Black & Tan Minstrels to play the racist role of the pickaninny, Topsy. She graduated to other minstrel shows such as the Florida Orange Blossom Minstrels and the Silas Green Show.

Meanwhile, vaudeville (from the French *voix de ville* or "voice of the city"), a new form of urban entertainment, arose and featured a variety of acts performing on a single bill. Vaudeville debuted on October 24, 1881, when entrepreneur Tony Pastor staged both white and African-American performers in a variety show that did not sell liquor and sought to appeal to "middle-class" families. Beginning in 1885, it expanded dramatically, when former circus employees Benjamin F. Keith and Edward Albee founded the Bijou Theater in Boston for their variety shows. Within a few years, a chain of theaters along the Eastern seaboard featured their acts and became known as the Keith-Albee circuit. Other vaudeville theater chains soon appeared. The Orpheum Circuit, established by Gustav Walter and eventually managed and owned by Martin Beck, boasted forty-five theaters in thirty-six US and Canadian cities. In 1902, Alexander Pantages, a poor Greek immigrant, opened operations in Seattle with the Crystal Theater and, by the twenties, controlled eighty-four vaudeville theaters nationally and in Canada. By the early twenties, many towns had access to a national review of performers who traveled between nearly two thousand vaudeville theaters. Although some African-American acts appeared on the white Orpheum circuit—including comedians Miller and Lyles and musical performers Noble Sissle and Eubie Blake—most did not have an opportunity to play the "finer" houses. In a racist climate, African Americans often were barred from attending vaudeville shows or could only attend on a special night.

To serve an African-American audience with African-American performers, in early 1909, twenty-five-year-old businessman Fred Barrasso opened the Amuse U Theater in downtown Memphis and, the next year, launched the Savoy in the same town. In June 1910, he tested the market for African-American theaters in nearby towns with Barrasso's Big Colored Sensation Company and met with success. By September 1910, the entrepreneur established the first African-American theater chain, the Tri-State circuit. According to Jelly Roll Morton, he created "the first Negro vaudeville circuit to play four houses in Grenville, Vicksburg, Jackson and Memphis" (Lomax 1950, 141). Shows at the theaters featured African-American comedians, snake charmers, juggling acts, and especially blues artists. In June 1911, while expanding his operations, Barrasso died suddenly.

While Barrasso was building his circuit, African-American vaudeville performer Sherman H. Dudley, known as the "Lone Star Comedian," founded an even larger theater empire. By 1909, Dudley had opened a string of venues around the Washington, DC, area and Virginia and, by 1916, had built houses in the South and the Midwest. The "Dudley Circuit," consisting of twenty theaters, almost exclusively promoted African-American artists to African-American crowds.

By the time female blues singers became popular, TOBA had been formed. Theaters hiring African-American performers for African-American customers had sprouted in more than forty cities at such venues as The Lyric in New Orleans, Cincinnati's Roosevelt, the 81 Theater in Atlanta, and the Monogram in Chicago. The Dream Theater, owned and managed by Ma Rainey, opened in Columbus, Ohio. TOBA formed in 1921 when Nashville businessman Milton Starr and African-American pianist Charles Turpin, the brother of ragtime pianist Tom Turpin, loosely organized the theaters into a national chain.

Though the TOBA circuit elicited criticisms from performers such as Ma Rainey, who complained that the acronym stood for "tough on black asses," the venues provided entertainment for and by African Americans in mostly African-American-owned theaters. "The audiences in the theaters on the Columbia, Keith, Orpheum and Poli circuits were either white or mixed but the T.O.B.A. audiences were strictly colored," explained Count Basie who played the show houses as a young man with blues singer Katie Crippen. "Some T.O.B.A. theaters were owned by white people, but most were operated by colored people," he added (Basie 1985, 92).

During the mid-twenties, female blues vocalists headlined the more than one hundred TOBA theaters. After her success with "Down Hearted Blues," Bessie Smith spent most of her time on the circuit with her troupe. In 1923 at the Frolic Theater in Birmingham, Alabama, she filled the house and attracted "hundreds and hundreds and hundreds" (Albertson 2003, 43). Clara, Mamie, and Trixie Smith and Ida Cox excited crowds at TOBA halls, and Ethel Waters and Lucille Hegemin spent time on the circuit. Through TOBA, female blues singers gained acclaim throughout the country.

The Expansion of the Record Business to Cater to the Blues Market

A wildly expanding record industry provided a context for the popularity of female blues singers. Within a five-year period from 1914 to 1919, phonograph sales exploded from $27.1 million to $158.7 million. In 1917, record companies sold twenty-five million discs and, four years later, peddled a hundred million records, more than half of them sold by the record giant, the Victor Company.

A new generation of record companies arose to serve more specialized audiences, once recording technologies became available to everyone. Initially, Victor held the patent for lateral-cut discs and sued the upstart labels, which had poached the inventions. Starting in 1919, fledgling Gennett Records battled Victor in court over the patents to laterally cut discs. On February 11, 1921, Gennett won a decision from Judge Augustus Hand of the US Circuit Court of Appeals, who allowed record companies to record laterally cut discs without a royalty to Victor and opened the floodgates for new recording firms.

Many of the dozens of emergent record labels refused to record African-American musicians. "I caught another glimpse of the same prejudice when I tried to introduce colored girls for recording our blues," W. C. Handy grumbled. "In every case the [record] managers quickly turned thumbs down. 'Their voices were not suitable.' 'Their diction was different from white girls.' 'They couldn't possibly fill the bill'" (Handy 1941, 207).

A few unprejudiced companies specialized in African-American entertainers. OKeh Records, the company that recorded Mamie Smith, signed and commercialized blues artists. In addition to records for Czech, German, Swedish, Yiddish, and Polish immigrants, it manufactured discs for African Americans. When Mamie Smith scored her unexpected hit "Crazy Blues," OKeh signed other female blues singers such as Sara Martin, Esther Bigeou, Ida Cox, and Alberta Hunter to its roster and recorded the W. C. Handy orchestra. The company hired pianist Clarence Williams as a talent scout for African-American musicians, who signed to a special line of OKeh discs called "the Original Race Records." The label felt that "the growing tendency on the part of white people to hear their favorite 'blues' sung or played" and the "already immense demand by the colored race for such records has made the Negro Record field more fertile than ever before" (*The Talking Machine World*, New York, August 15, 1923). "Who first thought of getting out Race records for the Race?"

rhetorically asked the company, when it published the *Blue Book of Blues*. "OKeh, that's right. Genuine Race artists make genuine blues for OKeh" (Oliver 1969, 95).

Other enterprising record executives such as African-American entrepreneur Harry Pace recorded blues talent. Studying at Atlanta University under African-American activist and NAACP founder W. E. B. Du Bois, Pace adopted the philosophy of his college mentor by contending that African Americans should focus upon business creation within the context of an African-American cultural identity. In 1903, Pace and Du Bois collaborated in an African-American-oriented printing business and, two years later, published the short-lived magazine *The Moon Illustrated Weekly*, which focused on African-American communities.

In January 1921, Pace left the publishing firm that he had started with W. C. Handy to form Black Swan Records by using $30,000 of his savings. The entrepreneur promised to record stellar African-American artists who he felt had been overlooked by white-dominated companies. "Companies would not entertain the thought of recording any colored musician or colored voice," he reasoned. "I therefore decided to form my own company and make such recordings as I believed would sell" (Ottley 1939, 234–38). Pace vowed to make a "serious bid for the Negro market in this field," recalled W. C. Handy (Handy 1941, 209). He named the company after African-American classical singer Elizabeth Taylor Greenfield, who had been nicknamed the "Black Swan."

W. E. B. Du Bois approved of Pace's business move. "We must develop a business organization to record and preserve our best voices," contended Du Bois, who served on Black Swan's board of directors along with a number of prominent African-American businessmen. "We are pleased to learn that such a company is now forming with adequate capital and skilled management of guaranteed integrity" (Suisman 2004, 1304).

Pace immediately identified and recorded African-American talent. Though hiring African-American classical composer William Grant Still as musical director and first releasing classical records, Pace quickly shifted to blues singers, when African-American classical artists failed to sell in a racist marketplace. He manufactured discs by blues singers Katie Crippen, Alberta Hunter, Lucille Hegamin, Trixie Smith, and, most notably, Ethel Waters. According to Pace's account, he discovered Waters singing in an Atlantic City cabaret and signed her. Waters recalled that "there was much discussion of whether I should sing popular or 'cultural' numbers. They finally decided on popular, and I asked one hundred dollars for making the record" (Waters 1951, 141).

During the summer of 1921, Pace recorded two numbers by Waters, "Down Home Blues" backed by "Oh Daddy." To promote the singer, Pace organized a national tour of the Black Swan Troubadours, headed by bandleader Fletcher Henderson, who also had attended Atlanta University. The record entrepreneur hired African-American newspaper columnist Lester Walton to manage the revue and landed rave reviews in major African-American newspapers. From fall 1921 to July 1922, as the Black Swan Troubadours tirelessly toured the United States, Black Swan sold more than a half million copies of the Waters record and, together with other releases, grossed more than $100,000.

Flush with success, Pace enlarged his operations. He moved his offices from the basement of his home to a building on Seventh and 135th Street in New York City, hired thirty African-American employees, and bought a record-pressing plant on Long Island, which shipped twenty-five hundred records daily. He entered the phonograph business by manufacturing such models as the "Swanola"; the Dunbar, named after African-American poet Paul Laurence Dunbar; and the L'Ouverture, in honor of Haitian revolutionary Toussaint L'Ouverture. In an understatement, Waters boasted that her record "proved a great success," and "got Black Swan out of the red" (Waters 1951, 141). For the next two years, Harry Pace continued to expand his enterprise until he overextended his finances, declared bankruptcy, and, in April 1924, sold his catalog to Paramount Records.

Paramount had already jumped into the blues arena when it took over the Black Swan catalog. Started on December 14, 1915, the company initially pressed German, Scandinavian, and Mexican music and recorded popular dance bands and vaudeville comedians. In 1922, amid fiscal troubles, chief executive Otto Moeser decided to offer "race" selections. "We could not compete for high-class talent with Edison, Columbia and Victor, and we had inferior records: so we went with race records," explained Moeser (Calt 1988a, 22). In July, Paramount signed Alberta Hunter, nick-named "Brown Sugar," who delivered the popular "Daddy Blues" and "Downhearted Blues." Encouraged by its success, the company followed with dozens of her songs.

In spring 1923, former professional football player and writer Mayo "Ink" Williams joined Paramount to fully exploit the blues mania as a record producer, talent scout, and head of the company's publishing arm, Chicago Music. The first African-American record executive in a white-owned company and a former Black Swan employee, Williams signed dozens of female blues vocalists to Paramount. Until bolting to Brunswick/Vocalion Records in mid-1927, he snagged such notable women blues singers as Ma Rainey, Edna Hicks, and Ida Cox. "I could have missed a whole hell of a lot of good singers because there were more artists than there were places to put 'em," he recalled (Calt 1989, 19). By the late twenties, after igniting an interest in male blues guitarists such as Blind Lemon Jefferson, Williams had transformed Paramount into one of the preeminent blues labels in the country that owned a recording studio and fifty-two record presses, which produced thirty-five thousand records a day. As Moeser admitted, "race records put us over" (Calt 1988b, 180).

Not to be outdone by small independent record labels, the more established Columbia Records capitalized on the blues craze, too. In 1922, it signed blues singers Edith Wilson, Dolly Wilson, and Leona Williams with moderate success. Early the next year, it achieved a massive breakthrough with Bessie Smith. Despite this triumph, Columbia never consciously focused on the blues market to the extent that OKeh and Paramount did. Its hits with Bessie Smith seemed a lucky anomaly more than a strategy.

Victor, the other major label, offered very few blues selections in its catalog. With the exception of several sides by blues singers Lena Wilson and Rosa Henderson, Victor contentedly churned out white orchestral versions of blues such as "Blue Hoosier Blues" by the Great White Way Orchestra, "Stack O' Lee Blues" by Fred Waring and his Pennsylvanians, and "Sobbin' Blues" by the Edgar Benson Orchestra of Chicago. As happened many times during the twentieth century, the major companies left stylistic innovations to small independent labels and focused on sure-selling pop.

The Great Migration of Southern African Americans to the North

A growing legion of African Americans in the major cities of the Midwest and the Eastern Seaboard represented a target market for blues records pressed by such companies as Paramount and Black Swan. As World War I progressed and the demand for industrial workers increased, African Americans from the South migrated to the North for jobs and a better life. They had been anxious to leave the harsh conditions of a Jim Crow South, which implicitly condoned regular lynching of African Americans during the post–Civil War era. Between 1891 and 1901, the typical African American in a Southern state would witness the lynching of friends and family members. During the World War I years, on average fifty-six African Americans a year were lynched by white mobs.

Many African Americans in the South hoped to leave racism behind when they migrated to the North. One woman in New Orleans dreamed about the "great chance that a colored person has in Chicago of making a living with all the privilege that whites have, and it makes me the most anxious to go" (Grossman 1989, 36). "They said it was a place of freedom," said "Georgia" Tom Dorsey. "I was looking for that" (O'Neal and Van Singel 2002, 7). "Take some of the sections from which the Negro is departing and he can hardly be blamed when the facts are known," reported the Houston *Observer* on October 21, 1916. "He is kicked around, cuffed, lynched, burned, homes destroyed, daughters insulted and oft times raped, has no vote nor voice, is underpaid, and in some instances when he asks for pay received a 2 × 4 [board] over his head."

In addition to a constant fear of death and racial discrimination, African-American sharecroppers endured natural disasters. Mississippi farmers experienced general devastation of their cotton crops when, in 1914, boll weevils ravaged their fields. Two years later, Alabama sharecroppers sustained a plague of weevils. Beset by ruined crops, African-American farmers found it difficult to get cash advances to plant crops for the next season. To add to their troubles, during the years before the First World War, African-American sharecroppers faced ruinous floods. In both 1912 and 1913, they saw the Mississippi River overflow, followed by severe drought in 1915.

Beaten down at home, African Americans in Southern states looked to the North as a land of promise. One migrant considered Chicago as "the mecca" (Grossman 1989, 4).

The *Chicago Defender* promulgated idyllic images of the Windy City. Established in 1905 by African-American entrepreneur Robert Abbott, the weekly newspaper quickly became the most-read African-American paper in the country. Distributed through African-American porters on the Illinois Central Railroad, by the end of 1916 the *Chicago Defender* boasted a circulation of fifty thousand, which mushroomed to one hundred twenty-five thousand within two more years. In addition to Chicago readers, it attracted people from more than fifteen hundred cities in the Southern states. In Laurel, Mississippi, a resident remembered that "people would come for miles running over themselves to get a *Defender*" (Grossman 1989, 79).

By 1916, the *Defender* was luring African Americans to Chicago. It told readers about "places for 1,500,000 working men in the cities of the North" (Grossman 1989, 85) and cast Chicago as a place "where every kind of labor is being thrown open" (35). The paper described an "exodus" and a migratory "epidemic" of African Americans traveling to Chicago and even scheduled a date for "a Great Northern Drive—May 15, 1917" for Southern African Americans to come to Chicago en masse. "Our chance is now," it encouraged its readers (35). "I bought a *Chicago Defender*," confessed one man from Memphis, "and after reading it and seeing the golden opportunity I decided to leave this place" (87).

Persuaded by the *Chicago Defender* and pushed from their lands by racism and natural disasters, African Americans flooded into Chicago and other Northern cities. Thousands saved cash for the two-cents-a-mile fare to the Windy City. Some rode for free with tickets from agents employed by major Northern manufacturing companies, which sent representatives to the South to recruit cheap labor. In Decatur, Alabama, during 1917, one remaining resident saw "hundreds of houses where mattresses, beds, wash bowls and pans were thrown around the backyard after the people got through picking out what they wanted to take" on their journeys to Chicago (Grossman 1989, 105).

Chicago, the terminus of the Illinois Central Railroad line, faced the greatest influx of African Americans. In 1910, the city had had 44,103 African-American residents out of a total population of nearly 2.2 million. By 1920, Chicago African Americans numbered 109,458, most of whom congregated in the city's South Side.

Other large Northern cities experienced similar exponential growth. From 1910 to 1920, New York City's African-American population increased from 91,709 to 152,467; Detroit's once-minuscule African-American community mushroomed to 40,838; and Philadelphia added nearly 50,000 African Americans.

Southern migrants thought that the railroad had transported them to a promised land. One newcomer to the Windy City began "to feel like a man. . . . My children are going to the same school with the whites, and I don't have to humble to no one. I have registered—will vote the next election, and there isn't any 'yes sir,'" he stated (Johnson 1930, 23). Another enthused that "you don't have to look up to the white man, get off the street for him" (Grossman 1989, 90, 167). Despite riotous clashes between lower-class whites and Southern migrants in Chicago and other Northern cities during the war years, most African Americans felt that they had made the correct choice to leave the rural South.

Most African-American newcomers found employment in their new hometowns. In Chicago, men worked in meat-packing plants and steel mills, which had mechanized and required unskilled laborers. "A Negro could always get a job in the stockyards" at such companies as Armour and Swift, asserted an African-American porter. Other African-American men labored at steel mills such as Illinois Steel. "They were hiring day and night," recalled one migrant. "All they wanted to know was if you wanted to work and if you had a strong back." During the great migration, workers in meat-packing houses and steel plants earned an average of $5.00 a day or 50 cents an hour compared to 65 cents a day in Southern cotton fields (Grossman 1989, 183–84).

African-American women who made the journey toiled as domestic servants and factory workers. In Chicago during World War I, almost half of employed African-American women worked as domestics and collected two dollars a day. Due to the wartime labor shortage, nearly fifteen percent of African-American women labored alongside their male counterparts in factories and received approximately the same wages as men. In all cases, African-American women earned more than they would at Southern field work.

The migrants, flooding into Northern cities and making more money than they had ever earned in the South, created a market for records by African-American performers. During World War I, W. C. Handy "was convinced that our people were lovers of music and they were great buyers. The market was definitely there, waiting to be tapped," he continued. "In Chicago, I had seen cooks and Pullman porters buying a dozen or two dozen records at one time. Not sophisticated music, of course, but oddities that appealed to them, and blues—always blues" (Handy 1941, 208). Clarence Williams, the talent scout who brought Bessie Smith to New York City and earlier had started a music-publishing business with Armand J. Piron, owned a record store on the South Side of Chicago, where "colored people would form a line twice around the block when the latest record of Bessie [Smith] or Ma [Rainey] or Mamie [Smith] came in" (Stearns 1956, 168).

Some songs by female blues singers specifically addressed the situation of African-American migrants. "Georgia Blues," related singer Ethel Waters, "told the story of a Southern gal who felt lost and homesick up North. The piece had universal appeal," she maintained (Waters 1951, 151).

The *Chicago Defender* heralded the blues singers with articles and advertisements. When Alberta Hunter signed with Paramount Records in 1922, it carried an article about the event and featured dozens of advertisements for her records. In May 1924, the *Defender* hosted a sweepstakes for readers on behalf of Paramount to name a Ma Rainey song, which the label called "Ma Rainey's Mystery Record." It awarded first prize to Ella McGill, who won a Roman-design console phonograph for her suggestion of "Lawd, I'm Down Wid De Blues" ("Mystery Solved" 1924).

In addition to advertising in the *Defender*, companies such as Paramount marketed blues to African Americans through a broad, multifaceted distribution chain. After producing discs for 1.5 cents apiece, the firms shipped them at 27 cents per record to wholesalers such as the St. Louis Music Company, which in turn sold them nationally for 45 cents to phonograph, candy, and jewelry shops, shoeshine parlors, and general department stores that peddled them at the 75-cent retail price. The labels also hired Pullman porters on the Illinois Central Railroad and door-to-door salesmen to hawk their wares. "You, too, can develop a profitable business of your own," urged Paramount in a *Defender* advertisement. "We start you—it's easy, pleasant work—full or part-time" (Calt and Wardlow 1990, 11). Through these tactics, in 1925 record companies sold more than seven million blues records to African-American consumers.

During the early twenties, an urban version of the blues captured the attention of Americans, especially African Americans who had recently migrated to Northern cities. Promoted through newspapers such as the *Chicago Defender*, vaudeville, and TOBA shows, and record labels such as Paramount, OKeh, and Vocalion, female singers became popular nationally with this blues form, which first appeared in the rural South at the turn of the century. By February 16, 1924, *Music Trades* magazine reported that "the sale of Negro records is becoming more and more of a volume proposition for phonograph dealers. . . . Dealers who can offer the latest blues by the most important of all colored singers of blues selections, are in a strategic position to dominate the sale of records in the colored population of their locality," it advised. Though discs by blues vocalists sold to a white audience as well, records such as Bessie Smith's "Gulf Coast Blues" became "popular among the younger set of her race in nearly every city," the magazine concluded (Albertson 2003, 64). The blues blossomed in Northern cities and appealed to thousands of Southern African Americans who took comfort in an urban variant of their rural past.

For Discussion and Further Study

Chapter Quiz

1. How did the blues develop in the rural South? What musical elements were influential in its development?

2. How did W. C. Handy popularize and commercialize the rural blues to form a new musical style?

3. How did the success of Mamie Smith's "Crazy Blues" pave the way for the popularity of female blues singers? How did her image and music reflect the new freedoms that women enjoyed in urban centers?

4. How did the image of the "New American Woman" lead to greater acceptance for blues performers like Bessie Smith?

5. What new performing and recording opportunities arose in the 1920s that led to the spread and popularity of the blues? What role did prejudice play in the initial reaction of recording executives to blues performers? How were records separately marketed to African-American and white consumers?

6. What role did the Great Migration of African Americans from the rural South to the urban North play in the popularity of the blues?

CHICAGO JAZZ AND TERRITORIAL BANDS

Hoodlums, Bootleg Booze, and Radio

During the 1920s and 1930s, Prohibition and the popularization of radio stimulated the development of jazz in Chicago and other Midwestern urban centers. In 1920, a new federal law banning the production and sale of alcohol launched the Prohibition era. Rather than end drinking, Prohibition allowed gangster Al Capone to control most of the Chicago-area nightclubs. It also fueled the power of corrupt Kansas City political boss Tom Pendergast, who permitted an illegal liquor trade to thrive in gang-operated nightclubs. By inadvertently pushing the control of nightspots to hoodlums and crooked politicians, Prohibition led to a flourishing, criminal-dominated jazz business in Chicago and Kansas City. Commercial radio, introduced in the 1920s, further bolstered jazz by broadcasting the music from nightclubs and prominent hotels to make it into a national phenomenon and transform several jazz musicians, such as Louis Armstrong, into stars.

At 11:00 p.m. on July 8, 1922, a twenty-one-year old trumpeter from New Orleans sat on board the Illinois Central train bound for Chicago. "When the conductor came through the train hollering, 'Chicago next stop,'" he recalled, "a funny feeling ran up and down my spine. I was all eyes looking out of the window. Anybody watching me closely could have easily seen that I was a country boy," he admitted (Reich 2016). Like most migrants to the Windy City, he "had no one to meet me," the trumpeter remembered. He hopped in a cab and went directly to the bandstand of the Royal Gardens nightclub. Louis Armstrong had arrived in Chicago (Shapiro and Hentoff 1955, 103).

During World War I and its aftermath, African-American jazz musicians, many of them from New Orleans, joined the migration of Southern African Americans to the North. Looking for higher pay and wider recognition, they flocked to Chicago, Kansas City, and New York City to perform their unique brand of jazz. By the early twenties, jazz musicians found employment in cabarets and dancehalls, where they entertained both African Americans and whites looking to hear an exciting new music. Benefiting from the new, dazzling technology of radio and recordings, they spread jazz across the country.

The Great Musical Migration to Chicago

African-American musicians followed the thousands of African-American share-croppers who moved to Northern cities. They migrated for greater opportunities and better salaries in the North, where a recently arrived clientele awaited them. Before the United States entered World War I in 1917, several dozen African-American musicians departed permanently from the South to Northern cities, especially Chicago. New Orleans bands, which performed in Chicago before the war, included groups led by bass player Montudie Garland (1911), trumpeter Natty Dominique (1913), and Bill Johnson's Creole band (1915). Other African-American jazz men arrived in Chicago during the war. "I'd been hearing so much about up North," related Sidney Bechet, "I was having an itch to go. We'd all heard about how the North was freer, and we were wanting to go real bad." In 1917, the saxophonist/clarinetist made the trip (Bechet 1960, 90, 96). From 1917 to 1930, more than 250 African-American musical performers from the South journeyed to the North, mostly to Chicago. They followed early migrants who enticed them with stories of more work and less discrimination.

Many musicians made the trek directly from New Orleans. Of the more than fifty African-American jazz musicians in Chicago during the twenties, half of them migrated from the Crescent City. The musicians, already having played together in various bands, connected with friends to perform in their new town. "I'd say, about 1917—that a whole lot of musicaners started to leave New Orleans for up North, mostly Chicago," remembered Sidney Bechet, "and they was all writing back to New Orleans that work was plentiful, telling the New Orleans musicaners to come up" (Bechet 1960, 116).

The closure of the Storyville vice district, directed by the United States Navy, forced some New Orleans musicians to head north. During late 1917 after the United States had declared war on Germany, the Navy pressured New Orleans city officials to shutter the largest and most prominent vice district in the country. In October, the "Navy started a war on Storyville," recalled Louis Armstrong, after several sailors had been killed and robbed in the District. "The police began to raid all the houses and cabarets" (Armstrong 1955, p. 75). Within a few weeks, the United States Navy, headed by Josephus Daniels, enforced a regulation banning prostitution within five miles of a military base.

On November 14, despite protests from New Orleans mayor Martin Behrman, the Navy officially closed Storyville. "The scene was pitiful," remarked one eyewitness. "Basin Street, Franklin, Iberville, Bienville and St. Louis [streets] became a veritable shambles of Negro and white prostitutes moving out. With all they had in the world reposing in two-wheel carts or on wheelbarrows pushed by Negro boys or old men, the once Red Light Queens were making their way out of Storyville." By nightfall, the reporter moaned, "the once notorious Red Light District was only a ghost—mere rows of empty cribs" (Shapiro and Hentoff 1955, 63–64). "It was sure sad to watch the law run all those people out of Storyville. It reminded me of a gang of refugees," Armstrong later wrote. "I have never seen such weeping and carrying on" (Armstrong 1955, 75). "The people of that section spread out all over the city" the trumpeter continued, "so we turned out nice and reformed" (Shapiro and Hentoff 1955, 65). Though not eliminating work for New Orleans musicians, the demise of Storyville severely restricted it and changed the character of the city.

African-American musicians from New Orleans who were displaced from Storyville traveled north for greater pay. "There was word there was lots of money in Chicago," remembered clarinetist Buster Bailey, who grew up in Memphis, moved to New Orleans, and in 1919 headed for Chicago. From 1910 to 1916, entertainers in the South earned several dollars per evening or approximately $20 to $25 a week. By 1920 in the Windy City, most jazz musicians received a salary of $40 per week. In 1922, when Louis Armstrong arrived in Chicago, union scale had climbed to $52.50 per week (Shapiro and Hentoff 1955, 78–79).

The Chicago Stroll: The Home of Chicago Jazz

During the twenties in Chicago, a red-light district spawned a burgeoning market for jazz musicians. Before the war, a twenty-square-block vice district known as the Levee offered Chicagoans illicit thrills. It contained five hundred saloons, six theaters, hundreds of "concert halls," fifty-six pool rooms, and five hundred bordellos, which housed three thousand prostitutes. In 1912, Levee vice establishments were closed after Mayor Carter Harrison, bowing to pressure by community activists, launched raids.

When African Americans streamed into Chicago's South Side during and after the war, a new vice district appeared with major entertainment venues. The action centered on a South State Street promenade from Thirty-first to Thirty-fifth Streets called "the Stroll" that featured prominent clubs. The *Chicago Defender* referred to the area as "a mecca for pleasure" (Kenney 1993, 15). The *Chicago Herald* warned that "they say the Levee is dead. Perhaps it is, but the ghost of the Levee is stalking about the streets and alleys of the South Side, manifesting unmistakable desires for resurrection" (Spillane 1998, 38).

The Dreamland nightspot on Thirty-fifth and South State streets was among the most prominent cabarets in the area. On October 7, 1914, it opened equipped with the newest electric lights and fans and a dance floor for more than eight hundred people. Three years later, the café reopened under the management of African-American entrepreneur William Bottoms. "The members of the Race who patronize cabarets have always taken pride in this particular resort as operated by Billy Bottoms," related the *Chicago Defender* on October 18, 1924. "Residents and businessmen of the Race throughout the city could feel safe" in the African-American-operated establishment. Like other cabarets in the area, the Dreamland offered drinking, dancing, and, for those interested, a female companion for hire.

When Bottoms remodeled the Dreamland in late 1920, patrons marveled at the opulence of the nightclub. "In the large dome center of the ceiling hangs a beautiful bunch of green foliage, in which blaze red, white and blue incandescent lights," raved the *Chicago Whip* on November 19, 1920. "On the outer edge of the dome are several dozen incandescent lights with the initial 'D.' Hanging from the ceiling there are four lights with shades, hand painted."

Two other Billy Bottoms–run venues flourished near the Dreamland. Smaller and more intimate than the Dreamland, the Deluxe Café offered similar fare and attracted a comparable audience. Located about four blocks from the Dreamland, the Royal Gardens dance hall accommodated a thousand customers. It boasted a "big crystal ball that was made of small pieces of reflecting glass and hung over the center of the dance floor," according to drummer George Wettling. "The ceiling of the place was made lower than it actually was by chicken wire that was stretched out, and over the wire were spread great bunches of artificial maple leaves" (Shapiro and Hentoff 1955, 100). The nightspot catered to a young neighborhood crowd and avoided prostitution by using dance chaperones.

Before the war, African-American businessman Henry "Teenan" Jones opened two vice-riddled cabarets on the Stroll. He first launched the Elite Café No. 1, which housed a bar, restaurant, and a dance floor for up to four hundred patrons. In 1915, Jones launched a second site, the after-hours Elite Café No. 2, which hosted TOBA shows in Chicago. He advertised it as "the most elaborate emporium on the Stroll. Fine wines, liquors and cigars; café and cabaret in connection" (Kenney 1993, 10). On January 23, 1915, the *Chicago Defender*, plugging the African-American-owned business, called it "a Mecca for High-Class Amusement."

The Apex club, another cabaret owned and operated by African Americans, provided after-hours entertainment. Formerly called The Nest, the café came under the ownership of Julian Black, manager and promoter of heavyweight boxer Joe Louis. During the war, when other cabarets closed around 1:00 in the morning, the Apex kept the party alive until sunrise.

Other cabarets, controlled by whites, operated on the Stroll. On South State and Thirty-fifth streets, patrons visited the Plantation Café. Diagonally across the street, party-seekers reveled at the Sunset Café, later managed by Joe Glaser. Established in 1921, the spacious café featured one hundred tables for up to six hundred patrons and a sunken dance floor in front of the bandstand.

White-owned cafés served both African-American residents and whites from other parts of town who wanted the excitement of drinking and dancing on the African-American South Side. The "slummers," as reformers labeled the white patrons, "are apparently pleased with the atmosphere of sensuality and find delight in seeing the intermingling of the races" (Kenney 1993, 24). Pianist Willie "The Lion" Smith—who in 1923 performed in Chicago—noticed a difference between the Chicago mixed-race cafés, called "black and tans," and the nightclubs in New York City: "Somehow it seems . . . that there was a lot more mixing of the races in Chicago at that time than there was in Harlem" (Smith 1978, 127).

Jazz, Prohibition, and Al Capone

Prohibition enhanced the allure of cafés on the Stroll. The drive to prohibit the manufacture and sale of alcoholic beverages in the United States originated with the progressive movement, which from the 1890s undermined political machines in emerging urban centers by instigating reforms that established more democratic control of the political process. The efforts of these activists, many of them women, led to such changes as the direct election of senators, women's suffrage, reform of the banking system by creating a Federal Reserve Bank, ensuring the quality of food through the Pure Food and Drug Act, advances in education, and a sliding-scale income tax.

Congregating on the West Coast and in Midwestern states such as Wisconsin, many progressives wanted to severely limit the consumption of alcohol to reduce the incidence of alcoholism and family abuse. The Anti-Saloon League, formed in 1893 by Howard Hyde Russell in Oberlin, Ohio, led the charge. By the early twentieth century, the group had created its own publishing house that distributed more than forty tons of anti-liquor leaflets a month and convinced some state legislators to ban the sale of alcohol within their borders. As the United States entered World War I, nearly 75 percent of all Americans lived in states that prohibited the sale of alcoholic beverages, and, in August 1917, the Lever Food and Fuel Control Act prohibited the production of alcoholic beverages during wartime.

During the war, the Anti-Saloon League and the progressives pushed for an amendment to the Constitution to institutionalize prohibition across the country. On December 18, 1917, Congress passed the Eighteenth Amendment to the Constitution and sent it to the states for ratification. Within a year, the states had approved the amendment and made it law. In late October 1919, both the House of Representatives and the Senate overrode the veto of President Woodrow Wilson to enact the Volstead Act, which enforced the new amendment. The act provided that "no person shall manufacture, sell, barter, transport, export, deliver or furnish any intoxicating liquor" except for scientific research. On January 17, 1920, the legislation went into effect and immediately changed the consumption of alcohol from a common pastime to an underworld activity controlled by hoodlums.

People streamed into cafés to surreptitiously procure alcohol. They ordered "tea," which consisted of alcohol. Alternatively, patrons came with bottles of liquor and ordered empty cups from the proprietor. They carefully shielded their alcohol from view in case a raiding party broke into the cabaret looking for booze. "It was Prohibition so they couldn't serve booze. You brought your own," one patron explained. "What you'd do is order fruit punch or something like that and they would bring you a setup and then you'd pour your own under the table" (Giddens 2001, 232).

In Chicago, gangs such as the Capone syndicate controlled access to illicit drinking. In 1919, at the age of twenty, Al Capone migrated from New York City to Chicago at the behest of gang boss Johnny Torrio. Torrio worked for prostitution king "Big Jim" Colosimo and urged his boss to enter into the fledgling bootlegging business. When Colosimo refused, on May 11, 1920, Torrio ordered Capone to assassinate the leader. Immediately after Colosimo's death, Torrio took over the gang with Capone as his right-hand man. When, in January 1925, gunmen shot and killed Torrio, a twenty-six-year-old Capone assumed leadership of the South Side gang.

Capone procured liquor from Canada or produced it himself. He used stores as fronts to bottle the booze into gallon jugs and sold it to cabarets or on the street. Capone purchased several cabarets to directly manage the illicit activity. The Capone syndicate reputedly bought the Plantation Café, closely worked with manager Joe Glaser at the Sunset, and controlled other venues near the city. Working at Tancil's cabaret, cornetist Jimmy McPartland remembered how "one night a bunch of tough guys [from the Capone gang] came in and started turning tables over to introduce themselves. . . . All over the place people were gashed and bleeding. The mobsters would break a bottle over some guy's head, and then jab it in his face, then maybe kick him," the cornetist continued. Two days later, authorities found proprietor and former boxer Eddie Tancil dead. "That was the beginning of the mob's moving into the night club business," maintained McPartland (Shapiro and Hentoff 1955, 129).

Gangland interests dominated bookings at many nightspots. Capone and his associates allied with Jules Stein, who by 1922 booked bands into cabarets. By 1924, the Capone-backed Stein joined forces with Ernie Young and Fred Hamm to establish the Music Corporation of America (MCA), which placed musicians in Chicago nightclubs. In June 1926, MCA opened an office in New York City to manage the bookings business in the Midwest and on the East Coast.

To protect his financial interest in the bands that he controlled, Capone frequently assigned bodyguards to key jazz performers. "When I went out on the road," recalled pianist Earl Hines, "Al Capone appointed two bodyguards to go with me, because he felt rival gangs might try to injure me to injure him" (Dance 1977, 61).

Reformers decried the spread of gang-controlled cabarets by focusing on the race mixing, which occurred in some of the clubs. The Committee of Fifteen reform group condemned the "black-and-tan," where "white and colored patrons mingled in intoxicated revels" (Grossman 1989, 170). In 1922, the *Chicago News* blasted the "South Side negro belt. Without a doubt this district is the foulest spot in Chicago," it told its readers. "Black and tan cabarets, buffet flats, soft drink saloons and every form of vice are flourishing" (Spillane 1998, 36). "To a public accustomed to the old and recognized pitfalls—the saloon and the brothel—the cabaret was a new and more intriguing form of moral hazard," Walter Reckless summarized in his 1933 study, *Vice in Chicago* (Reckless 1933, 101).

Despite fears over racial integration, city officials in Chicago supported gang-infested cabarets and allowed them to flourish. Mayor William Hale "Big Bill" Thompson was indebted to African-American voters for their political allegiance and vowed to ensure that clubs could operate with minimal interference. "Thompson's cops were on the take and managed to look the other way whenever something was happening, regarding the Prohibition law," chuckled Willie "The Lion" Smith (Smith 1978, 122–23). "Sixty percent of my police [were] in the bootleg business," confessed Chicago police chief Charles Fitzmorris (Kobler 2003, 69). Actively undermined by the mayor and challenged by Al Capone, the 134 federal agents who had jurisdiction over the broad territory of Illinois, Iowa, and eastern Wisconsin had the thankless and impossible task of enforcing Prohibition.

The Ebullient Chicago Brass Bands

During the early twenties, cabarets in Chicago featured music by small brass bands, unlike the piano-driven cafés in New York City. "Chicago cabarets were a brass player's paradise," explained Willie "The Lion" Smith. "They had the bands and the good horn men out in Chicago, while we had piano men [in New York]" (Smith 1978, 124, 129). Though featuring a floor show consisting of a master of ceremonies, a line of chorus girls, and sometimes singers, Chicago nightclubs highlighted brass bands, which played multiple sets separated by an intermission pianist.

Brass bands showcased a complex combination of popular tunes, ragtime, and a heavy dose of the blues, which became increasingly prominent after the success of the female blues singers. "The one thing those instrumentalists could do was play the blues so that you could dance on a dime," enthused Willie "The Lion" Smith. "The bands proved to be a real treat because we hadn't heard groups in the East that could play the blues and stomps like these guys in the Middle West" (Smith 1978, 129, 123).

Like bands in New Orleans, Chicago outfits accepted a variety of requests from the dancers. "From some of the stuff that's in the jazz history books you'd think we didn't play anything but 'Royal Garden Blues' or 'King Porter Stomp,' but we played the popular tunes of the day," related the Lion. "We played what the customers asked to hear and in those days everyone had a windup phonograph" (Smith 1978, 126).

Café goers danced to the brass bands. They gyrated to the ragtime two-step, the one-step, the shimmy, and the Fox Trot. By the mid-twenties, patrons of nightspots were stepping to the lively Charleston. Twenties brass-band jazz propelled the high-powered Charleston and reflected the high-energy urban life. "Jazz has come to stay because it is an expression of the times, of the breathless, energetic, superactive times in which we are living; it is useless to fight against it," remarked classical conductor Leopold Stokowski in 1924 (Ogren 1989, 7). The same year, Irving Berlin, composer of "Alexander's Ragtime Band," compared jazz to the "rhythmic beat of our everyday lives. Its swiftness is interpretive of our verve and speed and ceaseless activity" (144). The dynamic brass bands and the wild dancing that accompanied them on the Stroll epitomized the shocking changes that had overtaken America and faced rural migrants to the Windy City.

Given the intimate connection between fast-paced jazz music and frenetic city living, writers called the decade of the twenties the "Jazz Age." In 1922, novelist F. Scott Fitzgerald coined the term in his collection of short stories, *Tales of a Jazz Age*. Nine years later in *Echoes of the Jazz Age*, he outlined the shifting definition of jazz as first "sex, then dancing, then music. It is associated with a state of nervous stimulation." By the mid-twenties, Americans had conflated jazz with the decade. Some talked about "jazz poetry," "jazz theology," "jazz drama," "jazz architecture," and "jazz management." In 1924, one newspaper in Pennsylvania even referred to a "jazz snowstorm" (Johnson 2011, 16).

King Oliver in Chicago

Joe "King" Oliver migrated from New Orleans to deliver high-powered jazz in Chicago. Born in Aben, Louisiana, in 1885, the non-Creole Oliver moved as a youth with his sister's family to New Orleans, where he worked as a butler and a gardener. He first studied trombone and then learned cornet in a children's band organized by Walter Ketchen. In 1907, the budding cornet player joined the Eagle Brass Band headed by Frankie Dusen, when Buddy Bolden left the outfit. "They were rough babies who drank a lot and really romped," laughed bass player George "Pops" Foster. After a few years, Oliver teamed with the Magnolia Brass Band, another uptown group of primarily African-American musicians, and then bolted to the Creole-dominated Onward Brass Band, with which he played second cornet behind leader Manuel Perez. "When he crossed Canal Street and became a member of the Onward Brass Band with Manuel Perez," remarked Foster, "then he got real good" (Brothers 2006, 118–19). Next, Oliver landed a job with Edward "Kid" Ory's band. "Kid Ory and Joe Oliver got together and made one of the hottest jazz bands that ever hit New Orleans," recalled Louis Armstrong (Armstrong 1955, 76).

In the spring of 1919, Joe Oliver migrated to Chicago. Harassed by racist police in New Orleans and courted by bandleader/clarinetist Lawrence Duhe, who by 1917 had already relocated to the Windy City, Oliver boarded a train and reached his new home. Upon arrival, he received offers from two bands, Duhe's group playing at the Dreamland Café and Eddie Vincent's band at the Royal Gardens. The cornetist joined both bands. Oliver played at the Gardens from 9:00 p.m. to 1:00 a.m. and left promptly for the Dreamland Café, where he performed until 4:00 in the morning.

An ambitious Oliver soon became a leading attraction in Chicago. On February 22, 1919, the manager of the Royal Gardens introduced the new Chicagoan and crowned him "King" with a golden paper crown. After several months, Oliver quit the Royal Gardens to assume leadership of Duhe's band at the Dreamland. By October 5, 1919, the Oliver band performed at Comiskey Park during the World Series between the Chicago Black Sox and the Cincinnati Reds.

Joe Oliver named his outfit King Oliver's Creole Jazz Band, even though few members, including the leader, claimed Creole heritage. During a tour of the West Coast, "some little smart guy in the audience said, 'I thought you said those guys were Creoles. These guys are no Creoles. They are niggers!'" recalled drummer Warren "Baby" Dodds (Dodds 1992, 34).

Coming from the Uptown section of New Orleans, Oliver and his mates delivered a mix of ragtime, popular songs, and a strong measure of the blues. He specialized in using such items as cups for trumpet mutes to achieve unique and different sounds—so-called freak effects. "He was the greatest freak trumpet player I ever knew," gushed fellow African-American trumpeter Mutt Carey, who also often employed mutes. "He did most of his playing with cups, glasses, buckets and mutes. He was the best gut-bucket man I ever heard" (Shapiro and Hentoff 1955, 42). In one song, remembered Louis Armstrong, Oliver made "his horn sound like a baby crying" (Armstrong 1955, 191). Sometimes, Oliver elicited gurgling sounds from his instrument by playing the trumpet submerged in a bucket of water. "Joe could make his horn sound like a holy-roller meeting," added Carey. "God, what that man could do with his horn!" (Shapiro and Hentoff 1955, 42).

Oliver and his blues-infused band dressed for success. When the Lawrence Duhe group joined the vaudeville act of Mabel Elaine, they dressed in farm clothes and acted like country bumpkins. In contrast, the Oliver outfit exchanged the standard New Orleans red undershirts and suspenders for tuxedos to look sharp in the city.

The well-dressed Oliver band gained acclaim in the Windy City, even among young whites who had been introduced to jazz by the New Orleans Rhythm Kings. "I had never heard any music so creative and exciting as this band played," Bud Freeman reminisced about the Oliver band. "I was not only hearing a new form of music but was experiencing a whole new way of life" (Freeman 1974, 7–8). Banjo player Eddie Condon described listening to the Oliver band as "hypnosis on first hearing . . . Freeman and [Jimmy] McPartland and I were immobilized: the music poured into us like daylight running down a dark hole" (Condon and Sugrue, 1992, 107). In 1922 during an Oliver performance, Louis Armstrong noticed that the Lincoln Gardens "was filled up with all the finest musicians from downtown including Louis Panico, the ace white trumpeter, and Isham Jones who was the talk of the town in the same band" (Armstrong 1955, 189). "Pretty soon," the trumpeter added, "all the white musicians from downtown Chicago would all come there after work and stay until the place closed" (Shapiro and Hentoff 1955, 104).

Louis Armstrong Arrives

In 1922, Louis Armstrong joined King Oliver's Creole Jazz Band on second cornet, likely because Joe Oliver had dental problems that made it difficult for him to play his horn all night long. Armstrong had been tutored by Oliver in New Orleans and idolized his elder, calling him "Papa." "It was my ambition to play as he did," confessed the young cornetist (Armstrong 1955, 77). "Everything I did I tried to do it like Oliver" (Brothers 2006, 110). Besides receiving informal lessons at Oliver's home in the Crescent City, Armstrong took Oliver's spot in the Kid Ory Band after his mentor's recommendation. When he took Oliver's seat with Ory, Armstrong "was doing everything just exactly the way I heard Joe Oliver do it."

Armstrong had been prodded by Oliver to come to Chicago. "He kept sending me letters and telegrams telling me to come up to Chicago and play second cornet for him," related Armstrong. In 1922, after he finished a stint on a riverboat, the young trumpet player "definitely accepted Joe's offer" and "hurried over to the Illinois Central station in New Orleans."

The twenty-one-year-old Armstrong eagerly accepted his second-cornet role in the band, even though he believed that "Joe wasn't in his prime like he was before he sent for me" (Brothers 2006, 130). Nonetheless, in coming to Chicago, Armstrong felt that he had "hit the big time." "I was up North with the greats. I was playing with my idol, the King, Joe Oliver," he wrote in his autobiography. "My boyhood dream had come true at last" (Armstrong 1955, 191).

Louis Armstrong meshed well with his tutor. As New Orleans African Americans from Uptown, both Oliver and Armstrong favored the blues. When he first heard Armstrong in New Orleans, fellow cornet player Mutt Carey felt that Louis "played more blues than I ever heard in my life" (Shapiro and Hentoff 1955, 46). One advertisement in the *Chicago Defender* on October 23, 1926, characterized an Armstrong tune as "the bluest, most tormenting blues number you've heard" (6).

Despite sharing a blues foundation with his mentor, Armstrong seldom produced the freak trumpet sounds that defined Oliver's approach. "Though Joe Oliver was Louis' idol and he wanted to play like Joe, that wasn't his style," explained Lil Hardin, the piano player in King Oliver's Creole Jazz Band and Armstrong's future wife. "He tried to play some of Joe's solos, but they sounded different. Joe always played with a mute, you know, and Louis played clear and straight" (Shapiro and Hentoff 1955, 101). Armstrong preferred the high register on his instrument while Oliver blew freak sounds in the middle range.

King Oliver's Creole Jazz Band. *Pictorial Press Ltd/Alamy Stock Photo*

LISTENING GUIDE 9

King Oliver and His Creole Band with Louis Armstrong

"DIPPER MOUTH BLUES"

On April 6, 1923, King Oliver and his Creole Band recorded "Dipper Mouth Blues" for Gennett Records. It was named after Louis Armstrong, who acquired the nickname of "Dipper Mouth" supposedly due to his unusually large embouchure or his wide smile. In June, the band re-recorded the song for OKeh Records. In May 1925, Armstrong and the Fletcher Henderson band waxed the tune. The composer of the song remains unknown. King Oliver claimed title to the song but Armstrong likely wrote at least parts of it.

As the title states, the tune is based on a standard twelve-bar blues. This performance, the original King Oliver version, contrasts the gut-bucket, novelty style of Oliver with the more precise, clear tone of Armstrong. It also highlights the introduction of instrumental solos by band members above the polyphony of the other instruments. Besides Oliver and Armstrong, the group includes Honore Dutrey on trombone, Lil Hardin on piano, Bill Johnson on banjo, Johnny Dodds on clarinet, and Baby Dodds on drums.

0:00–0:05	Introduction of a trumpet duet by Oliver and Armstrong with rhythm by the banjo in the background. Note the importance of the banjo as a rhythm instrument during this time period.
0:06–0:20	The first three-bar theme of the song by the ensemble with Baby Dodds on woodblocks and the remainder of the band playing multiple melodies (polyphony) in the style of many New Orleans outfits.
0:21–0:37	Restatement of the three-bar theme with clarinetist Dodds soaring above the ensemble.
0:38–0:55	Clarinet solo by Johnny Dodds with the rest of the band playing a stop-time rhythm, which allows a soloist to enter during the "stops" of the polyphony.
0:56–1:05	Second solo by Dodds.
1:06–1:22	Ensemble again provides its interesting polyphony with an un-muted Armstrong and Dodds taking the lead against slightly softer melodies by the others.
1:23–1:36	Gut-bucket, muted, syncopated solo with blues slurs by Joe Oliver above the polyphony of the band.
1:37–1:50	Second solo by Oliver that connects to the first.
1:51–2:08	Third solo by Oliver, ending when the banjo player shouts "let's play that thing."
2:09–2:26	Multiple melodies come from the ensemble for an end, otherwise known as the coda, to the song.

Within a few months, the two-cornet version of King Oliver's Creole Jazz Band made jazz history by becoming one of the first well-known African-American bands to cut a jazz record. On April 6, 1923, the group ventured to the studios of Gennett Records in Richmond, Indiana. "It was something none of us had experienced, and we were all very nervous," confessed drummer Baby Dodds. "We were all working hard, and perspiration as big as a thumb dropped off us. Even Joe Oliver was nervous" (Dodds 1992, 69). In addition to the leader, Armstrong, and drummer Dodds, the outfit included Johnny Dodds on clarinet, bassist Bill Johnson, and Honore Dutrey on trombone. It also featured pianist Lil Hardin, one of the first well-known female jazz instrumentalists. Under the guidance of Gennett engineer Ezra Wickemeyer, who carefully positioned the musicians at the correct distances from recording horns, the band waxed twenty-seven numbers, which included blues such as "Chime Blues" and "Canal Street Blues" and rags such as "Snake Rag" and "Weatherbird Rag." In January 1924, after nearly nine months, the Creole Jazz Band hit with a song from the session, the Oliver-Armstrong–penned "Dipper Mouth Blues." King Oliver's Creole Jazz Band continued to record for Gennett, OKeh, and Paramount and sold discs to an expanding African-American urban market.

Drummer Warren "Baby" Dodds. *Photograph by William P. Gottlieb. William P. Gottlieb/Ira and Leonore S. Gershwin Fund Collection, Music Division, Library of Congress*

Kansas City, Territory Bands, and the Pendergast Machine

During the early twenties, Kansas City, Missouri, underwent social changes similar to those in Chicago and fostered a blues-based jazz. Like other cities throughout the United States during the World War I era, Kansas City acted as a magnet for Southern African Americans. In 1920, after African Americans streamed there from the South and Southwest, the African-American population in Kansas City had jumped to thirty thousand and more than 10 percent of the population. Kansas City welcomed the Walder family, including future musicians Herman and Woodie, who migrated from Texas to Kansas City for a better life. "My dad didn't want us to be raised like he was raised," asserted Herman, who later played alto saxophone with the George E. Lee Famous Novelty Orchestra (Rice 2002, 288).

As in Chicago, where Big Bill Thompson ruled with an iron fist, Mayor Thomas Pendergast controlled Kansas City. In 1876, his brother, James Pendergast, moved from St. Joseph, Missouri, to a fledgling Kansas City, and opened the Climax Saloon, where he offered gambling and high-interest loans to customers. In 1892, the saloon owner won a spot in city government as an alderman on the City Council and, in 1900, helped elect Democrat James Reed as mayor. In 1911, when James Pendergast became ill, he asked his younger brother Thomas to take over the political machine he had built.

Tom Pendergast aggressively expanded his brother's political base through favors to special interest groups and the poor. He doled out contracts to his supporters, aided gambling interests, and during Prohibition actively supported the manufacture and importation of liquor. To secure votes, he distributed clothing, food, and other items to the poor unexpectedly or through Democratic social centers, which he created. Every Christmas, Pendergast bankrolled a turkey dinner for twenty-five hundred poor men, women, and children from his North Side ward. "He did a lot for the poor people," recalled Henry McKissick, boss of the predominantly African-American Second Ward, which usually delivered the majority of its twenty thousand votes to the Pendergast machine. "They'd come up in his office day after day; he'd give them a five or get some help and get 'em in the hospital or something" (Pearson 1987, 87–88).

Free-wheeling cabarets, clubs, and saloons arose in Kansas City thanks to Pendergast's support of the liquor business during Prohibition. Pianist Mary Lou Williams came to the city late in the decade with her husband, saxophonist John Williams. She found "music everywhere in the Negro section of town, and fifty or more cabarets rocking on Twelfth and Eighteenth Streets" (Shapiro and Hentoff 1955, 287). William "Count" Basie, who first came to Kansas City in 1925 with blues singer Katie Crippen, described Kansas City as "a marvelous town. Clubs, clubs, clubs, clubs, clubs, clubs, clubs" (Pearson 1987, 108). "We came to the corner of Eighteenth Street and wham! Everything along the street was all lit up like klieg lights. It was one of the most fantastic sights I have ever seen in my life," Basie added (Basie and Murray 1985, 64).

Gangs controlled the clubs and cabarets, which offered illegal liquor, gambling, and, at times, prostitution. Like Johnny Torrio and Al Capone in Chicago, Johnny Lazia dominated most of the illicit activity. Born in 1896, a young Lazia began as a street tough and graduated to organizing for the Pendergast political machine. By the early twenties, the gangster had infiltrated Kansas City cabarets and clubs and had bought a number of them.

In 1926, Pendergast formed an alliance with Lazia. In exchange for seven thousand votes from the Italian section of the North End, Pendergast agreed to give Lazia free rein to operate his liquor, gambling, and prostitution enterprises. "You know, the laws in [Kansas City] were a little lax," winked trumpeter Wilbur "Buck" Clayton. "Most of the policemen had been crooks, and everything was wide open, particularly a lot of prostitution and gambling" (Pearson 1987, 91). By the time Mary Lou Williams arrived in town, she noticed that "most of the night spots were controlled by politicians and hoodlums, and the town was wide open for drinking, gambling and pretty much every form of vice" (Shapiro and Hentoff 1955, 288).

The Kansas City mobsters employed and protected jazz musicians who worked in the vice-ridden clubs and cabarets. "In Kansas City all them big clubs were [run by] them big gangsters, and they were the musician's best friend," divulged saxophonist Buster Smith. "They give you a job, and something to eat, and work regular" (Pearson 1987, 95). "Those gangsters would always treat everybody right," agreed guitarist Eddie Durham. "If you touched a musician or one of the girls, you'd go out on your ear. Nobody ever harassed musicians" (94–95).

Kansas City musicians singled out several club owners who provided regular assistance to them. "Felix Payne and Piney Brown and Ellis Burton," insisted pianist Sam Price, "were the fellows that really helped to sponsor jazz." Saxophonist Eddie Barefield felt that Brown—who operated a numbers racket from his club— "was like a patron saint to all musicians. If you needed money to pay your rent he would give it to you and take you out and buy booze," he added (Pearson 1987, 97). "Chief" Burton, owner of the "rough" Yellow Front Saloon and a political power in Kansas City, dispensed charity to many musicians. "If you went up to him and didn't have a job, that was right up his alley," related Sam Price, "cause he'd help you get a room, give you some food, give you some money, and really help you" (99). Trumpeter Ed Lewis called "The Chief" a "humanitarian, and we all loved him for what he did for us" (Driggs 1959a, 24).

 LISTENING GUIDE 10

Bennie Moten's Kansas City Orchestra

"MOTEN SWING"

During the twenties and early thirties, Bennie Moten represented the most prominent Kansas City bandleader. In 1929, he recruited Bill "Count" Basie on piano and recorded the best examples of his work before Moten's premature death.

This song, recorded on December 13, 1932, had its origins five years earlier when Buster Moten and trombonist Thamon Hayes composed an earlier version, "Moten Stomp." It features four beats to the bar and an AABA form that continues for thirty-two measures. It showcases a thirteen-member band, which includes Basie, trumpeter Oran "Hot Lips" Page, tenor sax

player Ben Webster, arranger/trombonist/guitarist Eddie Durham, alto saxophonist/clarinetist Eddie Barefield, and bassist Walter Page.

The Moten band, much like the subsequent Basie bands, based their songs on head arrangements, which generally refers to a sparsely composed introduction and ending or theme of the music that allowed maximum room for soloists to improvise unlike more highly composed scores.

The Moten band also relied heavily on the blues as well as riffs, or short, melodic bursts, in its songs.

0:00–0:08	An eight-bar rhythm section introduction with the sparse piano of Basie.
0:09–0:18	Basie launches into a stride piano section, which demonstrates Basie's debt to stride masters such as James P. Johnson.
0:19–0:27	The band explodes with call-and-response by the brass and reeds, which trade riffs.
0:28–0:36	Basie returns with a striding piano with a rock-steady left hand and the syncopated melody on the right hand.
0:37–0:57	In the second part, the sax section takes the lead for two quick choruses with background work from Basie. The saxes offer wonderful dynamics, when the section begins quietly and then erupts with more volume.
0:58–1:05	Eddie Durham solos on guitar by chording rather than picking single notes, assisted in the background by the rolling piano of Basie.
1:06–1:15	The sax section takes the lead again with Basie as rhythm.
1:16:–1:46	In the third section, Eddie Barefield solos on alto saxophone in between riffs by the saxophone section in a manner similar to the stop-time of New Orleans bands such as King Oliver. Starting at 1:38 until the second part of the section, the stop-time ceases and only Basie provides the background.
1:47–1:56	The entire band plays the theme.
1:57–2:16	In the fourth section, trumpeter Hot Lips Page solos with background by Basie. He begins with almost a King Oliver–type freak, slurred note.
2:17–2:26	Ben Webster solos with backing from Basie.
2:27–2:36	The trumpet returns. Again, Page almost uses a King Oliver style of slurred blue notes.
2:37–3:21	The entire ensemble enters with bursts of riffs to state the melody or head until the ending. Basie provides a few flourishes in the background during the last few seconds.

The Kansas City jazz musicians played a slightly different variant of Chicago small-band jazz. Like King Oliver's Creole Jazz Band, they based their music on ragtime, the blues, and popular songs. Unlike their Chicago peers, Kansas City jazz artists emphasized a distinctive, swaying 4/4 blues beat, which originated in the African-American church and entailed a distinctive role for the rhythm section. Bassist Gene Ramey likened it to "an old-time revival, like an old camp meeting." The "trumpets are going one way, the saxophones another way, the trombones are still going a different way, and that rhythm section is just straight ahead," he explained (Pearson 1987, 115).

During the early twenties, African-American Bennie Moten and his band best captured the sound that epitomized early Kansas City jazz. After taking lessons from two former Scott Joplin students, Moten began his career as a ragtime pianist. In winter 1918, he teamed with drummer Dude Lankford and blues singer Bailey Hancock to form the B. B. & D. trio (Rice 2002, 286). For four years, the threesome performed at several of the more than three hundred social clubs such as the Elks and the Knights of Pythias that knit together the African-American community of Kansas City like the clubs in New Orleans. By September 1922, Moten had expanded the band to six members, who performed at various dance clubs and eventually landed a steady gig at the Panama Gardens.

Unlike Chicago outfits, Moten's band and many other Kansas City groups were organized around the "commonwealth" concept. Band members shared equally in the money that they earned rather than a leader hiring sidemen for a set price. "The take would be counted and Bennie would take the expense money off the top, and the rest would be divided into equal parts," explained Count Basie, who joined Moten later in the decade. "A lot of territory bands used to do that. But nobody made it work any better than Bennie. It was just like a beautiful family," the Count added (Basie 1985, 124, 18).

In September 1923, only a few months after King Oliver recorded for Gennett, Moten and his Five Jazz Hounds entered the OKeh studio in Chicago. Prodded by record-store owner and African-American entrepreneur Winston Holmes, the band recorded eight songs, including two instrumentals, "Elephant's Wobble" and "Crawdad Blues." On the other six songs, they backed blues singers Mary Bradford and Ada Brown, both of whom had migrated from Kansas City to Chicago and returned to their hometown.

Moten's records embodied the striding rhythms of sanctified church music. "If Bennie would lose his left hand, wouldn't be no Moten style," trumpeter Booker Washington mentioned. "That's the key to that. His rhythm combined with the percussion, the bass especially" (Pearson 1987, 129). The propulsive rhythm gave the music a swinging feeling that defined the Kansas City sound.

Moten partly owed his success to the Tom Pendergast machine, which controlled the cabarets and the musicians who worked in them. "Bennie was a businessman first and last," explained trumpeter Oran "Hot Lips" Page. "He had a lot of connections out there, and he was a very good friend of Pendergast, the political boss. Through contacts of this kind, he was able to control all the good jobs and choice locations in and around Kansas City" (Shapiro and Hentoff 1955, 297). "Bennie was very strong politically in those days," agreed Ed Lewis, who stayed with Moten for six years. "Pendergast was for him, and so was Judge Holland and Tommy Gershwin, the prosecuting attorney" (Driggs 1959a, 24).

The George E. Lee Famous Novelty Orchestra competed with Moten for dominance in Kansas City. Forming in 1920, the band featured singer Lee and his younger sister Julia on piano along with such standouts as saxophonist Herman Walder. It generally entertained customers at the Inglenook cabaret near the Panama, where Moten performed. Like the Moten group, Lee's outfit periodically backed blues singers on record.

Rather than blues-inflected, swinging instrumentals, the band concentrated on popular songs. Trumpeter Hugh Jones "liked George Lee's band best because it played more popular music" (Pearson 1987, 149). Lee's outfit added a vaudeville-type variety show to enhance the musical entertainment. "They did novelties, like sing different songs and get us to do little acts," recalled violinist and bandleader Clarence Love.

In 1920, pianist Jesse Stone launched the Blues Serenaders, which delivered a sound similar to Moten's style. The group evolved from a school band in St. Joseph, Missouri, where the group met. Adding members constantly, during the late 1920s Stone moved to Kansas City and packed cabarets with customers, but never rivaled the prominence of Moten or Lee.

During the early 1920s, Walter Page and his Blue Devils attracted attention in and around Kansas City. Page, educated at Kansas State University, periodically joined Moten for concert dates. "Bennie was paying for my food and transportation, so when I'd finished a weekend I'd made me $20.00 and had a ball," remembered the bassist (Driggs 1958, 13). In 1923, Page took a job as head of Billy King's Road Show, which toured the TOBA circuit. Two years later, when the show disbanded, Page kept the group together as Walter Page's Original Blue Devils and used King Oliver as his model. The leader, known as "the Big 'Un," popularized the "strolling" or "walking bass," which accentuated all four beats rather than the two-beat approach of most other bands to further define the driving Kansas City sound.

Because Kansas City had a small population compared to Chicago, most Kansas City bands found steady work by traveling from their home base to specific geographic territories in other states. "We went all through Oklahoma, trailing Bennie Moten, and he's trailing us," mentioned Herman Walder of the George E. Lee orchestra (Pearson 1987, 150). "At those places like Oklahoma," agreed trumpet player Booker Washington who played with Moten, "we exchanged two cities. George Lee played one week in one town, in Tulsa, and we'd play a week in Oklahoma City. Then George would go to Oklahoma City, and we'd go to Tulsa." Sometimes, the Moten band "left Oklahoma and made a tour through the South, Texas and Louisiana" (126). Branching out, Lee played "ballrooms all up through the Midwest and down South, as far out as Arizona and North Dakota," related saxophonist Budd Johnson. "We used to play all the state fairs, two or three days at a time, in these little towns" (Zwerin 1968, 19).

Other bands grabbed different territories. Jesse Stone's Blues Serenaders journeyed to the "wilderness," according to Ed Lewis, "around Sioux Falls [South Dakota], and Lincoln, Nebraska" (Driggs 1959, 23). Walter Page and the Blue Devils traveled in two seven-passenger Cadillacs, towing an equipment trailer mostly in the region from Wichita, Kansas, to Oklahoma City but at times trekked as far as Tennessee, Colorado, and Texas. "Mostly we would be playing one-night stands," asserted Basie about the Blue Devils. "We'd come in and play a dance and move on to the next town on our schedule" (Basie 1985, 20).

The movement of territory bands extended the Kansas City sound through a large geographic area. "The Kansas City influence first spread within a radius from Texas to Oklahoma and into Missouri," asserted drummer Jo Jones. "Men based in Kansas City would do one-nighters through all those territories" (Shapiro and Hentoff 1955, 296).

Louis Armstrong Becomes a Star

As territory bands spread across the Midwest and the Southwest, Louis Armstrong broke from his mentor Joe Oliver and set his sights on New York City. Within two years, he became the first African-American jazz soloist to create a national stir.

Armstrong's wife, Lil Hardin Armstrong, who in 1921 joined King Oliver's Creole Jazz Band and three years later married Armstrong, convinced the trumpeter to break with his idol, Joe Oliver. "I thought the main thing to do was to get him away from Joe," asserted Lil. "I encouraged him to develop himself, which was all he needed. He's a fellow who didn't have much confidence in himself" (Shapiro and Hentoff 1955, 101). New Orleans trombonist Preston Jackson, who sporadically played in the Oliver band, felt that "if it wasn't for Lil, Louis would not be where he is today. Lil is the cause of Louis leaving Joe Oliver's band, where he was playing second trumpet, and going out for himself, and thereby gaining a little recognition," Jackson contended (95).

Prodded by his wife, in autumn 1924 Louis Armstrong left the King Oliver Creole Jazz Band and Chicago. When he landed in New York City, Armstrong connected with the orchestra of Fletcher Henderson. "Knowing the way that horn sounded, I had to try to get him for my band that was scheduled to open at the Roseland Ballroom," Henderson reminisced (Shapiro and Hentoff 1955, 203).

When Louis joined the Henderson band in October, he immediately attracted attention. "When he left Joe and joined Fletcher Henderson," contended Preston Jackson, "he became known here and abroad" (Shapiro and Hentoff 1955, 102). "Nobody had ever heard so much horn-blowing before. [Armstrong] almost caused a riot," vividly recalled Duke Ellington, who had landed in New York before Armstrong (Firestone 1993, 112). "Louis Armstrong hit town!" declared Rex Stewart, who became a trumpet star in Ellington's band. "I went mad with the rest of the town. I tried to walk like him, talk like him, eat like him, sleep like him. I even bought a pair of big policeman shoes like he used to wear and stood outside his apartment waiting for him to come out so I could look at him" (Shapiro and Hentoff 1955, 206).

In November 1925, a restless Louis returned to Chicago. In the Windy City, the trumpeter signed a management contract with Joe Glaser, the mob-influenced music entrepreneur who owned the Sunset Café. With Glaser's help, Armstrong worked briefly with the smooth-sounding orchestra of Erskine Tate at the Vendome Theater, where he furnished music for silent films and live shows such as Giacomo Puccini's three-act opera, *Madame Butterfly*. By April 1926, the

Louis Armstrong in New York City. *Photograph by William P. Gottlieb. William P. Gottlieb/Ira and Leonore S. Gershwin Fund Collection, Music Division, Library of Congress*

trumpeter moved to the six-hundred-seat Sunset, where he performed in the band of Carroll Dickerson, which included pianist Earl Hines. Soon, the Glaser-backed Armstrong assumed leadership of the band. "He played shows at the Sunset with a sixteen- or seventeen-piece band," explained the cabaret manager. "Besides the band we had twelve chorus girls, twelve show girls and big name acts" (Shapiro and Hentoff 1955, 108).

At the Sunset, the "eccentric" dance team of Brown and McGraw performed with Armstrong who honed his improvisational skills by accompanying the dance act. Professional dancers such as Earl "Snake Hips" Tucker, Jigsaw Jackson, and Rubberlegs Williams perfected a speedy, extremely variable, and athletic style of dance known as "eccentric" dancing. During the World War I era, eccentric dancers were accompanied by many jazz bands to forge a century-long connection between jazz and dance. In 1915, Morgan Prince danced to the beats of the Creole Orchestra, and Joe Frisco accompanied the Tom Brown band.

Herbert Brown and Naomi McGraw were well-known African-American eccentric dancers. In 1919, they married and, two years later, quit their jobs for stage careers. The duo developed a dance routine that they performed at vaudeville theaters and on the TOBA circuit. In 1924, the couple settled in Chicago and danced at local cabarets such as the Lincoln Gardens and the Plantation Café. After taking their eccentric dance act to New York City, the team returned to Chicago. On October 14, 1925, *Variety* described their routine as a "million twists and turns, grimaces and floor fol-de-rol plus the time step, which clicks all the way."

Starting in summer 1926, Louis Armstrong performed with the Brown-McGraw team at the Sunset. Whenever the dance duo moved, Armstrong followed on his horn. "They did a jazz dance that just wouldn't quit. I'd blow for their act, and every step they made, I'd put the notes to it," recollected the trumpeter (Shapiro and Hentoff 1955, 106). Adolphus "Doc" Cheatham, a trumpeter and bandleader who frequented the Sunset, saw Armstrong play to "every step they made" (Harker 2008, 89, 96). After a year of soloing to the furious dancing, Armstrong had sharpened his improvising skills beyond any other jazz instrumentalist.

Armstrong took his perfected skills into a Chicago studio with a small band that he assembled for recording, which featured his wife on piano, trombonist Kid Ory, Johnny Dodds on clarinet, and Johnny St. Cyr on banjo and guitar. On November 12, 1925, Louis Armstrong's Hot Five cut three songs: "Gut Bucket Blues," "My Heart," and "Yes I'm in De Barrell." In February the next year, the group recorded four more songs, which included such tunes as "You're Next," and "Oriental Strut." Replacing Lil Hardin with Earl Hines and sometimes adding other members to create Louis Armstrong's Hot Seven, the ever-changing outfit continued to record and, by the end of 1928, produced forty-eight more songs, many of which became jazz standards.

Armstrong introduced "scat" singing to jazz with the now-classic "Heebie Jeebies." On the morning of February 26, 1926, Armstrong entered the studio to wax the Boyd Atkins-penned ditty. When he supposedly forgot the words, the trumpeter spouted gibberish to the beat of the music and accidentally pioneered scat singing, which captured the imaginations of jazz vocalists for the next century. "That's the way it started," contended manager Joe Glaser. "Louis forgot the words and just sang sounds. That's the way it really started." "Louis forgot the words and started scattin'," corroborated Kid Ory, who played on the date. "We had all we could do to keep from laughing. Of course, Louis said that he forgot the words, but I don't know if he intended it that way or not. It made the record, though" (Shapiro and Hentoff 1955, 108, 109).

LISTENING GUIDE 11

Louis Armstrong and His Hot Five

◁)) **"HEEBIE JEEBIES"**

Louis Armstrong launched jazz scat singing with this song. Supposedly unable to remember the words, he blurted out nonsense syllables expertly to the rhythm to initiate a wild, classic tune.

According to clarinetist/saxophonist/jazz scenester "Mezz" Mezzrow upon hearing the record, "we thought we were dreaming when we heard him begin singing the words—'I got the heebies, I mean the jeebies'— and then sail into a sequence of riffs that sounded just like his horn-playing. He started a musical craze that became as much a part of America's cultural life as Superman" (Mezzrow 1946, 117, 119).

Reed player Boyd Atkins, who like Armstrong had played in bands under Fate Marable on Mississippi

riverboats, wrote the song. A year after the smashing success of "Heebies Jeebies," he joined the Armstrong band at the Sunset Café in Chicago.

The term "heebie jeebies" had been coined in 1923 by cartoonist Billy DeBeck in his popular comic strip *Barney Google* to denote anxiety about a certain person or place. In a short period of time, it appeared as the title of a song recorded by Lovie Austin and her Blues Serenaders, as well as providing the name for a Chicago South Side magazine and the title for a movie.

In addition to Armstrong, the personnel on this 1926 recording included Lil Hardin Armstrong on piano, Kid Ory on trombone, Johnny Dodds on clarinet, and Johnny St. Cyr on banjo.

0:00–0:10	Brief, relatively simple piano introduction by Lil Hardin Armstrong.
0:11–0:39	The trumpet of Armstrong swoops into the music and the band starts in a typical New Orleans style with the polyphonic interplay of the horns.
0:40–0:58	Armstrong offers a solo with rhythm backing from the banjo.
0:59–1:25	Johnny Dodds solos on clarinet with backing from St. Cyr.
1:26–1:53	Armstrong burst into his vocals, singing about the heebie-jeebies dance with backing from St. Cyr on banjo.
1:54– 2:12	At this point, Armstrong forgets the words and breaks into his scat singing to make jazz history. He ends with the words about the heebie-jeebies dance. His vocals mimic the sound of his trumpet.
2:13–2:21	Armstrong starts to sing the words again about the heebie-jeebies dance.
2:22–3:00	The ensemble breaks into typical New Orleans jubilation. Before the ending or the coda at 2:48, St. Cyr strums the banjo twice and someone shouts "got the heebie jeebies." At 2:54, St. Cyr strums the banjo twice again and Louis responds, "I just have to have the heebies" in a playful manner. At 2:58, St. Cyr offers two more banjo strums and in a response the band as an ensemble ends the song to complete the call-and-response ending.

Armstrong's Hot Five scored with several tunes. In July 1926, the Hot Five hit with "Muskrat Ramble." The next year, Armstrong and his compatriots followed with "Potato Head Blues," "Big Butter and Egg Man," and "Keyhole Blues." In 1928, the Hot Five recorded the popular "West End Blues" and "Hotter Than That."

Jazz Moves from Chicago to Harlem

Federal Prohibition agents forced the bustling and successful Chicago jazz scene to relocate to New York City. In 1927, federal agents successfully cracked down on Chicago cabarets and shuttered many of them. Prodded by reformers and disregarding protests from Chicago mayor Big Bill Thompson, in March agents raided and closed Chicago's Plantation Café. A few months later, they shut down three other nightspots that featured jazz music, such as the Sunset. In February 1928, when the Supreme Court refused to hear an appeal from club owners, Prohibition enforcement agents closed eight more clubs. "Chicago was once the hottest café town in the United States, famous for sizzling music, torrid night life, [it was] a great little spot for the little guys," moaned *Variety* in March 1928. "But that's history now. Night by night it gets tougher for the cabarets. One by one, Chicago's night clubs are biting the dust," the magazine concluded. By May, Prohibition officials had displaced 250 cabaret entertainers and 200 musicians. On March 2, 1929, the *Chicago Defender* pessimistically reported that "most of the night clubs using small orchestras have been closed on account of prohibition violations, making it pretty tough on our musicians."

Gang violence in nightclubs exacerbated the troubles of Chicago musicians. The Italian South Side mobsters, headed by Al Capone, and his North Side Irish nemesis, George "Bugs" Moran, bitterly fought one another to control the bootlegging business in the Windy City. In November 1924, Capone assassinated the head of the Irish mob, Dion O'Banion in a North Side flower shop. In retaliation, Moran, the new head of the North Siders, attempted to murder Capone twice. By late 1927, the war between rival gangs led to bombings of the Capone-owned Plantation Café and the Café de Paris. *Variety* warned that the Plantation Café had "turned rough—even for those seeking high-power[ed] . . . thrills" (Kenney 1993, 149). On February 14, 1929, the five-year feud between Capone and Moran climaxed with the "St. Valentine's Day Massacre." Gunning for Moran, Capone's cronies executed five members of the North Side gang with Tommy guns in a garage. "It looked to me like the whole continent was being drowned in a bath of blood," remarked Milton "Mezz" Mezzrow (Mezzrow 1946, 159).

The closing of many cabarets and mob-instigated violence drove many musicians from Chicago to New York City. Garvin Bushell, the clarinetist who played in Chicago with Mamie Smith and many New Orleans transplants, left for New York and eventually joined Elmer Snowden and Fletcher Henderson. "You could sit in your house any night in Chicago and hear a huge explosion down the block," he related. "I couldn't stay in Chicago. Couldn't take it" (Peretti 1992, 147). As early as April 1927, Joe Oliver left the city for New York, when the Plantation Café closed.

Louis Armstrong, the most visible jazz star, likewise permanently left the Windy City for New York City. By June 1929, he performed in a Broadway revue, *Hot Chocolates*, which had been bankrolled by gangster Dutch Schultz (b. Arthur Flegenheimer) and conceived by brothers Conrad and George Immerman, who operated Connie's Inn in Harlem. Later in the year, Armstrong signed a contract to play at Connie's Inn. "New York seemed to be stricken with the same fever regarding jazz that Chicago had experienced five or six years before," related white Chicago pianist Joe Sullivan at the end of the decade (Shapiro and Hentoff 1955, 269).

The Dawn of the Radio Age

Radio transformed Louis Armstrong from a leading jazz man into a national sensation. Radio was originally developed through the work of several inventors. In late 1900, Reginald Fessenden combined telephone components, a high-frequency spark transmitter, and a thin wire dipped in nitric acid to obtain a partial, broken-voice transmission of a human speaking. In a few years, he converted vocal sound into higher, more powerful frequencies so it could be carried over long distances and then returned to lower frequencies that could be heard by the human ear. On December 24, 1906, Fessenden conducted the first clear, long-distance radio transmission by broadcasting a record by George Handel, playing "O, Holy Night" on the violin and wishing everyone a merry Christmas. Within two years, Hugo Gernsback, later a radio and science-fiction magazine publisher, manufactured a ten-cent crystal radio, which within four years allowed more than four hundred thousand Americans to listen to broadcasts.

In 1919, General Electric launched a national radio business named the Radio Corporation of America, or RCA for short, under David Sarnoff, a Russian immigrant to New York City. Rather than simply facilitating point-to-point transmission, Sarnoff hoped to "make radio a household utility in the same sense as the piano or phonograph. The idea," he speculated, "is to bring music into the house by wireless" (Balk 2006, 33).

On October 27, 1920, Westinghouse Electric and Manufacturing Company, a rival to RCA, received a license for the first commercial radio station, KDKA, in Pittsburgh. A few days later, it broadcast the presidential election results. In addition to election returns, Westinghouse broadcast records, live band performances, news, and farm reports. In early 1921, it hired the first full-time radio announcer, Harold Arlin, and transmitted play-by-play accounts of boxing matches and Pittsburgh Pirates baseball games.

In July 1921, RCA countered by obtaining a license for a station and immediately broadcast the heavyweight championship boxing match between

An early radio, 1925. *Library of Congress Prints and Photographs Division*

Frenchman Georges Carpentier and American Jack Dempsey from Jersey City to three hundred thousand listeners. At the same time, RCA effectively cornered the radio market by joining forces with Westinghouse in a series of negotiations. By the end of 1921, the company had laid the groundwork for the commercialization of radio by gathering all the important patents for radio manufacture under its control.

By 1922, America had fully embraced radio. Consumers spent more than $60 million on radio sets. "So rapid has been the spread of the fad that dealers in radio apparatus report that they will be unable to supply the orders for several months," announced *Variety* on March 10. "The rate of increase in the number of people who spend at least a part of their evening in listening in is almost incomprehensible," *Radio Broadcast* informed its readers in May. "The movement is growing in some kind of geometrical progression" (Balk 2006, 41).

Technological advances enhanced the quality of the radio experience to heighten the popularity of the new medium. In 1922, loudspeakers replaced headphones to allow several people to listen to a radio simultaneously. By 1925, electrification permitted many Americans to easily plug radios directly into an outlet in their homes and dispense with a heavy battery.

Sales soared with streamlined and affordable radios. In 1923, when Sears, Roebuck and Montgomery Ward began to carry a line of inexpensive radios in their catalogs, more than four hundred thousand American homes owned a radio. By 1926, more than five million American homes, or almost 20 percent of all households, enjoyed radio broadcasts. Given that on average five people per family listened to a single radio set, twenty-five million Americans tuned into their favorite station every week. By the end of the decade, more than eleven million families, or 41 percent of all households, had purchased a radio, and annually were spending $843 million on radio sets.

Many national businesses used the rising medium to advertise products. Dodge automobiles sponsored a *Dodge Victory Hour*, named after a new car model. Champion Spark Plugs, Maxwell House Coffee, and the battery-producing American Ever Ready Company enticed listeners with ads. Albert Lasker of Chicago's Lord and Thomas advertising agency "recognized [radio's] great potential [for marketing] at the outset" and convinced such clients as Pepsodent toothpaste, Palmolive soap, Lucky Strike cigarettes, and Kleenex tissues to sponsor programs, including music shows, on radio stations (Balk 2006, 89).

National networks magnified the influence exerted by radio over consumers. In September 1926, RCA incorporated the National Broadcasting Company (NBC) as a network with twenty-five affiliated radio stations. The affiliates paid NBC to use common programming for designated time periods, while NBC shared ad revenues with its affiliates. With a much larger geographic reach, NBC attracted more advertisers, which paid to be heard on broadcasts to thousands of people. On November 15, 1926, NBC aired a four-hour comedy and music extravaganza on its affiliate stations. The next day, the *Washington Post* proclaimed that radio "has put aside its swaddling clothes and has become a potential giant." By June 11, 1927, when Charles Lindbergh returned from a transatlantic flight to receive the Distinguished Flying Cross in Washington, DC, NBC broadcast the ceremony and accompanying parade on fifty stations in twenty-four states.

Not to be outmaneuvered, the Columbia Phonograph Company bought a financially troubled Chicago station and changed its name to the Columbia Phonographic Broadcasting Systems, with sixteen affiliates from Boston to St. Louis. On Sunday afternoon, September 18, 1927, the network premiered from WOR in Newark with an hour-long spectacular. A year later, when the record company divested itself from the network, William S. Paley, the son of a Philadelphia cigar magnate, bought the network and changed its name to the Columbia Broadcasting System, shortened to CBS.

Besides helping companies to sell their products to a national market, the consolidation of the radio industry helped homogenize America. Networks ensured that people from across the country heard the same shows on the same day and learned about the sports players, news figures, comedians, singers, and musicians who became shared American cultural icons. Though some stations catered to specific population niches, national networks reached across the country to develop a standardized American culture and a national identity.

Radio Catapults Jazz into the National Spotlight

Network radio resulted in a national platform for music. Though including spoken-word commentaries, farm-related reports, ethnic and religious shows, and educational programming, most broadcasts focused on music. Stations spun popular discs and aired a varied array of live concerts from orchestras to kazoo recitals.

In 1928, the merger of RCA with Victor Records to establish RCA Victor cemented the close connection between music and radio. RCA had previously bought the largest vaudeville booking and theater chain, the Keith-Albee-Orpheum enterprise. The two acquisitions allowed the company to dominate the "amusement" business. "The Radio Corporation, its subsidiaries and affiliated companies will comprise a group of properties completely equipped to participate in every branch of popular entertainment," declared the front page of the *New York Times* on December 13.

Jazz music and radio rose together. In 1921, the first commercial station, KDKA, broadcast a program of male baritone vocalist Lois Deppe and pianist Earl Hines, a future band mate of Louis Armstrong and for nearly a dozen years the bandleader at the Al Capone–operated Grand Terrace Ballroom in Chicago. "The broadcast caused a lot of excitement, especially in the colored neighborhood [in Pittsburgh] because this was 1921. A lot of people had crystal radio sets, and there was a radio buff on Wylie Ave. who had a loudspeaker sticking out his window," remembered the singer. "The street was all blocked with people, and we were just mobbed when we came back" (Dance 1977, 134).

Other jazz musicians hit the airwaves. In 1921, Paul Whiteman started a long career in radio by airing on the New York station WJZ. The next year, Kid Ory's band premiered on radio from Los Angeles, and in May the *New Orleans Daily Item* arranged for the Black Swan Troubadours accompanied by blues singer Ethel Waters to broadcast a concert, which reached five states and Mexico. In October 1923, Memphis station WMC broadcast Bessie Smith and "her crack jazz orchestra" from the Beale Street Palace. The singer "known from coast to coast as a singer of blues that are really blue, gave the air some currents that it will not forget, as long as a cloud is left in the sky," exclaimed the *Chicago Defender* (Albertson 2003, 45). The next January, WMC again featured Bessie, who the *Memphis Commercial Appeal* characterized as a "colored singer of deep indigo blues" (65).

In 1924, Nils Granlund broadcast from several nightclubs to thrust jazz into the radio limelight. As the publicist for theater magnate Marcus Loew and manager of the Loew-owned station WHN, Granlund rented telegraph lines to connect the Roseland Ballroom and WHN for remote broadcast of the Fletcher Henderson Orchestra. By the end of the next year, Granlund had wired more than thirty New York clubs and cabarets to remotely broadcast jazz live to radio audiences. In early 1924, the *Outlook* noted that "you can scarcely listen in on the radio, especially in the evening, without hearing jazz. This has been called a Jazz Age, and the United States is a Jazz Country" ("Jazz" 1924, 382). When the decade ended, jazz had "become the piece de resistance in the musical diet of the radio listener," contended the *New York Times*. "In these days when the majority of programs include jazz it would seem that jazz was the wine of music that stimulates every musical taste," observed the *Chicago Defender* on August 31, 1929.

Louis Armstrong successfully rode the wave of radio to become a household name. When he moved to New York City in September 1924 to join the Fletcher Henderson band, he could be heard on the radio thanks to Nils Granlund's having wired the Roseland Ballroom. The trumpeter attracted throngs of fans who listened to him on the radio. "Louis Armstrong had come to New York and joined Fletcher," remembered Count Basie. Though never hearing the band in person, the Count "heard the records, and I heard him on the radio" (Basie 1985, 7).

When Armstrong returned to Chicago in late 1925, he received more airplay. On February 27, 1926, he participated in an OKeh Records extravaganza, which radio station WGN broadcast live. "Come Along! Come Along!" to the "OKeh Race Records Artist Night" at Fort Dearborn Lodge, proclaimed an advertisement in the *Chicago Defender*. Though not headlining the event, Armstrong received air time during the radio spectacular, which promised "Jazz—Joy—Pep." Starting in April 1928 and ending in June 1929, when he played with the Carroll Dickerson Orchestra at Chicago's Savoy Ballroom, Armstrong could be heard on WMAQ nightly. Along with record sales, Armstrong made the leap from popular cabaret player to national star through countrywide radio exposure. The trumpeter, protected by gangs during Prohibition, and backed and supported by fellow migrants to the North, took advantage of new technology to transform jazz from a novelty to a national pastime.

For Discussion and Further Study

Chapter Quiz

1. What role did Prohibition play in the development of jazz during the 1920s and early 1930s?

2. Why did Joe "King" Oliver leave New Orleans for Chicago? What impact did his band have on local white musicians there? What was unique about his trumpet style?

3. How did Bennie Moten's band set the standard for Kansas City groups? What elements of his style were widely copied by other musicians?

4. What role did Lil Armstrong play in promoting her husband's career? How did Louis Armstrong further his success by partnering with the mob-connected manager Joe Glaser?

5. Why did many musicians leave Chicago toward the end of the 1920s? What opportunities were offered to them in New York City that they didn't have in Chicago?

6. How did radio play a role in the growth and popularity of jazz?

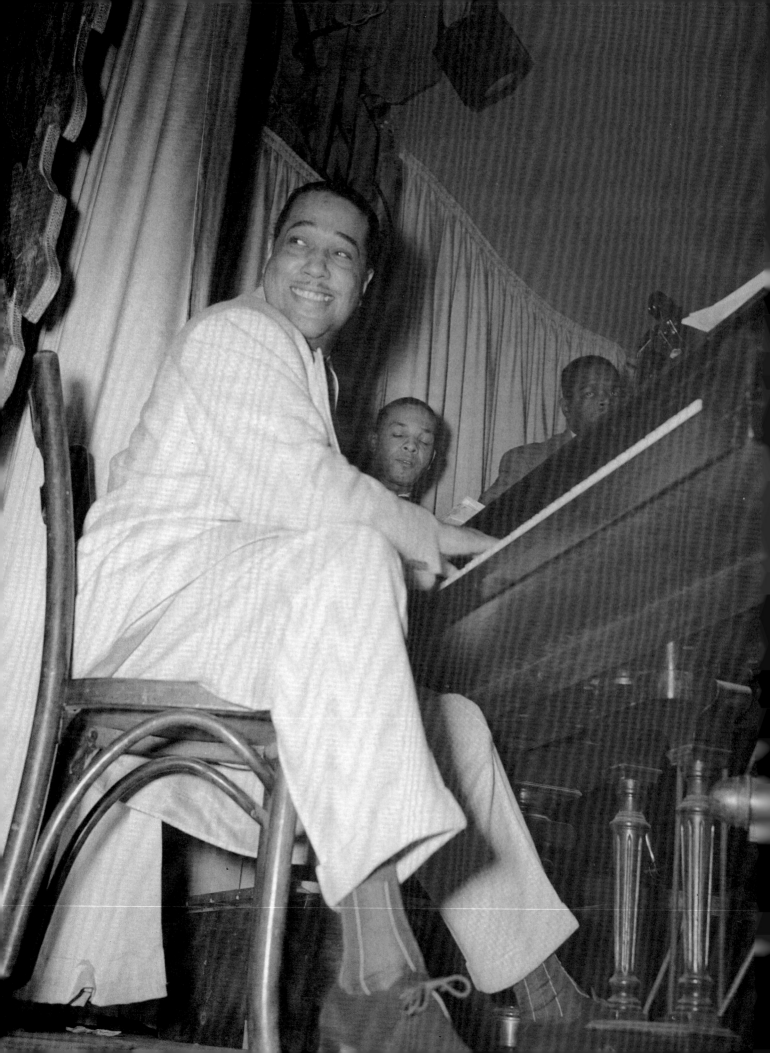

6

NEW YORK JAZZ, 1927–1932

Duke Ellington, the Mob, the Harlem Renaissance, and the Media

T his chapter deals with the jazz business, the importance of new technology, and the complexities of race. It describes the rise of Duke Ellington through the help of mobster Owney Madden and manager Irving Mills, and his appearances on the relatively new media of radio and films with sound. The text also illustrates the complicated racial identity of Ellington who, like other members of the Harlem Renaissance, strove to elevate the African-American position in the arts yet played "jungle" music to please the racist, thrill-seeking audiences who "slummed" at such Harlem venues as the all-white Cotton Club.

On Sunday evening, December 4, 1927, a young white socialite couple put on their best party clothes, bundled into their heavy coats, and hailed a taxi on a street in downtown New York City. The couple jumped into the warm back seat and instructed the driver to head north to the African-American section of town, a place called Harlem in uptown Manhattan. They had heard about the frivolity and forbidden pleasures that the area held from a book they had read the year before, Carl Van Vechten's *Nigger Heaven*. Having enough money to experiment and being young enough to lust for adventurous experiences, the couple hoped to find new and exciting ways to enjoy themselves. The taxi sped toward 142nd Street and Lenox Avenue for the opening of a new revue at the Cotton Club called the *Cotton Club Parade Rhythm-Mania*.

The suave Duke Ellington. Photograph by Gordon Parks, Farm Security Administration Collection, Library of Congress Prints and Photographs Division

As the couple rode toward Harlem, they looked forward to an exhilarating, all-African-American show. They had heard about the Harlem-based, vaudeville-type revue, which featured a line of light-skinned, scantily-clad, African-American chorus girls who needed to be at least five-feet-six-inches tall and under twenty years of age, dance acts such as the Berry Brothers and Earl "Snake Hips" Tucker, comedians such as Butterbeans and Susie, singer-showgirls such as Aida Ward, and a jazz band. "They were top-flight performers designed to appease the appetite of a certain type of African-American performance, the smiling black, the shuffling black, the black-faced black, the minstrel, coon-show atmosphere which existed," explained Cotton Club dancer Howard "Stretch" Johnson (Cohen 2010, 54).

At nine o'clock, when the couple finally arrived at the Cotton Club, they paid a cover charge of two dollars and walked up a long set of stairs. A waiter dressed in a red tuxedo seated the couple at a table covered with a red-and-white-checked gingham tablecloth. As the couple took in the exhilarating sights of the club, they noticed nearly seven hundred other whites seated at tables in the back and along the walls, which had been decorated in a jungle motif with palm trees and bongo drums. One bandleader remembered the club's scenery as a "Southern mansion with large white columns and a backdrop painted with weeping willows and slave

The Cotton Club. *Science History Images/Alamy Stock Photo*

quarters. I supposed the idea was to make whites who came to the club feel like they were being catered to and entertained by black slaves," he added (Calloway and Rollins 1976, 88).

From their table, the couple had a clear view of the stage where the smartly dressed, ten-piece house band, the Duke Ellington orchestra, was performing. The band, previously a mainstay at the downtown Kentucky Club, had just moved uptown to the Harlem club at the last moment, after both King Oliver and Sam Wooding refused the job. The couple heard the orchestra, led by the dapper Ellington, play such songs as "East St. Louis Toodle-Oo" and "Black and Tan Fantasy," which the group had recorded earlier in the year. Between sets by the other performers, the young socialites listened to the band deliver their unique combination of gut-bucket blues and symphonic music.

After watching the band and the all-star revue, the young couple hailed a cab to head back downtown. Though tired from the excitement, they chatted about the night, the performances, and Duke Ellington's band.

Duke Ellington Gets His Start in Music

Edward "Duke" Ellington had worked hard to secure the coveted Cotton Club engagement. As a youth, Ellington took piano lessons and became enamored with music, when, at age fourteen, he heard a ragtime pianist. "I cannot tell you what that music did to me," he confided. A friend echoed that "he was set on fire by the rolling rhythm and entrancing treble of ragtime." Before long, the young pianist could play ragtime progressions and showcased his abilities at the local soda fountain, where he worked part time.

At age sixteen, Duke became a professional musician. Turning down a graphic-art scholarship to the Pratt Institute sponsored by the NAACP, he joined a local orchestra that played at various social functions. Onstage, Ellington drew inspiration from the flashy tricks of stride master Luckey Roberts, whose performances he frequently saw as a boy at the Howard Theater in Washington, DC. When Duke mimicked Roberts, "the kids around the band were screaming with delight and clapping for more. In two minutes the flashy hands earned me a reputation and after that I was all set" (Nicholson 1999, 15).

By 1919, an enterprising Ellington started his own band, Duke's Serenaders. He placed a one-inch advertisement in the phone book that offered to provide "irresistible jass" to "select patrons" (Nicholson 1999, 19). Within a few weeks, Duke was rushing between two or three jobs at a time and averaging about $150 to $200 a week. By 1922, Duke had cemented his reputation around Washington, DC.

Ellington Travels to New York

Accompanied by saxophone player Otto "Toby" Hardwick and drummer Sonny Greer, in March 1923 Ellington and his band mates traveled to New York City. There, they joined Wilbur Sweatman, an experienced African-American vaudeville orchestra leader and clarinetist who began his career by performing in circus bands as a teenager.

Sweatman's experience dated to the beginning of jazz. He played with W. C. Handy and Mahara's Minstrels and, by 1902, led his own outfit in Minnesota that recorded popular rags. In 1908, Sweatman moved to Chicago and, three years later, joined the vaudeville circuit headlining as a novelty act by playing three clarinets simultaneously. In 1916, Sweatman recorded "Down Home Rag" and became close friends with ragtime innovator Scott Joplin. Two years later, he landed a lucrative recording deal, and by 1920 had released twenty-two songs. By 1929, Sweatman's Jazz Band had sold more than a million copies of releases such as "Everybody's Crazy" and "Kansas City."

After a few months with Sweatman, a restless Ellington headed back to his hometown with Greer and Hardwick. He joined a band led by banjo player Elmer Snowden with Art Whetsel on trumpet. "It was just about the most popular band in town," Snowden gushed (Nicholson 1999, 33).

The Ellington Band

Soon, Ellington again became a bandleader. In June 1923, he initially returned to New York City as a member of Snowden's Washingtonians. With the assistance of Willie "The Lion" Smith, the band found work at Barron's Exclusive Club, which had been opened in 1915 by Barron Wilkins.

By September 1923, the Hollywood Café in Times Square at West Forty-ninth Street was hosting the band. A small venue with a bandstand large enough for only a few musicians, the basement club had a low ceiling and featured floor shows aimed primarily at white audiences. According to Duke, the venue showcased "a colored chorus, about six girls, all pretty chicks" as well as singers and a comedian. The band played two sets a night, backing the showgirls and playing dance music (Nicholson 1999, 49). The club became a hangout for celebrities such as white bandleader Paul Whiteman and actress Joan Crawford. By the summer of 1924, the Hollywood Club reopened as the Kentucky Club with the Washingtonians as one of its regular attractions.

Early in 1924, Ellington took over leadership of the outfit after a dispute with Snowden over money. "It didn't take long before we thrust leadership on Duke," explained Sonny Greer. "He didn't want it, but his disposition was better and more balanced than ours" (Nicholson 1999, 40).

Under Ellington's leadership, the Washingtonians began to attract attention. In the Kentucky Club, Ellington ensured that radio broadcasts from the nightspot expanded from one night a week to a nightly program. "Station WHN was just opening up around then and they started broadcasting us every night after two a.m.," remembered Ellington. "All the air time helped build up our name" (Nicholson 1999, 43).

During the summers of 1926 and 1927, the bandleader also scheduled one-night engagements throughout New England. Ellington and his group "packed the ballrooms nightly" in Massachusetts, Connecticut, Rhode Island, and Maine with the help of Charles Shribman, who owned the Charleshurst Ballroom in Salem, Massachusetts, and helped form a circuit of New England theaters with other ballroom managers (Tucker 2000, 26). By late 1927, when the Washingtonians left the Kentucky Club for the Cotton Club, they had built a regional reputation. "Duke and the boys are slowly and surely becoming New England's favorite dance orchestra," reported the *New York Tribune* (27).

The Symphonic Blues

During Ellington's tenure at the Kentucky Club, respected African-American classical violinist and composer Will Marion Cook helped Ellington formulate a new style, which combined symphonic music and the gut-bucket blues of New Orleans brass bands. Cook had studied at the National Conservatory of Music under Antonín Dvořák, composed music for nearly a dozen African-American Broadway plays, and in 1918 organized the forty-piece New York Syncopated Orchestra. By the time he met Ellington in 1925, Cook sported a mane of white hair and had gained the esteem of music publishers throughout New York for his compositional mastery. The two musicians, one revered for his classically based skills and the other just starting in the business, often rode in a taxi together across the city. During the rides, confided Duke, "I would get my lessons" (Nicholson 1999, 46).

Armed with a better understanding of musical theory, Ellington began to write music. "During my first few months in New York I found out that anybody was eligible to take songs into the music publishers on Broadway," he related. After partnering with Joe Trent to sell a song for a fifty-dollar advance, Ellington got "hooked in writing MUSIC" (Nicholson 1999, 44). In 1924, he scored several songs of the *Chocolate Kiddies* revue for the Sam Wooding band and started to compose for his own group.

Ellington increased his knowledge of classical music on trips to the symphony. "Practically every afternoon we'd go to one of the movie houses where they had a symphony orchestra in the pit, they had many of them on Broadway," recalled Duke. "You'd sit and you would listen to the symphony through two or three shows and you'd go to the Kentucky Club and try to make your six-piece band sound like a symphony," he revealed (Nicholson 1999, 58). "Six pieces sounded like twelve, and we played so smooth, we were never loud, very soft, beautiful," pointed out Sonny Greer (Crouch 1979).

Duke Ellington Band, 1926, with Duke at far left. *Everett Collection Historical/Alamy Stock Photo*

Ellington likened his music to the symphonic sound of one of his inspirations, Paul Whiteman. "Paul Whiteman was known as the King of Jazz and no one yet has come near [to] carrying that title with more certainty and dignity," he asserted (Ellington 1974, 103). Unlike others who disparaged Whiteman for diluting jazz, Ellington praised him: "Don't let them kid you about Whiteman. He had been a big man in our music. He's done a lot for it" (Nicholson 1999, 199).

In 1923, Duke added a bluesy element to his symphonic jazz band. Trumpeter James "Bubber" Miley, influenced by those "Holy Roller churches, where they sing, and everybody's clapping hands, and passing out," as fellow band member Albany "Barney" Bigard noted, joined the outfit and contributed a growling, low-down trumpet sound based on the style of his idol, King Oliver (Dance 1970, 85-86). "He used to growl all night long, playing gut-bucket on his horn. . . . Our band changed its character when Bubber came in," related Ellington (Nicholson 1999, 47). The band complemented the growls of Miley with the muted trombone of Charles "Plug" Irvis, who had played with Willie "The Lion" Smith and blues singer Lucille Hegamin. "He was strictly a gutbucket trombonist," related the more melodic Otto Hardwick, noting that "the word gutbucket must have stemmed directly from Irvis' style and his use of a real bucket for a mute. He and Bubber got together on duets after growling at each other for a few days, and thus set the style of the band," said Hardwick. Together, they growled back and forth, achieving a "wah-wah," call-and-response effect. When Irvis left the outfit in June 1926, Ellington hired Joe "Tricky Sam" Nanton who likewise adopted the gut-bucket New Orleans style (Nicholson 1999, 48).

The unique combination of the small-band symphony with blues growls became known by the racist term "jungle music" to many whites who listened to it. "I don't know whether it was Paul Whiteman because he idolized Duke, or Gershwin," commented Sonny Greer, but "George Gershwin says to Paul, 'I know what that is, that's Jungle Music.' And it stuck with us" (Crouch 1979). The label fit with the racist Southern-plantation décor of the Cotton Club.

Ellington soon recorded his new sound. In November 1924, he took his six-piece outfit into the studios and recorded four sides, and the following year four more. In November 1926, Duke Ellington and His Kentucky Club Orchestra recorded the now famous "East St. Louis Toodle-Oo" and, in April 1927, "Black and Tan Fantasy," one of his first extended pieces.

Duke at the Cotton Club

By the time Ellington took his group into the Cotton Club, he had expanded the band to ten pieces to achieve a fuller, more symphonic sound. Duke recruited Louis Metcalf, a mellow-sounding trumpeter who acted as a foil to the exuberant Bubber Miley. In June 1927, the Louisiana-born Wellman Braud joined the orchestra with his percussive, string-slapping style on the upright bass, an instrument that began to replace the tuba in jazz outfits. Around the same time, Ellington hired the Boston-bred teenager Harry Carney, who played baritone sax and clarinet. A few months later, Ellington recruited New Orleans–born clarinetist/saxophonist Barney Bigard, who had been tutored by noted New Orleans teacher Lorenzo Tio Jr., and had played with King Oliver and then the Luis Russell band. In 1928, Art Whetsel returned to the band. By the end of the year, Ellington had stabilized an enlarged unit, when the Boston-born alto/soprano saxophonist Johnny Hodges and the flamboyant trumpeter Freddie Jenkins joined the orchestra.

LISTENING GUIDE 12

Duke Ellington and His Kentucky Club Orchestra

"EAST ST. LOUIS TOODLE-Oo"

One of Ellington's first commercial successes, "East St. Louis Toodle-Oo" exemplified the style called "jungle music." Initially recorded by Ellington on November 29, 1926, for Vocalion Records, "East St. Louis" begins with an orchestral introduction followed quickly by the bluesy trumpet of co-composer Bubber Miley, who used a plunger mute to achieve his unique effect. Bubber continued his growling with a light background by the ten-man ensemble.

Miley, raised in New York City, became enthusiastic about mutes when he heard a performance by King Oliver. He joined Ellington in 1923, when he started to experiment with the plunger mute, basically a rubber sink or toilet plunger removed from its handle. By moving the mute in and out of the trumpet's bell, Miley was able to create exciting new sounds.

On the record, a brief trombone solo by Tricky Sam Nanton follows Miley. "Bubber and Tricky were the first to get really wide recognition for the plunger thing," explained Ellington (Dance 1970, 7). Then, likely Prince Robinson offers a clarinet solo before the entire ensemble takes over. At the 2:47 minute mark, Miley again unleashes his trumpet for the finale.

As a strategy to retain control of his music, Ellington re-recorded "East St. Louis" numerous times. On March 14, 1927, he waxed the song for Brunswick Records; the next week the orchestra did the same for Columbia; and near the end of the year the band recorded the tune for Victor. The following year, Ellington and his band mates cut "East St. Louis" for a bevy of budget labels.

The name "East St. Louis Toodle-Oo" may refer to a dance popular among African Americans at the time known as the "toodle-oo" or "todalo." In a 1962 interview, Ellington described it as a "broken walk" like an elderly man might make; others described it as a hip-shaking step (Tucker 1988, 88–91).

This original version of the song included Ellington, Louis Metcalf and Bubber Miley on trumpets, Joe Nanton on trombone, Prince Robinson on clarinet and saxophone (likely), Edgar Sampson and Otto Hardwick on alto saxophones, Fred Guy on banjo, Sonny Greer on drums, and Mack Shaw on bass.

0:00–0:10	The ensemble provides a swaying introduction.
0:11–0:35	A muted trumpet by Bubber Miley states the theme with the orchestra backing him. Many critics at the time called the mute a novelty or an effect. King Oliver helped originate such effects.
0:36–0:47	The trumpet delivers a new melody, ending with Greer knocking woodblocks together.
0:48–1:00	The trumpet returns to the main theme and again ends with Greer's woodblocks to denote the beginning of a new section.
1:01–1:26	Tricky Sam Nanton on trombone solos around the theme with Greer's and Guy's banjo backing him.
1:27–1:48	The clarinet, likely Prince Robinson, solos with rhythm backing that includes a periodic cymbal crash by Greer.
1:49–2:19	The brass restates the introduction, starting with six quick bursts from the group and cymbal crashes from Greer to denote the beginning of the section. It ends with three quick bursts.
2:20–2:32	The reeds create an airy solo, accented by Greer's cymbals and ending with three quick bursts from the group and Greer.
2:33–2:46	The entire ensemble once again combines efforts to restate the theme.
2:47–3:03	Bubber Miley restates the initial section on the muted trumpet with the swaying orchestra backing him.

LISTENING GUIDE 13

Duke Ellington Orchestra

 ### "BLACK AND TAN FANTASY"

First recorded on April 7, 1927, "Black and Tan Fantasy" recreated the mood found in "black-and-tan" jazz clubs, which catered to both whites and African Americans.

The twelve-bar blues begins with a lilting, muted duet by co-author Bubber Miley and Tricky Sam Nanton. After a half minute and punctuated by a cymbal crash delivered by drummer Sonny Greer, Toby Hardwick contributes a sweet saxophone solo backed by the ten-piece unit. Nanton then interjects another plunger-muted improvisation. At the two-minute mark, Ellington assumes control with a stride-style piano followed by Tricky Sam making full use of the plunger. Miley returns with several blues-drenched measures, sharply accented by the band. The trumpeter and the orchestra ends with a humorous quote from Frédéric Chopin's "Funeral March," otherwise known as the

Piano Sonata #2 in B-flat minor, Opus 35 (1839). Like his other works at the time, Ellington combined classical references with the blues for a distinctive sound.

Ellington repeatedly re-recorded the song, including two more versions in fall 1927. Two years later, Duke and his men performed the song in the film *Black and Tan*, staring Fredi Washington.

The personnel on this date included Ellington, Bubber Miley and Louis Metcalf on trumpets, Joe "Tricky Sam" Nanton on trombone, Otto Hardwick on alto saxophone, Rudy Jackson on tenor saxophone, Harry Carney on baritone saxophone, Fred Guy on banjo, Wellman Braud on bass, and Sonny Greer on drums.

Structurally, the song consists of a twelve-bar blues with a sixteen-bar verse at a slow to moderate tempo or time.

0:00–0:24	Haunting, muted duet by the trumpet (Miley) and the trombone (Nanton), the melody of which came from the "The Holy City" (1892), a sacred song, which Miley's mother sang.
0:25	A cymbal crash by Sonny Greer to announce the end of the first section and the beginning of the second section.
0:26–0:39	Sweet, silky solo by sax man Toby Hardwick to begin the second section that contrasts with the opening and was written by Ellington.
0:40–0:44	Full band emerges as dominant to answer Hardwick in a descending fashion to connect to the next section called a turnaround.
0:45–0:57	Hardwick continues with his melodious sax.
0:58–1:00	Horns play in unison and then another cymbal crash by Greer.
1:01–1:54	Miley holds a B-flat note for four beats and then delves into a brilliant solo chock full of effects, including growls and slurs.
1:55–2:20	Ellington interjects a stride-based solo on piano.
2:21–2:46	Tricky Sam offers muted solo on trombone, which includes a wah-wah effect and the imitation of a whining horse similar to the ODJB in "Livery Stable Blues."
2:47–3:12	Miley offers a muted trumpet solo with quick bursts from the band in response until the band joins him in harmony at 3:05.
3:13–3:22	The band ends with a nod to Chopin's "Funeral March" and a clash of Greer's cymbal.

Initially, mixed reviews greeted the orchestra. Covering the opening of the Cotton Club, on December 7, 1927, *Variety* magazine stated that "the big[gest] attraction, of course, are the gals, 10 of 'em, the majority of whom in white company could pass for Caucasians." It devoted almost no space to the Ellington orchestra. Even the band's manager Irving Mills realized that "the first show was kind of weak" (Nicholson 1999, 72). However, the band shed its nervousness and became more polished as its tenure at the club continued. Other bandleaders such as Don Redman and groups such as the Mills Brothers covered Ellington's songs for hits, and the band became nationally known.

African-American Harlem

The success of the band at the Cotton Club stemmed from several factors, including many new, mob-protected jazz venues, which opened in Harlem to serve white audiences. Before 1920, Harlem clubs catered almost exclusively to the more than one hundred thousand African Americans who streamed into the area during and after World War I. In 1920, the Garden of Joy, an open-air club built upon a hill and lit in the evenings by Japanese lanterns, opened its doors for Harlem locals. Near 133rd Street and Lenox, the Nest showcased the bands of Sam Wooding, Elmer Snowden, and Luis Russell. Nearby, party goers frequented Tillie's Chicken Shack and Mexico's. According to Willie "The Lion" Smith, "133rd Street was IT. Things were swinging to beat all hell on 133rd between Lenox and Seventh Avenues in the mid-twenties. . . . It must have been the busiest street in the world," he marveled (Smith 1978, 158).

By the mid-1920s, nightspots dominated Harlem. In a thirty-four block area, more than three dozen cabarets, clubs, and dance halls enticed customers with entertainment. From 142nd Street to the north, 126th Street to the south, Seventh Avenue to the west and Fifth Avenue to the east, jazz could be heard from the late afternoon until noon the next day.

Most of these new nightspots served the local African-American population. "In those days," remembered Willie "The Lion" Smith, "white people hadn't gotten to coming around" (Smith 1978, 89). Only a few clubs such as the Nest attracted both African-Americans and whites to its shows.

The Mob Invades Harlem

The patrons of Harlem clubs changed when the Owney "The Killer" Madden mob moved into the area and offered whites illegal liquor and protection. In 1923, after serving nine years of a twenty-year sentence, Madden became a kingpin of the illegal alcohol business created by Prohibition. He entered this emerging market when he joined with the preeminent bootleggers in New York City: Italian mobster Frank Costello and Big Bill Dwyer, a fellow product of Hell's Kitchen and a former dockworker. The trio headed a bootlegging operation with a fleet of steel-plated speed boats and ships, the largest of which could carry twenty thousand cases of liquor. In 1925, Madden took over the business with Costello after Dwyer was convicted of bribing the Coast Guard to allow free access of his liquor into the country. Madden also operated an illegal brewery through a front on West Twenty-sixth Street and Tenth Avenue named the Phoenix Cereal Beverage Company, where he churned out thousands of barrels of beer called Madden's No. 1.

Madden delivered much of his beer and hard liquor to his more than twenty Harlem jazz venues, including the Cotton Club. His clubs allowed him to largely control the Harlem bootlegging business during Prohibition and dominate the uptown jazz business. Madden's gang also used their nightspots to launder funds. "It was a way to turn the money over, a good front," explained Ellington's son, Mercer (Nicholson 1999, 82).

Before Prohibition, "the guys who ran the places were Negroes and kept order," emphasized Willie Smith. "That is, up until 1920 when things changed and the hoodlums, who furnished the booze, came and took over" (Smith 1978, 88).

Duke Ellington and the Mob

To ensure that their venues consistently featured top-flight performers, mobsters such as Owney Madden hired and protected bands such as the Duke Ellington outfit. At the Club Kentucky, the Ellington band had its first introduction to organized crime. "The Club Kentucky was something," related Sonny Greer. "We had all the gangsters, all the big gangsters you read about, Legs Diamond, Lucky Luciano and all the Brooklyn gang. They'd rendezvous" there (Nicholson 1999, 51).

Owney Madden used his menacing gangland tactics to manage the Cotton Club and protect Ellington. In 1920, the club initially opened as an intimate supper club, the Club Deluxe. It was run by African-American heavyweight boxing champion Jack Johnson, who had become an icon in Harlem after his victories over several notable white opponents in the ring. Three years later, Madden forced Johnson to sell the nightclub and reopened it as the Cotton Club. In 1925, after federal authorities temporarily closed the club for violation of Prohibition, he hired crony Herman Stark as stage manager, who became the face of the nightspot. Madden also ordered one of his notorious henchmen, George "Big Frenchy" DeMange, to oversee his investment. To bring Ellington to New York, Owney needed to free him from a previous commitment made with Philadelphia booker Clarence Robinson. He sent "a suggestion [to Robinson] he couldn't ignore . . . 'Be big,' Clarence was told, 'or be dead'" (Cooper 1990, 54–55).

Madden's gang ensured that the Cotton Club would not have any close competitors. In 1930, Cabell "Cab" Calloway and his Missourians were slated to open a new venue, the Plantation Club, on 126th Street near Lenox. "The Plantation people really intended to get their share of some of those big dollars from the people downtown who were coming uptown to enjoy the Harlem moon and get their kicks," recalled Calloway. Cab and his orchestra worked "like dogs" to prepare for the first show. A few hours before opening night, they entered the venue and "found it in shreds. Everything had been torn up. . . . Even the dance floor was chopped up." "The Cotton Club mob," concluded Calloway, "had decided they didn't want any competition" (Travis 1983, 226).

Madden's influence extended well beyond Harlem. In Chicago, during the summer of 1931, James Petrillo—then the head of the Chicago musicians union—tried to lecture Ellington in his dressing room about bookings in Chicago. To teach Petrillo a lesson, Ellington called Owney Madden and informed him of the situation. The now-anxious union leader asked drummer William "Sonny" Greer who Ellington was calling. "The man who owns our band," recalled Sonny Greer. Ellington told Petrillo to speak directly to Madden, who instructed the contrite union leader to give the bandleader "no more trouble" (Crouch 1979). A few years later, Madden assigned a personal bodyguard to Ellington. The thug got "Duke from the theater with his machine gun between his legs, and they had bullet-proof glass [in the car]," chuckled band member and clarinetist Barney Bigard (Willard 1976).

At one point, Madden squelched an attempt to kidnap Ellington in Chicago by calling his fellow gangster Al Capone for help (Dance 1970, 88).

Whites Descend upon Harlem

Offered top talent, a protected environment, and illegal alcohol by the mob, whites started to flock to Harlem clubs, which by the mid-1920s catered to a mostly white clientele. The expensive Smalls' Paradise was opened on October 26, 1925, by Edwin Smalls, a former African-American elevator operator turned entrepreneur. Charles Johnson's Paradise Orchestra, a floor act of twenty-five showgirls, and dancing waiters entertained mostly white socialites in their evening gowns and suits. At a time when the average laborer earned between six and eight dollars per week, fifteen hundred partygoers typically spent four dollars for an evening at the cabaret. "Smalls' Paradise was one of the biggest cabarets in America. The crowds were 80 percent white at least, maybe more, 90 percent," noted saxophonist Benny Waters, who played there with the Charlie Johnson band (Deffaa 1990, 32–33).

Two years earlier, Conrad Immerman, called Connie by his friends, had established Connie's Inn on 131st Street and Seventh Avenue with his brothers George and Louie. The three-hundred-capacity club, procuring its booze from gangster Dutch Schultz, a friend of Madden's, admitted only white patrons. "Connie's Inn catered to whites and featured light-skinned Negroes [as performers and dancers]," observed John Hammond, the music impresario and jazz fanatic who later discovered Benny Goodman, Bob Dylan, and Bruce Springsteen (Hammond 1938, 55).

The Cotton Club, probably the most well-known Harlem club and Owney Madden's prime jazz venue, likewise admitted only whites. The gangster specifically chose the name of the club to attract whites and charged an admission fee of three dollars to keep out neighborhood African Americans. The choreographer for the nightspot, Althea Fuller, told one of the chorus girls that "Mr. Madden doesn't want the races mixin'" (Bruno 2012). "Harlem Negroes did not like the Cotton Club and never appreciated the Jim Crow policy in the very heart of the dark community," remembered noted African-American poet and author Langston Hughes (Cohen 2010, 54).

In 1927, after a five-year absence from New York, Rudolph Fisher, a novelist and physician who lived in Harlem and a frequent cabaret customer, noticed the difference in clientele at the venues. Upon walking down the narrow stairs of his favorite basement cabaret, Fisher looked around the club and thought, "'What a lot of ofays [slang for "whites"]!'" as he noticed the patrons in the nightspot. He "grew puzzled and began to stare," then wondered if he was in the right place. "I suddenly became aware that, except for the waiters and members of the orchestra, I was the only Negro in the place." Fisher found the same situation in other clubs throughout Harlem. After "wandering in a daze," he visited other nightspots such as the Nest, Smalls' Café, Connie's Inn, and the Cotton Club. Fisher concluded that "the best of Harlem's African-American cabarets have changed their names and turned white" (Fisher 1927, 393).

Whites flocked to Harlem clubs to experience a "primitive" African-American culture, as it was described in popular newspapers and literature. Curious about rumors concerning an unrestrained and wild African-American lifestyle, they wanted to experience a more exciting way of life. As white Chicago residents did, when they frequented black-and-tan clubs, white New Yorkers wanted to taste the forbidden fruits of African-American culture. "Harlem had a tremendous reputation, everyone expected blaring trumpets, squirming girls, every night was Saturday night and everyone had rhythm," shrugged Duke Ellington (Nicholson 1999, 78). On November 6, 1926, an advertisement in the African-American newspaper the *New York Age* promised a "slumming hostess" to guide "inquisitive Nordics" through Harlem. "Your season is not completed with thrills until you have visited Harlem."

The sensationalist view of Harlem, replete with wild parties, drugs, and all-night music, became even more pronounced with the 1926 publication of white novelist and amateur photographer Carl Van Vechten's novel, *Nigger Heaven*. The book derived its title from the phrase used to refer to the segregated balcony of a theater, where whites forced African Americans to sit to avoid intermixing. Reinforcing stereotypes of African Americans, the novel delved into the secret workings of Harlem nightlife by using Smalls' Paradise, one of the author's hangouts, as an example of the typical Harlem nightspot, renamed the "Black Venus" in his book. Though Edwin Smalls, the club owner, permanently banned Van Vechten from his club for his lurid and unbalanced description of the cabaret, whites nonetheless assumed that *Nigger Heaven* accurately portrayed Harlem nightclubs. The phenomenal sales of the book spread an inaccurate but alluring image of Harlem culture despite outcries by African-American Harlem luminaries who viciously denounced it. After the publication, stated author Van Vechten, Harlem slumming parties "became quite a rage" (Osofsky 1965, 235).

Irving Mills and the Media

In addition to the interest of whites in Harlem nightlife, the efforts of manager Irving Mills, who strategically positioned his client with radio, film, and the record industry, helped Ellington became increasingly popular. Mills started as a song plugger, founded a song publishing business with his brother, Jack, and later established a record label to record emerging African-American blues and jazz artists. "Everybody thought I was crazy in the early days," laughed Mills. "Who went for race records then? The black people" (Cohen 2010, 47).

In November 1926, Mills agreed to manage the Ellington band. After hearing Duke and his band at the Kentucky Club, he invited the bandleader to his office, where Ellington signed a contract that gave Mills nearly half of all profits from the orchestra for his management services.

Mills immediately started to work on the media to popularize his client. After concluding that Ellington needed more exposure, the manager added a radio wire in the Kentucky Club to broadcast the music on station WHN. For the 2 a.m. airtime, he tapped Ted Husing, the fast-talking New York announcer who later pioneered modern-day sportscasting, to serve as the broadcaster. When Ellington moved to the Cotton Club, Mills ensured that Husing hosted the band three evenings a week on WHN. "He did such a terrific job that our band soon became widely known," Ellington contended (Shapiro and Hentoff 1955, 232–33). By March 21, 1928, *Variety* exclaimed that "one of the hottest bands on the air is Duke Ellington's from the Cotton Club Monday midnights." By the end of the decade, the Ellington outfit became "the most prominent Negro broadcasters on the air," reported the *Daily Mirror*. They were "the only Negro broadcasting stars to receive a rating." In 1931, a flyer advertising the band read: "Now-a'days when you turn on the old radio, the first thought is Duke Ellington. When you don't find Duke, well, you turn it off again. . . . There are but few persons indeed who have not heard [Ellington] over the radio" (Cohen 2010, 57).

In addition to radio, the emerging industry of talking motion pictures promoted Ellington. First introduced in Paris at the Exhibition of 1900 and perfected in 1919 by Lee de Forest, movies with sound became viable when Western Electric developed moving-coil loudspeakers that could fill an area the size of a theater. In 1927, Warner Brothers premiered the first successful film with sound, *The Jazz Singer*. Starring popular vaudeville song-and-dance man Al Jolson as a rebellious Jewish youth who leaves his family to sing jazz in a cabaret using blackface, the film grossed more than $2.6 million and won an Honorary Award in the first Academy Awards ceremony. By the end of 1929, Warner's film profits skyrocketed from $3 million to $14 million.

Warner's growing success spurred other studios into action. In November 1928, Paramount, the largest studio, premiered its first feature with complete dialogue, *Interference*. Three months later, Columbia became the last major studio to release a talking motion picture. By 1931, nearly all of the twenty-two thousand theaters in the country offered movies with sound. Every week ninety-five million Americans, or 78 percent of the entire population, paid admission to watch their favorite film stars act out their fantasies, and movies accounted for 16 percent of all recreational spending.

As part of his efforts to promote Ellington in as many media as possible, Irving Mills marketed Duke Ellington through the new and lucrative film industry. In 1929, only three years after Hollywood launched talking films, the manager secured a movie appearance for Ellington and his band in the short film *Black and Tan*. The director, Dudley Murphy, cast Ellington as a debonair, intelligent jazz artist and his sharply dressed orchestra as skilled musicians who performed band hits such as "Black and Tan Fantasy" and "Black Beauty." Rather than portraying popular stereotypes of African Americans as comedic buffoons, Ellington and his band portrayed high-class African Americans.

The next year through the efforts of Mills, the full-length comedy, *Check and Double Check*, which starred Amos 'n' Andy, included the Ellington Orchestra. In the film, whites Freeman Gosden and Charles Correll, who in 1928 had introduced the characters in one of the most successful shows on radio, smeared on blackface to play two stereotyped African-American characters modeled on earlier minstrel shows. Though based on a racist premise, the movie featured an African-American band for the first time in a full-length film. It relegated the Ellington outfit to the background until the camera zoomed in on the band during its performance of "Old Man Blues." Offering a mixed racial message, which typified the portrayal of Ellington at the time, director Melville Brown forced two of the light-skinned band members to use cork to blacken their faces, but nevertheless showed a nattily dressed and well-groomed orchestra in performance without any comic relief.

Mills also tackled the recording industry. To provide his client maximum flexibility and the ability to record his compositions multiple times, Mills counseled Ellington to record for a variety of labels rather than enter into a long-term contract with a single company. Between 1927 and 1930, the Ellington Orchestra released discs for almost all major and many smaller labels, including Vocalion, Victor, Brunswick, OKeh, Columbia, Pathé, and Cameo.

The manager promoted the sound as "jungle music" to tie it to the success of the Cotton Club and differentiate it from other orchestras sprouting up in Harlem at the same time. In his "advertising manual," he instructed his staff to refer to the band's music as "primitive rhythms! Weird melodies!" (Nicholson 1999, 159). Mills encouraged a willing Ellington to reinforce the jungle image by the names of a few of his compositions: 1929's "Jungle Jamboree" and 1930's "Jungle Blues" and "Jungle Nights in Harlem."

To reconcile Ellington's high-class symphonic sound with the "jungle beat," the manager told the press that the orchestra "can play 'sweet' and discreet jazz in the manner of Mr. [Paul] Whiteman, then turn about and twist their music into weird and primitive strains with all the barbaric rhythms of the jungle" (Nicholson 1999, 156).

The Ellington Image

Despite using the "jungle music" tag, Mills portrayed his client as a high-toned artist. As a self-proclaimed "hound on publicity," he developed a detailed marketing plan, which he referred to as his "exploitation campaign." It "was aimed at presenting the public a great musician who was making a lasting contribution to American music," related Mills. He wanted Ellington to be accepted as "an authentic artist because I made his importance as an artist the primary consideration" (Cohen 2010, 63; Nicholson 1999, 150).

To achieve his goal, Mills hired six public relations men and instructed them to refer to Ellington as "Harlem's Aristocrat of Jazz" and the band as "Duke Ellington and His Famous Orchestra" (Cohen 2010, 59–60). The manager stressed "Ellington's genius as a composer," and the admiration of Ellington by such authorities as Leopold Stokowski, famed conductor of the celebrated Philadelphia Orchestra, and Paul Whiteman, who Mills characterized as "synonymous with jazz" (Nicholson 1999, 13).

Mills encouraged Ellington to record "serious" music that spanned both sides of a 78 record and jockeyed with record companies to place Ellington's records alongside those of white classical composers. On December 20, 1928, the manager enlisted the help of Matty Malneck's white classical musicians and ten members of the Hall Johnson Choir to join Ellington in a recording of "St. Louis Blues" for Victor. To have the track released on the prestigious "Red Seal" label—reserved for classical music—Mills intended to "put the white band and the African-American band together as one." Within a few days, the manager was alerted by Victor executives about "a big problem, and the problem was that I ought to know better than to put a black and white band together." Rather than buckle under the pressure, Mills responded that "as long as Duke Ellington is on the black label [reserved for African-American artists] and it's under the counter when . . . he's a big hit on radio, . . . we won't make any more records." By his threatening tactics, Mills successfully forced Victor to promote the record alongside releases by its white classical music artists (Nicholson 1999, 88).

Mills ensured that the Ellington band projected a decorous image as it toured the country. Unlike most African-American bands of the time, Ellington's orchestra traveled in its "own Pullman car, had our own baggage car, we had full possession of the diner," remembered Sonny Greer. "When we went to the gig, we'd have a fleet of cabs wait to take us, bring us back," he continued. "We were traveling like kings" (Nicholson 1999, 162–63). "The moneys that I spent on Duke for photographs, for clothes, for publicity," boasted Mills, "I don't think that anybody ever spent on anybody what I did for Duke" (Cohen 2010, 63).

Through Mills's ceaseless efforts, the press enthusiastically promoted the orchestra's sophisticated public image. After the band played Chicago's Palace Theater in May 1930, *Variety* contended on May 21 that the concert increased Ellington's "standing among the colored race in modern music" and compared him to African-American classical composer and bandleader James Reese Europe. The same year, the *Herald Tribune* reported that the bandleader made "jazz seem an end in itself and not merely an invitation to dance" (*Variety*, April 2, 1930, in Nicholson 1999, 105). The African-American *Pittsburgh Courier* newspaper applauded Irving Mills for building "high-class attractions with colored talent" (Nicholson 1999, 150). Through Mills's help, Ellington became known as a leader of serious music in the United States. His brand reflected the emphasis on the upwardly mobile, intelligent, and accomplished artist who could succeed in a white world that characterized the Harlem Renaissance.

The Harlem Renaissance

This new movement, which emphasized African-American achievement and self-esteem, dovetailed with the image of Duke Ellington as a serious musician. African-American writers, poets, and artists hoped to combat racial prejudice by showing whites that African Americans could compete with them in the white conception of the arts without compromising their unique African-American culture. In his controversial essay "Criteria of Negro Art," W. E. B. Du Bois felt that African-American art could "be just as beautiful, and beautiful largely in the same ways, as the art that comes from white folk, or yellow, or red [and], until the art of the black folk compels recognition, they will not be rated as human" (Suisman 2004, 1305).

Many Harlem Renaissance writers such as poet Langston Hughes advocated a uniquely African-American viewpoint on the white-conceived arts that instilled a sense of African-American self-pride. "The younger Negro artists who create now intend to express our individual dark-skinned selves without fear or shame. If white people are pleased, we are glad. If they are not, it doesn't matter. We know we are beautiful," he proclaimed in his 1926 manifesto, "The Negro Artist and the Racial Mountain." Hughes challenged fellow African-American writers to shed "the urge within the race toward whiteness," a concept he defined as "the racial mountain." Rather than assimilation into a homogenous American culture, Hughes and his colleagues promoted the idea of cultural diversity, which merged mainstream America with unique ethnic cultures, including the African-American perspective (Hughes 1926).

Langston Hughes concentrated his writings on the dignity and travails of the average African American and criticized class divisions based upon economic standing. He focused on "the low-down folks, the so called common element" who "have their nip of gin on Saturday nights and are not too important to themselves or the community, or too well fed, or too learned to watch the lazy world go round. . . . They are the majority," he exclaimed. "May the Lord be praised" (Hughes 1926). In his writings, Hughes rejected the notion of nurturing the most talented individuals in the

Harlem Renaissance writer Langston Hughes, 1943. *Photograph by Gordon Parks. Farm Security Administration/Office of War Administration Black-and-White Negatives, Library of Congress Prints and Photographs Division*

African-American population that had been espoused by W. E. B. Du Bois and instead captured beauty and grandeur in everyday life.

Other Harlem Renaissance figures devoted their attention to commonplace activities of African Americans in the neighborhood, including the interest in jazz. Claude McKay described Harlem nightlife in his influential novel *Home to Harlem* (1928). The illustrations of artist Aaron Douglas depicted scenes of everyday African-American life in *The Crisis*, the official publication of the NAACP founded by W. E. B. Du Bois in 1910, and *Opportunity: A Journal of Negro Life*, the official periodical of the National Urban League. Harlem native Rudolph Fisher turned to Harlem nightlife for his fictional subjects in works such as *City of Refuge* (1925). Zora Neale Hurston, one of the few women among the Harlem Renaissance writers, vividly described jazz in her autobiographical essay "How It Feels to Be Colored Me" (1928) as a way to describe the difference between herself and a white friend.

Though extolling the lives of ordinary African Americans, the educated writers and artists of the Harlem Renaissance only lived the conventional life of the African American vicariously or by choice and took pride in their noteworthy academic and literary achievements. Alain Locke earned a PhD from Harvard, attended Oxford University, and by 1912 became a faculty member at Howard University; Langston Hughes entered Columbia University and eventually attained a BA from Lincoln University, the first historically black university; Aaron Douglas graduated from the University of Nebraska in 1922; poet Countee Cullen, author of *Color* (1925), which explored racial identity and racism, graduated from New York University (BA) and Harvard (MA); and Jamaican transplant poet Claude McKay attended Kansas State University for two years before returning to New York City.

By the mid-twenties, the constant stream of writing and art from the educated Harlem residents had attracted public attention. In 1925, the *New York Times* announced that "we are on the edge, if not in the midst, of what might be called a Negro Renaissance" (Nicholson 1999, 27). In 1926, Langston Hughes witnessed a "present vogue in things Negro." A year later, Rudolph Fisher noticed "this sudden, contagious interest in everything Negro. . . . Negro stock is going up and everybody's buying," he reported (Fisher 1927, 398, 396). "Harlemites thought the millennium had come," mused Hughes. "They thought the race problem had at last been solved through art" (Osofsky 1965, 232).

Ellington and the Harlem Renaissance

From an early age, Ellington embodied the Harlem Renaissance ideal of a cultured African American with a sense of racial pride. Ellington grew up in Washington, DC, in a middle-class family, which spoiled him. His father, James, acted like a "Chesterfieldian gentleman who wore gloves and spats, and [was] very intellectual," recollected Ellington's younger sister Ruth. Ellington recalled his father teaching him "how to be a fine, upright, clean-living gentleman" (Nicholson 1999, 4–5).

As a youth, Ellington became conscious of class distinctions among African Americans in Washington, DC. "I don't know how many castes of Negroes were in the city at the time," he related, "but I do know that if you decided to mix carelessly with another you would be told that one just did not do that sort of thing" (Ellington 1974, 17). As a middle-class African American, the future bandleader learned lessons about upward mobility promoted by Booker T. Washington. In school, Ellington recalled the importance placed upon "being a representative of a great and proud race," and added that in public "your behavior is what the race depends upon to command respect" (Nicholson 1999, 7).

As a teen, Ellington strived to represent his race by carrying himself with aplomb. Considering himself "a pretty fancy guy," he affected an upper-class demeanor by wearing well-chosen clothes and affecting high-class speech. Ellington "was sharp as a Gillette [razor] blade," intimated drummer Sonny Greer about the musician as a teenager, and by high school his friends called him "Duke" because of his classy ways.

Rising to fame in New York City in the midst of the Harlem Renaissance, the sophisticated Ellington perfectly fit the profile of the successful, upwardly mobile African American who excelled in the arts without losing his racial identity. He considered his music a dignified symphonic effort to hoist his compositions and his race to a high level of esteem. "We have developed a kind of symphony music that, no matter what you think, is different and distinctive, and that lends itself to the playing of the peculiar compositions of our race," he argued (Cohen 2010, 27). "It is my firm belief that what is still known as 'jazz' is going to play a considerable part in the serious music of the future," he told *Rhythm Magazine* in March 1931.

Ellington embodied the ethos of the Harlem Renaissance in more than his music. Dressed in sharp suits, ties, white linen shirts, and shining shoes with spats, Ellington ensured that the band projected an elegant image to earn respect for their race. "We had fines in the band for coming late, and dressing, of course, that was the thing," explained the bandleader (Nicholson 1999, 83).

As much as the music, the Ellington image impressed some African Americans. In 1930, reed player Jack Kelson, then eight years old, went with his father to an Ellington concert. As he recalled, "It wasn't the music that grabbed me. It was the Ellington presence. I remember very clearly, they wore black tuxedo pants, a cummerbund, and a [formal] Eton jacket . . . every man a picture of sartorial elegance. Well, it reflected Ellington: race pride, black pride and all of that" (Bryant 1998, 208).

Ellington's sense of style was not limited to clothes. He insisted that the members of his band reflect racial pride in their speech and demeanor and relied on trumpeter Art Whetsel to instill racial self-respect among the group. Whetsel "would speak up in a minute on the subject of propriety, clean appearance and reliability," smiled Ellington. "If and when any member of our band made an error in grammar, he was quick to correct him. He was aware of all Negro individuals who were contributing to the cause by *commanding respect*" (Ellington 1974, 54). Due to the efforts of Ellington and Whetsel, the band exemplified the Harlem Renaissance ideal of upward mobility in a white society. "We carried the flag and the prestige of my people," proudly asserted drummer Sonny Greer (Crouch 1979).

Ellington as a Maturing Composer

As white interest in Harlem peaked, Duke Ellington paid homage to and promoted the New York neighborhood and its nightclubs through his compositions. In 1927, Ellington recorded "Harlem River Quiver" and in January 1928 renamed "East St. Louis Toodle-Oo" as "Harlem Twist" for OKeh. In early 1929, the band cut "Harlemania" and "Harlem Flat Blues," and, the next year, delivered "Cotton Club Stomp." Throughout his career, Ellington continued to mine the Harlem theme on such songs as "Blue Harlem," "Harlem Speaks," and "Take the 'A' Train."

LISTENING GUIDE 14

Duke Ellington Orchestra as the Harlem Footwarmers

🔗 "MOOD INDIGO (DREAMY BLUES)"

Ellington claimed that he composed "Mood Indigo" while waiting for his mother to cook dinner for him. "I needed another number [for a radio show that evening]. I'd better scratch something out while I wait. So I did the orchestration in fifteen minutes," he recalled (Tucker 2000, 340). It was "the first tune I ever wrote specially for microphone transmission," he added. On October 13, 1930, when he broadcast the number, the bandleader remembered that "wads of mail came in raving about the new tune" (Hasse 1995, 134).

Ellington originally named the tune "Mood Indigo" against the advice of manager Irving Mills. "I wanted to call it 'Mood Indigo,' but Irving said that wasn't commercial enough!" He laughed. "We'll call it 'Dreamy Blues,'" instructed Mills. When asked about the name of the song on the air in 1930, Ellington blurted out "Mood Indigo," which became the permanent title of the song, even though the first two recordings of it carried "Dreamy Blues" on the disc.

Barney Bigard, the star of "Mood Indigo," had a different story about the genesis of the song. Growing up in New Orleans, the Creole clarinetist learned his instrument from famed teacher, Lorenzo Tio Jr. According to Bigard, during 1930 in New York City, he met Tio, who suggested several tunes to him. "There was one I liked, and I asked him if I could borrow it," related the clarinetist. Tio had learned the song "Dreamy Blues" while playing in Armand Piron's band. "I took it home and kept fooling around with it. I changed some of it around . . . and got something together that was mostly my own but partly Tio's" (Bigard 1986, 64). Bigard gave the song to Ellington, who reworked it as he sometimes did with material that other band members gave him and took songwriting credit. Eventually, Bigard sued Ellington and was awarded rights as co-composer.

Regardless of its origins, "Mood Indigo" became the first popular tune of the Ellington orchestra. "This was

our first big hit," the bandleader asserted (Nicholson 1999, 113).

On October 14, 1930, seven members of the band recorded the song for OKeh Records. They started with a three-horn delivery backed by the steady beat of Freddie Guy's banjo, but with a new twist. Unlike the usual practice, Ellington dispensed with the block section of one instrument (e.g., a trombone section) and instead used three different instruments as a group: the trombone, trumpet, and clarinet. Supposedly to accommodate the studio microphones, he inverted the registers of the instruments and placed the trombone and trumpet in the high register and the clarinet on the lower level to produce a haunting, ethereal effect. Both trumpeter Art Whetsel and trombonist Tricky Sam Nanton relied heavily on mutes. After the mood had been established, Bigard took an airy solo on clarinet followed by a trumpet solo. Ellington and his band released this version of the song as the Harlem Footwarmers.

Three days later, to cater to listeners, the group recorded the tune for Brunswick Records as the Jungle Band to reflect the popular but racist conception of their music as "jungle music." The Jungle Band released at least twenty other sides, including "Cotton Club Stomp," "Creole Rhapsody," and "St. Louis Blues."

On December 10, 1930, Ellington released yet another version of the song for RCA Victor with an expanded band. In 1931, at the urging of Irving Mills, Mitchell Parish wrote lyrics to "Mood Indigo," which became a standard that many jazz artists subsequently recorded.

This version of the song is the first version of the song for OKeh Records as the Harlem Footwarmers. It includes Arthur Whetsel (trumpet), Joe "Tricky Sam" Nanton (trombone), Barney Bigard (clarinet), Duke Ellington (piano), Fred Guy (banjo), Wellman Braud (bass), and Sonny Greer (drums).

0:00–0:43	The horns—trombone (Tricky Sam Nanton), trumpet (Art Whetsel)—and clarinet (Barney Bigard), state the melodic four-part theme in an inverted order, in which the clarinet plays in the lowest register and the trombone plays in the highest. Banjoist Fred Guy strums a rhythm in the background to create an overall dreamy effect. At 0:22, Nanton can be briefly and faintly heard with a muted growl.
In part one (0:00–0:09)	The horn trio plays the main theme; they follow by repeating the first part but deliver a descending set of notes at the end (0:10–0:21); in the third part (0:22–0:31), the three horn men play a different passage with some growls by the trumpet (0:23–0:24); and in the fourth part (0:32–0:43), the trio repeats the first part of the theme.

0:44–1:26	Bigard unleashes a tasteful clarinet solo, which builds upon the melody and includes a wavering tremolo, extended notes (e.g., 1:12–1:15), and blue notes (e.g., 0:50 and 1:07) with backing from Guy.
1:27–2:09	Whetsel solos on trumpet with the solid 4/4 backing from the banjo and piano. His four-part solo complements the previous passage by Bigard but includes several fast, multinote runs (e.g., 1:52 and 1:57–1:58), New Orleans–style gut-bucket blue notes (1:55), and extended notes (2:06).
2:10–2:20	Duke Ellington takes an innovative solo over two measures that breaks from the main melody to somewhat jar the listener.
2:21–3:02	The inverted horns reenter with the banjo backing them and restate the four-part theme from the beginning (0:00–0:43).
3:03–3:08	The song ends when the horn trio sustains a note and Ellington plays two concluding notes with them.

Throughout the remainder of his career, Ellington continued to write standards such as "Sophisticated Lady" (1933), "In a Sentimental Mood" (1935), and "Black, Brown and Beige," (1943) to secure his stature as a major figure in jazz and American music.

The Cotton Club Legacy: Cab Calloway and Jimmie Lunceford

Other bands associated with the Cotton Club such as the Cab Calloway and Jimmie Lunceford orchestras played music and assumed an image similar to Ellington's. Raised in Baltimore's middle-class Sugar Hill district, Cab Calloway attended Crane Junior College (now Malcolm X College) in Chicago, where he became interested in jazz after frequenting and singing at various clubs, including the Dreamland Café. In March 1930, Calloway signed with Moe Gale, an agent and co-owner of the Savoy Ballroom. As part of the deal, Cab received $100 a week for ten years and assumed leadership of the Missourians, the house band at the Savoy that originally had come from Kansas City.

After a few gigs around New York City, Calloway and his band succeeded Ellington at the Cotton Club while Duke and his band toured the country. As Calloway told it, after a set at the Crazy Cat in New York, "the club was empty by then and four guys were sitting there with their coats and hats on. I could tell from the look of them that they were from the mob." They asked the twenty-two-year-old Calloway to perform the next day at the Cotton Club to cover for Ellington who began a special tour. "The Cotton Club mob had just bought out my contract the easy way. Pure muscle" (Calloway and Rollins 1976, 86–87). In the process, Mills earned a 45 percent share of the Calloway band as booking agent, Mills' lawyer held an additional 10 percent, and Duke Ellington snagged another 10 percent, leaving Calloway with 35 percent of his band's profits.

The entertaining bandleader Cab Calloway. *Photograph by William P. Gottlieb. William P. Gottlieb/Ira and Leonore S. Gershwin Fund Collection, Music Division, Library of Congress*

At the Cotton Club, the Calloway band continued the tradition of Ellington's lush orchestrations and snappy appearance. The flamboyant leader dressed in a top hat and tuxedo and demanded that his musicians look and act professionally. The band entertained the Cotton Club clientele with a version of Ellington's symphonic jazz with less emphasis on blues-based growls from the trumpets and trombones. Aided by radio coverage in the Cotton Club, in 1931 the orchestra scored with the smash "Minnie the Moocher."

Jimmie Lunceford rode the spirit of the Harlem Renaissance to success. In high school, Lunceford learned music theory from Wilberforce Whiteman, the father of Paul Whiteman, and continued his studies at Fisk University. In 1929, when forming his first band, he recruited three of his classmates from Fisk: pianist Edwin Wilcox, saxophonist Willie Smith, and trombonist Henry Wells.

The Oklahoma-raised Lunceford offered his version of the Ellington sound. After forming an orchestra in 1929, Lunceford toured for five years until he landed a spot at the Cotton Club. The orchestra backed singer and showgirl Adelaide Hall

LISTENING GUIDE 15

Jimmie Lunceford Orchestra

"MOOD INDIGO"

The Jimmie Lunceford orchestra, following Ellington into the Cotton Club, recorded a series of Ellington compositions. On September 4, 1934, and again on November 7, the band cut such Ellington standards as "Sophisticated Lady," "Solitude," "Black and Tan Fantasy," and a version of "Mood Indigo."

Unlike the original Ellington recording of "Mood Indigo" that featured a seven-man ensemble, the Lunceford version featured a fourteen-member band, including the leader. With a larger unit and without Ellington's unique piano contribution, Lunceford's "Mood Indigo" focused on the ensemble and the arrangement, which Lunceford mainstay Willie Smith developed after working with Sy Oliver. Rather than the dreamy, nuanced original of Ellington, Lunceford crafted a powerful, surging, dance-oriented version of "Mood Indigo," which pitted sections of the orchestra against one another and presaged the onrushing swing era.

The Lunceford variant begins with the brass stating the theme, with clarinet and saxophone sections delivering the staccato rhythm that banjo player Freddie Guy provided to the Ellington original. At 0:55, a trumpet solo by Eddie Tompkins takes over, followed at 1:31 by the New Orleans–sounding trumpet of Sy Oliver with a staccato saxophone section in the background. After the brass and reeds weave around one another, the reeds state the theme again. Only during the final section does a mixed-horn group recreate the bluesy, subdued mood offered by Ellington's version, which Lunceford ends by an ascent of the instruments for a powerful finale.

Although Ellington failed to initially chart with the song, Lunceford scored a hit with his arrangement. He did the same with "Black and Tan Fantasy," recorded on the same day. In late 1934, Lunceford hit with the jumpy "Rhythm Is Our Business," which also augured the swing era that exploded the next year with Benny Goodman.

For this song, the band included Sy Oliver, Eddie Tompkins, and Tommy Stevenson on trumpets; Laforet Dent on alto saxophone; Willie Smith and Earl Carruthers on alto and baritone saxophones and clarinet; Moses Allen on bass; Joe Thomas on clarinet and tenor saxophone; Jimmy Crawford on drums and vibes; Al Norris on guitar; Edwin Wilcox on piano; and Henry Wells and Russell Bowles on trombones.

0:00–0:43	In a startling departure from the Ellington version, the muted brass section states the theme, backed by a clarinet section and the saxophones, which play the melody in three octaves and a bouncy stop-start rhythm. In nearly a call-and-response, the brass interplays with the other two instrumental sections to create an unexpected, jumpy version of the song.
0:44	A burst from a trombone and two notes from the piano signal a new section of the song.
0:45–0:49	A muted trumpet by Eddie Tompkins plays a very brief lead.
0:52–0:54	A short plunger-growling trombone solo by Henry Wells follows.
0:55–1:30	Trumpeter Tompkins takes a shaky extended solo accompanied by five saxophones and a bass, which interrupt in staccato, New Orleans–like stop-time.
1:31–2:09	On trumpet, Sy Oliver begins with a smooth, lyrical style and then transitions to a New-Orleans–style trumpet with slurs and almost King Oliver–esque freak sounds to end the section. A staccato saxophone section with the bass backs him and gives the solo punch.
2:10–2:28	The brass and reed sections weave around each other and the main theme of the song as the sections politely battle in a style that anticipates the swing era, which flourished a year after this recording.
2:29–2:35	The reed section sways with the main theme.
2:36–2:45	As a nod to the Ellington original, Lunceford adds an inverted horn section of trumpet, trombone, and clarinet backed by very short bursts from the brass for an exciting rhythm.
2:46–2:50	Unlike the Ellington variant, the song ends by a swift ascent in pitch of the instruments for a powerful finish.

in the club's revue, called "As Long as I Live." Based upon its success at the well-known venue, the orchestra hit with two Ellington compositions, and the next year followed with "Rhythm Is Our Business." The Lunceford Orchestra, favoring a two-beat rhythm (one, two; one, two) rather than the standard four beats (one, two, three, four; one, two, three, four), relied on arranger Sy Oliver to develop a distinctive version of symphonic jazz. By the early thirties, it and other well-dressed, symphonic-sounding bands had followed Duke Ellington to stardom.

A Race Riot and the End of the Harlem Club Scene

By the mid-thirties, a race riot in uptown New York City sent the Cotton Club and Harlem jazz into a tailspin. On Tuesday afternoon, March 19, 1935, spurred by rumors that a teenager had been beaten to death for shoplifting a knife in a Kress five-and-ten department store across from the Apollo Theater, thousands of African Americans stormed the business district. They burned and looted shops and broke more than two hundred store windows. After five hundred police officers quieted the disturbance a day later, three African Americans had died and 121 had been arrested, and $2 million worth of property had been destroyed. Adam Clayton Powell Jr., then the assistant pastor of the Abyssinian Church and later a member of the US House of Representatives, blamed the conflagration on the substandard living conditions of African Americans in Harlem. "Continued exploitation of the Negro is at the bottom of all this trouble," he exclaimed, "exploitation as regards wages, jobs, working conditions. . . . The trouble seems to be over for the time being but it may break out in a week, or even in a month, unless our people get some assurance of economic adjustment to end the discrimination against them," Powell warned. A day after the riot, the New York Times observed that "Harlem's sidewalks, stoops and apartment house windows were alive with resentful Negroes" ("Mayor Starts" 1935, 16).

In the wake of the riot, uptown club owners relocated to downtown New York City to cater to fearful whites who would no longer frequent Harlem for their entertainment. Due to a declining number of patrons, in September 1936 the Cotton Club closed its doors and reopened downtown on Broadway and Forty-eighth Streets away from any possible rioting. For opening night, the club featured Cab Calloway and, by March 1937, had rehired its mainstay Duke Ellington. Only Harlem clubs with a primarily African-American clientele such as the Savoy Ballroom and the Apollo Theater remained open. The heyday of jazz in Harlem had passed.

During the late twenties and early thirties, the Ellington, Lunceford, and Calloway bands set the tone and image for jazz. Bankrolled by gangsters, they performed regularly at such swank Harlem venues as the Cotton Club and attracted droves of curious white audiences who sought the thrills of a forbidden African-American culture. Assisted by savvy entrepreneurs such as Irving Mills, they reached homes across the country through the emerging technologies of the day: records, radio, and films with sound. To achieve respectability amid the racist environment, the orchestras customized and repurposed the symphonic jazz of Paul Whiteman and dressed and acted in a highly cultured manner. As with other African-American artists who formed the Harlem Renaissance, they combated racial prejudice by demonstrating that they could succeed in white society on its own terms without sacrificing a uniquely African-American culture. Ellington and his contemporaries wrenched jazz from the low-down barroom and placed it solidly within mainstream American culture while retaining its African-American identity.

For Discussion and Further Study

Chapter Quiz

1. How did Duke Ellington's background and education influence the development of his musical style? What elements of African-American and white music did he combine in his work?

2. Why were Ellington's early compositions called "jungle music"? What elements were incorporated into it that were supposed to represent the "primitive" nature of African-American jazz? How did this attitude among white listeners color how Ellington and his music were received?

3. What role did the mob play in the operation of Harlem nightclubs like the Cotton Club? Why did these clubs attract well-to-do white audiences? How did these audiences influence the music that was performed in these clubs?

4. What role did manager Irving Mills play in promoting Ellington's music and career? How did he use popular media like radio to spread Ellington's sound? Why did Ellington need a white manager to succeed in the popular music world?

5. How did ideas about racial pride and African-American self-expression develop during the Harlem Renaissance and influence Ellington's career?

THE GREAT DEPRESSION AND THE GROWTH OF RADIO

The Rise of the Soothing Crooners

D uring most of the 1930s, a severe economic depression and radio both had a major impact on jazz. Amid the most serious depression in modern American history, urban Americans stood in bread lines to get food, jazz clubs suddenly lost their customers, and record sales plummeted as discretionary income disappeared. In this bleak period, the relatively inexpensive medium of radio provided the most constant and affordable form of entertainment to most Americans. It became even more alluring with the invention of new microphone technologies, which fostered a new, smooth, intimate style of singing known as "crooning" by vocalists such as Bing Crosby, who became major stars amid the economic gloom.

In 1921, Edgar Harburg—nicknamed "Yip" by his friends—graduated from City College in New York City. After a brief stint working as a journalist in South America, he partnered with a friend to establish the Consolidated Electrical Appliance Company. "I never liked the idea of living on scallions in a Left

Bank garret," he joked. He had learned at an early age from his Yiddish parents, the Hochbergs, who had emigrated from Russia, that prosperity came only to those who worked long hours. Although business flourished under the capable Harburg, the fortunes of the new company suddenly turned sour. "A thing called the Collapse, bango! socked everything out. 1929. All I had was a pencil," he recalled. The Great Depression bankrupted Yip, who had a wife and two children and a $70,000 debt.

Yip's experience mirrored the fate of most Americans in the Depression era. "We thought American business was the Rock of Gibraltar," he explained. "Suddenly the big dream exploded. The impact was unbelievable." The roaring, carefree twenties had crashed into pieces and left huddled, unemployed, and desperate masses, who scrambled to survive.

Over the next few months, an unemployed Harburg scuffled to make a living. Like many New Yorkers at the time, he joined the lines of the recently unemployed, who waited on New York City streets for bread and soup that was being handed out by philanthropic groups. "You'd see the bread lines," he recollected. "The biggest one in New York City was owned by [millionaire newspaper mogul and former U.S. Representative] William Randolph Hearst. He had a big truck with several people on it, and big cauldrons of hot soup, bread. Fellows with burlap on their shoes were lined up all across Columbus Circle, and went for blocks and blocks around the park, waiting."

On the corners of other New York streets, men, women, and children begged for anything that they could get. "The prevailing greeting at the time, on every block you passed, by some poor guy coming up, was 'Can you spare a dime,' or 'Can you spare something for a cup of coffee,'" Harburg recalled. "'Brother, can you spare me a dime,' hit on every block, on every street." Americans who had been successful entrepreneurs just a few months earlier had fallen on hard times with a resounding crash.

Armed only with a pencil, and having nothing else to do, Harburg wrote songs. He teamed with songster Jay Gorney and landed a job with a revue sponsored by Broadway theatrical producer and theater owner Earl Carroll, who became famous for his scantily clad showgirls. In 1932, the duo collaborated on a show, *Americana*, that focused on the hardships of the Great Depression. As part of the show, the duo wrote the song, "Brother, Can You Spare a Dime?" which described the tough economic times.

Striking a heartfelt chord with many Americans, the song swept the country. "Everybody picked the song up," remembered Harburg. "Bands were playing it and records were made. When Roosevelt was a candidate for President [in 1932], the Republicans got pretty worried about it," he intimated (Terkel 1970, 19–21).

The Great Depression

The Depression began in America with the stock market crash in October 1929. During the twenties, Americans had speculated frenetically in stocks. The market climbed higher and higher over those nine years until March 1929, when the Federal Reserve privately met and cautioned the government about imprudent and wild market gambles. An initial panic occurred late that month, during which speculators traded nearly six million shares and sent stocks plummeting. However, the downward trend quickly reversed, when Charles E. Mitchell, president of the National City Bank of New York and a member of the Federal Reserve Board, promised that his bank would loan $25 million in credit to distressed borrowers. With confidence restored, the market temporarily stabilized. By September 3, the Dow Jones Industrial Average topped 381, an all-time high.

On October 24, 1929, the market crashed again after more than a thousand investors traded frantically on "Black Thursday." When the traditional gong sounded at 3:00 p.m., more than twelve million shares had been traded with a paper loss of $5 billion. At the end of the day, a *New York Times* reporter saw "tired brokers, their faces streaming perspiration, their collars torn, leaning against the posts. Others, their hands full of unexecuted orders, stood as though dazed."

To quell the tide, a group of bankers dumped millions of dollars into the market and pledged to steady the financial freefall. President Herbert Hoover immediately calmed Americans by reassuring them that the market drop represented only a

Soup line in Chicago opened by Al Capone, 1931. Records of the US Information Agency, 1900-2003. *National Archives*

temporary decline. "The fundamental business in the country, that is the production and distribution of commodities, is on a sound and prosperous basis," he proclaimed (Hoover 1929).

Despite these attempts to reverse the trend, the downward spiral continued. On Black Monday, October 28, 1929, stocks fell even lower. In unfettered trading, the market plunged 22.6 percent in one day. On Tuesday, the market fell another 12.8 percent. "Stock prices virtually collapsed yesterday, swept downward with gigantic losses in the most disastrous trading day in the stock market's history. Billions of dollars in open market prices were wiped out as prices crumbled under the pressure of liquidation," read the *New York Times* on October 30. "Hysteria swept the country and stocks went overboard for just what they would bring at forced sale." *Variety* aptly described the event in a now-famous, front-page headline on October 30: "Wall St. Lays an Egg."

The Depression deepened as the banking industry restricted the money they lent to new and existing businesses. By curbing lending, the banking industry reduced the number of entrepreneurs who could start companies and blocked existing businesses from expanding, which drove the gross domestic product downward. Bank failures worsened the economic malaise. Holding portfolios of heavily discounted stocks, many banks declared bankruptcy. Between 1929 and 1933, 10,763 of the 24,970 commercial banks in the country became insolvent. In 1933, the failed banks held approximately $7 billion in frozen assets.

Herbert Hoover tried to stabilize wages by appealing to major businesses to bolster wages in the hope that well-paid workers would fuel the consumer-driven

Unemployed workers in New Jersey, 1934. *Photograph by Mark Benedict Barry, Library of Congress Prints and Photographs Division*

economy. As a result, many business leaders kept wages the same for their workers, but balanced budgets by severely reducing their workforces and causing unemployment to skyrocket. In 1929, just more than 3 percent Americans were unemployed; in two years, the jobless rate in the United States stood at nearly 16 percent. By 1933, unemployment neared an all-time high of 25 percent, and the number of part-time workers who wanted full-time jobs comprised almost another third of the population.

Shocked by the magnitude of the depression and fearing an unending financial crisis, Americans stopped spending and sent the consumer-based economy into a tailspin. Jobless and struggling to repay loans for items that they had purchased on credit during the booming twenties, they patched old clothing rather than buying new garments, delayed repairs on homes, and did not purchase new appliances. Between 1929 and 1930, automobile sales declined by more than 20 percent, department-store purchases fell by 16 percent, and mail-order sales dropped by nearly 36 percent. After 1929, American consumers reduced overall yearly expenditures on average by 10 percent.

The Entertainment Industry during the Depression

When American consumers restricted spending, the music industry confronted sinking record sales. In 1927, record companies sold 104 million discs. Three years later, during the Depression, they peddled a mere 10 million records. By 1932, record production in the United States had sunk to 6 million discs valued at $2.5 million. "You couldn't sell anything in 32," complained Brunswick Records salesman Harry Charles (Calt and Wardlow 1990, 23). One executive feared that the business "seemed to be experiencing not a slump but a final collapse" (Erenberg 1998, 14). Many small jazz and blues labels closed amid the crumbling economy. In 1930, Gennett Records stopped production. Three years later, Paramount Records ceased operations. In 1935, OKeh stopped pressing discs.

Herbert Yates, a businessman who had amassed a fortune in the tobacco industry and owned Republic Motion Pictures, viewed the depressed music industry as an opportunity to sell cheap records. In October 1929, amid the stock market crash, the entrepreneur purchased the American Record Corporation (ARC), a conglomeration of budget labels. In a novel marketing ploy, Yates produced custom labels for the larger retailers. He churned out Romeo discs for S. H. Kress & Company's five-and-dime department stores, Challenge and Conqueror records for Sears, Roebuck and Co., and Oriole 78 platters for J. G. McRory's dime-store outlets. He absorbed the catalogs of various labels such as Columbia, Brunswick Records and Vocalion over the following two years.

While Yates built a cut-rate record business in the United States, two major companies emerged in Great Britain. In 1929, Edward Lewis established Decca Records. The carbon microphone summer 1934, he bought two American pressing plants and incorporated an American offshoot of Decca. As president of the American branch, the record magnate hired Jack Kapp, who had successfully expanded the jazz and blues roster of Brunswick Records. Within a few months, Kapp arranged more than two hundred recording sessions.

In March 1931, Electric and Musical Industries, Inc. (EMI) emerged from a merger of the British branches of Columbia and Victor. Reeling from gross-revenue losses of more than 80 percent in two years, the two companies joined forces to survive. The newly established company invested heavily in radio, built a studio on Abbey Road, launched a mail-order business, and sold record players at a loss to stimulate disc sales. By 1934, EMI joined Decca, ARC, and Victor as the major companies that controlled the record industry.

While the record industry contracted and consolidated, nightclubs experienced hard times. Harlem nightspots no longer attracted footloose clientele who had lost their savings in the stock market crash, and the Harlem scene deteriorated. On February 21, 1931, the *New York Daily Mirror* observed that "with the exception of the Cotton Club—and possibly Connie's Inn—the rest of the black belt cafes have gone pretty much to the doggies."

On December 5, 1933, a further blow to nightclubs came, when federal and state governments ended Prohibition with the adoption of the Twenty-first Amendment. "With repeal of Prohibition folks no longer had to come to speakeasies to buy liquor sold by racketeers," explained bandleader and clarinetist Cecil Scott. "Harlem's hot music suddenly cooled off because the patrons could buy a bottle and drink at home far cheaper" (Shapiro and Hentoff 1955, 197). "The Depression for musicians in New York," summarized banjoist and guitarist Danny Barker, "was a bitch" (196).

In other major cities, jazz clubs closed and left many musicians unemployed. In Chicago during June 1932, the *Defender* found jazz venues "scarce as hen's teeth." Saxophonist Budd Johnson found "things were really difficult. This was the Depression. You could see the bread lines and people sleeping in the park" (Zwerin 1968, 20; Kenney 1930, 154). In Detroit, formerly a nightclub haven, only one nightspot survived.

Irving Mills somehow escaped the decimation of the Depression-era music industry. He ensured that his clients found employment and record deals. Mills often underwrote the cost of recording his artists such as Cab Calloway. Amidst the worst of the downturn, Mills also bolstered his major client, Duke Ellington. "We worked clean through the Depression without ever knowing that there was one," boasted clarinetist Barney Bigard, who worked with Ellington throughout the era (Stowe 1994, 103).

The Jukebox and Radio

The jukebox and radio replaced most live jazz shows for Americans. Starting in 1927, jukeboxes—automated record players that were installed in taverns, restaurants, soda fountains, and other places that people gathered—were stocked with the hit songs of the day and could be played for as little as a nickel. By 1934, during the height of the Depression, more than twenty-five thousand jukeboxes manufactured by such companies as Seeberg and Wurlitzer blasted forth across the country and replaced more expensive live music. By 1938, more than a quarter million jukeboxes stuffed with thirty million records entertained the public and accounted for nearly half of all record sales.

Americans who did not have the time, inclination, or money to plug nickels into jukeboxes to hear the hits listened to their favorite music on the radio. In 1930, 50 percent of all urban families, both white and African American, listened to a radio in their homes. As deflation pushed the average cost of a radio down from $139 in 1929 to just $47 four years later, Americans snapped up radio sets like wildfire.

Advertising revenue permitted stations to broadcast programs at no cost to listeners and transformed radio into a ubiquitous communications medium during the crushing Depression (Firestone 1993, 73). Corporations used radio advertising to reverse skidding sales and hired well-known musicians, comedy acts, and dramatic actors to build their brands. Tobacco companies, trying to counteract negative publicity generated by a 1932 report that linked cancer to cigarettes, sponsored programs such as Lucky Strike's *Your Hit Parade*, Camel's *Caravan*, Chesterfield's *Moonlight Serenade*, and the *Old Gold Hour*. Food companies launched *Kraft Music Hall* and Maxwell House coffee's *Show Boat*. By 1933, during the worst of the Depression, the two major networks—NBC and CBS—and smaller, unaffiliated stations together raked in more than $60 million in advertising dollars. "No Depresh for Radio" proclaimed a headline in *Variety* (Firestone 1993, 73).

The Condenser Microphone

The condenser microphone made it easier to enjoy music on the radio. It replaced the carbon microphone, which generally produced a muddy, scratchy sound that failed to adequately capture low-end frequencies by distorting the bass, acoustic guitar, drums, and high-pitched vocalists. The carbon microphone best showcased big-voiced, booming vocalists such as opera star Enrico Caruso and popular Irish tenor John McCormack.

The condenser microphone revolutionized broadcast music. Widespread by the late twenties, it clearly captured the sound of guitar, bass, and drums. "The [condenser] microphone is particularly sensitive to guitar music," explained Tony Colluci, a staff guitarist for the NBC orchestra, in an October 1930 *Metronome* article. "It reproduces all the richness and depth of tone brought out by guitarists who are in constant demand for so many programs on the air" (Spring 1997, 194). Due to its clarity and wider range of frequencies, the new microphone paved the way for baritone crooners who softly cooed and coaxed listeners and replaced the forceful tenors of the previous two decades.

Bing Crosby: The Advent of the Crooner

Harry "Bing" Crosby possessed a soothing, melodious bass baritone voice. He exploited the benefits of the condenser microphone to achieve national stardom as the first jazz singer who did not double on an instrument. Born in Tacoma, Washington, and raised in the eastern part of the state, Crosby displayed an early interest in singing after he saw vaudeville sensation Al Jolson perform. He joined a variety of singing groups near his home in Spokane, and, in October 1925, traveled with a friend, Al Rinker, to Los Angeles to find fame and fortune. They called on Rinker's sister, Mildred Bailey, then a rising blues and jazz singer, who recommended them to Paul Whiteman. On December 6, 1926, the duo joined Whiteman and added singer/pianist Harry Barris to perform as Paul Whiteman's Rhythm Boys. Crosby thought it "incredible" that they had been signed by Whiteman who, according to the singer, "in 1927 stood out above other American band leaders as Mount Everest stands out above other mountains" (Crosby 1953, 38).

The Rhythm Boys sang in a jazz-based vocal style. Learning from Louis Armstrong (who eventually became a close friend of Crosby's), the trio developed a pop-jazz approach that fit perfectly with the popular jazz symphonies of Whiteman. They created "an entirely new style of singing pop songs. We were far more jazz oriented than any other singing group of that time," insisted Al Rinker. "We were greatly influenced by the great jazz musicians we had heard and were working with" (Giddens 2001, 161). The group gravitated toward jazz even more after Whiteman hired many former Jean Goldkette–band jazz stars, who especially influenced Bing. "I listened and learned," confided Crosby. "Bix [Beiderbecke], [Bill] Challis, even Frank Trumbauer would make suggestions to me for my vocalizing, and I'd give it a try" (171).

The three dashing young men, singing in a jazz-infused style, particularly appealed to women. On August 15, 1928, *Variety* considered the group a hit "with the younger generation, particularly the flaps [flappers]." The trio, especially Crosby, similarly charmed African-American women. "There were just as many colored people 'buying air,' raving over Bing's recordings, as much as anyone else," revealed Louis Armstrong. "The chicks were just a swooning and screaming when Bing would sing" (Giddens 2001, 181).

After the Rhythm Boys generated a fan base, Whiteman asked leader Bing Crosby to solo on a few of the band's many records. In 1927, two selections featuring Bing's sonorous baritone were best sellers. The next year, Whiteman showcased Crosby as star soloist on seven songs, which swept the nation, including "Ol' Man River." In 1929, the Whiteman orchestra highlighted Bing on five hits. The next year, as the Depression engulfed the United States and as Whiteman's musical prominence eroded, the bandleader scored three times with his singing sensation.

Crosby projected a soft, intimate style. Accommodated by the wider frequency range of the condenser microphone, he replaced the pomposity of operatic tenors with a relaxed, friendly baritone. "He employed a completely new and different style, which sounded more natural and effortless than any I'd ever heard," singer/songwriter Johnny Mercer explained (Giddens 2001, 170). To Louis Armstrong, "Bing's voice has a mellow quality that only Bing's got. It's like gold being poured out of a cup" (Crosby and Firestone 1984, 224).

Crosby's laid-back voice provided a welcome, soothing antidote to the harsh realities of everyday life for Depression-era Americans. In 1931, *Metronome* linked the Crosby phenomenon to the gloomy mood of the country. The magazine believed that the "soft and subdued melody" of Crosby reflected the somber mood of a nation in the grips of a Depression. "That feverish decade following the world war has come to an end," it asserted. "People are tired of raucous jazz, hysteria, stark reality and other concomitants of the post war age" (Wald 2009, 99).

In 1930, Crosby and the other Rhythm Boys left Whiteman to hone their jazz sound in the Gus Arnheim band, which the year before had scored with "Sleepy Valley." "Bing and his Trio were really romping . . . at the Cocoanut Grove Hotel in Hollywood," remembered Louis Armstrong, who at the time performed at the nearby Cotton Club in Los Angeles. "Bing and Gus Arnheim and Company would broadcast first every night and leave the ether wave sizzling hot." When the bands finished their sets, continued the trumpeter, the Rhythm Boys "would haul ashes over to the Cotton Club where we were playing and swing with us, until 'Home Sweet Home' was played." In August 1930, on an off-night from the Arnheim band, the trio partnered with Duke Ellington on the song, "Three Little Words" for the film *Check and Double Check* (Giddens 2001, 234).

In 1931, Crosby left the Arnheim band and the Rhythm Boys for a solo career. In March, Bing released a debut record under his own name, "Out of Nowhere," which quickly became a best seller. Later in the year, Crosby scored with two more top-selling numbers and, in his first year as a solo recording artist, amassed an amazing total of twelve hits.

William S. Paley, the president of the Columbia Broadcasting System network, noticed Crosby's phenomenal recording success and signed the singing sensation to a radio contract. In late August 1931, CBS and Bing agreed to stage a fifteen-minute show nightly from Monday through Saturday that would be broadcast to network affiliates across the country. The network paid Bing $1,500 per week, a large sum at a time when many stood in bread lines. On September 2, the network aired Crosby's solo radio debut with the theme song, "When the Blue of the Night (Meets the Gold

LISTENING GUIDE 16

Bing Crosby and the Lennie Hayton Orchestra

"BROTHER, CAN YOU SPARE A DIME?"

During the depression, Bing Crosby dominated the jazz market and became the first significant jazz singer who did not play an instrument. He encapsulated the period with this song, which told the tale of Depression-era pain and suffering.

On October 25, 1932, during the depths of the Depression and three weeks after "Brother, Can You Spare a Dime?" appeared on Broadway, the crooner recorded his version of the song for Brunswick Records with the orchestra of Lennie Hayton, who had played with Crosby in the Paul Whiteman band and continued to tour and back the singer during the early Thirties. Bing insisted that jazz men Eddie Lang (guitar) and Joe

Venuti (violin) play in the orchestra. Within two weeks after recording the tune, Crosby scored with the timely and top-selling song.

Crosby demonstrated his propensity toward jazz with "Brother, Can You Spare a Dime?" He effortlessly slid over and between notes and delivered multiple notes over a single syllable. As with jazz instrumentalists, the crooner extended the tempo of a phrase to produce varied and interesting rhythms within a line. Tellingly, in the studio immediately after recording this song, Crosby launched into a stride-like version of "Sweet Sue, Just You," in which he scat-sang a passage of a 1928 Bix Beiderbecke solo.

0:00–0:11	A highly orchestrated, lush introduction to the song that has been embellished with strings. The introduction begins with a strummed chord by Lang.
0:12–0:34	Bing starts his smooth, lilting vocals in the first verse about a farmer who has served in the war and now has fallen upon hard times. In a jazz and blues tradition, Crosby slides over a note and back again at 0:16, and at 0:20 quickly hitting multiple notes on one syllable in a stunning vibrato. He repeats these techniques throughout the song.
0:35–0:56	Second verse with vocals in an ascending pitch. Again, he repeats his vocal techniques from the first verse. At 0:52 ("just waiting for bread"), he employs an interesting time change by extending the phrasing of his vocals much like jazz men do with their instruments.
0:57–1:16	Third verse with a gradual backing of the orchestra, which dynamically builds volume. At 1:16, Crosby improvises by singing a note, jumping forward, and then back again on one word ("dime").
1:17	The trumpets play a bar to signal the beginning of a new verse.
1:18–1:30	The next line chronicles the Depression-based trouble of a railroad worker.
1:31–1:39	Crosby delivers the next line about a down-and-out construction worker. At 1:38, he again generates multiple notes on the word "dime."
1:40–2:01	Next verse, Crosby builds volume and intensity as he describes the problems of an ex-serviceman from World War I. At 1:48, he weaves an improvised vocal solo with several notes over a syllable, much like an instrumentalist might do with a horn. After 1:51, the trumpet enters with a secondary melody to denote the military service of the subject of the lyric.
1:59–2:00	When Crosby hits the word "drum" in an ascending lyric, the drum beats for a bar.
2:02–2:20	Crosby goes to the next line. At 2:05, Crosby extends the rhythm in the word "Al" to give it punch. At 2:16, Crosby sings multiple notes on the word "pal."

2:21–2:25	The orchestra enters with a 4/4 march rhythm to accentuate the military service of the subject of the lyric.
2:26–2:45	Crosby goes to the next verse with prominent drum rolls in the background to further accentuate the subject's military service. At 2:34, Crosby again vocalizes multiple notes over a syllable.
2:44–2:46	In dramatic fashion, Crosby sings in a higher pitch and slides from one line of lyrics to the next one.
2:47–2:58	He continues to use the vocal techniques just described.
2:59–3:12	Backed by the full orchestra, Crosby dynamically increases the volume of his vocals to increase the pathos and again vocalizes multiple notes on "dime" at the end of the song, which finishes at 3:12 with a cymbal crash.

of the Day)." The format consisted of three vocals and one instrumental by the house band, which included at Bing's insistence such jazz players as guitarist Eddie Lang (b. Salvatore Massaro) and violinist Joe Venuti. Between songs, announcer Ken Roberts hawked cigars for sponsor Certified Cremo (Giddens 2001, 268).

Bing Crosby in a publicity photo, 1930s.

Almost instantly, Crosby achieved radio stardom. Fan letters poured into the station, and the press requested interviews. "The show was an immediate success," gushed Ken Roberts. "Tremendous. He was a real star." When dropped by Cremo cigars, the singer was eagerly snapped up by Chesterfield cigarettes, which signed him to a thirteen-week contract at $2,000 for two shows per week. On his new program, Crosby sang in front of Lennie Hayton's band, which spotlighted future jazz bandleaders Artie Shaw and Tommy Dorsey (Giddens 2001, 266).

Crosby changed the music industry by shifting the emphasis from the song to the singer. Directly challenging Tin Pan Alley songwriters, who for years determined popular hits for bands and vocalists, Bing squarely placed the singer in control. "With Bing," contended Roberts, "it was no longer the song that sold records, it was the artists" (Giddens 2001, 266).

Crosby's shining star shone brighter when he conquered the new medium of sound films. In the same year that he became a radio sensation, Bing released short movies with Educational Pictures, owned by Mack Sennett, who directed and discovered such silent-film comedy stars as Buster Keaton, Charlie

Chaplin, and Harold Lloyd. During the summer months, Crosby played dramatic roles to rave reviews in four shorts, including *I Surrender Dear*. In September, *Photoplay* reported that the Sennett shorts "not only get over the Crosby voice, but the Crosby personality, which seems to be quite sumpin.'" When reviewing the films early the next month, the *Motion Picture Herald* nicknamed Crosby "the baron of the baritones," and believed that he "can act sufficiently to put over his songs" (Giddens 2001, 253).

Emboldened by his success with Sennett and his high-profile radio presence, in 1932 Crosby agreed to a five-picture deal with Paramount Pictures for $300,000 over a three-year period. In October, he appeared as a good-natured radio singer in *The Big Broadcast*. The next year, he starred in *College Humor* and *Too Much Harmony*, which both reinforced the Crosby image of the laid-back, well-meaning, good-humored, and upstanding entertainer who represented the average American. He fortified his clean-cut image in more than fifty films, which culminated in his Academy Award–winning performance as a priest, Father O'Malley, in 1944's *Going My Way*.

Bing Crosby crooned to the top of the jazz echelon through the relatively new technologies of condenser microphones, radio, and sound films. In 1932, Bing racked up eight top-selling entries, including the Depression-defining "Brother, Can You Spare a Dime?" The following year, he scored with thirteen hit songs, including the smash "Shadow Waltz." During the thirties, Crosby sold two million records a year and registered 101 hit singles, nineteen of which became major hits. Artie Shaw, soon to be a noted bandleader, considered Bing "the first American jazz singer in the white world. Bing was an enormous influence. You couldn't avoid him . . . he was the first hip white person in the United States" (Giddens 2001, 265, 260). By the end of his career, which increasingly became pop oriented, Crosby finished with 152 top-ten hits, of which thirty topped the chart, and sold more than a half billion records worldwide.

By 1932, Crosby and a spate of other crooners dominated the music scene. On December 6, 1931, the *New York Times* reported that "the mushroom growth of the radio crooner has been nothing short of phenomenal. . . . Turn the dial to the right or the left and you hear the crooner's plaintive voice. The listener may take them or leave them but he cannot elude them."

The Sweet Bands: Guy Lombardo

During the Depression years, "sweet" bands such as Guy Lombardo and the Royal Canadians entertained Americans with the more comforting style of jazz pioneered by Bing Crosby. Hailing from London, Ontario, from an Italian immigrant family, young teen violinist Guy Lombardo (b. Gaetano Alberto) headed a group with brothers Carmen, Lebert, and Victor. In the early twenties, the band moved to Cleveland, where they first became popular.

In 1927, Lombardo and an expanded band landed a stint for $1,600 a week at Chicago's gang-operated Granada Café, which featured music and dancing on the first floor and a small gambling room upstairs. Despite a reluctant club manager, Lombardo insisted that the club install a radio wire and, in November 1927, convinced newly established station WBBM to broadcast the band. Scheduled for a fifteen-minute spot, the Royal Canadians immediately generated hundreds of accolades from listeners, "and the word came back, keep playing all night until the club closes" (Lombardo and Altshul 1975, 61). The next day, Lombardo received offers from the Wrigley Chewing Gum Company and Florsheim Shoes to headline a half-hour radio program aired from the Granada. "In a few weeks," boasted Lombardo, who somewhat overstated his Chicago success, "the combination of our unpaid broadcasts from the Granada and the Florsheim and Wrigley programs made us not only the most celebrated band in Chicago, but probably the whole country" (62).

The Royal Canadians played music that matched the reassuring style of Crosby. The bandleader "liked the slow tempo which enabled them [customers] to dance; the soft sound that permitted a swain to whisper endearments his girl could hear; the sweet, rich tones of Carmen [Lombardo's] sax and Lebe [Lebert Lombardo's] trumpet" (Lombardo and Altshul 1975, 63). He focused on "the melody because we didn't dress [the music] up with fancy embellishments" (80). In 1928, after listening to the band at the Granada Café, Louis Armstrong characterized the Lombardo sound as "the sweetest music this side of heaven." He especially liked "their beautiful tones (the most essential thing in music), their beautiful way of phrasing" (78).

Inspired by the success of Bing Crosby with the Paul Whiteman orchestra, in 1927 Guy Lombardo convinced his brother Carmen to sing. Though detesting the role, Carmen nonetheless complied with his brother's wishes. "Carmen Lombardo's voice was now as much a part of our identity as his sax and Lebe's trumpet," asserted Guy (Lombardo and Altshul 1975, 65).

Prodded by booking agent Jules Stein of the MCA group, the band moved to New York City to repeat their Chicago success. "We wanted to get to New York before other bands caught on to the tempo and diminished one of our trademarks," reasoned Lombardo (Lombardo and Altshul 1975, 88). On October 3, 1929, just days before the stock market crash, the Royal Canadians arrived in New York City. They landed a job for $2,000 a week at the Roosevelt Grill in the Roosevelt Hotel. On opening night, related the bandleader, "all the heads of the music publishing firms had reserved tables. So had, it seemed, the entire segment of New York's show business community. Wall Street had sent a large representation of stock brokers, most of them in white ties" (93). *Variety* praised the band for their "soothing quality." However, within three weeks, attendance at the Roosevelt Grill dropped precipitously. "The stock market had crashed," lamented Lombardo. "The Roosevelt Grill was no longer filled with gay, happy, paper-rich patrons. Even those without money in the market hardly felt like dancing" (99).

Radio saved the Royal Canadians. Upon arriving in New York City, Lombardo snagged three remote broadcasts per week on WABC. In 1930, as the Depression deepened, the orchestra nabbed a half-hour, nationally broadcast program on Monday nights from 9:00 to 9:30. "At the start of the Depression, [radio] was all we needed to become one of the major show business attractions in the nation," explained Lombardo. "We had staked our future on radio," he admitted. "But we never anticipated that a terrible recession would make the medium the dominant force in the entertainment business. How could we know that the day would come that few people could afford a speakeasy, a nightclub, a night of dining and dancing in a hotel?" Depression-era Americans, Guy concluded, "never abandoned their quest for entertainment. They turned now to the cheapest way they could get it—in their own living rooms" (Lombardo and Altshul 1975, 102).

The Royal Canadians turned into a national sensation through radio. In 1930, the band registered fourteen hits, including the bestselling "You're Driving Me Crazy! (What Did I Do?)." The next year, it delivered ten top-selling entries. From 1930 to 1938, throughout the worst of the Depression, the Royal Canadians scored sixty-seven hit songs, including seventeen top-selling smashes.

Bands looking for a formula to stardom replicated the sweet music of Guy Lombardo. "We had helped create the demand for more and more dance orchestras, and now in the early thirties combinations were being organized with the sole purpose of duplicating the Lombardo sound," sniffed the bandleader (Lombardo and

Altshul 1975, 161). From 1933 to 1938, the Indiana-born Jan Garber—a classically trained violinist who acknowledged his debt to Lombardo—racked up nineteen best sellers, including three major hits. Bandleader Sammy Kaye instructed his men to station themselves behind the Royal Canadian bandstand so they could listen and then imitate Lombardo's sound. Throughout the thirties, sweet bands such as the Royal Canadians and smooth vocalists such as Bing Crosby consoled a shocked and poverty-stricken America. "The wild jargon called jazz blended into a hushed melodic rhythmic type of music in slower tempo and softer cadences," summarized the *New York Times* on December 6, 1931.

For Discussion and Further Study

🔗
Chapter Quiz

1. How did the Great Depression affect the entertainment industry? What changes occurred that were particularly difficult for jazz musicians?

2. What was the impact of new entertainment technologies such as the jukebox and radio on the music industry? How did these new technologies help spread jazz?

3. How did crooners like Bing Crosby use the newly developed condenser microphone to develop a new vocal style? Why was this style particularly suited to radio?

4. What is "sweet" music? Why do you think it had a strong appeal to Depression-era audiences?

8

BIG-BAND SWING

The New Deal, Jitterbugs, and Racial Integration

In July 1935, the Benny Goodman band left New York City for a tour across the country that ended in a month-long stay at the Palomar Ballroom in Los Angeles. Goodman and his band mates had low expectations for the series of one-night stands along the way, some of which paid as little as $250. "There wasn't a whole lot of optimism about what might happen when the tour hit the road," remembered pianist Jess Stacy, who had started with Paul Mares of the New Orleans Rhythm Kings and gained a following in Chicago before joining Goodman (Firestone 1993, 144).

The engagements began reasonably well. Stopovers in Pennsylvania and Ohio drew adequate crowds, and a two-night stand in Milwaukee attracted a number of musicians from Chicago. Hordes of fans, however, never materialized. "I began to wonder what happened to all those radio listeners who'd written us fan letters," recalled Goodman, who referenced the coast-to-coast, late-night Saturday NBC radio program, *Let's Dance*, which was broadcast on fifty stations.

When the Goodman band reached Denver, it played at Elitch's Garden, a ballroom on the outskirts of town, to customers who expected a sweet waltz orchestra. When they heard Goodman's music, many attendees demanded refunds. During the three-week engagement, Benny modified his style by selecting more sedate numbers, but had little success. He entertained only a smattering of dancers while most people frequented a nearby dance hall to listen to Kay Kyser's band, which offered a combination of dance music, Kyser's "Kollege of Musical Knowledge" quizzes, and the comedic routine of cornetist Merwyn Bogue, otherwise known as Ish Kabibble. "It was a fiasco, a terrible fiasco," reflected Helen Ward, the singer in the band. "And it really got to Benny. He was so heartbroken he stayed alone in his hotel room in downtown Denver all day" (Firestone 1993, 146). The normally tight-lipped, twenty-six-year-old Goodman referred to the Denver gig as "about the most humiliating experience in my life" (145). "I remember thinking after Denver, 'Oh well, that's the end of this goddamn thing.' Meaning the whole business of leading a band," he revealed. "I was really down" (Sudhalter 1999, 561).

On August 21, 1935, the unexpected happened when the band started its month-long engagement at the Palomar Ballroom. After a rather quiet first set that lasted nearly an hour, the band "dug in with some of the best playing I'd heard since we left New York," recalled Goodman. "Screw this—let's play," instructed the bandleader. "So we started playing Fletcher Henderson arrangements of 'King Porter Stomp' and 'When Buddha Smiles.' To our complete amazement, half the crowd stopped dancing and came surging toward the stand. The first big roar of the crowd was one of the sweetest sounds I ever heard in my life, and, from that time on, the night kept getting bigger and bigger, as we played every good number in our book" (Sudhalter 1999, 561; Firestone 1993, 149). After the band finished, Taft Schreiber, the West Coast representative for Goodman's booking agency, Music Corporation of America (MCA), hurriedly called his bosses in New York about the good news. "The band is the biggest thing that ever hit the West Coast!" he exclaimed (Firestone 1993, 149).

After the near riot, the Goodman band continued to play to hordes of teens and young adults who thronged the large, redecorated dance floor of the ballroom, which had been wired for nightly radio broadcasts. *Metronome* reported that "the dancers literally swarmed the platform and, though they came to dance, they stood around to listen and applaud." "It was unbelievable," related saxophonist Hymie Schertzer. "They stood in front of the band by the hundreds." The Goodman band, delivering dynamic big-band music, had tapped into a new teenage market and captured the optimism of Americans who had started to emerge from the worst economic crisis in US history. Though most prominent swing leaders except Count Basie were white and played to white audiences, Goodman and his peers built their music upon African-American innovations and many times championed African-American musicians to start the slow process of racial integration in jazz (Firestone 1993, 150).

Benny Goodman and Big-Band Swing

A style of jazz known as "swing" became popular after Goodman's performance at the Palomar. Swing had always been an important part of jazz. From the days of ragtime, jazz had been at least partly defined as syncopated or swinging music. More than three years before Goodman's Palomar success, Duke Ellington had recorded "It Don't Mean a Thing If It Ain't Got That Swing," a phrase that manager Irving Mills claimed to have suggested to Duke. In late 1937, Ellington asserted that "eighty percent of the so called 'swing' music is of Negro creation, even though we can see all types of music combined in the integrated unit we call swing or jazz" (Nicholson 1999, 186).

Despite the long-lasting connection between swing and African-American-inspired jazz, the music press marketed a crop of young musicians as a new jazz trend by dubbing Goodman and his cohorts as "swing musicians" and the group as a "swing band." On August 3, 1935, *Melody Maker* first mentioned swing music in the article, "Debunking the Frankenstein of Jazz . . . Swing!" Three months later, *Variety* launched the column "Swing Stuff." In 1936, the press began to refer to Goodman as the "King of Swing." In January, *Metronome* selected the Goodman band as "the outstanding swing band as well as the sensation of the year" and hailed "the hot-sweet 'swing' style'" of the orchestra (Firestone 1993, 158). "I don't mean that Benny Goodman started swing," explained George Simon in *Metronome*. "Sure, Ellington and Henderson and Redman and Goldkette and others had been there first, but so far as swing's acceptance and, in many ways, its greatness go, it's all pretty much Benny" (Simon 1971, 1).

Goodman half-heartedly accepted the "swing" moniker. He considered the word as "a tag that would associate us with something definite in the public mind." Benny begrudgingly felt that "there was no way of avoiding it, so we had to go along with what the public wanted to call us." When asked about the term, the bandleader believed that "swing" could only be recognized but not defined (Firestone 1993, 158).

Despite Goodman's reluctance to embrace the term "swing," from 1935 through 1938 swing had a general meaning to the average American. It referred to big bands, most of

Benny Goodman at work, 1930s. *Photograph by C. M. Stieglitz. Library of Congress Prints and Photographs Division*

LISTENING GUIDE 17

Benny Goodman Orchestra

◁))) **"KING PORTER" (ALSO CALLED "KING PORTER STOMP")**

On July 1, 1935, Benny Goodman and his band recorded the Fletcher Henderson arrangement of this song for Victor to help jump-start the swing era. The orchestra featured the trumpet of Bunny Berigan as part of the fourteen-piece ensemble.

The song likely had been written by Jelly Roll Morton between 1905 and 1910, and was first recorded in 1923 by Morton as a piano solo and the next year as a duet with King Oliver. Morton composed it for his friend and Florida pianist Porter King. Before Goodman, Fletcher Henderson's band as well as Cab Calloway, the Edgar Benson Orchestra, Claude Hopkins, and Isham Jones waxed the tune.

The song demonstrates the basis of swing: tight arrangements of the orchestra sections (brass and reeds), which interplay in call-and-response in both loud and softer textures; hot improvisational soloists (especially Goodman and Berigan in this case); and an insistent 4/4 beat. It paved the way for other tunes and bandleaders who followed this formula to success.

On this song, the band included Goodman (clarinet); Bunny Berigan, Nate Kaizbier, Ralph Muzillo (trumpets); Sterling Ballard, Jack Lacey (trombones); Toots Mondello, Dick Clark, Hymie Schertzer, Adrian Rollini (saxophones); Frank Froeba (piano); Allan Reuss (guitar); Harry Goodman (bass); and Gene Krupa (drums).

0:00–0:20	The version begins with an innovative trumpet solo by Berigan.
0:21–0:32	The full band enters with a shout and accompanies Berigan for a few more bars of his solo.
0:33–0:38	The full band provides a few measures as a transition to the next section.
0:39–0:57	The sax section takes over and repeats the theme twice in a somewhat subdued manner to add to the dynamics of the song.
0:58–1:42	Benny Goodman takes a swooping, floating, brilliant solo with accompaniment from the trombones in unison and a crashing cymbal from drummer Krupa.
1:43–2:01	Berigan enters for another hot solo, which the trumpet player based upon Jimmy Harrison's solo in the 1928 version of the song by Fletcher Henderson. In one stretch, Berigan hits six high D flats.
2:02–2:22	Jack Lacey weaves a trombone solo.
2:23–2:42	The saxophone section plays the melody twice while the brass section answers in short, exciting staccato bursts until the end of each measure, when the brass takes the lead.
2:43–3:07	In a perfect transition from the previous section, the brass maintains the lead with the reed section offering the bursts, which sound like train whistles. In a call-and-response established in the previous section, the two sections battle one another for a propulsive, swinging effect that exemplifies the best of swing jazz.

them white, with at least fourteen members who played surging, finger-snapping, tightly arranged music punctuated by a few well-rehearsed solos.

Less blues-based than New Orleans groups, white swing bands swayed to popular tunes written by Tin Pan Alley songsmiths by pitting one section of instruments against others in a version of call-and-response. During the early twenties, large bands generally featured one section of instruments at a time playing a group solo. Beginning with Ellington and the Don Redman–arranged Fletcher Henderson band, swing orchestras matched one section of instruments such as the saxophones against other sections such as trumpets to produce a throbbing, propulsive feel. "Now, with one section playing against another section, and within the riffing of phrases, and by using jazzmen who gave the music a hot, driving tone, the whole band swung," explained Max Kaminsky, who had played in Chicago Dixieland groups and in 1936 transitioned to a job with Tommy Dorsey's big band (Ward and Burns 2000, 240).

The New Deal and the Easing of the Great Depression

The 1932 election of Franklin Delano Roosevelt as president and his promise of a New Deal engendered an optimistic mood among Americans that the energetic swing music reflected. During the election, Roosevelt hammered on President Herbert Hoover for his antiquated financial policies and his insistence on Prohibition. On November 8, 1932, Roosevelt won the presidency by one of the largest margins in history, earning nearly 60 percent of the popular vote and taking forty-two of forty-eight states.

The new president embodied hope to the American people, who had been devastated by the Depression. At his inauguration in January 1933, the *New York Times* reported that Roosevelt symbolized "change to millions yearning for any kind of change." The incoming president embodied "some form of relief to all—the hungry and the thirsty, those in business and those out of employment, the mortgaged and the mortgage holder, the farmer and the factory worker," the *Times* editorialized (McCormick 1933, 1).

During his first hundred days in office, Roosevelt did not disappoint his supporters. To address high unemployment, he created the Public Works Administration, which between 1933 and 1939 pumped more than $6 billion into building schools, highways, bridges, and hospitals. Roosevelt pushed for a Civilian Conservation Corps (CCC) to provide unemployed young men with clothing, food, shelter, and a minimal wage to reforest America, control floods, and carve out parks from wilderness lands. In its nine years, the Corps employed more than three million workers who built eight hundred parks. Roosevelt also secured the homes of many Americans through the Home Owners' Loan Corporation, which enabled 40 percent of American homeowners to pay off home loans over an extended period rather than the typical five to ten years.

Between 1935 and 1938, during the second phase of the New Deal, a Roosevelt-friendly Congress continued to help Americans. In July 1935, Congress approved the National Labor Relations Act, which granted workers the right to collective bargaining and launched the National Labor Relations Board to ensure fair-labor practices. Three years later, a maximum forty-hour work week, guaranteed overtime, and a minimum wage were established, while dangerous child-labor practices were ended. The Social Security Act addressed endemic poverty and the financial sting of old age by allocating universal pensions to the elderly, unemployment benefits, and supplemental income to the needy and disabled.

The Works Progress Administration (WPA) further expanded opportunities for the unemployed. Beginning in 1935, the WPA provided jobs to eight million unemployed Americans who built and refurbished 650,000 miles of highway, 20,000 miles of water mains, and 125,000 public structures such as the San Francisco–Oakland Bay Bridge, the Lincoln Tunnel, and LaGuardia Airport. The WPA also supported 40,000 artists, including painters Jackson Pollock and Mark Rothko, actors such as Burt Lancaster and Orson Welles, and writers such as Ralph Ellison, John Cheever, and John Steinbeck. The Federal Music Project, headed by Nikolai Sokoloff, a former conductor of the Cleveland Symphony Orchestra, employed 16,000 musicians, mostly classically trained, who gave free public performances and musical instruction.

Unemployment hurtled downward and the economy improved due to Roosevelt's programs. By 1936, record-high, Depression-era unemployment of 25 percent had shrunk to around 9 percent. Under Roosevelt's presidency, the gross domestic product increased on average 8.5 percent annually, the highest rate in history. Fueled by investor confidence, by 1934 the money supply skyrocketed from $32.2 billion to $45.7 billion. By any measure, the country was headed from the depths of Depression toward prosperity.

Exuberant swing music reflected the better times. "Swing began to take hold in a national way about the time this country gave evidence of pulling itself out of the ruck," contended *Metronome* in March 1938. "The economists call it recovery. But the effect on the mass mind is one of loosening up" (Stowe 1994, 24–25).

Franklin D. Roosevelt on the radio, a medium he used well and wisely, 1938. *Photograph by Harris & Ewing. Harris & Ewing Collection, Library of Congress Prints and Photographs Division*

The Teenage Jitterbugs

Coupled with the renewed optimism that the New Deal engendered, an emerging audience of teens contributed to swing's success. The energetic, sometimes unruly mob of teenagers who crowded the bandstand at the Palomar in Los Angeles represented a new force in America that embraced young swing-band members as heroes.

A new generation of jazz players, many of them too young to remember ragtime, populated swing bands. In 1935, when Louis Armstrong celebrated his thirty-fourth birthday, Ellington turned thirty-six, Bing Crosby was thirty-two, and Goodman and his colleagues were still in their twenties: Goodman, saxophonist Hymie Schertzer, and Gene Krupa were twenty-six; Bunny Berigan was a year older; trumpeter Harry James, who joined Goodman in early 1937, was nineteen; lead alto sax player Toots Mondello was twenty-four; and singer Helen Ward and trumpeter Pee Wee Erwin were twenty-two. Of the mainstays in the first Goodman band, only pianist Jess Stacy had reached thirty.

The teens who flocked to the young Goodman band experienced a much different life than the generation that preceded them. Before the Great Depression, most young people entered the labor force at an early age. In the 1909–1910 school year, less than 20 percent of youth between the ages of fifteen and eighteen enrolled in school, and a mere 9 percent graduated from high school. Instead, they worked in sometimes dangerous factories, as domestics, or on farms. At the onset of the crash, more than half of seventeen-year-old boys had already entered the workforce or looked for work; less than 40 percent attended school full-time.

When the Depression engulfed the United States and adult breadwinners begged for jobs, teens had fewer places to work, so many more attended high school. During the 1929–1930 school year, 30 percent of teens graduated from high school and, ten years later, more than 50 percent received a high school diploma. Interacting with one another in high school, a majority of teenagers forged common interests, including shared music preferences. Receiving some money from their parents as the economic picture brightened, they represented a new consumer market for radio advertisers, dance promoters, and record companies, which had dropped prices on most discs to an affordable thirty-five cents.

Youth developed a distinct subculture around swing bands. Some serious fans, called "Okays," stood transfixed on their heroes in front of the bandstand. They sported crew cuts, wore sharp, conservative clothes, and traveled miles to see their favorite groups. Other teens, dubbed "Ickies," mobbed the stage and danced like whirling dervishes to the surging beat. Male Ickies slicked back their hair and parted it down the middle. They donned vibrant, loose-fitting suits, called drapes or zoot suits, which likely originated at the Savoy Ballroom. The zoot suits, sometimes called jitterbug suits, consisted of long coats with oversized shoulders and pleated, peg-legged pants that measured twenty-six-inches in circumference at the knees and narrowed to fourteen or even twelve inches at the ankle. Girls preferred black-and-white saddle shoes, prim jackets, and long, pleated, flowing skirts that billowed as they twirled on the dance floor.

The young swing fanatics spoke a distinctive language by using swing slang to express themselves. They called drums "skins," referred to fast, exciting songs as "killer-dillers," considered melodic, non-syncopated pop music as "schmaltz," and belittled lukewarm swing fans as "alligators." In the swing lexicon, enthusiasts nicknamed female singers "canaries," labeled a well-executed performance as "solid" or "out of this world," and complimented fellow swingsters as "hep cats."

To *Time* magazine on January 20, 1936, the swing maniacs "discuss their hobby in terms which often sound like high-flown nonsense."

Hot Clubs served as gathering spots for some swing devotees. First conceived by European jazz fanatics in 1934, Hot Clubs quickly spread to the United States. In 1935, the United Hot Clubs of America was founded with branches in New York City, Chicago, Boston, Los Angeles, Cleveland, Birmingham, and New Haven and linked with its European counterpart in the International Federation of Hot Clubs. "The time has come when a worldwide organization of Hot Clubs, exercising a tremendous influence for the betterment of swing music along many fronts, is no longer an idle dream," proclaimed Marshall Stearns, a professor of English literature at Yale University and secretary of the Federation. The group sought the "universal progress of swing music" and named French jazz critic Hugues Panassie as president and *Downbeat* writer and record producer John Hammond as head of the American branch. For a two-dollar membership fee, Hot Club inductees received special Hot Club–produced recordings, a lapel pin, the Hot Club–published journal *Jazz Hot*, and discounts on musical instruments (Stowe 1994, 81).

Two jazz magazines promoted swing to its adherents. Established in July 1934 by insurance agent Al Lipschultz, who in a few months sold it to his music-savvy editor Glenn Burrs, the Chicago-based *Downbeat* helped market the rise of swing by enlisting as writers such Hot Club leaders as John Hammond, Marshall Stearns, Helen Oakley, George Frazier, and Leonard Feather. The ten-cent magazine especially praised the exploits of rising swing star Benny Goodman, who first appeared in *Downbeat's* second issue. In 1939, *Metronome*, an older publication that had been launched in 1881 to cover classical artists, swung toward swing, when Hot Club devotee George T. Simon assumed the post of editor.

The jitterbug, first labeled the Lindy Hop, became the official dance of swing enthusiasts. It resembled an older dance, the Texas Tommy. According to one youth, "you have to sway, forwards and backwards, with a controlled hip movement, while your shoulders stay level and your feet glide along the floor. Your right hand is held low on the girl's back, and your left hand down at your side, enclosing her hand" (Stearns and Stearns 1968, 330). By late 1927, through the efforts of hoofers such as George "Shorty" Snowden, the dance spread throughout the Eastern Seaboard. To commemorate Charles Lindbergh's first-ever nonstop solo transatlantic flight from New York to Paris in 1927, the athletic dance became known as the Lindy Hop.

The Savoy Ballroom in Harlem became the home of the Lindy Hop. Opened on March 12, 1926, by Moe Gale (b. Moe Galewski), his brother Charles, real estate tycoon Charles Buchanan, and entertainment mogul I. Jay Faggen, the dance hall occupied the second floor of a building that stretched an entire block from 140th Street to 141st Street on Lenox Avenue. The ten-thousand-square-foot ballroom featured a dance floor 200 feet long and 50 feet wide. Accommodating more than four thousand African-American and white patrons, it flaunted a pink interior, mirror-covered walls, padded booths, overstuffed chairs, and colored lights that shone on dancers. The Savoy had two bandstands, which hosted two orchestras each night for musical battles. Tagged "home of happy feet" by actress Lana Turner, the ballroom served as home base for professional dancers who introduced steps such as the Lindy Hop.

Dancers incorporated physically challenging aerial acrobatics during the breakaways of the Lindy Hop. Hoppers such as Frankie Manning, Norma Miller, Al Minns, and Leon James threw their partners overhead or to the side and flipped backward to stun onlookers. "The lindy-hoppers at the Savoy even began to practice acrobatic routines, and to do absurd things for the whites, that probably would have never entered their heads," wrote Harlem Renaissance luminary Langston Hughes in 1941's *The Big Sea* (Hughes 1981, 226). The African-American dancers displayed "a remarkable amount of improvisation and personal specialty," observed John Martin in the *New York Times.* "Some of it is acrobatic and strenuous, some of it superficially erotic, and all of it full of temperament and quality" (Martin 1943, 5). Starting in 1935, Herbert "Whitey" White enlisted stars at the Savoy to form the dance troupe Whitey's Lindy Hoppers that showcased the increasingly wild dance numbers on national tours and in films such as the Marx Brothers movie, *A Day at the Races* (1937).

Malcolm X, then a fifteen-year-old African-American teenager named Malcolm Little, described a typical Lindy Hop dance at the Roseland State Ballroom in the Roxbury section of Boston, where he lived: "*Showtime!* People would start hollering about the last hour of the dance. Then a couple dozen of really wild couples would stay on the floor, the girls changing to low white sneakers." Just like a ring shout, the other dancers formed "a clapping, shouting circle to watch that wild competition." They transformed the ballroom into a "rocking ship," and the "greatest lindyhoppers" competed until a winner had been declared (Malcolm X 1973, 51, 64).

By the early thirties, the Lindy Hop had overtaken America. In late 1932, Thomas Parsons, a correspondent for the magazine *American Dancer*, initiated a radio broadcast to instruct listeners about ballroom dancing. "From the very first broadcast of my dancing class I was besieged with requests to teach the Lindy Hop over the air," he later wrote. After ignoring the suggestion for more than a year, Parsons finally "commenced a series of radio lessons of this dance. For three months my fan mail soared to a record-breaking amount." Soon afterward, he taught a Lindy Hop class at the Roseland Ballroom in New York City that enrolled a thousand students (Spring 1997, 190–91).

By the mid-1930s, when Benny Goodman reached California, young and nimble swing fans were dancing the Lindy Hop, which had been renamed the "jitterbug" after Cab Calloway's song, "Call of the Jitter Bug" (1934). Rather than exhibiting the graceful moves of African-American dancers at the Savoy, white teens released tension by spontaneous jerks and spasmodic flailing to show their approval of the band. "The white jitterbug is oftener than not uncouth to look at, though he may be having a wonderful time," mused the *New York Times* (Martin 1943, 5). "The bugs, literally glued to the music, would shake like St. Vitus with the itch," laughed Benny Goodman who saw the dancers from the bandstand. "Their eyes popped, their heads pecked, their feet tapped out the time, arms jerked to the rhythm." One typical youth at a Goodman concert "went slightly off his conk. His eyes rolled, his limbs began to spin like a windmill in a hurricane—his attention, riveted to the rhythm, transformed him into a whirling dervish" (Goodman and Shane 1939, 12, 11). "Looking back on it, though," reasoned Detroit dance master George Wendler, the jitterbug "did eventually open up dancing for white people. The sophisticated mask was discarded, you were permitted to get with it and be carried away" (Stearns and Stearns 1968, 329).

Ballrooms, which usually charged less than a dollar for admission, attracted huge crowds of dancers. In addition to the Savoy and Roseland in New York City and the Palomar in Los Angeles, long-standing Chicago dance halls hosted swingsters. The Trianon Ballroom was distinguished by an opulent décor and accommodated more than three thousand dancers. The nearby Spanish-style Aragon Ballroom featured an octagonal dance floor ready for five thousand dancers, a grand salon, and three stages for music. Ballrooms also catered to young dancers in other cities. The Archer chain of dance halls opened in such Midwest states as Iowa, Indiana, Nebraska, Minnesota, and the Dakotas. The Eagles Ballroom welcomed swing dancers in Milwaukee. The Shribman Brothers network of ballrooms operated in New Jersey, Pennsylvania, and throughout New England. Baltimore's Alcazar Ballroom, the Arcadia in Detroit, and the Ali Baba in Oakland likewise attracted swing fanatics. By the thirties, large dance halls greeted jitterbugs in most major cities of the United States.

During the swing era, theaters provided a venue for jazz. Many theaters had been established in large cities during the latter part of the vaudeville era. When vaudeville declined in popularity, theater owners switched to cinema to fill their houses. Before films with sound, most theaters located bands or at least a pianist in the pit under the movie screen to provide music and sound effects to accompany silent films and live stage shows. In his hometown of Red Bank, New Jersey, Count Basie remembered that "in those days of silent movies the Palace Theater used to have a house piano player who used to provide the musical background for what was happening on the screen" (Basie 1985, 32). In 1925, during the "days of silent films," recalled Louis Armstrong, the Vendome Theater in Chicago hired the Erskine Tate Orchestra, which featured Armstrong, "to play for the films" (Shapiro and Hentoff 1955, 256). In 1926, the year before films with sound became prevalent, theaters hired twenty-two thousand musicians, or 20 percent of the American Federation of Musicians. However, by 1930, when sound films had become popular, cinemas employed only five thousand of the union's members.

Ironically, after firing pit musicians, theaters hired swing bands to entertain teens during intermission between a double-feature of two films. By 1936, in New York City's Times Square, the Paramount Theater presented big bands between movies. Owners of the Fox Theater in Detroit, Shea's in Buffalo, the Hippodrome in Baltimore, and the Palace in Cleveland booked bands as part of the cinematic experience. By the end of the decade, theaters in nearly every major city showcased big bands.

During the swing craze, teens and preteens too young to drink alcohol in nightclubs attended shows at movie theaters for as little as twenty-five cents before noon just to hear a band. "Early shows were the norm everywhere, because our music was the entertainment of youth," mentioned Woody Herman who in 1936 took over the Isham Jones band and, three years later, scored with the million-seller, "Woodchopper's Ball." "Kids would skip school to hear us before the prices changed after noon" (Herman 1990, 36).

On March 3, 1937, raucous teens flocked to the Paramount Theater in New York City to hear swing favorite Benny Goodman. By 7:00 a.m., as the band practiced for the first morning intermission show, several hundred teens congregated in front of the box office. To Benny, "it was exciting, but also a little frightening—scary" (Firestone 1993, 198). Within minutes, swing maniacs gobbled up the 3,664 tickets and streamed into the theater for the first film, the *Maid of Salem*, which starred Claudette Colbert. As the film reel rolled, remarked Goodman, "there were noises and whistling coming through from the house."

After the film, Goodman's orchestra met a nearly uncontrolled response. The band ascended from the pit of the theater to the stage in dramatic fashion by an elevator. "When we got to the stage the first time the audience was in such a hysteria and so enthusiastic we couldn't play, so we just sat there for four or five minutes and said, 'When you get through applauding, well—we'll play,'" remembered Goodman (Firestone 1993, 200). After the noise subsided, the theater's manager and band manager/agent Willard Alexander noticed "a couple of youngsters [who] got up and started to shag [jitterbug] in the aisles. Then a few more started to climb over the rail towards the orchestra, and [the manager] jumped up and rushed out, yelling 'Somebody's going to get hurt there any minute. They'll be a panic'"

(Shapiro and Hentoff 1955, 315–16). Later, reported the *San Francisco Chronicle*, "a few more of the enthusiastic swingdings tried to climb on the stage, lured irresistibly forward by the Pied Piper of the clarinet" and began "shagging on the stage with the audience beating out a vast rhythm with their palms" (Erenberg 1975, 46). "The crowds were crazy," smiled saxophonist Jerry Jerome. "Crazy!"

The mayhem persisted during the remainder of the Goodman two-week engagement. Some lucky youth who witnessed the first performance refused to leave their seats and stayed for multiple shows, forcing others to wait outside for hours in brisk, forty-degree weather before they could enter the theater. By the end of the day, twenty-one thousand teens had wedged into the Paramount for five, forty-five-minute performances, which started at 10:30 in the morning and ended at 10:30 p.m. By the end of the week, they had paid $58,000 in admission charges and concession-stand purchases, twice the amount spent during Guy Lombardo's stint the week before. "I don't think that any of us realized how strong a hold [the band] had on the youngsters until a certain day in March 1937," Benny admitted (Shapiro and Hentoff 1955, 315).

The Goodman outfit met a frenzied reception in theaters located in other cities. A few weeks after the Paramount spectacle, the band opened at the Metropolitan Theater in Boston. "Yesterday," reported the *Boston Globe* on May 21, 1937, the theater "appeared to hold every boy and girl in greater Boston who could beg a school 'absent' excuse from a tolerant parent. Benny Goodman, King of Swing, is in town, which means that the youngsters of the city are in their seventh heaven of rapture," the newspaper announced.

By the end of the decade, teens had forged an unbreakable link with swing bands. One young man from Boston, converted to swing in 1937, confessed that "every aspect of my life and that of my friends revolved around big bands, jazz, dancing, jitterbugging." After discovering "the music of our time," he felt that "our heroes, our dress, look, styles, morals [and] sex lives" emanated from swing bands and "the lives they showed us" (Erenberg 1975, 39). On February 26, 1939, the *New York Times* equated swing with "the voice of youth striving to be heard in this fast-moving world of ours. Swing is the tempo of our times" ("Letter" 1939, E9).

The Business of Swing

Radio programs and theater concerts turned a few swing bands into profit centers. By 1935, radio had become the most important communication medium in the country. The proportion of radio-equipped families rose to nearly 67 percent, and the average listener tuned in four hours a day and could sample programming from nearly six hundred stations, depending upon his or her location.

Advertisers such as cigarette and food companies sponsored nationally broadcast programs of popular bands from the NBC and CBS studios. In the midst of the Depression, Old Gold cigarettes backed Fred Waring and his Pennsylvanians, one of the bestselling dance bands on the Victor label with thirty-two hits between 1923 and 1932. Camel cigarettes funded the Casa Loma Orchestra, a cooperative outfit eventually headed by Glen Gray, which during the decade registered twenty-three top-selling selections (Firestone 1993, 92). Though many jazz bands appeared prominently on radio, only major stars snagged spots on sponsored, network-based radio programs.

High-profile hotels promoted less-well-known bands through non-sponsored or sustaining programs. Such swanky locations as the Pennsylvania Hotel and the

Lincoln Hotel in New York City wired radio connections into dance rooms that linked late-night, live music to the major broadcasters at no cost to the networks.

Swing musicians earned little money from hotel broadcasts. Typically, a bandleader paid each of fourteen musicians and a singer $150 per week for a total cost of $2,250. The band had additional expenses of $900 for a press agent, personal and road managers, a booking agent, arranger's fees, photos, press books, and other items. The outfit paid a 10 percent "traveling-band" levy to the union if it ventured from its home base. On the road, a band also needed $400 for transportation. In total, a swing group generally spent nearly $3,850 a week. On average, an orchestra earned between a $2,000 minimum and no more than $4,000, which forced most swing bands to accrue debt for each week of a hotel stint. "There's no money in any hotel engagement," bitterly complained Artie Shaw (b. Arthur Jacob Arshawsky), whose band topped the chart in 1938 with "Begin the Beguine." "There isn't a hotel in the country able to afford more than four thousand dollars for music" (Shaw 1939, 67).

The older, well-heeled clientele at hotels frustrated young bands that wanted to swing. When the Benny Goodman orchestra performed at the Roosevelt Hotel, remembered singer Helen Ward, "the place was impossible for what we were trying to do. How softly can you play 'King Porter Stomp'? The people were absolutely, totally unnerved. They were used to sweet music, and now they couldn't hear each other over dinner" (Firestone 1993, 130).

Despite substandard wages and reserved audiences, most bands still fought for spots at radio-wired hotels. The orchestras, explained Artie Shaw, aggressively pursued hotel dance rooms "to get a precious radio wire. Some of them even lose money playing a hotel, but if your name and music go out coast-to-coast, four or five times a week, you're getting publicity that would cost a fortune to buy. Radio, more than anything else," concluded Shaw, "is responsible for this frantic fight to tie up wired hotel spots. The Great God Microphone is deity to the bandsman and he worships at its shrine" (Shaw 1939, 67).

Booking agents handled the coveted wired hotels. Three booking agencies—the Music Corporation of America (MCA), the largest agency that controlled 63 percent of white swing bands; the William Morris Agency; and the General Amusement Corporation—cornered the hotel market. "These three booking offices *are* the music business, and every leader knows it," music writer Irving Kolodin asserted. "The agencies represent the hotels of the nation, where promotional campaigns for orchestras are launched and reputations cultivated" (Kolodin 1941, 72). "All the choice spots with radio wires are tied up by contract to three or four booking agencies," agreed Artie Shaw. "Although a hotel may want my band badly enough to offer a comparatively high price, I can't ordinarily be booked unless my [agency] controls the hotel," he grumbled (Shaw 1939, 67).

Bookers championed their clients and secured hotel jobs for them to support their careers. In 1935, Willard Alexander, a young, ambitious agent with MCA who had led a band himself, pleaded with his bosses, company president Jules Stein and vice president Billy Goodheart, to work with Benny Goodman. After much wrangling, Alexander signed Goodman to a contract with the firm. Later in the year, the agent found a five-night-a-week job for the Goodman band at Chicago's Congress Hotel, which had wired its ballroom to local radio station WGN. By the end of the year, MCA obtained a sustaining NBC show for the orchestra from the locale. "It wasn't until the engagement at the Congress that it really became established," recalled trumpeter Pee Wee Erwin about the early Goodman outfit. "All of a sudden a national reputation began to develop, and it was obvious from all the activities that were going on, it was getting to be a whale of a popular band"

(Firestone 1993, 159). By 1936, MCA had transformed Goodman into the "Man of the Hour to thousands of jazz fans," according to *Time* on January 20. The agency booked two more sponsored radio programs for Goodman. In March 1936, it convinced the Elgin Watch Company to sponsor a three-month, live radio show called the *Elgin Review*. The agency then booked Goodman on the *Camel Caravan*, a cigarette-sponsored radio program, which for three years had been under contract to the Casa Loma Orchestra.

MCA thrust Goodman into a nearly iconic status after booking him for seven months at New York's influential Pennsylvania Hotel, which hired its acts exclusively through MCA. In October 1937, Willard Alexander scheduled the Goodman band at the Pennsylvania for six nights a week, three of them aired nationally. Coupled with sponsored airtime from the Congress Hotel, the Pennsylvania Hotel job thrust Benny firmly into the national limelight. Alexander "became as important to Benny Goodman's early career as anyone," explained John Hammond, by then a friend and major supporter of Goodman (Firestone 1993, 127). "By now all Willard Alexander had to do was pick up the telephone and say, 'Benny's available April 13th for a week,' and everyone would jump at the top price," recalled Goodman's saxophone player Jerry Jerome (238). MCA agents performed the same service for other swing clients, including the orchestras of Tommy Dorsey, Harry James, and Bunny Berigan.

To make money from publicity generated by hotel appearances, nationally recognized swing bands performed in large theaters booked by the agencies. The orchestras earned up to $9,000 a week from theaters, which grossed as much as $60,000 for a week-long engagement.

Well-known swing outfits collected reasonable salaries on the road. If a band earned a reputation through radio, it commanded a premium when it toured. Bands such as the Goodman unit received $2,000 a night, when playing ballrooms and for proms. In a 1937 tour across the country, Benny grossed nearly $90,000 for two months of work.

Bands receiving little or no radio play could demand much less salary. These unlucky musicians—numbering between thirty to forty thousand according to one estimate in the mid-thirties—performed a seemingly endless series of one-night stands in cities throughout the country for $250 a night. Artie Shaw remembered "two weary years on the road, playing every hamlet in New England and the Middle West, making six-hundred-mile jumps overnight to earn a top fee of two hundred and fifty dollars—for five or six hours of playing in a stuffy hall or an ex-barn from which the cows had only recently been evicted" (Shaw 1939, 68).

While most bands toiled in obscurity, a star system of top bandleaders emerged. Orchestra leaders became celebrities who were discussed in gossip columns and adored by their fans. "Name bands were the greatest thing you could be part of in those days," explained drummer Mel Lewis, who at the time was a high school student aspiring to be a musician. "That was the star thing in those days. You were either a movie star or a bandleader in the 30's and 40's" (Rusch 1990c, 7). Rather than the entire orchestra, the front man received the attention. "The people who lined up to hear Benny Goodman couldn't have cared less about who was playing first alto," sax player Jerry Jerome confessed. "Those kids were screaming their heads off when I stood up to take a solo, but they didn't know me" (Firestone 1993, 238).

Successful bandmasters raked in the money. Benny Goodman, the son of two immigrants who was raised near Maxwell Street in the Chicago ghetto, earned more money than he ever imagined. In 1937, he collected the princely salary of $100,000, when most Americans struggled to eke out a living on an average annual

The exuberant Gene Krupa, June 1946. *Photograph by William P. Gottlieb. William P. Gottlieb/Ira and Leonore S. Gershwin Fund Collection, Music Division, Library of Congress*

income of $1,788. At the height of his popularity, Artie Shaw amassed a fortune. "My lawyer and business manager tell me my net income for 1939 will be in the neighborhood of a quarter of a million dollars," he revealed. "When America dances, it pays its pipers well."

The star system encouraged exciting soloists, many from the Goodman outfit, to break from their leaders and start their own bands. In February 1938, after three years with the irascible Goodman, Gene Krupa quit his mentor. "Eat some shit, Pops!" Krupa screamed at his boss one night after Benny relentlessly chided him (Rusch 1988a, 11). Krupa established a big band and scored with four major sellers before a drug charge derailed his career. Trumpeter Harry James, who had begun his career by performing with his parents in circuses, left Goodman more amicably. Debuting with Benny in January 1937, James exited two years later with a line of credit from Goodman. In return, James agreed to pay his former employer 30 percent of his net earnings for ten years. Bunny Berigan, the fiery trumpeter who died at the age of thirty-three from alcoholism, departed from the Goodman band after a short stint. In 1937, he assembled an outfit and hit with "I Can't Get Started." Goodman's African-American pianist Teddy Wilson formed a unit, which performed during his off time from Benny's quartet. With help from John Hammond, he landed a contract with Brunswick Records and, in 1936, scored six best sellers and ten more the next year, including the blockbuster "Carelessly." Only brothers Tommy and Jimmy Dorsey, former members of the Jean Goldkette band who co-led an orchestra for a year before splintering into two bands in 1935, did not revolve around the Benny Goodman orbit. By July 5, 1939, *Variety* noticed the "hysterical activity in the forming of new orchestras." "Never before in the history of dance bandom have so many new orchestras sprung up as now," echoed *Metronome.* "The enthusiasm of former sidemen who are willing to take a risk for greater glories is exceeded only by promoters in booking offices who see newer ways toward bigger shekels without the risk" (DeVeaux 1997, 131).

Prominent bandleaders enjoyed celebrity status through films, which one agent called "the greatest source of publicity ever developed for bandleaders" (Erenberg 1975, 173). Following the lead of Bing Crosby, Goodman and his orchestra grabbed a guest spot in *The Big Broadcast of 1937* and, in January 1938, captured a role in *Hollywood Hotel.* During the next decade, the band surfaced in six more full-length features, including *Sweet and Low-Down,* which cast Benny in a dramatic role as himself. Starting in 1941, Tommy Dorsey and his band appeared in ten movies and, during the forties, his brother Jimmy made five films. Gene Krupa's band played in *Ball of Fire* (1941). Artie Shaw portrayed himself in the Fred Astaire film *Second Chorus* (1940) and, the same year, he married the shapely and well-known actress Lana Turner, subsequently wedding Hollywood knockout Ava Gardner in 1945.

That same decade, Harry James snagged nine movie spots and married actress and pinup Betty Grable, the dream girl of every GI during the war.

Count Basie and Kansas City Swing

The Count Basie Orchestra, perhaps the most well-known African-American swing band, rose to fame through the help of Benny Goodman. Idolizing the stride masters, Bill Basie left his New Jersey hometown for New York City, where he studied informally with such pianists as Willie "The Lion" Smith and Fats Waller. In 1926, Basie toured the TOBA circuit with the vaudeville act Gonzelle White and the Big Jazz Jamboree. Two years later, he joined the Oklahoma City–based Walter Page and his Blue Devils and, in 1929, bolted to the premier Kansas City band headed by Bennie Moten.

After Moten died unexpectedly during a tonsillectomy, Basie started a nine-piece group and performed at a small Kansas City nightspot, the Reno Club, where patrons bought beer for a nickel and scotch for fifteen cents. "It was like a club off the street," laughed Basie. "But once you got inside, it was a cabaret, with a little bandstand and a little space for a floor show, and with a bar up front, and there was also a little balcony in there. There were also girls available as dancing partners" for a small fee, a practice referred to as a "taxi dance" (Basie and Murray, 157). As a bandleader, Bill Basie assumed the "Count" moniker to match the royal-sounding names of Duke Ellington, King Oliver, and Paul "The King of Jazz" Whiteman.

The band played differently than the tightly arranged big-band fare of the day. It primarily used "head arrangements," which constituted a series of improvised solos within a simple, informal structure that band members memorized rather than read from a composed sheet of music. "The Basie band had the feel of a small band," explained drummer Jo Jones. "The arrangements were almost all 'heads' and no matter how many men we had at any one given time, there was all the freedom and flexibility of a small unit. This was not true of the other large bands contemporary with Basie" (Shapiro and Hentoff 1955, 303).

The Count and his cohorts, though forced to perform commercial music and pop tunes for dancers, used their open-ended format to focus on the blues. "We had our own thing, and we could always play some more blues and call it something," related the leader (Basie 1985, 165). "I never get tired of playing the blues, or listening to the blues," he added (Pearson 1987, 136).

Radio propelled the Basie Orchestra into the national spotlight. A radio connection from the Reno Club to local station W9XBY broadcast the band's performances across a wide geographic region. "They used to bring a pickup in there at least a couple of times a week, and people used to hear us from as far away as Minneapolis and Chicago and the East and all the way down to the Gulf States," remembered

Count Basie at the piano, New York City, 1946. *Photograph by William P. Gottlieb. William P. Gottlieb/Ira and Leonore S. Gershwin Fund Collection, Music Division, Library of Congress*

the Count (Basie 1985, 160). Saxophonist Lester Young heard the group from Minneapolis, where he played at the Nest Club. "Used to hear the Basie band all the time on the radio and figured they needed a tenor player," insisted the twenty-six-year-old Young, who became known as the "President," a name conjured up by Billie Holiday, when she sang with Basie. Lester sent Basie a telegram offering to play with the outfit and joined the band. A radio broadcast prompted Fletcher Henderson to send Basie a few arrangements (Harris 1949, 38).

In early 1936, jazz promoter John Hammond heard the group on a broadcast from the Reno Club. He began praising the band in *Downbeat* and in one article asked Basie to contact him. After Basie responded, Hammond appeared unannounced in Kansas to see the band. "It was a Sunday night and we were on the air, and this very young cat just came right on up there and sat on the bench beside me," recalled the Count. Hammond "really dug it. He stuck around to talk some more after we finished our last number, and we went out to some other spots that were still open" (Basie 1985, 165–66).

An enthusiastic Hammond rushed back to Chicago and told Benny Goodman, his friend and future brother-in-law, about his new find in Kansas City. Sitting in Hammond's car, which was equipped with a special twelve-tube Motorola radio, Goodman and Hammond picked up a weak signal from Kansas City and listened to a Basie broadcast. Goodman "was interested enough to make a special trip to Kansas City to hear the group in person," related the Count. "When Benny came to the Reno Club in the spring of 1936 to hear the band," continued Basie, "none of us was aware that he was digging us. Benny went back to Chicago and phoned his own booker, Willard Alexander of Music Corporation of America, in New York. In the meantime, John mentioned us to Willard" (Shapiro and Hentoff 1955, 300). Alexander then journeyed to Kansas City and signed the band.

Under the guidance of MCA, the Basie band procured more jobs with radio wires and attracted greater attention. The Count expanded his nine-piece unit into a standard fourteen-piece big-band orchestra by adding trumpeter Buck Clayton and the full-toned sax of Herschel Evans, who many times battled the more relaxed Lester Young for dominance. The group, called Count Basie and his Fourteen Barons of Rhythm, landed a record deal with Decca to cut twenty-four songs in three years and snagged a sustaining radio program from the Grand Terrace Ballroom in Chicago that gave the band national exposure. "Those broadcasts were good for our reputation," maintained Basie (Basie 1985, 182). In early 1937, the band aired nightly from the swank William Penn Hotel in Pittsburgh. Through the help of MCA, the next year, the Count and his Rhythm Barons played on Fifty-second Street in New York City at the Famous Door, a well-known jazz nightclub, which arranged a CBS-network wire that sent the band to homes across the nation. "That was the very best thing that could happen for the band because we had excellent airtime, and that was when radio was it," gushed the bandleader. "People used to tell us how they would go out and drive through Central Park listening to us on their radios in their cars, and those jitney cab drivers out in Chicago used to run up and down South Parkway digging us on their radios, too" (217).

A radio performance gave Basie his biggest hit, "One O'Clock Jump." In 1937, after extemporaneously composing a song during a broadcast, the announcer asked for its title. "Well, it just had no title so it was up to someone to pick one out in a hurry," recalled the Count. "I glanced up at the clock. It was almost one o'clock. 'Just call it "One O'Clock Jump,"' I told the announcer" (Shapiro and Hentoff 1955, 301). The successful song solidified the reputation of the Basie band. By the end of the decade, radio, MCA, and the sponsorship of Benny Goodman had catapulted Basie to fame.

 LISTENING GUIDE 18

Count Basie Orchestra

"ONE O'CLOCK JUMP"

In 1937, during a radio performance, Count Basie created one of his most enduring hits, the twelve-bar blues "One O'Clock Jump." On July 7 the same year, he recorded the song for Decca and subsequently waxed the tune for Columbia. Basing the song on his riff-style or "head arrangement" in which each section improvises on a loosely conceived, general structure, Basie allowed such master jazz men as sax players Lester Young and Herschel Evans, trumpeter Buck Clayton, and bassist Walter Page to take the lead. After his initial success with "One O'Clock Jump," Basie closed most shows with the tune for nearly fifty years. Basie hit with this version of the song for Decca, which guitarist Eddie Durham and saxophonist Buster Smith helped compose.

Overall, the song followed a twelve-bar-blues format like many of Basie's other numbers and offered most of the space for soloists to improvise.

Personnel for this song included Basie (piano); Buck Clayton, Ed Lewis, and Bobby Moore (trumpets); George Hunt and Dan Minor (trombones); Earle Warren (alto saxophone); Herschel Evans and Lester Young (tenor saxophones); Freddie Green (guitar); Walter Page (bass); and Jo Jones (drums).

0:00–0:11	Basie begins with an eight-bar boogie-woogie–like left-handed vamp (defined as a short, repeated figure), backed by the rhythm section.
0:11–0:27	Basie establishes the melody with his right hand with single notes and receives especially excellent backing by guitarist Freddie Green.
0:28–0:44	Basie embarks on the second piano chorus, rapidly shaking the notes in tremolo fashion.
0:45–1:02	Herschel Evans solos on tenor saxophone backed by the muted brass, which plays a five-note riff. The riff, a brief, repeated pattern of notes, characterized much of Basie's music and represented a mainstay of swing. It also represented a call-and-response of a soloist or leader and a section of the band.
1:03–1:19	Trombonist George Hunt solos with the saxophones riffing on a five-note pattern in the background.
1:20–1:35	The light-toned saxophonist Lester Young, the foil to the full-bodied Evans, solos over the muted brass riffs with drummer Jo Jones playing bass-drum accents after the third beat of every other measure.
1:36–1:52	Trumpeter Buck Clayton solos with a repeated and descending riff by the saxophones.
1:53–2:09	With backing from Basie, Walter Page solos on bass. Unlike many previous bassists, Page turned the instrument into a vehicle for solos.
2:10	The saxes and the brass each play riffs in a call-and-response duel.
2:27–2:43	The saxophones change chords to deliver the main melody of the tune as the brass continue its riff in the background.
2:44–3:00	The saxophone section returns to a four-note riff and battles the brass, which maintains its riff. Jo Jones hits the snare drum every two measures to accent the battle of the two sections. This riff-based song ends amid the riffing.

Swing and the Beginning of Racial Integration in Jazz

Other African-American jazz artists such as Teddy Wilson found an advocate in Benny Goodman who at least partially eased racial discrimination in the white big-band world. On May 14, 1934, at the urging of singer Mildred Bailey, Teddy Wilson joined the Goodman band on a record date. Wilson had studied at the Tuskegee Institute and idolized Earl Hines. Like Bing Crosby, Wilson benefited from the condenser microphone, which enabled him to more easily execute a dazzling series of right-hand piano runs. "When I came up," he explained, "the microphone was being used to amplify the piano, so it wasn't necessary to have all the power that [Earl] Hines used. This enabled me to do a lot of running in the right hand." The microphone "inspired me to get into the kind of running thing that a saxophone does, more cascading passages," rather than the octave-based, punchy, trumpet-sounding keyboard style, which had been perfected by Earl Hines "to be heard above the other [band members]" (Lyons 1983, 63; Dance 1977, 26).

John Hammond, a staunch advocate of racial integration, convinced Goodman to continue the collaboration with the innovative Wilson. "To me, Teddy was the ultimate chamber music player, and chamber music was my great love," intimated Hammond, who had been a symphony viola player. "I knew that, with his education, he was going to be the guy to break down racial barriers. He had the musical skills, the technique, the reading ability—and the manner" (Firestone 1993, 135–6).

Goodman took Hammond's advice. To repay Wilson for work on his record, on July 2, 1935, Benny played on an otherwise all-African-American session with an eight-piece band that included Wilson, sax stylist Ben Webster, and singer Billie Holiday. Less than two weeks later, Goodman formed a trio with Wilson and drummer Gene Krupa. On April 12, 1936, after performing publically between sets of Goodman's larger band at the Congress Hotel, the trio became a permanent fixture of the Goodman act. "There had been a lot of interracial record sessions. But this—playing in public with Benny—was a breakthrough," reminisced Teddy Wilson. "I knew of the pressures that were pulling Benny the other way. Guys in the music business were telling him he'd ruin his career if he hired me" (Firestone 1993, 166).

African-American vibes player Lionel Hampton joined Goodman's small group to make it a quartet. Hampton started performing as a drummer for the *Chicago Defender* newsboys' band. During the late twenties, he moved to the Les Hite Orchestra, which had a residency at the mob-supported Los Angeles Cotton Club. For nine months there in 1930, Hampton and his band mates performed behind Louis Armstrong and recorded with him. On July 21, during one session, Hampton volunteered to play the vibes on "Memories of You," a hit for Armstrong. When Louis and then Hite left the band, Hampton assumed leadership of the Cotton Club Orchestra.

One night in August 1936, during a chance meeting, Hampton emerged into the spotlight. While playing vibes on stage, he heard a marvelous drummer, pianist, and clarinetist behind him. When he looked over his shoulder, Hampton saw the Benny Goodman trio: Teddy Wilson, Gene Krupa, and the King of Swing himself. Initially hearing about Hampton from John Hammond, Benny seemed "carried away, so he asked me would I go and join him and make a recording session with him that same morning," recalled an incredulous Lionel. The vibes player immediately agreed and rushed to the studio. On November 11, 1936, Hampton permanently joined the Goodman quartet. "Black and white had [almost] never played together [in public]," explained the vibraphonist. "This was integration and it was all a total success." Hampton considered it his contribution to "social change in the United States" (Tompkins 1983a).

LISTENING GUIDE 19

Benny Goodman Quartet

"MOONGLOW"

Recording this song on September 9, 1936, Goodman, pianist Teddy Wilson, vibes player Lionel Hampton, and drummer Gene Krupa made history by debuting as a racially mixed quartet. A year earlier, Goodman and Krupa had previously recorded with the African-American Wilson to integrate jazz musicians on record, pre-dating by more than a decade the entry of African-American Jackie Robinson into major league baseball.

The combo's size also had significance. During the swing era, when bands usually had fourteen members, the small-group concept harkened back to the small New Orleans brass bands. More significantly, it pre-saged small bebop combos, which featured artists who played rapid-fire solos.

The song, "Moon Glow" (also called "Moonglow" or "Moonglow and Love"), was written by composer and bandleader Will Hudson in 1933 as a theme song for his band. First recorded by Joe Venuti, the thirty-two-bar tune had a 4/4 beat and a structure of AABA, which consists of one eight-bar strain (A) played twice, an eight-bar bridge (B), and a return to the initial theme (A). It became a hit for the Goodman quartet as well as Artie Shaw (1941) and Harry James (1946), and has been recorded by hundreds of jazz bands. Eddie DeLange wrote lyrics to the song.

Spotlighting the impact of technology on musicians' performance-style choices, Teddy Wilson uses quick runs of right-handed single notes, which the condenser microphone made possible, versus the less sensitive carbon microphone, which necessitated more of a block-chord approach. Notably, Wilson came to the attention of Goodman, when the bandleader heard the pianist perform a version of "Moonglow."

0:00–0:08	Wilson opens the song with a quick run of right-handed single notes.
0:09–0:25	Goodman on clarinet establishes the calming melody. In the background, Hampton answers Goodman's clarinet in a subdued call-and-response, and Krupa offers an uncharacteristically restrained accompaniment on drums.
0:26–0:42	Goodman repeats the melody with backing from the drums and vibes, which gives the song an otherworldly sound.
0:43–1:01	Wilson plays a brilliant syncopated solo that sounds almost boppish with its single-note runs, which highlight each note of a chord (also called an arpeggio), and creative use of rhythm.
1:02–1:20	Goodman again states the initial melody with the same rhythmic background from the vibes and drums.
1:21–2:23	Hampton takes an extended solo on vibes, an instrument that had only recently been introduced to jazz. He generates a stellar passage that, like Wilson's solo, looks forward to bop with its rhythmic and harmonic complexity. He plays chromatically (defined as music in half steps or notes on a chord outside the European diatonic scale) on several passages.
2:24–2:55	Goodman takes a solo with call-and-response from Hampton and backing from Wilson and Krupa. Unlike Wilson and Hampton, he plays a passage that focuses more on the melody.
2:56–3:12	Goodman restates the melody with rhythm backing.
3:13–3:22	Hampton delivers a brief riff, which Goodman answers with backing from Wilson on piano. Hampton ends the song with a sustained note on vibes.

Other members of the Goodman band accepted Wilson and Hampton. "There were Southerners in the band and Italians and Jews, but we were all like brothers. The whole outfit was as solid as a family. And we were all very much aware of what was going on," asserted Teddy Wilson. "It was completely different from what Jackie Robinson had to put up with when he joined the Brooklyn Dodgers [in April 1947] and had to fight the guys on his own team" (Firestone 1993, 182–3).

John Hammond helped integrate Goodman's small group even further, when he discovered African-American electric guitarist Charlie Christian. During summer 1939, he saw Christian's six-piece band in Oklahoma City and witnessed the guitarist play fluid Lester Young–influenced solos with an electric guitar that he had recently introduced to be heard easily over a brass section. The writer observed, these were as "exciting improvisations as I have ever heard on any instrument, let alone the guitar" (Firestone 1993, 265). Convinced that Christian could fit well with Goodman's small group, Hammond secretly took the guitarist to a Goodman performance at the Cocoanut Grove in Los Angeles and snuck the guitarist's amplifier and loudspeaker on stage while Benny ate dinner. When the bandleader returned, Hammond ushered Christian from the kitchen to the stage.

Bewildered and angry, Goodman tried to stump the young uninvited guitarist. He called out "Rose Room," which he suspected Christian never heard. Reared on the song, Christian reeled off more than twenty choruses to the wild pleasure of the crowd. "Everybody got up from the tables and clustered around the bandstand," remembered Hammond, "and there could be no doubt that perhaps the most spectacularly original soloist ever to play with Goodman had been launched" (Firestone 1993, 266). Goodman hired Christian immediately and, on August 19, 1939, featured the guitarist on his *Camel Caravan* NBC network show. Benny permanently enlarged his quartet to a sextet, which for the next two years included Christian and his hollow-body Gibson ES-150 guitar.

Fletcher Henderson, an African-American bandleader who for nearly a decade filled the prestigious slot at the Roseland Ballroom in New York City, rounded out the Goodman sextet. Though a gifted and popular musician, the mild-mannered Henderson never mastered the art of leading a band and failed to properly discipline his men. "Everybody knew he was an easygoing guy, and the greatest harm he ever did to anybody was to himself by being too easy with his musicians," revealed his brother Horace, a noted pianist and bandleader. In 1928, after Fletcher survived a serious automobile crash, he became less organized. By the winter of 1934, with the business of his outfit in disarray, Henderson dissolved the band.

Looking for work, Henderson found a champion in Benny Goodman. Urged by John Hammond, he agreed to write for Benny who wanted more punch in his arrangements. Fletcher gave Goodman the existing arrangements from his band such as "King Porter Stomp" that infused the Goodman band with the needed snap it lacked. For nearly a year, Henderson arranged dozens of other songs for the Goodman band. "As far as I know it was the first time [the Henderson arrangements] had been played by a white orchestra," guessed Goodman. In 1935, Fletcher reformed a band and, after his outfit disintegrated in 1939, rejoined Goodman as a writer and a pianist in the big band and sextet.

Henderson and Goodman both benefited from the partnership. Henderson secured a highly visible position at a low point of his career. "I'm telling you that nobody could have done more than John [Hammond] and Benny," claimed Fletcher's wife, Leora. "Benny did everything he could do to build up Fletcher's name" (Shapiro and Hentoff 1955, 222–23). For Goodman, the band profited from a much-improved sound. "Fletcher's ideas were far ahead of anybody else's," he contended. "Without Fletcher I probably would have had a pretty good band, but it would have been something quite different from what it eventually turned out to be. I really thought he was a genius," he added (Firestone 1993, 117).

When Henderson temporarily left the Goodman outfit, African-American arranger Jimmy Mundy came into the Goodman fold. The classically trained Mundy had been a saxophonist and arranger for the Earl Hines band, which for more than a decade performed at the Al Capone–controlled Grand Terrace Ballroom in Chicago. From 1935 to 1938, he generated more than four hundred charts for the Goodman band. His work included exciting "jump" arrangements, which jitterbugs referred to as "killer-dillers," including the exuberant "Sing, Sing, Sing."

In 1938, at a Carnegie Hall concert, Benny demonstrated his policy of musicianship over race. Like an updated version of Paul Whiteman's performance in 1924 at Aeolian Hall, Benny promised "Twenty Years of Jazz" from its inception to swing. On January 16, a nervous Goodman band took the stage. "I feel like a whore in a church," quipped trumpet player Harry James about the revered venue (Firestone 1993, 212). The band peered at the audience, mostly youth who paid 85 cents to $3 for one of the 2,860 available seats, then launched into "Don't Be That Way" to the delight of fanatics who abandoned their seats to jitterbug in the aisles. As he addressed the various stages of jazz history, Goodman broke with the Whiteman tradition by showcasing such African-American musicians from the Ellington band as trumpeter Charles "Cootie" Williams and saxophonists Johnny Hodges and Harry Carney. For a special jam session, he invited Basie, saxophonist Lester Young, and trumpeter Wilbur "Buck" Clayton to join. Goodman ended the evening with an unrestrained version of "Sing, Sing, Sing," which drove the audience wild.

By 1939, Benny Goodman had helped integrate jazz. Though his groundbreaking efforts hardly eliminated racial discrimination, he "opened the door a giant crack," according to Teddy Wilson (Firestone 1993, 183). "I truly feel that the Benny Goodman quartet opened the door for Jackie Robinson coming into major league baseball," agreed Lionel Hampton. "The integration of musicians started a lot of things happening" (Blumenthal 1994, 19).

Other bandleaders combated racial segregation. In April 1941, Gene Krupa employed African-American trumpeter Roy Eldridge as part of a small group and then as a member of the full-fledged orchestra. Artie Shaw later convinced Eldridge to leave Krupa for his outfit. In March 1938, Shaw lured Billie Holiday to his orchestra. "It was a desperate chance but I wasn't thinking in terms of that," related the bandleader. "I needed a good singer and couldn't find one," he continued. "I hired her, and finally she was the right singer for that band" (Ruhlmann 1992, 30). During the early forties, Charlie Barnet, who in 1940 scored with "Where Was I?" and waxed a popular version of "Cherokee," hired such African-American jazz men as Detroit trumpeter Howard

Billie Holiday in action at the Downbeat, 1947. *Photograph by Carl Van Vechten. Van Vechten Collection, Library of Congress Prints and Photographs Division*

McGhee, bassist Oscar Pettiford, trumpeter Dizzy Gillespie, and trombonist James "Trummy" Young.

Big bands fraternized on stage through battles between bands, regardless of color. On May 11, 1937, in a now-famous contest, Benny Goodman and Chick Webb attracted ten thousand swingsters who crowded and pushed to buy four thousand tickets at the Savoy Ballroom in New York City for an event billed as the "Music Battle of the Century." Goodman started with the killer-diller "Peckin'" and traded musical jabs with Chick Webb, the drummer who led the regular band at the Savoy. After two sets and a "torrid battle," both outfits left exhausted. According to *Metronome*, the audience informally proclaimed Webb the winner (Erenberg 1975, 60). The next month in Chicago, Goodman competed with the Roy Eldridge orchestra. Roy's band, according to Eldridge's sax player Dave Young, "blew the ceiling off that place." Not to be outdone, Goodman "went right through the ceiling and the crowd went with them. Those white boys were playing those black arrangements with a togetherness you wouldn't believe," conceded Young (Firestone 1993, 204).

Many African Americans in white big bands felt the stress and pain of their pioneering efforts. During her stint with Artie Shaw, Billie Holiday was forced to enter through the back doors of clubs, use the freight elevator, and eat in the kitchens rather than the dining rooms. Like most African-American performers, she relied on select hotels and private homes, which serviced an African-American clientele. From 1936 to 1966, Holiday and others relied on *The Negro Motorist Green-Book*, which published the names of hotels, restaurants, and other establishments that catered to African Americans. "I saw that Billie was not going to be able to handle it for long," explained Shaw. "It got to be very tough" (Ruhlmann 1992, 34). On November 19, 1938, Holiday left the band.

Roy Eldridge likewise suffered the scourge of inequality. In one instance as a member of the Artie Shaw band, he appeared at a club before the other musicians to get ready for a concert. Because of his color, Eldridge was refused entry by the doorman until Shaw's then-wife, Ava Gardner, explained the situation to the manager. By the time Eldridge finally took his seat on the bandstand, he "was just too ticked off. I threw my mutes and things around; I began to cry" (Korall 1987, 112). Though tormented by racial prejudice, African Americans in white big bands blazed a trail that had a far-reaching impact on jazz and the rest of America.

Swing's the Thing

By the late thirties, white-dominated swing music and its well-recognized bandleaders, especially Benny "the King of Swing" Goodman, became ubiquitous in the United States. "Whether or not you regard it as good news, swing is thriving," reported the *New York Times* on August 14, 1938. "It has lent its name to toys, notions, games, women's clothing, jewelry and coiffure. It has been accepted in the lives of a sufficient portion of the population to have affected its mores and language. It has been reflected in the nation's literature, and has inspired novels, biographies, mystery stories, scholarly dissertations, countless magazine articles and newspaper features. It has served as a theme for Hollywood," the article concluded (Gilbert 1938, 6). "There will be no post mortem on swing this year," declared *Metronome* in early 1938, "and if times are propitious, for some years to come" (Firestone 1993, 241). Jazz had become the popular music of the United States and an integral part of American culture.

Jazz record sales and revenues reflected the public fascination with swing and the rebounding post–New Deal economy. In 1938, 8.4 million jazz discs sold. The next year, the record industry peddled $36 million worth of music, much of it swing oriented, and the business of swing, which included records, concerts, and radio revenues, amounted to more than $110 million.

Benny Goodman, the most visible swing bandleader and the central figure in the swing era, assumed iconic status. In 1939, a thirty-year-old Goodman sold millions of records, commanded top prices for concerts, appeared constantly on radio, and published a brisk-selling autobiography written with *New York Times* critic Irving Kolodin, titled *The Kingdom of Swing*. "Benny Goodman was, at one time, probably more famous than the President of the United States—all over the world," remarked vibes player Terry Gibbs, who played with several big bands including the Goodman outfit (Rusch 1988e, 13).

From 1935 through 1938, an energetic, ebullient swing and the central figure of Benny Goodman transformed jazz into the most popular American music of the decade. It reflected the optimism of Franklin Roosevelt's New Deal and publically broke down racial barriers. Amid a recovering economy, it capitalized on the emerging teen market, the jitterbug craze, and the marketing power of radio to capture America from coast to coast.

For Discussion and Further Study

Chapter Quiz

1. How did African-American "swing" become associated with Benny Goodman and other white big bands? What does this suggest to you about the way African-American musical styles have been co-opted by white performers over the decades?

2. How did the rise of a new teenage audience influence the reception of big-band jazz? What was the impact of jazz's association with new dance styles like the jitterbug?

3. What role did radio, ballrooms, and theaters play in promoting swing? How was swing marketed to the new teenage audience? What opportunities were opened to leading swing performers—in contrast, how did the working but less well-known swing musicians fare in this system?

4. What role did Count Basie play in promoting the Kansas City swing style? How was his band successfully promoted to the growing white audience?

5. What role did Benny Goodman play in integrating his bands? How did Goodman's efforts lay the groundwork for other white ensembles to include African-American musicians?

WORLD WAR II AND JAZZ

Sentimental Bands, All-Female Big Bands, and a New Musical Idol

This chapter deals with the effects of World War II, the role of women, and the jazz business. It shows how World War II fundamentally affected jazz by depleting the ranks of big bands through the draft; making record pressing more difficult because of the lack of natural materials; shifting the dominant sound of jazz from a frenetic exuberance to a crooning sentimentality; and allowing a number of female jazz artists to rise to prominence as performers for the first time through all-female touring bands. The war also created a group of young, lonely women, separated from their husbands and boyfriends, who had the money to spend on heartthrobs such as Frank Sinatra, who became a celebrity amid a ban on recording instrumental music.

In September 1942, Glenn Miller, the most popular civilian bandleader from 1939 to 1942, volunteered for the Navy at the age of thirty-eight. Initially, he had been rejected as being too old. Not dissuaded, a persuasive Miller convinced the army to allow him to establish a "modernized" army band. "America means freedom, and there's no expression of freedom quite so sincere as music," he asserted (Erenberg 1975, 191). The new recruit formed an updated version of a marching band, which broadcast a weekly radio show, *I Sustain the Wings*. During summer 1944, Major Miller received permission to create a fifty-piece Army Air Force band, which performed more than eight hundred concerts for service men and women and recorded special V-discs ("V" for "victory") produced to bolster the morale of the troops.

On Friday, December 15, 1944, Glenn Miller sat in a car on a runway at Twinwood airfield near London. He was waiting to fly across the English Channel for an upcoming Christmas concert to entertain GIs who had recently liberated Paris. Miller watched the pilot, a twenty-year-old who just a few months earlier passed his final flight tests, taxi his one-engine transport aircraft down the strip and pull beside the car. "Sorry I'm late," the pilot shouted over the whirr of the engine. "I ran into heavy squalls, but the weather is supposed to be clearing over the continent" (Twinwood Airfield Bedfordshire, n.d.). The bandleader waved at his manager, who intended to join his boss the next day with other orchestra members. In less than a minute, Miller took off for Orly Field in Paris at 1:55 in the afternoon.

Weather conditions looked menacing. Ominously, the thin layer of clouds at the airfield turned into heavy, full cloud cover at 1,500 feet over the English Channel that obstructed the view. As the plane climbed to escape the clouds, the temperature fell below freezing. The carburetor likely seized, which forced the plane to spiral out of control. It plunged into the freezing waters of the English Channel, killing the pilot and Miller.

The day after the crash, Allied forces battled the Germans, who launched their last major offensive in what came to be known as the Battle of the Bulge. Occupied with one of the most brutal, large-scale battles of World War II, military commanders never noticed that Glenn Miller's plane had disappeared. On December 18, Orville A. Anderson of the US Eighth Air Force received notification of the downed aircraft and exclaimed, "They've had it. I can mount a search but it won't matter." The American Armed Services officially announced the bandleader's death the day before Christmas. A few days later, Nazi propaganda minister Joseph Goebbels concocted a story that the straight-laced Miller—who had married his school sweetheart and recently adopted two children—had been found dead in the arms of a Parisian prostitute.

More than anyone else, Glenn Miller had exemplified the mood of America from mid-1939 until his untimely death. The soothing music of the "King of Velvet Swing," as some called him, provided Americans an escape from the tumultuous realities of the most massive war in history.

World War II

World War II dramatically changed America. The war officially began when Germany attacked Poland on September 1, 1939. Three days later, France and Great Britain declared war on Germany. The Soviet Union, attacking Poland from the east, initially joined Adolf Hitler's Nazi Germany in the Axis alliance, which also included Italy, headed by dictator Benito Mussolini, and an expansionist Japan.

Axis forces proceeded quickly. On April 9, 1940, Germany overran Denmark and Norway, and, on May 10, attacked France, Belgium, the Netherlands, and Luxembourg. By late May, the German army had trapped French and British forces. The British retreated to Dunkirk and, aided by a massive flotilla of military and civilian craft, escaped largely intact across the English Channel. On June 22, the French formally surrendered to Hitler. Starting in July 1940, the Fuehrer authorized incessant air strikes on British ports, airfields, and airplane factories. By the end of October, however, the British Royal Air Force (RAF) had survived the Luftwaffe's constant battering, and the German blitz across Europe had been at least temporarily halted.

Although not officially entering the war until after the Japanese attack on its Pearl Harbor naval installations on December 7, 1941, the United States mobilized for the Allied war effort much earlier. On October 4, 1939, Congress approved the sale of weapons to European democracies. In May 1940, as the Germans encircled Allied troops in France, the United States authorized $1 billion for the production of fifty thousand fighter planes. On September 16, 1940, after heated debate, Congress passed the first peacetime draft in history, which required men between the ages of 21 and 36 to register for military service. On March 11, 1941, Congress enacted the Lend-Lease policy, which allowed the United States to provide weapons and supplies to allies in Europe and Asia at no cost to the recipients, and which ended any pretense that the United States would remain neutral during the war.

The Office of Price Administration (OPA) readied America for war. Established on August 28, 1941, the office set prices for consumer goods to ensure adequate supplies for a possible war and to avoid inflation, which New Dealers considered a major threat to the economy. It instituted maximum prices for nearly every consumable good, including toast and doughnuts at five cents each; a hamburger at fifteen cents; a half pint of milk at seven cents; and even a breaded pork cutlet at thirty-five cents. The OPA limited the amount of gasoline, coffee, clothing, and basic commodities a person could purchase. At the gas station, it required car owners to use a coupon to buy a monthly allotment of gasoline.

On Dec. 7, 1941, at 7:48 in the morning, the Japanese Imperial Navy dispatched 353 fighter planes and bombers from six battleships to the Pearl Harbor naval base in Hawaii. In a surprise attack, the Japanese sunk four of eight US battleships in the harbor, damaged three cruisers, and destroyed 188 aircraft. When the smoke cleared, 2,403 Americans lay dead and 1,178 were wounded. The Japanese lost only twenty-nine planes. The next day, President Roosevelt appeared before Congress, which responded with a declaration of war. The War Production Board (WPB) immediately redirected manufacturing toward wartime purposes. The Board converted the production of materials used for consumer goods—such as automobiles, silk stockings, and home appliances—to wartime supplies such as jeeps, tanks, parachutes, and weapons. By war's end, the concentrated effort of the WPB resulted in the production of 86,000 tanks, nearly 300,000 airplanes, 17 million rifles, 315,000 pieces of field artillery, 4.2 tons of shells, and 41.4 billion rounds of small-arms ammunition.

In addition to major changes in consumption and production, the war caused a seismic shift in the American workforce. Between 1941 and 1945, more than sixteen million Americans, mostly men, entered the armed services, which still remained racially segregated. Of these, nearly ten million were drafted, and 405,000 perished. As men streamed into the armed forces, the once-pressing problem of unemployment nearly vanished overnight. By 1942, the unemployment rate dropped to 4.7 percent and, for the remainder of the war years, hovered at less than 2 percent.

With men at war, women stepped into the labor force to take their place. From 1941 to 1944, the female workforce in the United States increased from 14 million to 19 million, and the percentage of working women over the age of fourteen increased from 27 to 37 percent. Women in the higher-paid manufacturing industries rose more than sixfold from 340,000 to nearly 2.2 million, and women in government jobs doubled. The iconic image of "Rosie the Riveter" symbolized the pivotal and new role women were playing in industry.

Jazz Goes to War: The Effect of World War II on Jazz

World War II fundamentally impacted jazz, just as it influenced nearly every aspect of American life. The draft depleted the ranks of big bands, which had proliferated during the Goodman era. In just four months after the declaration of war, bandleader and trombonist Jack Teagarden—who typified the wartime experience—lost seventeen of his men to the war effort. By August 1942, every major big band similarly had lost between one-quarter and one-half of its personnel. Even undrafted musicians, restricted from travel by draft boards, found it difficult to stay with a band. "Fewer draft-age musicians are now able to get a free traveling hand from their respective draft boards," related *Billboard* in September 1943. They "must remain within convenient calling distance" ("Units Feel Pinch" 1943).

Some patriotic bandleaders folded their civilian outfits and went off to war. In a "Band Leader's Honor Roll" from March 15, 1943, *Downbeat* tallied 61 former band maestros in uniform.

Other bandleaders, desperate for players, hired inexperienced musicians. "Our band was really 'sad' until after the war," complained Hayes Pillars, co-leader of the Jeter-Pillars band, "because it was hard to recruit fellows, you know, because everybody you could get—they were either in the Army or had to go" (Floyd 1983, 46). During the war, when Tommy Dorsey lost forty-two musicians to the armed services, he dryly observed that "I'm paying some kid trumpet player $500 a week, and he can't even blow his nose" (Ward and Burns 2000, 296).

Some bands signed talented teenagers to keep their orchestras afloat. Red Rodney (b. Robert Chudnick), then a Harry James enthusiast and later a bop trumpeter, recalled that "all of the good trumpet players were drafted. So the big-name bandleaders were looking for kids who weren't old enough or were draft exempt" (Sidran 1992, 20). As the war worsened, men between the ages of eighteen and twenty-one became eligible for the draft, which significantly reduced available teens for big bands.

Naval recruiters enlisted African-American musicians as members of military bands, which further devastated civilian big bands. From 1942 to 1945, the United States Navy enticed more than five thousand African Americans to join military orchestras. Bandleader Howard Funderberg recalled naval agents coming into town and heading straight to the "main music store, and say[ing], 'Who are the bands and who are the musicians here?' A guy came to my house to talk about the musicians, and when we played the next dance, he was there to listen to the musicians, and told them what the Navy was offering" (Floyd 1983, 43).

Many African-American recruits landed in North Chicago at the Great Lakes Training Station. After a few months rehearsing there, twenty-five-man bands were formed to tour naval bases around the world. Three units, one headed by trumpeter Clark Terry, remained at the Great Lakes Training Station for the duration of the war to train incoming recruits.

Though rooted in discrimination, the policy to use African-American service-men as musicians rather than as combat troops had advantages. At Great Lakes, recruits practiced their instruments all day and sometimes even rented apartments in the city. Trumpeter and arranger Gerald Wilson was stationed at the naval base after playing with the Jimmie Lunceford band. Compared to other soldiers, he felt that "we were very privileged people. We lived in Chicago. In fact," he added, "I never slept another night on the base after I got out of boot camp" (Bryant 1998, 331). Marshal Royal—who for three years headed a Navy band at St. Mary's College—confessed that "I didn't do anything but entertain, play for dances, play for regimental parades. I didn't even live on base" (46).

The number of big bands dropped precipitously amid the draft. "The mortality among name and semi-name bands continues to rise as the draft makes further inroads" contended *Billboard* on July 18, 1942.

All-Female Jazz Bands

While African-American and white male musicians flooded into the armed forces and many big bands dissolved, more than one hundred all-female civilian orchestras were formed to expand the pioneering efforts of a few earlier all-female bands such as Ina Ray Hutton and the Melodears.

The International Sweethearts of Rhythm came together at the Piney Woods Country Life School for African-American children, located near Jackson, Mississippi. In May 1941, after a performance in Washington, DC, at the Howard Theater, the International Sweethearts officially broke with their school after they learned that some band members would not graduate. The Sweethearts enlisted Eddie Durham and then Kansas City–bred pianist/orchestra leader Jesse Stone to mold them into a professional unit. By 1943, the group played opposite established male bands at large venues such as New York's Apollo Theater, where they performed seven shows a week. At Detroit's Paradise Theater, the orchestra drew diehard fans who stood in pouring rain to buy tickets. "I've never seen a bunch of people stand out for Duke Ellington like that," chuckled Jesse Stone, who roomed with Ellington for four months and wrote arrangements for the Chick Webb and Jimmie Lunceford bands. By the end of the war, boasted Stone, the Sweethearts had "a bigger and more lasting name than any other female group in the country" (Placksin 1982, 134).

The Darlings of Rhythm were another popular all-female band. Organized in Harlem during 1943 by saxophonist Lorraine Brown, the African-American orchestra toured the country to packed houses. In April 1944, the *Chicago Defender* reported that "this all-girl orchestra compares with any in the business . . . these famous girls have broken attendance records in more than a dozen cities and are receiving requests for return engagements galore" (Tucker 2000, 211). A month later, the paper named the band "America's number-1 all-girl orchestra" and gave special notice to such stars as alto saxophonist Josephine Boyd (212).

By 1943, as the war dragged on, women jazz outfits proliferated. After leaving the International Sweethearts of Rhythm, Eddie Durham established the African-American, twenty-member All Star Girl Orchestra, which featured such musicians as trumpeter Jean Starr. Other successful female outfits included the all-white big band, Ada Leonard's All-American Girl Orchestra, and such African-American groups as the Texas Playgirls, the Queens of Swing, and the Prairie View College Co-Eds. "They were glad to have females who could play," recalled trumpeter Clora Bryant who joined the Prairie View Co-Eds. "We'd play all the large cities in Texas.

We did one-nighters up and down the coast . . . from Florida to New York. We ended up playing the Apollo Theater!" (Bryant 1998, 344–45).

The expanding number of female jazz bands found it difficult to meet popular demand. "The hunt for girl musicians is gaining new proportions," reported *Billboard* in September. "Agents show little optimism in the hope of finding enough new fem combos to fill the diminishing supply" ("Units Feel Pinch" 1943).

Some women found jobs in formerly all-male bands. In 1941, trumpeter and vocalist Billie Rogers joined Woody Herman as the only "girl musician" in the group. Trumpeter Fran Shirley connected with the Charlie Barnet Orchestra, and bassist Lucille Dixon played with Earl Hines. When her husband, Dick Stabile, went to war, Gracie Barrie took over leadership of his band. Valaida Snow led the gender-mixed Sunset Royals, who performed at such venues as the Apollo Theater and the Savoy. Women even cracked into studio orchestras.

Women in the jazz bands felt a new sense of empowerment with their expanded roles. Many agreed with Viola Smith, drummer and leader of the Coquettes Orchestra, when she wrote in *Downbeat* that "the girls of today are not the helpless creatures of an earlier generation" (Stowe 1994, 171). "Girls work right along beside men in the factories, in the offices, in nearly every trade," a female drummer told *Downbeat* in 1942, "so why not in the dance bands?" (Stowe 1994, 169).

Despite the strides taken by female jazz artists during the war, sexism persisted. *Downbeat*, though liberal on racial issues, lambasted jazz women. "Good jazz is a hard masculine music with a whip to it," it declared in 1941. "Women like violins, and jazz deals with drums and trumpets" (Placksin 1982, 128). When drummer Pauline Braddy performed with the International Sweethearts of Rhythm, she encountered an "Oh, no, not a girl" attitude. She heard some men muttering that women "should stay home and learn to cook" (136). In one instance, when the Sweethearts appeared at the Apollo, some male musicians in the audience refused to believe that women could play so well and asked then-manager Eddie Durham for permission to go backstage to check. "It's a pantomime, they gotta have a band back there," they chided him. "Ain't no girls can play like that" (133).

Wartime Rationing

The rationing of natural resources, along with the draft and the emergence of female bands, transformed the big-band business. Gasoline, needed to fuel tanks, planes, and jeeps, became difficult to procure for bands, which constantly traveled to one-night stands. Especially in the Midwest, where orchestras traveled longer distances between jobs, the gasoline shortage caused a 40 percent decline in business. Trombonist Benny Morton complained that "we couldn't use gas for the big buses to move the bands around" (Tompkins 1975, 1).

The rationing of shellac devastated the record industry, which used the material to manufacture discs. After the Japanese blocked the shellac trade route in India and Thailand, the US government diverted the remaining shellac to the military for engine repair. Initially, the WPB limited record companies to 30 percent of the shellac that the labels had used during the previous year. On November 2, 1942, however, the WPB entirely eliminated new shellac for record production.

Record labels relied on scrap-shellac programs to produce new titles. In 1942, Victor launched recycling campaigns to buy used and broken records, which the label melted to manufacture new discs. A few months later, Columbia Records mimicked the Victor program by staging "disc nights" at venues such as the Roseland Ballroom in New York City, where dancers received 2.5 cents in credit for every worn or unwanted disc that they brought with them. Although these efforts

Watch Valaida Smith perform "Patience and Fortitude"

generated some shellac, the companies only had limited supplies of the essential material and only selectively produced new discs.

The limitation on new records created problems for bands. For years, orchestras had used discs for promotion. In August 1939, *Downbeat* stated that "the leader knows that once his records are released . . . his band will be exploited via a dozen methods, and over hundreds of radio stations in the hinterlands—all which adds up to publicity which, in many cases, the leader himself couldn't buy in a lifetime on his own" (Stowe 1994, 113). Coupled with the draft and wartime rationing, the smaller number of new records made it difficult for many bands, especially lesser-known ones, to survive.

With only a handful of bands available, the cost of orchestras soared for ball-room owners. "The salaries of name bands are reaching boom heights," reported *Billboard* on September 12, 1942. Harry James, who had formerly accepted $5,500 a week to play the Paramount, now earned $10,000. Glenn Miller, hired by a the-ater in Detroit, raked in a "dazzling" $21,000 for a week's work by contracting for a base salary as well as a percentage of gross revenues. The inflated salaries forced many theaters to close. "It became too big a speculation for ballroom owners to stay open," insisted Benny Morton. "They rented some of [the venues] out as storage places to the Government" (Tompkins 1975, 1).

Glenn Miller: Sweet and Sentimental

During the war, the style of big-band jazz shifted. Rather than playing hyperkinetic dance music for jitterbugs, a sweet-and-sentimental jazz became popular. Led by trombonist Glenn Miller, the soothing sounds comforted a tense nation at war.

Born Alton Glenn Miller in rural Iowa on March 1, 1904, he constantly moved with his family and eventually settled in Colorado, where he played trombone in the town band. After a brief stint at the University of Colorado, he joined several local bands and then played for stage shows. In 1925, Miller secured a job with Ben Pollack's orchestra, which at the time included Benny Goodman, followed by stints with the Dorsey Brothers and British bandleader Ray Noble.

In 1937, Miller founded his own group, which featured a new sound. He fo-cused on elegant arrangements and harmony by featuring the clarinet of Wilbur Schwartz as a fifth member of the saxophone section that played an octave above the saxophones. He joined the reed section with the brass (trombones and trum-peters), which many times played with mutes to produce an overall velvety, pastel-like sound. "The years of serious study I've had with legitimate teachers finally is paying off in enabling me to write arrangements employing unusual, rich harmo-nies, many never before used in dance bands," he explained to *Downbeat*. "Har-mony comes first," he insisted (Stowe 1994, 120).

Despite musical innovations, the Miller band struggled to survive. The outfit trudged through a string of low-paying jobs that barely covered expenses. In June, at New Orleans's Roosevelt Hotel, Miller earned $5.75 a week for himself. After a few weeks, a drunken band member wrecked one of the band's two cars. "In late 1937, before his band became popular, we were both playing in Dallas," recollected Benny Goodman. "Glenn was pretty dejected and came to see me. He asked, 'What do you do? How do you make it?' I said, 'I don't know, Glenn. You just stay with it'" (Spink 1985). By the end of the year, Miller had lost $18,000 on the orchestra, which he disbanded in early January 1938.

Two months after dismantling his first group, Miller assembled a second band by borrowing $10,000 from Tommy Dorsey. In June, the band performed at New York's Paradise Restaurant and, by September, landed a recording deal with

RCA Records. However, in February 1939, after a tour in North Carolina, a disillusioned Miller nearly quit the bandleader role.

Then Miller's fortunes suddenly brightened. He landed a gig at New Jersey's Meadowbrook Club, which had a national radio wire. During the summer of 1939, the band moved to the swank Glen Island Casino in New Rochelle, New York, which had launched the careers of many big bands. By the conclusion of the engagement, Miller had scored the major hit "In the Mood" and followed with twenty-four more best sellers, including his signature "Moonlight Serenade." In less than a year after dejectedly disbanding his first outfit, Miller broke attendance records at the Kansas City Convention Hall, where he drew nearly 7,800 jazz fanatics and earned $4,680 for the one-night stand. "It's an inspiring sight to look down from the balcony on the heads of 7,000 people, swaying on a dance floor—especially when you are getting $600 for every thousand of them," Miller joked (Kolodin 1941, 78).

Miller ascended to the heights of big-band music through radio. In October 1939, Miller signed a contract for $250,000 a year with Chesterfield cigarettes for a sponsored radio program. Replacing the Paul Whiteman orchestra, the band broadcast three fifteen-minute spots a week to a national audience. "Radio made Glenn Miller," asserted his drummer Moe Purtill. The bandleader wanted to "go on the air as much as we can. We just did about twenty tunes at first, played those same twenty tunes over and over. Pounded them into you on the broadcasts," the drummer added (Erenberg 1975, 168).

At the end of a momentous year, *Time* crowned Miller the new King of Swing. "At first Miller's was rated as just another good swing band. But last summer" reported the magazine, "things began to happen. Within five months Glenn Miller's band was causing more rug-dust to fly, making more phonograph records, and playing more radio dates than Goodman and Shaw together." The magazine calculated that "of the twelve to twenty-four discs in each of today's 300,000 U.S. jukeboxes, from two to six are usually Glenn Miller's" ("New King" 1939, 58).

Until enlisting in late 1942, Miller delivered a rapid-fire string of top hits. In 1940, his first full year of stardom, Miller grossed $630,000 from *Chesterfield Hour* broadcasts, twenty-five weeks of hotel engagements, sixteen weeks of one-nighters, ten weeks in theaters, and two record dates a month for RCA Victor. Among his biggest successes was "Tuxedo Junction."

Even African Americans snapped up Miller discs. "I remember thinking how nearly the whole evening's music at [the segregated] Mason High School dances [in Lansing, Michigan] had been Glenn Miller's records," recalled Malcolm Little, soon to become civil-rights activist Malcolm X. "What wouldn't that crowd have given, I wondered, to be standing where Glenn Miller's band was actually going to play?" (Malcolm X 1973, 42).

In addition to hit records and sold-out performances, Miller conquered the silver screen. In 1941, he appeared as bandleader Phil Corey in the movie *Sun Valley Serenade*. The next year, he starred in *Orchestra Wives*, which prominently featured the Miller band and its hit records. When he donned a uniform, Miller traded a nearly $20,000-a-week salary for military pay.

Miller's success can be at least partly attributed to the times. His romantic, sweet music provided a much-needed counterpoint to a tense, brutal war. "Escapist radio entertainment is apparently hitting a new high," observed *Billboard* on November 14, 1942. Americans flocked to "radio listening as a means of temporary 'escape' from world events" ("Listeners Favor Escape?" 1942, 6). "Entertainment and sports are the greatest antidote against hysteria, and we need them to win the war!" agreed *Downbeat* (Stowe 1994, 146).

Miller encouraged Americans to escape through his smooth, soothing sound. "War workers like to dance for relaxation," recalled Ray McKinley, who drummed

LISTENING GUIDE 20

Glenn Miller Orchestra

"TUXEDO JUNCTION"

This song, written by bandleader/trumpeter Erskine Hawkins and a group of others, became a theme of the Erskine Hawkins Orchestra, which performed at the Savoy Ballroom opposite Chick Webb. The title referred to an area near Birmingham, Alabama—Hawkins's hometown—which showcased a club by the Nixon Building and Tuxedo Park.

On February 5, 1940, Miller slowed down the tempo of the song to make a recording for Bluebird Records that sold 115,000 discs in the first week of

its release. He featured trumpeter Johnny Best as soloist.

The Bluebird version of the song included Miller, Frank D'Annolfo, Howard Gibeling, and Paul Tanner (trombones); Clyde Hurley, Dale McMickle, John Best, and Legh Knowles (trumpets); Al Klink and Tex Beneke (tenor saxophones); Hal McIntyre and Jimmy Abato (alto saxophones); Wilbur Schwartz on clarinet and alto saxophone; Rollie Bundock (bass); Mo Purtill (drums); Dick Fisher (guitar); and Chummy MacGregor (piano).

0:00–0:18	A dynamic, 4/4 introduction that builds from a barely audible level to mid-volume. A unified trombone unit, backed by rhythm, repeats a riff in a sound that mimics a train coming closer and closer to the Tuxedo Junction. The section fulfills the role of the trumpeter in the New Orleans brass band who created freak sounds with his instrument. Miller has been noted for his broad dynamics.
0:19–0:33	Johnny Best plays a riff on trumpet, which responds to the call of the smooth reed (saxophones with the added clarinet) section. The reed section, playing in unison, became a trademark for Glenn Miller and achieved its smooth, airy sound through the addition of a clarinet as a fifth member of the section.
0:34–0:49	The muted brass section and the reed section trade riffs in a call-and-response, which provides a stark contrast to the two textures, one somewhat harsh (trumpets) and the other velvety (reeds).
0:50–1:07	The trumpet unleashes a slow, bluesy trumpet solo with silky reed riffs in the background.
1:08–1:25	Johnny Best takes a second solo with the constant riffs of the reeds behind him.
1:26–1:42	A restatement of the soft riff-based, train-sounding introduction.
1:43–1:59	The brass bursts through the soft-sounding riffs with considerable volume and battles the reeds with riffs that provide a stark contrast. The section ends with a familiar figure by the brass.
2:00–2:03	The piano enters for a few bars and with the drums signals an end to the section.
2:04–2:21	Another restatement of the rhythmic introduction by the brass.
2:22–2:35	The silky reed section joins the riff-based section to contrast with the brass, which increases its volume.
2:36–2:40	The piano and drums again signal an end to the section.
2:41–2:59	Another restatement of the soft, trombone choir introduction.
3:00–3:15	A loud burst from the trumpet contrasts with the slow passage immediately before it and initiates the call-and-response between the brass and the reeds.
3:16–3:23	Full orchestra ends the tune.

for Glenn Miller in his wartime band. "Neither minds nor bodies could relax to any but sweet music" (Stowe 1994, 154). Miller keenly understood the need for calming music during turbulent times. "When we started out three years ago, none of the big bands played pretty," he asserted in 1940, "and the majority of people like to hear pretty tunes" (Erenberg 1975, 186).

Miller's appearance and age projected a comforting image. "Bespectacled and scholarly looking," he "was a commanding guy, youthful but mature" who "looked like security," remarked Miller's press agent (Erenberg 1975, 187). When finally achieving commercial success, the thirty-five-year-old Glenn Miller looked like an adult compared to the more youthful Benny Goodman. Miller seemed like an even greater symbol of steadiness when he turned away from fame and fortune to enlist in the armed forces. "I, like every patriotic American, have an obligation to fulfill," he declared, "to lend as much support as I can to winning the war" (Erenberg 1975, 181).

From his induction to his untimely death, Miller supported the war effort by soothing the troops with sentimental memories of home. He catered to the typical serviceman who yearned "to hear things that remind them of home, that bring back something of those days when we were all happy and free and when we used to be able to put on a Miller record or listen to a Miller broadcast." The bandleader created a "dream world" and an "avenue of escape" for fighting men who daily faced death (Stowe 1994, 155). To General James Doolittle of the Army Air Force, Miller represented the best morale builder for the troops, next to a letter from home.

The comforting, romantic ensemble sound of Glenn Miller captured the country and gently nudged the frantic, optimistic, hot swing of the New Deal from the forefront. The "average campus kid wants his music grooved for 'smooth' dancing," revealed a May 1942 survey of 158 college campuses. "The harum-scarum jitter-hopping is definitely a thing of the past" ("Collegians Like It Smooth" 1942).

The Dorseys: Sweetly Swinging Sounds

Many swing bands emulated Glenn Miller's success by offering a romantic, calming sound. One of the most successful was led by Jimmy and Tommy Dorsey. The brothers had been raised in Pennsylvania by bandleader Thomas Dorsey Sr., and learned music at an early age. During the early twenties, they worked in the Scranton Sirens territory band. From 1924 to 1927, they played with the California Ramblers and then the Jean Goldkette outfit, before landing with the prestigious Paul Whiteman Orchestra. Sax man and clarinetist "Jimmy went first [to Whiteman] and then sent for Tommy," recalled their mother. "That's the way it's always been. Whenever Jimmy joined a band, he'd always tell the leader about the kid brother, the trombone player" (Sudhalter 1999, 360).

During the late twenties and early thirties, the brothers informally recorded together. In 1928, they scored with their first hits, "Coquette" and "Dixie Dawn." The next year, the Dorseys charted with "Let's Do It (Let's Fall in Love)" and, during the following four years, enjoyed three more record successes. Between freelance recording dates, they performed with such bands as the Victor Young Orchestra and the symphonic-sounding Sam Lanin unit.

Closely linked and respecting each other's musical talent, the brothers nevertheless fought mercilessly. In 1928, when they played with Sam Lanin, recalled saxophonist Arnold Bilhart, "they were on the floor, a real knock-down, drag-out fight right there on the stand. . . . Tommy got up and jumped all over Jimmy's brand new saxophone. Made scrap metal of it. Jimmy grabbed his brother's trombone and just wrapped it around his knee, slide and all. Ruined it" (Sudhalter 1999, 360).

Despite physical confrontations, in spring 1934 the two brothers assembled an eleven-piece band, which for much of the first year included the multi-talented Glenn Miller as an arranger, trombonist, and musical director. That summer, they debuted to rave reviews at the high-class Sands Point Bath Club on Long Island, New York, and, during the fall, moved to New York's Palais Royale. In September, the Dorseys signed to the newly established Decca Records and, during the next four months, cut nearly sixty songs. They immediately had a major success with "What a Difference a Day Makes," and soon followed with more bestsellers.

The Dorsey brothers based their sound on the relaxed, lightly swinging style of Bing Crosby. "Bing was the biggest thing around in those days," remembered Dorsey band drummer Ray McKinley. "There was nobody who sang like him. The Dorseys often had played for Bing, and they felt . . . that they could achieve something if they pitched their sound like his" (Sudhalter 1999, 375). While Benny Goodman stormed the Palomar with his hot music, the Dorseys crafted smoother music that retained remnants of the symphonic jazz popular a few years earlier. *Metronome* characterized the band as "one of the slickest, most exciting musical aggregations ever to enter our musical lives" (376).

Just as it achieved success, the band imploded. On May 16, 1935, the orchestra started a summer residency at the Glen Island Casino. On May 30, as Tommy blew the first few bars of the newly recorded "I'll Never Say 'Never Again' Again," Jimmy criticized Tommy for his fast tempo. An incensed Tommy stomped off the stage and refused to return. "He didn't say anything wrong. He just bawled me out with his eyes," fumed Tommy to Corky O'Keefe when the agency owner tried to reconcile the brothers (Sudhalter 1999, 378). Though Tommy eventually fulfilled his contractual obligations, he left his brother to launch his own unit. Jimmy kept the band and, for the next two years, backed Bing Crosby on the *Kraft Music Hall* radio program.

Tommy approached Joe Haymes about taking over his band. "It was a very good band," pianist Paul Mitchell asserted, but "Joe really had no leadership qualities and was about to go broke" (Ruhlmann 1994, 19). In summer 1935, Tommy assumed leadership of the fifteen-piece band from a desperate Haymes and immediately signed with the prominent booking agency MCA and RCA Records. In early fall, the band snagged an engagement at New York's French Casino and entered the studio for their first recording date.

Tommy vacillated between two different styles of jazz. In a subset of the orchestra, the Clambake Seven, which Dorsey likely modeled after the Goodman Trio and Quartet, he concocted a Dixieland-influenced version of swing. For his full orchestra, Dorsey fashioned a smooth, nearly symphonic sound, which was enhanced by vocalists such as Edyth Wright and Jack Leonard. In 1937, the band landed a Wednesday-night, half-hour radio spot sponsored by Raleigh-Kool cigarettes. Marketed by radio, Dorsey registered with one of his most well-known hits, the Irving Berlin–penned

Tommy Dorsey spinning discs, 1947. *Photograph by William P. Gottlieb. William P. Gottlieb/Ira and Leonore S. Gershwin Fund Collection, Music Division, Library of Congress*

ballad "Marie," which sold one hundred fifty thousand copies when a hit equaled sales of twenty thousand.

During the forties, Dorsey produced romantic ballads interspersed with a sporadic swinging tune. In 1940, he tallied eight top hits and replaced the Clambake Seven with Tommy Dorsey and His Sentimentalists. The next year, Tommy appeared in the feature-length film *Las Vegas Nights* and starred in four more movies during the next two years. In 1942, he added a string section to the orchestra to further emphasize his silky approach. During the war years, the press referred to Dorsey as the "King of Sentimental Swing."

Harry James: From Hot to Sweet

During the late thirties, Harry James adopted a sweet, nearly symphonic sound. When playing trumpet with Goodman, James earned a reputation as a lightning-fast soloist who brought jitterbugs to the dance floor. In January 1939, determined to establish a band, James borrowed $7,000 from Benny Goodman in exchange for one-third of his net earnings over the next ten years. To ensure a swinging sound, he hired Andy Gibson, an African-American arranger and trumpeter who had worked with Duke Ellington, Count Basie, and Charlie Barnet. The trumpeter inked a deal with Brunswick Records and debuted with swinging mayhem at the Benjamin Franklin Hotel in Philadelphia.

The swinging James band met resistance from ballroom owners eager for more subdued fare. In August 1939, the band performed at New York's Roseland Ballroom and seemed "just about the most rhythmic white band dancedom has yet known" to an enthusiastic *Metronome*. Despite pleasing the jitterbugs, James nearly lost the engagement, when the ballroom manager demanded slower numbers (Firestone 1993, 234).

Amid the Glenn Miller craze, James switched direction by adopting a lyrical, full vibrato (a slight fluctuation of the pitch) on his trumpet, adding strings, and recording ballads and classically oriented numbers.

By 1942, James and his sentimental sound overtook America. He registered his first top hit with the romantic, string-enhanced "Sleepy Lagoon" and followed with a sixty-piece orchestral version of "I Had the Craziest Dream." The bandleader headlined the *Spotlight Bands for Coca-Cola* radio show on Monday nights, replaced Glenn Miller on the *Chesterfield Hour*, and periodically appeared on comedian Jack Benny's popular radio program. He starred in two Hollywood films, *Springtime in the Rockies* and *Private Buckaroo*. By the end of the year, James had grossed $750,000 from film appearances, concerts, and record royalties. In late September 1942, *Time* magazine aptly

Harry James during a Coca-Cola radio show rehearsal, 1946. *Photograph by William P. Gottlieb. William P. Gottlieb/Ira and Leonore S. Gershwin Fund Collection, Music Division, Library of Congress*

summarized James's turnaround. "A semi-failure at first, bandleader James began tasting success only when he laid away his ambitions as a 'hot' man, and developed a simple sweet style that features the clear, cool James trumpet against a mass of soft strings. Wartime fans, tired of pure heat, now want their heartstrings twanged" ("Horn of Plenty").

In 1943, the phenomenal rise of Harry James continued. On April 10, when the *Chesterfield Hour* announced that James would broadcast from Chicago twice a night for six nights, nearly two hundred thousand fans requested tickets for the shows, which could seat forty-eight thousand ("James Ork Follows" 1943). On April 21, when the Paramount Theater booked James, lines gathered at 6:00 a.m., and by the 8:30 a.m. entrance time "the crowd was so thick that the plate-glass window at McBride's Ticket Agency next door to the theater was smashed by milling youngsters," reported *Billboard*. After the first show, teens refused to leave the theater until James distributed a thousand of his photos. By the evening, twenty-five thousand jazz fans had purchased tickets to see the newest craze ("Harry James—Paramount" 1943, 1, 11). On May 22, *Billboard* announced that Harry James had won its annual College Music Poll: "Shooting up from third place last year and no place at all the year before, Harry James went ahead of all contesting band leaders" and edged out Glenn Miller, who had won the poll the previous three years (Crennard 1943, 1). Collegians, the magazine contended, "prefer their music smooth and languid" (23).

Throughout the remaining war years, James coasted on the sentimental wave. In 1944, he scored six bestsellers, including "I'll Get By (As Long As I Have You)." The next year, he released the major success "It's Been a Long, Long Time," which perfectly captured the sentiment of a nation that had been gripped by war for nearly three years.

Artie Shaw's Sweetened Jazz

Artie Shaw floated on a sweet, symphonic cloud to stardom. He started on clarinet with Austin Wylie's Golden Pheasant Orchestra in Cincinnati. Faced with competition from Benny Goodman on clarinet, Shaw switched to saxophone and landed jobs with radio studio bands, which he considered "boring, mind-numbing garbage. I developed the kind of lead alto sound you needed to cut through in radio," he contended (Sudhalter 1999, 574).

On May 24, 1936, Shaw won a slot in "New York's First Swing Concert" staged at the Oynx Club. Trying something new, the clarinetist composed "Interlude in B-Flat" and enlisted two violins, a cello, a viola, and a rhythm section to accompany him as Artie Shaw's Swing String Ensemble. As he did throughout much of his career, he employed the clarinet as another string instrument. "Often, I was trying to sound like a violin, especially like [Jasha] Heifetz," he confessed (Sudhalter 1999, 583). At the concert, Shaw impressed fellow musicians and, based upon the performance, snagged contracts from Brunswick Records and the Rockwell-O'Keefe booking agency.

Shaw formed a twelve-piece band around the string octet. "I always felt that a string background for a hot clarinet would wed the best of sweet and swing," he said. On June 11, 1936, he took the orchestra into the studio and recorded "Japanese Sandman," a 1920 hit for Paul Whiteman, who served as an inspiration for forties sweet-jazz bands. A few months later, Shaw eliminated the brass to form Artie Shaw and His Strings (Shaw 1939, 16).

Amid the craze for hot swing bands, the string-heavy big band attracted few fans. It opened at New York's Hotel Lexington and moved to the Paramount

Theater with "mediocre success," according to Shaw. The Shaw orchestra received even a worse reception during a series of one-night stands (Shaw 1939, 16). It reached its nadir at the Adolphus Hotel in Dallas. "You could have shot deer in the place," Shaw sarcastically joked (Sudhalter 1999, 580). In March 1937, Shaw disbanded the group. "Musically, it had everything," complained the bandleader, "but the shaggers wanted hot brass and wild drum solos. There was no audience for it" (Ruhlmann 1992, 26).

Dejected, Shaw assembled a more traditional band. "I was so disgusted that I made up my mind to give the public what it eventually wanted—which was . . . 'the loudest band in the whole goddamn world!' I decided, okay, if they want noise, I'll give 'em noise." In April 1937, Shaw unveiled a fourteen-piece band without strings at Boston's Raymor Ballroom. Shaw retained violinist Jerry Gray as arranger and, on April 2, 1938, added Billie Holiday after trying a dozen other singers. For nearly eighteen months, Shaw and his band trudged around the country in a series of one-nighters. He described it as "two years of seasoning and heartbreak—when a hotel room was a luxury shared by three brass players, a drummer and their instruments. We'd finish at Scranton, Pennsylvania, at two in the morning, grab a bite to eat, crowd into the truck and two used cars we had picked up, and make Youngstown, Ohio, three-hundred-and-fifty miles away, by noon the next day" (Shaw 1939, 17).

Shaw's fortunes changed with the mood of the country. In late June 1938, "Begin the Beguine," a Cole Porter tune, was recorded by the band. Released that September, the ballad showcased Shaw's high-register clarinet floating over the swaying brass. By 1944, it had racked up a million sales. A perfect sentimental antidote to troubled times, the disc vaulted Shaw's band to the top of the jazz ranks. "I joined the band three weeks after 'Begin the Beguine' became available in the stores," remembered trumpeter Bernie Privin. "Before I knew it, the band was the hottest thing in the country. The record was played everywhere. Because of it, Artie suddenly became a major celebrity." "Overnight I found I had 'arrived'—which in show business means a complete metamorphosis," Shaw explained. "One moment you're barely making ends meet—barely managing to meet your expenses, such as payroll for your men, agency and management fees, [and] publicity expenses. . . . The next moment you find yourself making thousands of dollars a week even after paying all these expenses" (Ruhlmann 1992, 34).

Shaw steamrolled to success. Starting October 26, 1938, he landed an engagement at the New York's prestigious Hotel Lincoln, which broadcast the orchestra over the radio. In December, the band scored with "They Say," sung by Helen Forrest. On Christmas, Shaw fittingly partnered with Paul Whiteman's Orchestra in a Carnegie Hall performance. In 1939, he had another top hit with "Thanks for Everything." Shaw topped a *Billboard* survey of college students, and portrayed himself in *Dancing Co-Ed* (1939), which starred an eighteen-year-old siren, Lana Turner, who Shaw married the next year.

On November 18, 1939, at the height of his popularity, Shaw shockingly retired from the music business. After suffering from pneumonia and a rare blood disorder, he abruptly left the stage in New York City. "I suddenly decided I'd had it," he recalled. "I walked off the bandstand, went up to my room, and called my lawyer. When I got him on the phone I told him I was leaving" (Ruhlmann 1992, 40). Shaw traveled to Acapulco, Mexico, where he "swam, fished, lay in the sun, loafed around, did absolutely nothing," and the band dispersed.

In 1940, a bored Shaw came out of retirement to once again conquer the entertainment business. He worked on the film *Second Chorus*, and then gathered a recording band, a thirty-two piece outfit, including strings. On March 3, he cut his biggest hit, "Frenesi," a tune by composer Alberto Dominguez that he had heard in Mexico. Emboldened by the chart topper, in summer 1940 Shaw organized a twenty-two-piece

LISTENING GUIDE 21

Artie Shaw Orchestra

"BEGIN THE BEGUINE"

This song came from a 1935 musical written by composer Cole Porter for the Broadway show, *Jubilee*. Inspired by a New Guinea folk song, it referred to the beguine, a dance found in Martinique that resembled a rhumba. Originally, it featured a Caribbean-tinged rhythm. Unlike many jazz songs, which featured an AABA structure, "Begin the Beguine," remarked Cole Porter, had "one theme of 16 bars repeated endlessly and then finished off with a new theme which is repeated twice."

On July 24, 1938, Artie Shaw recorded the song for RCA's budget-label Bluebird with an arrangement by violinist Jerry Gray (b. Generoso Graziano), who admired classical composer Claude Debussy and honored the Spanish-based rhythm of the original. Shaw who

"worked very closely with Gray," insisted on the standard swing 4/4 beat but kept most of Gray's chords. "It was arranged in a beguine rhythm—bhum bhum, bhum pah bhum—and Artie wouldn't stand for that," recalled guitarist Al Avola. By the end of his career, Shaw sold 6.5 million copies of the disc and recorded a total of nineteen Cole Porter songs, which he favored due to the shift between major and minor chords.

Personnel: Shaw (clarinet); John Best, Chuck Peterson, and Claude Bowen (trumpets); George Arus, Harry Rodgers, and Russell Brown (trombones); Les Robinson and Hank Freeman (alto saxophones); Tony Pastor (b. Antonio Pestritto) and Ronnie Perry (tenor saxophones); Les Burness (piano); Al Avola (guitar); Sid Weiss (bass); and Cliff Leeman (drums).

0:00–0:06	Shaw introduces the rhythm with four-bar bursts from the trumpets that are answered by the smooth-sounding saxophones. Composer Ronald Hunt had suggested that Shaw "let your lead sax or brass take the pick-up. You will find this an excellent intro."
0:07–0:35	Shaw, one of the all-time best clarinetists in jazz, states the melody fluidly and flawlessly. He has backing from the saxophones, which continue the rhythm from the introduction, and the rhythm section. At the end of the section, the brass enters to signal a change.
0:36–0:59	The warm saxophones take the melody with rhythmic accompaniment from the rhythm section and the muted trumpets, which provide a contrast.
1:00–1:02	Shaw interjects his clarinet to signal a transition in the music.
1:03–1:29	The open, non-muted trumpets alternate the melody with the reeds and receive rhythm backing from the snare drum, bass, and guitar.
1:30–1:49	Tony Pastor takes a melodic solo on tenor saxophone with backing from the rhythm section. Note especially the cymbal crashes of Leeman and syncopated riffs from the brass.
1:50–1:53	The silken saxophone section finishes the melody.
1:54–1:57	Shaw again signals a change with his clarinet.
1:58–2:18	An open brass section restates the melody against a subdued, fluid saxophone section and the rhythm section.
2:19–2:24	Shaw notes another transition by playing a fragment of the melody on his clarinet. The passage ends with Leeman's cymbal crash.
2:25–2:38	The brass reenters with the melody. In this passage, Shaw joins the saxophones to add power to the section.

2:39	A cymbal crash signals a transition.
2:40–2:46	The trombones, which had recently expanded to a trio, continue the melody.
2:47–2:49	Shaw restates the melody with the rhythm section.
2:50–2:59	The brass answers Shaw and then the saxophones answer the trumpets and complete the melody.
3:00–3:14	Shaw returns to state the melody and then ascends in pitch to reach a high note as a climax to the tune. The smooth saxophones and then the entire band back him to end the song.

orchestra with nine strings and two arrangers, African-American William Grant Still and Lennie Hayton, both of whom had composed for Paul Whiteman. "I took some studio men to try an idea, which was whether strings and woodwinds could be used within the context of a dance band or a jazz band," he explained. "And I found it could be" (Rulhmann 1992, 40). "A large orchestra with strings gave you a lot of new tone colors," he explained (40). In September, the band opened at San Francisco's Palace Hotel. A month later, Shaw recorded "Star Dust," a Hoagy Carmichael song that had been a top hit for Isham Jones a decade earlier, which established him as a sweet-jazz icon. "I remember being on tour in 1943 as a young horn player and hearing Shaw's 'Star Dust' on every juke box in every restaurant—three years after the record was issued," recalled Gunther Schuller, author and Third Stream jazz pioneer.

In summer 1941, after studying orchestration with Hans Burns, who had conducted the Berlin Opera, the bandleader assembled yet another group, Artie Shaw and his Symphonic Swing. The orchestra mixed a fifteen piece string section along with several jazz veterans. Shaw wanted to prove that "any distinctions we draw between 'jazz' and 'concert music' are arbitrary and quite unnecessary" (Sudhalter 1999, 595). He continued to score top sellers with his new group. By April 1942, when he left for the armed forces, Artie Shaw had helped define the sweet sound of the war years.

Sinatra, an unlikely teen idol, New York City, 1947. *Photograph by William P. Gottlieb. William P. Gottlieb/Ira and Leonore S. Gershwin Fund Collection, Music Division, Library of Congress*

The Rise of Frank Sinatra

During the war, many big-band singers became solo acts. As big bands dispersed and a recording ban quashed instrumental music, they sang smooth ballads to enthusiastic, hormone-driven teenage girls in theaters and ballrooms. A young voice from New Jersey named Frank Sinatra led the wartime crooners to the top of the jazz world and, like the sweet bands, fulfilled a need for a comforting sound among war-distressed youth.

Frank Sinatra rode a long, bumpy road to success. In his hometown of Hoboken, New Jersey, he sang at parties, halftime festivities for a high-school football game, weddings, and social clubs. "I performed anyplace that people would listen to me," he remembered (Summers 2005, 31).

A Bing Crosby show convinced Sinatra to sing professionally. "After Crosby went off the stage," smiled his Aunt Josie, "Frank turned to Nancy [Barbato, his then-girlfriend, who he married in early February 1939] and said: 'I'm going to be a singer.' When they got home that night he announced it, very seriously." "Most people think [Bing's] just a crooner. But they're wrong. He's a troubadour. He tells a story in every song," asserted Frank. "He makes you feel like he's singing just for you" (Summers 1939, 31).

Like Crosby, Sinatra strove for an intimate style, which relied on the condenser microphone. "I discovered very early that my instrument wasn't my voice. It was the microphone," he confessed. With condenser microphones, "you can sing as if you're singing in someone's ear, you can talk to a buddy in a bar, you can whisper sweet nothings to a woman" (Summers 1939, 33).

Frank traveled to nearby New York City for voice lessons to expand his range and eliminate his thick New Jersey accent while singing. He joined the group the Hoboken Four, which embarked on a tour in 1935 that was sponsored by radio amateur-hour host Major Edward Bowes. They also worked at the Rustic Club in Englewood Cliffs, New Jersey, just across the river from New York.

In 1938, the Rustic Club hired the twenty-three-year-old Sinatra as a waiter, emcee, and part-time singer for $15 a week. The bar featured a Saturday-night radio hook-up. As with other jazz hangouts, it attracted a mob clientele, which included Willie Moretti and Joe Adonis, both henchmen of New York gang kingpin, Charles "Lucky" Luciano. According to one observer, Moretti watched Frank audition for the job and "took a liking to Sinatra" (Summers 2005, 49).

To supplement his salary, Sinatra sang for local radio stations. "I was running around doing every sustaining radio show I could," he explained. "Sustaining—that meant no sponsor, and you better believe it that routine sustained everyone but me. . . . Sometimes I had it planned so I'd be on the air someplace or another every three hours all through the day. Don't think I was doing all this work for nothing—I got seventy cents car fare from Jersey to the Mutual studios," he joked (Ruhlmann 1991, 11).

Sinatra ultimately longed to be a singer in a big band, the most prestigious position for a vocalist at the time. "I simply dug the big band sound around me," he maintained (Ruhlmann 1991, 11). He approached Glenn Miller, who was still scuffling for work. "I walked up to him and I said, 'Glenn, I want a job,'" recalled Frank. "He said to me in essence, 'Don't call me, I'll call you.'" He next auditioned for Tommy Dorsey at Charlie's Grill in New Jersey, a joint owned by Moretti, but Sinatra froze at the microphone and could not sing a word.

Sinatra's breakthrough came in June 1939, when trumpeter Harry James heard him at the Rustic Cabin. Waiting tables when James arrived, Sinatra took off his apron, ascended the stage, and sang Cole Porter's "Night and Day." After a few bars of the song, James "felt the hairs on the back of my neck rising" (Summers 2005, 57). On June 30, 1939, Frank joined the band for an engagement at Baltimore's Hippodrome Theater for $75 a week. Sinatra's delivery fit well with the lush orchestrations of the James band. "He was always thinking of the lyrics," asserted the bandleader. "If it was a delicate or pretty word, he would try to phrase it with a prettier, softer type of voice." James felt that "he could sing the wrong melody and it would still be pretty" (Ruhlmann 1991, 12).

LISTENING GUIDE 22

Tommy Dorsey Orchestra with Frank Sinatra

🔗 "I'LL NEVER SMILE AGAIN"

In June 1939, Canadian songwriter/pianist Ruth Lowe wrote this song, when her husband, music publicist Harold Cohen, died unexpectedly in surgery a year after their wedding. In 1936, Lowe had been recruited by Ina Ray Hutton to join her all-female band, the Melodears, and played with the group until her marriage in 1938. In the Irving Mills–managed orchestra, Lowe performed with other such notable female jazz musicians as trumpet player Frances Klein, saxophonist Jane Cullum, and guitarist Marian Gange. Lowe also composed a Frank Sinatra signature song, "Put Your Dreams Away" (1944).

On April 23, 1940, and again a month later, Sinatra sang "I'll Never Smile Again" with the Tommy Dorsey Orchestra on Victor Records for his first number-one hit, which launched his career. He chanced upon the song when Ruth Lowe gave the sheet music to a member of the Dorsey band. Sinatra received backup help from the four-person Pied Pipers, a vocal quartet that featured Jo Stafford, who later scored as a single act. In 1941, Dorsey, Sinatra, and the Pied Pipers performed this song in *Las Vegas Nights*. Fred Stucle arranged this version of the song in an ABAC pattern.

The song elicited a response from war-fearing Americans when a rumor circulated that Lowe's husband had been a British Royal Air Force pilot who had been shot down by the Germans. It captured the anguish and trepidation of a nation preparing for war.

Personnel: Fred Stulce, Johnny Mince (b. John Muenzberger), and Hymie Schertzer (alto saxophones); Sid Weiss (bass); Buddy Rich (drums); Clark Yocum (guitar); Joe Bushkin (celesta); Don Lodice and Paul Mason (tenor saxophones); and Tommy Dorsey (trombone).

0:00–0:03	A tinkling introduction with Joe Bushkin playing the piano-like celesta.
0:04–0:36	Sinatra and the Pied Pipers enter with smooth, silky vocals and Bushkin's celesta in the background to create an ethereal feel. The vocals stay very close to the melody.
0:37–0:49	Sinatra takes the lead vocals with the celesta in the background.
0:50–1:01	Sinatra keeps the lead as the Pied Pipers start to harmonize with him.
1:02–1:30	Sinatra and the Pipers sing as a group to the constant background of the celesta.
1:31–1:32	The silky, high-pitched, almost quivering trombone of Dorsey signals a change.
1:33–1:43	Sinatra retakes the lead vocals with backing from Dorsey and the sax section, which provide a velvety, achingly slow background.
1:44	The Pied Pipers reenter to back Frank as he slides across notes, much like his idol, Bing Crosby.
1:45–1:58	Frank and the Pied Pipers sing in unison to the smooth-as-silk reeds.
1:59–2:26	In an instrumental section, Dorsey's almost violin–sounding trombone offers a melodic solo against the backdrop of the saxophone section and the slow-tempo rhythm section.
2:27–2:40	Frank again takes the lead with his vocals backed by the reed section and the celesta. At the end of the section, Sinatra again glides over the notes to make a seamless transition in the lyric. His breathing technique, at least partly learned from Dorsey—who seemingly never took a breath—allowed him to combine phrases and sing a song such as "I'll Never Smile Again" at an extremely slow tempo.
2:41–2:55	Pied Pipers again enter the song with the celesta in the background.
2:56–2:59	Another instrumental break by Dorsey and the saxophones.
3:00–3:10	Frank and Pied Pipers enter to end the song.

Although armed with a new singer, the band still struggled to earn a reputation. While performing at a club on Hollywood's Sunset Strip, "the manager came up and waved his hands for us to stop," related Sinatra. "He said Harry's trumpet playing was too loud for the joint and my singing was just plain lousy, and fired Harry, me and the entire band on the spot. He said the two of us couldn't draw flies as an attraction, and I guess he was right—the room was as empty as a barn."

That December, Tommy Dorsey approached Sinatra about joining his band. The month before, Dorsey had fired Jack Leonard, who since 1937 had sung with the band on two hundred songs. Tommy offered the singer $100 a week. "When Sinatra had the Dorsey offer, I said: 'Well, go ahead,' because we were barely making enough money to even eat," James said (Tompkins 1963c, 2). Sinatra considered the Dorsey band as "number 1 in the United States" and thought Dorsey "was like a god," so he eagerly accepted the offer (Summers 2005, 62; Kelley 1986, 51).

On January 26, 1940, Sinatra officially left James and, a few days later, recorded "The Sky Fell Down" with Dorsey's band. In late May, Sinatra delivered his first hit, the ballad "I'll Never Smile Again," which reflected the somber mood of a nation headed toward war. The recording stayed in the top spot for a dozen weeks. During the next year, Frank contributed to fourteen of seventeen Dorsey Top Twenty chart entries, including the number-one hit "Dolores" (April 1941).

Sinatra's fortunes changed following the success of his hit singles. In early May 1940, Sinatra had been listed as the twenty-second-best vocalist in *Billboard's* annual College Music Poll. In the next poll, Sinatra topped the list. By the end 1941, Frank had displaced Bing Crosby at the top of the annual *Downbeat* poll for singers.

Sinatra refined his style under Tommy Dorsey to achieve an enhanced smoothness. "It was in early 1940 that I really began developing a style of my own," he told *Life* magazine. "The thing that influenced me most was the way Tommy played his trombone. He would take a musical phrase and play it all the way through seemingly without breathing, for eight, 10, maybe 16 bars. . . . It was my idea to make my voice work like a trombone or a violin—not sounding like them, but 'playing' the voice like these instruments" (Ruhlmann 1991, 14).

To achieve an apparently effortless, flowing delivery, Sinatra exercised for better breath control. He ran track and swam in public pools, "taking laps under the water and thinking song lyrics to myself as I swam, holding my breath." He soon "was able to sing six bars, and in some songs eight bars, without taking a visible breath. This gave the melody a flowing, unbroken quality and that—if anything—was what made me sound different," Sinatra explained (Ruhlmann 1991, 14).

In September 1941, an ambitious Sinatra became restless and left the Dorsey band. "I'm going to be big, real big, bigger than Crosby, bigger than anybody," he boasted. "I'll leave the rest of the singers in the dust" (Kelley 1986, 61). Sinatra alerted Tommy Dorsey that he intended to pursue a solo career. "I'm giving you a year's notice," he told Dorsey. "He looked at me and said, 'What?' He didn't believe me. He thought I was kidding. Six months later I asked him if he wanted me to look for another singer. He got the message then," related Frank (Kelley 1986, 61). The singer received $17,000 from a re-signed Dorsey in exchange for nearly half his income for the next decade. On September 10, 1942, Sinatra gave his final performance as part of the Tommy Dorsey band. By the time of his departure, he had recorded eighty-four songs with the orchestra.

Sinatra Mania

Sinatra's solo career began with a bang. On Wednesday, December 30, 1942, New York's Paramount Theater booked Benny Goodman to headline a show with singer Peggy Lee. As a late addition, Sinatra was added to the bill. After Goodman played two numbers with his band and Peggy Lee sang a few songs, Sinatra nervously strode on stage in front of Goodman's orchestra. When Sinatra came into view, "the sound that greeted me was absolutely deafening. It was a tremendous roar," Frank remembered. "I couldn't move a muscle." Goodman "turned around, looked at the audience and asked [Sinatra], 'What the hell is that?' [Frank] burst out laughing and gave out with 'For Me and My Gal'" (Shaw 1965, 19–20). "I thought the goddamn building was going to cave in," recalled Goodman. "People running down to the stage, screaming." The theater manager heard teens yelling, "F-R-A-N-K-I-E-E-E-E-!" between the singer's four songs and four encores (Summers 2005, 78).

Goodman and Sinatra performed at the Paramount for another month to wailing fans. "We used to lean out the windows of the dressing room to see the crowd of swooners, like swarms of bees down there in the street, just waiting for the sight of Frankie," related Peggy Lee (Firestone 1993, 318). After Goodman left the Paramount for another job, Sinatra remained for an additional month, usually singing nine shows a day. The two-month Sinatra engagement at the Paramount signaled the beginning of a new trend in jazz that focused on the singer.

By late the next year, teenage fans had dispelled any reservations cast by Sinatra skeptics. On Tuesday, October 10, 1943, when Frank returned to the Paramount, a few dozen girls camped in front of the box office the night before his first performance despite a 9 p.m. curfew for teens. When Frank arrived for a 6:00 a.m. rehearsal, the line of skittish girls and a few boys had grown to nearly a thousand. By seven in the morning, thousands of fans stretched for blocks and waited for the doors to open at 8:30 a.m. After the Paramount finally admitted the teens, girls

Female fans at the Paramount Theater, waiting to see Frank Sinatra, October 12, 1944. *Photograph by Edward Lynch. Library of Congress Prints and Photographs Division*

ignored the featured film and chanted "We want Frankie! We Want Frankie!" When Sinatra took the stage, they screamed relentlessly until he pleaded with them for their attention so he could begin his set.

On the next day—Columbus Day, when most elementary and high-school students had a vacation from school—mayhem broke loose around the Paramount. Before the box office opened, a line of ten thousand girls, six abreast, filled the sidewalks and blocked traffic; another twenty-five thousand wild-eyed, breathless teens milled around Times Square. The girls destroyed the ticket booth, smashed nearby shop windows, and shoved New Yorkers who were on their way to work. The Chief of Police diverted two hundred cops from the Columbus Day parade and reinforced them with 421 police reserves, twenty radio-equipped cars, seventy patrolmen, fifty traffic cops, and two emergency trucks to quell the disturbance. When the theater doors finally opened, more than 3,600 girls crammed into the Paramount, shrieking and swooning for their heartthrob. Only 250 of the diehards left after the first show, creating an even greater frenzy outside among the waiting throngs.

Unbridled hysteria erupted in other cities. Near Chicago, fanatical teens smashed the window of a train that was carrying Sinatra. Teens banded together in more than two hundred Sinatra fan clubs with colorful names including the Subjects of the Sultan of Swoon, Frankie's United Swooners, Our Swoon Prince Frankie, and Bobby Sox Swoonerettes (Kahn 1995, 44). *Variety* characterized the Sinatra phenomenon as a "Sinatrance" (Shaw 1965, 26). By the end of 1944, the mass frenzy surrounding Sinatra's image had translated into $20,000-a-week performances and an annual salary of $1.1 million.

The Teenage-Girl Market Makes Sinatra an Idol

Emerging amid a wartime labor shortage, a new teen market helped propel the youthful Sinatra to stardom. During the war, many youths found jobs in companies desperate to find adequate labor to meet the demands of a wartime boom. Between 1940 and 1944, youth in the workforce increased by two million; conversely, teens between the ages of fifteen and eighteen who attended high school decreased by 1.2 million or 24 percent. In April 1944, aided by laws that allowed minors to work, 20 percent of fourteen- and fifteen-year-old boys and 40 percent of sixteen- and seventeen-year-old boys entered the labor market. A third of girls between the ages of sixteen and eighteen found employment. "Millions of youngsters have taken full-time jobs. Others have added jobs on top of school work," read a National Go-To-School Drive pamphlet in 1944 (Modell 1989, 168–69). With their disposable income, they bought soft drinks at soda fountains, cigarettes, and 78 rpm records, which usually cost thirty-five cents.

Teenage girls constituted a specialized market. They read periodicals such as *Seventeen* magazine, founded in 1944, to learn about proper etiquette, fashion, and sexual behavior. They went to movies to see screen idols and bought cosmetics to improve their appearances. For the first time, teenage girls represented a large, identifiable consumer market.

Girls snapped up records and attended concerts by Frank Sinatra, who served as a substitute for the sixteen million GIs. According to an observer at one of the Paramount shows, "four-fifths of those present are of the feminine sex, and of these, at least fourth-fifths belong to the bobby-socks brigade, age perhaps twelve to sixteen" (Bliven 1944, 592). Sinatra realized the source of his popularity. "It was the war years, and there was great loneliness," he explained. "And I was the boy in every corner drugstore, the boy who'd gone off, drafted, to the war" (Ruhlmann 1991, 16).

The lonely female legion felt a sexual attraction to Frank. "When he looked at you, you melted and screamed and clutched your heart," recalled a fan. "The attraction was definitely sexual" (Erenberg 1975, 196). *Downbeat* suggested that the singer "knows his feminine audience and fires romance—moonlight moods—at them with deadly aim" (Shaw 1965, 23).

As an object of sexual desire for young teenage girls, Sinatra understandably drew catcalls from boys. When Sinatra escaped the draft due to a punctured ear drum, men criticized the singer. One GI believed that "Sinatra was the most hated man of World War II, much more than Hitler" because "we were in the Pacific, had seen no women at all for two years, and there were photographs of Sinatra being surrounded by all these enthusiastic girls" (Erenberg 1975, 197).

Sinatra deflected complaints about his draft status by supporting the war effort. The singer performed at war rallies, bond fundraisers, and military bases, and helped raise money for a war-loan drive by auctioning some of his clothes. Frank cut more than ninety V-discs, which were records manufactured solely for men in the military.

The liberal Sinatra appealed to African-American teens by championing racial integration. In 1946, he visited the newly opened Benjamin Franklin High School in New York City in a primarily Italian neighborhood that bussed in African Americans. "When we first started going down there it was like an invasion of black kids into an Italian neighborhood," recalled Sonny Rollins, one of the students and a future saxophone great. "This caused rioting. People would throw stuff at us as we walked down the street toward the school." To quiet the racial troubles, Frank Sinatra performed a concert at the school auditorium. "He admonished the kids for fighting, especially the Italian kids," related Rollins. He said, "Cut it out and learn how to be good neighbors" (Nisenson 2000, 24). The incident, one of several attempts by Sinatra to quell racial upheaval in schools, impressed African Americans such as Rollins who became diehard Sinatra fans.

The Recording Ban

The American Federation of Musicians (AFM) instituted a recording ban in August 1942 that also benefited Sinatra. The AFM had been established in 1896 to represent the interests of musicians. In 1922, James Petrillo—the son of a sewer foreman who grew up in the slums on the West Side of Chicago—began his ascent to power in the union, when he took over its Chicago branch. Petrillo attacked technologies such as records, radio, and jukeboxes, which increasingly displaced club musicians and pit bands. Beginning on February 1, 1937, he issued an edict that forbade any musician in his jurisdiction from cutting a record.

In mid-1940, Petrillo was elected president of the national union, and set his sights on radio networks, which mostly broadcast recorded or "canned" music instead of featuring live musicians. Considering this practice a creeping menace to working musicians, the AFM sued major radio networks several times over the issue.

In late July 1940, a court decision undermined the union strategy. In a suit instigated by bandleader Paul Whiteman, the court ruled that musicians had no rights to their recorded materials after its sale. In essence, the court awarded broadcasters the unlimited right to freely use discs on the air.

After the union lost its battle against radio, Petrillo attacked record companies. He demanded a fixed fee from record labels for each disc sold and every time a jukebox used a record. To force the record industry to bow to his demands, Petrillo announced a ban on recording new material to begin on August 1, 1942.

Rather than acquiesce to Petrillo, major record companies tried to cope with the upcoming ban by stockpiling music. *Billboard* described "the high-pressure goings-on in record studios during late June and July, when diskers had bands working 24 hours a day" ("New Disks Running Out" 1942). Despite their efforts, the companies had little new product. In 1944, Columbia manufactured only sixty-two new discs compared to 2,360 selections four years earlier.

Though unable to record material by bands, record companies released new vocal tunes and re-released older songs by singers such as Frank Sinatra, who as a group did not come under the jurisdiction of the AFM. Until late June 1943, when singers agreed to abide by the AFM ban, companies recorded, publicized, and marketed new material by vocalists.

The government tried to pressure Petrillo into submission. The Department of Justice, the Senate Interstate Commerce Committee, the War Labor Board, and even President Roosevelt, sensing adverse public opinion toward the strike, threatened the union. Despite government intervention, the strike continued ("No Law To Stop" 1944).

Having depleted its backlog of discs and unable to record new material, the recording industry finally surrendered. On September 30, 1943, Decca Records, hoping to gain commercial advantage over its rivals, settled with the AFM. A few weeks later, the newly formed Capitol Records accepted Petrillo's demands. On November 11, 1944, after the ban had been in effect for more than twenty-eight months, Victor and Columbia acquiesced to AFM terms, which generated an annual fund of $4 million for unemployed and underemployed musicians (Gould 1944, 1). Though the strike had ended, for more than two years the labels had heavily promoted singers such as Sinatra who vaulted to prominence.

Other Major Jazz Vocalists

During the war, other male and female singers joined Sinatra in the vanguard of jazz. During the late thirties, Ella Fitzgerald started her rise to fame. Fitzgerald, a preeminent vocalist of the swing era, grew up poor in New York City. In 1932, at the age of fifteen, when her mother died, she shuffled between orphanages and ended up homeless on the New York City streets. Two years later, she debuted at Harlem's Apollo Theater. Though scheduled to dance, a nervous Ella sang instead and impressed the audience at the theater's famed Amateur Night. In 1935, while singing for the Tiny Bradshaw band, she met drummer Chick Webb, who hired the eighteen-year-old singer. In 1938, in front of the Webb band, Ella hit with "A-Tiskit, A-Tasket," a song based on a nursery rhyme that Fitzgerald co-wrote. On June 16, 1939, when Webb died, Fitzgerald assumed leadership of the band as Ella and Her Famous Orchestra.

In 1942, Fitzgerald dissolved the band for a solo career. She signed with Decca Records and hired Decca producer Milt Gabler as her manager. During the recording ban, she teamed with the male vocal group, the Ink Spots, for two number-one entries, "I'm Making Believe" and "Into Each Life Some Rain Must Fall." She continued on a long and successful solo career by refining scat singing with Dizzy Gillespie's bebop big band and collaborating with promoter Norman Granz.

Helen Forrest (b. Helen Fogel), an admirer of Fitzgerald, progressed from big-band singer to vocal star. While living at home, she became interested in singing after encouragement from her piano teacher. At sixteen, she quit high school and earned a spot as "Bonnie Blue" on the CBS radio show, *Blue Velvet Hour*. Forrest next sang with bands led by Artie Shaw, Benny Goodman, and Harry James. In 1944, disgusted with the limited role of a singer in a big band, Helen embarked on a solo career and increased her salary by nearly ten times. During the recording ban, she neared the top with "Time Waits for No One." She also scored with five Top Ten hits such as "Long Ago (and Far Away)" and "I'll Buy That Dream" by teaming with ex–Tommy Dorsey/ex–Harry James vocalist Dick Haymes, who complemented his recording career with wartime films.

Amid the Sinatra craze, former Tommy Dorsey singer Jo Stafford went solo. During the recording ban, she issued eleven Top Twenty entries. Stafford appealed to a sense of loneliness among young GIs as Sinatra did with girls back home. "A lot of the kids in the war wrote me letters, talking about my haunting quality," she explained. "They said it made them homesick—and happy to be unhappy. They could identify with it. It made them lonesome for their girlfriends" (Gourse 1984, 114).

African-American pianist and vocalist Nat "King" Cole (b. Nathaniel Coles) crossed color barriers to singing stardom. During the late thirties, the Earl-Hines–inspired Cole began performing with a sextet headed by his brother, Eddie, and cut his first record. Rather than front a big band, in 1937, Nat founded "King Cole and His Swingsters" with guitarist Oscar Moore and Wesley Prince on bass and snagged spots on several radio shows, including NBC's *Swing Soiree* and *Old Gold Hour*.

Cole favored piano but gravitated toward vocals when he received wild receptions from crowds for his singing. "I started out to become a jazz pianist; in the meantime I started singing," he explained, admitting, "At first I hadn't anticipated singing at all" (Gilliland 1969; Tynan 1958).

In 1943, as Sinatra took the Paramount by storm, King Cole entered the mainstream. His trio signed with Capitol Records, which had been founded the year before. With the help of music impresario Irving Mills, the same year, the trio landed a song and an appearance in the film *Here Comes Elmer*. After topping the R&B chart in 1944, the group scored with the Top Ten "Straighten Up and Fly Right." During the next two years, the smooth vocals of Cole drifted onto the charts and culminated in the 1948 megahit, "Nature Boy."

Billy Eckstine, another African-American crooner, moved from big-band conductor to a showcased soloist and bandleader. The son of a Pittsburgh chauffeur, he first performed at a church bazaar at the age of eleven and, in 1930, won a talent contest by imitating his hero, Cab Calloway, which led to a job with a big band in Washington, DC. In 1939, the twenty-five-year-old singer joined the Earl Hines band in Chicago and gained acclaim after singing on the Hines crossover hit, "Stormy Monday Blues" (1942). "Billy was a big star," contended band mate and saxophonist Budd Johnson, who had recruited the singer to the Hines orchestra (Zwerin 1968, 41). In 1943, Eckstine quit the band and, within a year, established a unit that showcased his vocals. *Time* called him the "sepia Sinatra." In 1945, Eckstine reached the Top Ten with "A Cottage for Sale"; the next year, he climbed there again with "Prisoner of Love." By 1948, reported *Time*, "the mail was pouring in, and the bobby-sox clubs were forming" with names such as "The Girls Who Give In When Billy Gives Out" ("Mr. B. Goes to Town" June 10, 1949).

The Decline of the Big Bands

The preeminence of big dance bands declined due to economic troubles and a second recording ban. Once wartime price controls had been lifted, inflation soared. By mid-1946, the inflation rate reached double digits and, by March 1947, hit almost 20 percent. Ballooning prices for basic goods constricted discretionary spending, which had fueled the wartime jazz-dance business. "The public," contended *Newsweek* in December 1946, "has apparently decided that it has only so much money to spend on music and entertainment, and that $2.50 and $3.50 a person for dancing does not fit the family budget" ("Strike Down" 1946, 76). Drawing smaller audiences, hotel owners and theater operators eliminated big bands as attractions. "What has happened to the band business is . . . typical of the overinflated wartime boom in dispensable commodities," explained *Newsweek* (75).

A wartime entertainment tax further undermined big dance bands. In April 1944, the federal government levied a 20 percent tax on New York cabarets that allowed dancing. "That meant that if an operator had a singer or a tap dancer, or even if there were public dancing in a room, he'd have to charge that extra 20 percent on top of the usual tax," explained drummer Max Roach (Gitler 1985, 77). "People began to sit down; they were sitting down listening to music because you couldn't dance in a club," he added (Gillespie 1979, 232).

In addition to the impact of television, the AFM initiated a second recording ban that undercut a recovering music industry. In 1947, union head James Petrillo needed to find work for more than forty thousand union members who had returned from the war. When Congress voided the agreement signed after the first recording ban, he also sought to reinstate royalties promised to the AFM. Met by an intransigent record industry, Petrillo vowed to start a second ban of new recordings on January 1, 1948 ("Petrillo Bans Recordings" 1947, 1, 5). "We're never going to make records, ever," Petrillo pledged ("Last Record Made" 1948, 1).

Unwilling to negotiate, music firms faced the ban on the scheduled date. The recording industry responded by stockpiling records of preeminent acts. The major companies, noted the *New York Times* on December 1, 1947, "are working on a hectic, round-the-clock schedule" and smugly announced that they "will have enough records to keep the country in tunes for three years" (Yokley 1947).

Yet during the second recording ban, the music industry crumbled. In 1947, nearly eight hundred record companies sold 350 million records, which retailed for $250 million. In 1948, during the ban, retail sales plummeted 40 percent to $150 million. On December 14, 1948, after nearly a year, record companies and the AFM struck a bargain, which routed 1 to 2.5 cents on each record sold to the union for a special fund. During the year-long ban and amid a postwar recession, big bands faded from prominence.

During the war, big bands led by Glenn Miller, Tommy Dorsey, Artie Shaw, and Harry James produced a soothing music that helped the nation cope with a bloody conflict. For the soldiers, their music represented an idealized vision of the peace and tranquility that they had left behind to fight on the battlefields. Similarly, crooners such as Frank Sinatra provided a smooth soundtrack for a burgeoning teenage market and, during a recording ban, became more important than many of the big bands that backed them. They built upon the success of Bing Crosby to elevate the status of the jazz singer to equal the importance of instrumentalists. After the war, amid economic troubles and a recording ban, the big-band business disintegrated. "The band business looks like it is finished," moaned one booking executive. "It will never again attain the prominence and earning capacity it enjoyed" (Erenberg 1975, 213).

For Discussion and Further Study

Chapter Quiz

1. What impact did World War II have on big bands and the music industry in general? How did this change the way jazz was performed and marketed to the public?

2. Why did all-female jazz bands become popular during the war years? Did women still face sexism as performing musicians despite gaining new popularity on the road?

3. How did Glenn Miller's and the Dorsey Brothers' music appeal to wartime audiences? What were the qualities that distinguished it from earlier big-band jazz?

4. How did Artie Shaw develop a big-band style that would appeal to audiences? What kinds of changes did he have to make in his music? Do you think this might have ultimately led him to give up performing?

5. How did the new teenage market make Frank Sinatra a major star during the war years?

6. What other vocalists achieved popularity in this era? Why do you think African-American singers like Nat King Cole and Billy Eckstine might not have been able to win as large a following as Frank Sinatra and other white singers?

THE BEBOP REVOLUTION

The Rise of African-American Pride

Thelonious Monk at Minton's Playhouse, 1947. Photograph by William P. Gottlieb. William P. Gottlieb/Ira and
Leonore S. Gershwin Fund Collection, Music Division, Library of Congress

Race serves as the main theme of this chapter. During and immediately after World War II, many young African-American jazz musicians began jamming together in after-hours clubs, where they exchanged new musical ideas. They developed a complex musical style called bebop that challenged most white musicians, who found it difficult to follow the rapid-fire chord changes and rhythmic patterns, and they demanded that audiences listen rather than dance. The young musicians, confronting the white jazz establishment, reflected the growing and general frustration among African Americans who supported the war against fascism abroad but still felt the pain of racism at home. They created a new type of African-American-centered jazz, which young fanatics embraced and small independent record labels released.

In 1938, saxophonist M. Henry Minton opened a new club, the Playhouse, near his home in Harlem. Minton's Playhouse occupied one room on 118th Street and St. Nicholas Avenue. In better times, the site had been the dining room of the Hotel Cecil. The club featured a long bar in the front backed by several tables for up to 125 customers. Between the rest rooms, a small, raised stage stood against a wall. The club charged no cover but required its clientele to pay two dollars to sit at tables that were covered with white linen tablecloths topped by glass vases.

In January 1941, saxophonist Teddy Hill became manager of the Playhouse. Hill led bands for eight years, landed a radio spot on the NBC network, and performed frequently at New York's Savoy Ballroom. Despite his successes, by 1941 Hill quit the band-leading role because he was tired of dealing with unscrupulous club owners. He trusted Minton as a fellow musician and eagerly accepted the managerial position. As one of his first moves, Hill asked a former sideman, drummer Kenny "Klook" Clarke, to assemble a band. Unwittingly, he helped usher in a new era of jazz called bebop.

A one-time member of trumpeter Roy Eldridge's orchestra, Clarke developed a new style of drumming while working with the Edgar Hayes big band. "In 1937, I'd gotten tired of playing like [Basie drummer] Jo Jones," he remembered. "I took the main beat away from the bass drum and up to the top cymbal. It was lighter and tastier," he explained. "That left me free to use my bass drum, the tom-toms and snare for accents. I was trying to lay new rhythmic patterns over the regular beat. Solo lines were getting longer. Soloists needed more help from the drummer—kicks, accents, cues" (Russell 1973, 133). On the advice of another former Hill sideman, trumpeter John Birks "Dizzy" Gillespie, Clarke accepted an offer from Hill to put together Minton's house band with the assurance that he would have free rein to follow his new approach.

Over the next few months, Clarke assembled a band. He snagged twenty-year-old trumpeter/vocalist Joe Guy (b. Joseph Luke) and hired Thelonious Sphere Monk, an unknown, twenty-four-year-old New Yorker who for two years had backed a traveling evangelist. On bass, Kenny chose Nick Fenton, a former violinist with an exceptional sense of time who recently had toured with Lester Young. "I thought it was a pretty good combo," Kenny smiled, "and as we started working together it emerged that we all had much the same idea of the direction in which we wanted to take the music." The band performed from 10 p.m. until four the next morning with an off-day on Tuesday (Hennessey 1990, 39).

The Birth of Bop

A young coterie of musicians working in Harlem nightclubs such as Minton's and Monroe's Uptown House developed bebop. They wanted to push beyond the somewhat constraining format of popular big bands, which by the end of the war had become somewhat formulaic. Through complex rhythms and a new harmonic vocabulary, they expressed the growing frustration of African Americans during postwar America by creating a music that few whites could play. Bebop pioneers such as Charlie Parker, Thelonious Monk, and Dizzy Gillespie redefined jazz for a new era and placed a distinctively African-American stamp on the music.

Many Harlem-based musicians flocked to Minton's, particularly on Monday nights, when major venues like the Apollo Theater were closed. Having Mondays off, musicians from Apollo's headlining bands gathered at the Playhouse at no charge to devour free ham hocks, fried chicken, black-eyed peas, barbecued ribs, candied yams, and hot biscuits, washing the food down with whiskey at twenty-five cents a shot. The jazz men listened to and sometimes jammed with the house band despite union regulations. "As a result, all the different bands that played at the Apollo got to hear the original music, and it got around," remembered Thelonious Monk (Hentoff 1956c, 15).

When the Jay McShann band worked the Apollo, a saxophonist from the outfit, Charlie Parker, wandered into Minton's for a free meal and jammed with the quartet. "He played alto at that time like Lester Young played tenor—and we enjoyed that very much because it was a higher sound, more penetrating," contended Clarke. "Being in Kansas City, I think Charlie picked up a lot from Lester, particularly in the

Thelonious Monk, Howard McGhee, Roy Eldridge, and Teddy Hill in front of Minton's Playhouse, September 1947. *Photograph by William P. Gottlieb.*

William P. Gottlieb/Ira and Leonore S. Gershwin Fund Collection, Music Division, Library of Congress

rhythmic sense—though he went a little further musically" (Hennessey 1990, 40). "Bird was playing stuff we'd never heard before," the drummer continued. "He was into figures I thought I'd invented for drummers. He was twice as fast as Lester Young and into harmony Lester hadn't touched. Bird was running the same way as we were, but he was way out ahead of us" (Russell 1973, 138). Parker made the Minton combo a quintet, when band members pooled their money to give him a job and Clarke gave him food and a place to sleep (138).

In autumn 1941, Dizzy Gillespie began regularly appearing on the bandstand. The fiery soloist eventually replaced Joe Guy, who had played behind Gillespie in the Cab Calloway Orchestra. Dizzy "gave us four key instruments—trumpet, alto, piano and drums. That, plus a good bass, was the band of the future," explained Clarke (Russell 1973, 139).

Other musicians repeatedly attended sessions at Minton's. Kansas City tenor-sax men Lester Young and Ben Webster participated in the sessions at Minton's. Webster, who played with Bennie Moten and later with Ellington, lived next door at the Hotel Cecil and often took the stage at the club. "We used to jam just about every night when we were off," he related. "Lester, [tenor-sax player Carlos] 'Don' Byas and myself—we would meet there all the time and, like, exchange ideas." Charlie Christian, a guitarist for Benny Goodman, jammed with the fledgling group. "Most of the time he just kept his amplifier in the Playhouse so that he could play with us every chance he got," Kenny Clarke reminisced (Hennessey 1990, 41). Christian "used to talk about the music at Minton's so much Benny Goodman used to come," boasted Kenny Clarke. Goodman "was all the rage at the time, and we always got a great deal of pleasure when he came in" (Shapiro and Hentoff 1955, 340).

When the music stopped at Minton's at 4:00 in the morning, Clark Monroe hosted musicians at Monroe's Uptown House. In 1938, with help from the mob, the dapper dancer and vocalist reopened the Harlem basement club on the site previously occupied by Barron's, where stride masters had reigned fifteen years earlier. He featured a song-and-dance act during the evenings and then catered to a late-night crowd by staying open until seven in the morning. Like Minton, Monroe "had a warm feeling for musicians, and he also used to feed us," recollected Dizzy Gillespie. "He didn't pay you any money, but you could eat, and he had a band there" (Gillespie 1979, 140). During summer 1942, Monroe asked Charlie Parker, who had quit the Jay McShann band and had attended jam sessions at the club since 1938, to regularly play at the Uptown House for tips in addition to his work at Minton's.

Many musicians flocked to Monroe's Uptown House. "After hours, I'd go to the Uptown House to jam," Dizzy Gillespie recalled. "There was as much creativity going on at Monroe's Uptown House as they had at Minton's. That's where we all used to go after hours, until daylight, to play" (Gillespie 1979, 141). "Musicians from all the big bands—I would say maybe Glenn Miller's, Harry James' band . . . they would all come down after work, and they would sit in," maintained bop-oriented pianist Al Tinney, who cemented the Uptown House band with saxophonist George Treadwell, lightning-fast trumpeter Vic Coulsen, and bassist Ebenezer Paul (Gitler 1985, 81).

During the war, the cast of characters at the embryonic Harlem music clubs changed. In 1943, as the war worsened, Kenny Clarke and Teddy Hill entered the armed forces. On August 18, the army nabbed bassist Nick Fenton. On September 30, 1944, Lester Young entered the army until, a few months later, his captain discovered several barbiturate pills, marijuana cigarettes, and some alcohol in the pockets of Young's uniform, and the army court-martialed him.

Despite personnel changes, young aspiring musicians crowded into Minton's and Monroe's to hear new sounds by band members such as Parker, Gillespie, and Monk who had escaped military duty. In September 1944, eighteen-year-old trumpet player Miles Davis journeyed from St. Louis to the Juilliard School of Music in New York City after being enticed by news of jam sessions at Minton's. "That's the *real* reason I wanted to come to New York," he intimated, "to get into the jazz music scene that was happening around Minton's Playhouse in Harlem" (Davis 1989, 52). When he quit Juilliard after a year, Davis used Minton's as an informal school. "We was all trying to get our master's degrees and Ph.D.'s from Minton's University of Bebop under the tutelage of Professors Bird and Diz," he insisted (61).

At the nightclub, Davis met many young jazz artists with similar goals. "Minton's was *the* ass-kicker back in those days for aspiring musicians," he recalled. "I ran into [trumpet player] Fats Navarro again up in Minton's and we used to jam up there all the time" (Davis 1989, 53–54). J. J. Johnson, a trombone whiz from Indianapolis who toured with Navarro in the Snookum Russell territorial band, joined the inner circle. Pittsburgh bassist Ray Brown left Snookum Russell's band with a one-way ticket to New York City, when he heard about new music brewing at the Playhouse. In 1942, on the advice of Dizzy Gillespie, trumpeter Howard McGhee visited Minton's, when he traveled through New York City with the Andy Kirk Orchestra (Gitler 1985, 86). Brooklyn-raised teenage drummer Max Roach became a regular fixture at the Harlem nightspot and met like-minded musicians who "became friends and started working together, playing together, jamming together" (76).

Many young novices gravitated toward Charlie Parker. For several years, Miles Davis trailed Parker, roomed with him, and eventually played with Bird on several record dates. "Bird himself was almost a god," Davis related. "People followed him around everywhere. He had an entourage" (Davis 1989, 68). "Charlie Parker was a dream. He was such a leader for us," enthused Walter Theodore "Sonny" Rollins. "We saw him as a Jesus Christ figure who got crucified for standing up for freedom" (Stern 1988, 93).

Some young bopsters stood in such awe of Charlie Parker that they switched from alto to tenor saxophone. "Rather than trying to compete with Charlie Parker," Philadelphia-native Jimmy "Little Bird" Heath "decided to change my instrument to tenor, and I could still play like Charlie Parker, but he wouldn't know it!" (Feather 1975, 18). "Sonny Rollins, Sonny Stitt, myself, Jimmy Heath and John Coltrane . . . we all started playing alto, but Charlie Parker was such a monster that we all gave up and switched to tenor," echoed New Jersey–bred Hank Mobley (Litweiler 1973, 28).

Though many emerging jazz men idolized Parker, they looked to Dizzy Gillespie for practical help and inspiration. "Bird might have been the spirit of the bebop movement, but Dizzy was its 'head and hands,' the one who kept it all together," explained Miles Davis. "He looked out for the younger players, got us jobs and shit, talked to us [about music]" (Davis 1989, 64). "Dizzy was really the catalyst of that period," summarized Max Roach. "Dizzy was much more outgoing, and he organized bringing people forward" (Gitler 1985, 137).

Other jazz aspirants shadowed Thelonious Monk, the reclusive piano genius at Minton's. Lightning-fast pianist Earl "Bud" Powell, a native New Yorker and nineteen years old in 1943, when he first performed at Minton's, found a champion in Monk. At first, asserted Monk, "no one wanted to listen to him." At his insistence, noted Monk, "the audience was forced to listen to Bud" (Kelley 2009, 81). Former Fletcher Henderson drummer Art Blakey many times tagged along with Powell for tutoring from Monk. "He'd take me and Bud Powell around, and

Dizzy Gillespie clowning at the Downbeat Club, 1946. *Photograph by William P. Gottlieb. William P. Gottlieb/Ira and Leonore S. Gershwin Fund Collection, Music Division, Library of Congress*

he'd stop the band and let Bud play, and let me play," the Pittsburgh native recalled. "He'd let you experiment all you wanted, and that was good. I learned a lot with him. Monk is largely responsible for me," he concluded (Tompkins 1963, 2; Enstice and Rubin 1992, 30).

Several teenagers who lived in the Sugar Hill section of Harlem and affectionately dubbed themselves the "Sugar Hill Gang" took informal lessons from Monk. The group consisted of sax player Sonny Rollins, drummer Art Taylor, saxophonist Jackie McLean, pianist Kenny Drew, and later Brooklyn-based pianist Randy Weston. "Every day after school I would go to Thelonious Monk's place and practice with the band," recalled Rollins. "All the guys would look at [the music] and say 'Monk, we can't play this stuff,'" he chuckled, "and then it would end up that everybody would be playing it by the end of the rehearsal" (Kelley 2009, 118–19).

LISTENING GUIDE 23

Thelonious Monk

"BLUE MONK"

Monk represents a central figure in jazz. Though usually lumped into the bop style because he helped frame bebop at Minton's, Monk spanned nearly the entire scope of jazz. He played twelve-bar blues, which he had learned as a youth in a traveling medicine show. He often quoted stride-piano masters in his solos and certainly exemplified the rhythmic complexity and harmonic progressions of bop. With his sporadic dissonance and percussive, double-key hits on the piano, Monk presaged the coming avant-garde. He also unexpectedly swooped down octaves on the piano, frequently leaving his sidemen feeling that they had just been pushed down an empty elevator shaft.

Though helping originate the bop movement, Monk differed in several significant ways from many boppers. Monk chose not to play at lightning speed but rather played deliberately. He never had standard big-band experience and seldom backed luminaries such as Parker and Gillespie on record. Unlike many bopsters who refashioned old standards in new ways, Monk

prolifically composed more than seventy songs, some of which became haunting standards such as "Round [about] Midnight." He wrote seemingly simple melodies and solo spots that many boppers and hard boppers found difficult. In one session with John Coltrane, Monk asked the saxophonist to play a passage. Bewildered, Coltrane asked Monk if the piece could be played on a saxophone. Monk responded that "the music's in the horn, play it."

On September 22, 1954, Monk first recorded "Blue Monk" for Prestige Records. For the record date, he assembled bassist Percy Heath and drummer Art Blakey. Written in the studio after Prestige owner Bob Weinstock complained that Monk seldom performed the blues, Monk developed this original composition by using part of the melody from Charlie Shavers's "Why Begin Again (Pastel Blue)" (1939), which Artie Shaw and His Orchestra performed. He composed the song as a twelve-bar blues in medium tempo and recorded it many times during his career.

0:00–0:03	Monk states the theme as a simple melody of an introductory note and a four-note motif, which he repeats in an ascending fashion.
0:04–0:06	In a variant of a twelve-bar blues, Monk responds to the first two four-note motifs with eleven notes that ping-pong back and forth until descending into a flatted blue note.
0:07–0:12	Monk repeats the first notes in a slightly higher pitch. He pauses slightly between 0:08 and 0:09 to change the rhythm and consciously hits two keys simultaneously at 0:10, which he will continue to do throughout the song.
0:13–0:19	Monk repeats a note five times, then lowers the pitch with the next note, and finally restates the eight-note theme twice.
0:20–0:26	Monk states a variant of the theme with a slightly different rhythm.
0:27–0:33	Monk restates the version of the theme above at a higher octave with rhythmic embellishments. At 0:28, he hits two keys to glide between notes and pauses slightly to shift the rhythm. At 0:31, he changes the rhythm by hitting the same note five times in stride fashion, and ends the passage in a major chord.
0:34–0:40	Monk transitions to the resolution of the twelve-bar blues and finishes the twelve-bar section.
0:41–0:47	The pianist plays a version of the theme in a highly syncopated, blue-note fashion.
0:48–0:54	Monk offers a five-note repetitious pattern three times before ending the section with two resolving notes.

0:55–0:59	Monk ends the section with a passage that answers the five-note motif in a call-and-response manner.
1:00–1:08	Monk repeats a six-note motif three times, increasing the pitch in the second iteration.
1:09–1:14	The pianist repeats the six-note motif above twice with a slight change in rhythm between them and ends with a similar four-note passage.
1:15–1:21	Monk answers the previous measures with a resolution to the theme.
1:22–1:28	Monk delivers a seven-note passage twice, separated by two notes.
1:29–1:41	Monk answers with another passage, which ends with a variant of the seven-note sequence above. Note the hitting of two keys simultaneously at 1:34.
1:42–1:48	Monk offers a highly syncopated passage, which vaguely resembles the previous passage at the end.
1:49–2:02	Monk plays a five-note passage separated by empty space.
2:03–2:09	Monk again states a variation of the theme.
2:10–2:16	In the second part of the twelve-bar measure, Monk moves back and forth between notes until repeatedly hitting a note.
2:17–2:22	Monk resolves the theme with a passage that leaps and falls, a characteristic of Monk's playing.
2:23–2:29	Monk begins with a flurry of notes before restating the theme.
2:30–2:43	Monk completes the section with a highly syncopated, staccato set of phrases, which change the rhythm.
2:44–2:57	Monk restates the theme twice with a highly improvised version.
2:58–3:05	The pianist completes the section with a blue-note filled section.
3:06–3:19	Monk moves from the previous section almost effortlessly to another improvisation on the main theme, in which he states the theme twice.
3:20–3:25	Monk completes the section with a rhythmically diverse passage.
3:26–3:40	Monk improvises on the theme twice, first with a rapid-fire series of notes (some repeated) and followed by a rhythmically varied passage at a lower pitch.
3:39–3:46	He completes the section with a quote from his song "Misterioso."
3:47–4:07	Monk states the skeleton of the theme by hammering on several notes repeatedly, then abruptly not playing, and repeating the syncopated passage at different pitches and rhythms with abrupt pauses in between them.
4:08–4:12	Monk plays the first part of another section in an angular, nearly dissonant, and heavily flatted manner.
4:13–4:19	Monk repeats a variant of the first part above.
4:20–4:27	Monk resolves the twelve bars with an innovative passage, which seems closer to the main theme by hitting on a note four times before selecting descending notes.

4:28–4:44	Monk plays a six-note sequence four times, which vaguely resembles the main theme.
4:45–4:47	Monk resolves the section by playing a note six times.
4:48–5:01	Monk delivers a four-note sequence four times, at a different pitch the third time, and always in different rhythms in a highly syncopated fashion. He ends on a minor note.
5:02–5:07	Monk completes the section with an improvisation on the main theme.
5:08–5:27	The pianist plays an entire three-part section very sparsely with only a few notes as the rhythm section keeps the beat.
5:28–5:48	Percy Heath takes a bass solo and stays along the major theme.
5:49–6:08	Heath continues his solo in a more improvisational manner.
6:09–6:10	Monk reenters as a bridge between the bass and drum solos.
6:11–7:06	Blakey plays a rhythmically complex, inventive solo loosely around the main theme.
7:07–7:34	Monk reenters to restate the theme in a straightforward manner similar to the introduction. He fades out by repeating a two-note figure embedded at the end of the theme four times.

Young, Gifted, and African American

The musicians who jammed at Minton's and Monroe's represented a youth movement in jazz. "Most of the musicians who played there were young," asserted a then twenty-seven-year-old Kenny Clarke. "I was one of the oldest and I was still under thirty" (Hennessey 1990, 47). In 1941, when Minton's and Monroe's started to percolate, Thelonious Monk, Dizzy Gillespie, proto-bop trumpeter Freddie Webster, and pianist Tadd Dameron were twenty-four; Nick Fenton was twenty-two; George Treadwell was twenty-one; Al Tinney had just turned twenty; and J. J. Johnson, Max Roach, and Fats Navarro were still teenagers. In its first full article about the new scene in Harlem, the *New York Times* focused on the "young men—and they are all young—who make this music" (Harman 1948).

The house band at Minton's presented a demanding style by playing at breakneck speed and introducing complex rhythms and harmonies. Kenny Clarke laid the foundation with a steady 4/4 beat, punctuated by unexpected "bombs" from the bass drum. "He'd play 4/4 very softly, but the breaks, and the accents on the bass drum you could hear," explained Dizzy. "We called them, dropping bombs" (Gillespie 1979, 137). Thelonious Monk effectively employed unique harmonies and half-steps. He introduced new chord substitutions and pushed other band members to change. "Monk's using accents and things made me play accents more myself, on the bass drum," declared Clarke (Hennessey 1990, 46). For his part, Gillespie furnished interesting rhythmic and harmonic elements to the music. "My own contributions to the new style of music at this point

Thelonious Monk,
American Composer

Charlie Parker in action, New York City, 1947. *Photograph by William P. Gottlieb. William P. Gottlieb/Ira and Leonore S. Gershwin Fund Collection, Music Division, Library of Congress*

were rhythm—Afro-American and Latin—together with harmony. I built most of the harmonic structure" (Gillespie 1979, 138).

Charlie Parker interjected unique chord changes at a blazing pace. "I'd been getting bored with the stereotyped changes that were being used all the time, and I kept thinking there's bound to be something else," explained Parker. "I was working over 'Cherokee,' and, as I did, I found that by using the higher intervals of a chord as a melody line and backing them with appropriately related changes, I could play the thing I'd been hearing" (Shapiro and Hentoff 1955, 354). Like his nickname, "Bird," Parker soared above the accompaniment with new chord changes in a flurry of sixteenth notes that Dizzy matched. It sounded like "Dizzy was playing a million notes in one bar," marveled pianist Mary Lou Williams, one of the few women who attended the jams at Minton's (Gillespie 1979, 150).

Just as Louis Armstrong had done with eccentric dancers Brown and McGraw, the modernists perfected their approach through interplay with dancers such as Baby Laurence (b. Laurence Jackson). "Rhythmically, the boppers were influenced by tap dancer Baby Laurence," maintained pianist Howard Anderson who worked with Gillespie and many of the young musicians. "He used to do a very high-speed syncopated type dancing. Charlie Parker and others used to listen to Laurence and play many of the figures that he would tap" (Royful 1989, 16). Gillespie, acknowledging the importance of dance to the new music, took pride in being a member of the exclusive 400 Club of athletic Lindy Hop dancers at the Savoy Ballroom, where he would "play one set with Teddy Hill's band, and dance the next set with the Savoy Sultans" (Tomkins 1973c, 2).

The band at Monroe's Uptown House generated a similarly difficult, rapid-fire music. Al Tinney blazed at the piano. Charlie Parker rose above the band with innovative chord changes. Trumpeter Vic Coulson, who had played with Parker in the McShann orchestra, delivered rapid-fire solos with intricate time changes, which Thelonious Monk contended "had a lot to do with our way of phrasing" (Alkyer and Enright 2000, 26). Some patrons asked Tinney, "'What the heck are these guys playing?' because it was different" (Gitler 1985, 81).

Gil Fuller, who arranged some tunes for Gillespie, outlined the technical aspects of the music in an essay that he handed to customers as they entered Minton's. "The conventional accents falling on the first and third beat of common time in the old two-beat era has now been superseded by accents falling on the second and fourth beats as well as the 'and' beats of a measure," he wrote. "A further development of the rhythmic structure appears by the super-imposition of various meters upon the four-quarter or common time, known as polyrhythms. These accents usually stimulate the listener because they have two-, three- and four-voice contrapuntal lines." Harmonically, he continued, "the dominant, tonic, and other diatonic chords in most cases are altered by adding the sixth, ninth, eleventh and thirteenth. These notes may be chromatically raised or lowered depending upon the taste of the individual. Diminished and whole-tone chords are almost extinct" (Myers 2013, 31–32).

As musicians swarmed to the Harlem nightspots, the young lions constructed progressively more difficult music to establish their dominance. "One night, after weeks of trying, Dizzy cut [outplayed] Roy Eldridge" who had been Dizzy's hero, related Kenny Clarke. "We closed ranks after that. To make things tough for outsiders, we invented difficult riffs" (Russell 1973, 139).

Kenny Clarke singled out the normally reserved Thelonious Monk for his disdain of musicians who failed to grasp new concepts. "We had musicians from all over New York wanting to get in on the act and eighty percent of them just couldn't play our music. We sure didn't want to sit and sweat and back up somebody who wasn't doing anything to inspire us," complained Clarke. To discourage the uninitiated, "Monk would play twenty chords and completely lose them. Sometimes he would say to them, 'Man, get off the stand—you're not playing right.' So the guy would say, 'But I thought we were playing the blues' and Monk would scowl and say, 'that's not the way we play the blues here; we changed all that'" (Hennessey 1990, 43–44).

The band at Minton's embarked on a mission to take music to a more advanced level. Clarke asserted that "a great change had to be brought about. Jazz had undoubtedly reached a stagnation point and it needed to move on to something more valuable and worthwhile—something comprehensive, but technically complicated—to raise the standards of musicianship" (Tomkins 1965e). For Thelonious Monk, modern music represented "a higher stage" of development (Tompkins 1965e, 3).

Almost exclusively, African Americans shaped the complex, difficult music in the Harlem clubs. All the leaders at Minton's and Monroe's and nearly every one of their disciples were African-American. Nineteen-year-old trumpeter Johnny Carisi, who later joined the Glenn Miller Army Air Force outfit, "was the only white boy up in Harlem playing at Minton's," contended Gillespie (1979, 139). Though infrequently allowing such whites as Benny Goodman to jam with them, the African-American groundbreakers conceived and constantly honed the new approach to jazz.

Looking for a snappy label to slap on the music that emanated from young African Americans in Harlem, the press called the new sound bebop after the scat singing of Dizzy Gillespie. The originators never endorsed the bebop tag. "I don't like to think of my music as bebop—but as modern music," complained Thelonious Monk ("Creator of Be Bop" 1948). "The music wasn't called bebop at Minton's," recalled Kenny Clarke. "We had no name for the music. We called ourselves modern. The bop label started during the war," the drummer insisted (Shapiro and Hentoff 1955, 350; Hennessey 1990, 26).

African Americans and World War II: The Quest for Victory Abroad and at Home

Wartime discrimination against African Americans, prevalent in the military, provoked bitterness and a resolve to action among the young modernists and helped to shape bebop. The armed forces were segregated into African-American and white units, with white officers many times commanding African-American companies. The War Department considered African Americans to be substandard troops who could not be trusted to perform well in action. Showing remarkable prejudice, one army psychiatrist commented that "the colored men offered me the greatest difficulty in diagnosis. Poor cultural, occupational and educational backgrounds often made it difficult to decide whether they were defective, preschizoid, or just colored" (Kelley 2009, 82). Rather than sending them into combat, the armed forces often relegated African-American recruits to service functions, including bands.

Initially, only the Army allowed segregated African-American units to participate fully in the war effort. In 1941, the Army Air Corps established the first all-African-American air group, the Ninety-ninth Pursuit Squadron, which was housed at Tuskegee University. On April 2, 1943, fifteen months after the United States entered the conflict, the War Department commissioned the unit to North Africa as the first African-American fighting troops. It ordered the group to prepare for the Allied invasion of Sicily scheduled for July. After the battle, command reports alleged that the unit performed poorly under battle conditions. Despite the bravery of the airmen, the account characterized the squad as cohesive "until jumped by enemy aircraft, when the squadron seemed to disintegrate" (Buchanan 1977, 92). Officials only commended the now legendary "Tuskegee Airmen" after the squad flew more than eight hundred sorties during the battle for Sicily.

Other branches of the military discriminated against African-American fighting troops. The War Department refused to accept African-American nurses except in "hospitals or wards exclusively devoted to the treatment of Negro soldiers." The Navy only authorized African Americans to participate as mess men until February 1943, when it permitted African Americans to fight in segregated units. The military declared that injured African-American soldiers could only receive blood from African-American donors due to a fear that blood from African Americans and whites differed biologically.

The difficult wartime experience of Jimmy Woode, who became a noted bass player with Charlie Parker, Miles Davis, and eventually Duke Ellington, exemplified the prejudicial treatment of African Americans. In 1945, after studying bass at Boston University, he volunteered for the Navy and landed in the Radar School at Point Lomar, California. After finishing in the top quarter of the class, Woode received a commission to teach at a base in Northern California and reported for duty. "The Commandant looked at my papers and said, 'very interesting Mr. Woode. But no nigger will ever teach on my base,'" Woode recalled. "As a result, I was relegated to making muster [i.e., appearing for roll call] with my class at 8 o'clock in the morning." He had the remainder of the day off while a "white of lesser rank taught my class" (Matthews 1997, 14–15).

African Americans readily understood the irony of a country that was battling fascism abroad but discriminated against African Americans at home. "The paradox of the American people fighting racist tyranny abroad while the majority sanction the doctrine of white supremacy and racial discrimination at home has seared the souls of African-American folk," pointed out a member of the Common Council for American Unity in late 1943 (Swan 1971–1972, 78–79).

A bitterness and rage erupted among many African Americans amid the reality of racial discrimination. During spring 1942, the Office of War Information conducted a survey of African Americans in Harlem to gauge their views about the war effort. It concluded that "resentment at Negro discrimination is fairly widespread throughout the Negro population." When asked if "you would be better off if America or the Axis won the war," a majority responded that they would have a better life under Japanese rule. By May 1943, Saville Davis, an African-American correspondent for the *Christian Science Monitor*, observed a "revolution in our social life . . . coming to the fore" (Finkle 1973, 697).

Angry African Americans banded together in organizations that sought to end discriminatory practices. During the war, membership in the NAACP increased by nearly ten times. In March 1942, James Farmer and forty-nine other African Americans founded the Congress for Racial Equality (CORE), which vowed to apply the nonviolent principles of Indian leader Mahatma Gandhi to the segregation problem in the United States.

Indignant over discrimination, many African Americans tried to avoid the draft. In 1943, trumpeter Buck Clayton was touring with the Count Basie band, when he received a draft notice. Trying to escape military service, he asked some African-American friends about the best ways to dodge induction. "Some would tell me, when I reported to the draft board or induction center, to eat soap," he recalled. "I also was told to break open a Benzedrine nasal spray and put the chemical used to make it in a bottle of Coca-Cola and drink it. . . . Then I was told to act gay and they wouldn't want me" (Clayton 1986, 115).

Some African Americans never reported to draft boards. By late 1943, African Americans composed 35 percent of nonreporting draftees but only 10 percent of the population, and more than two thousand African Americans were imprisoned for violating the Selective Service Act. Reflecting a general feeling among African Americans who refused to comply with the draft, one draftee said he resisted induction due to "the various crimes committed against my Race in the name of democracy" (Finkle 1973, 709).

Acutely aware of the general anger among African Americans, African-American leaders hoped to leverage the war effort to end segregation. They formulated a plan to simultaneously help the Allies and wipe out discrimination by applying World War II rhetoric about freedom to the home front. In January 1942, the African-American newspaper, the *Pittsburgh Courier*, first articulated the strategy, when it described the Double Victory campaign. Let "colored Americans adopt the double VV for a double victory," it asserted. "The first V for victory [will come] over our enemies from without, the second V for victory [will defeat] our enemies from within. Our two wars are inextricably intertwined," the paper concluded (Finkle 1973, 705). In early 1942, the *Crisis*, the official periodical of the NAACP, proposed a "new world which not only shall not contain a Hitler, but no Hitlerism. And to thirteen millions of American Negroes that means a fight for a world in which lynching, brutality, terror, humiliation and degradation through segregation and discrimination, shall have no place—either here or there" (Buchanan 1977, 113). By mid-1944, twenty-five African-American organizations had demanded a "Negro Bill of Rights."

Riots in Detroit and New York City

Some angry and bitter African Americans in Detroit and New York City, not content with the Double Victory strategy, took to the streets to voice their discontent. More than one hundred fifty thousand African Americans had recently streamed into Detroit from the South and many landed jobs in defense factories. "The war inevitably improved the financial lot of the Negro," observed sociologists Alfred Lee and Norman Humphrey in 1943. "His labor became an essential part of the manpower pool, and he is being rewarded more adequately than ever before in his experience" (Lee and Humphrey 1943, 9–10).

Because of their improved standing, African Americans confronted heightened racial bigotry from jealous whites. The "sudden gain in status, which violates one of the underlying prejudices of millions of Americans, evokes a powerful reaction" of intolerance, Lee and Humphrey reported. In the Detroit area, African Americans confronted the venom of such white racist firebrands as Father Charles E. Coughlin of the Christian Front; Frank Norris, "the hell-shouting Negro-hating preacher"; and Gerald L. K. Smith (Swan 1971–1972, 80).

In Detroit, growing racial tension first surfaced over dismal housing options for African Americans, who poured into the city in record numbers. According to one observer, the housing for African Americans "was indescribably overcrowded, congested and unyielding in its boundaries" (Guzman 1947, 237). On February 27, 1942, after the Detroit Housing Commission opened the Sojourner Truth public housing complex for African Americans in a primarily white neighborhood, whites burned a cross near the project, and two hundred protesters armed with clubs and baseball bats demanded that African Americans be banned from the area. In April, the mayor mobilized more than a thousand city and state police officers and sixteen hundred National Guardsmen to protect the families who relocated to the housing project. "We are here now and let the bad luck happen," vowed thirty-five-year-old African-American defense worker Walter Jackson, who rented one of the apartments with his wife and children. "I have only got one time to die and I'd just as soon die here" (Guzman 1947, 242).

Two months later, on Sunday evening, June 20, 1943, a riot started on the bridge to the Belle Isle Recreational Park. A fistfight occurred when an African American reputedly insulted a white sailor's girlfriend. The confrontation escalated

White racist sign at the Sojourner Truth Housing Project in Detroit, February 1942. *Photograph by Arthur S. Siegel. Farm Security Administration/Office of War Information Black-and-white Negatives, Library of Congress Prints and Photographs Division*

among the hundred thousand people in the park and, fueled by rumors, spread to the city, where white and African-American gangs prowled the streets. Angry youths overturned cars and burned them, looted buildings, and randomly shot passersby. The conflict overwhelmed authorities who pleaded with President Roosevelt to intervene. On June 22, after government troops appeared on the streets in armored vehicles and quelled the mayhem, 34 people lay dead, 461 suffered injuries, and 1,883 rioters, mostly African American, had been arrested. More than two million dollars in property, representing four hundred businesses, smoldered in ruins.

A few weeks later, residents in Harlem turned violent. During the war, Harlemites faced "poor housing, residential segregation, employment discrimination and poor facilities for common living," noted an eyewitness (Guzman 1947, 242). "Still barred from many defense industries in the area because of color, with dark memories of the depression years when seventy percent of Harlem was on relief, hemmed in a ghetto where they are forced to pay disproportionately high rents for rat and vermin-infested apartments," explained NAACP head Walter White, African Americans in Harlem reached a boiling point (White 1943, 221).

On August 1, 1943, a riot exploded. The disturbance started when white police officer James Collins confronted an African-American woman who complained about abusive treatment at the disreputable Hotel Braddock, formerly a hangout for jazz musicians. African-American military-police officer Robert Bandy witnessed the harassment in the hotel lobby, intervened, and stopped Collins when he tried to club the woman. During the ensuing melee, the irate officer shot the soldier, who in turn wounded the policeman.

Violence escalated when rumors spread that a policeman had shot and killed an African-American soldier. By 9:00 in the evening, more than three thousand people were congregated at the hospital, where the two were sent for treatment of their injuries. Small gangs of the larger crowd formed, roamed through Harlem, and broke windows. "Food stores were entered and all useful food—especially war-scarce sugar, meats and coffee—taken," read one report. "Liquor stores were completely 'cleaned out.'" Rioters especially targeted white-owned shops (Guzman 1947, 243).

Mayor Fiorello LaGuardia sent police officers to the site of the turmoil and personally established headquarters in a Harlem police station. The mayor toured the neighborhood in a car outfitted with a loudspeaker to reassure Harlemites that Bandy had been injured, not killed. LaGuardia allied himself with two respected African-American leaders, Max Yergan of the National Negro Congress and Ferdinand Smith, vice president of the National Maritime Union. In two days, after five million dollars' worth of damage had been done, the Mayor pacified the rioters, five of whom had been killed, more than five jailed, and nearly six hundred treated for injuries. Racial violence had ripped apart Harlem, the home of bebop.

Bop and the African-American Experience

Bop musicians in Harlem reflected the wartime ferment over racial bigotry and attempted to establish a sense of racial pride. Like African-American jazz men before them, young modernists encountered racial prejudice. In 1942, when Dizzy Gillespie worked in an otherwise all-white Charlie Barnet band, he performed at the Circle Theater in Indianapolis, where "colored people weren't even allowed to come in." One night, as he approached the theater and tried to enter, Dizzy met a security officer who stopped him and asked him where he was going. "To the band room," responded the trumpeter. Incredulous, the adamant guard only allowed Dizzy access after a fellow orchestra member confirmed Gillespie's identity (Gillespie 1979, 157).

The same year, Gillespie felt the blind rage of segregationists in Pine Bluff, Arkansas. After a show, thinking that everyone had exited the club, Dizzy went to the "white-only" restroom. "As I was coming out," he related, "this bottle was coming at my head. . . . The guy caught me in the back of the head," he continued. "I reached on the table and picked up one of those big bottles, a magnum bottle. I turned around and was just getting ready to hit this guy when about five guys grabbed me. And about this time, the blood, oh, the blood was coming from my head." Band mate Charlie Parker rushed Gillespie to the hospital, where he received nine stitches for the wound (Gillespie 1979, 177).

Parker clearly understood the barriers of bigotry. One night, he performed at a club to great acclaim. During intermission, the saxophonist went around the corner to a bar. "The paradox of his life was brought into focus when the bartender asked him what he wanted and addressed him as a 'nigger,'" related Irving "Duke" Jordan, who played regularly with Parker. He "was bugged at the fact that, being a Negro, he could go just so far and no farther" (Reisner 1962, 126).

Coming of age amid the wartime rhetoric of global freedom, young boppers became radicalized by discriminatory experiences. "Bird felt deeply about the African-American-white split," remembered pianist Hampton Hawes, who during the forties became a devotee of Parker. Charlie was "the first musician I met who understood what was happening to his people," Hawes insisted. "He talked to us about things I wasn't to read until years later in books by Malcolm X and [Black Panther Eldridge] Cleaver" (Russell 1973, 324).

Dizzy Gillespie wanted to address the issue of racial intolerance. Despite his happy-go-lucky exterior, Gillespie "refused to accept racism, poverty or economic exploitation. If America wouldn't honor its Constitution and respect us as men, we couldn't give a shit about the American way," he argued (Gillespie 1979, 287).

Angry over narrow-minded prejudice, leading young modernists refused to serve in the military. Charlie Parker escaped wartime service by reportedly protesting segregated practices in the armed forces at his draft board hearing. According to family lore, Thelonious Monk was classified as 4-F or unfit for service after railing against slavery and racism to the local draft board. In September 1943, when appearing before his board, Dizzy Gillespie met an army psychiatrist who asked about his views on fighting. "'In this stage of my life here in the United States, whose foot has been in my ass?'" the trumpeter countered. "'The white man's foot has been in my asshole, buried up to his knee in my asshole.' I said, 'Now, you're speaking of the enemy'" (Gillespie 1979, 119–20).

Other modernists responded to racial bigotry by converting to Islam, a religion that forbade racial discrimination, and shedding names that slave owners had given their ancestors. In 1942, drummer Art Blakey adopted the Muslim faith and changed his name to Abdullah Ibn Buhania after he endured a severe beating in Albany, Georgia, for not addressing a police officer as "sir." "After that experience," he related, "I started searching for a philosophy, a better way of life" (Boyer 1948, 31).

Others in the Blakey band and the extended jazz community soon followed Blakey's example. Pianist Walter Bishop Jr., a Blakey band member, followed his leader into Islam and became Ibrahim Ibn Ismail. Blakey trumpeter McKinley "Kenny" Dorham, who also played with Charlie Parker and Max Roach, assumed the name of Abdul Hamid. Others followed, including Kenny Clarke (taking the name Liaquat Ali Salaam), Blakey sax man Edmund Gregory (Sahib Shihab), and pianist Forrest Argonne Thornton (Sadik Hakim). In 1948, reed player Bill Evans became Yusef Lateef and read the Koran daily as well as consistently incorporating the prayer and dietary dictates of the religion into his life. The converts "are extremely serious about their new faith," contended the *New Yorker* in 1948. "They read translations of the Koran, study Arabic, which some of them can even write, and proselyte unceasingly" (Boyer 1948, 31).

Though not following fellow boppers who turned to Islam, Dizzy Gillespie seriously considered switching religions. In 1948, he told *Life* magazine that "on my trips through the South, the members of my band were denied the right of worshipping in churches of their own faith because colored folks couldn't pray with white folks down there." When asked if he intended to become a Muslim, the trumpeter proclaimed, "Don't say I'm forsaking Christianity because Christianity is forsaking me—or better, people who claim to be Christian just ain't. In Islam," he concluded, "there is no color line. Everybody is treated like equals" (Gillespie 1979, 293).

Young boppers who converted to Islam were no longer considered "colored" by many whites. "If you join the Muslim faith, you ain't colored no more," some recent converts told Gillespie. "You get a new name and don't have to be a nigger no more." Gillespie remembered that trumpeter Idrees Sulieman (b. Leonard Graham) "could go into these white restaurants and bring out the sandwiches to the other guys because he wasn't colored—and he looked like the inside of the chimney." Even police identification papers listed Muslim musicians as "white." Kenny Clarke proudly showed Dizzy his police card emblazoned with a large "W" rather than a "C" for "colored," proclaiming, "See, nigger, I ain't no spook; I'm white" (Gillespie 1979, 291).

While they wished to escape racial prejudice, bop musicians drew deeply on their African-American musical roots, including the blues. "The modern jazz musicians always remained very close to the blues," maintained Dizzy (Gillespie 1979, 294). Charlie Parker, reported trumpeter Howard McGhee, "could make more tunes out of the blues than any musician who ever lived" (Russell 1973, 196). Bird "had that blues feeling. He never lost that. I don't care how fast, how slow, or whether it was a ballad, a polka, a tango, anything he played, he retained it," insisted saxophonist Lou Donaldson (Tompkins 1981). Thelonious Monk, apprenticing with an evangelist, approached the blues through the African-American church. During the forties, when Miles Davis listened to Monk, "it was like watching and listening to sanctified church music" (Davis 1989, 79).

To guard and extol an African-American identity, modernists developed a complex blues that they hoped whites could not replicate and appropriate. Thelonious Monk wanted to "create something that they [whites] can't steal because they can't play it" (Shapiro and Hentoff 1955, 340–1). Dizzy Gillespie believed that the new music flowed directly from an African-American culture. When bandleader Jimmy Dorsey heard Dizzy, he exclaimed "Boy! That shit you're all playing. I sure would like to hire you for my band. But you're so dark." Dizzy retorted, "Well, if I wasn't like this, I wouldn't be able to play like this. Do you know anybody else who plays like this, [who is] your color," he lectured Dorsey (Gillespie 1979, 210).

Modern music revealed the awakened wartime and postwar African-American consciousness. "I think it was the start of the revolution, the civil rights movement . . . because that's what the music is talking about," observed sax man Dexter Gordon. "This is all the young generation, a new generation at the time. And they're not satisfied with the shit that's going down," he concluded. "It was a time of change, and the music was reflecting this" (Gitler 1985, 311). "Bebop symbolized a rebellion against the rigidities of the old order, an outcry for change in almost every field, especially in music," echoed Dizzy Gillespie. "The music proclaimed our identity" (Gillespie 1979, 201, 291). Between the late thirties, when Joe Louis outboxed German Max Schmeling, and 1947, when infielder Jackie Robinson broke the color barrier in major league baseball, young boppers served as an example of a newfound African-American determination to erase racial inequality.

Big-Band Bop

The bop creators initially plied their trade working in swing bands. Kenny Clarke had stints with the Edgar Hayes and Teddy Hill orchestras. Before 1943, Dizzy Gillespie worked in the bands of Teddy Hill, Cab Calloway, and Charlie Barnet. Charlie Parker started his career with territory bands led by Harlan Leonard and Buster Smith, one of his idols. During summer 1937, Bird ceaselessly practiced in the Ozarks with Kansas City mainstay George E. Lee. He learned chord progressions in the orchestra of the classically trained Tommy Douglas before joining the Jay McShann group. Of the bop pioneers, only Thelonious Monk never had experience in a big band before developing his style.

While playing in these bands, the boppers were exposed to the many popular songs that made up a large part of the bands' repertoires. Knowing the chord progressions of these tunes, they used them as the basis for their own new music. They transformed the Gershwin standard "I Got Rhythm" into "A Dizzy Atmosphere," "Red Cross," and the "Fifty-second Street Theme." The young boppers converted the Paul Whiteman hit "Whispering" into "Groovin' High." They transmuted the 1930 Leo Reisman hit "What Is This Thing Called Love?" into "Hot House"; Charlie Barnet's barn-burning "Cherokee" into "Ko Ko"; and "How High the Moon," a Broadway show tune from 1940, into "Ornithology." "We would make numbers up, but with standards, we'd change them around, put in new melodies and have a new tune," explained Dizzy Gillespie (Stern 1992, 51).

In late 1942, after the draft depleted the ranks of professional jazz musicians, pianist Earl Hines hired several modernists for his band, which functioned as a prototype of big-band bop. He snagged Dizzy Gillespie and asked Charlie Parker to play tenor sax. On January 15, 1943, Hines's band opened at the Apollo Theater and then crisscrossed the country on the TOBA theater circuit. On a package tour sponsored by Pabst Blue Ribbon beer, the band visited army camps in the South and the Midwest. On April 23, when the orchestra returned to the Apollo, Hines hired singer Sarah Vaughan, a nineteen-year-old who learned her gospel-drenched style in the Newark Zion Baptist Church and had just won the Apollo Amateur Hour contest. By late spring 1943, Gillespie and then Parker had left the band.

Billy Eckstine, a debonair vocalist who had sung for Hines, founded his own big band that featured a modern sound. In May 1944, prodded by his agent, he employed many modernists from the Earl Hines outfit. Eckstine "chose Dizzy as musical director because I didn't see anybody more apt at that particular time," the singer reasoned. "And that was the style of music we wanted to play" (Gillespie 1979, 182). The singer then hired Charlie Parker, seven other former Hines Orchestra members, and two veterans of the Jay McShann band as well as such budding boppers as trumpeter Fats Navarro, Chicago sax whiz Gene Ammons, and saxophonist Dexter Gordon. After the army drafted drummer Rossiere "Shadow" Wilson and saxophonist Tommy Crump, Eckstine turned to drummer Art Blakey and twenty-year-old, Detroit-raised sax man Eli "Lucky" Thompson. He also recruited singer Sarah Vaughan to the outfit. "That was the beginning of bebop," enthused Vaughan. "People would stand around and stare at us a lot because this music was so new" (179).

Unlike most other bands, the Eckstine outfit allowed members to improvise on complex chord changes rather than cater to dancers. "Our type of music was more or less a concert style of jazz," the bandleader explained. "People would start to dance, and then they'd turn around and listen. Sometimes our tempos were almost not danceable." About their arrangement of "Max Is Makin' Wax," Eckstine quipped, "You couldn't dance . . . at all" (Gillespie 1979, 190, 198).

Linking jazz with dancing, the public never accepted the Eckstine outfit. "[Club owners and patrons] were not thrilled by us coming in; young, wild, crazy cats playing this style. . . . People weren't ready at this particular time for a concert style of jazz," he concluded (Gillespie 1979, 190). After less than a year, the band unraveled.

Despite the commercial failure of the Eckstine group, in 1945 Dizzy formed a big band of boppers. He hired drummer Max Roach, trumpeters Freddie Webster and Bennie Harris, and, in the sax section, Charlie Parker and tenor man Charlie Rouse, who followed Gillespie from the Eckstine band. As an arranger, he enlisted the help of Walter "Gil" Fuller, who previously worked with Jimmie Lunceford as well as Eckstine. "We wanted to sound in the same idiom as the small bop unit with Charlie Parker," maintained Gillespie. "With a big band, a lot of musicians, instead of just a few, could play our music and make some money" (Gillespie 1979, 253, 223).

The band immediately headed South on an ill-fated tour. "To attract a mass audience to bebop," thought Gillespie, "we had to first establish a feeling for the music among the large black population of the South." Gillespie found the crowds unresponsive. "The orchestra and our style of playing, generally, was geared for people just sitting and listening to the music; nearly all of our arrangements were modern, so imagine my chagrin and surprise when I found out that all we were playing was dances" (Gillespie 1979, 223). Dizzy folded the band when he returned to New York City.

The next year, an undaunted Gillespie fronted another band of modernists. He built the foundation of the unit on vibraphonist Milt Jackson, bassist Ray Brown, and saxophonist Edward "Sonny" Stitt (b. Edward Boatner Jr.), a twenty-two-year-old Bostonian who matched the speed and ideas of Charlie Parker. Gillespie expanded the group by recruiting Bud Powell and then Thelonious Monk on piano, Kenny Clarke on drums, and trumpeter Dave Burns, a teenager who had met Gillespie at Minton's.

The bebop band offered intricate music for listening. John Lewis, a pianist who met Kenny Clarke in the army and eventually joined the Gillespie big band, characterized the sound of the orchestra as "virtuoso music" (Gillespie 1979, 266). Though persisting until 1950, the outfit never achieved national recognition. "For commercial reasons," noted Gillespie, "I had to abandon my big band, which all of us who loved modern jazz knew was a great artistic success" (357). The audiences would "just stand around the bandstand and gawk, so the dance-hall operators stopped sending for us" (Stowe 1994, 219). After the war, big-band bop and large orchestras in general gave way to small combos of modernists who entertained fans at cramped clubs in New York City.

The Flowering of Bop

During the mid- and late forties, jazz groups congregated around Fifty-second Street in New York City, called "The Street of Dreams" or simply "The Street" by hipsters. From early in the evening to four in the morning, combos entertained patrons who drifted from club to club within a three-block area to hear a potpourri of jazz styles. Jazz groups, observed *Billboard* in November 1943, flourished on Fifty-second Street, which "has in the past few months been the proving ground for smaller units, and this change in format is seen as one of the deciding factors in the unprecedented prosperity of many clubs on that lane" ("52nd Street Now Develops" 1943).

Though some nightspots featured older styles, many Fifty-second Street clubs spotlighted small groups of modernists who played music for listening rather than

Fifty-second Street in New York City during its heyday, summer 1948. *Photograph by William P. Gottlieb. William P. Gottlieb/Ira and Leonore S. Gershwin Fund Collection, Music Division, Library of Congress*

dancing. Some played at Kelly's, where the sawdust floors provided no option for dancing. Other boppers performed at the basement club, the Three Deuces, which was designed for the serious jazz fan with three rows of tables on each side of a center aisle and a tiny bandstand to the right. "The Street's aficionados were knowledgeable, sophisticated, generally well-fixed people who came to listen," noted club proprietor Art Jarwood, who owned an interest in several nightspots (Shaw 1971, 323).

The size of the bandstand, constricted by the many tables club owners crammed in for maximum revenue, necessitated a small group. "The bandstand couldn't hardly hold a five-piece combo, let alone ten or twelve people," explained Miles Davis. "So this kind of club created a new musician, who was comfortable in a small-band setting" (Davis 1989, 72).

Most boppers placed a premium on extended solos, so they found quartet and quintet formats ideal. Charlie Parker "wanted to play in small groups where he could solo like he wanted to, when he wanted to," confided Buster Smith, one of Parker's first bandleaders and a man he called his "dad" (Reisner 1962, 214).

White club goers on Fifty-second Street embraced racial integration by readily welcoming African-American artists. Especially after 1943, "color was no hang up," recalled pianist Billy Taylor (Shaw 1971, 173). "It was one of the first downtown streets where the racial thing didn't mean a thing," corroborated Art Jarwood. The patrons "didn't care whether a cat was black or green. They were carried away by the music" (Shaw 1971, 323). "Among the clientele on Fifty-Second Street there was very little racist feeling. That was one spot in New York where there was not too much discrimination," echoed Dizzy Gillespie (1979, 210).

With a friendly audience accustomed to listening to music that showcased soloists, modernists readily accepted engagements on Fifty-second Street. In 1942, boppers first appeared on the Street at Kelly's Stable during Sunday jam sessions. Early the next year, Kenny Clarke and his bop group snagged an engagement at the club through manager Ralph Watkins. Starting in October for six months, Dizzy Gillespie and bassist Oscar Pettiford co-led a quintet at the Onyx Club on the Street. "Our music had developed more into a type of music for listeners," Gillespie explained. "People sat at the tables, with no dance floor. They had another area where you didn't have to buy drinks. You could just sit there and listen to the music" (Gillespie 1979, 202).

In 1943, after rioting in Harlem, African-American club owner Clark Monroe moved the Uptown House to Fifty-second Street, and the next year established a second, nearby club, the Spotlite, where he opened with a Charlie Parker trio. Monroe also hired Dizzy Gillespie and Thelonious Monk as attractions. Through performances at the nightspot, Monroe helped "spread our message to a wider audience," insisted Gillespie (1979, 202).

Gillespie organized the definitive bop group at the Three Deuces. He recruited bop master Charlie Parker, African-American bassist Dillon "Curley" Russell, drummer Max Roach, and white pianist Al Haig. Opening on April 19, 1945, the band pulled jazz fanatics to Fifty-second Street until July, when the engagement ended. Gillespie called the combo "the height of our music" (Gillespie 1979, 231). In July and August, Parker brought a quintet into the club and replaced Dizzy with saxophonist Don Byas.

The Charlie Parker quintet at the Three Deuces on Fifty-second Street, August 1947. L to R: bassist Tommy Potter, Charlie Parker, Miles Davis, and Duke Jordan (at the piano). Drummer Max Roach not pictured. *Photograph by William P. Gottlieb. William P. Gottlieb/Ira and Leonore S. Gershwin Fund Collection, Music Division, Library of Congress*

West Coast Bop

During the 1940s, African Americans migrated to Los Angeles to work in defense plants. Many frequented clubs on Central Avenue, the hub of the African-American community. They heard jazz at the Club Alabam, the largest nightspot on the avenue. It "had tables all around the dance floor, maybe three deep, and they had a balcony . . . I think you could get nine hundred people in there," recalled Lee Young, a drummer and brother of Lester (Pepper and Pepper 1979, 48). Revelers could move across the street to the Hi-De-Ho. Some preferred the Streets of Paris or the Double V, named after the African-American strategy to end segregation. "Central Avenue was probably the closest thing to Fifty-Second Street than anywhere else that I know of," asserted pianist Gerald Wiggins who played at clubs on both streets (Bryant 1998, 323).

Gangsters controlled and operated many of the nightclubs. "The mob owned practically all the clubs the musicians played in," explained Britt Woodman, the Los Angeles trombonist who, with his brothers, William and Coney, formed the backbone of the Los Angeles music scene (Bryant 1998, 115).

Art Pepper, then a fifteen-year-old white sax aspirant who frequented Central Avenue, vividly described the scene on the street. "It was a festive time," he recalled. "The women dressed up in frills and feathers and long earrings and hats with things hanging off them, fancy dresses with slits in the skirts, and they wore black silk stockings that were rolled, and wedgie shoes. The men wore big wide-brimmed hats and zoot suits with wide collars, small cuffs, and large knees, and their coats were real long with padded shoulders. They wore flashy ties with diamond stick pins; they wore lots of jewelry; and you could smell powder and perfume everywhere" (Pepper and Pepper 1979, 41).

In late 1945, bop arrived on the pulsating Central Avenue. On Monday, December 10, until early February the next year, Gillespie and Parker played an engagement at the racially integrated Billy Berg's. Besides the leaders, the sextet included whites Al Haig and drummer Stan Levey as well as African Americans Ray Brown and Milt Jackson. "We were the first mixed band ever to play in California in a nightclub," Levey reminisced. "People were looking at us, 'What the hell? What's going—what's this?'" (Gillespie 1979, 248). "You could go to Billy Berg's out in Hollywood and be accepted as a person there," remarked Marshal Royal. "Segregation was still going on, but that [club] was open" (Bryant 1998, 47).

The sextet attracted most jazz musicians in the Los Angeles area. "Opening night was fabulous," recalled Buddy Collette, then a twenty-four-year-old budding sax player. "The place was packed with people. It must have attracted most of the L.A. musicians" (Bryant 1998, 146). "Almost 99 percent of the younger guys really loved this new music," agreed trumpeter Art Farmer, then seventeen, who attended the opening-night performance at Berg's (271). Bird and his group "turned L. A. on its musical ear" (Farmer 1957, 29).

Many young modernists stalked Bird around town. After listening to his idol, sax player William "Sonny" Criss marched to the First Street Hotel, where Parker stayed, and "went to the desk. They told me what room. Then I knocked on the door. No answer. Then I knocked. I was really determined. I was still at school. No answer. So I wouldn't give up. I kept knocking because they told me he was there. Finally, he peeped out of the peephole" (Gitler 1985, 170).

Though initially drawing sizable crowds at Berg's, the bop sextet saw business wane after the first few weeks. Unlike the progressive musicians, the general public did not understand bop. "The music wasn't well received at all," recalled sextet member Ray Brown. "They didn't know what we were playing: they didn't understand it, and a guy asked us to sing" (Gillespie 1979, 249). More direct, Charlie Parker felt that "nobody understood our music on the coast. They *hated* it"

 LISTENING GUIDE 24

Charlie Parker's Ri-Bop Boys

"KO KO"

Charlie Parker immortalized "Ko Ko" with one of the premier jazz solos of all time. According to pianist and critic John Mehegan, "if jazz critics ever established inflexible standards of evaluation allowing for two or three five-star jazz records a year, they might use 'Ko Ko' as an absolute" (Mehegan 1956).

Parker, who began to play the tune with the Jay McShann Orchestra, plays this version at near blinding speed (300 beats per minute) and, at the same time, puts forward an incalculable number of ideas.

On November 26, 1945, at 5:00 p.m., Parker and the group recorded the song for Savoy Records. He had assistance from bassist Curley Russell; drummer Max Roach, who weaves a blazing, tempo-defying drum solo; and Dizzy Gillespie, who matches Parker's speed and precision. Parker had chosen Miles Davis for trumpet on this session, but Gillespie happened to wander in during this recording and took Davis's place. Gillespie doubled on piano for the recording of the song when Bud Powell failed to make the date.

The song is loosely based on the chords to "Cherokee," which was written in 1938 by English composer, actor, and bandleader Ray Noble and became well-known the next year through a rendition by the Charlie Barnet band. In 1939, the tune also was waxed by the Count Basie Orchestra. It has little in common with the Duke Ellington song of the same name.

The 1945 Parker recording consisted of a thirty-two-bar introduction: an eight-bar head, an eight-bar trumpet part, an eight-bar sax section, and an eight-bar head. Next, it showcases two brilliant solos by Charlie Parker, a twenty-eight-bar drum solo by Roach, and then a general restatement of the introduction.

Distinctively, this rendition has only the vague hint of a melody rather than an obvious melodic core. Unlike a traditional "song," it focuses on harmonic progression or a series of chords and chord substitutions played in a pattern. As a cluster of chords, "Ko Ko" serves as a vehicle for jazz virtuosos to demonstrate their mastery rather than a song for dancing, signaling a significant break from the jazz past.

0:00–0:05	The thirty-two-bar introduction in B flat begins with Gillespie and Parker playing in octaves with rhythmic accompaniment by Max Roach on snare drum, which denotes a change at the end of the passage.
0:06–0:11	Gillespie solos with a flurry of notes on muted trumpet.
0:12–0:18	In a call-and-response to Gillespie, Parker unleashes a lightning-fast improvised solo with rhythm background from Max Roach, who heavily accents several beats to "drop bombs" in typical bop fashion.
0:19–0:22	Gillespie and Parker reunite to play in harmony with Roach's heavy beats as an accompaniment.
0:23–0:24	Gillespie and Parker briefly play in unison. Roach's loud snare-drum beat signals a change in direction at the end of the passage.
0:25–0:28	Parker starts a solo with rhythm backing from drums, bass, and piano, the last which Gillespie likely played.
0:29–0:31	Parker repeats a four-note phrase twice before letting loose with an inventive solo.
0:32–0:49	Parker continues with his solo, constantly shifting the rhythm by stops and starts through unexpectedly resting on a certain note to create an innovative, exciting, and syncopated rhythmic complexity as compared to much of big-band jazz. Roach accompanies Parker lightly in the background with intermittent accents.

0:50–1:04	Parker attacks the bridge of the song in a new key to give the song a bluesy element. He starts by repeating a phrase in different pitches (0:50–0:55), changes chords, and then solos until he reaches the original key. The rest of the rhythm section also backs Parker.
1:05	Roach provides two quick accents to signal a new phrase by the saxophone.
1:06–1:15	Parker continues his blazing solo with Roach dropping bombs sporadically. The drum signals a change at the end of the passage.
1:16–1:19	Parker quotes the well-known piccolo solo in the New Orleans song "High Society" by Alphonse Picou.
1:20–1:22	Parker returns with a version of the passage that he played at 0:50.
1:23–1:40	Parker returns to his improvisation.
1:41–1:47	Parker moves to the bridge with a somewhat disguised version of "Tea for Two," his second musical quote in the song.
1:48–2:07	Parker launches into a harmonic progression with backing from the piano, which follows by chording the changes. Roach continues to drop bombs and the bass provides a steady beat. Near the end of the improvisation, Parker slides across a bluesy note to demonstrate his blues base.
2:08–2:11	Max Roach solos by generating rapid-fire beats that shift time constantly much like polyrhythmic African drumming. He begins with a call-and-response between the bass drum and the snare drum.
2:12–2:18	He continues with rolls on the snare drum and only sporadic bass drum beats.
2:19–2:30	The drum rolls intensify and accentuate several rhythms in a complex polyrhythmic pattern.
2:31–2:35	Gillespie and Parker play in unison similar to the introduction.
2:36–2:42	Gillespie solos on muted trumpet. An insistent drum beat signals a change at the end of the solo. At 2:41, Gillespie abruptly changes the rhythm by holding a note much like Parker does throughout his solos.
2:43–2:49	Parker solos by again responding to Gillespie in a call-and-response manner. Once again, drummer Roach indicates a change at the end of the passage.
2:50–2:53	Parker and Gillespie play together and restate the theme from the very beginning of the song. Accompanied by the rhythm section, they end the song with a syncopated "ch-bop" rhythm on the final two beats.

(Feather 1955, 6). "They were *so* hostile to us there," agreed Dizzy Gillespie (Boyer 1948, 29).

By February 3, 1946, Dizzy headed back to New York City, and Parker remained in California to gig at clubs near his hotel and at Billy Berg's Sunday matinees. By the end of July, Bird suffered a drug-induced mental breakdown, walked naked through the lobby of his hotel, and ended in Camarillo State Hospital for five months.

The Bop Cult of Hip Teens

In 1947, the fortunes of the modernists improved after several engagements at renowned concert halls. In September, Dizzy Gillespie and his cohorts performed at the prestigious Carnegie Hall and returned there the next two years. Two months later, Gillespie, Parker, and other boppers gave a concert at Symphony Hall in Boston, which signaled that bop had finally attracted a serious and sizable audience.

The next year, the Royal Roost on Broadway presented and promoted bop, which slowly shifted away from Fifty-second Street. In April, the club hosted a "bop concert" staged by promoter Monte Kay and disc jockey "Symphony Sid" Torin, who since 1937 had acquired a reputation as a premier radio personality. "I was convinced that there was an audience for bop," recollected Kay. On a Tuesday night, the Roost offered a concert with Bird, Miles Davis, Fats Navarro, and Dexter Gordon (Shaw 1971, 272). The concert targeted youth who paid ninety cents to "sit in the 'bleachers' and listen to the show without buying a drink of any kind," explained Kay. "Such a crowd showed up that we had to call the cops," smiled club owner Ralph Watkins. "I turned the spot into a progressive jazz joint" (272, 215). Watkins installed a radio wire in the club for Friday broadcasts, hosted by Symphony Sid, to spread bop across the region. Soon, the Roost was called the "Metropolitan Bopera House," a nickname referring to the nearby Metropolitan Opera House. In 1948, Watkins launched the eight-hundred-seat Bop City on Broadway at West Forty-ninth Street to accommodate the overflow of bop fanatics from the Royal Roost.

Birdland catered to boppers on Broadway after the success of the Royal Roost. The swank club was opened in 1949 by Morris Levy, his brother Irving, and Oscar Goodstein. The nightspot, decorated with plush carpet, imitation-leather booths, and large oil paintings of jazz celebrities, accommodated nearly five hundred patrons. The club owners constructed a heavy, plate-glass sound studio for nightly, thirty-minute radio transmissions emceed by Symphony Sid. Like the Royal Roost, Birdland focused on teenagers who paid a low admission, sat on bleachers, and sipped soda. "Not only did teenagers enjoy the jazz of that period, but they knew all the players and their records," observed pianist Billy Taylor, who performed at Birdland for nearly two years (Shaw 1971, 172).

Bop records, available nationally after the war, firmly established the reputations of modernists among jazz aficionados. On November 26, 1945, Savoy Records—a small label in Newark, New Jersey, founded three years earlier by Herman Lubinsky—recorded Parker, Dizzy, pianist Sadik Hakim, bassist Curley Russell, and Max Roach. It issued such classic recordings as "Billie's Bounce," "Ko Ko," and "Now's the Time."

Los Angeles–based Dial records signed Charlie Parker. In March 1946, it brought Parker, trumpeter Miles Davis, and several other modernists into the studio to record "Moose the Mooche," Gillespie's "A Night in Tunisia," "Ornithology," and "Yardbird Suite." Until December 1947, Dial's owner Ross Russell repeatedly waxed the music of Parker and his band mates and dedicated his label to modern music.

In 1946, Dizzy Gillespie signed a three-year contract with RCA. The next year, the trumpeter worked with the label to wax "Manteca," which displayed the influence of Cuban music on his compositions. In the song, he included syncopated Latin bass lines and featured the conga and vocals of Chano Pozo, who repeatedly shouted the title that was Cuban slang for marijuana.

 LISTENING GUIDE 25

Dizzy Gillespie Septet

 "A NIGHT IN TUNISIA"

During 1941 and 1942, Gillespie conceived of this song during a tour with the Benny Carter band. When experimenting with thirteenth chord changes on the piano, he "looked at the notes on the chords as I played the progression and noticed that they formed a melody. The melody had a very Latin, even oriental feeling, the rhythm came out of the bebop style," which he defined as a "heavily syncopated rhythm in the bass line" (Gillespie 1979, 171). On January 27, 1945, the trumpeter recorded the song with the Boyd Raeburn band and subsequently played it during stints with Earl Hines and Billy Eckstine. In 1946, Charlie Parker recorded the tune with Miles Davis on trumpet.

Gillespie first called the song "Interlude" and then "A Night in Tunisia" on the advice of Earl Hines. "One of his numbers became famous as 'Night in Tunisia,' a title I suggested because World War II was raging and there was a lot of action in Tunisia," recalled Hines (Dance 1977, 90).

On February 22, 1946, Gillespie recorded the tune for RCA Victor with a seven-piece group, which included Milt Jackson on vibes, guitarist Bill DeArango, bassist Ray Brown, drummer J. C. Heard, Don Byas on sax, and Al Haig on piano. The group released the version below.

0:00–0:04	The song begins with a complex, melodic bass line rather than the standard walking-bass line, which provides a steady beat as it connects the chords.
0:05	The piano enters to back the bass.
0:06–0:07	The heavily accented drums of J. C. Heard begin.
0:08–0:09	Milt Jackson on vibes enters the group and answers the bass.
0:10–0:12	Don Byas enters on saxophone with a six-note riff as the rhythm continues to build tension and add a mysterious mood to the piece.
0:13–0:34	Dizzy enters with his trumpet to complete the group and plays the main theme twice.
0:35–0:45	Dizzy plays an interlude to the main theme on muted trumpet with Byas playing harmony and the rhythm section in the background.
0:46–0:56	Dizzy repeats the main theme.
0:57	Milt Jackson hits his vibraphone to indicate a change.
0:58–1:05	Saxophonist Byas restates the interlude with Jackson in the background. Drummer Heard indicates the completion of a measure by a drum roll, and the bassist provides the rhythm.
1:06–1:12	Dizzy joins Byas in the interlude, playing in harmony with him.
1:13–1:36	Dizzy takes a high-pitched, unmuted, and fast solo. Typical of bop, he plays in a highly syncopated fashion in a stop-start manner by unexpectedly holding or not inserting notes to build tension.
1:37–1:41	Gillespie states the passage that he played in the interlude but in a higher pitch.

1:42–1:47	Gillespie continues his improvisation with a flurry of notes in rapid-fire succession.
1:48–1:49	Gillespie states a variant of the main theme.
1:50–1:56	Dizzy continues his frenzied, high-pitched solo.
1:57–1:58	Gillespie loosely states the main theme.
1:59–2:04	Byas states the main theme as he climbs octaves.
2:05–2:28	Byas improvises on the chord changes and swoops around an ascending and descending set of notes as he demonstrates his mastery of the blues. Like Gillespie, he creates rhythmic complexity by suddenly stopping or changing speed to jar the listener.
2:29–2:38	Jackson solos on vibes. Like the other bop virtuosos, he adds a rhythmic, syncopated complexity to his solo work by holding notes longer than expected.
2:39–2:47	The full band enters and revisits the main theme twice with Gillespie on muted trumpet.
2:48–3:00	Dizzy offers a brief solo with rhythm-section backing.
3:01–3:05	As Dizzy holds a note, Byas enters, Jackson then plays a bar on vibes, and Dizzy ends the song on a single, held note.

Blue Note Records provided an outlet for the music of many boppers. It had been established in 1939 as a classic jazz label with an investment of $100 by German immigrant and record collector Alfred Lion and his boyhood friend and photographer Frank Wolff. "We started with Dixie, then we went to swing, and then we drifted to modern," confessed Lion ("Those First 20 Years" 1959, 10). In September 1947, the label brought pianist Tadd Dameron and trumpeter Fats Navarro into the studio and, the next month, captured the first recorded performances of Thelonious Monk as a leader. "We couldn't give Monk away," explained Alfred Lion. "But we made some records. . . . And I liked it so much we made some records again! The hell with it," he thought as he marketed the pianist as the "Genius of Modern Music" (Fox 1986, 109). Near the end of the year, the Blue Note owners followed with such other boppers as Art Blakey and his group, saxophonist James Moody and his Bop Men, the Howard McGhee–Fats Navarro Boptet, Bud Powell and His Modernists, and the Max Roach quartet.

Prestige Records also jumped on the bop bandwagon. Twenty-year-old jazz collector Bob Weinstock started in the music business by selling records from his family's apartment in New York City. He opened a jazz record store that attracted many customers, including drummer Kenny Clarke. "He told me that if I started a record company he would get all the jazz greats to record for me," reminisced Weinstock (Schudel 2006, 2). In January 1949, the budding entrepreneur launched the company with a family loan to record modern jazz music. During the first year of operation, Prestige snagged Fats Navarro, trombonist J. J. Johnson, and sax men Sonny Stitt and Wardell Gray.

In late 1948, Ralph Watkins, announcer Symphony Sid, ex–Savoy record producer Teddy Reig, and concert promoter Monte Kay started Royal Roost Records as an offshoot of the Broadway club. According to Reig, one night, when the four men "were stoned to the bone," they each contributed one thousand dollars to fund the label (Pullman 2012, 117). Within a year, Reig took over the company and recorded such budding boppers as Bud Powell (39). Along with other small, independent record labels, Roost trumpeted the music of bop across the country.

Many young jazz fans who lived outside New York City first discovered modernist music through records released by the independents. "We used to play those records," confided bassist George "Red" Callender. "We'd get in a room and live with them all night. It was unbelievable. Something from outer space" (Gitler 1985, 146). After saxophonist Art Pepper left the army at the end of 1946, a friend spun two bop records for him. "Sonny Stitt was first, and that just made me ill," he enthused, "and then when I heard Bird I just got deathly sick" (153). Los Angeles sax man Sonny Criss asked his mother to buy two Charlie Parker discs on a trip to Chicago. "When I heard those records just like my mind was popped," he said (168). In a survey of high school students in June 1945, nearly half of the respondents knew about the Savoy label, which had only been established three years earlier, and 37 percent had heard about Blue Note Records.

Jazz promoter, label owner, and civil-rights activist Norman Granz further popularized the new music. In early 1946, the twenty-eight-year-old jazz impresario added bop star Charlie Parker to his second Jazz at the Philharmonic national tour, which showcased some of the best jazz talent such as Coleman Hawkins and Lester Young in staged jam sessions. Two years later, Granz signed Charlie Parker to a deal for his Clef Series on Mercury Records and continued to highlight Bird on his concert tours.

In the late forties, the press declared that bebop had arrived. *Metronome* magazine crowed that "a new era began in jazz in 1947, that modern jazz had come to stay, had even come to pay" (Pullman 2012, 89) and proclaimed 1948 as the Year of Bop. In January 1948, the *Saturday Review* categorized Dizzy Gillespie, Charlie Parker, and Kenny Clarke as "stars" and applauded "their bizarre fashion" of music (McKean 1948, 50). Six months later, the *New Yorker* reported that "this music, which the knowing refer to simply as bop, has shaken the world of jazz" (Boyer 1948, 28).

Hip teens embraced the lifestyle of musicians hardly older than themselves to create a bop cult. Many bop fanatics, mostly male, donned loose-fitting suits called drapes or zoot suits much like the outfits that the jitterbugs favored. They wore dark, horn-rimmed sunglasses even in the evenings to look professorial and sported berets of the anti-Nazi French Resistance, dress styles that were popularized first by Thelonious Monk and then Dizzy Gillespie. Those old enough to grow facial hair displayed goatees like the one preferred by Dizzy, who used it to cushion his mouthpiece. To mimic Gillespie, wrote the *New Yorker*, bop diehards "try to walk with his peculiar loose-jointed, bow-legged floppiness; [and] try to force their laughter into a soprano squeak" (Boyer 1948, 28).

Most bop adherents spoke in hipster slang, much of it originating with such disc jockeys as Daddy-O Daylie from Chicago, who "would always try and use the bop phrases to help sell the music, to showcase modern music" (Gillespie 1979, 281). Bop zealots called their friends "homeboys" and "baby" and their enemies "Jim," a term denoting the discriminatory Jim Crow laws. When listening to music, they would "catch some riffs" at a "hip" local nightspot and "flip their wig" and "dig" or appreciate it. After they "split" from the club, the aspiring hipsters retreated to their "cribs" for a "nod." In 1949, Babs Gonzales (b. Lee Brown), a jazz vocalist who headed Three Bips and a Bop, codified the new language in a twenty-two-page *Be-Bop Dictionary and History of Its Famous Stars*. When high school opened in September 1949, observed *Time*, "school children in Chicago and elsewhere were ready. Their jeep-hats bobbed in school corridors, their scat-talk filled the classrooms, some of their jackets bore the inscription, 'Bebop is spoken here'" ("Ready or Not" 1949).

By the end of the decade, bop had become a teenage subculture. "The bebopper cult had reached its zenith. I looked around and everybody was trying to look like me," noticed Dizzy. "These were black and white people alike, by the tens of thousands, willing to stand up and testify for bebop. At concerts, they would let the ones who wore berets, goatees, and horn-rimmed glasses sit up on the stage with the band. A lot of them were teenage girls who had their goatees painted on with grease paint. From 1948 through 1949, America seemed definitely thrilled by our music, its eyes were agog and its ears wide open" (Gillespie 1979, 342).

Attracting white and African-American youth, modern music promoted racial integration. "Bop has been a dominating factor toward racial harmony, not only among musicians and show people, but also among the general following," contended Babs Gonzales in 1949.

Despite the success of bop, the mainstream press mercilessly ridiculed the bop subculture. *Time* magazine defined bop as "hot jazz overheated with overdone lyrics full of bawdiness, references to narcotics and doubletalk" ("Be-bop Be-bopped" 1946). It referred to bebop as "carefully disorganized music" and "shrill cacophony" ("Bopera on Broadway" 1948). Journalist Robert Ruark tagged the modernist style as "a kind of musical outrage for which some people profess a fondness. It is played by people who wear goatees and berets. Its language has been compared to that spoken by Cro-Magnon man, obviously the mental equal of the modern bopster" (Stowe 1994, 208–9). "The impulse of most first listeners to bebop is to run," reported *Collier's* magazine in March 1948. "Some obey that impulse" (Henderson and Shaw 1948, 17).

Because bop appealed to teens, some critics linked it to juvenile delinquency. In 1950, the Milwaukee Catholic archdiocese barred young boppers from school, identifying them by their "gangster tendencies." A police officer warned that bebop fans inevitably would be plagued by "drinking, marijuana smoking, shop lifting and illicit sex relationships" (Stowe 1994, 209). In April 1946, Ted Steele, a Los Angeles disc jockey, banned bebop from station KMPC because it represented "a contributing factor to juvenile delinquency" (Myers 2013, 40). By 1949, *Downbeat* lamented that the term bop "is being kicked around so loosely in the columns of newspapers that it is just a matter of time until it will be employed to designate juvenile delinquents" (Stowe 1994, 209).

Established musicians blasted bop. Louis Armstrong said that "it's not jazz—all them variations—it's more an exercise" ("Louis the First" 1949, 60). Bandleader Artie Shaw felt that "Bach did more bebop in one piece than those guys have ever done" ("With a Nail File" 1949). In 1948, jazz giant Fletcher Henderson maintained that "of all the cruelties in the world, be-bop is the most phenomenal" (Stowe 1994, 223). Even the normally broad-minded record producer, John Hammond, considered bop to be "a collection of nauseating clichés, regurgitated ad infinitum" ("B.G. and Bebop" 1948).

Some fans of New Orleans jazz, classifying themselves as "moldy figs," disdained bebop. In 1946, the *Record Changer* represented the figs by declaring that "every single year there is a new crop of phonies trying to pervert or suppress or emasculate jazz. This year it's Diz Gillespie" (Feather 1987, 87). Writer

Leonard Feather, defending the modernist camp, likened classic jazz fanatics to fascists. On March 5, 1949, Rudi Blesh, writer and record label owner, organized a jazz concert at the Metropolitan Opera House, which pitted a traditional group against modernists. On the side of classic jazz stood Sidney Bechet, clarinetist Buster Bailey, Sidney de Paris on trombone, Walter Page on bass, drummer George Wettling, and pianist Ralph Sutton. They battled Charlie Parker, pianist Al Haig, Kenny Dorham on trumpet, drummer Max Roach, and bassist Tommy Potter. Blesh, a self-proclaimed "moulde fygge," felt that the traditionalists had triumphed. The next day, the *New York Herald Tribune*, which funded the event, affirmed that "classic jazz has won a complete and undisputed victory!" (Reisner 1962, 53).

Despite the criticisms, some established musicians incorporated bop into their styles. Lester Young "perfected a more relaxed, listenable form that we call relaxed bop" (Stowe 1994, 213). Bandleaders such as Jimmy Dorsey added bop elements into their repertoires by asking Gillespie to write arrangements for them (Gillespie 1979, 168). By 1948, most jazz bands integrated shreds of bop into their music. "The style had influenced nearly every band in the land," insisted the *New York Times* in December (Harman 1948).

Bandleader Woody Herman especially gravitated toward bop. During the early forties, Herman asked Dizzy to write arrangements for his band and hired musicians who wanted to try the modern style. Unlike other bands Gillespie helped, noted the trumpeter, "Herman's band came at it more naturally. All the trumpet players in the band wanted to play like me, all the drummers wanted to play like Kenny Clarke or Max Roach and so on. Woody had a band that was trying to sound like us" (Gillespie 1979, 169). In October 1947, after being inactive for a year, Woody assembled a largely white, bop-influenced orchestra known as his "Second Herd." The band spotlighted a Charlie Parker–influenced saxophone quartet that included Stan Getz, Zoot Sims, Herbie Steward, and baritone man Serge Chaloff. In late 1947, Al Cohn joined the group, first as an arranger and then as part of the sax section, when Steward left the band. On December 27, 1947, the Woody Herman outfit waxed the bop-based tune "Four Brothers" to give a name to the bop-inflected saxophone section.

Though attracting attention from the press and emulated by fellow musicians, bopsters never realized much money or acclaim for their innovations. In May 1945, for a Town Hall performance, Gillespie and Parker only received twenty-five dollars each. At the time, no bop records entered the charts. The boppers never interested a general audience, which thought of them in negative terms. "The average layman, or the average listener, they thought bop was only associated with people that were on drugs, . . . and led a dirty life," remarked sax player and bandleader Charlie Ventura, who blended bop into his music (Gitler 1985, 232). Boppers received little recognition from the average African American despite the modernists' reflection of the general African-American indignation over racial discrimination and their attempt to forge an African-American identity. Charlie Parker as "a symbol to the Negro people? No," asserted Art Blakey. "A symbol to musicians, yes" (Reisner 1962, 51).

The Bop Mania Subsides

By the end of 1949, the bop mania subsided, when the music changed and many boppers fell prey to drugs. Charlie Parker, who had become increasingly interested in such classical composers as Béla Bartók and Igor Stravinsky, realized one of his dreams by recording an album with string arrangements. On November 30, he went into the studio with conductor Jimmy Carroll, four jazz men, and seven classical musicians, including oboist Mitch Miller. "When I recorded with strings, some of my friends said, 'Oh, Bird is getting commercial,'" he asserted in 1953. "That wasn't it at all. I was looking for new ways of saying things musically. New sound combinations" (Woideck 1998, 80). After the release of the album early the next year, Bird supplemented his bop group with violins for engagements at Birdland and the Apollo Theater in New York and clubs in Chicago, Detroit, and Washington, DC.

Hooked on heroin at an early age, Parker unwittingly infused hard drugs into the bop subculture, especially among young musicians who followed the star saxophonist's example. When Parker joined the orchestra of Tommy Douglas, remarked the bandleader, "he was about fifteen then and he was high then" (Reisner 1962, 82). In 1942, Bird lost his job with Jay McShann on the "day we had to carry him off the bandstand and lay him on a table. We couldn't feel no pulse. 'Bird, you've got back on your kick again, and so I've got to let you go,'" McShann apologized after Parker had been revived (150). During his time with the Billy Eckstine band, Parker continued to indulge in heroin and regularly fell asleep on the bandstand. In small combos, he shot heroin until one day he collapsed, a shell of himself, during a Dial recording session.

Despite the dangers, young boppers hoped to emulate their idol in every way and became hooked on heroin. "I think Charlie Parker influenced alotta young musicians and old ones too, introduced them to alotta hard drugs," explained saxophonist Budd Johnson. "Because they say, 'What! This guy can play like that? This stuff must do something!'" (Gillespie 1979, 285). "The idea was going around that to use heroin might make you play as great as Bird. A lot of musicians did it for that," echoed Miles Davis (1989, 96). "Some of the younger guys like Dexter Gordon, Tadd Dameron, Art Blakey, J. J. Johnson, Sonny Rollins, Jackie McLean, and myself—all of us—started to get heavily into heroin around the same time" (129). "That was our badge. It was the thing that made us different from the rest of the world," explained Bird devotee and trumpeter Red Rodney about heroin use (Gilter 1985, 282).

Ralph Watkins, owner of Kelly's Stable, the Royal Roost, and Bop City, summarized the history of jazz by the drugs musicians in each era preferred. "The Dixielanders were alcoholics," he maintained, probably referring to the alcohol-induced deaths of such luminaries as Bix Beiderbecke and Freddie Keppard. "In the swing era, it was marijuana. With modern jazz, an awful lot of the kids went to hard drugs" (Shaw 1971, 220).

Drugs contributed to the swift decline of bop, when many boppers suffered the consequences of repeated heroin use. "Dope, heroin abuse, really got to be a major problem during the bebop era, especially in the late forties," explained Dizzy Gillespie (1979, 283). By the end of 1950, in an article titled "Dope Menace Keeps Growing," *Downbeat* warned that heroin "has become a major threat and unless Herculean effort is made by everyone concerned to halt its spread, it may well wreck the business. We are not talking about marijuana, Benzedrine or Nembutal," it cautioned. "We are referring to real narcotics, heroin, principally" (Pepper and Pepper 1979, 118). In a study of more than four hundred white and African-American jazz musicians in New York City from 1954 to 1955, heroin had been tried once by 53 percent of the respondents, twice by another 24 percent, and had hooked 16 percent of the musicians. The heroin users, mostly in their twenties, consumed the drug "on the basis of some kind of magical identification with their heroes and the assumption that they would play better if they, too, were drug users" (Winick 1959–1960, 246).

Nightclubs shied away from boppers who seemed undependable amid the growing drug problem. "Established nightclubs would not touch the new music because of the narcotics problems," intimated George Wein, who owned Storyville, a nightspot in Boston, and later organized the Newport Jazz Festival (Gillespie 1979, 400). By 1949, Babs Gonzales addressed the heroin epidemic in an article entitled, "What's What with Bop."

Thelonious Monk suffered the consequences of hard drugs. In August 1951, Monk and Bud Powell were stopped in Monk's car, where police found a bag of heroin that Powell had tossed near Monk's feet. Refusing to expose Powell, Thelonious served two months at Rikers Island jail, which New York constructed in 1932 as a men's prison. After a second arrest, Monk lost his livelihood for a year when police revoked Monk's cabaret card, a police identification paper required since 1931 that permitted musicians to work in New York City.

Other boppers ended in jail, too. In 1948, Sonny Rollins used heroin to imitate his idol, Charlie Parker, and, two years later, became hooked on the drug. "I was stealing from my house, my family. I was a heroin addict," he painfully remembered. "I got involved with a robbery and a revolver" for drug money and ended up at Rikers (Spencer 1990, 156; Hawes 1972, 32). "Everybody was trying to out-junkie Charlie Parker," explained saxophonist Frank Morgan, then a teenager in Los Angeles who idolized Bird and became involved with heroin until 1953, when he landed in jail (Isoardi 1992–1993, 23). "Cats were always getting 'busted' with drugs by the police, and they had a saying, 'To get the best band go to KY.' That meant the 'best band' was in Lexington, Kentucky, at the federal narcotics hospital," mentioned Dizzy Gillespie (1979, 283).

Charlie Parker, the star soloist and symbol of the bop movement, suffered the ultimate effects of heroin use. On March 12, 1955, Parker, bloated from alcohol and broken by years of drug abuse, passed away at the age of thirty-four.

Though the bop mania subsided, modernists had created a new, complex jazz in small combos that started at Minton's and Monroe's and spread to most major cities. Radicalized by continued racial discrimination after World War II, they developed a decidedly African-American style with breakneck speed, complicated rhythms, and innovative harmony that few whites could replicate. Though no longer a rage, bop created a musical language that fundamentally changed jazz and has continued into the twenty-first century.

For Discussion and Further Study

Chapter Quiz

1. Who were the key musicians in the development of bebop? What new innovations did they introduce in the music?

2. How did the experience of African-American soldiers in World War II affect their feelings about their music and lives when they returned home? How did some African-American leaders try to use the war effort to help end segregation?

3. What elements of bebop were developed by African-American musicians specifically to avoid being co-opted by white performers? How did this affect their music?

4. How were the clubs along Fifty-second Street different from earlier night-clubs that catered to white audiences? Why was this important to bop musicians?

5. How did the young white audience emulate their favorite bop performers? What influence did bop have on fashion, language, and the broader "hipster" culture?

11

JUMPIN' THE BLUES

Boogie Woogie, Deejays, and the Second Great Migration

D uring the post–World War II years, changes in the music industry led to the rise of rhythm and blues (R&B). The introduction of influential disc jockeys or "deejays," who promoted new records on radio and independent record labels dedicated to African-American music, led to an explosion of small jazz ensembles, which delivered upbeat entertainment. Drawing on the boogie-woogie tradition, R&B catered to younger African Americans who trekked from the South to find work in Northern industries and wanted an electrifying dance music rather than the more cerebral bebop.

In late 1945, seventeen-year-old saxophonist Cecil McNeely shadowed Charlie Parker when he descended upon Los Angeles with the new sound of bop. Along with members of Cecil's band, which included saxophonist Sonny Criss and pianist Hampton Hawes, he "jammed with Bird and Miles and all the guys" (Bryant 1998, 184–85). He even took Parker "home, and my mother would wash his clothes." From Parker, Cecil learned "how to write changes, progressions, in numbers rather than chord structure. That way you could transpose" (185). After Bird left Los Angeles, McNeely continued with his fledgling bop group and learned to read musical notation. "I learned how to play very legit," he pointed out.

Lionel Hampton at the vibes, New York, 1946. Photograph by William P. Gottlieb. William P. Gottlieb/Ira and Leonore S. Gershwin Fund Collection, Music Division, Library of Congress

On December 13, 1948, McNeely suddenly reversed direction. When Ralph Bass, West Coast talent scout for Savoy Records, asked him to record a Glenn Miller selection, he completely abandoned complex bop for a stripped-down, "very simple" arrangement. "I forgot about everything that I learned and just went and played soul, so to speak. Soul. One note. Don't try to play a lot of notes," he explained. He said to his band members, "'Let's just drop everything and just blow,' and that's what happened. Like a light turning on and off, it was that much [of a] drastic change." Pleased with the result, Savoy owner Herman Lubinsky asked the sax player, "What's your name?"

"Cecil," the saxophonist responded.

"Do you have a nickname?" Lubinsky inquired.

"Yeah, Jay," answered McNeely.

Lubinsky, an astute marketer, exclaimed "Big Jay," which became Cecil's stage name (Bryant 1998, 186–87).

The song Big Jay McNeely refashioned from the Glenn Miller tune, renamed "The Deacon's Hop," topped the R&B chart. It featured a honking, swaying, straightforward sax with a boogie-woogie beat accentuated by hand clapping and an occasional burst from the band in the background. "I think I was the one who cut the new ground," asserted Big Jay. "I think the style that I was creating was more backbeat and drive; more or less like Hamp [Lionel Hampton] was doing, a little swing, hard swing type of thing. I always thought of myself as a jazz musician who was playing for people who wanted to dance," he maintained (Myers 2009a).

In performances, McNeely supplemented the propulsive rhythm with a wild stage act by walking on the bar while honking and playing the sax on his back. "I got on my knees; nothing happened," he recalled. "I lay on the floor and that did it" (Bryant 1998, 188). One fellow musician remembered that "Big Jay McNeely used to get up on the bar, lay on his back. He'd walk outside, and people would follow him. He'd walk down the street, they would come on back" (111). "The showman-ship just came into the fold," McNeely admitted (187). With one quick decision, Big Jay had scored a chartbuster by deserting bebop for a gut-bucket, swinging, and danceable sound mixed with theatrics that became known as jump blues. As big bands receded from popularity, he helped develop a style for small combos that offered an alternative to bop.

The Boogie-Woogie Craze

A boogie-woogie beat and big-band swing served as the major inspirations for jump blues. The expression "boogie-woogie" likely originated from West African words such as "boog" from the Hausa people in Nigeria and "booga" from the Mandingo tribe in Sierra Leone that meant "to beat." Referring to a driving, percussive cluster of eighth notes in standard 4/4 time usually produced by the left hand on a piano, a boogie-woogie rhythm resulted in a rolling, bass-heavy effect.

The boogie-woogie piano style probably originated in Texas. Eyewitnesses first heard it in the northeastern part of the state near Marshall, which served as a major hub of the Texas and Pacific Railway. During the early 1870s, itinerant African-American pianists in the area played the rolling-bass piano blues for workers in lumber and turpentine camps by mimicking the sounds and rhythm of a chugging locomotive moving down the tracks. Huddie Ledbetter, otherwise known as Leadbelly, who used rolling-bass lines on the guitar, remembered hearing the rhythm near the Caddo Lake area of northeast Texas in 1899. A few years later, when traveling to Shreveport, Louisiana, Leadbelly encountered the same style. "Boogie woogie was called barrelhouse in those days," he recalled. "One of the best players was named Chee-Dee. He would go from one gin mill to the next on Fannin Street [in Shreveport]. He was coal black and one of the old-line players, and he boogied the blues" (Wolfe and Lornell 1992, 35). Around the same time, pianist Jelly Roll Morton came across the boogie-woogie beat near New Orleans.

African-American George Thomas and his younger brother Hersal brought the boogie rhythm to Chicago. Born in 1883, the Texas-born George sang in the choir and played piano and organ at the Shiloh Baptist Church, where his father served as deacon. After performing in pit bands around Houston, in 1914 George moved to New Orleans, where he teamed with Clarence Williams to establish a successful music publishing business. The next year, he sent for his brother Hersal and his sister, singer Beulah "Sippie" Wallace, and arranged work for them in clubs around the Crescent City and throughout the South. In 1916, George composed and published "New Orleans Hop Scop Blues," arguably the first published song that used the boogie-woogie beat. In 1917, when the Storyville district closed, George traveled to Chicago and sent again for his brother and sister. In 1922, he collaborated with Hersal on "The Fives," a song credited as the beginning of the genre.

In 1929, Clarence "Pine Top" Smith popularized the boogie-woogie style. Born in Troy, Alabama, and raised in Birmingham, he started on the TOBA vaudeville circuit as a singer, comedian, and pianist and sometimes backed blues singer Ma Rainey. On the advice of fellow pianist and talent scout Cow Cow Davenport, Pine Top moved to Chicago and signed to Vocalion Records. On December 29, 1928, under the guidance of African-American producer Jay Mayo "Ink" Williams, he recorded the successful "Pine Top's Boogie Woogie," which gave the style a name. Tragically, before a second scheduled recording date a few months later, Smith died from gunshot wounds at the age of twenty-four.

Two Chicago pianists brought boogie-woogie to a national market. Boyhood friends Meade Lux Lewis and Albert Ammons learned piano in the Ammons household and became intrigued by "The Fives." After parting ways, in 1924 Lewis and Ammons by chance met each other again and found that they both worked for the Silver Taxicab Company in Chicago and still played piano. The friends started to perform together in various clubs and at parties. In 1927, Lewis recorded a rudimentary boogie-woogie tune, "Honky Tonk Train Blues," for Paramount Records. During the following decade, he re-recorded the song for several companies and, in June 1936, waxed "Yancey Special" for Decca in honor of influential barrelhouse pianist, Jimmy Yancey, who regularly appeared in Chicago but never recorded until 1939. In 1934, Ammons opened his own nightspot, the Club DeLisa, and, for the next two years, showcased his talent there. By January 1936, the pianist had landed a contract with Decca Records, and with the group the Rhythm Kings issued "Early Morning Blues" and Pine Top Smith's "Boogie Woogie Stomp."

Working together as a duo, pianist Pete Johnson and singer Joe Turner from Kansas City further promoted boogie-woogie. Born in 1904, Johnson began as a drummer but switched to piano and found work at local bars. Meanwhile, while still a teenager, Joe Turner listened to the pianist from outside a Kansas City club. "One time," chuckled Turner, "I put on my daddy's long pants, and made me a mustache with an eyebrow pencil and stuff and slipped in there." He returned "every chance I got" (Kiefer 1991, 15). As he grew to six-feet-two and three hundred pounds, "Big Joe" sang in nightclubs and tended bar. He was hired at the Sunset Tavern, a Kansas City establishment managed by Piney Brown that featured Pete Johnson on piano. Turner would "go up to the bandstand and sing, and then come back down, get right back behind the bar [to pour drinks]" (15–16). Sometimes, "while Joe was serving drinks, he would suddenly pick up a cue for a blues and sing it right where he stood, with Pete [Johnson] playing piano for him," recalled pianist Mary Lou Williams, who at the time performed and arranged for Andy Kirk's Twelve Clouds of Joy. "I don't think I'll ever forget the thrill of listening to Big Joe Turner shouting and sending everybody while mixing drinks" (Shaw 1978, 47).

Unlike smooth crooners or low-down blues singers, Turner bellowed the blues in a style that complemented the barrelhouse piano style of Pete Johnson. "Everybody was singin' slow blues when I was young," reasoned Turner, "and I thought I'd put a beat to it and sing it up-tempo" (Kiefer 1991, 16). He defined his approach as "jumper blues" (Gourse 1984, 75). "Pete Johnson and I got together, and we worked at that pretty good for a long time, and we finally got pretty good at it. So we used to do it in a nightclub and it went over so good, we just kept it up," explained the shouter (Kiefer 1991, 16).

In early 1936, music writer John Hammond traveled to Kansas City to hear Count Basie, when he spotted Turner and Johnson. He invited them to New York City to perform on a bill with Benny Goodman. Despite the break, the duo attracted little attention and returned home.

However, two years later in 1938, Hammond cast a national spotlight on boogie-woogie with a concert, "From Spirituals to Swing." In mid-December, the entrepreneur wrote an extended *New York Times* article, which somewhat arrogantly contended that "not only the American music lover, but even the American musician himself knows next to nothing about the authentic music of the American Negro." To remedy the deficiency, Hammond pledged to assemble "unfettered Negro musicians of the South and Southwest as well as the best sophisticated dance musicians in a concert at Carnegie Hall." He promised to showcase "boogie-woogie blues pianists whom the writer has dug up in many arduous years of talent-scouting for phonograph companies" (Hammond 1938, 9–10). In addition to acoustic blues and the swing of Count Basie and the Benny Goodman Sextet, the program heavily advertised Joe Turner and the leading boogie-woogie pianists. On December 23, Hammond staged the event for a racially integrated audience. The next day, the *New York Times* enthused about the "boogie-woogie piano playing—it relies heavily on what the art calls 'the big bass.' . . . It needs to be seen as well as heard," reported the newspaper, "especially Albert Ammons, Meade 'Lux' Lewis and Pete Johnson, all from the West, live their music" (Taubman 1938, 13).

After the Carnegie-hosted milestone, record companies rushed to press boogie-woogie discs. On December 30, less than a week after the concert, Columbia subsidiary Vocalion Records recorded Meade Lux Lewis with "Boogie Woogie Prayer." The same day, the company waxed Big Joe Turner and Pete Johnson with "Roll 'Em Pete" and Albert Ammons's "Shout for Joy." Two weeks after the concert, Blue Note Records began recording Lewis and Ammons and followed with material from Johnson. In 1940, Decca issued Pete Johnson's "Kaycee on My Mind" and Joe Turner's "Piney Brown Blues," which honored the Sunset Tavern manager who gave the shouter and Johnson a start. In only a few months, record companies had distributed boogie-woogie discs across the nation.

Barney Josephson, owner of the Café Society, highlighted boogie-woogie pioneers who remained in New York City after the "From Spirituals to Swing" concert. He had established the club to support racial integration and left-wing political causes and considered the venue as a "political cabaret with jazz," much like nightspots he had seen in Prague and Berlin. In early 1939, the proprietor introduced the anti-lynching song "Strange Fruit," to singer Billie Holiday, who performed it at the club.

Josephson allowed Hammond and Benny Goodman to stock the club with artists, including boogie-woogie practitioners from the Carnegie Hall concert (Wilson 1988). "At Café Society, Albert Ammons and Meade Lux Lewis were there first, and then they brought in Pete Johnson and I," explained Joe Turner (Kiefer 1991, 16).

Boogie-woogie stars also appeared in movies. In 1941, the short animated film, *Boogie-Doodle*, highlighted the music of Albert Ammons, and, three years later, Ammons appeared as himself in the full-length *Boogie Woogie Dream*. Joe Turner snagged a part in the Los Angeles revue scored by Duke Ellington, *Jump for Joy*, and secured a role in several three-minute promotional films called soundies, which were played on a special jukebox. By the end of World War II, boogie-woogie had been firmly established as a popular style in America.

Pete Johnson at the Café Society nightclub, August 1946. *William P. Gottlieb/Ira and Leonore S. Gershwin Fund Collection, Music Division, Library of Congress*

Watch Billie Holiday perform "Strange Fruit"

The Big-Band Boogie of Lionel Hampton and Lucky Millinder

As boogie woogie swept America, big bands mixed the boogie beat into their music. Trombonist Will Bradley (b. Wilbur Schwictenberg) and his orchestra, performing at the Famous Door in 1940, specialized in boogie-woogie titles. Showcasing Freddie Slack on piano and Ray McKinley on vocals and drums, the band hit the Top Ten with "Beat Me Daddy (Eight to the Bar)," "Scrub Me, Mama, with a Boogie Beat," and "Cryin' the Boogie Blues." In August 1942, when Slack launched his own outfit, he scored with "Cow-Cow Boogie" along with other boogie tunes.

Others caught the boogie fever. In 1941, the Andrews Sisters, a trio of Minnesota siblings who eventually sold more than seventy-five million records, harmonized to "Boogie Woogie Bugle Boy." Earl Hines embellished a standard for "Boogie Woogie on St. Louis Blues"; Tommy Dorsey offered "Boogie Woogie"; and, at the beginning of the craze, Glenn Miller joined the boogie crowd with "Booglie Wooglie Piggy."

While others featured boogie tunes as novelties, Lionel Hampton and his band fully adapted the boogie-woogie beat to their music. After September 1940, Hampton left Goodman with financing from Louis Armstrong's manager Joe Glaser to establish an orchestra, which generated a rock-steady, boogie-woogie beat on such tunes as "Hamp's Boogie Woogie." Hampton increasingly incorporated theatrics into his act. "I put that little showmanship in it to go along with the playing," he stated (Tompkins 1983a).

Saxophonist Jean-Baptiste "Illinois" Jacquet joined the Hampton band and became the archetypical one-note honker, in contrast to Charlie Parker who wove a flurry of sixteenth notes into a complex fabric. Jacquet had grown up in Broussard, Louisiana, the son of a bandleader who headed a New Orleans–style group that battled visiting territorial outfits. He idolized Texas sax man Herschel Evans, who he heard "with Troy Floyd's [territorial] band when they were battling my father, and that sound really stuck with me" Jacquet declared. "Later on I heard him with Lester Young in Basie's band, and then I heard Chu Berry with Cab Calloway's band. I was still playing alto, but when I heard those tenors, I knew that was the sound" (Birnbaum 1988, 77).

In 1940, eighteen-year-old Illinois toured with Hampton, who discovered the sax player through Nat King Cole. Less than two years later, Jacquet soloed on a recording of "Flying Home," a tune written by Lionel and Benny Goodman. The saxophonist later recalled that "I said to myself, 'this is my first record, and I'd better not sound like Herschel or Prez [Lester Young.]' For the first time, I'd better get myself and try to get *me* in there" (Birnbaum 1988, 78). To differentiate himself, Illinois honked and moaned on the saxophone by embellishing one note with repeated squeals to take the song to the Top Twenty. "When I played that solo, nothing could happen for at least half an hour," the sax man smiled. "You couldn't play another number, because they weren't going to listen to it" (78). "We had the crowd going wild, jumping up and down to the beat and screaming," enthused Lionel Hampton. "We had them going crazy" (Shaw 1978, 83).

Illinois Jacquet flying home in the studio, 1947. *Photograph by William P. Gottlieb. William P. Gottlieb/Ira and Leonore S. Gershwin Fund Collection, Music Division, Library of Congress*

Jacquet complemented his howling tenor with nearly unrestrained histrionics. He walked across the stage, moved his horn in unison with his squawks, and swayed to the boogie beat. "We've always been in show business," he asserted. "By me having been a dancer first, when I started playing the saxophone I had to move around; I couldn't stay still in one place like most of the guys. And being in your twenties, man, you're going to do things," he added (Tompkins 1973d). To intensify the excitement, many times Jacquet faced off against band mate and saxophonist Dexter Gordon. The dueling, explained Gordon, "all started in Hamp's band with Illinois and myself. We had a number called 'Pork Chops' or, as they say in the vernacular 'Po'k Chops,' and that was designed as a duel for our tenors" (Tompkins 1962, 2).

In 1942, when an exhausted Illinois left the Hampton outfit, the bandleader settled on wailing saxophonist Arnett Cobb who, during the thirties, had played with Jacquet. Armed with Cobb's blasting Texas tenor,

 LISTENING GUIDE 26

Lionel Hampton Orchestra with Illinois Jacquet

"FLYING HOME"

Lionel Hampton wrote this showstopper with Benny Goodman, when the two men played in the Benny Goodman Sextet. Supposedly, Hampton whistled the tune during his first flight on an airplane. On November 6, 1939, the Goodman Sextet recorded the song, which featured solos by Hampton and guitarist Charlie Christian. In 1940, after he started his own orchestra, Hampton recorded the song. On May 26, 1942, he waxed the definitive version of the tune, when Illinois Jacquet let loose a wild, unrestrained saxophone solo on the song.

Hampton asked pianist Milt Buckner to arrange this version of the song.

Personnel: Karl George, Ernie Royal, Joe Newman (trumpets); Fred Beckett, Sonny Craven, Harry Sloan (trombones): Marshall Royal (clarinet, alto saxophone); Ray Perry (alto saxophone); Dexter Gordon and Illinois Jacquet (tenor saxophones); Jack McVea (baritone saxophone); Milton Buckner (piano); Irving Ashby (guitar); Wendell Marshall (bass); George Jenkins (drums); and Lionel Hampton (vibraphone).

0:00–0:04	A brief introduction by Hampton on vibes.
0:04–0:15	The trumpets provide a swooping introduction to the saxophone section, which states the theme three times. The brass section ends the passage with a punchy accent.
0:16–0:25	The saxophone section again states the theme three times. At the end of this section, the saxophone section finishes the passage.
0:26–0:34	Hampton solos briefly with backing in a steady 4/4 beat by the drummer.
0:35–0:44	Hampton continues his solo with backing from the saxophone section, which provides a riff as rhythm.
0:45–1:23	Illinois Jacquet starts his solo with a punchy, chugging backing from the brass section. As he solos, Jacquet slides over sustained notes to create a bluesy feel to the music in a style reminiscent of the Basie Orchestra.
1:24–1:35	Jacquet fastens upon one note and repeats it twelve times until he ends it with a phrase. The propulsive rhythm continues with the brass section riff.
1:36–1:43	Jacquet repeats his honking.
1:44–1:53	Jacquet weaves a solo above the riffing brass.
1:54–2:02	Jacquet repeats his honking in modified form by blowing a note, pausing for the riff of the brass, and then blowing the note twice more. He repeats this passage twice until ending his solo with a brief improvisation. The note from Jacquet's sax and the response of the brass section constitutes a call-and-response that creates a swaying, toe-tapping effect.
2:03–2:05	A two-second introduction by Hampton's vibes provides a transition to the next section.
2:06–2:25	In another call-and-response passage, the sax section provides the rhythmic riff behind the upward sliding sound of the brass section.

2:26–2:35	In an exciting call-and-response, Hampton trades three-bar and four-bar measures with the high-pitched, open trumpet of Ernie Royal, who imitates the honking of Jacquet and ends the passage with a sliding effect that mimics a roller-coaster.
2:36–2:44	The brass section plays a riff, which a sliding saxophone section introduces and backs.
2:46–2:56	Hampton exchanges single notes with the screeching trumpet of Ernie Royal, first in 4/4 time and then in double time. The two end the passage by playing together in double time.
2:57–3:07	The brass section riffs against the riffing saxophone section to create a driving finish.

Hampton waxed "Flying Home No. 2," which almost duplicated the sales of its successor. By the mid-forties, the Hampton band served as a model for a boogie-woogie big band.

The wild Lionel Hampton and honker Arnett Cobb, 1946. *Photograph by William P. Gottlieb. William P. Gottlieb/Ira and Leonore S. Gershwin Fund Collection, Music Division, Library of Congress*

The Lucky Millinder band provided the final ingredient needed for jump blues, when it grafted Joe Turner-like, shouting vocals into the mix. Lucius "Lucky" Millinder, an atypical band boss who could not play an instrument, began as a master of ceremonies and dancer and eventually led several bands. "Lucky couldn't read a note, but if you gave him a bunch of guys who could read, in a week's time, he'd have them sounding like a band that had been organized for a year," pointed out Panama Francis, who drummed in one of Millinder's orchestras (Shaw 1978, 59). In 1938, Lucky partnered with boogie-woogie pianist Bill Doggett to form an outfit, which secured a residency at the Savoy Ballroom in New York City and, by the middle of 1941, snagged a record deal with Decca. The band specialized in pile-driving, swaying tunes such as "Apollo Jump" and "Rock Me."

Blues shouter Wynonie Harris added propulsive vocals to the Millinder orchestra to create an even greater stir. A native of Omaha, Nebraska, Harris traveled to Kansas City, where he heard the shout-vocal style of Joe Turner. In 1944, after moving to Chicago, he was spotted by Lucky Millinder, who offered him a position in his band. In June 1945, Harris and the Millinder group entered the Top Ten for eight weeks with "Who Threw the Whiskey in the Well," a rousing number with Harris belting the blues complemented by hand clapping in the background. By the end of the war, the shouting vocals, honking sax, and boogie-woogie beat of jump blues had arrived.

The Second Great Migration of African Americans

During World War II, African Americans who streamed into Northern cities and earned higher wages in defense plants provided a market for jump blues. They had been pushed from the Southern cotton culture, which for nearly two centuries had dominated the region, when brothers John and Mack Rust invented the mechanical cotton picker, which in one hour could harvest 400 pounds of cotton—the equivalent to four days of work for an African-American cotton picker ("Picker Problems" 1936, 59). By 1947, African-American sharecroppers had largely been replaced by the new machine.

The North looked attractive to Southern African Americans who saw their livelihood disappearing. As the United States geared up for war, the need for workers in Northern and West Coast industrial factories offered many African Americans a chance for jobs, which paid much more than manual labor in the South. "With the commencement of World War II, the extraordinary demand for labor in industries speeded up the movement of Negroes from the agricultural South to the urban areas," explained one observer (Guzman 1947, 8).

African Americans streamed into Chicago. During the forties, 214,000 Southern African Americans arrived in the Windy City and increased the African-American population by 77 percent in a decade. About half the migrants came from the Mississippi Delta region, which stretched 200 miles from Memphis to Vicksburg. They paid $15 for the day-long trip on the Illinois Central Railroad to the Windy City, the home of the widely read, African-American-owned newspaper the *Chicago Defender*, which encouraged Southern sharecroppers to migrate to the North.

African Americans traveled to other Northern cities, too. During the forties, the African-American population skyrocketed in New York City, Cleveland, and Philadelphia. "Detroit became a haven for a lot of the immigrants from the South, like people from Alabama, Georgia, parts of Florida, [and] Mississippi," observed African-American songwriter Billy Davis, who lived in the Motor City (Broven 2009, 320). In April 1945, the *Chicago Defender* characterized "the great Negro march on freedom northward of the present war period" as "a chapter as significant in the life of mankind as the ancient Hebrew migration out of Egypt" (Conrad 1945, 13).

The African-American migrants found jobs in factories and shipyards and "made more money than they ever thought existed in their lives," maintained Los Angeles–based Marshal Royal, an alto sax man who played for Count Basie. "Some of them worked two eight-hour shifts a day, making that dough" (Bryant 1998, 47). "A lot of people [were] coming in from the South, going into defense plants," agreed saxophonist William "Sonny" Criss. "There was new money. People hadn't had that kind of money before" (Gitler 1985, 168).

After the war, the federal government ensured continued good times. To fuel the economy, President Harry Truman and Congress rebuilt war-torn Europe. Between 1945 and early 1948, the United States allocated nearly $14 billion to stabilize Europe. In April 1948, Congress passed the Marshall Plan, named in honor of Secretary of State George C. Marshall, which authorized an additional $13 billion to bolster the European states. During the late forties, the government stimulus resulted in record-high employment levels for the 1.5 million African Americans who headed North during the decade.

Jump blues targeted African Americans who had migrated from the South and were looking for an upbeat, energetic, and stimulating sound that reflected a hustle-bustle urban environment and good times. They embraced the urban jump blues rather than the more sullen country blues or the complex bebop, which they did not understand. "The African-American people," stated Los Angeles music entrepreneur Art Rupe, "looked down on country [blues] music. Among themselves, the African-Americans called country blues 'field nigger' music. They wanted to be citified" (Shaw 1978, 182–83).

Louis Jordan and Jump Blues

Near the end of World War II and into the postwar era, small-combo jump blues, also called rhythm and blues (R&B), became the rage. As big bands faded from prominence and as the recording ban lifted, small groups dispensed a hyper-charged, beat-laden music that emphasized a boogie-woogie beat, a screaming, honking sax, and shouted vocals. The small-combo format afforded club owners and record producers a relatively inexpensive way to hire talent yet retain the excitement of a larger ensemble. Unlike the cerebral, complex bop, which reflected a growing militancy among African Americans, jump blues provided entertainment and a chance to dance.

Louis Jordan epitomized the small-combo jump blues. Born in Brinkley, Arkansas, in 1908, a teenaged African-American Jordan started in his father's band and toured with the Rabbit Foot Minstrels. In 1932, he settled in Philadelphia and lent his alto sax and energetic vocals to a band fronted by Philadelphia native and trumpeter Charlie Gaines. Four years later, he landed a place in the Chick Webb Orchestra, a mainstay at the Savoy Ballroom in New York City.

In 1938, when Chick Webb died, Jordan formed his own combo and signed with Decca Records. "I loved playing with a big band. I loved singing the blues" he explained. "But I really wanted to be an entertainer—that's me—on my own. I wanted to play for the people, for millions, not just a few hep cats." He initially established a nine-piece outfit and then reduced it to a sextet, later adding a guitar. First focusing on ballads, Jordan called the group, Louis Jordan: His Silver Saxophone and Golden Voice (Shaw 1978, 66). Within a year, he changed the name to Louis Jordan and His Tympany Five, because drummer Walter Martin many times used the tympani kettle drum. His first recordings focused on standard fare and slow boogie-blues numbers, which Jordan sang in a clear, almost crooning voice.

Jordan did not attract much attention until he applied the boogie-woogie beat to novelty numbers. At the Fox Head Tavern, a beer joint in Cedar Rapids, Iowa, Jordan turned to more topical and amusing selections. He recalled that "it was there I found 'If It's Love You Want, Baby, That's Me' and a gang of blues—'Ration Blues,' 'Inflation Blues,' and others" (Shaw 1978, 67). Jordan agreed to try these novelty songs, many of which were written by his bassist Dallas Bartley, due to the remote location of the nightspot. "They were not in New York or Chicago. They were not known, and they could make fools of themselves," recollected the band's manager Berle Adams. "That was where they developed all the novelty songs that later made Jordan. When they came back to the Capitol Lounge [in Chicago], they had a wealth of material and became a smash overnight" (78).

The sax player/vocalist hit the charts with his novelties sung in a spirited style. In 1942, he first hit the top of the R&B chart with "What's the Use of Getting Sober (When You Gonna Get Drunk Again)." In 1944, he scaled the chart with two war-related tunes, the Top Ten R&B "Ration Blues" and "G.I. Jive," which hit the top spot on the pop and R&B charts. He followed with the smash, "Is You Is or Is You Ain't (Ma' Baby)."

LISTENING GUIDE 27

Louis Jordan and His Tympany Five

"CALDONIA"

"Caldonia" was inspired by the earlier "Old Man Ben" (1938) by Hot Lips Page, which introduced the notion of a hard-headed woman. It supposedly referred to a strong-willed, lanky lady named Caldonia who lived in Memphis and constantly challenged men in a gambling den. In 1944, Jordan composed the song around the fragment about Caldonia in "Old Man Ben" on the advice of Page and published the song under the name of his then-wife Fleecie Moore because he had signed to another publishing company and wanted free rein with the song.

Ironically, other bandleaders recorded the tune shortly before Jordan. On February 26, 1945, Woody Herman and His Herd waxed an up-tempo version for Columbia after he heard Jordan perform the song and,

by May, nearly topped the chart with it. A week later, Erskine Hawkins scored with a number-twelve pop hit of "Caldonia," which *Billboard* described on April 21, 1945 as "right rhythmic rock and roll music." On April 19, 1945, Louis Jordan recorded the song for Decca that entered *Billboard* and eventually reached number six on the pop chart. He also produced a short film of the song to promote his public appearances that reached both white and African-American audiences. Almost immediately after the hit, Jordan completely restocked the Tympany Five with new members.

Personnel: Al Morgan (bass), Bill Austin (piano), Alex "Razz" Mitchell (drums), Idrees Sulieman (trumpet), Freddie Simon (tenor sax), and Louis Jordan (vocals and tenor sax).

0:00–0:15	The songs starts with a boogie-woogie piano passage by Bill Austin. As with boogie-woogie piano in general, the pianist plays eight bars to the beat with the left hand to give the rhythm a propulsive, driving feel.
0:16–0:34	The band enters by playing a four-bar riff three times in a twelve-bar blues.
0:35–0:50	The group chooses another riff, repeats it five times, and then resolves it in a final measure for an ending. The boogie-woogie beat of the piano continues throughout the passage and the remainder of the song.
0:51–1:08	Jordan's vocals start backed primarily by the boogie-woogie beat of the piano.
1:09–1:13	In a high pitch, Jordan repeats "Caldonia" twice and then sings the phrase "what makes your big head so hard" in a twelve-bar-blues format. At the end of the passage, Jordan sings an insistent "now" to signal the upcoming section.
1:14–1:24	Jordan continues with the vocal line, again backed by the pulsating piano.
1:25–1:40	Jordan's gravelly saxophone trades measures with the punchy, insistent riff of the trumpet in a call-and-response. At 1:36, Jordan inserts a blue note in his solo.
1:41–1:59	The trumpet enters, playing a gut-bucket, braying, almost New Orleans–style novelty or freak riff and trades six bars with the saxophones. The exchange simulates the sway of a big band and re-emphasizes the importance of call-and-response to jump blues and jazz in general.
2:00–2:15	Jordan proceeds with his humorous vocals in an almost spoken-word style.
2:16–2:22	Jordan restates the Caldonia section of 1:09–1:13, still backed by the boogie-woogie piano.
2:23–2:33	The group restates the riff from 0:16–0:34, repeats it three times, and then resolves it to finish the passage.
2:34–2:38	The group plays four syncopated beats to end the song.

Watch Louis Jordan and His Tympany Five perform "Caldonia"

In 1945, Louis Jordan and His Tympany Five unleashed a different kind of sound that defined jump blues. On April 19, the band waxed "Caldonia" in the Decca studio. Unlike his previous, more deliberate boogie-woogie blues, he accelerated the tempo, abandoned his near-croon for a shout, and honked and squeaked on his sax to help define a new genre. "Hey boy," he shouted to his bassist, who started the tune with an insistent, speeded-up, boogie-woogie beat in one performance, "that ain't the beat we supposed to play. Well," Jordan shrugs his shoulders, "I guess I better get on in here with it" as he blasts his sax in time to the rhythm. "*I made the blues jump*," he exclaimed (Shaw 1978, 74). In a month, the song shot up the R&B chart to number one and registered on the pop Top Ten.

The Tympany Five repeated their jump-blues triumph. In 1946, the group sold two million copies of the propulsive "Choo Choo Ch'Boogie" and a million discs of "Buzz Me." Three years later, Jordan scored with "Saturday Night Fish Fry (Parts 1 and 2)." From 1945 to the end of the decade, Jordan and his band racked up a

Louis Jordan (far right with saxophone) and his band, circa 1947. *Photograph by William P. Gottlieb. William P. Gottlieb/Ira and Leonore S. Gershwin Fund Collection, Music Division, Library of Congress*

remarkable thirteen number-one R&B hits, entered the R&B Top Ten thirty-six times, and scored with five Top Ten pop entries. "All over the country he had, like in most jukeboxes, 7 or 8 hit records at one time," marveled organist Wild Bill Davis who played with Jordan (Rusch 1988g, 26). Based upon their recording success, the group performed at the downtown Paramount Theater and at the Apollo Theater twice a year. On November 4, 1947, the Jordan band attracted seven thousand wild adherents to the Oakland Auditorium and, the next February, grossed $70,000 for a two-week engagement at the Golden Gate Theatre in San Francisco.

Jordan supplemented his highly charged music with a flashy stage show. Tenor sax player Paul Quinichette—who briefly played with Jordan and later established his reputation with Count Basie—remembered "sequined Christmas-tree-type uniforms, red pants, vivid green coats, sequined ties and boots" of the Jordan outfit (Chilton 1992, 144). "What Louis was trying to do was to present his audiences with a Technicolor picture of a live band, getting the musicians to imitate a movie on stage," recalled Aaron Izenhall, who played trumpet in the band during the forties. "The wild colors, the movement, the exaggerated gestures, the whole thing came over like a scene from a movie" (124).

Understandably, Jordan used films to market his records. The band made "motion picture short[s] in which we would introduce new songs," related manager Berle Adams, who teamed with Jordan in 1941. "We would then book these shorts into theaters in black communities" so "they would be able to see Jordan perform new material on the screen" (Shaw 1978, 80). Starting in 1944, Jordan appeared in full-length features such as *Follow the Boys* and *Meet Miss Bobby Sox*. In the two years following World War II, he starred in films geared for African-American audiences, including *Beware!*, *Look Out Sister*, and *Reet, Petite and Gone*.

The jump blues appealed primarily to African Americans. "A lot of Jordan's material dealt with black situations in a comical way," Berle Adams observed (Shaw 1978, 84). In addition, many white disc jockeys refused to spin Jordan records and introduce the Tympany Five to a broad white audience. "Most Jordan hits were in the R&B field. It was impossible to get airplay from white jockeys on the big stations," Adams maintained (85).

Despite being boycotted by white radio, Jordan sometimes reached white listeners. "After my records started to sell," he contended, "we drew mixed audiences to clubs. I was trying to do what they told me: straddle the fence" (Shaw 1978, 67–68). "Louis Jordan's big sale was African-American," clarified manager Berle Adams, but "some of them carried over to white. The original 'Is You or Is You Ain't (Ma' Baby)' was a big white seller, 'Choo Choo Ch'Boogie' was a big white seller, 'Ain't Nobody Here but Us Chickens' was a big white seller, and a number of others" (Broven 2009, 29; Shaw 1978, 85).

The Rise of Independent Record Companies

Small, independent record companies spread jump blues across the nation. After the war and the lengthy recording ban, major companies—RCA, Decca, and Columbia—rushed to record star artists and largely ignored new talent, especially budding African-American musicians. Entrepreneurs saw a market for jump blues among African Americans who had migrated to major urban areas and established new labels to cater to this audience.

The introduction of the reel-to-reel tape machine revolutionized the recording process and encouraged the growth of independent companies. Rather than the cumbersome process of recording a musician in a studio by depressing a stylus onto wax, it permitted quick access to recording technology for anyone who could afford the machine. Along with the rise of independent pressing plants that were not owned by the major labels, the new technology enhanced the ability of small labels to start with minimum funding.

In July 1943, African-American pianist and composer Leon Rene established Exclusive Records. Rene, composer of the pop smash "When the Swallows Come Back to Capistrano," established the Los Angeles–based company because he and his brother Otis "found it difficult to get the big record companies to record our material. You just couldn't sell a colored artist to any of the majors," he maintained (Shaw 1978, 152). While his brother founded Excelsior Records for pop and blues titles, Leon held his first session with jump-blues pianist/vocalist Joe Liggins and His Honeydrippers to wax "The Honeydripper." "Phew! We had people lined up around the block to hit the stores to buy that record," remembered Leon (Broven 2009, 38). The disc "put Exclusive Records solidly in the recording business" (Shaw 1978, 154). After issuing seven more Top Twenty hits by Liggins, Exclusive Records "became the nation's number one independent R&B record company," boasted the label owner (154–55).

Other entrepreneurs, emboldened by the success of Exclusive Records, launched record labels. During the forties, Art Goldberg traveled from his home-town of Pittsburgh to Los Angeles, changed his name to Art Rupe, and established Juke Box Records. Conducting a market analysis of current hits, he found that many chartbusters included "boogie" in their titles, so he decided to focus on jump-blues artists. As he told it, "there was a tremendous demand for this type of record. The majors weren't supplying music of this type. With the wartime shortage of shellac and other materials, their pressings went mostly to pop music" (Shaw 1978, 180). Given the vacuum created by larger record firms, Rupe concentrated on "an area neglected by the majors and in essence took the crumbs off the table of the record industry" (182).

Impressed by the Lucky Millinder band, Rupe searched for a small group with the same sound. "I couldn't afford eighteen pieces, so I ended with two small acts," he explained. Spending a start-up budget of six hundred dollars, he released two boogie numbers: "Kansas City Boogie" by George "Blues Man" Vann and the Sepia Tones's "Boogie #1," which sold 70,000 copies in a year and a half (Shaw 1978, 184). In late 1945, Rupe hooked jump-blues singer/drummer Roy Milton, who had founded the Solid Senders a dozen years earlier. Three days before Christmas, the label owner recorded Milton's "R. M. Blues," which nearly topped the R&B chart and entered the pop Top Twenty, and featured the honking sax of Buddy Floyd. "No attempt was made at hard technical swinging. Just sheer emotion," noted tenor man Jack Kelson, who joined Milton five years later (Bryant 1998, 229). During the next ten years, Rupe released more than seventy-eight Roy Milton sides, of which nineteen hit the Top Ten R&B chart.

In late 1947, twenty-five-year-old R&B guitarist/vocalist Jimmy Liggins signed with Rupe, who by then had changed the name of his label to Specialty Records. Brother of the Honeydripper and a former professional boxer, Liggins delivered an even more raucous version of jump blues than his brother. Jimmy and His Drops of Joy highlighted a frantic, honking sax and up-tempo rhythm, which accompanied Jimmy's shouting vocals on such party anthems as "Saturday Night Boogie Woogie Man" and "Night Life Boogie." By the turn of the decade, Art Rupe's Specialty Records successfully had released dozens of small-group jump blues and, in 1955, unveiled Little Richard (b. Richard Penniman), who transitioned jump-blues jazz to rock and roll through a furious, pulsating, unrestrained version of the jump-blues style.

In 1945, brothers Leo and Eddie Mesner entered the jump-blues sweepstakes. Operating a Los Angeles record store, the Philharmonic Music Shop, the duo founded Philo Records, later renamed Aladdin Records. In July, the brothers recorded Illinois Jacquet, who had started a five-piece outfit with his brother Russell on trumpet, and young bassist Charles Mingus to recreate the exuberance of the Hampton big band with a small combo. They waxed two versions of Jacquet's signature "Flying Home" to launch the label. In September, the Mesners released the first solo recordings of jump-blues singer Wynonie Harris, who assembled a band after quitting Lucky Millinder.

In December 1946, nineteen-year-old Houston pianist Amos Milburn signed with the Mesners. Milburn had been inspired by "some early Louis Jordan numbers," he related. "I took piano lessons but was into things like Tommy Dorsey's 'Boogie Woogie' and the Albert Ammons, Pete Johnson, Meade Lux Lewis stuff" (Kiefer 1991, 12). By the time he left the armed forces and recorded for Aladdin, he had perfected the propulsive jump blues. In 1948, Milburn scored with his best-selling tune, "Chicken Shack Boogie," and followed with nineteen Top Ten R&B hits. Milburn and the Chicken-Shackers released more than a hundred tunes on the label.

Sax player/vocalist Chuck Higgins recorded for Vernon "Jake" Porter's Combo Records. After a stint in the Air Force, Higgins attended the Los Angeles Music Conservatory, playing the trumpet. In 1950, he formed a combo with sax man Johnny Parker that performed in the lounge of the Club Alabam on Central Avenue. When the owner of the nightspot asked Higgins to downsize his band, Chuck learned to play the saxophone in two weeks. In 1951, Higgins ventured to Jake Porter's rudimentary home studio and taped "Pachuko Hop" and "Motor Head Baby," which featured Higgins on saxophone performing in a definitive jump-blues style. "I couldn't move around on the sax, like I could on the trumpet—remember, I learned to play sax in two weeks," confessed Higgins, "so I developed that thing of hitting the one note over and over—dooo, dooo, dooo, dooo! I was raising so much hell with that, though, that the other guys started copying me. Big Jay [McNeely] and Joe Houston won't admit it, but I think the reason they started to honking was to keep up with me" (Dawson 1992, 24). To add excitement to his stage act, Higgins hired a "big girl, about 250 pounds, and she'd travel with the band," he intimated. "She'd come up during the show and tear my shirt off and clown at me . . . That always got the crowd going," he smiled (26).

Jumpers such as Hal Singer and Paul Williams recorded for Herman Lubinsky, the owner of Savoy Records who first recorded Big Jay McNeely. In June 1948, Savoy waxed Hal Singer, who started with such territory bands as Tommy Douglas before joining Jay McShann. After some session work with Savoy, he signed with Lubinsky and hit the top R&B spot with the honking "Cornbread." Later in the year, the Detroit-raised Williams recorded "The Hucklebuck," a reworking of the 1928 Andy Gibson song, "D-Natural Blues," which ignited a dance craze throughout the nation. When he left Savoy in late 1951, Williams had recorded thirty-six jump-blues tunes for the label.

De Luxe Records unearthed jump bluesman Roy Brown. Established in May 1944 by brothers David and Jules Braun in Linden, New Jersey, the label discovered Brown by a twist of fate, when, in 1947, Brown offered his idol Wynonie Harris the song "Good Rockin' Tonight." When Harris refused the tune, De Luxe asked Brown to record the song and scored a minor hit with it. Sensing the potential of the song, Syd Nathan of King Records—who had just bought a majority share of De Luxe—asked Wynonie Harris to sing a more upbeat version of the selection for King. The Harris version vaulted to the top of the R&B chart and inspired a young Elvis Presley, who covered the song seven years later.

The Dawn of the Disc Jockey

The jump-blues sound received a plug from disc jockeys, a relatively new profession. During the early days of radio, station managers broadcast live performances with quick and terse introductions, read stock and farm reports, and interviewed local notables with minimal intrusion. Most stations seldom spun records, on orders from the American Federation of Musicians, which frowned on broadcast of pre-recorded material.

Al Jarvis fundamentally changed the role of the announcer and the spinning of discs on the air. After graduating from the University of Southern California, he answered an ad in the newspaper that stated: "Man wanted to talk on the radio." Hired by Los Angeles station KFWB, Jarvis initially read from newspapers and randomly spoke about anything that might interest listeners. One day in 1932, he brought a Victrola into the studio, played records, and informed the audience about the musicians on the discs. Within a few months, the innovative announcer was spinning several records by an artist in quick succession, trying to recreate a live broadcast from a ballroom. He modeled his strategy after the sixteen-inch electrical transcription discs, which contained live recordings punctuated by announcements and proved useful to small radio stations that needed material to fill empty time slots. Jarvis called his show, *The World's Largest Make Believe Ballroom*. Though a breakthrough, the new program generated little attention outside the Los Angeles area.

Martin Block popularized the format that Jarvis had created. A former salesman, Block started his radio career in Los Angeles, where he heard the Jarvis program. To better support his family, in late 1934 he moved to New York City, where he found a position at station WNEW. The station had just secured exclusive rights to broadcast the trial of Bruno Richard Hauptmann who, two years earlier, had been accused of kidnapping and murdering the twenty-month-old child of famed aviator Charles Lindbergh. Because WNEW's on-site reporter relayed only periodic updates rather than continuous coverage, Block convinced his boss to adopt Jarvis's format and snagged Retardo diet pills as a sponsor for the program.

On February 3, 1935, Block launched his own *Make Believe Ballroom* with reports from the courtroom of the Hauptmann trial interspersed between records. He introduced the discs with patter, which made it appear that he had bandleaders in the studio. Trying to "develop his own personality" on the air (Block 1954), he called his turntable a revolving stage and referred to his studio as the "crystal ballroom," likely a reference to the crystals used in many radios at the time. After the first broadcast, six hundred orders poured into Retardo, and, within a week, nearly four thousand customers flooded the company with requests for diet pills. In four months, the announcer captured four million listeners. Soon, Block was spinning fifteen-minute segments of records by well-known bands, which lobbied him to play their discs. Initially, the radio personality used Charlie Barnet's "Make Believe Ballroom" as a theme song, then updated it in 1940 with Glenn Miller's "Make Believe Ballroom Time" for his permanent theme.

The influence of Block's program spread. In 1940, *Make Believe Ballroom* went into national syndication. In April 1942, *Billboard* enthused over the "fabulous" program and referred to Block as the "world's greatest salesman. His word is gospel to untold thousands of consumers in the [New York] Metropolitan area; a kind word from him about a record is sufficient to boost its sales through the roof. There has, in fact, never been anyone quite like him," the magazine concluded (Block 1954). By the end of the war, Block earned the princely sum of $22,000 a week and picked between sponsors, which offered to support the show.

After the success of Block, broadcasters who regularly and continuously spun records dominated the airwaves. On August 13, 1941, *Variety* coined the term "disc jockey" to describe a radio announcer who primarily played records. Prominent deejays included Henry Louis in San Diego; Nashville's Frank Bow, who broadcast records at a 50,000-watt station that reached thirty states; and Santa Monica's Joe Adams, a protégé of Al Jarvis who aired jazz records. By the end of the war, radio announcers across the country had become personalities, known for slick salesmanship and particular musical tastes.

African Americans also landed jobs as disc jockeys. In 1939, Hal Jackson, the first African-American announcer, hosted a show on Washington, DC station WINX. Beginning in 1945, Al Benson (b. Art Leaner), a one-time member of a vaudeville troupe and storefront church preacher, jockeyed on station WGES in Chicago. Within three years, he switched to WJJD and became the most popular announcer in the Windy City. In 1947, *Ebony* magazine identified sixteen African-American jockeys throughout the country and gushed that because "a voice has no color . . . new vistas [have opened] to Negroes in radio." Eight years later, more than five hundred African Americans were spinning platters on the air (Brewster and Broughton 2000, 30).

Many radio personalities, both African-American and white, championed jump blues. In 1947, white Los Angeles announcer Hunter Hancock spun R&B records for station KFVD. Hancock premiered the show *Harlematinee*, followed by *Huntin' with Hunter*. In 1949, Bill Randle hosted the *Interracial Goodwill Hour* on Detroit station WJLB before moving to Cleveland on WERE, where he continued to play jump-blues discs. In October 1949, Harold Ladell introduced the *Mr. Blues Show* on WHBI in New York and then on WNJR in Newark "to create exposure" for jump blues. "I played five records" over and over, he recalled. "Amos Milburn's 'Chicken Shack Boogie' was one of them" (Broven 2009, 218).

In 1946, Gene Nobles joined station WLAC in Nashville to spin R&B records. He rotated platters from 11:00 p.m. until midnight on *The Dance Hour*, sponsored by a company that sold baby chickens for three dollars per hundred. In February the next year, the jive-talking jockey who had been a carnival barker and bingo dealer met Randy Wood, who owned a nearby record store. He convinced Wood to sponsor his radio show for twelve dollars an hour to attract more customers. After two weeks, Wood received a barrage of letters asking for records by the jump-blues artists on the radio. By summer 1947, Nobles had enlisted two other local record dealers in his scheme. Reaching an audience in thirty states with the powerful WLAC signal, Nobles created a national market for R&B and for records in Nashville record stores, which increasingly specialized in a mail-order business (Broven 2009, 99).

In 1948, African-American record-store owner John Dolphin promoted jump blues on his radio program. Dolphin owned the largest R&B record shop in Los Angeles and began to broadcast from the window of his shop. He ceaselessly publicized upcoming R&B acts and aired R&B records, which his shop sold twenty-four hours a day. Dolphin hired such white disc jockeys as Hunter Hancock and Dick "Huggy Boy" Hugg to sell jump blues. "Every day, for years, he'd play my records two or three times a day on his radio show," recalled Chuck Higgins about Dolphin. "He kept me hot because his store was where you bought race records in those days" (Dawson 1992, 26).

Independent distributors paid attention to the disc jockeys. "The disc jockeys were a pipeline to the jukebox operators; the boxes made the hits," explained record salesman Lester Sill about the four hundred thousand jukeboxes that accounted for 50 percent of all sales. "In San Diego, after I saw the dee-jays on Sunday, I visited the jukebox [operators] on Monday and all through the rest of the week. Selling them was easier if I could say, 'Listen to [disc jockey] Henry Louis, and you'll hear the new [jump-blues record]'" (Shaw 1978, 196).

Record labels gave added incentives to disc jockeys to play specific records. Sometimes, they gave the jockeys cash. "We never wrote a check to a dee-jay," remarked Joe Bihari of Modern Records, which recorded Joe Turner and howling sax man Joe Houston. "We paid them in cash." Bihari considered the pay-out "like a marketing expense." Other times, salesmen slipped five hundred to a thousand records to radio announcers in exchange for their interest in a disc. "We took certain dee-jays and said, 'Look we're gonna send you free records. Get yourself a little record store,'" confided the straightforward Bihari (Broven 2009, 301). Sometimes a deejay was listed as a "coauthor" of a song so he could enjoy a piece of the royalties.

Jump Blues on Top

Near the turn of the fifties, the popularity of jump blues became apparent to other jazz musicians. In 1947, Dizzy Gillespie, one of the originators of bop, noticed the frenzy over jump blues when on tour with Illinois Jacquet. "He was playing what the people, the masses of blacks, wanted," he recalled. "We played behind him and he became a big star. The same thing happened with Louis Jordan, a small group, five pieces, the Tympany Five. Our band got a lotta publicity, but the money didn't roll in like the publicity. We didn't play that kind of music" (Gillespie 1979, 309). Bop pianist Gerald Wiggins observed "it was the blues with the guitars wanging away, and the tenor honking and the drums had a heavy backbeat. You know, it wasn't music at all," he complained. "But it took the public's fancy, and they ate it up. In fact, guys like myself were saying, 'Well, this won't last.' [But] it got bigger and bigger and bigger" (Bryant 1998, 320).

An incident on Central Avenue in Los Angeles vividly displayed the contrast between the cerebral bop and the more popular, emotionally laden jump blues. During the late forties, bop trumpeter Art Farmer and tenor saxophonists Dexter Gordon and Wardell Gray performed at the Downbeat Club across the street from the Last Word, which hosted Big Jay McNeely. Big Jay "came out in the street with his horn and came all the way across Central Avenue and walked into the Downbeat with his horn, playing it, honking, whooping and hollering," remembered Farmer. "Part of his act was complete, total abandon. It was like somebody who had become completely possessed by the music. He throws off his coat and throws that down, then he jumps on his back, and he's playing the horn, puts his legs up in the air, and he's playing all the time" (Bryant 1998, 275–76). After witnessing the wild audience reaction to McNeely's act, a few weeks later at the Olympic Theater in Los Angeles, "Dexter decides that he's going to pull a Big Jay," related Farmer. "All of a sudden he starts to come out of his coat, and Wardell . . . takes the coat and very civilly folds it and puts it on his arm. There's Dexter, and he's a honkin' a la Big Jay, and he finally gets down on his knees a la Big Jay. And these people in the audience, these kids, these teenagers, are looking up there like, 'Gee, when is he going to do something?' . . . He stayed down there on his knees like he's praying, like he didn't know what to do then," laughed the trumpeter. "So finally he got up off his knees, and the show went on" (276).

Rather than play bop, saxophonists wailed to get work from club owners who demanded honking. In 1951, twenty-five-year-old John Coltrane, then a saxophonist in Philadelphia, played on the weekends at local clubs. In one venue, he asked the owner, "What do I have to do to please people?" The proprietor briskly replied, "Honk more than you play, you're not honking enough." Coltrane, studying advanced musical theory at the Granoff School of Music on weekdays, promptly scaled the bar counter, walked forward, and swayed back and forth, all the while honking and squealing on his sax (Thomas 1980, 56). "They had me walking the bar, playing like a honking tenor player and all that. That was the thing of the day and all of us did it," confided Seldon Powell who favored a bebop style. "This was the thing that was selling in those days, and that's what you did" (Rusch 1989b, 6).

By the turn of the decade, *Billboard* acknowledged the power of jump blues. In 1942, it launched a Harlem Hit Parade chart. Four years later, on June 25, 1949, it switched the chart designations of "race" and "sepia" to "R&B." It made jump blues, a raucous variant of jazz, into a distinct, important style, which could be measured in terms of hits and sales.

The Moondog Coronation Ball in Cleveland signaled a high point of jump blues but also hinted at its eclipse. Conceived by WJW disc jockey Alan Freed and concert promoter Lew Platt, the event brought together on one stage notable jump-blues artists such as Paul Williams and His Hucklebuckers who Freed promoted on his radio show. Scheduled for March 21, 1952, from 10 p.m. to 2 a.m., the Ball drew nearly twenty-five thousand white and African-American teenagers who packed the Cleveland arena, which seated only ten thousand. The crushing mob broke doors, fought, and screamed until a startled and scared fire department turned on the lights to stop the show and police used fire hoses for crowd control. Though canceled, the dance convinced Freed that only the wildest acts would satisfy hormone-driven teens. During the next three years, small-combo jump blues evolved into a more agitated, youth-based music, which Freed called rock and roll.

For Discussion and Further Study

Chapter Quiz

1. What is boogie woogie? How did it develop? Who were the key performers in this style and how did they achieve popularity? What influence did this music have on the small jazz ensembles of the late forties/early fifties?

2. How did band leaders like Lionel Hampton and Lucky Millinder adapt boogie-woogie rhythms and stylings into their big bands? How did this further popularize and spread the musical style that was now called jump blues?

3. What role did Louis Jordan play in catering to the new, younger African-American audience, which migrated from the South seeking employment and freedom from segregation in the North? How did he help establish the small-combo, jump-blues style?

4. How and why did independent record companies arise in the postwar years? What impact did they have on recording and promoting African-American jazz?

5. How and why did deejays become major forces on radio? What role did they play in promoting jazz?

12

JAZZ IN THE POSTWAR YEARS

Anticommunist Paranoia, the GI Bill, and the Long-Playing Record

I n post–World War II America, a fervent anticommunist sentiment, the GI Bill, and the introduction of the long-playing record (LP) shaped jazz. Immediately after the war, an anticommunist paranoia swept the country and sometimes targeted jazz musicians. At the same time, the GI Bill offered musicians who returned home from war the chance for a free college education. This exposed many of them to classical theory that complemented their jazz knowledge. Together, the anticommunist obsession and the GI Bill led to a classically tinged, tension-filled, jagged jazz, exemplified by the Stan Kenton band. Many of these recordings were much longer than typical three-minute popular songs. The new technology of the twelve-inch LP with its longer play time accommodated this new, complicated music and allowed jazz to reflect an era of anxiety.

During the forties, Hazel Scott originally became popular at Café Society, the nightclub in New York's Greenwich Village that attracted a progressive, racially mixed audience. By 1950, she had established herself as a popular, contemporary jazz pianist, singer, and civil-rights activist. Early in the year, Scott headlined a show on a local New York television network that in July was syndicated countrywide to become the first national television show hosted by an African American.

Within weeks after her national premiere, Scott was listed as a communist in the pamphlet *Red Channels: A Report on Communist Influence in Radio and Television*, which

The sultry June Christie, late 1940s. Photograph by William P. Gottlieb. William P. Gottlieb/Ira and Leonore S. Gershwin Fund Collection, Music Division, Library of Congress targeted more than 150 suspected communists in the entertainment business. To try to save her program, in September 1950 Scott volunteered to testify in front of the House Un-American Activities Committee. Although she had been an ardent advocate of civil rights, she forcefully denied being a member of the Communist Party or sympathizing with its activities. Despite her renunciation of communism, within a week the *Hazel Scott Show* was dropped by the network. The musician struggled to attract an audience and, by the late fifties, had emigrated to Paris. Like many others, Scott had fallen victim to the anticommunist paranoia that gripped America.

Anticommunist Paranoia

From the late forties to the early fifties, many Americans fell into a fit of suspicion and began looking behind every corner for a communist fellow traveler. In 1947, transplanted English poet W. H. Auden won the Pulitzer Prize for *The Age of Anxiety,* which encapsulated the mood of the country. Two years later, composer Leonard Bernstein used the poem as the basis for his Symphony No. 2, and a year later choreographer Jerome Robbins used the Bernstein composition for a ballet. Only a few years after US soldiers joined Russian compatriots in defeating Hitler, an anticommunist, anti-Soviet fear gripped the nation and hardened into an icy stand-off with the Soviet Union called the Cold War. The tension-filled political climate shaped jazz, as exemplified by the brittle-sounding Kenton orchestra.

On March 21, 1947, a Loyalty Order instituted by President Harry Truman helped launch the anticommunist fervor by scrutinizing federal personnel for purported communist tendencies through anonymous testimony from witnesses who the accused might never confront. The Loyalty Order also spurred the Attorney General to create a list of supposed subversive organizations, which the Federal Bureau of Investigation, headed by arch-conservative J. Edgar Hoover, monitored to expose communist infiltrators in government.

The House Un-American Activities Committee (HUAC), established in 1938 but made into a permanent standing committee in 1945, whipped up anticommunist hysteria. First it unleashed an investigation of the motion picture industry, as suggested by the conservative Motion Picture Alliance for the Preservation of American Ideals, established in 1944 by Walt Disney, Clark Gable, John Wayne, Ronald Reagan, and a host of other right-wing Hollywood stars and producers. In October 1947, HUAC started proceedings and, within six weeks, cited for contempt ten Hollywood professionals whom the Motion Picture Alliance promised to fire or never hire again. HUAC broadened its scrutiny to other areas of the entertainment industry and eventually damaged the reputations of music professionals such as songwriter Yip Harburg and bandleader Artie Shaw.

In 1950, amid the HUAC hearings, pro-business Republican senator Joe McCarthy from Wisconsin further fanned the flames of suspicion. During a speech in Wheeling, West Virginia, he contended that 205 current members of the State Department were members of the Communist Party. Though the committee dismissed his accusations, McCarthy continued his scare tactics by attacking the communist sympathies of a mysterious government official, only named "Mr. X," with no evidence (White 1950). The next year, he leveled his sights on George Marshall, Army Chief of Staff during World War II and then Secretary of Defense. On June

14, 1951, McCarthy baselessly charged that Marshall and Secretary of State Dean Acheson had hatched a plot "to weaken the United States for its conquest by the Soviet Union." In a three-hour harangue, the senator described a "conspiracy so immense, an infamy so black, as to dwarf any in the previous history of man" (Hinton 1951, 3)

Jazz Goes to College on the GI Bill

During the aftermath of World War II, a brittle but brash, sometimes dissonant jazz reflected the nervous tension in America caused by the fear of a communist threat. The music sprang from jazz men who returned from the war and enrolled in government-subsidized college music programs, which taught them the latest in musical theory. The resulting "progressive" music, mixing jazz with the classical avant-garde, extended the boundaries of jazz and expressed the nerve-racking times.

In June 22, 1944, Congress enacted the Servicemen's Readjustment Act, commonly known as the GI Bill. The law prepared the country for the end of war by offering several benefits for returning soldiers who had been on active duty, including low-cost mortgages for easy home purchases, low-interest loans to start small businesses, and one year of unemployment compensation at twenty dollars a week. Possibly most important, the law authorized payment of tuition and living expenses for four years to veterans who wanted to attend college or vocational training.

Higher-education institutions welcomed the returning hordes of servicemen. In 1945, veterans represented just 5 percent of college enrollment. Within twelve months, college-attending vets accounted for 48 percent of students. By the end of the program, more than 2.2 million of the sixteen million World War II veterans had enrolled in higher education through the GI Bill, and more than 50 percent successfully graduated.

Lennie Niehaus, a sax player and arranger who attended college after the war, described a typical college classroom. "In 1946, I had just turned 17 years old and started college [at Los Angeles City College] right after [high-school] graduation," he recalled. "World War II had just ended, and a lot of the vets were studying on the G.I. Bill. In classes, they'd give me looks like, 'What's this kid doing in college?' . . . The classes were made up mostly of 25-year-old guys," he remembered (Myers 2009f, 1).

White veterans predominantly filled the classroom seats. During the 1946–1947 academic year, returning African-American servicemen represented only 4 percent of vets who entered college through the GI Bill. In 1947, two researchers for the nonprofit Public Affairs Committee discovered that the African-American veteran "wants very simple things in life: A good job, educational and vocational guidance, better housing, and a little self-respect. He knows that returning veterans were supposed to find these things. He knows they exist in this land of ours. But he does not find them" (Onkst 1998, 535).

Many white musicians who left the armed forces congregated in several music colleges across the country to learn music theory and classical structures. The enrollment of veterans in the summer program at the highly competitive Juilliard School of Music in New York City expanded from twenty-one in 1945 to 650 the next year. In 1947, others flocked to the school after reading an advertisement in *Metronome* that offered "training for professional musicians in all branches of music" (Myers 2013, 58). Teo Macero, saxophonist, composer, and eventually a producer at Columbia Records, attended Juilliard after the service and studied saxophone with Vincent "Jimmy" Abato, who had a seat in the prestigious Metropolitan Opera Orchestra but also had performed with Paul Whiteman, Glenn Miller, and Tommy Dorsey. Enrolled in Juilliard from 1948 to 1949, and again from 1952 to 1953, Macero earned a diploma, onto which the school stamped "GI."

The Schillinger House in Boston also admitted veterans. Founded in 1945 by Lawrence Berk and eventually becoming the Berklee College of Music, faculty at the school tutored students in the Schillinger system of harmony and composition, which had been developed by Joseph Schillinger, a Russian composer and music theorist who had taught George Gershwin and Benny Goodman. The music school initially took fifty students but, by 1949, expanded to five hundred attendees to accommodate the influx of returning veterans. Schillinger alumni included veterans such as sax player Charlie Mariano, who graduated in 1951.

African-American pianist John Lewis chose the Manhattan School of Music. Lewis began classical lessons at age seven and graduated from the University of New Mexico. In 1945, after leaving the army and moving to New York City, Lewis enrolled in the school, which had been founded in 1917 by pianist and philanthropist Janet Schenck. In 1953, he earned his master's degree.

Other decommissioned jazz men attended schools in California. "When I came back from the service, which was about 1946, there was a big change," remembered sax player Buddy Collette. "There were schools opening up then and many of them music schools. The Central Avenue players, even before, were not into a lot of schooling. There were more new musicians in town, like Bill Green from Kansas City, and many had the G.I. Bill for studying" (Bryant 1998, 146–47). Collette enrolled in the Los Angeles Conservatory of Music and Art. "I got four years of study for free, as well as books, metronomes, reeds," he recalled (174).

The Westlake College of Music attracted many prominent musicians from the big bands. Newly opened in 1945 by Alvin Learned near Westlake Park in downtown Los Angeles, the school admitted Clifford "Bud" Shank, many Tommy Dorsey band members, Duke Ellington's sidemen Britt Woodman and John Anderson, and Buddy Collette. Westlake enrolled sax player/arranger Bill Holman who "definitely was a different musician coming out than when I went in. I learned to write and arrange, thanks largely to my studies" (Myers 2013, 65). "The G.I. Bill covered two years of my musical training as well as private lessons. When I finished I could sight-read music, compose and arrange," related Holman (49). Other Westlake students included saxophonists Bob Cooper, Bill Perkins, and Bob Gordon and French horn player John Graas, who had played with the Indianapolis and Cleveland symphony orchestras.

The Westlake College taught a standard music curriculum enhanced by several unique experiences. Based upon the Schillinger system, the course of studies included ear training, pitch, and sight-reading through the solfeggio method, harmony, conducting, writing, and arranging with two one-on-one lessons per student per week. One unique course offered discussion of composition for big band, followed by a performance of the composition at the end of the class.

Teachers at Westlake included classical luminaries such as Peter Jona Korn, a German-born composer who in 1941 fled the Nazis and, seven years later, founded and conducted the New Orchestra of Los Angeles. In 1945, Alfred Sendrey—a Hungarian conductor who trained at the Academy of Music in Budapest and assumed many prestigious conducting posts throughout Europe before migrating to the United States—took a position at Westlake. The same year, Russ Garcia, who trained with such noted classical composers as Ernst Toch and Mario Castelnuovo-Tedesco and had been a staff composer for NBC before the war, joined the faculty. "I taught my classes at Westlake all the tricks I knew, including polytonality, tone row writing, rhythmic curves, Schillinger techniques and contrapuntal techniques," he explained. "In my classes were most of the musicians in Kenton's and Les Brown's bands as well as some of Woody Herman's alumni and lots of the greatest studio musicians. Many were there on the G.I. Bill" (Myers 2013, 65).

Some veterans enrolled at other California colleges. In 1946, after his discharge from the Navy, drummer/vibes player Cal Tjader (b. Callen Tjader Jr.) registered in the music program at San Francisco State College. The same year, sax player Jimmy Giuffre transitioned from the Army Air Force to the University of Southern California, where he earned a master's degree. In 1940, trumpeter Chesney "Chet" Baker moved to Glendale, California, where he used the GI Bill at the newly established El Camino Junior College to major in music.

The quasi-mystic Wesley LaViolette offered private lessons to students on the GI Bill. LaViolette was an American composer with a penchant for the lyricism of Chopin and Eastern philosophy. In books such as *The Creative Light* (1947) and *The Crown of Wisdom* (1949), he outlined a theory of artistic mastery through meditation. "To be genuinely creative, the artist must exist on a level—both conscious and subconscious—that can only be achieved through serious meditation," explained trombonist Milt Bernhart, who attended the Westlake College of Music and then became a disciple of LaViolette. "The way to meditate is suggested by LaViolette in thought patterns, which over a period of time would become virtually automatic. In the case of Jimmy Giuffre and [trumpeter] Shorty Rogers [b. Milton Rajonsky]," Bernhart contended, "this did happen" (Spencer 2013, 57–58). LaViolette "gave us a common language," insisted French horn player John Graas, who studied with the composer. "Dr. LaViolette has been a major influence on all of us. He's a composer and teacher and has a wonderful way of communicating the knowledge of form—especially counterpoint—to a musician regardless of the musician's background" (Shapiro and Hentoff 1955, 396).

Many returning veterans shifted their musical ideas after GI Bill–funded education by applying classical training and music theory to jazz for a new sound. The college-educated jazz men experimented with polytonality or the use of two keys simultaneously, a variety of complicated time signatures, different instrumentation, and counterpoint, which involved combining two connected melodies at the same time. "The G. I. Bill of Rights was a tremendous force in this cross-fertilization," insisted jazz-classical composer Gunther Schuller. "Classical and jazz were segregated then. One didn't mention that you had a classical teacher. For jazz, it was too square." After jazz men studied under the GI Bill, "in a very short time, jazz steadily became much more intricate and developed" (Myers 2013, 66).

Buddy Collette summarized the effects of a classically based education on the sound of jazz: "Formal study changed me as a musician. I studied the Schillinger system on flute, clarinet and saxophone. I was also composing and writing." In his view, "by 1948, many jazz musicians gradually began to realize that classical music was something also great and that there was nothing to be ashamed of. It was a great music that had been kept separate from jazz, and jazz had been separate from classical. That all began to change after the war," he concluded. "There was respect and awe and cross-pollination" between the two types of music (Myers 2013, 68).

Stan Kenton and His Jagged Music

Stocked with many returning veterans who attended college under the GI Bill, the Stan Kenton band delivered a sound that embodied a tension-filled postwar America. A tall, lanky pianist from California, Kenton started his music career during the thirties by playing in the big bands of Vido Musso and Gus Arnheim. In 1941, Stan formed his own fourteen-piece orchestra and performed at the Rendezvous Ballroom in Balboa Beach, California, which nationally broadcast the band three times a week. Despite stints at the Roseland Ballroom in New York City and at Meadowbrook in nearby New Jersey, the orchestra failed to attract much attention.

On September 21, 1943, Kenton's fortunes changed, when he was hired to appear on comedian Bob Hope's popular, longstanding radio program. For more than eight months, the band appeared weekly from 10:00 p.m. to 10:30 p.m. on the show, which attracted an audience of more than forty million listeners. Through publicity from the program, the Kenton orchestra scored its first Top Five hit in September 1944 with "And Her Tears Flowed Like Wine" with the sultry, hip singer Anita O'Day (b. Anita Colton), who had begun her career with Gene Krupa. The next year, the orchestra neared the top with the swinging novelty tune "Tampico," sung by June Christy (b. Shirley Luster), who lent her silky vocals to several big bands as a teen before joining Kenton earlier in the year. In 1946, the outfit continued its string of Top Ten hits.

In spring 1947, Kenton made a dramatic shift. At the height of a long-sought commercial success, he suddenly and unexpectedly disbanded his orchestra and headed out on the highway in his Buick. Tormented by a failing marriage and exhausted by a long tour of the South and Southwest, he set out in search of a new life. In one small Arkansas town, he saw "some guys sawing and hauling wood. It looked nice. About like the nicest job I could have had then. Whereupon I applied for work and got turned down" (Alkyer and Enright 2000, 30). Kenton then toyed with the idea of becoming a psychiatrist.

After a few months of soul-searching, Kenton returned to music with a purpose. In *Downbeat*, he blasted "the so-called sweet bands," which manufactured "the old 'drone' chords," and promised a "progressive jazz based upon [the latest] classical music. I think the greatest composer is Stravinsky, with [Darius] Milhaud a close second," he argued. "The generation that makes my band known will make Stravinsky's music as popular as Beethoven's" (Alkyer and Enright 2000, 31).

Like the boppers, Kenton wanted to create serious music more fit for concert halls than ballrooms. "I don't think jazz was meant to continue as dance music," he asserted. "Jazz has to develop; it can't always remain just functional dance music" (Shapiro and Hentoff 1955, 388). He vowed to abandon traditional clubs, hotels,

Kenton in front of one of his posters, 1947. *Photograph by William P. Gottlieb. William P. Gottlieb/Ira and Leonore S. Gershwin Fund Collection, Music Division, Library of Congress*

and ballrooms for more respectable venues such as Carnegie Hall, Boston's Symphony Hall, and the Chicago Civic Opera House. He pledged "to devote his time to establishing 'Halls of Jazz' around the country" (Harman 1948).

Kenton chose some recent attendees of Los Angeles and San Francisco music schools to staff his new band. He picked drummer Shelly Manne, tenor sax man Bob Cooper, and Milt Bernhart on trombone. As an arranger, Kenton retained the Italian-born Pete Rugolo who, after his army service, studied with Milhaud at Mills College. "I would do some daring things with time signatures or dissonances, or classical things," admitted Rugolo (Gioia 1992, 149).

Recorded between September and December 1947, *A Presentation of Progressive Jazz* revealed Kenton's edgy, surrealistic approach. The disc, maintained Kenton, hoped to create "a tonal picture of the American way of life . . . everyday sounds put to music" by combining somewhat dissonant modern classical music and jazz (Alkyer and Enright 2000, 30). It featured such selections as the symphonic "Impressionism" and the innovative, brittle "Fugue for a Rhythm Section," which began with aggressive lines by bongos, followed by maracas, and then guitar and piano in counterpoint laced with polytonality. "Monotony" highlighted a tension-filled, repetitive bass line throughout, interrupted by a guitar, piano, and then the full swaying band, which played in multiple keys. June Christy delivered the eerie, spoken-word vocal on "This Is My Theme." Amid the nerve-jangling rat-tat-tat of bongos, "Lament" showcased the dissonant runs of Brazilian classical guitarist Laurindo Almeida, who laced the music with Afro-Cuban and samba rhythms. "Laurindo had the right feel for Afro-Cuban music and for the neo-classical approach Stan was developing," remarked band mate Bud Shank who, six years later, collaborated with Almeida on samba-jazz experiments (Myers 2008e). "The long-awaited Kenton album of progressive jazz" will "stir up a boiler factory of comment ranging from wild enthusiasm to downright vilification," *Downbeat* mused in a review of the record. The jittery, raw sounds signaled a "radical change" from the "conventional swing-band lines" of Kenton's previous efforts (Vosbein, n.d.).

During the next several years, Kenton developed a dissonant modern-classical/jazz combination. Expanding his orchestra to nearly forty members including a sixteen-man string section, he selected such GI Bill recipients as French horn player John Graas and trumpeter Shorty Rogers, who had been steeped in current classical theory. The "Innovations" band, as Kenton called it, extended the jagged progressive-jazz experiment. Reviewing a free concert by the band at the Los Angeles Philharmonic Auditorium on February 11, 1950, *Billboard* noted that "some of the numbers deserved cheers for their originality in concept, refreshing instrumentation and novel rhythmic treatment. Others were too abstract to be properly grasped at first hearing." The magazine concluded that "as a whole, the new book offers a fresh slice of Kentonia, which borders closely to the modern symphonic school." The song "Mirage" "would not be out of place on a symphony program"; "Conflict" "is more on the abstract side, in which unorthodox harmonic combinations are intensified by equally strange instrumentation to create a restless, nervous setting"; and "Incident in Sound" "is no mere incident, but a wild frenzied piece that works up to a white heat" ("Boff Hands" 1950).

Kenton used saxophonist Bob Graettinger, another Westlake College graduate, to venture into even more challenging musical territory. In 1947, the bandleader hired Graettinger to compose a piece, "Thermopylae," which showed the influence of Graettinger's time in Benny Carter's band. Satisfied with the piece, Kenton asked for more material from the composer, who responded with a four-piece tone poem, entitled *City of Glass*, which Graettinger wrote while studying with Russ Garcia. In 1948, the Kenton Progressive Jazz band premiered the four-movement work at the Chicago Civic Opera House to a stunned and only mildly appreciative audience.

The serious Bob Graettinger at work, 1946. *Photograph by William P. Gottlieb. William P. Gottlieb/Ira and Leonore S. Gershwin Fund Collection, Music Division, Library of Congress*

In December 1951, the Kenton orchestra recorded a reworked version of the composition, which Graettinger described as "abstract and non-objective" (Graettinger 1952). Rob Darrell of *Downbeat* referred to the record as an "adventure in new sound" and "probably the most exciting, maybe one of the most vital and certainly the noisiest symphonic experiment yet achieved by a jazz composer and conductor. It's out of Schoenbergian and Bartokian bloodlines, perhaps, as far as the music itself goes, but all dolled up with the very latest in Graettinger and Kenton-style innovations where the frenzied but dazzling interplay of sonorities is concerned" (Vosbein, n.d.). Kenton believed that *City of Glass* provided "an example of the kind of music jazz is going to become" (Shapiro and Hentoff 1955, 387).

Kenton felt that the new music reflected the mood of the nation. In November 1947, he contended that "dissonances are required" at a time when "the world needs psychiatry for its present neurosis" (Alkyer and Enright 2000, 31). Early the next year, he maintained that "the human race today may be going through . . . nervous frustration and thwarted emotional development, which traditional music is entirely incapable of not only satisfying but representing" ("He Calls It Progress" 1946). In early 1950, he thought that "people hear music and they don't know what the hell they like about it, but it creates a certain turmoil, a certain insecurity, certain things that are with us today" ("Certain Turmoil" 1950).

The bandleader had accurately captured the prevailing temperament of the country. In 1947, the orchestra and individual band members filled the top slots in *Downbeat* polls. The next year, Kenton won first honors in the annual *Billboard* survey of disc jockeys, and almost unbelievably *Billboard* named *A Presentation of Progressive Jazz* as the number-one pop album of the year. In April 1948, in *Billboard's* tenth annual poll of college students, the Kenton band won the top slot. The same year, though characterizing Kenton's music as "Duke Ellington with the D.T.s [delirium tremens resulting from alcoholism]" and "screeching blotches of sound," *Time* magazine begrudgingly admitted to a Kenton "craze" and described one performance at Carnegie Hall, when Kenton "fans ripped the place wide open" ("He Calls It Progress" 1946). At the end of 1948, "the "progressive kick," contended the *New York Times*, had "influenced every band in the land" (Harman 1948). By December 1952, even the jumpy, skittish *City of Glass* nearly topped the pop chart and remained in the Top Ten for a mind-boggling three months.

The Long-Playing Record

The long-playing record, popularly called the LP and perfected by Columbia Records, facilitated the success of Kenton's orchestral jazz. In 1938, Edward Wallerstein joined the Columbia Broadcasting System after working for RCA. He convinced CBS president William S. Paley to purchase Columbia Records and its pressing plant in Bridgeport, Connecticut. On January 1, 1939, Wallerstein was installed as president of the record label, and work commenced on a research project to create a record that could play much longer than the three- to four-minute 78 rpm shellac disc.

RCA, Columbia's arch-rival, had already introduced but discarded the twelve-inch record. On the evening of September 17, 1931, the company unveiled a long-play, twelve-inch disc that played at 33-1/3 revolutions per minute. "A new two-sided phonograph record that plays for half an hour and in that time reproduces an entire symphony or a complete vaudeville act with manual attention only at the fifteen minute mark, was introduced last night," heralded the *New York Times*. "This long-playing disk records in its finely spaced grooves as much music as four ordinary [78 rpm] phonograph records." RCA first used the format to release a classical session of Beethoven's *Fifth Symphony* by Leopold Stokowski with the Philadelphia Orchestra and followed with thirty-four more long-playing discs ("Phonograph Disks" 1931). Less than two years later, RCA withdrew the long-play record from the marketplace because the rigid needles then available created a noisy sound and destroyed the record grooves after a few plays. Edward Wallerstein, then general manager of RCA's Victor Record division, instituted the recall. "The complaints from customers all over the U.S. were so terrific that we were forced to withdraw the LPs," he confessed (Wallerstein 1976, p. 56). Although it commissioned engineers to improve the sound and durability of the twelve-inch disc, RCA eventually abandoned the project.

In 1939, while at Columbia, Wallerstein reignited experiments to create long-play records to better capture an extended classical composition. "Columbia invented the twelve-inch LP for classical music, which ran long and had required multiple 78-rpms to fit all the music of a symphony," mentioned George Avakian, then head of the company's pop division. "The LP reduced the cost, weight and inconvenience of the 78-r.p.m. albums" (Myers 2010f). To reach his goal, Wallerstein assembled a team of engineers to spearhead the project. Though beginning in 1939, they discontinued the research to devote attention to the war effort, and renewed work in 1945 after Columbia signed such classical giants as the New York Philharmonic Orchestra and the Chicago Symphony. Once they developed a heated stylus, automatic variable pitch control, and a variable-reluctance cartridge, the team produced longer-playing discs that could be commercially viable.

By the end of 1946, the engineering department demonstrated their results, to the chagrin of Wallerstein. "It was a long-playing record that lasted seven or eight minutes," complained Wallerstein, "and I immediately said, 'Well, that's not a long-playing record.' They then got it to ten or twelve minutes, and that didn't make it either. This went on for at least two years." Paley, confessed Wallerstein, "got a little sore at me, because I kept saying, 'That's not a long-playing record,' and he asked, 'Well, Ted, what in hell is a long-playing record?' I said, 'Give me a week,

Record man George Avakian at home with a new twelve-inch record on the turntable. *Photograph by William P. Gottlieb. William P. Gottlieb/Ira and Leonore S. Gershwin Fund Collection, Music Division, Library of Congress* and I'll tell you'" (Wallerstein 1976, 58). Within the week, Wallerstein measured the time of most recorded classical symphonies and "came up with a figure of seventeen minutes to a side," recalled the executive. "This would enable about 90 percent of all classical music to be put on two sides of a record. The engineers went back to their laboratories" (59).

By fall 1947, after Columbia had spent $250,000 on research, the engineering team developed a disc that contained twenty-two minutes of music per side at frequencies between 50 hertz and 10 kilohertz or a range of 7.5 octaves with approximately 1,500 feet or one-third of a mile of grooves. It was made using a vinyl compound that featured "quiet surfaces [that] made it an ideal material for the purpose," contended Wallerstein (1976, 57). After years of hard work, the team achieved the "foundation of the long-playing record: low distortion, extended frequency range, low surface noise, and—last, but not least—uninterrupted playing of pieces which were meant to be played that way" (Goldmark 1954, 78).

Philco, a company that had become a leader in radio and television production, partnered with Columbia to commercialize the twelve-inch disc. It rapidly perfected a "balanced fidelity reproducer"—an armored crystal cartridge, hermetically sealed from moisture, with a steel, replaceable needle, which placed only one-fifth of an ounce of pressure on the disc. "Its tracking pressure is so low and so stable that it has ten times greater ability to respond to the minute variations of the microgroove," reported *Billboard*. "It gives a wider range of 'highs' and 'lows' than ever before but attains an alleged almost complete freedom from surface noise and record scratch" ("Columbia Diskery" 1948, 21). The company initially priced the new "reproducer" at $29.95 but then quickly lowered the cost to $9.95.

On June 19, 1948, Columbia and Philco announced their new products at a press conference at the Waldorf-Astoria Hotel in New York City. "As I stepped up to the podium to address the fifty-odd representatives of the press," remembered Wallerstein, "on one side of me was a stack of conventional 78-r.p.m. records measuring about eight feet in height and another stack about fifteen inches high of the same recordings on LP. After a short speech I played one of the 78-r.p.m. records for its full length of about four minutes, when it [stopped], as usual, right in the middle of a movement [of a classical composition]. Then I took the corresponding LP and played it on the little Philco attachment right past that break," he continued. "The reception was terrific. The critics were struck not only by the length of the record, but by the quietness of its surfaces and its greatly increased fidelity. They were convinced that a new era had come to the record business" (Wallerstein 1976, 60).

The debut of the ten-inch record was also announced by Wallerstein. Unlike its twelve-inch counterpart, which had been reserved for classical releases, the ten-inch was slated for popular artists and included up to twenty-five minutes of music per disc. "Since pop songs were relatively short, the thinking at first was that the genre really didn't need a twelve-inch disc," explained George Avakian. "A ten-inch LP meant fewer tracks—and fewer royalties to pay, which meant lower overhead. There were no [composer] royalties to pay on classical recordings" (Myers 2010f).

Columbia rushed 105 selections of classical music to the market. As the first twelve-inch release, it issued Nathan Milstein's violin performance of Mendelssohn's Concerto in E Minor with the Philharmonic Symphony of New York. Columbia sold the record for $4.85, which represented a savings to the consumer who previously needed to buy multiple 78- rpm discs to listen to an entire classical work. The pop department followed with titles in a ten-inch format, which sold for $3.85. "Once we decided to move forward with the ten-inch LP, we needed a complete catalog of pop LPs in a hurry," remembered Avakian. "I developed around 100 titles relatively quickly," including a series of jazz reissues (Myers 2010f).

Alex Steinweiss designed attractive, poster-like covers for the discs. In the initial rush to market, graphic artists created thin paper covers with block lettering on a one-color background, called "tombstones," to package the LPs. In 1948, thirty-one-year-old Steinweiss received a commission for a better design of the new product. A graduate of the Parsons School of Design and a former assistant of renowned poster designer Joseph Binder, he had joined the company ten years earlier as part of the advertising department. For the new LP, Steinweiss suggested a hard, protective cardboard cover with representative art to sell the contents. "An album cover is designed, not merely to be a pretty picture or an artist's personal conception of what music is about, but rather by its simple, direct design and bold use of color, it is projected at once as a powerful poster as well as an attractive package," he told *American Artist*. "The design elements are composed in a simple dynamic style and are chosen for their ability to convey to the onlooker enough about the nature of the music to arouse in him a longing to perhaps listen to one record" (Steinweiss and McKnight-Trontz 2000, 38). The graphic designer used both realistic and abstract designs and, pressed for time, many times hand-lettered the copy for the covers to introduce a new typeface called the "Steinweiss scrawl." He designed covers with enticing visual images, which increased sales dramatically.

In answer to Columbia, RCA first adopted a combative approach. It concentrated its efforts on the development of the seven-inch, 45-rpm record, which it hoped would displace the LP. Executives at RCA believed that boxed sets of 45s offered even greater fidelity than the LP format. Though the vinyl 45 became the leading format for jukeboxes, on January 4, 1950, RCA started to produce LPs. By one estimate, it lost $4.5 million during the two years that Columbia dominated the market.

Other companies quickly developed long-playing, "microgroove" records advertised by graphically striking covers. In 1949, Capitol Records, the home of Stan Kenton, became the first company to press 33-1/3 rpm records after Columbia. In 1950, the company released six ten-inch Kenton albums, including reissues of 78s as well as the concept LP, *Innovations in Modern Music*. Two years later, it marketed *City of Glass*, which, like classical titles, needed a longer-playing format to be best appreciated. By 1953, Capitol had released six more ten-inch Kenton records. By permitting extended solos and more intricate compositions, the long-playing record helped to change jazz from arrangements of three-minute popular tunes to the style delivered by the Stan Kenton band, which incorporated the classical avant-garde. It allowed jazz to reflect the nervousness of a culture buffeted by the winds of a fervent anticommunism and the anxiety-producing prospect of a prolonged Cold War.

For Discussion and Further Study

Chapter Quiz

1. How did the anticommunist hysteria of the 1950s affect the careers and lives of prominent jazz musicians?

2. How did the GI Bill play a role in spreading jazz to college campuses? Did African-American veterans equally receive these benefits?

3. What influences helped shape Stan Kenton's approach to creating a new type of big-band music? How did this music reflect the changing cultural and social climate of the day?

4. What opportunities did the new long-playing records offer to jazz musicians? How did the ability to create entire albums of music—as opposed to individual songs released on 78s—change the way composers and performers approached recording?

COOL, CLASSICAL, AND RESPECTABLE

Jazz Goes Mainstream

During the 1950s, jazz entrepreneurs successfully promoted a cool, classically based jazz to mainstream America. Festival promoters such as George Wein, record executives such as George Avakian, and small labels such as Pacific Jazz and Fantasy Records marketed the relaxed, cool jazz of college-educated, California-based musicians, the modal innovations of Miles Davis, and the Third Stream of Gunther Schuller to college campuses and other primarily white audiences. The jazz businessmen proved so successful in merchandising jazz as a dignified and acceptable art form for average Americans that the State Department used jazz as a tool in the Cold War to present a sanitized image of American culture to the wider world.

In 1951, saxophonist Art Pepper made a change. After eight years with the experimental Stan Kenton, he quit the band. "The traveling got to be unbearable," he recalled. For nine months of the year, he would "finish a job, change clothes, get on the bus, travel all night long to get to the next town in the daytime, check in and try to get some sleep, and then go and play the job" (Pepper and Pepper 1979, 115).

Pepper chose a more balanced life. After a Kenton tour ended in California, he stayed in the Golden State and started a quartet with drummer Joe Mondragon, vibes player Larry Bunker, and pianist Hampton Hawes. Using a low-interest,

The young Art Pepper in action, 1947. *William P. Gottlieb/Ira and Leonore S. Gershwin Fund Collection, Music Division, Library of Congress*

low-down-payment loan from the GI Bill, Pepper bought a house and left the frantic road life behind. "I had finally gotten to know my daughter," he reminisced. "We had a little white poodle named Suzy, and I had a car." From his perspective, "everything was perfect" (Pepper and Pepper 1979, 116).

In search of a better life, many other Kenton band members exited the orchestra with Pepper. "Most of us had been on the road so long that we just wanted to get off the road and get into a little different lifestyle," recalled trumpeter Shorty Rogers (Tompkins 1983c). French-horn player John Graas remembered that "we all decided we wanted to stay on the Coast, we wanted to live in California" (Shapiro and Hentoff 1955, 396).

Many former Kentonians who remained in California settled "on the outskirts of Los Angeles in the suburbs, in [one-story] ranch houses [with large yards]," noted Lennie Niehaus, a Kenton alumnus and jazz arranger/sax player (Myers 2013, 116). "We all have our own homes and the payments are less than the rent would be [in an East Coast apartment]," enthused John Graas (Shapiro and Hentoff 1955, 399). They joined a legion of other Americans who left the lower class for middle-class status and felt that they had realized the American dream.

The ex-Kentonians enjoyed the warm, sunny weather and the relaxed attitude of Southern California. "The weather out here was great, and many musicians wanted to move here," explained bassist Howard Rumsey, who helped popularize West Coast jazz (Myers 2009c). "Out here in the early 1950s, the outdoors was a big thing," noted Lennie Niehaus. "You had wide-open spaces, a lot of foliage, and the coastline and the surf. Everything was easier going. It was the opposite of New York [City]. On the West Coast, everyone was a little cooler" (Myers 2013, 116). "You don't get panicked like in New York," echoed Graas. "For musicians life is freer, more relaxed" (Shapiro and Hentoff 1955, 399). In 1955, drummer Shelly Manne regularly woke "up in the morning and maybe I'll go out and take a shovel and start to dig in the ground or, maybe I'll talk to my neighbor," he explained. "There is no tension. It's an easier way of doing things. You enjoy more in life" (Manne 1955).

Jazz musicians found sunny California especially attractive due to available work in film and television. "Myself and all the guys were starting to be used in some film projects," recalled Shorty Rogers. "Previous to that time it was kind of unheard of." Rogers pinpointed the change with the 1953 cult classic, *The Wild One*, starring Marlon Brando, which Rogers helped score, and *The Man with the Golden Arm* (1955), which included on the soundtrack such West Coast ex-Kentonians as Rogers on flugelhorn, trumpeter Conte Candoli, drummer Shelly Manne, and sax men Jimmy Giuffre, Bob Cooper, and Bill Holman (Tompkins 1983c). Others made money in the thriving television industry, which by 1955 had grown into a billion-dollar business. "A lot of us have more financial security

A relaxed Shelly Manne at work, January 1947. *Photograph by William P. Gottlieb. William P. Gottlieb/Ira and Leonore S. Gershwin Fund Collection, Music Division, Library of Congress*

here what with film studio work, radio and TV," summarized John Graas about Southern California (Shapiro and Hentoff 1955, 400).

Most jazz musicians like Art Pepper, demanding creative control of their work, formed small combos. Connected by a newly constructed, 715-mile maze of California highways, they banded together and merged jazz with light-hearted classical sounds in a respectable, palatable style called cool jazz.

The Relaxed California Sound

During the fifties, jazz reflected the buoyant, sunny, middle-class California life-style. "What we were exposed to in the landscape and lifestyle was integrated into the sound," explained Niehaus. "Artists are products of their environment, and out here back in the Fifties, there was more horizontal space. It was a different pace that was centered on pausing and taking your time" (Myers 2013, 116). "It was the music of happy," stated Howard Rumsey simply (Myers 2009c). "When you hear West Coast jazz, you're hearing the happiness we were feeling," agreed sax player Dave Pell, then in Los Angeles (Myers 2013, 115). "We woke up happy, drove around optimistic, and ended the day content. It would only make sense that the jazz many of us played would sound the way we felt. We were blessed" (Myers 2013, 94).

Musically, West Coast jazz men favored a lighter sound steeped in the classical theory that they had learned in college after the war. Unlike the classical-avant-garde-tinged jazz of the Kenton Orchestra, indicated Lennie Niehaus, "the West Coast sound featured more counterpoint"—combining two or more melodies, played simultaneously. "We also used more linear pieces. Much of this came from the classical classes that many of the guys were taking" (Myers 2013, 116). "Once I discovered counterpoint," revealed sax man Jimmy Giuffre, "this was my direction. . . . Counterpoint is music's salvation" (Gioia 1992, 233; Manne 1955, 21).

To arrive at a cool sound, sax players emulated the lilting style of Lester Young. Sax man Art Pepper described Young as "one of the greatest saxophone players that ever lived in this world." He considered him "better than Charlie Parker" (Gioia 1992, 286). "A whole generation of tenor players were influenced by one man—Pres," proclaimed Bill Perkins about Young (Tomkins 1987). Brew Moore summarized the feelings of most young, white saxophone players on the West Coast when he asserted that "anyone who doesn't play like Lester is wrong" (Gioia 1992, 106).

Unlike boppers who dropped "bombs," many West Coast drummers used brushes and a light touch. The Los Angeles–bred

The revered Lester Young at the Famous Door in New York City, 1946. *Photograph by William P. Gottlieb. William P. Gottlieb/Ira and Leonore S. Gershwin Fund Collection, Music Division, Library of Congress*

Foreststorn "Chico" Hamilton, one of the preeminent West Coast drum men, "played light and firm" (Myers 2013, 113). He approached the drums as "a very melodic instrument, very soft, graceful in motion as well as sound: a sensuous feminine instrument" (Gioia 1992, 186). Drummer Shelly Manne, who played with Kenton intermittently from 1946 to 1952 before settling near Los Angeles, "felt that the drums have a great melodic potential." "If a drummer must play an extended solo, he should think more about melodic lines than rudiment lines," he asserted (Gioia 1992, 270–71). Drummer Larry Bunker, who played with Gerry Mulligan, "reached a point where I didn't even have a pair of drumsticks. It was all brushes" (Gavin 2002, 65).

Sax player Jimmy Giuffre dispensed with drums altogether. He favored "jazz with a non-pulsating beat. The beat is implicit but not explicit; in other words, acknowledged but unsounded. I've come to feel increasingly inhibited and frustrated by the insistent pounding of the rhythm section," he confessed in 1955 (Gioia 1992, 234–35).

During the fifties, many West Coast jazz men experimented with different instrumentation. Unlike the standard bop combo of a rhythm section and a horn or two, they used instruments usually reserved for classical orchestras. Bob Cooper played English horn and oboe; Bud Shank performed flute–oboe duets with Cooper; Fred Katz, who had studied with classical giant Pablo Casals, played cello in the Chico Hamilton combo; and John Graas performed on the French horn. West Coast groups such as the Gerry Mulligan Quartet dispensed with the piano altogether in quest of new sounds.

Following a long tradition, West Coasters employed different rhythms, especially Latin beats, which had been wedded to jazz since its origins. In New Orleans, jazz players liberally utilized the five-stroke clave, an Afro-Cuban rhythm pattern. On the advice of multi-instrumentalist Mario Bauza, Dizzy Gillespie partnered with Cuban percussionist Chano Pozo (b. Luciano Pozo Gonzalez) who taught Dizzy "multi-rhythm" and helped compose the song "Manteca" before the conga player's untimely death from a gunshot wound in late 1948 (Gillespie 1979, 319).

West Coast jazz men flirted with Latin sounds into the fifties. In 1953 and 1954, former Kenton band mates Bud Shank and Laurindo Almeida introduced a conglomeration of samba and jazz with two releases on Pacific Jazz Records under Almeida's name. "In 1953, Laurindo was working on the Sunset Strip in Hollywood with jazz bassist Harry Babasin as a duo," explained Shank. The twosome added Shank and drummer Roy Harte who had co-founded Pacific Jazz Records to form a quartet and record their groundbreaking work (Myers 2008e).

Cal Tjader preferred the Cuban mambo, a musical rhythm and dance derived from the contradanza or habanera. In 1954, after leaving pianist George Shearing, the drummer/vibes player formed his own mambo quintet. "One of the chief compensations of being with Shearing," he contended, "was that back East I got to hear a lot of mambo leaders such as Machito [b. Francisco Raúl Gutiérrez Grillo], Tito Puente, and Noro Morales. Those bands had a tremendous effect on me. Immediately I wanted to reorganize a small combo along the same lines, only with more jazz feeling incorporated in the Latin format" (Tynan 1957a, 17). By March, Tjader and his quintet recorded for Fantasy Records, which released the album *Cal Tjader Plays Afro-Cuban: Ritmo Caliente* that featured Armando Peraza on congas. Tjader's Modern Mambo Quintet followed with a series of albums, which included such Latin stalwarts as pianist Manuel Duran, Carlos Duran on bass, and a series of Latin percussionists.

The Lighthouse

Howard Rumsey assembled many jazz men who favored a light, Latin-tinged sound at the Lighthouse at Hermosa Beach, a 180-seat, rectangular club decorated with Polynesian trappings and a photo of Stan Kenton on one end of the building. Bassist Rumsey, an original member of the Kenton band, had been raised in California. In January 1949, he received permission from John Levine, owner of the Lighthouse tavern and fourteen other bars in the Los Angeles area, to stage jazz concerts at the venue on sparsely attended Sunday afternoons. Rumsey also secured approval to spin jazz records on Tuesdays and Thursdays (Myers 2009c). "There was a fifteen percent state tax in California on entertainment that featured singing or was for dancing," Rumsey related. "Customers saw the extra hit in their bills, and clubs passed it along to the state. But instrumental music was not taxed," Rumsey related (Myers 2009c). "I had seen people just sitting and listening to a small jazz group rather than dancing. This was a new concept out here in the early 1940s," he recalled. "I thought that concept might work at the Lighthouse" (Myers 2009c).

Rumsey, who confessed that "Kenton was a god to us," hired several ex-Kentonians and opened for business. He chose Art Pepper, Bob Cooper, Shorty Rogers, Milt Bernhart, Jimmy Giuffre, and Shelly Manne. The bassist also added local pianists such as Frank Patchen (Gioia 1992, 199). On May 29, 1949, Rumsey launched his experiment. "I put together a fine combo, opened the front door—there was no p.a. [public address] system, but we kept the music loud enough to roar out into the street," he fondly remembered, "and within an hour Levine had more people in the room than he'd seen in a month" (Feather 1980, 168).

The venue allowed the group to try new musical ideas that the musicians had learned in college. "It was a place of learning, of experiment, of creativity, of study, and amongst all the funny and crazy things that went on, it offered a structure, a framework for creativity that probably will never be equaled again," remembered Bud Shank, who played at the Lighthouse (Shipton, p. 710). The music at the Lighthouse focused on counterpoint, remembered Shorty Rogers. "I used it some. Jimmy [Giuffre] used it more than me. We looked at the old masters: Bach, Beethoven, Mozart" (Shipton 1999, 711).

The adventurous group drew a young, college-age audience rather than the standard dock hands and aircraft-industry workers who had previously frequented the club. "The audiences were growing larger and getting younger," maintained Rumsey. "When the college kids came in, they wanted a new sound, and we responded to their excitement" (Myers 2009c). "A great many of the UCLA, SC [University of Southern California] and L.A. City College crowd headquarter here, which may account for the uncommonly high percentage of classy good-looking girls," reported Dick Williams of the *Los Angeles Mirror* in 1954. "The average age is in the mid-20s" (Howard Rumsey's Lighthouse All-Stars 1957).

Rumsey increased interest among college-age listeners by booking the band at various local colleges. "The way I spread the word was to hold concerts at all the Southern California colleges," he explained. "I was out at El Camino College several times with the All Stars [the name he chose for the combo], playing one-hour concerts. I played eight to nine schools every semester. I built clientele that way. I loved to play and groove. We even played high schools. We would wind up connecting with younger audiences and older guys who were in college on the G.I. Bill," he concluded (Myers 2009c).

By 1952, Howard Rumsey and his men landed a recording contract. On July 22, the group waxed four songs in the studio of Contemporary Records, a label headed by Lester Koenig, a former movie producer who had been blacklisted during the

McCarthy scare. The next year, the combo recorded four times to establish the Lighthouse name. In 1954, the Lighthouse All-Stars teamed with Shelly Manne and Lennie Niehaus for several more efforts.

West Coast Jazz

Other West Coast players, many of them ex-Kentonians, rode the coattails of the Lighthouse All-Stars. When Contemporary Records recorded the All-Stars, remembered Rumsey, "the bigger record companies started picking off the All Stars, like Shorty Rogers" (Myers 2009c). In 1952, the trumpeter signed with the California-based Capitol Records. He issued six sides with such ex-Kenton men as Art Pepper, Shelly Manne, Jimmy Giuffre, and John Graas for his first release, *Modern Sounds*. The next year, Rogers signed with RCA and released two more records with his group, the Giants.

In June 1951, an unemployed and penniless Gerry Mulligan, a baritone sax player who had arranged for Kenton, hitchhiked to California with his girlfriend. After reaching the Golden State, he walked into a bar and met drummer Chico Hamilton, who he approached about forming a band. Mulligan, Chico, and bass player Keith "Red" Mitchell rehearsed in Hamilton's living room and found work at a downtrodden local nightspot, The Haig, which had been converted from an old bungalow into a club that seated eighty-five people. During a performance, Mulligan received a recording offer from twenty-five-year-old Dick Bock, a student at Los Angeles City College who did publicity for the venue and had been a talent scout for the Los Angeles–based Discovery Records. Photographer William Claxton, then a UCLA undergraduate who helped chronicle the West Coast jazz scene, overheard the proposal and asked Bock, "Do you have a record company?"

"No," replied Bock, "but I will have one by morning" (Nolan 2006). True to his word, Bock used $400 dollars in savings and partnered with Claxton and Roy Harte, a drummer and owner of Drum City music store, to start Pacific Jazz Records.

Mulligan became the first artist on the new label. In August 1952, after a few preliminary sides, he settled on a quartet with trumpeter Chet Baker, drummer Chico Hamilton, bassist Von "Bob" Whitlock, and no piano, which Mulligan believed to be an instrument of "such tremendous capabilities" that it reduced the role of the "solo horn to a slave." He considered the acoustic "string bass to be the basis of the sound of the group, the foundation on which the soloist builds his line. . . . Because the bass does not possess as wide a range of volume and dynamic possibilities as the drums and horns," he felt that his group needed "to keep the overall volume in proportion to that of the bass" for a softer sound. "Gerry wanted everything as light as a feather," recalled bassist Whitlock. "A nice airy sound, clear and clean, that we kept the extraneous bullshit away." Mulligan hoped to deliver the soft "listenable music" to "the widest possible audience" (Mulligan and Bock 1952).

Within six months of forming, the group released the first, self-titled ten-inch record. During the next two years, Mulligan and Chet

Gerry Mulligan at a European press conference, 1957. *Dutch National Archives, Photograph by Eric Koch*

LISTENING GUIDE 28

Gerry Mulligan Quartet

🔊 **"LINE FOR LYONS"**

Mulligan recorded this tune on September 2, 1952, at the Black Hawk club in San Francisco, where the group opened for the Dave Brubeck quartet. He delivered the song for Fantasy Records with trumpeter Chet Baker, bassist Carson Smith, and drummer Chico Hamilton. The saxophonist titled "Line for Lyons" in honor of influential disk jockey Jimmy Lyons, who hosted the NBC program *Discapades* and in 1958 founded the Monterey Jazz Festival. At the same session, Mulligan named another song for deejay Don Barksdale. "Gerry wasn't above kissing a little ass, when it was convenient," laughed Carson Smith about the song titles (Gavin 2002, 58). Marketed via constant plays by the two radio announcers, the Gerry Mulligan Quartet with its "Line for Lyons" established the band as a jazz leader on the West Coast and became one of the first often-played songs of the quartet.

The Mulligan quartet demonstrated the basic elements of what became known as West Coast cool: soft, relaxed dynamics, delicate brush drumming, and two horns, which played with each other in counterpoint much like horns in New Orleans brass bands.

On the practice of "improvised counterpoint" in the quartet, Mulligan explained that "the contrapuntal idea had always been there. It certainly existed in the early days of New Orleans music, each one of the lines of the instruments having its own function within the ensemble, playing separate lines. That's counterpoint. . . . In Dixieland," he added, "you had the clarinet riding on the top; the trumpet (or cornet) playing around the melody, establishing the lead line; and the trombone playing in an accompanying way, establishing the chord relationship that connects it with the rhythm section." In the Mulligan quartet, counterpoint developed as the two horns played different but complementary melodies over the bass and drums (Josephson 2015, 28, 58).

0:00–0:22	Mulligan and Baker play the theme twice largely in unison with delicate brush drum work and a relaxed bass line.
0:23–0:35	The quartet moves to the third part of the theme, in which Baker states the melody and Mulligan answers him in a call-and-response fashion.
0:36–0:46	The quartet restates the main theme from the first section.
0:47–1:11	Mulligan improvises around the main theme with smooth lines and inventive rhythm changes.
1:12–1:35	Baker takes the lead with a solo, which centers around the melody with smooth backing from Mulligan, who takes the place of the piano in this piano-less quartet.
1:36–2:02	Mulligan leads the way until 1:39, when Baker enters and plays counterpoint to Mulligan, effectively developing two interrelated melodies at the same time around the main theme, and helping to establish counterpoint as a major element of the cool sound of the West Coast.
2:03–2:12	At this point, Chet Baker takes the lead again with the trumpet and states the main theme with Mulligan as a backing horn. Mulligan adds counterpoint near the end of the passage.
2:13–2:20	Baker and Mulligan play the main melody, largely in unison, with only a hint of counterpoint.
2:21–2:31	Baker and Mulligan both play the six-note ending of the theme three times and fade out for the ending.

Baker recorded ceaselessly for Bock to establish the two horn players as nationally recognized artists.

Mulligan possessed the same penchant for jazz infused with classical structures as most West Coast–based jazz players. In February 1953, *Time* magazine reported about his use of polyphony [music with many parts or voices, each having its own melody] and "Bach-like counterpoint. As in Bach, each Mulligan man is busily looking for a pause, a hole in the music, which he can fill with an answering phrase." The periodical identified his "favorite composers—Stravinsky, Ravel, Prokofiev and Bach" and enthused over the new type of jazz instrumentation in his group ("Counterpoint Jazz" 1953). "People used to call us the Chamber Music Society of Lower Wilshire Boulevard," joked bassist Whitlock. "The beauty was the counterpoint" (Myers 2012c, 8).

During fall 1953, Bethlehem Records opened its doors to record West Coast jazz. Label owner Gus Wildi had originally focused on blues reissues but then turned his attention to the West Coast Kentonians. "We had to do something or go out of business," he confessed ("Bethlehem Started in Pops" 1956, 10). He waxed sax player Charlie Mariano, a graduate of the Schillinger School of Music via the GI Bill, who was joined by other Kenton players such as trombonist and Lighthouse All-Star Frank Rosolino and trumpeter Stu Williamson. Bethlehem teamed classically trained pianist Claude Williamson with trumpeter Conte Candoli, another former member of the Kenton and Howard Rumsey bands. In 1955, Bethlehem issued *Four Horns and a Lush Life* with ex-Kenton men. Along with other jazz labels, Bethlehem helped publicize the talents of many West Coasters.

To sell their records, the labels used artwork and album titles that connected the musicians with their West Coast environs. Pacific Jazz pictured Chet Baker playing trumpet as he hung onto the mast of a sailboat next to his laughing session mates on *Chet Baker and Crew*. For a Bud Shank/Shorty Rogers album with Bill Perkins, the label used an aerial shot of Los Angeles, which highlighted the bustling freeways. For the cover of trumpeter Stu Williamson's first release as a leader, Bethlehem Records used a photo of the blue-tinted Pacific Ocean crashing against the banks of the West Coast.

By 1955, the labels had successfully equated a college-based, classically infused jazz with a "West Coast sound." When Dick Bock of Pacific Jazz Records decided to release an anthology of his artists, he asked photographer William Claxton about a title. "Why don't we call it *Jazz West Coast* to accompany my first book?" Claxton suggested. "And out of that came the term West Coast jazz, which the news media picked up. At first," the photographer continued, "musicians on the East Coast said, 'Bull, there's no such thing as West Coast jazz, that's all nonsense.' Which in a sense was true. A lot of the big West Coast stars, like Brubeck in San Francisco and Mulligan in L.A., were from other parts of the world. But the name didn't go away," he concluded. "The term just stuck after that" (Claxton n.d., 11).

To reinforce the image of a West Coast jazz, some companies consciously staged illusionary battles between West Coast jazz men and their East Coast counterparts. RCA blatantly divided jazz by coast with *East Coast–West Coast Scene* (1955), which pitted Shorty Rogers for the West Coast against saxophonist Al Cohn and his group for the East Coast contingent. MGM Records issued *West Coast vs. East Coast: A Battle of Jazz* (1956), which matched Kentonians such as Pete Rugolo against such Basie men as Frank Wess and Thad Jones. "Part of the East Coast-West Coast jazz feud really started with the A&R [talent scout] guys," summarized Creed Taylor who at the time produced records for Bethlehem Records. "Back then, the major labels had an East Coast producer and one on the West Coast. Both were competing for promotion dollars, exposure and dominance" (Myers 2013, 114).

By the mid-fifties, the record labels had successfully marketed the notion of West Coast jazz. "Once upon a time, the jazzman's capital was New Orleans; later came Chicago and Manhattan's 52nd Street," *Time* magazine declared. "Today, the liveliest center of developing jazz is California, where a cluster of youngsters, still mostly in their 20s, are refining the frenzies of bop into something cooler, calmer and more coherent" ("Listen to Those Zsounds" 1954).

The Modern Jazz Quartet: East Coast Cool

Though branded as West Coast jazz by the promotion departments of record companies and the popular press, the calming, classically tinged jazz of the fifties also surfaced on the East Coast. "The main difference between West Coast jazz and East Coast jazz," quipped drummer Shelly Manne, who played on both coasts, "is that there are thirty-five hundred miles between the Ranch Market and Charlie's Tavern. We're all heading in the same direction. All may be going to heaven. But one is going by route 66 and the other is going by [route] 90," Manne added (Manne 1955).

The New York–based Modern Jazz Quartet joined the primarily Southern California cool-jazz movement by offering a classically inflected variant of cool jazz, which some critics called chamber jazz. In 1946, as a side project of Dizzy Gillespie's big band, pianist John Lewis, drummer Kenny Clarke, vibes player Milt Jackson, and bass player Ray Brown started to perform as a quartet. In 1952, when Percy Heath replaced Brown, the group named itself the Modern Jazz Quartet. By February 1955, its personnel stabilized after drummer Connie Kay (b. Conrad Kimon) replaced Clarke.

The Modern Jazz Quartet consciously created a dignified image that mainstream America could embrace. Patterning themselves after Duke Ellington, the group dressed sharply in black suits, white shirts, and ties. The band sometimes used French titles to give their compositions gravitas. "We've proved that we can be respectable, dignified, and gentlemen," insisted Milt Jackson. "A lot of people think jazz musicians are dope addicts, drunks and sex fiends, and you're branded with that. But we've proved it isn't so" (Goldberg 1965, 118). "This is what jazz needs—cultured people. Rich people's groove is opera and symphony. We integrate the two," Jackson concluded (DeMichael 1961a, 20).

The Modern Jazz Quartet and its brand of respectable cool jazz came into the spotlight through the Newport Jazz Festival, which had been organized by jazz pianist, club owner, and music entrepreneur George Wein and bankrolled by tobacco heirs Elaine and Louis Lorillard. In July 1954, the quartet performed at the first Newport Jazz Festival to seven thousand fans in the swank, exclusive, and ultra-conservative resort town of Newport, Rhode Island. "The four musicians, looking young, intense and intellectual, played a few numbers and the audience listened solemnly to their subtly swinging beat, characterized by off-beats and cross-rhythms," noted one member of the audience (Ross 1954, 46). As bassist Percy Heath commented, he wanted to get "jazz out of the tavern" (Feather 1980, 92).

By the end of the event, the national press felt that jazz had become respectable. "When you consider the raffish background from which sprung a great deal that is the earthiest and most precious in jazz, you realize how extraordinary is the leap to a full-blown festival in, of all places, Newport," observed the *New York Times* a week after the event. "How respectable can jazz get? Will it be in Buckingham Palace next?" it asked (Taubman 1954). "The jazz festival changed the perception of jazz to the general public," insisted George Wein (Wein, interview with author).

In 1955, the Quartet released its first full-length album, *Concorde*, which featured a light, swinging, classically influenced sound. In the liner notes, jazz writer

Ira Gitler focused on the classical aspects of the music. "All the pieces display different use of contrapuntal techniques," he observed. "The counterpoint played by Milt, John and Percy Heath is improvised and interdependent." He noted that the group's introduction and finale to "Softly as a Morning Sunrise," a composition by Austro-Hungarian composer Sigmund Romberg, "are one of the extracts from Bach's *The Musical Offering*." He classified the title track on the LP as a "fugue (the height of the use of counterpoint)" and gushed over the Gershwin medley on the album.

A few days after the group recorded *Concorde*, the quartet solidified its stately image at the second Newport festival, which attracted leaders of the music business and more than twenty thousand fans. The combo played "fugues and something like a theme and variations in the style of [French composer Gabriel] Fauré," remarked the *New York Times* (Schoenberg 1955b). "The wheel has come full turn," the newspaper excitedly reported. Jazz "has come of age" (Wein 2003, 147).

In 1956, the Modern Jazz Quartet fortified its reputation when it accepted a residency at the recently opened Music Inn, a French provincial structure that had been purchased by Stephanie and Philip Barber, near the open-air, summer classical performances of the Boston Symphony at Tanglewood, Massachusetts. During the final three weeks in August, the MJQ had "an opportunity to prepare new material, rehearse, and explore new ideas and to take a physical and spiritual breather." The group headed five round-table discussions about "improvisation, composition and rhythm." Pianist John Lewis suggested that the Barbers establish the Music Inn School of Jazz, an annual, three-week course under the aegis of Lewis that consisted of classes about jazz composition and techniques for various instruments. At the end of the year, the Modern Jazz Quartet released the classically inspired *At Music Inn* with cool saxophonist Jimmy Giuffre as guest soloist. "It's a long trip from dingy backroom dives in New Orleans to a sun-bathed, verdant hillside in the Berkshire mountains of Massachusetts, but jazz has made the journey," concluded critic John Wilson (all quotes from album liner notes, Wilson 1956a).

After exposure at Newport and the Music Inn, the Quartet captivated a general audience. "The MJQ was big on the music scene then," recalled trumpeter Miles Davis. "The kind of 'cool' chamber thing they were doing was getting over big" (Davis 1989, 175). At a concert in Carnegie Hall on September 15, 1956, announced the *New York Times*, the audience "seemed to hear and respond to the Modern Jazz Quartet with more intense interest than to any other instrumental group on the program." The quartet, the newspaper stated, offered a "combination of delicacy and ruggedly propulsive swing that it has made almost its own" and performed with a "relaxed assurance" (Wilson 1956b).

The Making of Miles Davis: Newport and George Avakian

Miles Davis, an originator of cool jazz, also catapulted to fame through his performance at the 1955 Newport Jazz Festival, which showcased the trumpeter's brand of understated, reserved modal jazz. In 1949, Davis had collaborated with Earnest Gilmore "Gil" Evans, a former arranger for the velvety, classically influenced second big band of Claude Thornhill. Davis, Evans, former Thornhill band members such as Gerry Mulligan, saxophonist Lee Konitz, and classically trained tuba player Bill Barber and a few other like-minded musicians worked together in Evans's New York City basement apartment to merge classical music and jazz. They wanted to produce a sound similar to the eighteen-piece Thornhill big band with a nine-piece group. "We were trying to sound like Claude Thornhill, but he had gotten his shit from Duke Ellington and Fletcher Henderson," maintained Miles Davis (1989, 116).

By summer 1948, the nine musicians had founded a racially mixed band. "Gil and Gerry had decided what the instruments in the band would be before I really came into the discussions," admitted Davis, who by then had completed a year of theory at the Juilliard School. "But the theory, the musical interpretation and what the band would play, was my idea. This whole idea started out just as an experiment, a collaborative experiment," insisted the trumpeter (Davis 1989, 116).

From 1949 to 1950, the group worked with Capitol Records to complete three sessions, which produced a fusion of jazz and classical music. In "Moon Dreams," explained classically trained nonet member and French-horn player Gunther Schuller, the group featured "counterpoint. There are five different layers of contrapuntal lines" (Myers 2010j). Pianist John Lewis, later of the Modern Jazz Quartet, who arranged "Move" and "Rouge" for the nonet, wanted "to find new ways to use the instrumentation of the nonet, which included tuba and French horn. So I tried to use the possibilities these instruments offered in a polyphonic way, so you'll hear a couple of melodies going on simultaneously with contrasting instrumental colors in my pieces for that group," he recalled (Shipton 1999, 696). "The whole idea was to try something more sophisticated than just a simple tune and improvising it," he added. "We were a little tired of that routine" (Lyons 1983, 78). Winthrop Sargeant, classical music critic at *The New Yorker*, likened the compositions to the work of an "impressionist composer with a great sense of aural poetry and a very fastidious feeling for tone color." He felt that "the music sounds more like that of a new [work by classical composer] Maurice Ravel than it does like jazz" (Gioia 1997, 283).

Capitol Records cared little for the recordings despite its innovative pairing of instruments and the moody, impressionistic compositions of the group. The label initially released only a handful of the sides and first issued all eleven instrumental selections of the nonet in 1957 as a Miles Davis record under the title *Birth of the Cool* to capitalize on the emerging success of the trumpeter.

After abandoning the classical-jazz experiment and laboring several years in a bop style, Miles Davis rose to stardom after he performed at the Newport Jazz Festival. In 1955, the trumpeter stunned the Newport audience with his rendition of a Thelonious Monk composition, "'Round About Midnight," when he played his trumpet with a Harmon mute, which contained a cork outer rim that forced all the air through the mute for a thin, ethereal sound, unlike the rapid fire delivery of bop. "Everybody went crazy. It was something. I got a long standing ovation," he recollected. "When I got off the bandstand, everybody was looking at me like I was a king or something" (Davis 1989, 191).

Upon hearing the reaction of the crowd at Newport, George Avakian of Columbia Records signed Davis as a popular ballad instrumentalist. "I was convinced that his ballad playing would appeal to the public on a very large scale," recalled the executive. "While his bebop playing had established his reputation among musicians and jazz bands, I knew that bebop would never connect on a large scale. I viewed him as a much bigger figure, a pop-jazz star" (Myers 2010f). "The real money was in getting to the mainstream of America, and Columbia Records served the mainstream of this country," Miles reasoned. "You could be a great musician, an innovative and important artist, but nobody cared if you didn't make the white people who were in control some money. As a musician and as an artist, I have always wanted to reach as many people as I could through my music" (Davis 1989, 205). In 1956, Avakian headed to Columbia studios with a Miles Davis group, which consisted of John Coltrane on tenor saxophone, pianist Red Garland, Paul Chambers on bass, and drummer Philly Joe Jones.

Avakian immediately molded Davis into a commercially viable product. He convinced Jack Whittmore of the Shaw Artists Corporation to book Davis into the best clubs. "Back then," remarked the executive, "the way you promoted yourself was in front of live audiences. If audiences liked you, they told others and bought your records" (Myers 2010f). Avakian constructed a respectable group image by prompting the band to "wear black silk suits with black neckties and white shirts. They looked terrific," remembered Avakian. "Miles established the look, and then I persuaded him to standardize it." As the record mogul thought at the time, "Hey, this is what's going to get [Miles] into *Time* and *Newsweek* and break him out of the jazz category" (Myers 2010h).

To ensure a broad audience, Columbia emphasized the cool aspects of Davis's music. After recording his first small-group LP, the label encouraged Miles to contribute to Gunther Schuller's album for the Jazz and Classical Music Society, and included a Davis selection on a jazz album compiled by the popular classical conductor Leonard Bernstein. In May 1957, the label paired Miles with Gil Evans for the classically based *Miles Ahead: Miles Davis + 19 with Gil Evans*, which included twenty-one musicians with such diverse instruments as flutes, a French horn, a tuba, and a bass trombone as well as Davis on flugelhorn. "I wanted to do something different that would establish Miles as a soloist and frame him in an orchestral setting," maintained Avakian (Myers 2010h).

The rich, full sound of Miles Davis coupled with his classy image spelled success. "It's really Miles' melodic playing that put him across with the public on a wide scale," Avakian pointed out. "That happened first with our album, *'Round About Midnight* in 1956 and on an even bigger scale with *Miles Ahead* in 1957, which sold a million copies and established him internationally" (Myers 2010f). "George Avakian finally got his way. Not only did this group make me famous, but it started me on the road to making a lot of money, too," agreed Davis. "Whenever we played, the clubs were packed, overflowing back into the streets, with long lines of people standing out in the rain and snow and cold and heat" (Davis 1989, 197).

George Russell inspired Miles's new musical direction. A composer, music theorist, and a former drummer for the Benny Carter band, Russell co-led classically based concerts at Brandeis University with Gunther Schuller. In 1953, while a sales clerk at Macy's department store, Russell published his landmark book, *The Lydian Chromatic Concept of Tonal Organization for Improvisation*. "I devoted the years 1950–53 to the production of a thesis," he stated. "It deals with the relationship between chords and scales. Its basic principle is that a major scale in its natural sequence is composed of two tetrachords. From this basic reasoning, an order of chords and scales and, finally, of all elements of tonality emerges that makes a very strong case for the Lydian scale being the more natural scale for modern music" (Cerulli 1958, 16). Three years later, Russell released the album *George Russell: The Jazz Workshop*, which jump-started an emphasis on modal jazz.

Miles Davis embraced Russell's theories and based his playing on modes, or a scale of distinctive whole and half steps, which replaced the standard chord progressions used by previous generations of jazz musicians. He abandoned the rapid-fire, single-note runs and complicated chord changes of bebop for more musical space and a "melodic understatement," a concept that he had learned from pianist Ahmad Jamal (Davis 1989, 190, 220). As the trumpeter explained, "modal music is seven notes off each scale, each note. It's a scale off each note, you know, a minor note. The composer-arranger George Russell used to say that in modal music C is where F should be. . . . What I had learned about this modal form is that when you play this way, go in this direction, you can go on forever," Davis continued. "You don't have to worry about changes and shit like that. You can do more with the

Miles Davis Group

 "SO WHAT"

Miles Davis popularized modal jazz. Rather than playing the bop standard of chord changes and a plethora of chord substitutions, he chose a mode that allowed him to improvise on an entire scale rather than a few notes on a chord. When asked about the song, Miles curtly responded that "all you do is play all the white keys on the outside, and all the black keys on the bridge" (Heath 2010, 94).

Recorded on March 2, 1959, "So What" provided the lead song on the influential album, *Kind of Blue*. A prime example of modal jazz, it starts with sixteen bars of the Dorian D modal scale, shifts to eight bars of Dorian E flat, and returns to eight bars of Dorian D in a thirty-two-bar AABA structure. It has a bass/piano call-and-response introduction, which was developed

by arranger Gil Evans for pianist Bill Evans and has some similarities with a version of "Pavanne" by pianist Ahmad Jamal, who Miles enjoyed. Supposedly, the name of the song derived from a conversation between Miles Davis and actor Dennis Hopper, when Hopper responded to a Davis question with "So what?" Though certainly not the standard cool jazz, "So What" presented a subdued, quiet, and delicate music that fit the times. It starkly contrasted the subdued rhythm section and the cool solo of Davis with the more bop-oriented improvisations of Coltrane and Adderley.

Personnel: Miles Davis (trumpet); John Coltrane (tenor saxophone); Cannonball Adderley (alto saxophone); Bill Evans (piano); Jimmy Cobb (drums); and Paul Chambers (bass).

0:00–0:12	Bassist Paul Chambers starts with two notes and pianist Bill Evans responds with three notes to create a melody in a slow tempo.
0:13–0:19	In unison, Evans and Chambers increase the tempo of the song.
0:20	Chambers strikes a note.
0:21–0:28	Evans offers a brief improvisation.
0:29–0:32	Chambers strikes the same note as 0:20 and then improvises briefly in the low register.
0:33–0:49	Chambers starts the melody with an eight-note riff, and Evans responds with a two-note chord in a steady rhythm for a call-and-response between the two musicians. Drummer Jimmy Cobb provides a light backing on cymbals, starting at 0:49.
0:50–0:59	The horns (Miles Davis on trumpet, Cannonball Adderley on alto sax, and John Coltrane on tenor sax) enter to play the same melody as Evans. Chambers continues the same eight-note riff, and Cobb plays the cymbals with more intensity.
1:00–1:02	Evans and Chambers repeat the same call-and-response from 0:33–0:49 to give the passage a dynamic texture.
1:03–1:11	The horns and Evans take the melody up a half step with the same backing from Chambers and Cobb and repeat it three times for the B section of the AABA structure.
1:13–1:15	Evans and Chambers repeat the same call-and-response from 0:33–0:49.
1:16–1:26	The horns and Evans drop to the original key and repeat the melody three times with the same backing from Chambers and Cobb.
1:27–1:30	Evans and Chambers repeat the same call-and-response from 0:33–0:49.

1:30	Cobb indicates a change with a cymbal accent.
1:31–1:37	Miles starts an extended, melodic, innovative trumpet solo. He initially receives backing from Cobb and Chambers, who state the same rhythm, and Evans, who answers Davis with the two-note chord as a call-and-response.
1:38–1:45	Davis continues the solo with backing only from Chambers and Cobb, who continue the same rhythm.
1:46–1:59	As Davis continues his solo, Evans reenters to answer Miles with a series of chords in the open spaces. The rhythm section persists with backing.
2:00–2:06	Evans takes the music up half a step with two chords and then a chord repeated four times, which Davis plays over; then he hits a series of minor blue notes to give the solo a blues-infused, midnight-at-the-club feel. Throughout the solo, in bop fashion, Davis unexpectedly stops and starts again to provide interest and tension in the rhythm.
2:07–2:13	Evans returns to the two-chord main theme in a quiet, almost imperceptible manner to accompany Davis, who continues the song with the rhythm section.
2:14	Drummer Cobb provides an accent to indicate a downward shift to the music.
2:15–2:55	Davis continues his lyrical solo with the two-note chord from Evans and rhythm backing from Cobb and Chambers. Davis slides his notes (called glissandos) throughout his solo to enhance the bluesy quality of his playing and extend the rhythm in places.
2:56	Davis unexpectedly moves high in the register in an interval jump, which jars the listener and signals a move to the B section of the song, which moves from the D-flat Dorian mode to the E-flat Dorian mode. Such an interval jump belongs more to a bop style than a cool jazz style, which generally stayed in the middle register.
2:57–3:09	Davis solos in the B section of the song.
3:10–3:25	Davis returns to the original key to complete his solo with a bluesy flourish.
3:26–3:38	After a drum accent by Cobb, Coltrane starts his solo in a restrained manner. Coltrane provides a crystal-clear, piercing tone that contrasts with the highly subdued, sliding sound of Davis. The rhythm section provides the same backing that it did for Miles.
3:39–3:51	Coltrane becomes more heated in his solo, and Evans changes his two-note riff to a four-note riff at a greater tempo to accommodate Coltrane. Coltrane repeats a phrase four times with variations in all four.
3:52–4:00	Cobb increases the volume slightly on the snare drum to follow the faster, more intense pace of Coltrane.
4:01–4:05	Coltrane hits a higher register of the saxophone.
4:06–4:20	Coltrane reaches down to the lower register of the horn and repeats a phrase four times with variants on it each time by embellishing it at the end.
4:21–4:26	Coltrane repeats a phrase twice with some differences.
4:27–4:40	Coltrane improvises a passage.
4:40–4:47	Coltrane repeats a passage twice in different pitches and slightly different rhythms.
4:48–4:59	Coltrane improvises a measure and repeats it three times with significant differences.

5:00–5:16	Coltrane finishes his two-chorus improvisation. At the final bar, the drum beat becomes louder to signal a new section of the song.
5:17–5:40	The warmer-sounding Adderley enters for a two-chorus solo as the rhythm section grows quieter.
5:41–5:55	Adderley shifts up a half step, and Evans responds with two different chords at a louder volume as a backdrop. In the solo, Adderley descends in pitch and then rises again. The rhythm section continues to provide relatively quiet support to Adderley.
5:56–6:02	Adderley shifts back a half step as he repeats a two-note passage.
6:03–6:09	Adderley continues his improvisation.
6:10–6:14	Adderley repeats the phrase from 5:56–6:02 with some embellishments.
6:15–6:22	Adderley continues his solo and plays a trill (two notes played alternatively and very rapidly) at 6:17 and at 6:19.
6:23–6:30	Adderley repeats a descending phrase three times.
6:31–6:38	Adderley lets loose a rapid succession of bop-style notes in stop–start fashion to change the rhythm sporadically.
6:39	Adderley slides across sustained notes much like Davis but unlike the more precise Coltrane. Adderley uses this technique repeatedly during his solo to give his improvisation a bluesy feel.
6:40–6:52	Cannonball continues his solo, repeating the phrase he used at 6:23–6:30.
6:53–7:05	Adderley ends his solo in a bop style as he slides across notes in the final two measures for a bluesy finale. Like Coltrane, Adderley's style contrasts with the more subdued, cool style of Davis.
7:06–7:33	Evans starts a slow, tasteful, sparse, and deliberate solo as the horns play the main theme in a call-and-response with the pianist. Cobb and Chamber play lightly in the background.
7:34–7:46	In the B section, the horns shift to the E-flat Dorian scale along with Evans. Evans begins to play more dissonant notes.
7:47–8:02	Evans continues his explorations by playing a phrase four times with significant differences.
8:03–8:15	Evans shifts to the two-note melody he used in the introduction and plays it four times, supported by drums and bass.
8:16–8:25	The horns join Evans in the main theme and play it three times.
8:26–8:29	For the fourth restatement of the theme, the horns stop and only Evans and the rhythm section play, similar to the introduction. The absence of the horns shows the importance of dynamics or a change in volume for the song.
8:30–8:39	Like the passage from 8:16–8:25, the horns and Evans restate the main theme with rhythm backing.
8:40–8:43	The horns quit playing and let Evans and the rhythm section state the main theme. It repeats the pattern at the beginning of the song and at 8:26–8:29.
8:44–8:55	In yet another repeat of the passages above, the horns state the theme three times with Evans and the rhythm section.
8:56–9:21	Again, the horns stop playing and Evans and the rhythm section state the theme. Unlike the previous sections, Evans and the rhythm section continue to play the theme themselves, getting progressively softer and softer until they fade out to end the song.

musical line. The challenge here, when you work in the modal way, is to see how inventive you can become melodically. In the modal way," he concluded, "I saw all kinds of possibilities" (225).

By 1958, Davis had incorporated the Lydian modal scale in his music. In February, he employed modes in "Milestones." During March and April 1959, Miles built a complete album, *Kind of Blue*, upon a modal foundation. He recruited two sax players, Cannonball Adderley and John Coltrane, for the session. "I felt that Cannonball's blues-rooted alto sax up against Trane's harmonic chordal way of playing, his more free-form approach, would create a new kind of feeling," he reasoned. He engaged Bill Evans for most of the piano duties. "I needed a piano player who was into the modal thing, and Bill Evans was," he recalled. "I met Bill Evans through George Russell, whom Bill had studied with. I knew George from back at Gil's [Evans] house on 55th Street" (Davis 1989, 225). "Bill brought a great knowledge of classical music, people like Rachmaninoff and Ravel," Miles added.

Released on August 17, 1959, the iconic *Kind of Blue* captured the possibilities of modal playing. Bill Evans wrote the liner notes for the LP and described many of its tracks using terminology that drew on Russell's work. Evans characterized "'So What' as a simple figure based on 16 measures of one scale, 8 of another and 8 of more of the first"; "'Blue in Green' is a 16 measure circular form"; "'Flamenco Sketches' is a 6/8 twelve-measure blues form that produces its mood through only a few modal changes"; and "'All Blues' is a series of five scales, each to be played as long as the soloist wishes." "Freddie Freeloader," a standard twelve-bar blues, represented the most traditional piece. *Billboard* lauded the LP by describing it as staying "within the confines of what might be called the 'interior' style of cool jazz" ("Kind of Blue Review" 1959).

The Triumph of Dave Brubeck: Colleges and Columbia Records

Pianist Dave Brubeck took the jazz–classical hybrid to its commercial zenith. Like many returning veterans, Brubeck jump-started his career with higher education. "Because of the G.I. Bill, I could go to Mills College" near San Francisco, asserted Brubeck, whose brother Howard had taken classes at the school. "We were pulled away from worrying about how to make a living," he observed (Myers 2013, 63). "Then we gradually had other friends, like Dave Van Kriedt, Bill Smith, Dick Collins, Bob Collins, Jack Weeks," Brubeck added (Panken 2007, 161).

Darius Milhaud, a French composer who emphasized polytonality or the use of more than one key simultaneously, tutored Mills students. Milhaud had been a member of Les Six—a group of composers working in Montparnasse outside of Paris during the twenties. He had collaborated with Paul Claudel, poet and French ambassador to Brazil, and in 1922 became interested in jazz when he heard it on a Parisian street. In 1940, Milhaud left France for California, fearing that the Nazis would detain him due to his Jewish heritage, and settled into a position at Mills College. Milhaud "was a great classical composer who loved jazz. Many jazz musicians in the San Francisco area were drawn to him," recalled trumpeter Dick Collins (Myers 2010b, 4). When Brubeck and his friends took a class from the composer, "he asked, 'Do any of you play jazz? Raise your hands.' So we raised our hands," laughed the pianist. "He said, 'I want you to write your fugues and counterpoint for jazz orchestration if you want to.' That's how the octet was born," chuckled Brubeck (Panken 2007, 161).

The Dave Brubeck Octet put theory into practice. It included Brubeck, Dick Collins, Cal Tjader, arranger/tenor sax man Dave Van Kriedt, the melodic Paul Desmond on alto, Bob Collins on trombone, Bill Smith on clarinet, and baritone sax/bassist Jack Weeks. The group played "a mixture of classical ideas put in jazz form," according to Dick Collins (Myers 2010b, 5). "From Milhaud's compositions and his classes I became more aware of polytonality and polyrhythms and the usage of Bach-like counterpoint in both classical and jazz," revealed Brubeck, who wrote many of the compositions for the band. Brubeck considered Milhaud "the true father of my octet" (Myers 2013, 63).

The octet first performed on college campuses. In March 1947, it debuted at Mills College. Two years later, the octet played the College of the Pacific, where Brubeck had earned a baccalaureate degree. "Then we started playing at University of California at Berkeley. But we didn't get enough work to really make it," recalled Brubeck (Panken 2007, 161).

In 1949, as the Dave Brubeck Octet searched for work, disc jockey Jimmy Lyons, who later founded the Monterey Jazz Festival with Brubeck, contacted the pianist with a job offer. He asked if the group's rhythm section would play in Oakland at the Burma Lounge. "It wasn't one of those things where anybody was going to say, 'Well, don't work. Don't leave us,'" remarked Brubeck. "We were trying to work wherever we could. And that's how the trio came about" (Tompkins 1963b). Brubeck, drummer Cal Tjader, and bassist Ron Crotty, who had studied at San Francisco State and Mills College with Darius Milhaud, took the gig and moved around California clubs to cobble together a living.

With Lyons's help, the trio landed a weekly, daytime radio program on NBC. "You could hear us clear out into the Pacific, and all up and down the coast," remembered Brubeck. "And when the sailors would come in, and they were always coming into San Francisco, they'd look for where I was playing. That really helped me in club work, the constant flow of sailors every week." The trio found a job for half the year at the Black Hawk, a San Francisco nightspot in the Tenderloin district that had been opened in 1949 by Guido Cacianti and Johnny and Helen Noga (Lees 1995, 52).

Attracting sizable audiences at the Black Hawk, the trio garnered attention from record labels. During late 1949 and 1950, the group waxed four sides for Coronet Records, a small San Francisco company owned by Jack Sheedy. When Sheedy failed to pay the band, Brubeck bought the masters for $350 and leased them to the Circle pressing plant owned by brothers Sol and Max Weiss. The trio appeared on two discs pressed by the Weiss brothers, who called their label Fantasy Records.

The brothers hired Brubeck as an informal talent scout because they cared little about jazz. "We weren't diehard jazz fans, never were, still aren't," confessed Max. "Anything that sold, we would sell. [We did] mainly jazz because that was the only thing that we were aware of that wasn't a flash in the pan" (Gioia 1992, 64). The brothers paid the leader of a session $80 and the sidemen $40 each and hoped that they could sell five thousand copies of a disc to turn a profit.

In 1951, Brubeck suffered an injury that changed his style. While working at the Zebra Lounge in Honolulu, Hawaii, the pianist suffered a devastating accident while on Waikiki Beach with his family. "I was showing my kids how to dive through an incoming wave," he recalled. "When I went through the wave, I hit the sandbar full force and nearly severed my spinal cord. Instead of hitting it head on as I should have, I turned." After twenty-one days in traction, he regained feeling "back into my limbs. But given the severity of the accident, I knew that when I started to play again, I'd need another solo instrumental voice in the group to help carry the load" (Myers, 2010a; Lees 1995, 53). "There was a period of a few years where I couldn't physically do much—I was almost paralyzed," he added. "I lost a certain amount of dexterity at that time, so I had to rely on chords" (Goldsmith 1977, 27). Rather than a single-note attack, Brubeck focused on a percussive, chord-based approach.

The disabled Brubeck scribbled a note to sax player Paul Desmond (b. Paul Breitenfeld), who had met Brubeck in the Army and had hired the pianist several years earlier. The pianist told him, "'I think it's time to form that quartet you've been pushing for.'" Because Tjader and new bassist Jack Weeks had found other work, and Crotty had been drafted into the Army, Brubeck urged Desmond "to find a rhythm section, which would give us a quartet. I had to write him in traction, with my hands over my head" (Myers 2010a; Lees 1995, 53).

Desmond had similar musical inclinations as Brubeck. The son of a pianist who played for silent movies, the alto sax man had attended San Francisco State College and "loved the vigor and force of simple jazz, the harmonic complexities of Bartók and Milhaud, the form (and much of the dignity) of Bach, and, at times, the lyrical romanticism of Rachmaninoff. You see a lot of us in contemporary jazz look for these qualities you find in classical musicians—but in an evolving jazz context," he asserted. "We both loved Bach and Stravinsky and a lot in between," echoed Brubeck (Enstice and Rubin 1992, 86).

Desmond agreed to join the pianist and find other band members if Brubeck ensured that he could never be fired and gave him 20 percent of all income. He agreed that Brubeck would be the leader of the combo. As other members of the band, Desmond chose bassist Wyatt Ruther, who had been educated at the Pittsburgh Musical Institute and played with the quartet until 1952, when Ron Crotty replaced him. The alto sax player located a series of drummers before settling on Joe Dodge.

The group displayed the classical bent of Desmond and Brubeck. Desmond played in a light, Lester Young–influenced tone. He "listened to more classical music than jazz. I really enjoy Stravinsky, obviously, and Bartók, Ravel, Debussy, Charles Ives—sort of what would be considered contemporary music," he confessed (Tompkins 1973e). Steeped in the classics, he played counterpoint against Brubeck's percussive piano. The pianist constantly referred to the "kind of counterpoint that Paul and I love to play" (Tompkins 1963b).

The Brubeck quartet first found large audiences on college campuses. Familiar with the college environment, Brubeck's wife, Iola, looked through the *World Almanac,* jotted down the names of schools on the West Coast with music departments, and sent them letters about her husband's quartet. "We offered to play free, or whatever they could afford to pay us. We'd play assemblies at high schools and junior high schools, too," the pianist reminisced. The group performed at the University of Oregon, traveled westward to the University of Idaho, and zigzagged back to the University of Washington. The quartet extensively toured other campuses across the country. "I think at about February, we started those college concert things," remembered drummer Joe Dodge. "We did sixty of them in a row, sixty one-nighters in a row!" (Gioia 1992, 97). Needing money, Brubeck even took a part-time position at the University of California, Berkeley, to teach a class about jazz in the extension division for $15.

The quartet recorded many of their college-campus performances. In 1953, the combo recorded *Jazz at Oberlin* in Ohio and, the same year, followed with discs recorded at Wilshire-Ebell College in Los Angeles and the College of the Pacific, Brubeck's undergraduate alma mater. The next year, the group waxed a performance at the University of Michigan and the University of Cincinnati for *Jazz Goes to College* and eventually released *Jazz Goes to Junior College* from gigs at Fullerton and Long Beach junior colleges near Los Angeles. "We created that audience ourselves and there's hardly a jazz musician alive today who hasn't benefited from what we did," boasted Brubeck about his jobs at colleges (Leikam 1992, p. 5). "I know that at the colleges where we've played, they've hired other groups because they liked us," bragged the pianist (Gleason 1957b, 14).

In mid-1954, Brubeck's fame spread beyond the jazz cognoscenti when he signed to Columbia Records. Early in the year, after George Avakian heard him at the Black Hawk, Brubeck signed with the label for an advance of $6,000. "Eventually Fantasy Records and I made some kind of decision that we were going to split up," explained Brubeck, who had been misled to believe that he owned part of the company in exchange for his talent-scout services. "I was penniless. At this point we were ten thousand in the hole to the government for taxes. So I did need the money" (Lees 1995, 54).

On November 8, 1954, a thirty-three-year-old Brubeck vaulted into the national spotlight when *Time* magazine devoted its cover to the pianist, the only jazz artist after Louis Armstrong to receive the distinction. At a time when the United States was waging a Cold War with the Soviet Union, Brubeck became *Time*'s poster boy for a clean-cut, acceptable jazz that could be embraced by mainstream America.

Referring to Brubeck and his colleagues as "modernists," *Time* focused on the "intense, quiet music," which "is neither chaotic nor abandoned. It evokes neither swinging hips [of swing] nor hip flasks [of jump blues]." From the perspective of *Time*, Brubeck contrasted starkly with "late'40s bop," which "became briefly fashionable, with its air-splitting protests against swing stereotypes" and its "offbeat spastic rhythms. . . . The jazz style called modern does not protest against anything very much except dullness," it enthusiastically contended.

The magazine emphasized the heavy dose of classical music that Brubeck and his like-minded musicians infused into jazz. "Once it starts swinging, it seems to move on to more interesting matters, such as tinkering up a little canon a la Bach or some discordant counterpoint a la Bartók or even a thrashing crisis a la Beethoven," it reported. Brubeck, observed *Time*, "picks a random theme and toys with it, reflectively trying it first on the white keys, then on the black, allowing traces of Mozart or John Philip Sousa to creep in." "When I play jazz I am influenced by classical music," it quoted the pianist. "And when I compose I am influenced by jazz." To the magazine, Brubeck and his colleagues ushered in "the birth of a new kind of jazz age in the U.S." ("Man on Cloud No. 7" 1954, 1).

Brubeck was cast as an all-American cowboy steeped in the ethos of the American West. Born in the small town of Concord, California, and raised on a ranch in nearby Ione, Brubeck "learned to rope, brand and vaccinate cattle. As his older brothers practiced their violin and piano, Dave protested against his own music lessons: 'Ma, you've got two musicians; I want to be a cattleman.'" Given Brubeck's background, *Time* characterized his music as "ruggedly individual" and highlighted such compositions as his "On the Alamo."

The magazine also portrayed Brubeck as epitomizing dominant American values. "While itinerant musicians are apt to dally with belles along the way," *Time* noted, "Dave is happily married and has four children (a fifth is on the way)." It described Brubeck's Presbyterian, "mildly religious upbringing," his service in World War II, and clearly pictured him as a Caucasian on its cover despite Brubeck's constant boasting of his Native American heritage. "In a business that has known more than its share of dope and liquor, Brubeck rarely drinks," related the magazine, "and, after seriously and philosophically considering the possible value of mescaline, [he] rejected the whole idea." As an ultimate sign of social purity, the magazine reported that "characteristically, Dave has several priests among his friends."

In sum, *Time* cast Brubeck as a respectable jazz man: white, classically based, college-educated, a near teetotaler, family-oriented, and a former GI who seemed beyond reproach. In an age that stressed conformity, the magazine designated

Brubeck as an example of the ideal musician who reflected traditional values of fifties America. It lauded Brubeck's cool jazz as a welcome relief from the swing jitterbugs, the complex African-American bop, and the boisterous jump blues ("Subconscious Pianist" 1952; "Man on Cloud No. 7" 1954).

The next year, Columbia Records embarked on a broad promotional blitz for Brubeck and its other jazz performers. On June 1, it launched "the biggest jazz promotion in our history" ("Columbia Girds" 1955). To increase sales and visibility of its artists, the record company started the Columbia Record Club, which gave members several free records when they joined and subsequently sent an optional selection on a monthly basis. Within a year, the club enrolled more than 15 percent of jazz fans as well as thousands of others (Feather 1956, 45). The record label also secured a spot for Brubeck at the second Newport Jazz Festival as a performer and symposium member with Gunther Schuller to cast a popular but respectable image. "It's a wonderful thing," remarked the *New York Times* about Brubeck's performance at Newport. "Jazz musicians are using learned contrapuntal dissonances and learned composers are using jazz" (Schonberg 1955a).

As part of a marketing campaign for Brubeck, Columbia inked an endorsement deal for the pianist with cosmetics manufacturer Helena Rubinstein, which created a Red Hot and Cool lipstick to coincide with Brubeck's album of the same name. It featured an ad in every drugstore window that pictured a beautiful model dropping ashes from her cigarette into a piano while Brubeck played. "The only reason I went for the lipstick deal was that it might promote the good of jazz among the people who might be strangers to it—the *Vogue* readers, for example," the pianist reasoned. "Some critics say the *Time* magazine cover piece was bad," Brubeck continued. "Well, I say the *Time* cover introduced a lot of people to jazz on different terms than they'd ever known. The lipstick promotion is doing the same thing" (Freeman 1956). "Musicians and fans all over America, when they saw the advertisement," effusively wrote *Downbeat* in 1956, "felt that jazz finally had arrived" (Feather 1956, 20).

Promoting Brubeck had its desired effect. Brubeck "outsold any single album by another kind of pianist named Liberace" with his first Columbia release, *Jazz Goes to College* (1954). The quartet earned $2,500 a week, and Brubeck grossed $100,000 annually. By January 1956, *Downbeat* referred to Brubeck as "a famous jazz musician" (Freeman 1956). In May, when *Billboard* published a sales chart of popular jazz albums, Brubeck captured both the second and ninth slots. The next year, *Downbeat* reported that Brubeck's "LPs have consistently outsold any other modern jazz artist. The effect of this," concluded the magazine, "makes him the undisputed king of record sales in jazz" (Gleason 1957a, 14). Two years later, the quartet almost topped the pop chart with *Time Out*, which included the hit "Take Five" and sold a million copies.

Dave Brubeck and his classically trained cohorts had ushered in a new acceptance of jazz among adults. According to *Downbeat*, the mid-fifties "may be remembered by posterity as the time of the great jazz gold rush," when companies released twenty new jazz albums a week (Feather 1956, 17). "Every record company, large and small, had plunged into the production of long-playing jazz discs" (18). "Jazz, which used to account for a tiny percentage of sales among the major record companies, has become a big moneymaker for the big labels," *Time* concluded ("Man on Cloud No. 7" 1954, 1). "In the press," lauded *Downbeat*, "there were developments that afforded jazz a new cachet. It was now not only newsworthy and respectable but even from the viewpoint of the women's magazines, downright chic. . . . Madison Avenue, the last commercial bastion," the magazine proclaimed, "had been stormed and conquered" (Feather 1956, 20).

Watch a live version of "Take Five"

LISTENING GUIDE 30

Dave Brubeck Group

 "TAKE FIVE"

Recorded on July 1, 1959, after Brubeck had already achieved some renown and had finished his State Department tour, this song encapsulates the Brubeck sound for the later part of his career. It showcases the pounding, percussive piano of Brubeck, the lilting, smooth saxophone of Paul Desmond, the rhythm section of bassist Eugene Wright and drummer Joe Morello, and distinctive time signatures. Featuring a Turkish/Bulgarian rhythm that Brubeck heard on the streets of Turkey during the overseas tour, the selection has a 5/4 time around an E flat minor structure.

On September 21, 1959, Columbia Records released the song as a single, which eliminated most of Morello's jolting drum solo that appeared in the version on the album *Time Out*. The label also issued the song as a 33-1/3 single to unsuccessfully try to move the singles market closer to the LP.

In May 1961, the song reached number twenty-five on the chart, when Columbia Records reissued it and producer Teo Macero spurred the Columbia promotion department by plotting with a Chicago DJ to order 5,000 advance copies of the disc. Though the full album had been released in late December 1959, this rerelease two years later pushed *Time Out* to number two on the pop chart.

Composed by saxophonist Paul Desmond, this song offers an interesting variation of cool jazz. Like most cool jazz, it features an understated rhythm section and the almost floating saxophone of Desmond. On the other hand, unlike most light-handed cool jazz pianists, Brubeck plays percussively.

0:00–0:06	The drum and bass establish the 5/4 time (boom, chuk-a, chuk, boom, boom), which Morello had used as a warm-up exercise.
0:07–0:20	Brubeck enters to replay six-note riff eight times to reinforce the rhythm against the light cymbal playing of Morello, who described himself as a "melodic drummer" (Clark 2019, 177).
0:21–0:34	Desmond's alto sax states the melody in two four-bar phrases: D–E–E–B and then D–E–B–E. Brubeck and the rhythm section continue to play the rhythm.
0:35–0:49	Desmond plays the bridge in two four-bar passages: C–B–A–G, then C–B–A–F.
0:50–1:03	The sax plays the melody twice, first in D–E–E–B and then D–E–B–E.
1:04–1:10	Desmond starts a rich, silky solo with swoops and stop-starts to create rhythmic interest.
1:11–1:17	Desmond repeats a phrase four times with slight variations each time.
1:18–1:25	Desmond improvises on a passage twice.
1:26–1:33	Desmond returns to the passage in 1:11–1:17 and again restates it four times. For the third and fourth statements, he increases the pitch significantly to a higher tone.
1:34–1:50	After several measures, Desmond returns to the passage immediately above and restates it four times in a variety of ways.
1:51–2:27	The rhythm section and Brubeck restate the rhythm from the introduction as drummer Morello gets progressively louder to signal the beginning of his solo.
2:28–4:20	Morello launches into a drum solo. Though somewhat rare in cool jazz and even for the Brubeck quartet, the solo presents a rather subdued Morello compared to such hot swing drummers as Gene Krupa. Throughout, the sparse solo never totally overpowers Brubeck and the rhythm section, which can be clearly heard throughout until Brubeck, the rhythm section, and the drummer fade away to end the solo. The solo did not appear on the single and seldom receives airplay as part of the song today.

4:21–4:35	The smooth-sounding Desmond restates the melody twice as D–E–E–B.
4:36–4:48	Desmond shifts to C–B–A–G, then C–B–A–F for the bridge (the middle part of the song) in an AABA structure.
4:49–5:04	Desmond states the melody in D–E–E–B, then D–E–B–E.
5:04–5:20	Desmond completes the song by repeating the last measure of the melody three times. In the third restatement, he plays at a higher pitch and sustains the note for the finale.

Brubeck as a Weapon in the Cold War

The United States government used the respectable and increasingly popular jazz of Dave Brubeck as a weapon in the Cold War against the Soviet Union. In 1955, President Dwight Eisenhower saw a need for "more than mere maintenance of military strength and success in foreign affairs" and considered funding for the arts as "the cheapest money we can spend in the whole area of national security." The President emphasized that "the Federal Government should do more to give official recognition to the importance of the arts and other cultural activities" by establishing a Federal Advisory Commission on the Arts (Carletta 2007, 119, 126).

Consumed with fear over the encroachment of communism, Congress heeded Eisenhower's call. In 1955, it offered temporary funding for arts-oriented trips abroad and followed a year later with legislation that provided permanent money for international cultural and trade-fair missions. The State Department sent choral groups, classical musicians, and even basketball teams to countries selected for their political importance. As the showcase for the program, it authorized racially integrated jazz groups to tour the globe to demonstrate the superiority and racially harmonious nature of American culture. Many legislators felt that jazz tours complemented the *Voice of America* radio broadcasts, which had been started in 1942 as part of the war propaganda machine and, by the mid-fifties, reached thirty million people in eighty countries to denounce the Iron Curtain of communism.

The State Department commissioned the respectable and classically influenced Dave Brubeck to solidify support among its allies. Following the international junkets of Dizzy Gillespie's and Benny Goodman's racially integrated bands, it hoped that Brubeck and his integrated quartet would demonstrate that the United States had a cultural superiority and conflict-free racial relations. "As a serious jazz artist with some classical training and background," a State Department representative maintained, "we believe Mr. Brubeck can add a new dimension in correcting certain overseas misconceptions on American jazz" (Crist 2009, 153).

Brubeck began his tour only four months after racial violence erupted in Little Rock, Arkansas, when students integrated a high school, and after the Soviets successfully launched the unmanned spacecraft, Sputnik. The quartet included African-American bassist Eugene Wright and three Caucasians: Brubeck, Paul Desmond on sax, and drummer Joe Morello. "The musicians in my group have always been selected for their musical ability and for no other reason," the pianist boldly asserted. "If they paid me a million dollars they couldn't get me to drop Gene because he's a Negro" ("Brubeck Stands Fast" 1959; Gleason 1960, 12). Only three days before the State

Department tour, Brubeck backed his words with action when he agreed to perform at East Carolina College in Greenville, North Carolina, only after college officials reluctantly agreed to allow Wright to perform as a member of the quartet.

On the most ambitious State Department tour to date, the group started in London on February 8, 1958, at the Royal Festival Hall to kick-off sixty-seven concerts in sixteen countries. The quartet continued with a whirlwind spin around Europe and its neighboring countries. Brubeck then geographically encircled Russia with performances in Poland, India, Turkey, Pakistan, Sri Lanka, and Afghanistan. The quartet had been scheduled to end the tour in April, but, when the Middle East became politically volatile, Brubeck and his colleagues headed into the maelstrom. In early May, they played a concert in Iran, then boarded a plane to Iraq without Desmond, who refused to participate in the politically charged Iraqi event.

After the group left Iraq, the country erupted into turmoil. On July 14, 1958, General Abd al-Karim Qasim attacked and took charge of Baghdad in a nationalist coup, which overthrew and killed Iraqi king Faisal II. Al-Karim Qasim assumed the roles of prime minister and defense minister, and allied the country with the United Arab Republic rather than the United States–sponsored Baghdad Pact countries. "Right after we left Iraq," explained Brubeck, "there was a regime change. The army tried to rescue the people from the hotel where we had been staying. But after they took everyone out, the trucks got stuck. Everyone was shot and killed. We were lucky to have left when we did" (Myers 2010a). The Iraqi coup shocked the United States, which responded by sending fourteen thousand troops to nearby Lebanon to maintain its influence in the area.

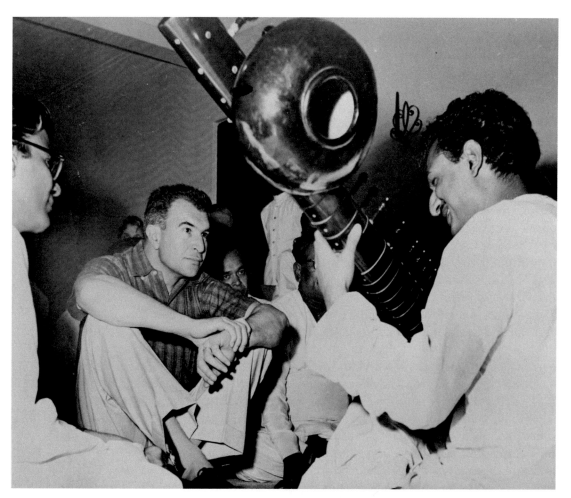

Brubeck watching sitarist Halim Abdul Jaffar Khan while on tour in India. *Holt-Atherton Special Collections, University of the Pacific Library*

During the tour, responsive audiences heaped effusive praise upon the classically infused, cool jazz of Brubeck and his group. In Warsaw, an embassy representative lauded the pianist's "horn-rimmed jazz." In Bombay, the combo's three performances "convinced hundreds of lovers of serious music that progressive American jazz is a musical form that deserves serious consideration." Indian music critic Sorab Modi proclaimed that "jazz has come a long way in the last 50 years" by moving "from the dives to the concert halls. Jazz," he concluded "has become respectable" (Crist 2009, 153).

The Brubeck quartet achieved State Department expectations. The group embodied "freedom" to Tomasz Stanko, an audience member at the concert in Krakow, Poland, and a future trumpeter. "Jazz was a synonym of Western culture, of freedom, of this different style of life" (Russonello 2018).

Though exploited by the State Department as a pawn in a violent and sometimes lethal political chess match, Brubeck harbored no regrets. He undertook the mission "out of a love of country" (Von Eschen 2004, 56), and upon his return wrote an extended article for the *New York Times Magazine* about the positive effects of the tour. Like Gillespie and Goodman, Brubeck felt that the junket proved that "jazz is color blind. When a German or a Pole or an Iraqi or an Indian sees white men and colored in perfect creative accord, when he finds out that they travel together, eat together, live together and think pretty much alike, socially and musically, the bad taste of Little Rock is apt to be washed from his mouth" (Brubeck 1958, 14). More generally, Brubeck thought that jazz, "the freest and most democratic form of expression," embodied and promulgated the American ethos in the fight against Communism" (14). "I don't like to use the word 'propaganda' in connection with it, although it is the easiest way to explain its value," he admitted about the purpose of his tour (31). During the mid-to-late fifties, jazz had become a respectable enterprise that served as an explicit tool in an ongoing Cold War.

The Third Stream of Gunther Schuller

Gunther Schuller, a participant in the Miles Davis–Gil Evans nonet and a former member of various orchestras, including the New York Philharmonic under Arturo Toscanini, expanded the cool-jazz integration of classical music into jazz in a style that he called the "Third Stream." "Back in 1957, there were two main streams of music—jazz and classical music," he explained during a lecture at Brandeis University. "I called one the First Stream and the other the Second Stream. The two streams got married, and they begat a child, like the Bible says, and a Third Stream was born" (Myers 2010l). Schuller believed that the Third Stream fused "the improvisational spontaneity and rhythmic vitality of jazz with the compositional procedures and techniques acquired in Western music during 700 years of musical development" (Lange 1993, 43).

To help promote the new style, Schuller and John Lewis started the Modern Jazz Society. "John and I founded the ensemble in 1955 because we felt we had to put teeth into what we were saying about jazz-classical fusion," insisted Schuller. "We soon renamed it the Jazz and Classical Music Society" (Myers 2010k). In 1956, Society members released *A Concert of Contemporary Music*, which featured Lewis, Schuller, Percy Heath, and Connie Kay from the Modern Jazz Quartet along with several other like-minded colleagues.

Schuller also wrote and conducted music to demonstrate Third Stream principles. While at Brandeis, he teamed with five composers on a commissioned piece for the Festival of the Arts. On three nights in June, Schuller conducted an orchestra, which performed the works for the Brandeis Jazz Festival in New York City that Columbia Records released the next year as an LP, *Modern Jazz Concert*. From

October 1956 until the next June, Schuller worked with Dimitri Mitropoulos to assemble and record a forty-four-piece orchestra that consisted of Jazz and Classical Music Society members such as former nonet players Miles Davis, John Lewis, Jimmy Giuffre, and Billy Barber; and newcomers such as pianist Bill Evans, who captured the classical-jazz mix perfectly. "Bill was unbelievable," Schuller enthused. "He had studied so much classical music that he was able to sight read all of this stuff" (Myers 2010k). In 1957, the group released *The Birth of the Third Stream* on Columbia Records.

African-American pianist Cecil Taylor also blended jazz with many modern classical concepts. Born in Long Island and starting classical piano and percussion lessons at the age of five, Taylor enrolled in the New York College of Music and then Boston's New England Conservatory, where he "took piano for the first three years along with arranging, harmony and advanced solfege" (Spellman 1966, 54). When in Boston, he frequented clubs, where he listened to such jazz men as Charlie Parker. He subsequently merged the styles of Duke Ellington and Thelonious Monk with the classical forms of Igor Stravinsky.

In 1951, the pianist heard Dave Brubeck in New York City. "I was very impressed with the depth and texture of his harmony, which had more notes in it than anyone else's," he remembered. "I was digging Stravinsky, and Brubeck had been studying with Milhaud. But because of my involvement with Stravinsky, and because I knew Milhaud, I could hear what Brubeck was doing" (Spellman 1966, 61).

In November 1956, after graduating from the New England Conservatory, Cecil landed a job at the Five Spot, a New York Bowery bar owned by brothers Joe and Iggy Termini. Cecil brought with him cellist Buell Neidlinger, who had attended Yale University and had become involved with Gunther Schuller's Third Stream experiments. For drums, he chose Dennis Charles, a transplant from the Virgin Islands and an Art Blakey enthusiast. In a few days, Taylor's student, the Monk-inspired saxophonist Steve Lacy (b. Steve Lackritz), who had attended the Schillinger School and the Manhattan School of Music, made the trio a quartet.

During the five-week engagement at the Five Spot, Cecil Taylor produced a percussive, classical-jazz fusion. Like Brubeck and some modern classical composers, Taylor used the piano as a percussion instrument by pounding the keys like a drum. "I asked him to please take it easy on the piano," recalled Joe Termini about the upright piano at the Five Spot. "And just as I asked him, two keys came flying off. Cecil, he's a piano tuner's delight" (Spellman 1966, 48). "Percussion had always been a big influence on my music," admitted Taylor (51). Sometimes, like classical composers John Cage and Christian Wolff, an enthusiastic Taylor even left the piano bench and plucked the strings inside his instrument.

Like some modern classical composers, Cecil edged toward atonality. "A small minority of jazz composer-performers are working primarily with the outer reaches of tonality, and

Cecil Taylor, 1966. *Photograph by Guy Kopelowicz*

have reached that borderline where their music often spills over into areas so removed from any center of tonal gravity that it can be thought of as 'atonal,'" wrote Gunther Schuller. "Foremost among these is Cecil Taylor" (Spellman 1966, 29).

Taylor released discs that demonstrated his classically permeated jazz. In 1958, Cecil released *Looking Ahead!*, on which he explained his theory of music. "I am not afraid of European influences. The point is to use them—as Ellington did—as part of my life as an American Negro," he asserted (Taylor 1959). He sought to utilize "the energies of the European composers, their technique, so to speak, *consciously* and blend this with the traditional music of the American Negro, and to create a new energy" (Goldberg 1965, 214–15).

Covering a concert on Saturday, March 7, 1959, at the Circle in the Square in New York City, the *New York Times* captured the essence of the pianist. Cecil Taylor delivered an "atonal potpourri compounded of leaps, lunges, sudden splashes of almost incredible virtuosity, fleeting reflections of Stravinsky, Gershwin and Tatum and suggestions of popular tunes that lurk tantalizingly just beyond the edge of recognition. Serving in an urgent, prodding, rhythmic role," the newspaper continued, he "plays with a jarring, jabbing attack, keeping a passionate accompaniment as he bobs and weaves over the keyboard." Taylor successfully combined the classical and jazz heritages into a style "that is completely his own" (Wilson 1959).

By the end of the fifties, cool jazz, modal jazz, and the Third Stream had effectively combined classical music and jazz into a popular hybrid. Though some jazz men such as Paul Whiteman, Duke Ellington, and Benny Goodman had previously blended classical music into their styles, many fifties jazz artists conspicuously integrated classical elements into jazz to transform it into a respectable music, which mainstream America embraced. "In a very short period of time," boasted Gunther Schuller, "jazz steadily became much more intricate and developed" (Myers 2010j).

For Discussion and Further Study

Chapter Quiz

1. What geographic and musical influences led to the development of cool jazz? Who were some of the prime players and composers in this new style?

2. What role did clubs like the Lighthouse play in nurturing cool jazz? What kind of audience did these clubs attract?

3. How did new West Coast labels promote the cool jazz style?

4. How did the East Coast–based Modern Jazz Quartet bring its own perspective to cool jazz? Did its racial makeup—an all-African-American group, compared to mostly white musicians from the West Coast—play a role?

5. How did promoters like George Avakian help build Miles Davis's national career?

6. How did Dave Brubeck play a role in spreading jazz to new audiences? Why do you think he might have been featured on the cover of *Time* magazine? How did he reflect continuing disparities in attitudes toward race in America?

7. How did musicians like Gunther Schuller and Cecil Taylor incorporate ideas from contemporary classical music into their own compositions and performances?

14

THE CIVIL-RIGHTS ERA

Hard Bop and Soul Jazz

This chapter focuses squarely on race. It shows how jazz artists endorsed the civil-rights movement and participated in the late-fifties and early-sixties drive for African-American equality. Bandleaders such as Max Roach and Art Blakey recorded compositions that specifically addressed civil-rights issues and felt a new connection to African culture. African-American musicians reflected and endorsed the growing pride in African-American culture, called "soul," and African-American jazz artists integrated musician unions across the country.

On February 1, 1960, at 4:30 in the afternoon in Greensboro, North Carolina, four African-American college freshmen entered a Woolworth's department store, part of a national discount chain with hundreds of stores across the country. The foursome—Junior Blair, Frank McCain, David Richmond, and Joe McNeil—had met in an algebra class at the North Carolina Agricultural and Technical College, an academic institution, which had been founded in 1891 as an "Agricultural and Mechanical College for the Colored Race." The four students sat at a lunch counter in the store. When waitresses at Woolworth's declined to serve them due to a white-only policy, the students refused to leave their seats until the store closed. "Others found out what we had done, because the press became aware of what was happening," recalled O'Neil. "So the next day we decided to go down again, I think we went down with fifteen [people], and the third day it was probably a hundred and fifty, and then it probably mushroomed up to a thousand" (Hampton and Fraser 1990, 56–57).

Protests spread to other Southern cities. Within a week, students in neighboring Durham and Winston-Salem, North Carolina, adopted the "sit-in" tactic at lunch counters to demonstrate for equal treatment of African Americans. Two weeks later, college students demanded equality in more than fifteen cities in South Carolina, Virginia, and Florida.

During 1960, the college-based sit-in movement grew. In April, students met at Shaw University in Raleigh, North Carolina, and founded the Student Nonviolent Coordinating Committee (SNCC) to formally challenge discriminatory policies with sit-ins. That October in Atlanta, students from historically black colleges, led by Martin Luther King Jr., staged a sit-in at the white-only lunch counter of Rich's Department Store. Over fifty people were arrested, and King was sentenced to four months on a chain gang, sparking national outrage. In seventy-eight cities throughout the South, students disrupted downtown businesses with the sit-in tactic. In Northern states, protesters erected picket lines around local outlets of discount chains that condoned discriminatory practices in the South. More than fifty thousand demonstrators, mostly African-American, entered stores, remained in their seats, and peacefully confronted police who dragged them to jail.

Many jazz artists reflected and joined the movement for African-American equality by explicitly expressing a sense of self-worth and a disdain for discrimination through their music. Building upon the musical principles of bop, African-American jazz artists developed the hard-bop and soul-jazz styles to join in the protest against a racially segregated America. "The Sixties was a turbulent time, and the music depicts what's going on," observed second-generation bop saxophonist Jimmy Heath (Panken 1995, 21).

The Birth of Hard Bop

During the mid-fifties, some African-American bop enthusiasts expanded the bop style by further emphasizing its blues basis. Art Blakey, a premier hard bopper, felt that blues formed "the basis of jazz." "We wanted to keep the blues sound firmly in the band," noted saxophonist "Blue" Lou Donaldson, who played with Blakey in the Jazz Messengers. "Blues had to be part of what we were doing so the music would stand out. Blues gives jazz its identity" (Myers 2010n).

The second-generation boppers also continued to expand on the harmonic changes initiated by the bop forerunners. Saxophonist Jimmy Heath and like-minded young musicians focused on "altered chords, what scales could be played on those chords, and how to enhance a composition by selecting certain notes to play the melody. These concepts were part of reharmonizing melodies," he concluded (Heath 2010, 79).

Although avid disciples of the bop pioneers, the second generation refined bop in several ways. Rather than rely on well-known tunes for rapid chord changes, they composed many of their own songs. The young jazz men also highlighted muscular drumming by Max Roach and Art Blakey, who pushed the groups they headed with propulsive, almost explosive beats. The horn men in the Blakey and Roach groups favored slightly jagged, angular lines in their extended solos to give the music a "hard" edge. Through their enhancements on bop, the young modernists developed a driving, harsher, more jarring sound than the ethereal bop, which Charlie Parker epitomized with his floating, bird-like style.

Journalists and record labels distinguished the younger boppers with the term "hard bop." Writer/pianist John Mehegan likely first coined the phrase in early 1957 in the *New York Herald Tribune*. Always eager for a new trend to market, record labels adopted the term. That year, Columbia Records released *Hard Bop* by Art Blakey and His Jazz Messengers. In 1958, Bethlehem Records produced Blakey's *Hard Drive*. The same year, Blue Note, a major purveyor of hard bop, characterized trumpeter Lee Morgan as *The Cooker* on his album. By the end of the fifties, writers and record companies had successfully established hard bop as a genre.

Max Roach at the Three Deuces, 1947. *Photograph by William P. Gottlieb. William P. Gottlieb/Ira and Leonore S. Gershwin Fund Collection, Music Division, Library of Congress*

Energetic drummers and combo leaders Max Roach and Art Blakey formed the centerpiece of the driving hard bop. During the late forties, young drummer Max Roach had been a prominent member of recording bands led by Charlie Parker and pianist Bud Powell. After a stint in California, he assembled a second-generation bop quintet in 1954 with bassist George Morrow, pianist Richie Powell (Bud's younger brother), the fleet-fingered trumpeter Clifford Brown, and eventually sax man Sonny Rollins, who attacked the music with sparse but complex solos. Roach drove this prototypical hard bop band until the untimely deaths of Brown and Powell in an automobile accident on June 26, 1956.

Art Blakey and various iterations of his Jazz Messengers typified the hard-bop approach. In 1947, the twenty-eight-year-old Blakey made an ill-fated attempt to gather sixteen fellow young bop aspirants into a big band called the Seventeen Messengers. Seven years later, pianist Horace Silver approached Blakey with sax man Hank Mobley, trumpeter Kenny Dorham, and bassist Doug Watkins and said, "I got these guys together, Art, and this is gonna be your group. . . . You can call it the Jazz Messengers," suggested Silver (Santoro 1987, 34). In 1955, the Jazz Messengers released their debut on Blue Note Records. A few months later, the band followed with two live albums recorded at the Café Bohemia, a Greenwich Village nightclub. After April 1956, when the Jazz Messengers signed to Columbia Records with its effective promotional machine and replaced Dorham with trumpeter Donald Byrd, the outfit epitomized second-generation bop by churning out chunks of hard-edged, bop-derived music propelled by its leader's driving, relentless drumming.

Just as Thelonious Monk had mentored him, Blakey tutored many third-generation boppers who helped define the hard-bop style. After Donald Byrd left the Jazz Messengers, the drummer employed a series of blazing trumpeters. He

Art Blakey in action, 1955. *Album/Alamy Stock*

snagged Bill Hardman for two years, then replaced him with twenty-year-old Lee Morgan, a follower of Clifford Brown who wove together an onslaught of rapid-fire notes backed by Blakey's driving drums. In 1961, Blakey hired Freddie Hubbard who also followed the Clifford Brown tradition by playing sensitive but rapid-fire solos (Woodward 1998b, 33).

Many young hard-bop sax men filtered through the Blakey outfit. In 1956, Jackie McLean joined the Messengers. Schooled by Bud Powell, McLean attended Benjamin Franklin High School with Sonny Rollins, who became his initial role model. When first hearing Bird, recalled the alto sax player, "[he] overwhelmed me." Jackie frequented Fifty-second Street clubs in New York City to hear bop groups and sporadically connected with Bird. "Any kind of exchange of words with him was enough inspiration for me to go home and practice the horn for a month," remembered McLean (Spellman 1966, 203, 206, 219). In 1951, the twenty-year-old McLean joined Miles Davis and Sonny Rollins on the album *Dig*, and remained with Miles and several other bop groups until he joined with Blakey, lending his off-center, passionate solos to the group.

Chicago-raised Johnny Griffin modeled himself after Johnny Hodges on ballads and Charlie Parker on up-tempo numbers. Hoping for a unique bop sound, he quit listening to Parker "in order to stop being influenced [by him]" (Gold 1958, 17). In 1957, after stints with Lionel Hampton and trumpeter Joe Morris, the "Little Giant," as his friends called him, found a perfect vehicle for his speedy bop delivery with the Jazz Messengers. "I like to play fast," he related. "I get excited" (DeMicheal 1961b, 20).

Tenor sax man Benny Golson was a Philadelphia native and close friend of John Coltrane. In 1958, he became a Messenger when Johnny Griffin embarked on a solo career. "When I look back on those days, my playing style wasn't that great. It was too smooth and silky," admitted the sax man. "Art Blakey taught me to put bite in the stuff. He taught me how to play forcefully" (Myers, 2008b, 2008d).

The next year, Newark-raised Wayne Shorter joined the group for a five-year stay. He had been introduced to bop through Martin Block's *Make Believe Ballroom* and Symphony Sid's radio broadcasts. "I heard Monk, Charlie Parker, Bud Powell, Dizzy; imagine hearing that on AM radio!" he declared. When reaching New York, Shorter worked for a year in a factory and jammed at night. After a stint in the armed forces, he met trumpeter Lee Morgan, who told him, "'We've been waiting for you to get out of the Army.' All these people I hadn't met were waiting for me," the sax man fondly remembered (Yanow 1986, 56–57). Shorter joined the Messengers and, as with other young hard boppers, came under the tutelage of Art Blakey, who encouraged an aggressive, powerful style to complement the leader's drumming.

On June 19, 1955, a little more than three months after the death of Charlie Parker, Julian "Cannonball" Adderley emerged as a new star, one of the few prominent hard-bop horn men who did not emerge from a Roach or Blakey band. After graduating from Florida A&M University as a music major, the Florida-born sax player got a job as band director at Dillard High School in Fort Lauderdale. In 1955, after deciding to attend summer courses at New York University to work on a master's degree, Adderley traveled to New York City with his brother Nat, who had played cornet with Lionel Hampton. Once in town, the two immediately headed to a show by bop bassist Oscar Pettiford at the Café Bohemia. Just before starting time, Cannonball noticed that sax player Jerome Richardson had not appeared and saxophonist Charlie Rouse had not brought his horn to the club. Adderley, horn in hand, was asked to come onto the stage by Rouse who, ready for a laugh, knew from a previous gig in Florida that Cannonball worked full-time as a high school teacher and only sporadically performed with local groups. Not hesitating, Adderley jumped on the bandstand and played "I Remember April" and "Bohemia After Dark." With each successive bop-inspired solo, he received greater and greater applause, which prompted the club owner to ask about the identity of the mystery saxophonist. "He comes from Florida, and he's called Cannonball," Nat blurted (Ginell 2013, 10).

The jazz community quickly heard the news about the wild reception for the high school teacher from Florida. Boppers such as alto player Jackie McLean and white saxophonist/Charlie Parker acolyte Phil Woods who attended the fateful performance told their friends about Cannonball. Less than ten days after this New York debut, Kenny Clarke—who had been drumming for Pettiford at the Café Bohemia—invited Cannonball and his brother to play on the album *Bohemia After Dark*

Cannonball and Nat Adderley in concert at the Concertgebouw, Amsterdam, April 1961. *Photograph by Dave Brinkman. Dutch National Archives*

on Savoy Records. On July 14, Savoy asked Cannonball to record an album as a leader with Clarke, Nat Adderley, pianist Hank Jones, and bass player Paul Chambers as the supporting cast.

A week after the Savoy sessions, Bobby Shad, director of artists and repertoire for Mercury Records, heard about the sensation from trumpeter Clark Terry and arranger Quincy Jones. Without listening to him play, the executive signed the new phenomenon to a five-year contract with Emarcy, the jazz subsidiary of Mercury. On July 21, Shad took Cannonball into the studio with a nine-man group arranged by Quincy Jones. Later in the year, he added strings to the mix for a second Cannonball offering. During summer 1955, Mercury transformed Adderley from a Florida high school teacher into a rising national jazz star by engineering a marketing campaign that promoted the saxophonist as the "new Bird." By August, *Downbeat* wrote about the rags-to-riches ascent of Cannonball and referred to him as "the greatest since Bird" (Ginell 2013, 11). "There were a lot of good players around like [saxophonist] Gigi Gryce and Phil Woods, but no one rose to a position of leadership after Bird's death," explained Adderley. "And I happened to be the right person at the right time. A fresh face, that's all, just a fresh face" (Wilson 1972, 12).

Hard Bop at the Lunch Counter

Young hard boppers understood the bop message as well as the music. During the late fifties and early sixties, "bebop reflected our alienation from the mainstream," contended saxophonist Walter "Sonny" Rollins. "My friends and I believed that bebop was the first musical movement to completely turn away from the minstrel image of most black entertainment. It was the complete opposite, and it was a new birth of freedom. It was more than music—it was a social movement" (Nisenson 2000, 28). "African-American people had fought and died in the war, and were tired of waiting to get on the front of the bus," continued Rollins. "This was the first generation that wouldn't go quietly to the separate hotel, the back of the bus, the separate food counter" (Santoro 2004, 55–56). Art Blakey believed the bop pioneers "didn't take no shit, they'd just as soon die as play the music" (Santoro 1987, 33).

Steeped in the bebop demand for equality, many young hard boppers identified with the emerging civil-rights movement in America and explicitly attacked the segregation around them. As early as September 1956, drummer Max Roach recorded a composition called "Mr. X." "'Mr. X' was dedicated to [Black Muslim leader] Malcolm X. He was very young at that time and just about to get on the scene," explained Roach. "He saw, at that young age, all the things that we saw happening to black folks around the United States of America, the racism that had been in existence for years. It was part of me, growing up in the United States of America, and being black, of course, to be conscious of all those things," he added (Sidran 1992, 38).

A twenty-eight-year-old Sonny Rollins hammered upon civil rights in his *Freedom Suite*. "I had thought black people had a little more freedom. But this wasn't the case," he related. "So *Freedom Suite* really comes from all these things, not just one incident, and it comes to a head for me by early 1958" (Myers 2013, 157). Rollins explained that "I was talking about social conditions in this country, and I got a lot of heat for that record" from the owners of Riverside Records, who "didn't want to put it out with the title 'Freedom Suite' and wanted to delete the commentary as to the purpose of the suite" (Penn 1996). Rollins had to settle for a brief, boxed section printed on the back of the cover that explained the intent of its title. "America is deeply rooted in Negro culture: its colloquialisms, its humor, its music," the saxophonist wrote. "How ironic that the Negro, more than any other people,

LISTENING GUIDE 31

Max Roach Group

"DRIVA' MAN"

Drummer Max Roach conceived of *We Insist! Max Roach's Freedom Now Suite* as a paean to the civil-rights movement and the move toward African independence. He wrote "Driva' Man" with songwriter, poet, playwright, and civil-rights activist Oscar Brown Jr., to exemplify the plight of African Americans under slavery. He used the theme of the patrol boss who pushed slaves in the field to squeeze maximum work from them and tracked escaped slaves to return them to their masters.

Recorded on August 31, 1960, Roach wrote the selection in 5/4 time in C minor and used a hit on the drum rim to imitate the crack of a whip.

Personnel on the album included Booker Little (trumpet), Julian Priester (trombone), Walter Benton and Coleman Hawkins (tenor saxes), James Schenck (bass), Max Roach (drums), Abbey Lincoln (vocals), and Nat Hentoff (supervisor).

0:00–0:03	The song starts with a shake of a tambourine and a hit on the drum rim to imitate the crack of the whip of the boss man in the fields. Roach uses the drum-rim hit throughout the song. The first few seconds also set the tempo, which resembles a chain gang slowly marching down a beaten path or a field holler.
0:04–0:58	Singer Abbey Lincoln (b. Anna Wooldridge), who Roach married in 1962 and who became a ceaseless civil-rights advocate, sings a cappella to start the song about the driva' man who pushed and corralled slaves in the American South. She sings in a call-and-response with Roach who continues his drum-rim hits and a shake of the tambourine.
0:59–1:37	After Lincoln has finished her vocals, the saxophones enter to state the twelve-bar blues theme in C minor amid the cracking of the driver's whip with rim shots and backing from the brass section. The combination of the slow tempo, the simple saxophone melody, and the brass backing gives the song an ominous feel.
1:38–2:12	Sax master Coleman Hawkins offers a blues-drenched solo in a twelve-bar format as he expertly extends phrases and merges notes together. He has accompaniment from Roach, who primarily plays the cymbals and rim shots, and a forceful pattern from the bassist.
2:13–2:32	Hawkins continues his solo, now with added backing from the horns, which play a riff within the twelve-bar blues format.
2:33–2:49	As he solos, Hawkins begins to hit blue notes, which give the song a sense of anguish and pain (example, 2:34).
2:50–3:22	The horns end their riff and Hawkins receives backing only from Roach and Schenck.
3:23–3:56	The horns reenter with a minor-note riff against Hawkins' solo that infuses the song with a dangerous feeling.
3:57–5:13	Hawkins completes his solo and Lincoln reenters with her almost spoken-word vocals, which describe the horrors of slavery. She again receives accompaniment from Roach and Schenck. At the very end of the lyrics, she breaks in a vibrato for a few seconds.

can claim America's culture as its own, is being persecuted and repressed, that the Negro who has exemplified the humanities in his very existence, is being rewarded with inhumanity" (Rollins 1958).

Other young jazz men voiced their opposition to racial discrimination. In 1957, John Coltrane recorded "Bakai" about the brutal murder of Emmett Till, a fourteen-year-old African-American Chicago boy who in 1955 had been brutally murdered on a summer vacation in Mississippi, when he supposedly insulted a white woman. Two years later, the volatile bassist Charles Mingus composed "Fables of Faubus" as a sarcastic ode to Arkansas governor Orval Faubus, who had blocked the integration of public schools in Little Rock two years earlier. In 1960, Mingus recorded "A Prayer for Passive Resistance." When questioned by a reporter, the bassist asked, "Why do you want to write about jazz musicians when there's a [civil-rights] war going on?" (Goldberg 1965, 149). Pianist Bobby Timmons released "The Sit-In" on his *Born to Be Blue* album. Multi-instrumentalist Yusef Lateef felt that "you couldn't avoid the civil rights movement back then. The scenes were in the newspapers and on TV all the time. My music was an expression of my feelings toward life and toward that struggle," he insisted (Myers 2013, 155).

In late 1960, when sit-ins were sweeping the country, Max Roach's hard-hitting *We Insist! Max Roach's Freedom Now Suite* reached the stores. The album cover pictured three African Americans sitting-in at a lunch counter without food and a white waiter glaring at them. The liner notes began with a quote from civil-rights leader A. Philip Randolph. "A revolution is unfurling," it read. "America's unfinished revolution. It is unfurling in lunch counters, buses, libraries and schools—wherever the dignity and potential of men are denied. Masses of Negroes are marching onto the stage of history and demanding their freedom now!" (Randolph 1960). A boxed section in the liner notes explained the importance of the student sit-ins, followed by a paragraph about the role of jazz musicians in the movement: "Jazz musicians, normally apolitical and unmindful of specific social movements, were also unprecedentedly stimulated by the sit-ins." It reported that hard boppers such as Roach and Art Blakey "declared public support for the sit-ins" (Randolph 1960). "Max told me that his motivation for recording the album had been the lunch counter sit-ins in Greensboro, North Carolina, in February 1960," remarked Nat Hentoff, who supervised the recording sessions. "For years since *Brown v the Board of Education*, there had been virtually no change in the progression of desegregation. Finally, with the sit-ins, here was a sense that there could be a revolution" (Myers 2013, 157). Roach and his band mates first performed the suite live at the NAACP Youth Council assemblies in Washington, DC, and Philadelphia.

Riding for Freedom

The Freedom Ride, another tactic of the civil-rights movement, gained support from hard boppers. In 1946, the Supreme Court banned segregation on buses and trains engaged in interstate travel. Fourteen years later in *Boynton v Virginia*, the court applied its ruling to bus and train terminals by arguing that segregation of the terminals violated the Interstate Commerce Act and desegregation could be enforced by federal intervention.

While riding on a bus to New York City during a snowstorm, Gordon Carey and Tom Gaither, two field secretaries for the Congress for Racial Equality (CORE) who had been conducting nonviolent workshops in South Carolina, decided to test the new law. They discussed "Gandhi's march to the sea" and "an analogous march to the sea in the South" that ended in New Orleans. Carey and Gaither devised a bus trip "inspired by the Journey of Reconciliation, which CORE and the Fellowship of Reconciliation had sponsored back in '47. Somehow the drama of the whole thing caught us up, and the two of us planned most of the Freedom Ride before we ever got back to New York City" (Hampton and Fraser 1990, 74–75).

The two friends pitched their idea to CORE director James Farmer, who supported a nonviolent "interracial group ride throughout the South. The whites in the group would sit in the back of the bus, and the blacks would sit in the front of the bus, and would refuse to move when ordered," explained Farmer. "At every rest stop, the whites would go into the waiting room for blacks, and the blacks into the waiting room for whites, and would seek to use all the facilities, refusing to leave." CORE hoped to "create a crisis, so that the federal government would be compelled to enforce federal law," emphasized Farmer (Hampton and Fraser 1990, 75).

On May 4, 1961, seven African-American and six white Freedom Riders of varied ages boarded buses in Washington, DC, destined for the South. One group traveled on a Greyhound bus, and the other contingent bought tickets from Trailways. They hoped to ride through Atlanta, then Alabama and Mississippi, and arrive in New Orleans on May 17 on the seventh anniversary of the *Brown v Board of Education* decision.

The groups confronted hostile crowds once outside the nation's capital. In Rock Hill, South Carolina, recalled Freedom Rider and future Georgia Congressman John Lewis, "we were met by a group of young white men that beat us and hit us, knocked us out and left us lying on the sidewalk in front of the entrance of the waiting room" (Hampton and Fraser 1990, 77).

Trouble exploded in Alabama. An angry mob of racists, armed with pistols, clubs, chains, and blackjacks, waited for the Greyhound bus at Anniston and slashed its tires before it left the terminal. The crowd stalked the damaged bus in cars until it reached the outskirts of town, where "the mob surrounded it, held the door closed and a member of the mob threw a firebomb into the bus while members of the Anniston police force mingled with the crowd," recalled James Farmer (Hampton and Fraser 1990, 79). At the Anniston station, remembered James Peck, who rode the Trailways bus, "a group of six Klansmen boarded our bus and bodily threw the black riders into the back seat" and "told the driver to drive on." When the bus reached Birmingham, which in fifteen years had been rocked by more than fifty racially motivated bombings, "twenty men with pipes" confronted the civil-rights advocates. "The mob seized us," remarked Peck, who the crowd mercilessly beat until he lay in "a big pool of blood" that required fifty-three stitches to his head (78). When the bus tried to leave the Birmingham terminal, Klansmen blocked its departure.

John Patterson, the racist governor of Alabama, had no sympathy for the riders. He thought that the civil-rights protesters "were deliberately doing this in order to create trouble, violence if necessary. I thought that the Freedom Riders should stay home and mind their own business," he declared (Hampton and Fraser 1990, 80–81).

The SNCC sent reinforcements to Birmingham as replacements for the wounded and battered original thirteen riders. When they arrived on May 17, the riders confronted Theophilus "Bull" Connor, commissioner of public safety, who arrested the civil-rights advocates, drove them to the Alabama–Tennessee border, and told them to return to their campuses. Undaunted, the SNCC sent additional riders who traveled to the bus terminal and progressed through Alabama to Mississippi. Arrested in Jackson, Mississippi, and sent to the Mississippi State Penitentiary at Parchman Farm for sixty days, the Freedom Riders suspended the march to New Orleans.

The federal government, embarrassed by the widely broadcast rage and violence of Southern segregationists against the Freedom Ride, moved into action.

 LISTENING GUIDE 32

Art Blakey

 "THE FREEDOM RIDER"

Ever since visiting Africa in 1947, Blakey had been interested and concerned with the civil-rights movement. He unabashedly showed his support of civil-rights protesters with the song "The Freedom Rider," which commemorated the brave whites and African Americans who rode in two buses through the South to integrate public bus stations. Like an African griot, he tells the story of the Freedom Riders through his drums.

This song illustrates the importance of the drums for an insistent hard bop. Recorded on May 27, 1961, it featured only drummer Blakey.

0:00–0:06	The song starts with a cymbal crash and an insistent drum roll and then another cymbal crash.
0:07–0:12	Blakey hits the drum five times and follows with a quick four beats. He repeats this pattern twice.
0:13–0:26	Blakey hits the drum once and follows with a drum roll and ends with a cymbal crash. He repeats this pattern four times.
0:27–0:41	In a call-and-response between two of his drums, Blakey establishes polyrhythm by hitting one drum twice, then hitting a different drum twice while playing a different rhythm on the cymbal. He repeats this pattern twelve times. The interplay between the two drums and the cymbal gives the pattern a very African feel and signals a bus rolling down the road.
0:42–0:51	Blakey establishes another rhythm, which he repeats three times with a hard hit at the end of each measure.
0:52–0:56	Blakey again changes the rhythm in an innovative transition from the previous pattern.
0:57–0:59	The drummer crashes his cymbal and then shifts the rhythm.
1:00–1:01	Three forceful cymbal crashes, which indicate gunshots or at least trouble for the Freedom Riders on the bus.
1:02–1:17	In a twelve-bar-blues format, Blakey establishes a pattern, repeated three times, that involves an insistent beat at the end of each measure. It constitutes a call-and-response with himself.
1:18–1:33	The drummer switches to another pattern, which nearly becomes a drum roll to increase the tension and speed of the song. He repeats the four-measure pattern twice.
1:34–1:46	Blakey builds upon the previous pattern in an innovative solo break and ends with a cymbal crash.
1:47–1:52	Returns to the pattern in 0:27–0:41.
1:53– 1:58	Five cymbal crashes twice indicate problems for the Riders.
1:59–2:11	Blakey returns to the rhythm pattern in 0:42–0:51.
2:12–2:17	The drummer transitions to another rhythm for a few measures and ends with a cymbal crash to signal a change.

2:18–2:34	The drummer transitions to the main four-beat pattern with background cymbals of 0:27–0:41, which sounds like the wheels of a bus moving. In this case, he heightens the tension by three cymbal crashes at the end of each sixteen beats, except for the last pattern. He makes the cymbal crash on top of the next four beats.
2:35–2:41	He repeats a descending pattern twice.
2:42–2:48	He repeats a pattern twice.
2:49–2:53	He repeats a pattern four times.
2:54–3:16	Blakey plays low-volume rolls with cymbals, which replicate a bus moving down the highway.
3:17–3:20	Blakey switches rhythm briefly.
3:21–3:31	Blakey plays his drum rolls louder with cymbal accents, which create a second rhythm. It signals that the bus is getting closer to a segregated terminal.
3:32–3:43	Restates basic beat from 0:27 in a slightly louder volume with the steady cymbal in the background that establishes a second rhythm. In true African tradition, Blakey creates an intricate polyrhythm throughout the song.
3:44–3:55	Blakey repeats the pattern in 2:18–2:34 with the three cymbal crashes at the end of each sixteen beats.
3:56–4:03	Back to the four-beat measures without the cymbal crashes as the bus continues on its journey.
4:04–4:12	Blakey solos with loud volume to indicate that the Freedom Riders have encountered trouble. He repeats a pattern three times.
4:13–4:20	He repeats a loud, drum-roll pattern twice, delivering an agitated sound.
4:21–4:31	Blakey loudly bashes his drum twelve times and then responds by hitting the drum at a much lower volume twelve times to develop an interesting dynamic. He repeats this pattern twice to indicate that trouble has come to the Freedom Riders. You can hear Blakey moaning in the background. He then approximates the sound of people running and ends the section with a cymbal crash to announce a change.
4:32–4:37	He repeats the basic four-bar beat of the bus rolling down the road with three loud cymbal crashes to increase tension.
4:38–4:45	Blakey returns to the rapid-fire gallop of the drums that he achieves by increasing the volume and changing the rhythm of the basic four-bar beat of the bus rolling down the road. Now, the bus is speeding down the road.
4:46–4:48	Blakey returns to the four-bar beat at a slower pace.
4:49–5:09	A return to a different, very syncopated rhythm of the basic four bars to indicate that the bus is speeding down the road and has been disabled in some way. A symbol crash indicates a change.
5:10–5:19	Blakey lowers the volume of the basic beat and increases the speed as the bus moves faster. To increase the tension, he crashes the cymbal once after every measure.
5:20–5:29	The drummer smashes the cymbal five times and, in a call-and-response, responds with beats on the drum. He repeats this pattern three times to indicate the problems confronting the Freedom Riders.

5:30–5:54	Blakey continues the basic sixteen beats, but on the last beat hits the bass drum to signal a gunshot or an explosion. The basic rhythm continues softly with repeated accents on the last two beats by the bass drum to indicate that the gunfire or explosions persist. At one point, the light cymbal charts the progress of the bus. A cymbal crash indicates a change.
5:55–6:10	Blakey reestablishes the basic beat of the bus with three cymbal crashes after eight beats (twice repeated) and then five cymbal crashes (twice repeated) to indicate continuing trouble.
6:11–6:15	The basic four-beat pattern returns.
6:16–6:29	Blakey establishes a new rhythm by hitting one drum and responding with another in a call-and-response. He repeats the pattern four times with an innovative ending the fourth time.
6:30–6:36	A heavy staccato beat repeated twice that sounds like gunfire.
6:37–6:39	He briefly restates the main beat of the bus rolling down the road.
6:40–7:08	After a few drum rolls, which might indicate explosions, the pace softens until only the cymbals keep the main rhythm with a very light drum roll in the background.
7:09–7:17	The drums get louder and louder in the basic four-beat pattern as the bus speeds down the highway in search of freedom.
7:18–7:24	To end the song, Blakey loudly beats the drums and crashes the cymbals.

In summer 1961, on the advice of US attorney general Robert Kennedy, the Interstate Commerce Commission crafted regulations to enforce the antidiscrimination decisions of the Supreme Court. "The feeling of people coming out of jail [in Jackson] was one that they had triumphed, that they had achieved, that they were now ready, they could go back home, they could be a witness," contended Cordy T. Vivian, who participated in the sit-ins and the Freedom Ride (Hampton and Fraser 1990, 96).

Hard-bop musicians supported the Freedom Ride with their music. Beginning on May 27, after the buses stalled in Jackson, Art Blakey recorded *The Freedom Rider*, which represented his "immediate reaction to the explosive growth of the civil rights movement." On June 28, 1961, Cannonball Adderley backed the riders by staging a benefit for them through CORE. In late 1961, hard-bop saxophonist Oliver Nelson waxed *Afro-American Sketches*, which traced the history of African Americans from Africa to the present and concluded with "Freedom Dance."

To further support racial harmony, Sonny Rollins integrated his group. In late 1961, after a two-year hiatus from the music business, the saxophonist formed a combo with two African-Americans, drummer Harry Saunders and bassist Bob Cranshaw, and white guitarist Jim Hall. He noted that "I definitely wanted to make a statement by having an integrated band. I took a lot of flak for it, a lot of flak. But you cannot say that it is all right to be racist as long as it's against white people," he reasoned (Nisenson 2000, 150–1).

Jazz, the March on Washington, and the Birmingham Bombing

As the civil-rights movement continued to grow, jazz musicians pushed for equality. On August 28, 1963, two hundred fifty thousand white and African-American civil-rights supporters converged on Washington, DC, for what would become known as the "March on Washington." "African-American people voted with their feet," recollected civil-rights leader Bayard Rustin, who had envisioned the march as early as 1941. "They came from every state, they came in jalopies, on trains, buses, anything they could get—some walked" (Hampton and Fraser 1990, 169). The protesters marched to the steps of the Lincoln Memorial to listen to ten civil-rights luminaries, including Martin Luther King Jr., who delivered his moving "I Have a Dream" speech, which the NBC and ABC television networks broadcast.

Some jazz artists directly supported the March on Washington. Before the March on August 23, Art Blakey, Thelonious Monk, and others staged an Emancipation March at the Apollo Theater in New York City. Two days later, Max Roach and others coordinated and performed at a benefit concert at the New York Polo Grounds to support the March.

Just before the transformational March on Washington, civil-rights organizers focused their efforts on Birmingham, Alabama. Earlier

March on Washington, August 28, 1963. *Photograph by Marion S. Trikosko. Library of Congress Prints and Photographs Division*

in the spring, high school students had marched against segregation. "A boy from high school, he can get the same effect in terms of being in jail, in terms of putting pressure on the city, as his father," reasoned civil-rights organizer Reverend James Bevel. "Yet, there is no economic threat on the family because the father is still on the job" (Hampton and Fraser 1990, 131). On May 2, using Birmingham's Sixteenth Street Baptist Church as a gathering spot, six hundred teens walked for a few blocks before Bull Connor arrested them. The next day, in the early afternoon, nine hundred students gathered around the church, chanted "Freedom! Freedom! Freedom!" and sang "We Shall Overcome" until Connor sprayed the protesters with pressurized fire hoses. "They're rolling that little girl there, right in the middle of the street," exclaimed a horrified David Vann, a white attorney sympathetic to the protesters. On May 4, one thousand teens marched into fire hoses and snarling police dogs. Within two more days, two thousand high school protesters had been jailed, antagonizing segregationist Alabama governor George Wallace, who proclaimed that Birmingham "was 'fed up'" with the demonstrations ("Wallace Says Birmingham" 1963). The extreme reactions of Bull Connor and Wallace swelled public support for the protesters, who forced the desegregation of some lunch counters and encouraged several store owners to hire African Americans as employees.

Just four months after the victory in Birmingham and a mere eighteen days after the transformational March on Washington, white racism reared its ugly head again in Birmingham. At 10:25 in the morning of September 15, 1963, as children attended Sunday school at the Sixteenth Street Baptist Church, a handmade bomb exploded. As the *New York Times* reported, a bundle of fifteen sticks of dynamite "blew gaping holes in the walls of the church basement." "Scores of young Negroes who had been attending Sunday school began pouring out of the entrances," the *Times* continued. "Some were bleeding, some were screaming and some were moaning" (Sitton 1963, 26; "Herbers" 1963). The explosion killed four children, who were found huddled together in the rubble. Fourteen other youths lay wounded. In the aftermath, police shot and killed a sixteen-year-old African-American boy, and a thirteen-year-old African-American child died after being shot while riding his bicycle. "I was shocked by the bombing. It happened right after the March on Washington," recalled Coretta King. "We had a feeling that the dream could be realized. And then, a few weeks later, came the bombing in Birmingham, with four innocent little girls [killed]" (Hampton and Fraser 1990, 176). Planned and executed by four Klansmen, the bombing represented the fourth in Birmingham that month and the twenty-first within eight years.

Saxophonist John Coltrane mourned the deaths of the African-American children in Birmingham. On November 18, 1963, he recorded "Alabama," which appeared on his *Live at Birdland* album. Less than a month later, he performed the song on the television show *Jazz Casual* to honor the youths. "It represents, musically, something that I saw down there translated into music from inside me," Coltrane explained (Jones, 1964).

Coltrane modeled "Alabama" on the cadences of the eulogy that Martin Luther King Jr. delivered three days after the bombing for those who died. He mimicked the civil-rights leader's intonations and the reactions of the distraught crowd to the speech. Like King, who started his speech by praising "these beautiful children of God," Coltrane began slowly, respectfully, and dirge-like. A third of the way through the song, the saxophonist matched the beats of King who explained that "these children—unoffending, innocent, and beautiful—were the victims of one of the most vicious and tragic crimes ever perpetrated against humanity" but that they "did not die in vain." Coltrane became more animated and forceful as he followed King's pattern as he preached to his increasingly agitated listeners. He ended the song with the sadness and pounding rage of drummer Elvin Jones, who crashed his cymbals repeatedly to signify the commitment of African Americans to the quest for equal rights (King 1963).

Martin Luther King Jr. acknowledged the importance of jazz musicians such as Coltrane to the civil-rights movement. "Much of the power of our Freedom movement in the United States has come" from "modern jazz," he insisted in the program for the 1964 Berlin Jazz Festival (King 2019).

A few hard boppers became so disgusted with racial discrimination in the United States that they relocated to Europe. In 1959, saxophonist Shihab Sahib permanently stayed in Europe after performing there. Two years later, pianist Kenny Drew moved to Paris and then settled in Copenhagen, and trumpeter Idrees Sulieman migrated to Stockholm. In 1962, saxophonist Dexter Gordon permanently moved to Europe. "With all the political and social strife during that time" in the United States, he recollected, he chose to live in Paris and then Copenhagen (Alkyer and Enright 2000, 176). In 1963, both drummer Art Taylor and saxophonist Johnny Griffen relocated to Europe. "They've got all the black musicians on the run," declared Griffin. "Black musicians all over Europe, running away from America" (Taylor 1993, 66).

Hard Bop and the African Heritage

While the civil-rights movement was occurring at home, many African nations rose up against years of colonial rule, further inspiring jazz musicians. Kwame Nkrumah, leader of the Convention People's Party in the Gold Coast, a British colony, started the liberation movement across the African continent. After working with British officials, on March 6, 1957, he secured independence for the renamed country of Ghana.

In 1960, as college students in the United States demonstrated for equality at segregated lunch counters, African liberation efforts spread like a bushfire. On January 1, the Republic of Cameroon proclaimed its independence from France. Between April and June, three more countries shed their colonial masters. In August, six more nations escaped from French shackles. On October 1, 1960, Nigeria established its independence. Within nine years, thirty-one countries had declared independence from France, Britain, and Belgium. Throughout the world, a black consciousness emerged to define the era.

Hard-bop musicians identified African struggles with the fight for equality in the United States. Sonny Rollins felt a particular affinity for Africa. While a youth, he marched with his grandmother "up and down Lenox Avenue in these parades with a flag that was at the time black, yellow and green" to show support for black nationalist Marcus Garvey. (Penn 1992, 19). "My grandmother had been a strong follower of Marcus Garvey and had served in several ancillary back-to-Africa movements," he recalled. "When I was a boy, I went to many rallies in our Harlem neighborhood for a range of different causes. I remember one in the mid-Thirties where we went to implore people to get involved in the early civil rights struggle" (Myers 2013, 146).

In 1953, as he thumbed through a *Life* magazine in a barbershop, a twenty-three-year-old Rollins chanced upon a photo that connected him to the African homeland and inspired a song. He noticed a photograph of Nigerian dancers in traditional costumes that "instilled in me a certain pride," he recalled (Myers 2013, 153). Deeply moved, Rollins dedicated a composition to the African country by calling it "Airegin." "Why did I spell Nigeria backward?" he rhetorically asked. "I guess it might have been too controversial to call a song 'Nigeria' at the time. Perhaps that would have been too blunt or blatant. Perhaps I wanted to make my message incomprehensible to white-owned record companies." On June 29, 1954, Rollins recorded the song with the Miles Davis quintet. "When we were done recording," he related, "I felt I had tossed my hat into the struggle. To me, 'Airegin' was a consequential thing. . . . I thought it would be an excellent way to instill civil rights and pride in blacks who listened to my music. When I wrote 'Airegin,' I hoped that greater consciousness for equality and freedom would be raised" (Myers 2013, 152–54).

Sonny Rollins (front) on an early date. *Album/Alamy Stock Photo*

"Most of the young black guys playing modern jazz were aware of these issues and we wanted our music, at least to an extent, to make a statement," Rollins added (Nisenson 2000, 62).

As the decade progressed, hard boppers issued dozens of albums that showed their interest in and affinity with the African independence movement. In 1955, trumpeter Kenny Dorham released the *Afro-Cuban* album with the selection, "Afrodisia." In 1956, Buddy Collette recorded his composition "Tanganyika" with the Chico Hamilton Sextet. The next year, Milt Jackson composed "Ghana" to commemorate the sovereignty of the new nation. In April 1957, John Coltrane cut "Dakar," a song dedicated to the capital of Senegal, and, in late June the next year, participated in Wilbur Harden's session, which included the songs "Dial Africa," "Tanganyika Strut," and "Gold Coast." In September 1960, sax man Jackie McLean teamed with tenor saxophonist Tina Brooks to record "Appointment in Ghana."

In 1960, after the sit-ins started, Max Roach's *We Insist!* outlined the connection between civil rights in the United States and African independence. The liner notes described the increasing "press coverage of the emerging, newly independent nations of Africa" and the impact of the reporting on "Negro students in the South [who] had been particularly aware of the impetus to their own campaigns for freedom given by the African examples. Jazz men," the notes observed, "have been becoming conscious and prideful of the African wave of independence. Several new original compositions were titled with the names of African nations, and some jazz men began to know more about Nkrumah than about their local Congressmen" (Randolph 1960). The record included two Afrocentric selections, "All Africa" and "Tears for Johannesburg," and a guest appearance by Nigerian drummer Babatunde Olatunji. From Roach's perspective, "we must decolonize our minds and re-name and re-define ourselves" (Roach 1972, 4).

The Afrocentric Randy Weston. *Photograph courtesy of Brian McMillen*

Randy Weston, a hard-bop pianist who idolized Thelonious Monk, clearly linked jazz, civil rights, and African decolonization. "My big awakening to Africa came as a result of my mother and father," explained the pianist. "Our entire neighborhood in Brooklyn was Pan-African," which encouraged the unity of all black peoples (Myers 2013, 159). "My dad always said that black people would never be free as a people until Africa is free: that's the only time we will be collectively strong, when Africa is strong," he recalled. "I was always upset about the separation of our people, the separation of those people who are considered part of the African diaspora from the Motherland itself" (Weston 2010, 82).

In 1960, Weston collaborated with trombonist/arranger Melba Liston and sax man Gigi Gryce to issue *Uhuru Afrika*, a Kiswahili phrase for "Freedom Africa." Weston asked

Babatunde Olatunji to lend his drumming to the effort. On the disc, Weston included "Uhuru Kwanza," "African Lady," "Bantu," and "Kucheza Blues" as well as a "freedom poem" by Harlem Renaissance writer Langston Hughes. "I wanted to write a suite dedicated to Mother Africa," Weston declared (2010, 83). "The whole point of *Uhuru Afrika* was to talk about the freedom of a continent; a continent that has been invaded and had its children taken away, the continent of the creation of humanity" (89–90).

The next year, Weston journeyed to Africa in search of his spiritual roots. "I wanted to find out why I played the way I played, so I went to Africa and discovered that I had never left the continent, spiritually" (Myers 2013, 159). As his plane flew over African territory, "I was so over the top in my excitement, I could swear I felt the rhythms of the plane engine," related the pianist. "At last, I was going back home" (Weston 2010, 103). Traveling with a delegation of twenty-eight African-American writers, musicians, scholars, and artists sponsored by the American Society of African Culture (AM-SAC), he journeyed to Nigeria, which had gained independence only a few months earlier. "The American and African counterparts in each art form got together and we saw similarities," he recalled about the ten-day visit. "I became more aware of African culture, West Indian culture, even more aware of the culture of the American Negro" (Gitler 1964, 36). Upon his return, Weston released the African-inspired album, *The Music of New African Nations*. Two years later, Weston returned to Nigeria for a twelve-day visit sponsored by AM-SAC.

After sit-ins mobilized African Americans, other jazz artists issued music devoted to African themes. In February 1961, Cannonball Adderley recorded *African Waltz*. The same year, Art Blakey, who two years earlier had cut "Africaine" with the Jazz Messengers, waxed "Afrique." Early the next year, he teamed with the Afro-Drum Ensemble for a series of African-based compositions. In 1961, John Coltrane released *Africa/Brass*, which was inspired by a record of African music he had bought. Coltrane "wanted the African sound," recalled trumpeter Freddie Hubbard, who played on the session (Kahn 2006, 52).

Soul Jazz and the African-American Identity

Some hard boppers inserted sounds from the African-American sanctified church into hard bop for a new style called "soul jazz." Conceived by record companies and the press, the term reflected the close connection of jazz to the more general feeling of African-American pride.

By the late fifties and early sixties, the term "soul" trumpeted the virtues of African-American culture. Though first coined in 1947 by Babs Gonzales (b. Lee Brown) in his dictionary of jazz slang, the word came into common usage amid the African-American struggle for equality. Among other things, it referred to food that African Americans had been compelled to eat during slavery such as chitterlings (pig intestines), ham hocks, collard greens, black-eyed peas, candied yams, and sweet potato pie. A reminder of past enslavement, "soul food" differentiated the African-American experience from the history of whites and built a sense of black community. Some even referred to good music as "greasy."

African Americans adopted a "soul" look by wearing African clothes and natural hairstyles. By the early sixties, some African-American men donned brightly colored, loose-fitting, dashiki shirts, and women favored long-sleeved, full-length kaftan tunics to imitate the current fashion of West Africans. Instead of straightening or "conking" their hair, African Americans sported long "Afros" by eschewing hair products and combing their hair away from their scalp in a large rounded shape. "We saw more and more sisters begin to wear natural hairdos, and more and more brothers begin to wear their hair in the new natural styles," remarked a Detroit bookstore owner during the sixties. Unlike early twentieth-century bluesman Big Bill Broonzy, who "never heard a black man or woman say, 'I'm proud to be black'" (Bruynoghe 1992, 145), many African Americans embraced the slogan, "black is beautiful."

Blacks in the United States even used a new word to define themselves, "Afro-American," which emphasized their African heritage. No longer content with being called "Negro," they asserted their independence from the segregated past and present. By 1967, Lerone Bennett Jr., the senior editor of *Ebony* magazine, found "a large and vocal group" that pressed with "an aggressive campaign for the use of the word 'Afro-American' as the only historically accurate and humanly significant designation of this large and pivotal portion of the American population." This group, he explained, "charges that the word 'Negro' is an inaccurate epithet which perpetuates the master-slave mentality in the minds of both black and white Americans." Some more fanatical Black Power advocates, he mentioned, favored the word "African-American" (Bennett 1967, 46).

Recasting the image of themselves and their culture, African Americans focused on a sense of self-worth by highlighting African-American achievements. They illuminated neglected accomplishments of their ancestors in the American Revolution and other wars, stressed scientific breakthroughs by African Americans, and spotlighted the contributions to American culture of African-American professionals, artists, poets, and writers. African Americans especially emphasized their advances in music by calling a distinctive blend of jazz, blues, and sanctified-church music "soul music."

Ray Charles (b. Ray Charles Robinson) was among the first "soul" musicians. A jazz pianist patterned after Nat King Cole, in the late forties Charles, who had been blind since childhood, unsuccessfully auditioned for Lucky Millinder's band, then traveled across the country from Tampa to Seattle looking for work. In early 1949, he cut his first disc, "Confession Blues," which nearly topped the R&B chart.

Ray changed his style from a muted jazz-blues to sanctified screams, which originated with his church upbringing. "Everybody in a small town went to church," he explained. "Sunday school in the morning, then regular services, home for dinner and back for BYPU [Baptist Young People's Union]. Then there were evening services, and you'd get home at ten at night" (Goldberg 1965, 176). As part of his church activities, Ray sang regularly at the Shiloh Baptist Church in Greenville, Florida.

Signing with Atlantic Records in June 1952, Charles merged his bluesy jazz with a passion for the sanctified church to scale the R&B chart. Ray took the Pilgrim Travelers' "I've Got a New Home" and reworked it as "Lonely Avenue" and changed "Nobody But You, Lord" to "Nobody But You." He transformed the gospel standard "This Little Light of Mine" to "This Little Girl of Mine," altered "I've Got a Savior (Way Over Jordan)" to "I've Got a Woman" for his first chart topper, and rejoiced on "Hallelujah, I Love Her So." "Now I'd been singing spirituals since I was three and I'd been singing the blues for just as long," explained Charles. "So what could be more natural than to combine them? It didn't take any thinking, didn't take any calculating. All the sounds were there, right at the top of my head." Bluesman Big Bill Broonzy criticized Charles for "cryin', sanctified. He's mixing the blues with the spirituals. He should be singing in a church" (Goldberg 1965, 176).

Saxophonists David "Fathead" Newman and Hank Crawford teamed with Charles to perfect a soul-drenched jazz. Idolizing Louis Jordan and playing with bluesman Lowell Fulson, in 1954 the Texas-born Newman joined the Charles outfit to unleash earthy, gritty wails to accompany his leader. Atlantic producer Jerry Wexler considered Newman to be the pianist's "alter ego on tenor" (Wexler 1993, 106). In 1958, saxophonist Hank Crawford connected with the Ray Charles band. "I started out playing in churches from the age of nine," he revealed. "I was playing in the Baptist church. My family was very much in the church, a very religious family" (Soonachan 2000, 22). After attending Tennessee State University in Nashville and forming a jazz combo, he joined the Charles group, with which for the next five years he integrated sanctified gospel into the band.

After the addition of Newman and Crawford, Ray Charles crossed over into the mainstream. In July 1959, he reached the pop Top Ten with "What'd I Say." During the next four years, Charles repeatedly hit the pop charts with such number-one blockbusters as "Hit the Road Jack" and "Georgia on My Mind." In 1960, he scored his first Top Ten album with *Genius Hits the Road* and, the next year, neared the top with *Genius + Soul = Jazz*. Amid the civil-rights unrest, he earned the titles of the "High Priest of Soul" and "Brother Ray."

Many hard boppers had experienced the African-American sanctified church music that propelled Ray Charles to stardom. Pianist Horace Silver, though raised Catholic, "was always enthralled with the black church" (Klee 1971, 16). "To know what jazz is, go to the Negro churches, the Baptist Church, the Revivalist Church," he asserted (Silver 1960). Charles Mingus recalled "swinging and clapping my hands in church as a little boy" (Mingus and Dorr-Dorynek 1960). "Holiness church," he asserted, "that's where my music came from" (Williams 1961). Mingus "made us play like the old, original blues with only two or three chords," revealed pianist Mal Waldron, who in February 1959 played with the bassist on the *Blues and Roots* album. "He brought in some gospel music, too, the first time that was done" (Goldberg 1965, 143).

Many hard boppers incorporated heavy doses of sanctified church music into their music to deliver soul jazz. Horace Silver described the difference in emphasis between hard bop and soul jazz: "Most of the groups, they came in, they played the head [main theme] and soloed and played the head on out and that was it," he explained about hard bop. "Whereas I thought to color it up a little bit and make the whole presentation more uplifting and desirable for people to listen to. You know, with an introduction and a few little interludes here and there. Maybe a shout chorus [from the church] or a tag ending." Soul jazz, he insisted, "was to bring happiness, joy, you know, so you can dance to it, you can, you know, pat your foot to it and uplift your spirits" (Sidran 1992, 63, 65). Silver infused such a sanctified, blues-based, back-beat rhythm in such songs as the aptly titled "The Preacher," which ended with a call-and-response from the band.

Horace Silver. *Photograph courtesy of Brian McMillen*

By the end of the fifties, the use of "soul" to distinguish and market a church-infused style had become common. In 1957, Milt Jackson released *Plenty, Plenty Soul*. "Everyone wants to know where I got that funky style. Well, it came from church," the vibraphonist explained (Hentoff 1957). "The music I heard there was open, relaxed, impromptu—soul music." Later in the year, Jackson and Ray Charles teamed for *Soul Brothers*. The next year, John Coltrane wailed on *Soultrane*. In 1959, organist Shirley Scott recorded *Soul Searching* and, the next year, followed it with *Soul Sister*.

In 1960, when sit-ins swept the country, the gates of soul jazz opened. Hank Mobley released *Soul Station*, and Johnny Griffin waxed *Big Band Soul*. Bassist Sam Jones released *The Soul Society*. As a tribute to the church, pianist Les McCann and his group recorded *The Shout*, which one critic felt established a "close relationship to the language of *soul*" (Gregory 1960). "I love gospel music, and I mean if you live next to a church all your life, what are you going to play?" rhetorically asked McCann, who as a youth sang in a church choir at the Shiloh Baptist Church in Lexington, Kentucky (Gleason 2016, 248). "An increasing number of Negro jazzmen are talking, thinking and playing 'soul' music," declared *Downbeat* in September 1960. "This is reflective, of course, of the ever-sharpening battle for a broader scope of civil rights for the Negro people" (Tynan 1960, 20).

Philadelphian Bobby Timmons emerged as a leader in soul jazz. Raised by his grandfather, who served as a minister, and starting as a church organist, the pianist became a mainstay of Art Blakey's Jazz Messengers and composed the sanctified jazz instrumental "Moanin.'" In 1959, he released a solo debut album, *This Here Is Bobby Timmons*, which especially promoted the soul-jazz tag. The title cut, "This Here," contended Cannonball Adderley, seemed to be "simultaneously a shout and a chant" and "related to the roots of soul church music" (Keepnews 1960). The next year, Timmons recorded *Soul Time*. During the next few years, the pianist issued *Sweet and Soulful Sounds*, *Little Barefoot Soul*, *Holiday Soul*, *The Soul Man!*, and *Soul Food*.

Some jazz artists futilely resisted attempts to label their music as soul. By 1959, complained Cannonball Adderley—who initially was tagged as "hard bop" by the press—"we were pressured quite heavily by [his record label] Riverside Records, when they discovered there was a word called 'soul.' We became, from an image point of view, soul jazz artists. They kept promoting us that way and I kept deliberately fighting it, to the extent that it became a game." Nonetheless, the saxophonist found that the liner notes to *The Cannonball Adderley Quintet in San Francisco* (1960) described the environment for his music as resembling "a church as much as a jazz club" (Gleason 1960). In 1963, Adderley discovered that a performance recorded in Japan on Riverside Records had been titled *Nippon Soul*.

During the late fifties and early sixties, "funk" or "funky" crept into the vocabulary to complement "soul jazz." Originally used to denote a bad odor but transformed by early New Orleans jazz men into a term of endearment, the expression became synonymous with "soul." In 1959, Riverside Records observed that "'soul music' is a prettier word than 'funky' but means just about the same thing" (Keepnews 1960). "'Funky' means 'earthy, blues-based,'" clarified Horace Silver. "'Soul' is the same basically, but there's an added dimension of feeling and spirit to soul—an indepthness" (Lyons 1983, 122). In May 1962, sax man Lou Donaldson covered both bases in his album *The Natural Soul*, which included "Funky Mama."

With a focus on the blues of the sanctified church, the much neglected organ became a staple of soul jazz. Though it had been played previously by such jazz stalwarts as Fats Waller, in the fifties the organ gained prominence with the

LISTENING GUIDE 33

Bobby Timmons Group

"DAT DERE"

Pianist Bobby Timmons epitomized the church-based, bluesy sound of soul jazz. In 1960, he wrote this song, which subsequently received lyrics from African-American composer and folk singer Oscar Brown Jr. The pianist incorporated many of the elements used in the sanctified church in the tune. For the title of the song, Timmons even used African-American vernacular language.

This song first appeared in Timmons' first solo album, *This Here Is Bobby Timmons* (January 1960), with Sam Jones on bass and drummer Jimmy Cobb. Three months later, Art Blakey included the song in *The Big Beat* with Timmons as the pianist for the Jazz Messengers. The song below comes from Bobby's first solo outing.

0:00–0:13	Timmons begins with an interesting call-and-response introduction on the piano as he responds to his left hand (bass) with lines from his right hand (treble) in a twelve-bar-blues pattern.
0:14–0:41	Timmons states the main melody of the song with light backing from the drums and bass.
0:42–0:55	The pianist states the B section or bridge of the song.
0:56–1:08	Timmons restates the melody.
1:09–1:23	The pianist launches into a boppish but subtle, slow, and bluesy solo. He states the melody on the left hand with chords while he plays single notes on his right hand.
1:24–1:36	Timmons adds blue notes to give the passage a bluesy feel.
1:37–1:50	Timmons solos around the bridge.
1:51–2:04	Timmons solos around the melody with single-note runs.
2:05–2:34	The pianist solos around the melody with a combination of single notes and chords, using trills to accentuate the sanctified, blues-based nature of the piece. The switch to chords also gives the song interest in the trio setting. At the end of the passage, Timmons accentuates the notes with a highly syncopated rhythm. He receives a relatively loud, steady, and persistent backing from the bassist through this entire section.
2:35–2:49	Timmons uses the same technique as above on the bridge of the song. Unlike hard boppers, the drummer provides a delicate accompaniment with the bassist.
2:50–3:02	Timmons returns to improvising around the melody with his chordal approach.
3:04–3:59	Sam Jones takes a bass solo with comping from Timmons and light drum accompaniment.
4:00–4:27	Timmons states the theme twice in a rolling, churchy piano style backed by a rock-steady, 4/4 base line and some subtle drumming. He liberally makes use of trills to get a sanctified-church effect.
4:28–4:40	Timmons restates the bridge pattern.
4:44–4:55	Timmons restates the same melody as he did in the beginning.
4:56–5:19	Timmons ends with the same self-contained call-and-response from the introduction with a few chordal flourishes at the end.

invention of the Hammond B-3. Patented in 1934 and manufactured the next year by Laurens Hammond and John Hanert, the B-3 was an electric organ that simulated the tone and range of the much more expensive pipe organ. Targeting religious groups, within three years Hammond sold the instrument to more than 1,750 churches. By 1966, the B-3 had been purchased by nearly fifty thousand houses of worship.

Jimmy Smith popularized the Hammond B-3 in jazz. "I was taught by playing for churches, being a Seventh Day Adventist. I learned a few hymns," related Smith, "so I'd be able to play in church and show off." By the age of nine, Smith had learned stride piano. By his teens, he had become a Bud Powell enthusiast and even visited Powell at his home in Willow Grove, Pennsylvania, located about six miles from Smith's house in Norristown. In 1947, after leaving the Navy, he used the GI Bill to hone his keyboard skills at the Philadelphia-based Ornstein School. In 1954, Smith permanently switched from piano to the Hammond B-3 after hearing a performance in Atlantic City by organist Wild Bill Davis, who had been a member of the Louis Jordan band. "I said, 'That's for me,'" recalled Smith. "When he finished playing, I snuck up on the bandstand to touch the action. It was so soft. I knew I could play it" (Ouellette 1995, 31).

Blue Note Records signed Smith and ceaselessly recorded and promoted his sanctified, organ-based jazz. For his first release in 1956, the liner notes stated that "his dexterity on the organ is comparable to Bud Powell's on the piano and he possesses the only 'Oklahoma funkish' style of comping on the blues since Charlie Christian" (Gonzales 1956). On his third vinyl offering, Blue Note dubbed him as the "incredible Jimmy Smith." By 1960, Blue Note had issued sixteen Jimmy Smith albums, including *The Sermon!*

Philadelphia-born organist Shirley Scott, an admirer of Jimmy Smith and Thelonious Monk, delivered a soul-drenched jazz. After teaming with gritty sax man Eddie "Lockjaw" Davis, in 1959 she signed to Prestige Records and released a series of soul-jazz albums, including *Soul Searching*. Becoming one of the most successful female instrumentalists in jazz, in 1961 on *Hip Soul*, she partnered with sax player and husband Stanley Turrentine, who had previously played with Jimmy Smith and Ray Charles.

Jimmy McGriff followed in the footsteps of Jimmy Smith, one of his childhood friends who informally tutored him. He became serious about the instrument when he met Philadelphia organist Richard "Groove" Holmes, who burst on the scene with *The Dynamic Jazz Organ*. "The first organ I sat and played was a B-3, and it was Groove Holmes' organ," McGriff remembered. "My younger sister got married, and he played for her wedding. And he told me to come on and play, and I said, 'Groove, I can't do nothing with this thing.' And he said, 'Don't say that, come on. I'll show you.' . . . And he showed me," maintained McGriff (Skelly 1992, 61). In 1956, he bought his first Hammond B-3 and studied at the Juilliard School. By 1962, McGriff landed a contract with Sue Records and waxed *I've Got a Woman*, which reached the Top Twenty with the title cut.

"Brother" Jack McDuff (b. Eugene McDuffy) mined the same sanctified blues vein as fellow organists. Raised by a minister, Brother Jack started as a pianist in a sanctified church. "My father wanted me to be a minister, and I guess the first time I realized that I wanted to be a musician was in the Navy," he related. "When I came home in 1946, I got my first musical job with 'Schoolboy' Porter" in Gary, Indiana. When sax man Willis Jackson asked him to join a jazz combo, McDuff switched from piano to B-3 organ. "Since that time, I guess, I have been influenced by one man, Jimmy Smith," he insisted. In 1960, McDuff signed with Prestige and recorded *Brother Jack*. "We feel this album is another step forward for the organ in jazz," the company claimed. "Jimmy Smith was one of the pioneers who introduced the organ to jazz and we feel pretty sure that he is proud of the increasing number of 'up and comers' who are following his lead," it added (Eyre 1960a).

By late 1959, the organ had become popular among budding jazz musicians. Hammond, the leader in the field, posted sales of nearly $28 million. "Manufacturers report that the electric organ, a relatively expensive instrument, has been outselling brasses, reeds, and strings with amateur musicians," *Downbeat* reported in October (Hoefer 1959, 26).

Ramsey Lewis brought soul jazz to white America. A Chicago-raised, classically trained pianist, Lewis begun playing for a church gospel choir. One day after the service, Wallace Burton, head of the seven-piece Cleffs, asked Lewis to join. Eventually, Lewis, drummer Isaac "Red" Holt, and bassist Eldee Young banded together as a trio and, starting in 1956, recorded for Argo Records, a jazz subsidiary of Chess.

For three days in May 1965, after moderate success with nearly twenty albums, Lewis and his trio performed at the Bohemian Caverns club in Washington, DC. The trio had practiced a version of "The 'In' Crowd," written by singer/songwriter Dobie Gray, a Texan who had been exposed to church music by his grandfather who served as a minster. Almost as an afterthought, Ramsey launched into the song at the end of the set. "All of a sudden," recalled Lewis, "the guys in the club are moving their shoulders, and the women are standing up and clapping and dancing. We just looked at each other," recalled Lewis. "In those days, did jazzers have hit records? What? Are you kidding?" remembered the pianist. "Soon enough, it was a bona fide hit that just kept selling." The band reached number five on the *Billboard* singles chart with "The 'In' Crowd" and almost topped the pop chart with the album of the same name. "It changed everything," confessed Lewis about the single. "That's African-American church music—getting down!" he exclaimed (Lyons 1983, 209). Soul jazz had become a national sensation (Staudter 2015).

Integrating the American Federation of Musicians

African-American jazz musicians faced prejudice not only in the world of bookings and recordings, but within the American Federation of Musicians (AFM), which had been segregated since its founding. The long fight of African-American jazz artists to integrate the union reflected the ongoing struggle for civil rights.

Trade unions for musicians sprouted up at the turn of the century just as ragtime developed. During 1896 in Cincinnati, the AFM was founded as the successor to the National League of Musicians. Although local chapters of the AFM in New York City and Detroit initially admitted all races to their ranks, most union locals excluded African Americans, who were forced to establish African-American-only AFM chapters. "Many of the members object to playing with a colored musician, but the chief objection is the appearance of a musical body composed of black and white musicians," wrote Thomas Kennedy, president of the white Chicago Local 10, in 1902. "To obviate the necessity for continual rulings it was decided to separate the two bodies and give the colored union a charter" of its own. (Halker 1988, 209). By 1910, forty-seven African-American chapters of the AFM had been established.

Both African-American and white locals provided many advantages to their members. They negotiated base salaries with concert halls and club owners, created unemployment funds, served as intermediaries with booking agencies, and set up credit unions for registered musicians. All chapters had representation in the national AFM convention.

Despite benefiting from many essential services, members of African-American locals suffered from discriminatory practices compared to their white counterparts. In Los Angeles, members of African-American Local 767 were largely excluded from work in the motion-picture industry. In other chapters, African-American musicians seldom found work in studio bands, radio, and some clubs. In post-WWII Boston, jazz musician Andy McGhee found that "black people worked this club and white people worked that club. Simple as that" (Boston Musicians' Association n.d.). "Segregation was a way of life," explained pianist/lawyer Marl Young, who during the thirties belonged to the African-American local in his hometown of Chicago. "It was just the way things were" (McLellan 2009).

Encouraged by the civil-rights movement, jazz musicians in some African-American locals demanded equal treatment. In Los Angeles, African-American Local 767 lobbied for a merger or amalgamation with white Local 47 to secure employment opportunities in the motion-picture industry and improved death benefits. By late 1951, "we started talking about getting rid of segregation," recalled Marl Young, who had moved out West. "If you're going to get any opportunities, you've got to be where the work is. And also, it's just basically wrong" (Bryant 1998, 388). After several battles and with help from several members of the white local, on June 25, 1953, the two unions combined.

During the late fifties and early sixties, other locals integrated. On January 14, 1958, the two local chapters of AFM in Seattle merged. During spring 1960, after the California attorney general threatened prosecution, African-American and white chapters in San Francisco consolidated. The same year, the two segregated musician locals in Denver came together. In 1962, Cleveland musicians amalgamated, and, the next year, Miami musicians ended discrimination.

Chicago, having the largest African-American local in the AFM with 1,300 members, begrudgingly headed down the road to integration. As early as the thirties, African-American Local 208 had unsuccessfully attempted to merge with white Local 10. In October 1963, the two unions, pressured by CORE, entered into "good-faith negotiations looking towards a merger" (Halker 1988, 219). When the white local balked at consolidation, the national AFM leadership placed the Chicago locals under receivership and forced a merger of the two groups. On January 11, 1966, the two chapters officially united. By the time of the Chicago unification, the American Federation under direction from AFL-CIO headquarters appointed James Petrillo to oversee integration of the remaining sixty segregated locals. Amid the civil-rights movement, African-American musicians across the country, many of them playing jazz, demanded equal treatment and reflected the assertion of African-American pride that hard boppers and soul-jazz artists embodied.

Chapter Quiz

For Discussion and Further Study

1. What impact did the civil-rights movement have on jazz musicians? How did it influence the music they created and how they performed it?

2. How was hard bop different from either cool jazz or bebop styles? How did it reflect a new interest in racial equality?

3. How did jazz composers and performers support civil-rights protests like sit-ins and the Freedom Riders? Do you think their work was influential on society's broader understanding of the need for an end to segregation?

4. How did the anti-colonial movement in Africa align with the civil-rights movement? What influence did it have on contemporary jazz musicians? How did they show the influence of African culture in their work?

5. What elements of soul jazz reflected a new interest in African-American pride?

6. How were jazz musicians influential in integrating the musicians' unions and other aspects of the music business?

15

FREE JAZZ
Asserting African-American Independence

During the 1960s, free jazz reflected African-American frustration at ongoing racism in the United States. As many cities erupted into riots and the Black Power movement aggressively sought equal rights for African Americans, a discordant, jarring free jazz symbolized the anger and bitterness of most African Americans. Several musicians formed collectives such as the AACM in Chicago to achieve independence and take control of their music from the white music establishment by creating record labels, staging concerts, and developing education programs about their African-American heritage. Others relied on small, independent labels to present their music. Besides expressing their resentment over racism, some free-jazz musicians such as John Coltrane hoped to use their music as a healing, spiritual force to attain racial equality.

In late 1964, Bill Dixon had an idea. He hoped to bring together many fledging jazz artists who had developed new sounds but who had found little commercial success. The trumpeter/pianist approached Peter Sabino, who managed the Cellar Café on Ninety-first Street near Broadway in New York City, about a four-day event for himself and fellow jazz players to prove that the public would flock to the new music if exposed to it.

Dixon had been raised in Harlem and had a history of organizing. After graduating from the Hartnette Conservatory of Music after the war, he worked as an administrator for the United Nations and, in 1953, founded the United Nations Jazz Society. Simultaneously, he lectured about jazz, taught continuing-education courses, and played trumpet with various outfits in New York City. In 1962, Dixon and Philadelphia saxophonist Archie Shepp released an album with one selection composed by Ornette Coleman, another by Leonard Bernstein, and two Dixon originals. The following year, Shepp and Dixon established the New York Contemporary Five. They recruited Los Angeles–raised trumpeter Don Cherry; sax man John Tchicai, who had been born in Denmark to a Danish mother and a Congolese father; bassist Don Moore; and drummer J. C. Moses. Within a two-year period, they waxed four discs.

Dixon realized the dream of a showcase for talented young jazz men who played what he loosely termed "the new thing." From October 1 to October 4, 1964, he scheduled more than twenty groups and solo performances at the Cellar Café that featured a new style of jazz. Over the four days, Dixon greeted more than seven hundred people who streamed into the club to listen to such emerging African-American jazz players as the John Tchicai quartet with drummer Milford Graves, the big band of composer/pianist Sun Ra, and the trio of bassist/composer Ali Jackson. Dixon's own sextet took the stand as well. Only avant-garde pioneer Ornette Coleman refused to participate, instead listening to the performances from the audience.

Believing that both African-American and white musicians suffered similar indignities, Dixon invited a few unknown white jazz musicians to the event. He featured pianist Paul Bley who, as early as 1957, was playing in Los Angeles with saxophonist Ornette Coleman and Don Cherry. The organizer also called Vienna-born trumpeter Michael Mantler and sax innovator Jimmy Giuffre. "They are treated significantly better, but not much better than are black musicians, and that is simply because they play jazz, which is looked on as something 'primitive,'" Dixon reasoned (Wilmer 1981, 214).

In most cases, the music presented by Dixon challenged the prevailing hard-bop, soul-jazz, and Third-Stream styles. In Dixon's combo, wrote the *New York Times,* a sax man "worked his way up and down the scales repeatedly while the other one produced sudden rolling phrases, shrill squeals and squeaks" (Wilson 1964). "There is often none of the formal organization found in most jazz—rhythm section and melody instruments, solo versus ensemble, strict time, etc.," contended *Downbeat* reviewer Dan Morgenstern. "Yet, the sound and feeling is often of a kind peculiar to jazz as we have become accustomed to it" (Morgenstern 1964, 33).

The jazz press regarded the event as a stunning triumph. Morgenstern deemed the concerts a "success" (Morgenstern 1964, 33). "Dixon proved there is an audience for the new jazz," asserted Martin Williams in *Downbeat.* "It is young. It is attentive. It is growing. And it wants to hear the music live. The new music is here," he added, "and any jazz journalists who don't like it—well, it looks like they can just lump it" (33).

Dixon scheduled additional performances in December based upon the success of the October series. Staging the concerts at Judson Hall in New York City, across the street from Carnegie Hall, the trumpeter organized four days of new jazz, including his group. "Mr. Dixon's quintet—two saxophonists, a bassist, a drummer and Mr. Dixon on trumpet played three selections, each approximately half an hour long," reported the *New York Times*. "Ensemble passages tended to consist of low, slow, moaning passages by the three horns backed by a very rapid cymbal" (Wilson 1964). Dixon invited other artists such as Archie Shepp, John Tchicai's group, the Sun Ra Arkestra, and the Free Form Improvisation Ensemble newly established by pianist Burton Greene and Harlem bassist Alan Silva to participate in the shows.

The new music, featuring cries on saxophones and trumpets and frenetic drumming, captured the growing militancy of the civil-rights movement. The first concerts were called the "October Revolution in Jazz," a nod to the Russian revolution, which started on October 25, 1917, in Petrograd. The new style was labeled "free" and "freedom," which harkened to the slogans of civil-rights marchers. To complement the music, the two four-day extravaganzas involved panel discussions about racial discrimination. In a *Downbeat* article about the concerts, Dan Morgenstern felt that "the 'new thing' is an expression of dissatisfaction with the status quo, a refusal to accept existing conventions, a restless, often furious assault on the present and most of the past" (Morgenstern 1964, 33). Dubbed free jazz, the new wave, the "new thing," and the avant-garde, the raucous, disjointed, and frantic music kept jazz in step with the tenor of the civil-rights movement.

Civil Rights and the Great Society

The angry feelings of disgruntled African Americans provided the context for the jazz avant-garde. No longer content to passively allow racists to oppress them, African Americans demanded an end to segregation by taking to the streets despite the passage of legislation that supposedly promised a better future.

On July 2, 1964, at the insistence of President Lyndon Johnson, Congress enacted the most sweeping civil-rights law since the Civil War. The Civil Rights Act instructed the attorney general to protect the voting rights of all citizens. It forbade discrimination in public places, established an Equal Employment Opportunity Commission and a Community Relations Service to solve racially based problems, forbade discrimination in federally funded programs, and funded school desegregation. Earlier in the year, Congress had ratified the Twenty-fourth Amendment to the US Constitution, which outlawed the poll taxes in federal elections that had made it more difficult for minorities to vote. In 1965, Congress passed a comprehensive Voting Rights Act.

President Lyndon Johnson also promised a "Great Society" of equality for all races and declared a "war on poverty." To achieve his vision, Johnson shepherded through Congress a series of programs such as a Job Corps for high school dropouts, a Neighborhood Youth Corps for unemployed teens, the Volunteers in Service to America to help in poverty-stricken urban areas, the Head Start Program for poor children, a food-stamp program, and Upward Bound to prepare disadvantaged children to attend college. He also pushed through the legislature such social programs as urban renewal and Medicare. Coupled with civil-rights legislation, the new laws of the Great Society offered African Americans hope for a better future and seemed to be a giant step toward realizing the dreams of Martin Luther King Jr.

There's a Riot Going On

Despite new legislation, African Americans continued to feel the scourge of discrimination. They lived in poor sections of towns with substandard living conditions and deficient school systems for their children. In 1965, African Americans found it twice as difficult to finds jobs as their white counterparts. They faced constant harassment and persecution from urban police forces, composed largely of white officers who targeted African-American residents. "The cops, they keep coming in here and busting heads," remarked one African-American inner-city resident in 1965 (Bart 1965a, 26).

The Watts section of Los Angeles exploded amid the brewing resentment and anger of African Americans. A 2.1-square-mile section of South Los Angeles, Watts became a predominantly African-American neighborhood when people poured into Los Angeles for work at aircraft and defense plants during World War II. Real estate covenants, which allowed home owners to discriminate against African-American buyers, excluded African Americans from moving into other areas of town or to the growing suburbs. By 1965, a congested Watts housed nearly a half million African-American residents.

Residents in Watts felt the sting of discrimination, poverty, and violence. In August 1965, reported the *New York Times*, the Watts "population follows the slum pattern of low income, high unemployment, above average school drop-out rate, an adult population of which two-thirds has less than a high school education." Nearly 30 percent of African-American males and 50 percent of African-American teenagers could not find jobs, and more than 60 percent of Watts inhabitants lived on government relief. "The crime rate in Watts far exceeds the city average," recounted the newspaper. "In the last three months, there were 1,000 crimes, including 98 murders, rapes and felonious assaults" ("Hot Summer" 1965).

Grass-roots programs tried to instill a sense of pride among the poverty-plagued Watts community. By 1965, recalled pianist Horace Tapscott, "we had all sorts of classes there and a breakfast program, which was later supported by the Black Panthers. We had youngsters in school and were teaching them about their history, as well as reading and writing. We had martial arts, [black] poetry and music classes outside of the regular schoolwork" (Tapscott 2001, 108). Tapscott and thirty compatriots in the Pan Afrikan Peoples Arkestra provided free music to the community.

Yet the confluence of impoverished conditions and a growing sense of African-American pride set the stage for violence in Watts. "We saw the anger," remembered Tapscott in 1965. "Some were screaming their poetry about black people and the police and dying. The tension was building, and it was just a matter of time before it exploded" (Tapscott 2001, 109). "What we didn't have in Watts wasn't civil rights," bitterly recalled one resident. "It was jobs, housing and education" (Szatmary 2014, 172).

On Wednesday, August 11, 1965, trouble erupted. Twenty-one-year-old Marquette Frye was speeding through Watts at eight o'clock on a hot, smoggy evening. California highway patrolman Lee Minikus stopped the youth and cited him for drunken driving. Frye's brother, a passenger in the car, dashed home to his mother, who rushed to the scene of the arrest to scold her son about his drinking. When Minikus drew his pistol, Frye's mother jumped on the back of the officer, and a crowd of twenty-five gathered on the street to witness the commotion. By ten in the evening, a group of two hundred African Americans pelted Minikus and a backup officer with rocks and concrete. In response, eighty policemen hurried to the scene and sealed off a sixteen-block area to control the outburst. Meanwhile, police took into custody the Frye brothers and their mother. When rumors circulated through Watts that police had brutally beaten Marquette Frye and assaulted a pregnant woman, larger crowds gathered on the streets of Watts.

The next day, the rioting intensified. "Within Watts, rioters ran loose, looting, burning, rampaging. They shot at helicopters flying over, sniped at policemen, set hundreds of major fires, which burned out of control when they blocked the entry of firemen," the *New York Times* told its readers ("Hot Summer" 1965).

By August 14, 3,900 heavily armed California National Guardsmen had rumbled into Watts to supplement more than a thousand Los Angeles police. The *New York Times* reported that "the Guardsmen were under orders to use rifles, machine guns, tear gas and bayonets." They traveled in jeeps equipped with machine gun turrets. One contingent of Guardsmen opened fire on a group of African Americans for ten minutes. "They've got weapons and ammo," scowled one Guard spokesman. "It's going to be like Vietnam" (Bart 1965b).

The rioters became even more incensed by the sight of the troops. They chanted "White devils, what are you doing here?" (Bart 1965b) and appropriated a slogan of Los Angeles disc jockey Magnificent Montague by screaming "Burn, baby, burn!" People "had lived through all that deprivation, and they were now uplifted," explained one rioter. When coming home from a party in Hollywood after playing a gig, pianist Hampton Hawes "saw what at first looked like a heavy blanket of fog till I noticed the flames spurting through. . . . Whole blocks were crackling with flames. Must have been the way Rome looked back then, except that these citizens were all a funny color and none of them were wearing togas. Never saw so many people on the street at one time in my life—and this is five in the morning" (Hawes 1972, 140).

On August 17, the rioting ended when the sheer force of the police action and an 8:00 p.m. curfew was imposed in Watts. During the six-day melee, nearly thirty-five thousand residents had caused $40 million in damage to 977 buildings. Thirty-four people, mostly African American, lay dead in the streets, and another 1,032 had been injured. Nearly thirty-five hundred rioters had been arrested.

Riots spread to other cities. On August 12, in Chicago, a protest march was held for an African-American woman who had been killed when she was struck by a fire truck. During the march, a skirmish broke out between police and African Americans. The confrontation escalated and lasted for two days until the governor mobilized two thousand National Guard troops. When the fighting subsided, sixty-seven African Americans had been injured and another 123 had been jailed. The next day, a riot engulfed Springfield, Massachusetts, where police faced off against protesters on the steps of city hall.

During the "long hot summer" of 1967, inferior living conditions sparked racial disturbances in dozens of major metropolitan areas. In Detroit, where nearly 30 percent of African Americans were unemployed, the worst civil disorder in twentieth-century America devastated nineteen square miles of the city, caused

Troops patrol the street in Washington, DC, after the King assassination riot, April 1968. *Photograph by Warren K. Leffler. Library of Congress Prints and Photographs Division*

an estimated $40 million in damage, and left forty-three dead, 2,250 injured, and 7,200 arrested. Said a twenty-two-year-old youth, "We're tired of being second class. We've been asking too long. Now it's time to take. This thing ain't over. It's just beginning" ("An American Tragedy" 1967, 27). During the first eight months of 1967, race riots disrupted more than 131 cities and left eighty-three dead, thousands injured, and blocks of burned-out buildings.

On April 4, 1968, turmoil swept the country after the assassination of Dr. Martin Luther King Jr. "When White America killed Dr. King," proclaimed African-American militant Stokely Carmichael—who had been a Freedom Rider and a former head of the SNCC—"she declared war on us. . . . We have to retaliate for the deaths of our leaders. The executions of those deaths are going to be in the streets" ("Take Everything You Need" 1968, 31). Almost immediately after the King assassination, racial violence exploded in Washington, DC. By the end of the week, racial violence had broken out in 168 cities, where almost two thousand shops were gutted; $40 million worth of property had been demolished; and forty-six people, mostly African-American, had been killed. The conflagrations took nearly seventy-three thousand US Army and National Guard troops to keep the peace.

Black Power

After the assassination of Martin Luther King Jr., civil-rights advocates such as Stokely Carmichael abandoned nonviolence for a militant stance. Carmichael coined the term "Black Power" to describe the new movement. He increasingly adopted the tenets of militants such as Malcolm X, who as a Black Muslim firebrand encouraged a separation of blacks from whites, and called whites inferior "white devils." By 1968, many young civil-rights organizers embraced confrontational rhetoric. "If America don't come around, we're going to burn America down," threatened H. Rap Brown, a former SNCC chair. "Violence," he added, "is American as cherry pie" (Pearson 1994, 152).

The Black Panther Party for Self-Defense, founded in October 1966 by Huey P. Newton and Bobby Seale, directly confronted the white-dominated power structure and advanced black nationalism. The Party initially aided African-American neighborhoods in the Oakland, California, area. Members advanced a ten-point program of "land, bread, housing, education, clothing, justice and peace" and proclaimed that "we want freedom. We want power to determine the destiny of our Black Community." The Panthers initiated free breakfast programs for children and health clinics in the inner city. To demonstrate their revolutionary intent, the Panthers wore black pants, black leather jackets, and black berets and toted loaded shotguns.

The Black Panthers became progressively radicalized. On May 2, 1967, the group occupied the California State Capitol in Sacramento to protest a ban on their weapons. Several months later, when Huey Newton admitted killing a police

officer, H. Rap Brown, the Panther Minister of Justice, described Newton as "our only living revolutionary. He has paid his dues," he contended. "How many white folks did you kill today?" Mimicking African revolutionaries, James Forman, the Panther Minister of Foreign Affairs, exclaimed that "we serve notice on our oppressors that we as a people are not going to be frightened by the attempted assassination of one of our leaders." He demanded "30 police stations blown up, one Southern governor, two mayors and 500 cops, dead" (Pearson 1994, 152).

Focusing on African-American self-determination, the Black Panthers grew exponentially. By 1968, the organization had established branches in nineteen cities, including Los Angeles, New York, and Boston, and boasted a national membership of ten thousand. More than a half million Panther supporters subscribed to the magazine, *The Black Panther*, which was edited by Eldridge Cleaver. By the end of the decade, the Panthers managed offices in sixty-eight cities with thousands of members.

The Black Arts Movement brought Black Power to the arts. In 1965, African-American writer Everett LeRoi Jones established the Black Arts Repertory Theater/School to give a name to the movement. In the poem "Black Art" (1965), he affiliated with Black Power activists by urging fellow poets to compose "poems that kill." Jones, then writing for *Downbeat*, expanded his notion of the Black arts by organizing a series of free-jazz

Black Panthers in front of the Lincoln Memorial, 1970. *Photograph by Warren K. Leffler and Thomas O'Halloran. Library of Congress Prints and Photographs Division*

concerts in lofts and coffee shops that featured performances by such artists as saxophonist Archie Shepp and reed man and founding SNCC member Marzette Watts (Jones 1971, 96). In 1967, a gun-toting Jones resisted arrest during a race riot in Newark and subsequently changed his name to Amiri Baraka to acknowledge his African heritage.

The Afrocentric Black Arts movement spread with the founding of several publications. Magazines such as *Freedomways* and the *Liberator* reinforced the tenets of Black Power, and journals such as *Black Dialogue* and the *Journal of Black Poetry* served as an outlet for rising African-American writers. According to African-American writer Ishmael Reed, "there would be no multicultural movement without Black Arts. Blacks gave the example that you don't have to assimilate. You could do your own thing, get into your own tradition and your own culture" (Salaam n.d., 1).

The Jazz Avant-Garde and Civil Rights

The sound and organization of the jazz avant-garde reflected a growing black militancy and contributed to African-American self-determination. "My generation, we went through [World War II] as teenagers. So there were great expectations in the black community in terms of fulfillment of what this country had to offer," observed Texas avant-garde saxophonist John Carter, who described the context for free jazz. "But we were in fact pretty disillusioned about the situation we found ourselves in" (Smith 1992, 8, 9).

The militant Archie Shepp, New York, 1967. *Photograph courtesy of Guy Kopelowicz*

Like other forms of racially motivated protest at the time, free jazz assaulted America with a discordant, almost hostile attack that could not easily be ignored. Unlike the finger-popping style of soul jazz, the avant-garde delivered a relentless, rhythm-based onslaught of cries that battered listeners. "The listener doesn't hear the regular thing he can pat his foot to and shake his head to," explained John Carter (Kofsky 1979a, 44). The sound of the avant-garde, commented African American poet and trumpeter Ted Joans, seemed "so rare and raw, like screaming the word 'FUCK' in St. Patrick's Cathedral on a crowded Easter Sunday." It sounded like "a pure black power of sounds" ("Albert Ayler Review" 1971).

The rebellious music of the African-American avant-garde reflected an increasing anger and discontent with American society and boiled over into aggression. "Music reflects the time and is also political," remarked avant-garde pianist Don Pullen. "When I teamed up with [saxophonist] Giuseppe [Logan in 1965] the air seemed charged, it was time for a change" (Macnie 1986, 20). Saxophonist Albert Ayler, a leader of the mid-sixties avant-garde movement, believed "that on tenor you could get out all the feelings of the ghetto. On that horn you can really shout and tell the truth" (Wilmer 1981, 100). African Americans "are beginning to see who they are," Ayler asserted in 1966. "I'm playing their suffering" (Backus 1976, 87). "I'm a Negro and I'm a jazz man," Ornette Coleman explained in 1965. "And as a Negro and a jazz man, I just feel miserable" (Spellman 1966, 150). Through music, Coleman expressed "the anger I feel as a Negro, the true anger I have to confront every day just in order to survive" (Morgenstern 1965, 17).

Saxophonist Archie Shepp probably best articulated the sentiments shared between African-American militants and new-jazz artists. In December 1965, he characterized the United States as "one of the most vicious, racist social systems in the world. . . . I have seen the tragedy of perennially starving families, my own. I am that tragedy" (Shepp 1965).

To Shepp, jazz music reflected the plight of African Americans and offered a way to address bigotry. "The Negro musician is a reflection of the Negro people as a social and cultural phenomenon. Jazz is American reality—total reality," he asserted (Shepp 1965). Shepp believed that a jazz musician should act "like a reporter, an esthetic journalist [to] liberate America esthetically and socially from . . . the inhumanity of the white American to the black American. I think the Negro people through the force of their struggles are the only hope of saving America, the political or cultural America," he emphasized (Jones 1965, 25). "I'm gonna sing it. Dance it. Scream it. And if need be, steal it from this very earth," he promised. "You can no longer defer my dream" (Shepp 1965). A few days after the assassination of Malcolm X on February 21, 1965, Shepp recorded the stark dirge of "Malcolm, Malcolm—Semper Malcolm" on *Fire Music* to memorialize the militant leader. Four years later, he recorded "Mamarose—Poem for Malcolm."

Other African-American members of the avant-garde believed that jazz could help solve the problems that plagued them. Drummer Sunny Murray contended that "if we are going to solve our problems, then the music has to live. The intensity of this music can really change things" (Levin 1979, 64, 58). Ornette Coleman fervently thought that he could "play to cure people of evil" (Santoro 1986, 41).

Believing they possessed a tonic against evil, many free-jazz musicians stressed the spirituality of their music. In his avant-garde album *A Love Supreme*, John Coltrane felt that he "experienced, by the grace of God, a spiritual awakening which was to lead me to a richer, fuller, more productive life. In gratitude, I humbly asked to be given the means and privilege to make others happy through music" (Coltrane, 1965). Albert Ayler's "music was about how music can heal the spirit," remarked pianist Don Pullen. "That's an important tradition in black music" (Johnson 1989). Fittingly, Ayler titled his masterpiece *Spiritual Unity* (1965) and the same year named a follow-up *Spirits Rejoice*.

Like battle-ready soldiers, the spiritually minded avant-garde trained physically by adhering to a healthy diet and scheduling exercise

Albert Ayler. *Photograph courtesy of Daniel Berger*

 LISTENING GUIDE 34

Albert Ayler Quintet

🔗 **"GHOSTS"**

Ayler always considered his music to be spiritual and healing. He delivered this song as a paean to the Holy Ghost. "The Holy Ghost has been favorable to me," Ayler stated in 1965. "The only way that I can thank God for His ever-present creation is to offer him a new music imprinted with beauty that no one, before, had heard" (Ayler 1965).

He directed his band, consisting of his brother Donald on trumpet, Michel Sampson on violin, William Folwell on bass, and drummer Beaver Harris, toward a spiritual salvation on this recording, which was cut live in Lorrach, Germany, on November 7, 1966. To solidify his quest, Ayler also released other titles such as "Spirits Rejoice" and "Prophet" on this date.

This song became one of Ayler's most well-known pieces. In late 1966, *Newsweek* called it "an unofficial anthem of the new music" (Zimmerman and Ross 1966, 108).

0:00–0:03	Albert starts the song with a slightly off-center, simple melody, which ends with a quaver and sounds like it came from the sanctified church. Before the wobbly end, Ayler overblows his horn for an interesting effect. Ayler many times utilized very basic melodies, almost folk melodies, upon which he would improvise with his full-bodied horn.
0:04–0:06	Donald Ayler answers his brother in a call-and-response, which represents a conversation so important in avant-garde jazz. Within the brief space of this exchange, Donald overblows his horn twice to signal the importance of overblowing an instrument in free jazz to expand the capabilities of an instrument. Within the background, violinist Sampson bows with a high vibrato (a wobble).
0:07–0:12	The vibrato-heavy violin comes to the foreground briefly.
0:13–0:26	Both Aylers and the violinist play competing melodies in a polyphony.
0:27–0:30	The violinist again takes center stage briefly and repeats part of the introductory pattern three times.
0:31–0:40	Both Aylers enter again to play competing melodies with the violin and each other in a polyphony somewhat reminiscent of New Orleans brass bands, but more adventurous.
0:41–0:49	The Aylers increase the tempo to establish a rhythm, but play different melodies for polyphony. The drummer and bassist enter to play other rhythms to create polyrhythm.
0:50–1:22	Unexpectedly, together Donald and Albert Ayler play a melody with a Latin-like rhythm and, in two instances, harmonize with one another on it (e.g., 1:09). The drums and the bass play different rhythms to maintain the polyrhythm, and the violinist establishes yet another rhythm and melody. At the end of this passage, the group slowly comes to a stop. Except for the two Aylers, all members of the group establish different rhythms in a group conversation—another essential element of the avant-garde and much of jazz in general.
1:23–1:29	Albert Ayler states the simple melody from the introduction in a very slow tempo. Meanwhile, his brother and the violinist play in a different rhythm.
1:30–1:32	Albert holds a single note and then slides downward with it, much like a blues musician. His brother and the violinist continue to play different rhythms.

1:33–1:36	The saxophone, trumpet, and violin all land on one note, which the saxophone and trumpet hold. The violin lands on the note and then repeats it as the others hold it.
1:37–1:49	Albert restates the introductory melody at a medium tempo. The trumpeter accompanies him with a riff, and the violinist continues with his own melody and rhythm.
1:50–1:56	Albert offers another simple melody while the trumpet, drums, and bass play different rhythms as the conversation continues.
1:57–2:21	Donald Ayler plays an almost march-like melody five times. Albert plays syncopated, staccato, almost sporadic notes and repeatedly overblows his horn to create new sounds. The drummer pounds out a loud rhythm, which contrasts with the melody and establishes polyrhythm.
2:22–2:35	Both Aylers start to play the melody together, and the violinist bows up and down the scale in a different rhythm. The drummer weaves a complex rhythm around the other group members.
2:36–2:50	The trumpet holds a note from the melody as the violinist continues to play an ascending pattern of notes that ends in a rapid-fire trill. The drummer temporarily ceases to play.
2:51–2:59	Both Aylers reenter along with the drums to converse with the violin. For a few bars, the violin states the introductory melody.
3:00–3:10	Albert and Donald quote several measures from the "First Call," which buglers play to start a horse race and perform as a first call to colors in the military. To end the song, each group member holds a note until only the trumpet plays a sustained note, which represents the final note in "First Call." For Albert Ayler, he inserts "First Call" at the end of the song to urge the "Ghost" to wake up and manifest itself spiritually.

regimens. During the sixties, John Coltrane regularly ate health food such as Tiger's Milk nutrition bars, beans, and raw vegetables, and kept a set of weights and a punching bag in his room for daily workouts. "Live cleanly," instructed Coltrane. "It's a duty we owe ourselves" (Gitler 1958, 17). Pharoah Sanders—who played sax with Coltrane from 1965 until Coltrane's death three years later—followed a similar diet, instructing everyone to "eat natural foods" (Rivelli and Levin 1979, 49). "We're not going to eat any pork, not going to take any drugs," vowed St. Louis sax man Oliver Lake (Looker 2004).

In training to battle evil, the avant-garde tried to refurbish the image of jazz. In 1965, the *National Observer* described the avant-garde as "jazz musicians who are determined to overthrow the image of the jazzman as a dissolute vagabond and jazz music as disreputable noise. They're determined to replace it with a new image of both music and musicians" (Ostermann 1965). "Jazz is Jim Crow. It belongs to another era, another time, another place," asserted Albert Ayler. "We're playing free music" (Ostermann).

The Sound of Freedom: Ornette Coleman

Ornette Coleman, a founding proponent of free jazz, typified the intense, rebellious avant-garde. In his formative years, he demonstrated a solid grounding in bop. During the late forties, he "could play those [tunes] that Bud Powell and

Charlie Parker had written. Anything that was melodically complicated I thought I had to learn," he recalled (Spellman 1966, 90–91).

Like most free-jazz men, Coleman also had experience in rhythm and blues. As a youth in Texas, Ornette backed Big Joe Turner for several months, joined the R&B outfit of Clarence Samuels, and worked with blues guitarist Pee Wee Crayton. He even toured with the Silas Green minstrel show. "If some rhythm-and-blues tune would come out, I would learn it on the horn and go right out and play it in a nightclub in a dance band," Coleman recalled. "That's the only style of music I would play in public" (Spellman 1966, 85, 95).

Coleman mixed and embellished his influences into an assertive sound that fit the defiant times. He borrowed the speed of bop for the typically breakneck, driving pace of his playing. His powerful tempo captured the rage of African Americans demanding change.

By extending the bop preoccupation with chord changes, Coleman nearly dispensed with the melody of a song structure altogether. One day, while playing at a dance, Ornette "was dragged because I could hear all these other notes that I could play to the changes of 'Stardust.'" While people slowly moved across the dance floor, he "just nutted out and started playing all the things I could think of to the changes without touching the melody. And then a guy hollered out, 'Get on the melody, get on the melody!' and then I realized: 'Why should I have to stick to the melody when I was already playing the melody and this guy didn't know it?' I know exactly what I'm doing. I'm beginning where Charlie Parker stopped," insisted Ornette (Spellman 1966, 93; Goldberg 1965, 243).

In addition to radically reshaping melody and harmonic progression, Coleman prolonged the unrestrained honks and overblown squeals of R&B saxophonists to

Ornette Coleman, August 1963. *Photograph by Guy Kopelowicz*

reflect the outrage among African Americans during the sixties. He encouraged the constant use of overtones (notes higher than an instrument's normal range) and multiphonics (playing two or more notes at once) to deliver dissonant, angry, and anguished cries.

Ornette's approach also fundamentally altered the role of rhythm in jazz. Rather than using the drums and bass as metronomes to keep time, Coleman suggested that each player should be "free to contribute what he feels in the music at any given moment" (Coleman 1960) and contribute equally to the rhythmic direction of the music. Building upon the polyrhythmic African roots of jazz, Coleman and his cohorts laced different rhythmic patterns over one another to weave a complex improvisational tapestry of beats.

With little melody, harmonic progression, or consistent rhythm, Ornette and the avant-garde nonetheless created a rapid-fire group conversation. The *National Observer* contended that "the 'New Thing' pushes improvisational playing toward its final point." Unlike virtuosos in bop quartets, "more and more group improvisation can be heard taking priority over the solo musician and his performance" (Ostermann 1965).

In a 1960 review of Ornette Coleman and his band, *Time* magazine pinpointed many elements of the new jazz. It described "wildly asymmetrical melodies, lurching and truncated rhythms, [and] tone colors as varied and highly personal as the sound of a human voice" ("Beyond the Cool" 1960). *Time* compared the music to the abstract-expressionist movement of artists such as Jackson Pollock that focused on spontaneous, automatic, and sometimes subconscious creation.

Ornette Coleman categorized his forceful, rhythmically complex, and at times dissonant style of jazz as "free." In 1958, on his debut *Something Else!!!! The Music of Ornette Coleman*, the sax man offered a music "as free and natural as is possible. . . . The creation of music is just as natural as the air we breathe. I believe music is really a free thing," he maintained (Hentoff 1958). The next year, composer Gunther Schuller identified the "most outstanding element in Ornette's musical conception" as "an utter and complete freedom. His musical inspiration operates in a world uncluttered by conventional bar lines, conventional chord changes and conventional ways of blowing or fingering a saxophone. Such practical 'limitations' did not have to be overcome in his music, they somehow never existed for him" (Williams 1959).

The jazz establishment initially rejected Ornette's music. When on November 17, 1959, Ornette Coleman landed a two-week stint at New York's Five Spot club, jazz columnists blasted the twenty-nine-year-old sax man. After attending a special preview of Coleman's music for the press, one journalist labeled him a "fake." Another snapped that "he has no form." Still another vowed to "go home and listen to my Benny Goodman trios and quartets." One charitable reporter felt that "I like him, but I don't have any idea what he is doing" (Hoefer 1960, 40).

Established musicians who attended Ornette's performances derided him. "I think he's jiving, baby. He's putting everybody on," grumbled trumpeter Roy Eldridge. "You know that I never like to criticize anyone publicly," echoed saxophonist Coleman Hawkins. "Just say I think he needs seasoning. A lot of seasoning." "Nothing's happening," moaned hard-bop pianist Red Garland. "Coleman is faking" (Hentoff 1975, 228–29). Max Roach, the innovative bop drummer who normally accepted new styles, became so incensed by Coleman that he followed Ornette into the kitchen of the Five Spot and punched him (Litweiler 1992, 83). Miles Davis blurted that Ornette "is all screwed up inside" (Goldberg 1965, 231).

Coleman responded to the sting of his peers' barbs. "When I arrived in New York, from most of the jazz musicians all I got was a wall of hostility," he remembered. "I guess it's pretty shocking to hear someone like me come on the scene when they're already comfortable in Charlie Parker's language. They figure that now they may have to learn something else" (Hentoff 1975, 231).

Ridiculed by the press and fellow musicians, Ornette Coleman faced professional and financial adversity. He received few offers from clubs and, distrusting the music business, refused to record for any label for two years. At one point, he unsuccessfully tried to open a club to air his new style. By the end of 1964, Ornette was scuffling for money and recognition.

Free Jazz Gets Organized: UGMA and the AACM

Free-jazz players in several cities coalesced into organizations that allowed the "new thing" to grow and prosper. Just as the civil-rights movement emphasized African-American empowerment, they managed and promoted free jazz themselves in the face of hostility from the press and much of the jazz community.

In Southeast Los Angeles, several years before Watts erupted into flames, pianist Horace Tapscott launched the Pan Afrikan Peoples Arkestra (PAPA). In 1961, Tapscott, alto sax man Jimmy Woods, and five others founded PAPA "to preserve music, our music, black music. We were trying to get our own people to realize what they have." Tapscott chose "'Pan Afrikan' because the music would be drawn from the African peoples around the world and 'Arkestra,' building off the word *ark* and Noah using it to save different parts of the world. We would preserve our music on the ark" (Tapscott 2001, 83). The Arkestra played on street corners, in schoolhouses, and regularly in the South Park neighborhood of L.A. Tightly knit, the band lived together communally and, within a few months, grew to nearly thirty members.

PAPA reflected the African-American quest for civil rights. After the Sixteenth Street Baptist Church bombing in September 1963, the band captured the horror of the incident in their music. "We almost went crazy," remembered Tapscott. "Everybody was going off, crying, and the music changed immediately. It had that low 'hummmm,' that channeled anger, and seemed to immediately affect the performance of all the cats" (Tapscott 2001, 92).

By 1963, Tapscott and his compatriots turned to social activism by establishing the Underground Musicians Association (UGMA). They scheduled classes in "reading, writing and spelling." The band brought in actors, poets, and dancers to teach and entertain the community. They visited schools "to get to the children as early as possible and start playing black music, and telling them stories about black folks in history, so they could have something to hook up with" (Tapscott 2001, 95). Tapscott taught a class about new jazz with trumpeter Bobby Bradford on Saturdays for the Black Student Union at California State University at Dominquez Hills. The Arkestra "were also talking against things that were happening to the community, like police brutality," explained Tapscott (88). The pianist believed that "if the political part of it gets together and the music part gets it together, the economic part of it gets together," and change will occur (Kofsky 1979b, 79–83).

The Association for the Advancement of Creative Musicians (AACM) had lasting success as an experiment in African-American self-reliance. In 1961, experienced musicians in Chicago formed a collective big band. "What I did was start rehearsing the band in my house," recalled pianist/composer Muhal Richard Abrams. Saxophonists "Roscoe [Mitchell] and Joseph [Jarman] were around then, so was [drummer] Jack DeJohnette. So we rehearsed regularly, and it became the Experimental Band" (Townley 1974b).

Ornette Coleman's music inspired the participants in the Experimental Band. "When Ornette first came on the scene, he really knocked us out because we didn't think there was another cat even thinking about stuff like that," revealed Abrams. "And he had his stuff so well together, too. Ornette definitely had an influence on just about every cat who came through at that time. The influence was more one of inspiration than of out-and-out copying," he added (Townley 1974b).

In May 1965, Abrams united with three other members of the Ornette-influenced Experimental Band to form the AACM. He recalled that "[pianist] Jodie Christian, [trumpeter] Phil Cohran, [drummer] Steve McCall and myself got together and formed an organization out of the Experimental Band" (Townley 1974b). Other early members included bassist Melvin Jackson, trombone player Julian Priester, sax men Gene Easton and Fred Anderson, and trumpeter Fred Berry. Some participants had previously met at Chicago's Kennedy-King Community College, such as alto saxophonist Henry Threadgill and Malachi Favors Maghostut, who dressed in traditional African costumes and wore face paint to show a connection to the African motherland.

The organization coalesced amid the 1965 riots that engulfed the Windy City. The group felt that "African-American people have now reached a juncture where they have assumed and/or rekindled a spirit of pride—an intelligent pride that has become infectious and inspiring" (Wilmer 1981, 125). Members established the AACM "to show how the disadvantaged and disenfranchised can come together and determine their own strategies for political and economic freedom, thereby determining their own destinies" (Lewis 2004, 50). By controlling their own fate, AACM participants safeguarded and nurtured the African-American cultural heritage. "It was, for us, a question of survival—African-American cultural survival," noted Abrams (De Muth 1978, 20). "Now that we're talking about change, we're talking about revolution and all that kind of stuff, so, well, we're doing it in the music," proclaimed Chicago-born-and-bred free-jazz violinist and AACM member Leroy Jenkins (Wilmer 1981, 115).

The founding members established a formal structure for the group. They elected a board of directors with Abrams as president and developed a nine-point agenda, which included free training programs, the cultivation of young musicians, and contributions to the Abraham Lincoln Centre—a local community assistance site in Chicago. The group especially wanted to offer concerts in formal settings to avoid the talkative, liquor-filled club atmosphere and be portrayed as African-American artists rather than as entertainers. "No, no, we're not working for club owners. Not this organization," argued Abrams in preliminary AACM meetings. "This is strictly concerts. See, there's another thing about us functioning as full artistic musicians. We're not afforded that liberty in taverns" (Lewis 2004, 54).

As an initial activity, the AACM staged several concerts in Chicago's African-American community. On August 16, 1965, at the South Shore Ballroom, the group sponsored the Joseph Jarman Quintet. A week later, it featured Phil Cohran's Artistic Heritage Ensemble. The organization handled all aspects of the performances, including promotion, renting the facility, preparing the brochure, and ticket sales. It followed with performances in churches, galleries, and other venues.

AACM members also released records. In 1966, Roscoe Mitchell signed to Delmark Records, a Chicago-based independent company, and issued *Sound*, which captured the activist spirit of the AACM. "The Roscoe Mitchell Sextet is armed and dangerous," read the liner notes. It reflected the "insistent dignity, the purposeful pride, the determination [of the musicians] to fulfill themselves as creative beings.

You can hear it in the music." The group exemplified the AACM, "[which] is the healthiest organism at work in jazz today. A large and benevolent family, it encourages individuality and freedom, yet has a remarkable spiritual unity" (Figi, 1966). For the album, Mitchell composed the Coleman-tribute song, "Ornette."

Other AACM members followed with discs. In December 1966, Joseph Jarman recorded *Song For* on Delmark. The next year, Phil Cohran waxed two seven-inch singles on his Zulu Records. In 1968, Muhal Richard Abrams debuted with *Levels and Degrees of Light*, and Chicago-born reed man Anthony Braxton released *3 Compositions of New Jazz*. "We're on the eve of the complete fall of Western ideas and life-values," Braxton warned. "We're in the process of developing more meaningful values, and our music is a direct extension of this" (Braxton 1968).

Free-jazz advocates from other parts of the country connected with the Chicago cooperative. In 1966, trumpeter Lester Bowie drove from St. Louis to Chicago to become part of the AACM. The next year, trumpeter Leo Smith journeyed from Leland, Mississippi, "to be completely free of any references to anything because that's the onliest way that I can create music" (Wilmer 1981, 114). Drummer Don Moye drifted into town after playing in the African Cultural Ensemble and the Detroit Free Jazz unit. Within three years, thirty musicians had flocked to Chicago to join the organization.

In 1967, four members of the AACM—Mitchell, Jarman, Lester Bowie, and Malachi Favors—established the Art Ensemble of Chicago and released a debut album under Bowie's name, *Numbers 1 & 2*. "The jazz pulse of Chicago stirs again," the liner notes stated. "Freedom, or more correctly the need, its discovery or rediscovery, is the dominant force in this revival. The signs of the revolution permeate most of jazz today, and in Chicago there are young musicians who, desiring freedom, are beginning to know how it is created" (Martin 1967).

The Black Artists Group

Several young African-American musicians in St. Louis formed a collaborative organization using the model of the AACM. In 1968, alto saxophonist Oliver Lake visited Chicago and was impressed by the AACM's music and structure. Lake suggested to a group of fellow musicians—including fellow alto player Julius Hemphill, trombonist Joseph Bowie, trumpeter Floyd LeFlore, and baritone sax man Hamiet Bluiett—that they become a branch of the AACM. Having a slightly broader vision, Hemphill proposed a group that would include a wide array of artists including poets, visual artists, and actors (Looker 2004). In collaboration with an African-American theater company headed by Malinke "Robert" Elliott, the musicians founded the Black Artists Group (BAG). "In the 1960s, we wanted to play a different kind of music than the music you'd hear in clubs all the time," mentioned Bluiett. "We were inspired by Ornette Coleman and wanted to stretch and play every day. So we got this organization together" (Bartlett 1997).

As a credo, BAG pledged to "synthesize the proud black past with the present, and to bring together many art forms into a unifying experience" (Looker 2004). In April 1968, Julius Hemphill, the first chair of BAG, became administrator of a $200,000 grant from the Danforth and Rockefeller Foundations. He used the funds to rent a building to serve as a site for music, dance, and art classes; an arena for concerts; and a practice facility for classes aimed at disadvantaged African-American youth (Parker 1992, 13). In July, the group premiered the play, *The Blacks,* by French playwright Jean Genet. By 1973, BAG released *In Paris, Aries* on a self-funded label.

BAG adopted an overt political stance. "There was so much politics, even the way BAG started, how it was named was political, because of the civil rights movement that was happening," recalled Oliver Lake (Looker 2004). Trumpeter Floyd Leflore noted that "we would bring in speakers . . . that came strictly from a political point of view. There were riots going on there. There was a great deal of unrest. There was a great deal of frustration with the whole scene, you know. So that was definitely reflected in the art-form and our attitude about it" (Parker 1992, 14).

BAG connected with the AACM through brothers Lester Bowie, who lived in Chicago and belonged to the AACM, and Joseph Bowie, who stayed in St. Louis with BAG. "We developed an exchange program with the AACM," explained Hemphill. "They would come down here, and we would go up there" (Smith 1988, 14; Looker 2004).

Jazz Collectives in New York City

Several collectives were formed in New York City to empower musicians to shape their own careers and play the music they wanted to explore. The Triumvirate consisted of John Coltrane, who had moved into the avant-garde; African drummer Babatunde Olatunji; and saxophonist/flautist Yusef Lateef. "Tunji, I'm tired of being taken and exploited by managers, club owners and concert promoters," Trane complained to the drummer. "I hate to see promoters manipulating one artist after another. We need to sponsor our own concerts, promote them and perform in them." On July 21, 1966, the threesome agreed to collaborate on bookings, rent halls and theaters in major US cities for performances, and teach "the music of our people" at universities and conservatories, "where only the European musical experience dominates and is being perpetrated." They used Olatunji's Center for Afrikan Culture as a base of operations. On Sunday, April 23, 1967, as part of an "Afternoon Happening" to "bring great black musical groups back to Harlem thus changing its tarnished image as well as improve and restore its cultural tradition and pride," the John Coltrane Quintet delivered two performances for "The Roots of Africa" program. Though Coltrane died less than three months after the show, he demonstrated an interest in collective action through the Triumvirate (DeVito 2010, 325–26).

Several new-wave jazz men in New York coalesced around the Collective Black Artists (CBA) group. In 1969, pianist Stanley Cowell; Reggie Workman, who played bass for Coltrane; trumpeter Jimmy Owens; drummer Warren Smith; and Don Moore, onetime bassist for Archie Shepp, banded together. "We decided we wanted to bring black artists more to the fore, in presentation and recording and so forth," explained Cowell. "We did a lot of concerts, took music into prisons, into schools" (West 2015). The group offered courses on the music business and established a big band, the CBA Ensemble, which periodically rented Town Hall to back such players as saxophonist Archie Shepp. For Cowell, it represented an attempt at African-American self-help.

In 1971, group members Cowell and trumpeter Charles Tolliver established a record label, Strata-East, to release the works of CBA artists. "We were black artists that did want to express cultural feelings, political feelings, coming from their experiences as black artists, as black people," explained Cowell. "Remember the inception of Strata-East is following on the urban upheaval of the late 60s—the assassination of King and Malcolm X and the urban upheaval in black communities across the United States" (Griffin 2015). The duo wanted artists to control their output. "Kind of a rebuilding thing, coming out of the need to take over our own

Pharoah Sanders, July 1968. *Photograph by Guy Kopelowicz*

resources," maintained Cowell (West 2015). "It's not really about success, it's about owning your own product," added Tolliver. "We've been able to put out our own music knowing that we own it, and that any benefits that we reap from it will go back into making more music" (Wilmer 1981, 228). Within three years, the label issued more than thirty records. "Without the efforts of Charles Tolliver and Stanley Cowell, probably none of us would have produced our first albums," contended drummer Warren Smith (Rusch 1988f, 13).

In 1969, several jazz men united in the Jazz and People's Movement (J&PM), likely the most visible collective. The group was led by Archie Shepp; trumpeter Lee Morgan, who by the late sixties had edged toward the avant-garde; and multi-reedist Rahsaan Roland Kirk, who spanned styles from hard bop to free jazz. Other members included avant-garde sax men Billy Harper and Pharoah Sanders; drummer Andrew Cyrille; and trumpeter Freddie Hubbard, who had played with Ornette on *Free Jazz*. They contended that "the media have been so thoroughly effective in obstructing the exposure of true black genius that many black people are not even remotely familiar with or interested in the creative genius within black society. The white man has partially succeeded once more in emasculating a facet of black culture and the black quest for freedom." To remedy the racial imbalance, the J&PM vowed to "help in the struggle to open the media and enable black artists to reach the positions of prominence that their artistry so deserves—to breathe new life into black culture" (Kruth 2000, 237–38).

The J&PM targeted popular television talk shows. It initially tried to schedule a meeting with talk-show host Merv Griffin to discuss the inclusion of more African-American jazz artists on his show. "How often do you see jazz musicians in front of the camera?" rhetorically asked Lee Morgan. After being ignored, on August 27, 1970, sixty musicians met at Griffin's studio during the filming of a show. Rahsaan Roland Kirk distributed police whistles to the group and instructed them to play them on his signal. Just as Griffin introduced a guest, the musicians blew the whistles and a few instruments that had been smuggled into the building. "This caught Merv by surprise," recalled one of the demonstrators. "We just kept blowin' these whistles. Everybody started looking around. We came out with the signs, 'More Jazz Music on TV,' [and] 'Honor American Jazz Music'" (Kruth 2000, 239). Kirk and Lee Morgan made their way to the stage and lectured the audience about their aim of more jazz music on American television. Eventually escorted from the studio, the group later met with the TV host about their grievances. "The next day, they had the chairman of the board down there to see us!" a triumphant Morgan proclaimed (Bourne 1972).

Kirk and his co-conspirators planned disruptions of other talk shows. They turned to *The Tonight Show Starring Johnny Carson*, one of the most popular programs on television. On an anniversary of the show, which New York mayor John Lindsay attended, fifty members of the J&PM rushed the door and gained entry when Kirk told police that he would blow the door down with his horn. When network executives promised to schedule discussions about booking more jazz on the air, the musicians quietly left the studio.

On October 13, the cooperative targeted *The Dick Cavett Show*. During the middle of an interview with British actor Trevor Howard, the group pulled out their whistles and blew. "The whistles were so loud that Dick Cavett put his hands over his ears. He didn't know where to go—the whole place was flooded with sound," remembered a participant. After an hour of mayhem, Cavett agreed to include a spokesman from the group on his show the following day.

As a final act of cultural disruption, the group set their sights on *The Ed Sullivan Show*, the premier program on television that had introduced Elvis Presley and the Beatles to America and had aired continuously since 1949. Before their threatened appearance, the J&PM negotiated with Sullivan, who promised to feature jazz musicians on his show. Kirk, Archie Shepp, and other members of the group agreed to play their rendition of a popular song by Stevie Wonder, "My Cherie Amour." On January 24, 1971, just before taking the stage for a generous five-minute time slot, Kirk blurted that "we're gonna burn it down! We're gonna burn the place down" (Kruth 2000, 245). Rather than playing the Wonder tune, the group stunned the audience with an explosive, free-jazz version of the Charles Mingus composition, "Haitian Fight Song," in one of the first avant-garde performances on national television.

Free Jazz on Independent Labels

In the quest for self-determination and recognition, free-jazz artists established their own independent record companies. As early as 1965, writer Amiri Baraka formed Jihad Productions, using the Arabic word for an Islamic term that means "to strive and persevere." He initially released *'S Time Now*, which featured the free-jazz royalty of drummer Sunny Murray, saxophonist Albert Ayler, bassists Lewis Worrell and Henry Grimes, and trumpeter Don Cherry. Baraka recited the poem "Black Art" for one of the selections.

The next year, pianist Don Pullen and drummer Milford Graves established SRP, short for Self-Reliance Project, to issue their records. The duo first waxed *In Concert at Yale University* with hand-painted album covers. They followed with *Nommo*. "Self-Reliance!," the liner notes read. "The watchword of new musicians and artists to do themselves. These musicians are now creating situations wherein those creative abilities, stagnant for so long because of repressive conditions, may now be fully realized" (Wilmer 1981, 228).

Other artist-owned labels appeared. In 1971, free-jazz sax player James Spaulding started East Records. He designed the logo for the label and released a 45-rpm single, "Uhuru Sasa," a Swahili phrase that translated into "Freedom Now" (Rusch 1989a, 14). The same year, Julius Hemphill created Mbari Records, a reference to the sacred visual art form of the Igbo peoples of southeast Nigeria. He launched the company with the album, *The Collected Poem—For Blind Lemon Jefferson*, which featured African artwork on its cover. Hemphill followed with *Dogon A.D.*, a nod to the Dogon people who lived south of the Niger bend in Mali.

In addition to artist-owned-and-operated labels, two small independents established by whites, ESP-Disk' and BYG Records, helped publicize the new music. Bernard Stollman, the innovator behind ESP, graduated from Columbia Law School and found work with the entertainment law firm of Flo Kennedy, where he assisted on several music-related cases such as the lawsuit over the estate of Charlie Parker. After leaving the firm and establishing his own practice, he provided legal services to Dizzy Gillespie, briefly managed Bud Powell, and worked with Atlantic Records on behalf of Ornette Coleman.

Stollman impulsively established a record label for spontaneous music. In 1963, during a snowstorm, he wandered into a popular piano bar, the Baby Grand, on 125th Street in New York City. During the middle of the set, "a small man in a gray leather suit, holding a large saxophone, brushed by me and jumped up on the stage. He had a black beard, with a little patch of white in it. He was not introduced and, ignoring the trio, began to blow his horn." Stollman watched the sax player solo "for twenty to thirty minutes, just a burst of music." Transfixed by the sounds, Stollman leapt from his seat after the performance and exclaimed that "your music is beautiful. I am starting a record label, and I'd like you to be my first artist," even though he owned no records or record player, and had never before thought of starting a record company (Weiss 2012, 21). Six months later, Stollman's phone rang. "This is Albert Ayler. I'm ready to record," the voice said. Stollman instructed Ayler to meet him at Varsity Arts Studio. On July 10, 1964, Stollman recorded Ayler, white bassist Gary Peacock, and drummer Sunny Murray (Weiss 2012, 21).

The enterprising lawyer plunged into the free-jazz scene. "I wanted to explore the new music," Stollman explained. "A few months later [after recording Ayler], the October Revolution in Jazz gave me an opportunity to meet the community. Archie Shepp stood on the steps outside, puffing his pipe; I invited him to record for the new label," he recollected. "I invited all of the artists I found. The artists I met at the Cellar Café [in October] who accepted my invitation to record them, became the nucleus of the label" (Weiss 2012, 22, 27). He wanted to nuture "an emerging community of composers" (26).

Stollman relied on an artist-friendly business model. "I saw the industry as an enemy to the creative process, and I drafted a new standard for the treatment of artists," he asserted. "Each production would be a collaborative undertaking, in which the artists would have full control over the repertoire and the recording process. Our slogan became 'The artists alone decide what you will hear on their E.S.P.-Disk'.'" Stollman pledged to surrender co-ownership of the material in perpetuity to the musicians (Weiss 2012, 31).

In September 1965, Stollman unveiled the label to help create a free-jazz movement. Along with the Albert Ayler album, it distributed a self-titled effort by Pharoah Sanders, a 1962 Town Hall performance by Ornette Coleman, and improvisations from the New York Art Quartet (saxophonist John Tchicai, bass player Lewis Worrell, drummer Milford Graves, trombonist Roswell Rudd, and LeRoi Jones, who spoke on the song "Black Dada Nihilismus"). During the next year and a half, the label released thirty-three albums by leading New York free-jazz practitioners to promote the new music. "He gave me a contract when nobody else in America would have dreamed of doing so," said alto saxophone player Noah Howard (Wilmer 1981, 233). "Without that company, a great part of the so-called avant-garde musicians wouldn't have been known," added John Tchicai (Weiss 2012, 93).

Radicalized youths in France provided a market for BYG Actuel, which also heavily supported free jazz. In May 1968, French student demonstrators exploded in rage. On May 2, after six weeks of trouble at the Nanterre branch of Paris University, students forced a closure of the institution. On May 6, twenty thousand students and faculty from the national student and faculty unions took to the streets near Sorbonne University. They burned cars, constructed barricades, and ripped cobblestones from roads to throw at police, who stood arm-in-arm to enclose the university and mercilessly beat students with rubber truncheons.

Sympathetic to students after the brutal police reaction, on May 14 workers who disliked the conservative policies of President Charles de Gaulle occupied factories and refused to work. A week later, more than ten million workers, approximately two-thirds of the French workforce, engineered strikes against employers and paralyzed the country. They asked for higher wages and better working conditions, and decried the regime of de Gaulle, who had been a war hero twenty-five years earlier.

Stunned, the government feared revolution. Prime Minister Georges Pompidou mobilized ten thousand reservists to ready for battle, and, on May 29, de Gaulle unexpectedly and secretly left the country with his family for a French military base in Baden-Baden, Germany. Upon his return, de Gaulle dissolved the government, called for a general election, and, early the next year, resigned from office.

The student protesters championed American free jazz and adopted it as their marching anthem. "The so-called 'free music' became the song of the young people's revolution in Europe—it had a heavy political connotation," recalled new-wave trumpeter Enrico Rava (Panken 2012, 40).

Capitalizing on an interest in free jazz among European youths, three friends—Fernand Boruso, Jean-Luc Young, and Jean Georgakarakos—founded a record company named BYG. In 1969, they invited several free-jazz artists to Paris for recording sessions. The trio launched the label with a release by Don Cherry and Ed Blackwell, *Mu, First Part*, and followed with the Art Ensemble of Chicago's *A Jackson in Your House*, Sunny Murray's *Homage to Africa*, and Archie Shepp's *Yasmina, A Black Woman*. Within two years, the company had released thirty-six free-jazz albums. By the end of the decade, BYG and ESP had established a foothold for free jazz in the United States and Europe.

The Avant-Garde Goes Mainstream

Just as important as African-American jazz collectives and independent record labels, the adoption of free jazz by established artists gave the new music credibility and respect. In April 1959, Sonny Rollins—a leading hard-bop saxophonist who had worked as a sideman for Thelonious Monk and Miles Davis—suddenly disappeared from the music scene. "I was getting a lot of publicity around '57, '58, and I didn't feel that I was good enough for what I was getting," Rollins revealed. "I wanted to go back and study. See, I've always considered myself a self-taught musician, and I've got this feeling of inferiority" (Spencer 1990, 230). Rather than continue along the path to hard-bop stardom, Rollins ceaselessly practiced on the catwalk of the Williamsburg Bridge, which stretched over the East River and connected Manhattan to Brooklyn. When reemerging on the scene in late 1961, Rollins showcased a different, freer sound. In the summer of 1962, he partnered with avant-garde trumpeter Don Cherry and Ornette Coleman drummer Billy Higgins for performances that pushed him toward a raw, angular approach. "When we were playing in the free style," explained the saxophonist, "we didn't play, say, a chord progression like C, F, G, C. What we played was phrases" (Nisenson 2000, 158). He released the live album *Our Man in Jazz*, recorded in late July at the Village Gate, that captured the furious music.

As the sixties progressed, Rollins delivered a relentless, extended shower of notes as he explored elements of free jazz. "Sonny was playing very long pieces," remarked avant-garde pianist Paul Bley, who recorded with Rollins in 1963 and 1964. "He would start a tune, play for an hour and fifteen minutes, and then turn to me and say, 'You got it!'" In one instance, the Rollins group performed a version of "This Can't Be Love" for four hours (Bley 1999, 82). "The main thing that affected me during this period was the change going on in this country with the civil rights movement," explained the saxophonist. "Things just reached a point where people wanted to say something about it. This was reflected in the music. People were trying to escape from the restrictions of society, all this racism and these kinds of things, so that in doing that, they felt that they should break down these song forms" (Nisenson 2000, 172).

Hard bopper Jackie McLean incorporated free jazz into his music. In 1962, as a nod to the civil-rights movement and free jazz, the former Charlie Parker disciple released *Let Freedom Ring*. "Ornette has made me stop and think," proclaimed the sax man (McLean 1963). The next year, he moved closer to the new wave with *One Step Beyond* and *Destination . . . Out!*, which included avant-garde trombonist Grachan Moncur III. "Staying away from a rut and finding newer and freer material is part of my inspiration to play and write," he asserted (McLean 1964). "Personally, I get tired of playing the same keys, chords changes and tunes over and over again. 'Freedom in jazz' is like a complete new field, new grazing grounds for all the cattle that want to go out and eat some new grass" (Gitler 1963, 24).

The shifting focus of pianist Herbie Hancock illustrated the general move toward the avant-garde. Born in Chicago, Herbie studied classical piano as a youth and attended Grinnell College, where he majored in electrical engineering and music. In 1961, he began working with bop trumpeter Donald Byrd and subsequently played with such hard-bop saxophonists as Jackie McLean and Hank Mobley. The next year, he waxed the single "Watermelon Man," which percussionist Mongo Santamaria took to the Top Ten, and which established Herbie as a force within the jazz community. In 1963, Hancock joined the Miles Davis band for a five-year stint.

In 1970, still reeling from the assassination of Martin Luther King Jr., two years earlier, Hancock turned to free jazz by establishing the group Mwandishi, which exhibited a sense of African-American pride. As band mates, he hired reed man Bernie Maupin, trombonist Julian Priester, trumpeter Eddie Henderson, drummer Billy Hart, and bassist Buster Williams. Each group member adopted a Swahili name on the advice of James Forman, otherwise known as Mtume, the son of saxophonist Jimmy Heath and a member of the black nationalist U.S. (United Slaves) Organization. Hancock assumed the name of Mwandishi, meaning "composer" or "writer." "We started wearing dashikis and African talismans, and I began to feel more connected than ever to the civil rights movement and to our shared, collective past as black musicians," noted Herbie. "This was a powerful transformation, and of course it affected our music" (Hancock 2014, 120).

The radicalized group delivered a nearly free-jazz sound. "I wanted to set everybody loose, to explore more deeply the avant-garde side of jazz music," Herbie insisted. "Everything was intuitive, in the moment. Nothing was planned. The more the group played, the further out the music got. [It had] evolved into this ferocious beast from outer space" (Hancock 2014, 126–27, 133, 124, 127). In 1971, the band released a self-titled debut, which "was as free as we could make it." It included "Ostinato (Suite for Angela)," an ode to Angela Davis, an African-American feminist and Black Panther leader (146).

John Coltrane as a Free-Jazz Symbol

John Coltrane best exemplified the transition of hard boppers to free jazz. Raised in High Point, North Carolina, Coltrane received an alto saxophone during his last year of high school. In 1943, amidst the mass migration of Southern African-Americans into Northern cities, Coltrane moved to Philadelphia and attended the Ornstein School of Music. Two years later, he entered the US Navy for a year.

After returning to Philadelphia from the Navy, Coltrane became a Charlie Parker fanatic. "When I first heard Bird, I wanted to be identified with him, to be consumed by him," revealed the saxophonist (DeVito 2010, 41). "On weekends, John and a bunch of young Philadelphia musicians would bring Charlie Parker records with them, discuss the music with . . . the other working musicians there, then sit in with us after hours," recalled tenor sax man Bill Barron (Thomas 1980, 34). During the late forties, when he landed jobs in the R&B outfits of King Kolax and Eddie "Cleanhead" Vinson, Coltrane changed from alto to tenor sax. "On alto, Bird had been my whole influence, but on tenor I found there was no one man whose ideas were so dominant as Charlie's were on alto," he intimated. "I drew from all the men I heard during this period on tenor, especially Lester Young" (Thomas, 42).

For three years from mid-1948, Coltrane found work in a variety of bands. He joined a group headed by Philadelphia trumpet player Mel Melvin that included the Heath brothers: Jimmy on alto, Al on drums, and Percy on bass. The tenor sax man bolted to bop trumpeter Howard McGhee's group, and, in 1949, played alto with the Dizzy Gillespie big band for a year. As the big-band era dissipated, Coltrane played tenor in a sextet organized by Dizzy.

In 1951, Coltrane returned to Philadelphia to study music. He enrolled in the Granoff School of Music, which had been founded in 1918 by Isadore Granoff, a Russian violinist who had performed at the 1913 premier of Stravinsky's *Le Sacre du Printemps*. Coltrane took lessons in music theory from Dennis Sandole, who taught him about polytonalities (using two keys at once), pedal point clusters (several drones, or low, sustained tones), and harmony derived from melodic lines, with no chord structure (Thomas 1980, 51). "He arrived an hour early, waiting on the steps for the school to open," remembered Granoff. "He used to work seven, eight hours a day at his instrument," a practice schedule that Coltrane continued throughout his life (DeVito 2010, 373). After his training at Granoff, Coltrane permanently switched to tenor to distinguish himself from Bird.

The tenor player again landed jobs with sundry jazz groups. For several years, he backed R&B acts such as Clarence "Bull Moose" Jackson and organist Shirley Scott, and joined the pop-oriented orchestra of Earl Bostic and Johnny Hodges's outfit. Late in 1955, John secured a spot with Miles Davis and recorded several discs with the leader. During the same period, he served as a sideman for such jazz men as Johnny Griffin, Paul Chambers, and Thelonious Monk, who in 1957 hired him for an extended engagement at the Five Spot club in New York City. At the same time, the productive Coltrane cut several hard-bop albums as a leader.

At the turn of the decade, Coltrane focused on his career as a solo artist. In 1959, he signed to Atlantic Records and, at the urging of Miles Davis's manager, engaged the Shaw Artists Agency to secure the best bookings possible. The saxophonist created his own publishing company, Jowcol, to retain control of composer rights. In May, Coltrane waxed the first album for his new label, *Giant Steps*, which the jazz community welcomed. "Along with Sonny Rollins, John Coltrane has become the most influential and controversial tenor saxophonist in modern jazz," stated critic Nat Hentoff (Hentoff 1960). In May 1960, the sax man gave notice to Miles.

Coltrane evolved musically by developing a rapid-fire style that critic Ira Gitler called "sheets of sound." Grounding his music on hard bop, he delivered a barrage of notes that engulfed the listener. The sax man sometimes played as many as three notes at a time through a false-fingering technique he learned from Monk. In his own words, he generated "a sweeping sound. I tried long, rapid lines . . . I was beginning to apply the three-on-one chord approach, and at that time the tendency was to play the entire scale of each chord. Therefore, they were usually played fast and sometimes sounded like [glissandos]" (DeVito 2010, 69). As Miles explained it, Coltrane "plays five notes of a chord and keeps changing it around, trying to see how many different ways it can sound. It's like explaining something five different ways" (Hentoff 1960). "Trane was the loudest, fastest saxophonist I ever heard," added Miles. "It was like he was possessed when he put that horn in his mouth" (Davis 1989, 222–23).

Though generating a passionate, almost ferocious music, Coltrane did not yet play free. He understood that his intense music might be difficult for listeners to grasp, so he tried to "make it presentable. I am worried that sometimes what I'm doing sounds like just academic exercises, and I'm trying more and more to make it sound prettier," he contended in 1959 (Hentoff 1960). "I realize I'm in the entertainment business and I'd like to be the sort of guy who can set audiences at ease," he stated two years later (Devito 2010, 121).

In 1960, Coltrane edged toward the avant-garde. That February, he received a soprano saxophone from Miles Davis, who bought it from a French antiques dealer. "After he got that horn, his style changed," claimed Miles. "He didn't sound like nobody but himself. He found that he could play lighter and faster on the soprano than he could on the tenor. When he played the soprano, after a while it sounded almost like a human voice, wailing" (Davis 1989, 224).

At the same time, Coltrane was heavily influenced by Ornette Coleman. "I heard Ornette who had abandoned chords completely and that helped me think clearly about what I wanted to do," maintained the saxophonist (DeVito 2010, 117). On June 28, 1960, Trane recorded with Ornette's sidemen—trumpeter Don Cherry, bassist Charlie Haden, and drummer Ed Blackwell—to cut *Avant-Garde*, which featured the soprano sax on some selections and revealed Coltrane's gradual shift in style.

The next year, Eric Dolphy, who had written the arrangements for Coltrane's *Ole* and *Africa/Brass* albums, pushed Coltrane closer to free jazz. Dolphy, a native of Los Angeles, studied with Buddy Collette and led the orchestra at Los Angeles City College. During 1954, in his hometown, he met Ornette Coleman who "taught me a direction" (Eyre 1960b). After playing in the bebop big bands of Gerald Wilson and Roy Porter, Dolphy joined Chico Hamilton and then Charles Mingus. In April 1960, he waxed *Outward Bound*. "This is right out of the Coleman dynasty, this is the sound of tomorrow, the sound of the Atlas missile, the sound of the Pioneer radio blip from outer space," proclaimed the liner notes (Eyre 1960b). Four months later, the saxophonist followed with *Out There*, which featured a surrealistic, space-age cover. "Something new's happening. I don't know what it is, but it's new, and it's good, and it's just about to happen," asserted Dolphy about the disc (Goldberg 1961). In December, he played bass clarinet on two Ornette Coleman albums, including the seminal *Free Jazz*.

John Coltrane, July 1965. *Photograph by Guy Kopelowicz*

Impulse! Records documented the collaboration between Coltrane and Dolphy. In 1960, only a year before signing Coltrane, Creed Taylor established Impulse! as a subsidiary of ABC-Paramount Records. He adopted "The New Wave of Jazz" as the slogan for the label. When Taylor left the company in the summer of the next year, Bob Thiele took the helm. As his first task, in May 1961, he recorded several sessions by Coltrane and Dolphy at the Village Vanguard club in New York City. "Since [Dolphy's] been in the band, he's had a broadening effect on us. There are a lot of things we try now that we never tried before," disclosed Coltrane. "We're playing more free" (DeVito 2010, p. 153).

Jimmy Garrison played bass on the Impulse! session. Initially a bebopper, the Philadelphia-raised Garrison switched to the the new wave when he heard Ornette Coleman. Garrison remarked that "prior to Ornette, bass players were more or less metronomic, and they weren't as atonal as you had to be playing with Ornette." In March 1961, the bassist joined Coleman on the album *Ornette on Tenor*. "I came up in the bebop school, so working with Ornette certainly changed my way of thinking about music and approaching the instrument," he recalled. When he landed the job with Coltrane seven months later, Garrison "felt that I could utilize what I had learned with Ornette" (Nolan 1974, 18).

At the Village Vanguard, Coltrane combined a burning interest in the complex music of India with the avant-garde. He described his exploration of new "approaches to music—as in India—in which particular sounds and scales are intended to produce specific emotional meanings" (Hentoff 1962). He also expressed admiration for sitar master Ravi Shankar.

When Dolphy left Coltrane in March 1962 to form his own group, Trane continued to move haltingly toward the avant-garde. On one hand, he released three mainstream records: a ballads album, a disc with Duke Ellington, and a session with singer Johnny Hartman. Yet the saxophonist increasingly relied on the soprano sax and experimented with new music. On July 7, 1963, he recruited avant-garde sax man Pharoah Sanders for a performance at the Newport Jazz Festival that Impulse! recorded as *Selflessness Featuring My Favorite Things*. He followed with the explosive *Coltrane Live at Birdland*. "When I make a change, I'm a little worried that it may puzzle people," mentioned Coltrane about the dichotomy of his recorded output. "Sometimes, I deliberately delay things for this reason. But after a while I find there is nothing else I can do but go ahead" (Thomas 1980, 195).

By late 1964, Coltrane stood firmly rooted in the avant-garde. On December 7, he recorded *Coltrane—A Love Supreme*, which encapsulated his spiritual direction and free-jazz leanings. In the liner notes, he admitted to a previous drug addiction, which he had overcome seven years earlier, when he "experienced, by the grace of God, a spiritual awakening. ALL PRAISE TO GOD," he testified like a Baptist preacher (Coltrane 1965). The music reflected the sanctified, thunderous, and unrestrained jubilation of a man unchained and received a lift from free-jazz tenorist Archie Shepp.

Coltrane continued along a spiritually infused, free-jazz path. In June 1965, he collaborated with avant-garde sax men Pharoah Sanders, John Tchicai, Archie Shepp, and Marion Brown on *Ascension* for a full-fledged, free-jazz assault. After completing the album, Coltrane phoned his friend Albert Ayler and excitedly told him that "I recorded an album and found that I was playing just like you" (Wilmer 1981, 107). The same month, Trane added Sanders to the mix on *Kulu Se Mama*. Later in 1965, he waxed *John Coltrane/Archie Shepp—New Thing at Newport*, *John Coltrane Featuring Pharoah Sanders Live in Seattle*, and the free-jazz album *Om*. The next year, until his untimely death on July 17, 1967, from liver cancer, Coltrane explored the outer reaches of jazz with such discs as *Interstellar Space* and *Cosmic Music*, the last dedicated to the memory of Martin Luther King Jr.

LISTENING GUIDE 35

John Coltrane and Rashied Ali

 "JUPITER" (FROM *INTERSTELLAR SPACE*)

During the final four years of his life, Coltrane slowly moved toward free jazz. He first incorporated several free-jazz elements and asked such free-jazz artists as Eric Dolphy and Don Cherry to perform and record with him. He then unleashed free-jazz solos within a more traditional format, in which each group member soloed individually. By the time of his death, the saxophonist had embraced the free-jazz concept of group improvisation.

Coltrane insisted that his music contained a spiritual message and, before his untimely death, concentrated on the outreaches of the physical universe in search of truth and beauty through free jazz. He recorded such albums as *Sun Ship* (1965), *Stellar Regions* (1967), and

Interstellar Space (1967). "My goal," he revealed in late 1966, "is to live the truly religious life and express it in my music" (Zimmerman and Ross 1966, 107).

Not released until September 1974, *Interstellar Space* consists of an extended suite about the planets: "Mars," "Venus," "Jupiter," and "Saturn." Recorded on February 22, 1967, only a few months before the tenor saxophonist's passing, "Jupiter" features only Coltrane and drummer Rashied Ali, who engaged in an intense, free-jazz conversation with only a hint of a melody. To Coltrane, the song demonstrated the "multi-directional rhythms all the time" of Ali that allowed the saxophonist to play "with maximum freedom" (Kahn 2006, 262).

0:00–0:12	Like the beginning of a church service, Coltrane starts the song with shakes of bells.
0:13–0:24	Drummer Ali enters with a dynamic pattern that builds volume, recedes, builds volume, recedes, and then builds volume again. Coltrane continues to shake the bells lightly.
0:25–0:38	Coltrane enters to play a two-measure pattern three times.
0:39–0:47	The saxophonist switches to another pattern and plays it three times. He then shortens the pattern, which he plays four times.
0:48–0:52	Coltrane delivers the first phrase of the two-measure main pattern, which he used to start the piece and ends in short blasts of the main theme.
0:53–0:55	The saxophonist starts to improvise around the main theme by taking two notes from the pattern and playing them at different pitches. To achieve new sounds, he overblows several of the notes to get a honking effect. Ali provides an intense, but solid rhythm as Coltrane begins to explore the pattern.
0:56–1:13	To build intensity, Coltrane rapidly plays a succession of three notes in a trill-like manner more than thirty times in an arrhythmic pattern to contrast with Ali and create polyrhythm. He still improvises around the main theme.
1:14–1:16	Coltrane plays a seven-note, almost melodic pattern.
1:17–1:21	The saxophonist seamlessly travels to the main theme, which begins as a five-note motif but then devolves into a two-note motif in a highly syncopated style. He overblows the last and then the first note in a creative improvisation.
1:22–1:38	Coltrane improvises on the main theme by playing the pattern in an ascending fashion and varies the number of notes played in the pattern. Near the end of the passage, he extends the range of the motif by overblowing three notes several times. Throughout this passage, Coltrane constantly changes the rhythm to contrast with Ali and maintain the polyrhythm. Coltrane's rhythmic complexity expanded upon the innovations of Charlie Parker and other boppers.

1:39–1:49	Coltrane improvises around a seven-note pattern.
1:50–1:54	Coltrane overblows beyond the register of the saxophone to unearth several interesting and startling sounds.
1:55–2:08	Coltrane returns with a variant of the main theme with a new ending note in every other measure. He repeats the motif four times and then (2:01) improvises on the pattern to produce a lightning-fast, twelve-note version of it, which he generally repeats four times with some small changes. As he plays, his speedy versions seem to ping-pong off one another to create a fascinating rhythm.
2:09–2:12	The saxophonist ends the above pattern with an innovative improvisation on it, which creates a shard of a melody.
2:13–3:17	At blazing speed, Coltrane creates an intense pattern, based loosely on the main theme, which he repeats more than thirty times. He varies the number of notes in each iteration to create a complex polyrhythm. Ali continues with backing on the drums with his own set of complex rhythms.
3:18–3:37	He significantly overblows the horn to generate interesting, high-register sounds, which exemplify free jazz. With his horn, Coltrane amazingly approximates the human voice and seems to be uttering cries of anguish or preaching to his followers.
3:39–3:51	Coltrane continues with the pattern, which started at 2:13, and plays at various rhythms by limiting the pattern to two notes or greatly expanding the number of notes.
3:52–3:58	Coltrane again overblows his horn to create human-like vocals.
3:59–4:12	Coltrane establishes another pattern, which he delivers in a sliding, descending manner.
4:13–4:27	Coltrane switches to a highly syncopated, staccato passage, which he ends by four times overblowing and sustaining a note. He created this passage by deconstructing the main theme.
4:28–4:35	Coltrane relaunches the above highly syncopated, staccato passage with a very different rhythm that more closely approximates the original theme.
4:36–4:45	Coltrane continues to improvise on the original theme at the beginning of the song at 0:25.
4:46–5:10	He begins to play call-and-response with himself by stating notes from the original theme motif and answering it with overblown notes. He varies the number of notes in the pattern to enhance the rhythmic complexity of the piece. This technique adds to the conversation within the music.
5:10	Coltrane abruptly stops, when Ali hits a cymbal. Ali continues his drumming.
5:11–5:14	Ali gives a drum roll and a cymbal crash and then stops.
5:15–5:21	To signal that the church of John Coltrane has ended, Coltrane starts to shake his bells, unaccompanied, as he did at the beginning of the song.

Devoted to peaceful coexistence, Coltrane ironically symbolized black militancy for many who heard his furious outpouring of music. "Trane's music and what he was playing the last two or three years of his life represented, for many blacks, the fire and passion and rage and anger and rebellion and love that they felt, especially among young black intellectuals and revolutionaries of that time," emphasized Miles Davis. "He was expressing through music what H. Rap Brown and Stokely Carmichael and the Black Panthers and Huey Newton were saying with their words, what the Last Poets and Amiri Baraka were saying with poetry. He played what they felt inside and were expressing through riots—'burn, baby, burn'—that were taking place everywhere in this country. Coltrane was their symbol, their pride—their beautiful, black revolutionary pride" (Davis 1989, 285–86). Trumpeter Charles Tolliver commented that "the whole push toward equality, along with John Coltrane's music, permeated everything we did for about five to eight years" (Ratliff 2007, 181).

John Coltrane appealed to students on radicalized campuses. While ESP-Disk' generally sold five hundred to a thousand copies of its records, *A Love Supreme* sold more than a hundred thousand without much airplay. "I was amazed, because I'd never heard much of his music on radio and wondered, 'Who's buying these records?'" asked Bob Thiele. "Then, I visited several colleges . . . and I saw almost all the student musicians had Coltrane records" (Thomas 1980, 178–79).

In addition to students, young hipsters and a more general, sometimes fanatical audience embraced Coltrane. "*A Love Supreme*—which was like a prayer—reached out and influenced those people who were into peace, hippies and people like that," remarked Miles Davis (Davis 1989, 286). During 1971, in San Francisco, Franzo and Marina King even established the One Mind Evolutionary Transitional Church of Christ devoted to the saxophonist. Changing the name of the church to St. John Will-I-Am John Coltrane African Orthodox Church in 1982, members played Trane's music on the radio every Tuesday and held mass every Sunday (Saint John Coltrane website, n.d.).

By the time of his death, Coltrane epitomized free jazz to the general public. "Trane was elected as the dean of free music," noted drummer Rashied Ali, who played with the saxophonist for three years (Ratliff 2007, 157). In December 1966, *Newsweek* proclaimed Coltrane as "the spiritual leader and father figure of the new jazz" (Zimmerman and Ross 1966, 107).

Free jazz, benefiting from the commercial success of Coltrane, became increasingly visible. Pharoah Sanders, Archie Shepp, and Albert Ayler signed to Impulse! Records. In 1965, the Newport Jazz Festival featured performances by Coltrane as well as Pharoah Sanders, Archie Shepp, and Paul Bley. Clubs such as Slugs in New York, which opened in 1966 as a hard-bop venue, changed to an avant-garde showcase. In November 1966, *Downbeat* declared that "it is obvious that the new jazz is here to stay" (Woodfin 1966, 19). The next month, *Newsweek* wrote an eight-page spread on "the new jazz," which it heralded as the "most dominant movement in jazz today" that embodied "racial pride, black consciousness, the frustrated anger of the exploited, [and] the cry for equality" (Zimmerman and Ross 1966, 101). By the late 1960s, contended pianist Kenny Barron, jazz musicians found it difficult to find work in New York City "unless you played 'free'" (Cutler 1989, 9). Though never reaching the *Billboard* charts, free jazz profoundly impacted jazz with its musical innovations and reflected the quest for African-American pride amid an increasingly militant civil-rights movement.

For Discussion and Further Study

Chapter Quiz

1. How did the continuing struggle for civil rights and an increase in black militancy in the mid-to-later 1960s influence the development of free jazz?

2. How did Archie Shepp describe his music? How does this compare to musicians like Albert Ayler's view of his music? How did both views reflect the tensions in the civil-rights and Black Power movements?

3. What role did Ornette Coleman play in developing and popularizing free jazz?

4. What role did musical collectives play in supporting free jazz? Why were African-American musicians particularly interested in forming these collectives? How did these organizations reflect the social and political turmoil of the day?

5. What was the role of independent and artist-owned labels in the free-jazz movement?

6. How did John Coltrane's musical style change during this period? What was the importance of his later work to jazz musicians?

JAZZ GOES ELECTRIC

Fusion, Jazz-Funk, and Smooth Jazz

Technological innovations and changes in the American economy significantly affected jazz from the late 1960s to the 1980s. The introduction of new technologies such as electronic instruments and the Moog synthesizer led many jazz musicians, especially Miles Davis and Herbie Hancock, to embrace jazz-rock and jazz-funk fusions. Beginning in the mid-seventies, an economic recession led many listeners to the softer sounds of "smooth jazz," which scaled the charts with the help of such entrepreneurs as Creed Taylor and such new media as MTV and smooth-jazz radio.

Jimi Hendrix, a rock guitar hero, wanted to meet Miles Davis. The guitarist had become increasingly interested in jazz after jamming with such players as Rahsaan Roland Kirk. He hoped to connect with the inventive Davis, who had played with Charlie Parker, shaped the hard-bop movement, been a cool-jazz originator, and had launched a commercial version of modal jazz with *Kind of Blue*. "Jimi liked what I had done on *Kind of Blue* . . . and wanted to add more jazz elements to what he was doing. He liked the way Coltrane played with all those sheets of sound, and he played guitar in a similar way," remembered Davis (Davis 1989, 292). Hendrix asked Alan Douglas, a friend of Miles's, to arrange a meeting.

In 1968, Miles and Jimi "started to get together," mostly at Miles's home. Because Hendrix could not read music, Davis would "play [an idea] for him on the piano or on the horn, and he would get it faster than a motherfucker. He had a natural ear for hearing music. So I'd play different shit for him, show him that way." Miles would play Hendrix "a record of mine or Trane's and explain to him what we were doing" (Davis 1989, 292–93).

Davis and Hendrix planned to cut an album together. On October 21, 1969, they sent a telegram to bass player Paul McCartney, asking the Beatle if he would record with them and drummer Tony Williams using Alan Douglas as the producer. Hendrix and Davis never heard from McCartney, who was out of town on vacation, so the album never materialized. In March 1970, Hendrix agreed that he would solo on "Hummin,'" a song on the Quincy Jones *Gula Matari* album. "He was dying to play jazz," asserted Jones. "He was saying 'Let's go do this thing. I'll meet you in Jersey,'" but never appeared for the session (Woodard 1990, 21). During the last days of August 1970, Miles and Hendrix both performed at the Isle of Wight outdoor concert festival. Miles and Jimi agreed to meet in London to discuss a joint album when the event concluded on August 30. Tangled in traffic jams, however, Hendrix failed to reach the meeting, and no joint Davis-Hendrix studio effort would ever take place due to Hendrix's premature death on September 18, 1970.

Miles Davis performing at the Isle of Wight Festival, 1970. *Pictorial Press Ltd/Alamy Stock Photo*

Though never recording together, Hendrix and Davis both benefited from their collaboration. Hendrix "started incorporating things I told him into his albums. It was great. He influenced me, and I influenced him, and that's the way great music is always made," contended Davis (1989, 292–93). After working with Hendrix, Davis integrated electronic instruments into his music and pioneered a jazz-rock music called "fusion."

Bitches Brew

Miles learned about new sounds made possible by electronics through his sessions with Hendrix. "Musicians have to play the instruments that best reflect the times we're in, play the technology that will give you what you want to hear," suggested Davis. "I was moving more and more to using electronic instruments to make up the sound that I wanted" (Davis 1989, 294–95).

By using electronic instruments, Davis hoped to reinvigorate jazz and his career. "Jazz seemed to be withering on the vine, in record sales and live performances," noticed Davis. "It was the first time in a long time that I didn't sell out crowds everywhere I played. *I* wanted to change course, *had* to change course for me to continue to believe in and love what I was playing. I wasn't prepared to be a memory yet," he sniffed (Davis 1989, 297–98).

As early as December 1967, Davis began an experiment. In a recording session, pianist Herbie Hancock "walked into the studio and didn't see any acoustic piano. I saw this little box [electric piano] sitting there, this little toy, so I said, 'Miles, where's the piano.'" Miles responded, "I want you to play this." A dumbfounded Herbie "tested it and heard this sound—this big mellow sound coming out—and I said, 'Oh, yeah, outtasight.' I liked it right away" (Townley 1974a, 16). Hancock, maintained Miles, "always liked electronic gadgets anyway, so he took to the Rhodes like a fish to water" (Davis 1989, 294). Miles wanted to use the Fender Rhodes, developed by Harold Rhodes after World War II and available commercially by 1965, to replicate the lush sound of a full orchestra in a small group.

Davis brought musicians into his band who were steeped in electronics. In summer 1968, he replaced Ron Carter—who did not feel comfortable using an electric bass—with young Czech bass player Miroslav Vitous and subsequently Englishman Dave Holland, who he spotted at Ronnie Scott's jazz club in London. "My interest was in finding an electronic bass player because of the sound it added to my band," insisted Davis (Davis 1989, 294). In September 1968, Miles hired Chick Corea (b. Armando Corea), a classically trained pianist who started with trumpeter Blue Mitchell and then drifted to the avant-garde. Along with Herbie Hancock, Corea added electric piano to the Miles album *Filles De Kilimanjaro*. After Hancock left to form his own band, Davis hired Austrian Joe Zawinul as a second keyboardist on organ and Fender Rhodes. "I heard Joe Zawinul playing electric piano on 'Mercy, Mercy, Mercy' with Cannonball Adderley, and I really liked the sound of the instrument and wanted it in my band," recalled Miles (Davis 1989, 294). When Tony Williams left to launch Lifetime, Davis turned to Chicago drummer Jack DeJohnette, who had briefly played with John Coltrane and members of the AACM. He also invited electric guitarist John McLaughlin to join the group. Keeping sax man Wayne Shorter, Miles had assembled an electric jazz band.

During late 1968 and early 1969, Miles took his outfit into the studio. With "In a Silent Way," written by Joe Zawinul, Davis "wanted to make the sound more like rock." Like rock bands, Miles spliced together bits of various takes to construct the album (also named *In a Silent Way*) rather than choose one complete take for each song on the album. He considered the song "a classic and the beginning of fusion" (Davis 1989, 296).

With a new record completed, the band toured for several months. In concert, Davis attached a wah-wah pedal to his "trumpet all the time so I could get closer to that voice Jimi had when he used a wah-wah on his guitar," explained Miles. "I had always played the trumpet like a guitar and the wah-wah just made the sound closer" (Davis 1989, 319).

Returning to New York, the electrified band gathered in the Columbia studio on Fifty-second Street and, for three days starting on August 19, 1969, recorded the jazz-rock breakthrough *Bitches Brew*. "Most rock musicians didn't know anything about music," reasoned Davis. "They didn't study it, couldn't play different styles—and don't even talk about reading music. But they were popular and sold a lot of records because they were giving the public a certain sound, what they wanted to hear." Given the sad state of rock, Miles concluded that "if they could do it—reach all those people and sell all those records without really knowing what they were doing—then I could do it, too, only better" (Davis 1989, 302).

At Columbia Records, Blood, Sweat & Tears and Chicago had blazed the jazz-rock fusion path before Davis. Organized in 1967 by guitarist/keyboard man Al Kooper (b. Alan Kuperschmid), Blood, Sweat & Tears generated a horn-based music, which featured jazz men such as trumpeter Randy Brecker and saxophonist Fred Lipsius. "When I first came to New York in 1967," intimated Brecker, "I joined the original Blood, Sweat & Tears. By then, jazz was already on the wane and you had to pay attention to pop and rock if you wanted to be part of a larger picture" (Myers 2013, 220). After other members forced Kooper out of the group in April 1968, the band recruited David Clayton-Thomas who added gritty, booming vocals to the jazz-rock mix for the top-selling *Blood, Sweat & Tears*. The group followed with two more chart toppers that featured Clayton-Thomas on vocals and jazz horn men such as saxophonist Joe Henderson and trumpeter Lew Soloff. Blood, Sweat & Tears, boasted drummer Bobby Colomby, will "make jazz part of our everyday culture" (Szatmary 2014, 215).

Chicago also mined the jazz-rock hybrid. In 1967, DePaul University classmates—guitarist Terry Kath, drummer Danny Seraphine, trombonist James Pankow, trumpeter Lee Loughnane, and saxophonist Walter Parazaider—founded the group. In April 1969, amid student revolts on campus, the band released a politically charged, jazz-rock album that included the voices of protesters at the 1968 Democratic National Convention and sold more than a million copies. By 1971, Chicago dispensed with radical politics and added a pop sensibility to achieve long-standing commercial success. The outfit reached the number-two position with *Chicago III* and, during the next four years, hit with five number-one albums. In 1970, trombonist James Pankow declared that "people are listening to better music in general. Rock 'n' roll is no longer 1-4-5; it's no longer simple music. It's becoming a legitimate music form" (McGrath and Quigley 1970, 2).

Columbia capitalized on the emerging buzz about jazz rock with *Bitches Brew*. Because Miles generally sold 60,000 copies of a record, Columbia president Clive Davis sought to push the trumpeter into a new sales bracket, where top producers sold a million platters. "He started talking to me about trying to reach this younger market and about changing," related Miles. "He suggested that the way for me to reach this new audience was to play music where they went, places like the Fillmore" (Davis 1989, 297–98).

LISTENING GUIDE 36

Miles Davis Band

"MILES RUNS THE VOODOO DOWN"

Ever the innovator, Miles Davis launched the fusion revolution with *Bitches Brew*, which included this song. He added electric instruments to the mix, added a few funk beats from Sly and the Family Stone, and focused on a rock rhythm to craft his entrée into fusion.

Recorded on August 20, 1969, "Miles Runs the Voodoo Down" included two electric pianos (Joe Zawinul on the left channel and Chick Corea on the right channel), John McLaughlin on electric guitar, two electric bassists (Harvey Brooks and Dave Holland), Wayne Shorter on soprano saxophone, two drummers (Don Alias on the left channel and Jack DeJohnette on the right), Bennie Maupin on bass clarinet, percussionist Jumma Santos, and, of course, Miles on trumpet. It was named by Miles in homage to Jimi Hendrix's "Voodoo Chile."

The tune featured a funky New Orleans rhythm. As drummer Don Alias told it, "Lenny [White] and Jack [De-Johnette] were playing and somehow things didn't jell. I had been practicing this drum rhythm while I was in New Orleans for Mardi Gras. I'm sitting there thinking, 'I've got the perfect rhythm for this tune,'" he continued. On the instruction of Davis, Alias sat at White's drum kit and played the rhythm, which Miles liked. "That's how I ended up being one of the drum set players on 'Miles Runs the Voodoo Down,'" Alias explained (Belden 1998, 125).

Miles plays on a single modal scale throughout the song with no chord progression. He adds variety to the tune by his dynamics (changes in volume) and his shift from a low to a high pitch or register on his horn. Like other fusion bands, which rely on electronic effects, Miles liberally makes use of echo on his trumpet in several key places.

Columbia, hoping to make Davis a pop star, issued the song as a single, which clocked in at the radio-friendly 2:49 and deleted saxophonist Wayne Shorter, who played on the extended version. The single version of the song, which also deleted solos by McLaughlin and Zawinul, has been analyzed below.

Personnel: Miles Davis (trumpet), Bennie Maupin (bass clarinet), Chick Corea and Joe Zawinul (electric pianos), John McLaughlin (electric guitar), Harvey Brooks and Dave Holland (electric basses), Don Alias and Jack DeJohnette (drums), and Jumma Santos, referred to as Jim Riley (congas and shaker).

0:00–0:04	Drummer Don Alias enters to establish a highly syncopated, basic groove.
0:05–0:13	Bassist Harvey Brooks softly complements Alias with a sustained note. Throughout the song Alias and Brooks supply its basic groove.
0:14–0:15	McLaughlin enters powerfully on electric guitar with a sustained note so typical of the funk style. A shaker plays softly in the background and will continue in several places throughout the song.
0:16–0:19	The guitarist plays a brief three-note pattern in the groove.
0:20	The drummer rolls his cymbal to the rhythm.
0:21–0:23	The second drummer, Jack DeJohnette, reinforces the groove, and McLaughlin hits several notes.
0:24	Bennie Maupin's bass clarinet enters to solidify the heavy-bass bottom of the groove.
0:27–0:33	McLaughlin plays a one-note riff four times with an embellishment on the last repetition.
0:34–0:38	Miles enters loudly and dramatically on a relatively low note, which he sustains and then slowly bends up and down in a quaver like a blues musician. He adds echo to enhance the effect.

0:39–0:49	Miles plays some well-chosen notes at a slow tempo mostly in a low register to the basic groove. He will use this motif as the main theme of his solo. At the end of the passage, Maupin plays a fast trill on his bass clarinet and Dave Holland enters (0:42) with a second bass to add depth to the groove. Maupin periodically contributes his trill-like pattern throughout the song.
0:50–0:53	The electric guitar plays a cluster of notes in response to Miles as the groove continues.
0:54–1:08	Miles hits a note in the high register and continues to solo in the high end of the horn by using a variant of the same theme as he stated in 0:34. He then switches to the middle register and finally to the low register. In the process, he dynamically plays softer and softer until he trails off by the end of this passage.
1:09	McLaughlin again hits a chord to signal a change.
1:10–1:13	Miles begins to play in the middle register of the horn with another improvisation around the main theme.
1:14–1:18	Miles lowers the pitch and volume of a note, which he sustains and bends to the groove.
1:19–1:25	Davis plays the same note, and then two others in an eight-note pattern in an almost hushed manner as the groove persists.
1:26–1:28	Miles returns to the main theme in a high register and sustains a note.
1:29–1:41	Miles continues his solo around the main theme as the electric pianos provide clusters of notes for support.
1:42–1:45	The groove continues without Miles.
1:46–2:00	Miles reenters with a solo in the upper range of his horn, overblowing as he begins. Again, he states the main theme. As he progresses, he lowers his tone until he reaches the lower end of the trumpet range and slides across notes before he stops. The band gets louder as they back Miles.
2:01–2:02	The groove temporarily proceeds without Miles.
2:03–2:04	Davis reenters in the middle register as he rapidly and repeatedly goes back and forth between a note to give the passage a quick motion. The technique is called tremolo.
2:05–2:06	The groove continues as Miles briefly pauses. These pauses, present throughout Miles's solo, indicate a rhythmic complexity, which Miles overlays on the basic funk groove.
2:07–2:16	After a high-pitch burst of six notes, Davis continues to rapidly and repeatedly play the same note as above but then uses tremolo in different pitches to ascend the scale and then descend the scale until he reaches the original note. Near the end of this section, an electric piano hits a cluster of notes to provide a slightly dissonant sound.
2:17–2:25	Davis returns to the main theme with louder backing from his band.
2:26–2:39	Miles solos with a flurry of notes, which ascend and then descend the scale.
2:40–2:47	Davis begins another variant of the main theme in the high register and then sustains a note, which he bends downward to finish this shortened version of the song.

The Fillmore Auditorium in the Haight-Ashbury District of San Francisco represented the epicenter of the sixties hippie subculture. Previously it had been a theater, which presented jazz and R&B acts such as Ray Charles. In July 1966, the Fillmore was reopened by entrepreneur Bill Graham (b. Wulf Wolodia Grajonca), a Holocaust survivor and Korean War veteran who settled in San Francisco, where he booked local rock bands such as the Grateful Dead. The venue also presented a wide spectrum of music including jazz acts ranging from Ornette Coleman to the big bands of Count Basie, Woody Herman, and Buddy Rich. In March 1968, the Fillmore East opened in New York City to complement the West Coast auditorium.

In the wake of *Bitches Brew*, Miles Davis presented his electric band at both Fillmore venues. On March 6 and 7, 1970, at the Fillmore East, Miles performed alongside blues rocker Steve Miller and electric singer-songwriter Neil Young. The next month, Miles appeared at the Fillmore in San Francisco on a bill with the Grateful Dead. "That was an eye-opening concert for me, because there were about five thousand people there that night, mostly young, white hippies, and they hadn't hardly heard of me if they had heard of me at all," recalled Miles. "After a while, they got quiet and really got into the music. I played a little something like *Sketches of Spain* and then we went into the *Bitches Brew* shit and that really blew them out" (Davis 1989, 300–1). Within a year, the trumpeter's group returned twice to the Fillmore West and one more time to the East Coast venue before both closed. "Those gigs I did for Bill [Graham] during this time were good for expanding my audience," concluded Davis. "We were playing to all kinds of different people" (301).

Attracting an expanded audience, Miles Davis reached a commercial apex. *Bitches Brew*, released on March 30, 1970, hit number thirty-five on *Billboard*, the best chart success of Miles's career, and sold more than two million copies. By incorporating electric instrumentation, Miles had again made jazz important to the masses of young music fans.

The Sobering Seventies

As the sixties melted into the seventies, youth seemed ready for the instrumental jazz of Miles Davis. Facing government guns and grim economic prospects, they turned from a rebellious, pounding acid rock to more sedate, complex, and apolitical music.

In early May 1970, the optimism of youth turned into a somber reality, when government troops gunned down students at Kent State. On May 2, shortly after President Richard Nixon announced the American invasion of Cambodia, students at Kent State University in Ohio assaulted police cars with bottles, broke store windows, and set trees on fire. Within two days, activists faced nine hundred National Guardsmen armed with M-1 rifles, submachine guns, and tear gas. On May 4, the third day of rioting, a group of students were cornered on a hill by sixteen Guardsmen who, without warning, pointed their guns at them and fired thirty-five rounds point blank into the helpless crowd. "It's about time we showed the bastards who's in charge," shouted one Guardsman. At the end of the massacre, four students had been killed and nine others had been wounded. "My God! My God! They're killing us," cried one Kent State freshman ("My God!" 1970, 32).

A few days after the killings at Kent State, African-American students at Jackson State College in Jackson, Mississippi, rioted. On the evening of Thursday, May 14, after hearing rumors that civil-rights leader Charles Evers had been killed, one hundred protesters gathered on Lynch Street and overturned cars. They confronted more than seventy-five police officers who advanced to within fifty feet of

Alexander Hall, suddenly fired 140 shots into the building, and killed two students and wounded twelve others. Though an FBI committee found no rationale for the gunfire, none of the policemen ever faced charges.

Colleges and universities across the nation erupted in violence after the murders at Kent State and Jackson State. Students targeted the ROTC buildings at the state universities of Utah, Nebraska, and Idaho; students at the University of California, Berkeley campus rioted for three weeks; and protesters at the University of Wisconsin took over the Army Mathematics Research Center and firebombed twenty buildings. Hundreds of colleges and universities closed for the remainder of the academic year. During May and June 1970 protests, which two-thirds of all students supported, mayhem exploded on more than five hundred college campuses.

After going home for the summer, many students felt powerless. Said one youth at the post–Kent State demonstration in Washington, DC: "The people here understand that we are surrounded by fully armed troops and that if we start anything, we'd be destroyed" ("Rebellion of the Campus" 1970, 29). Another activist believed that the government "had put up with us protesting, marching in the streets, but now they were just going to kill us" (Peck 1985, 240). "For me it was the turning point," insisted a student at Kent State. "Just shoot a few and it changed the whole world. Everybody straightened up and went home" (Reynolds 2009, 42).

An economic downturn created further anxiety. In 1969, US unemployment rose from 3.5 percent to 6.2 percent. The same year, inflation jumped to nearly 6 percent. Throughout the country, fear of a recession seized Americans who previously had experienced a near unprecedented prosperity.

Music reflected the fearful and tentative mood of youth who deserted hard-driving rock for more cerebral jazz rock. "The fading out of ear-numbing, mind-blowing acid rock [and metal]," *Time* reported in early 1971, "is related to the softening of the youth revolution. Its decline is variously viewed as a symptom of either progress toward harmony and thoughtfulness or a tragic slide from activist rage to a mode of 'enlightened apathy'" ("James Taylor" 1971, 45). "The times you live in have to do with what you produce," maintained drummer Tony Williams, who helped pioneer jazz-rock fusion. "The '70s for a lot of people were a reaction to the '60s" (Milkowski 1998, 147).

The Offspring of Miles: Fusion Explodes on the Scene

Several members of the *Bitches Brew* band followed in the footsteps of their leader by founding jazz-rock groups. Chick Corea compared Miles to a father who inspired "the rest of the family, and they would try to become like him" (Kart 1969, 21). "It was like he was stirring a big, black pot of notes and it stands as the foundation of a lot of what's going on right now," Billy Cobham, an uncredited drummer on *Bitches Brew*, explained about Miles (Smith 1975a, 13).

Many Davis disciples represented a new, young generation of jazz players. In mid-August 1969, when the band recorded *Bitches Brew*, most members who congregated around the forty-three-year-old Davis had not yet celebrated their thirtieth birthday. At nineteen, drummer Lenny White was the youngest of the group. Other musicians on the record included twenty-three-year-old Dave Holland; bassist Harvey Brooks and drummer Billy Cobham at twenty-five; guitarist John McLaughlin and drummer Jack DeJohnette at twenty-seven; and pianist Chick Corea and reed man Bennie Maupin at twenty-eight. Only saxophonist Wayne

Shorter at thirty-five, and thirty-seven-year-old pianist/composer Joe Zawinul, approached the age of the leader.

Coming of age during the fifties and sixties, Davis group members had a background in rock and roll to supplement a jazz base. Brooks (b. Harvey Goldstein) had played with Bob Dylan when he first turned on an electric guitar at the Newport Folk Festival in 1965, was a founding member of the band Electric Flag, and backed the Doors in the studio. John McLaughlin began his career with such British blues-rockers as the Graham Bond Organization and Alexis Korner. "We love the Beatles but we also love Coltrane," explained Larry Coryell, a Hendrix enthusiast and one of the few fusion pioneers who did not appear on *Bitches Brew*. "We love the Rolling Stones, but we also love Miles. I felt that it was only a matter of time before somebody who liked [drummer] Elvin Jones could also like [Beatle] George Harrison," he recalled (Milkowski 1998, 167; Coryell and Friedman 1978, 112).

Powerful drummer Tony Williams, who split with Miles less than a year before *Bitches Brew* to establish the band, Lifetime, described his dual allegiance to jazz and rock. "For a long time I realized that I had been living in two worlds," he remembered. "I was living in one world where I was making friends in grammar school and in high school, going to parties with them, listening to rock and hanging out on corners. And then I got a chance to go out with my father and play [jazz]" (Woods 1970, 18). Williams played with Cecil Taylor, Eric Dolphy, Sam Rivers, and Jackie McLean. Just before joining Miles, the young drum whiz "started hearing a lot of electricity. The first thing I remember," he recalled, "was Jimi Hendrix's first record, and the sound of it, with all that electricity. That started to excite me, and I wanted to hear more of that. My drumming became more aggressive and that was the direction I wanted to follow. The energy of the music is happening, but it's rock and roll, and because I'm a drummer, I'm attracted more to [rock's] power kind of drumming, and the emotional kind of drumming" (Fellezs 2008, 19, 2).

Innovative drummer Tony Williams. *Photograph courtesy of Brian McMillen*

Guitarist Larry Coryell. *Photograph courtesy of Brian McMillen*

Like the *Bitches Brew* group, most Davis sidemen who formed bands created interracial outfits. Miles always chose band members on the basis of talent and suitability, not race. In 1958, when he hired white piano player Bill Evans, "many blacks felt that since I had the top small group in jazz and was paying the most money that I should have a black piano player. I don't go for that kind of shit," exploded Miles. "I have always just wanted the best players in my group and I don't care whether they're black, white, blue, red or yellow. As long as they can play what I want, that's it" (Davis 1989, 231).

The bands that sprouted from *Bitches Brew* likewise mixed African Americans and whites, some of whom came from Europe. In 1970, two white former Davis sidemen who had been raised in Europe—keyboardist Joe Zawinul and Miroslav Vitous—joined with two African Americans—ex-Miles saxophonist Wayne Shorter and drummer Alphonse Mouzon—to found Weather Report. The next year, white British guitarist John McLaughlin established the Mahavishnu Orchestra and chose Irish-born bassist Rick Laird, Czech-born keyboardist Jan Hammer, white violinist Jerry Goodman, and African-American drummer Billy Cobham.

In 1972, the Italian/Spanish Chick Corea formed Return to Forever. After briefly exploring Latin music, the group turned to jazz rock with a racially integrated lineup. On *Hymn of the Seventh Galaxy*, the leader tapped African-American bassist Stanley Clarke, who "as a kid, grew up listening to Hendrix, James Brown, Miles Davis, John Coltrane" (Woodard 1991, 31). He swapped white drummer Steve Gadd for African-American Lenny White, when Gadd decided not to tour. To expand his sound, Corea added white guitarist Bill Connors. After Connors's departure, Corea selected white guitar man Al Di Meola, then a student at the Berklee College of Music who revered the Beatles.

In 1973, Larry Coryell established The Eleventh House. For the racially integrated unit, he chose African-American drummer Alphonse Mouzon, who had recently left Weather Report, along with whites Mike Mandel on keyboards and bassist Danny Trifan. He also tapped white trumpeter Randy Brecker who had played in Blood, Sweat & Tears and Dreams, an early fusion group.

The newly invented modular synthesizer distinguished most jazz-rock units from other jazz bands. In 1963, Robert Moog and Don Buchla developed the synthesizer simultaneously. Demonstrated by Moog the next year at the Audio Engineering Society, the original synthesizer consisted of several modular or subdivided circuits that emitted electrical signals, which controlled pitch, timbre, and amplitude. By patching the circuits in different arrangements, the synthesizer changed the tone, resonance, and modulation of the music to arrive at an orchestral array of sounds.

Musicians quickly adopted the synthesizer. By 1967, such diverse rock bands as the Monkees, the Doors, the Rolling Stones, and the Beatles used the synthesizer on top-selling albums. By 1970, when Robert Moog introduced a more affordable, solid-state, and portable Minimoog that no longer needed patch cords to function fully, the device became widespread in jazz.

Joe Zawinul had embraced the synthesizer by the second Weather Report album. On *I Sing the Body Electric* (1972), he introduced the electronic instrument to replicate the orchestral sounds that Miles approximated in his music. The keyboardist felt that the synthesizer "replaced all the many, many instruments you find, for instance, in a symphony orchestra, which a small group of musicians (for example, a quintet like Weather Report) could never accomplish before. It produces an incredibly full and versatile sound," asserted Zawinul. "It's like a dream world. I've heard orchestra sounds my entire life, and now I can do it myself because of a machine," he raved (Coryell and Friedman 1978, 187; Lyons 1983, 288).

Other jazz-rock artists experimented with the synthesizer. On *Birds of Fire* (1973), John McLaughlin expanded the sounds of the Mahavishnu Orchestra with the Moog played by keyboardist Jan Hammer. "Once you get down to serious business with the synthesizer, you realize that the possibilities are endless," enthused Hammer (Coryell and Friedman 1978, 157). The next year, Larry Coryell added the synthesizer of Mike Mandel to the electric mix of The Eleventh House. In 1975, Chick Corea supplemented Return to Forever with the synthesizer, which was used by both himself and Stanley Clarke. "I like the synthesizers because I like having the ability to bend a note, modulate a tone, and do things with timbres that the piano doesn't offer," Corea contended (Lyons 1983, 266). "I feel that synthesizers are playing a major role in most modern music," insisted the group's guitarist Al Di Meola (Coryell and Friedman 1978, 116).

The synthesizer-enhanced sound of fusion heralded a new era for many young players. "Technology had progressed and when it progresses there's a point where new musics can be formed," asserted drummer Lenny White, who for three years assumed drum duties for Return to Forever. "Music is a reflection of the times," he reasoned. "Now there's a new kind of music where you improvise more, like the traditional jazz music, but you use different instruments" (Coryell and Friedman 1978, 85).

The new fusion bands, following in the footsteps of Miles Davis, quickly obtained recording contracts. "After we recorded *Bitches Brew*," mentioned Joe Zawinul, "Columbia was immediately interested in [Weather Report]" (Coryell and Friedman 1978, 187) and signed the group as well as the Mahavishnu Orchestra and Return to Forever.

After witnessing the commercial success of *Bitches Brew*, young fusion artists sought mass appeal. Saxophonist Joe Farrell, who played with Return to Forever, "aimed at reaching a wider audience. You're still playing the same way, but instead of playing to thirty people in a club, you're reaching thirty-five hundred" (Coryell and Friedman 1978, 239). "I had felt that it was really very possible to make music that had a very high quality to it, and actually communicate it broadly to many people," echoed Chick Corea. "That was my goal with [Return to Forever]" (Rosen 1993, 42).

Most fusion players wanted to enjoy the financial rewards that large audiences brought. "When I hear people talk about commercialism versus artistic something, it sort of makes me think that there is possibly some sort of weird computation behind that," snipped electric bassist Stanley Clarke, who for four years performed in Return to Forever before starting his own band. "I sell records, so my music is commercial. Also, my music has a lot of artistic integrity to it" (Coryell and Friedman

LISTENING GUIDE 37

Mahavishnu Orchestra with John McLaughlin

"BIRDS OF FIRE"

In 1971, when John McLaughlin left Miles Davis and established the Mahavishnu Orchestra, he abandoned any leanings toward funk and launched an all-out jazz-rock attack. He recruited electric bassist Rick Laird, electric violinist Jerry Goodman, drummer Billy Cobham, and Jan Hammer on the synthesizer/Moog.

On "Birds of Fire," the lead track to his second album issued on January 3, 1973, he generates a blistering, driving attack, which combines jazz improvisation and variable time signatures with a rock sensibility. The guitarist, an avid fan of Jimi Hendrix, used a Gibson EDS-1275 double-necked guitar, which had six-string and twelve-string fret boards to give him more possibilities on the instrument.

The song was never issued as a single but appeared as the first track on the album of the same name, which hit number fifteen on the chart to become McLaughlin's most commercially successful LP. Generally, it has a time signature of 18/8 that has been derived from a *tala* in the Indian classical tradition. The title came from a poem, "Revelation," by Indian religious leader Sri Chinmoy, who taught meditation and instructed McLaughlin.

Personnel: John McLaughlin (guitar), Rick Laird (bass), Jerry Goodman (electric violin), Jan Hammer (keyboards/synthesizer), and Billy Cobham (drums).

0:00–0:17	A gong rings three times at low volume to start the song and establish an Eastern tone.
0:18–0:41	McLaughlin picks out a riff repeatedly with the gong continuing in the background. Bassist Laird gives backing with bass to establish a theme for the song. As McLaughlin and Laird play, the volume gets louder.
0:42–0:51	Goodman enters on electric violin and replicates the theme started by Laird, increasing the volume dramatically.
0:52	Cobham, who played with Miles Davis on *Bitches Brew*, unleashes a powerful drum pattern to complement the rhythm. The gong, which began as a light, almost delicate sound, now crashes with the increased volume in a dynamically interesting introduction.
0:53–1:04	The band continues with the increasingly loud groove.
1:05–1:25	In a call-and-response with himself, McLaughlin unleashes a powerful riff, then repeats it in a lower pitch and sustains the final note. He restates this riff twice. Backed by the band, the riff provides a driving, propulsive sensation to the song.
1:26–1:32	McLaughlin repeats a blinding-speed, two-note riff four times, using sustain to innovatively change the rhythm.
1:33–1:39	McLaughlin changes to a fast four-note riff, which he expertly varies by sustain, brief pauses, and pitch increases.
1:40–1:41	McLaughlin screams with the guitar by repeatedly hitting a note, sustaining it, and then bending the note up the fretboard.
1:42–1:48	McLaughlin descends the scale with a series of notes.
1:49–1:57	Amazingly, the guitarist increases the tempo by rapidly repeating three notes until he hits a high note and sustains and bends it.

1:58–2:00	McLaughlin again cries with his guitar as he did at 1:40.
2:01–2:08	The guitarist plays a variant of the main theme interspersed by high-pitched piercing screams on the guitar.
2:09–2:18	As the intensity increases, McLaughlin screams with his guitar repeatedly, only interrupted by a few notes of the main theme.
2:19–2:46	McLaughlin turns to the main riff, which he established beginning in 1:05.
2:47–2:59	In a quick series of ascending notes, the guitarist begins another pattern that ascends and then descends in pitch. Cymbal crashes by Cobham near the end of this passage signal a change.
3:00–3:02	The synthesizer provides several note clusters.
3:03–3:11	The electric violin, the bass, and other members of the band state the theme of the song without McLaughlin.
3:12–3:16	Jan Hammer on synthesizer, who up to this point has played fills behind McLaughlin, takes center stage with a solo, which approximates McLaughlin's improvisation. At the end of this section, he bends a note much like McLaughlin did on guitar.
3:17–3:30	Hammer plays a four-note riff ten times and then improvises around it.
3:31–3:34	On synthesizer, Hammer replicates the screams on guitar, which McLaughlin produced, that ping-pong back and forth by the end of the passage.
3:35–3:42	Hammer plays a rapid series of ascending notes until he drops back to mid-range.
3:43–4:00	The synthesizer rapidly repeats four high-pitched notes in tremolo fashion, varying the rhythm by adding a few notes between the four-note riff. Behind Hammer, Cobham provides muscular drumming.
4:01–4:10	More simulated screams from the synthesizer.
4:11–4:39	An energetic restatement of the main theme by the band that moves rapidly upward at the end with McLaughlin in the lead.
4:40–4:52	Return to the pattern that began at 2:47.
4:53–5:39	Return to the main theme with the guitar, violin, and bass in the lead backed by Cobham's pounding drums and crashing cymbals, which signal an end to each statement of the theme. Hammer provides a riff behind the theme. The band fades out while playing the theme.

1978, 8). Larry Coryell, putting it bluntly, hoped "to be a star and make a lot of money. I had a large family and a lot of debts to pay off" (Stamataky 1972, 18).

Many fusion outfits scaled the *Billboard* chart. In 1973, the Mahavishu Orchestra reached number fifteen with *Birds of Fire*. The same year, drummer Billy Cobham cracked the Top Thirty and topped the jazz chart with *Spectrum*. He nearly replicated his success with two follow-ups. In 1974, Return to Forever neared the Top Thirty with *Where Have I Known You Before,* and Weather Report landed in the Top Fifty with *Mysterious Traveller.* The next year, electric bassist Stanley Clarke hit the chart with *Journey to Love* with help from rock-guitar master Jeff Beck. Just as Miles had done with *Bitches Brew,* the first generation of fusion bands wrenched jazz from a largely specialty market and took it to a broad-based audience.

Jazz-Funk Fusion

As the seventies progressed, many young fusion artists inserted a funk element into the jazz-rock hybrid. Led by Miles Davis, they incorporated a hard, insistent funk into their music to push the funky texture of soul jazz to a new level.

James Brown unleashed funk on the world. In late 1964, after mixing his gospel roots with spirited rhythm and blues, Brown edged toward a new genre that became known as "funk" with the single "Out of Sight." On the track, Brown related, "you can hear the band and me start to move in a whole other direction rhythmically. The horns, the guitars, the vocals, everything was starting to be used to establish all kinds of rhythms at once . . . I was trying to get every aspect of the production to contribute to the rhythmic patterns" (Brown 1986, 149).

The next year, Brown perfected a rhythm-heavy style. "I emphasized the beat, not the melody, understand?" maintained Brown. "Heat the beat, and the rest'll turn sweat." Unlike R&B artists who accented the second and fourth beats, Brown used powerful, insistent bass-guitar figures to accentuate the first beat of a four-beat measure. "I changed the upbeat to the downbeat," he explained, "Simple as that, really" (Rose 1990, 59). To accompany and embellish the downbeat, Brown delivered his cries and screams over the staccato, punchy "rhythm hits" of horns to create an intense, one-chord groove. He generated a new sound that harkened back to the polyrhythms of Africa and the hollers in the cotton fields.

If James Brown perfected funk, Sly Stone (b. Sylvester Stewart) disseminated it to the white mainstream by merging funk with rock and roll. In November 1966, Stewart formed the racially diverse and gender-integrated Sly and the Family Stone, which took psychedelic funk to the top of the charts. In 1968, the band hit with "Everyday People." During the next year, the group scored with "Hot Fun in the Summertime," "Thank You (Falettinme Be Mice Elf Agin)," and the Top Ten album *Stand!* "It was Sly who first cracked the barrier between black-and-white rock," maintained George Clinton, a former staff songwriter for Motown and doo-wopper who turned to funk with the groups Parliament and Funkadelic.

Miles Davis, ever the innovator, incorporated funk into his sound. After *Bitches Brew,* "I was moving closer to the funk groove in my head," he recollected. "I was getting interested in seeing the black sound develop and that's where my head was moving toward, more rhythmic stuff, more funk rather than white rock," he continued. "I had met Sly and he had given me one of his albums." By 1972, Miles changed directions. "It was with Sly Stone and James Brown in mind that I went into the studio in June 1972 to record *On the Corner,*" he revealed. "It was actually a combination of some of the concepts of [English composer] Paul Buckmaster, Sly Stone, James Brown, and [German composer Karlheinz] Stockhausen, some of the concepts I had absorbed from Ornette's music, as well as my own" (Davis 1989, 320–1).

To fully integrate funk, Miles "decided to go electric all the way." He enlisted the help of electric guitarist John McLaughlin, organist/synthesizer player Harold Williams, the electric piano of Herbie Hancock, the Fender Rhodes of Chick Corea, electric bassist Michael Henderson, and even the electric sitar of Collin Walcott.

"I had to play my trumpet against that," Davis explained. "So then I got an amplifier hook-up with a microphone on my trumpet. That's how the groove thing got started with me" (Davis 1989, 323).

Miles hoped to further expand his audience with the updated sound. "I really made an effort to get my music over to young black people," Miles asserted. "They are the ones who buy records and come to concerts, and I had started thinking about building a new audience for the future" (Davis 1989, 324).

Weather Report followed Miles into jazz-funk territory. By its third release, *Sweetnighter* (1973), the band changed from atmospheric waves of improvisation to a funky groove. "*Sweetnighter* was a kind of getting down," commented saxophonist Wayne Shorter. "We sort of half-intentionally wanted to stay away from the ethereal. We've seen a lot of sitting down in nightclubs," he continued. "The third album was more, y'know, let's see some people dance. As soon as it came out, we started to see people dance" (Logan 1974, 38). The next year, the group hired ex-Sly drummer Greg Errico for a tour to promote *Sweetnighter*. On the next record, *Mysterious Traveller*, Weather Report replaced founding bassist Miroslav Vitous with the funkier Alphonse Johnson. By *Tale Spinnin'*, the band became a full-fledged, jazz-funk outfit.

Other fusion artists went in a funky direction. Between stints with Weather Report and The Eleventh House, drummer Alphonse Mouzon waxed chunks of funk such as *Funky Snakefoot* (1973). He asserted that "being from the South, I dig funk. What I'm trying to do is combine the contemporary sound with funk" (Hohman 1975, 16). During the mid-seventies, Michael and Randy Brecker released several albums, which Randy considered to be "funk stuff" (Milkowski 1992, 17). By 1975, Return to Forever turned at least partially to funk with *No Mystery*, and Billy Cobham released *A Funkyhide of Sings*. "It's my interpretation of playing some R&B with a lot of electronics," the drummer explained. "I'll give them a couple of 1-4-5 chords for ten minutes with a beat that is always in the same place, and everybody can dance to it" (Smith 1975a, 40). Bassist Stanley Clarke embraced funk on his records, which included such electric keyboardists as Chick Corea, George Duke, and Jan Hammer and electric guitarists Jeff Beck and John McLaughlin. In 1976, his *School Days* neared the Top Thirty.

The Crusaders exemplified the transition from hard bop to funk. In 1958, four teenagers from Houston—pianist Joe Sample, Wilton Felder on sax, Wayne Henderson on trombone, and drummer Nesbert "Stix" Hooper—moved to Los Angeles. In 1961, the four teens, called the Jazz Crusaders, signed with Pacific Jazz Records and released a hard-bop paean to the civil-rights movement, *Freedom Sound*. Two years later, Sample journeyed to New York City, where he "found all these jazz players were dressing in African clothing and many of them were changing their names to African names or Muslim names. The new hip term for this style was 'out to lunch.' I just thought, 'this is stupid, man.' Free jazz went against almost everything that I thought of as good about jazz," he maintained. Rather than shift to a freer approach, the quartet continued along the hard-bop route (Smith 2013).

In 1971, the group switched styles. The band shortened its name to the Crusaders and largely abandoned bop for a blues-based fusion. "The music that was inside us came from our community, from what we heard in the Fifth Ward [in Houston], what we heard in our little Creole church," related Joe Sample. "When we were writing songs for *Pass the Plate* [1971], we were very conscious of how much of this is jazz, how much comes from our knowledge of classical music and blues. It was a mixture" (Smith 2013).

Throughout the seventies, the band drifted increasingly toward funk and commercial success. In 1972, it signed to Blue Thumb Records and progressively relied on the electronic keyboards of Joe Sample and electric guitarist Larry Carlton for a funky sound. "Why am I holding back who I am? I am funky," insisted Sample. "When we played funky, it was *really* funky" (Zimmerman 2008, 68). Armed with funk, the band approached the Top Thirty with *Southern Comfort* (1974).

Donald Byrd (b. Donaldson Toussaint L'Ouverture Byrd II) also transitioned to funk. The Detroit-born trumpeter started his career as a hard-bopper. After a stint in the service and studies at Wayne State University and the Manhattan School of Music, he accompanied such hard boppers as Kenny Clarke, Cannonball Adderley, and Jackie McLean. In August 1955, he recorded his debut as a leader, *Byrd-Jazz*. In April 1956, the trumpeter joined Art Blakey's Jazz Messengers for a two-year stretch. After backing several artists on Blue Note, Byrd signed a contract with the label and, beginning in December 1958, recorded more than a dozen hard-bop albums.

Amid the trend toward electric instrumentation in jazz, Byrd moved to a funk-jazz fusion. In 1970, he hired Duke Pearson on electric piano. Three years later, the trumpeter enticed Crusaders Joe Sample and bassist Wilton Felder as well as Freddie Perren on synthesizer to appear on *Black Byrd*, which cracked the Top 100 on the pop chart. "People like James Brown," he asserted, "are much more meaningful to me, in my life, than a lot of so-called very big historical jazz figures." During the next few years, Byrd dished out several funky offerings such as *Street Lady* and *Stepping into Tomorrow* (Feather 1980, 104).

Grant Green also converted to funk. The St. Louis–born guitarist, idolizing Charlie Parker, first adopted bop. In late 1960, when he signed with Blue Note Records, Green crafted a straight-ahead hard-bop session. Within a few months, after sit-ins disrupted lunch counters across the country, Grant unleashed a bluesy, sanctified soul jazz. In 1961, he recorded with Hammond organists, including Big John Patton, Roosevelt "Baby Face" Willette, and Brother Jack McDuff, on such selections as "Soul Walk," "Sanctified," and "Soul Meetin'." The next year, he delivered *Feelin' the Spirit*, which consisted of jazz interpretations of spirituals such as "Go Down Moses" and "Joshua Fit de Battle of Jericho." "Many of his compositions have their origin in blues or gospel," commented jazz writer Joe Goldberg. "One of his favorite instrumental techniques is likewise one encountered vocally in Negro church music: the repetition of a single, often simple melodic phrase over and over again with gathering intensity" (Goldberg 1963).

During the late sixties, Green incorporated funk into his sanctified sound. "He used to wake me up and tell me, 'I want you to hear something. Listen to this,'" recalled Thomas Basir, a drummer who performed with Green and roomed with him. "And it would be somebody else's record, especially James Brown. IIe liked James Brown and the P-Funk [Parliament-Funkadelic of George Clinton], too. . . . We listened to all the funk groups, every last one of them" (Green 1999, 130). By August 1970, Green recorded the funky "Sookie Sookie," written by soul men Don Covay and Steve Cropper. Two years later, he released the unadulterated jazz-funk of *Live at the Lighthouse*.

Herbie Hancock scored the biggest commercial success with jazz funk. After dissolving the avant-garde group Mwandishi, Hancock underwent a dramatic shift. As he chanted in a daily Buddhist ritual, he heard the Sly Stone song, "Thank You (Falettinme Be Mice Elf Agin)," "ringing in my ears as I chanted! That's the moment I decided to start a funk band," he exclaimed (Hancock 2014, 173). "It was time to funk out" (174). To build a new band, Herbie recruited reed man Bennie Maupin, percussionists Harvey Mason and Bill Summers, and bassist Paul Jackson. He pledged to "take on playing synthesizers myself, so they would definitely be part of our new sound" and prototyped the Arp Odyssey and Pro-Soloist models (175). He called the band the Headhunters.

The Headhunters blended jazz with funk. As Hancock explained it, "our melodies had a sense of familiarity, so even though the band was stretching, the listeners didn't have to. We played around with harmonies and rhythms, but the untrained ear could still follow the music" (Hancock 2014, 178). "We were able to create an instrumental palette, a combination of jazz and funk with some very specific rhythmic elements that people could feel," added Bennie Maupin (183). When the band appeared in clubs, related Hancock, "everybody just flipped out! People were dancing, laughing, and having fun, just completely letting loose as we played. It was a party, and people loved the groove" (179).

Hancock's new funky direction generated a commercial sensation. The crowds and venues for the music "were much bigger, and they weren't necessarily jazz fans," recalled Hancock. "We were a jazz-funk outfit now, and I was stepping out from the piano to play giant synthesizers" (Hancock 2014, 183). In October 1973, the group released its first, self-titled album, which sold seventy-eight thousand copies in the first week. When the funksters headlined a sold-out show with the rock group Santana, band manager David Rubinson told Hancock, "Herbie, you have a big hit record now. They're here to see *you*." The pianist felt that "it really was like a dream" (182). Within six months, *Head Hunters* reached number thirteen on the pop chart and, by the end of the decade, registered sales of a million, making it one of the bestselling jazz records of all time. The next year, the band followed with the equally successful *Thrust*.

In 1972, Sonny Rollins released the funkified *Sonny Rollins' Next Album* after a six-year layoff. He explained the new fascination with a funk-jazz fusion: "The fact that Donald Byrd or Miles or Herbie Hancock were doing it—well, to me they were just trying to play where the energy at that time was. That was what I was into. It would have been ridiculous for me to play [like] the straight-ahead guys. They had reached a dead end. Everything they played was predictable. I really do enjoy playing funk," he gushed. "I like the freedom. You see, it's an easier beat to play with" (Nisenson 2000, 193). By the mid-seventies, jazz funk had arrived.

Smooth Jazz in a Declining Economy

During the seventies and eighties, hard times afflicted many Americans. When the Vietnam War drew to a close and officially ended on April 30, 1975, the American economy descended into a free fall. Unemployment escalated from an annual low point of 3.5 percent in 1969 to 8.5 percent in 1975 and, in December 1982, reached a high-point of 10.8 percent. At the same time, inflation rose precipitously from a low 1.6 percent in 1965 to 11.1 percent in 1974, and an even higher 13.5 percent in 1980.

The grim economic outlook especially affected the seventy-six million baby boomers who had been born between 1946 and 1964. In 1982, of the age cohort between 18 and 19, more than 22 percent could not find jobs. Slightly older boomers aged from 20 to 24 faced a 15 percent unemployment rate. The boomers in the 25-to-29 age bracket experienced 11 percent unemployment. Of the oldest boomer group, aged 30 to 34, nearly 10 percent could not find jobs. Except for teens, all other age groups had a less than 10 percent unemployment rate, and the parents of the boomers had less than a 5 percent jobless rate. Without work and facing higher prices for most purchases, baby-boom Americans needed music that soothed their nerves rather than jangling them.

Creed Taylor helped comfort baby boomers with smooth jazz. Taylor had a long history in the music business, including jobs at Bethlehem and ABC-Paramount Records. In 1962, at Verve Records, he introduced the bossa nova craze to the United

States by recording the Charlie Byrd/Stan Getz collaboration, *Jazz Samba*, and, the next year, releasing "The Girl from Ipanema," a collaboration by Getz, Brazilian songwriter-guitarist João Gilberto, and singer Astrud Gilberto.

In 1967, Creed formed a new jazz label, CTI, short for Creed Taylor Incorporated, to make jazz more palatable to a broader audience. To appeal to the masses, Taylor fused jazz with pop material. "Pop music is the music of the moment," he reasoned. "If you can use it as a vehicle for what you're doing, then a lot of songs can be turned around. That was my thinking at CTI." He strove for jazz "without the imposition of elongated passages" (Myers 2013, 184).

Creed laced melodic pop jazz onto rich orchestration for a smoother, more acceptable sound. He hired the concertmaster for the New York Philharmonic to create lush orchestral backups for his recordings (Panken 2005, 61). Taylor surrounded such established jazz artists as saxophonist Paul Desmond, vibes player Milt Jackson, and cornetist Nat Adderley with violins and cellos to make their music more palatable to mainstream America.

An expert promoter, Creed built a marketing machine to publicize orchestrated pop jazz. To establish a standard look for CTI records, he hired photographer Pete Turner and graphic designer Sam Antupit to create distinctive album covers: an art photo framed by a bold, single-color border with the name of the artist and label prominently displayed. Taylor strategically bought radio time and print ads to advertise his stable of artists.

CTI artists appreciated the efforts to promote their music. "I felt that CTI had one of the best promotion and distribution outlets for what I wanted to do," commented vibes player Milt Jackson (Lyons 1983, 15). "One thing CTI did was set a precedent as far as promotion was concerned," agreed soul-jazz saxophonist Stanley Turrentine, who signed with the label. "Before that, record companies never did buy spots, especially for jazz musicians. CTI got the musicians exposed, they did a great job of packaging" (Nolan 1975, 12, 39).

Wes Montgomery [b. John Montgomery] became one of Creed Taylor's first projects. The Indianapolis guitarist, who idolized Charlie Christian, had played with Lionel Hampton and in a group with his brothers, pianist Buddy and bassist Monk. By the time he signed with Taylor, Wes had already recorded nearly twenty-five albums as a leader. He featured a signature sound of single-note runs, followed by octaves (playing the same note on two guitar strings one octave apart) and then a series of block chords. He achieved an even more unique sound by using the side of his thumb rather than a guitar pick.

Taylor propelled the innovative guitarist onto the charts. In 1967, recalled Creed, "I picked up the Beatles' *Sgt. Pepper's* [*Lonely Hearts Club Band*] as soon as it hit the stores in June and called Wes and [arranger] Don Sebesky to my office." After the three men carefully listened to the disc, they "agreed that the last track on the second side—'A Day in the Life'—was appropriately bluesy and would be ideal for the title track of Montgomery's new album" (Myers 2013, 183). He gave the guitarist another Beatles tune, several pop songs, and a few standards to accompany an original composition by Montgomery. To make the music even more acceptable, Creed embellished the session with twelve violins, two violas, two cellos, and a harp. The resulting pop-jazz album, *A Day in the Life,* reached number thirteen on the chart. Montgomery and Taylor collaborated on two more chart entries before the guitarist's untimely death from a heart attack on June 15, 1968.

When fusion gained popularity, Creed Taylor integrated electronic instruments into the production mix. As early as 1970, he paired Herbie Hancock's electric piano and Ron Carter's electric bass with trumpeter Freddie Hubbard on *Red Clay.* Taylor recorded the electrified sax of Fats Theus and added the electric keyboard of Lonnie

Liston Smith to a record by sax man Stanley Turrentine. The next year, on *Beyond the Blue Horizon*, the producer asked guitarist George Benson, bassist Ron Carter, and organist Clarence Palmer to plug into amplifiers. During the next several years amid the fanfare over fusion, Taylor increasingly relied on electronic instrumentation for CTI artists.

Grover Washington Jr., led the move toward smooth jazz through CTI. Washington, a saxophonist who majored in music at Trenton State College, "stayed in the classical field for a long time doing concerts, small quartet things, saxophone, and woodwind ensembles." During the late sixties, after leaving the armed forces, he worked for a local record distributor, where he "got to check out people like Jimi Hendrix, Jethro Tull and John Mayall" (Coryell and Friedman 1978, 261). In 1970, Washington connected with Philadelphia organist/keyboardist Charles Earland in a soul-jazz band. By the time he signed with CTI in 1971, he enjoyed "doing all kinds of music, from [singer-songwriter] Carole King to Weather Report, [classical composer Sergei] Prokofiev to [Motown sensation] Stevie Wonder" (Mandel 1975, 15).

CTI stumbled to Washington largely by accident. The label first hired him as an arranger and backup saxophonist. In September 1971, when Hank Crawford, a soul-jazz alto sax player and musical director for Ray Charles, failed to appear for a session, Creed Taylor settled on recording Washington instead. He surrounded the saxophonist with twelve violins and cellos and chose pop songs by such stars as Marvin Gaye ("Inner City Blues" and "Mercy Mercy Me") and Bill Withers ("Ain't No Sunshine") and such standards as Hoagy Carmichael's "Georgia on My Mind." CTI released the album, *Inner City Blues*, which unexpectedly reached number sixty-two on the chart. "As luck would have it," recalled the saxophonist, "the record was a smash" (Mandel 1975, 15).

Emboldened by success, Creed Taylor repeated his formula for Washington. In February 1975, he used strings to back the saxophonist for the Top Ten *Mr. Magic*. "What it basically comes down to is that everybody is looking for something just right in the middle," maintained Washington. "They don't want to get too far out; they don't want to get too far in" (Coryell and Friedman 1978, 262). During the next five years, the label replicated its middle-of-the-road recipe for Grover Washington Jr., who placed six more albums in the Top Thirty. By 1980, Washington had jumped to Elektra Records for the number-five *Winelight*.

George Benson also rode the chart with the CTI formula of pop jazz enhanced by strings. The Pittsburgh guitarist started his career by playing with soul-drenched organist Jack McDuff. In 1968, using the approach that had succeeded for Wes Montgomery, Benson interpreted pop singles such as the Monkees' "Last Train to Clarksdale" backed with strings for *Shape of Things to Come*. During the next seven years, Benson assaulted the chart five times with pop jazz, including the *The Other Side of Abbey Road*, a commercially successful disc of Beatles songs with sumptuous orchestration.

In May 1976, Benson and smooth jazz conquered the mainstream. Signing to Warner Brothers, he picked several pop songs and composed one original for his major-label debut. As he had done for CTI, Benson supplemented his guitar with electric piano, Minimoog synthesizer, and orchestration, arranged by Claus Ogerman. At the last minute, the guitarist added his vocals. At first, his "producer didn't want to do it, as it was going so well as an instrumental album. He said, 'I don't know if we need that vocal now.'" Benson, who idolized Nat King Cole, persisted. "After all the trouble you went through to get me to do this, we should do it at least one time. If it comes out okay, we'll use it, if not, we won't," the guitarist insisted. In the final mix, Benson included his soulful, silky vocal for "This Masquerade," a tune penned by soul-rocker Leon Russell on the disc, *Breezin'*, which sold three million copies and vaulted to the top of the chart, the first jazz album to reach number one. "The album has catapulted me into another category," boasted the guitarist. "Now you might find me in the pop listings at the record store, where before I was only put in the jazz category" (Tompkins 1978). During the next four years, Benson racked up four more Top Ten smooth-jazz efforts.

Trumpeter Chuck Mangione scored with smooth-jazz hits. He began playing with his sibling Gap on piano as the Jazz Brothers. In 1966, he realized his boyhood dream by joining Art Blakey and the Jazz Messengers. In 1970, Chuck founded a group and recorded moderately successful records such as *Friends & Love . . . A Chuck Mangione Concert*, which featured the Rochester Philharmonic Orchestra. Though continuing to wax albums, in 1975 Mangione revealed that "I don't make any money yet" (Underwood 1975, 13).

Mangione's fortunes brightened considerably soon thereafter. In early December 1977, the trumpeter/flugelhorn player released *Feels So Good*, which relied on electronics to get a brassy but silky-smooth sound. "I like all the unique possibilities electronics allow us," he explained (Coryell and Friedman 1978, 50). Mangione reached the number-two spot on the chart with the album and nearly topped the chart with a single of the same name. In two years, he followed with the Top Ten *Fun and Games*.

Mangione described his melodic sound as feel-good music. "Most people want to go out and have a good time," he asserted. "I spent seven years being hip and now I'm having a good time, just playing music that feels good," the trumpeter conceded (Schaffer 1973, 19).

Saxophonist Kenny G likewise leapt to the top with smooth jazz. Born Kenny Gorelick, the Seattle native idolized smooth-jazz pioneer Grover Washington Jr. "I wanted to be the white Grover Washington, Jr.," he disclosed. "Grover could play melodically, but he had a soulful sound to him, and nobody else ever played like that" (Panken 2002). In 1973, while in high school, he landed a position with the deep-voiced, romantic soul-singer Barry White, and, in 1980, joined the Jeff Lorber Fusion band, which reached the lower end of the album chart. From 1982 to 1985, Kenny G released several albums that barely cracked the Top 100.

In 1986, two new media lifted Kenny G to stardom. On January 1, 1985, Viacom Media Networks launched a video channel for artists who might appeal to an audience in its thirties. VH1 aimed at this older demographic to complement the success of Viacom's youth-oriented MTV. In addition to reigniting the careers of established rock acts such as Eric Clapton, Billy Joel, and Rod Stewart, VH1 molded Kenny G into a television personality. "When VH1 launched," recalled record executive Peter Baron, "I made a Kenny G video for $30,000 ["Don't Make Me Wait for Love' (1986)]. People began walking into record stores and asking for the album by 'that sax player by the beach'" (Tannenbaum and Marks 2012, 229).

Smooth-jazz radio further fueled the popularity of Kenny G. As early as 1976, stations such as New York's WRVR-FM and WLOQ in Orlando, Florida, adopted a smooth-jazz format. During the late seventies and early eighties, the number of smooth-jazz stations grew exponentially and broadened the reach of the genre to a national audience, which strengthened sales of an already recognized style. By 1983, "adult contemporary" channels focused almost exclusively on smooth-jazz artists. Four years later, Los Angeles station KTWV launched "The WAVE" as a smooth-jazz format and hired Frank Cody, who helped popularize the term "smooth jazz." Cody promoted smooth-jazz on "The WAVE" and through his research firm, Broadcast Architecture, spread the smooth-jazz sound to other cities. From 1987 to 1993, the format snagged a 140 percent increase in a largely upscale audience to make smooth jazz a major market force.

LISTENING GUIDE 38

Kenny G

"DON'T MAKE ME WAIT FOR LOVE"

Rather than being a jazz innovator or fleet-fingered soloist, Kenny G delivers a precise, full-toned, extremely listenable smooth jazz. On this song from the *Duotones* album, he accompanies soft, gospel-based soul singer Lenny Williams, formerly the lead singer for the funky Tower of Power. He climbed the chart with this song, which benefited from a video of the same name that can be found on YouTube (https://www.youtube.com/watch?v=cGHnB8epj54). In his career, the sax player released twenty videos.

The tune, written by Walter Afanasieff, Preston Glass, and Narada Michael Walden and released on August 10, 1986, reached number fifteen on the singles chart and propelled the album to the number-two spot.

Personnel: Kenny G (saxophone); Lenny Williams (lead vocals); Walter Afanasieff (keyboards); Preston Glass (drum programming, background vocals, and synthesizers); Randy Jackson (synth bass); Karen Brewington, Gina Glass, and Yolanda Glass (background vocals).

0:00–0:11	The album-length song, slightly longer than the single, begins with a silky synthesizer riff, which establishes the relaxed beat backed by the drum machine.
0:12–0:15	The pitch rises from the synthesizer.
0:16–0:25	Kenny G enters on the beat to establish the velvety melody. An echo enhances Kenny's silky sound.
0:26–0:48	Lenny Williams starts the vocals, which are punctuated by the synthesizer in the background (e.g., 0:35–0:37), in a call-and-response with the vocalist. The synthesizer also identifies the break between the two-measure lyrics. On the single version of the song, Kenny G on saxophone replaces the synthesizer, which remains in the background.
0:49–0:56	Williams launches into a higher pitch and then drops to the original pitch.
0:57–0:58	Trained in gospel, Williams embellishes the word "away" by a quavering tremolo as he slides around the word.
0:59–1:22	Williams sings the hook or bridge as the synthesizer plays louder. After Williams delivers the lyrics, the synthesizer complements him. The female background singers lightly assist Williams on the hook and continue to do so throughout the song to lend texture and dynamics. On the single, Kenny G plays in a call-and-response with the synthesizer.
1:23–1:33	Kenny G restates the melody in a pure tone with little improvisation, in a manner similar to his first solo (0:16–0:25).
1:34–1:55	Williams goes to the next verse with backing from the synthesizer and drum machine. On the single, Kenny G also provides backing to Williams.
1:56–2:06	Synthesizer-generated violins enter to back Williams.
2:07–2:29	A return to the hook with Williams backed by the synthesizer. On the single, Kenny G leads the hook with Williams.
2:30–2:51	Williams repeats the hook with synthesizer backing. This repeated hook has been deleted from the single.

2:52–3:10	Kenny G starts to solo around the melody, sustaining a note (2:58–3:00) to provide dynamics and power to his solo.
3:11–3:14	Kenny G plays a quick succession of notes as Williams reenters.
3:15–3:34	Williams restates the hook. As he sustains notes (e.g., "baby" at 3:16 and "love" at 3:19), Williams sings the bridge in a higher pitch than the first version of the hook. The difference in pitch makes the song more interesting and dynamic. Kenny G plays when Williams pauses in a call-and-response pattern. The synthesizer plays in the background.
3:35–3:36	The singer and Kenny G play in unison to generate power as the song starts to close.
3:37–3:44	Williams again restates the hook with Kenny G and the synthesizer providing backing.
3:45–3:48	The singer breaks into a gospel shout—"ohhhh oh."
3:49–3:55	Williams again restates the hook with the synthesizer backing him.
3:56–4:00	Kenny G unfurls a rapid-fire succession of notes and ends on a sustained note to create tension in the song.
4:01–4:22	Williams yet again restates the hook while Kenny G answers him on the saxophone. This time, Williams sings in a pleading, highly syncopated voice, sometimes soaring into a falsetto.
4:23–4:32	Kenny G delivers another melodic solo with his mellow, echo-laden saxophone.
4:33–4:38	Kenny G again sustains a note to provide power to the song.
4:39–4:42	As Kenny G continues his solo with synthesizer in the background, the song fades out.

Promoted on both VH1 and smooth-jazz radio, Kenny G scaled the chart. In July 1986, he released *Duotones*, which featured drum machines, a synthesizer, and lush string arrangements and sold five million copies. Two years later, the saxophonist repeated his success with the Top Ten *Silhouette*, which sold four million copies. In 1992, Kenny G issued the number-two *Breathless*, which registered more than twelve million in sales and transformed the saxophonist into a pop star.

By the eighties, Americans had embraced smooth jazz and fusion, which resurrected jazz from an insider's music to a style popular among the general public. In a 1982 survey conducted by the National Jazz Service Organization, almost fifty-four million American adults, or 26 percent of the United States population, indicated a preference for jazz. The number of jazz fans compared favorably to enthusiasts of other genres such as rock, which 36 percent of Americans favored.

Jazz fans represented a specific demographic. They encompassed all ages, with the strongest inclination toward jazz existing among baby boomers between the ages of 18 and 34. Jazz aficionados consisted almost equally of men and women who had at least some college education, generally lived in urban areas, and possessed enough discretionary income to buy records that they heard on the radio. Though nearly half of African Americans favored the music, in sheer numbers whites predominated among jazz lovers. "The relative youth of this audience and its broad racial base suggest a strong potential for expanding the reach of this truly American art form," the report concluded (Horowitz 1986, iv).

Though the survey sample expressed interest in all types of jazz, it clearly conveyed an affinity for fusion and smooth jazz, which at the time of the survey dominated sales and media coverage. Combined with sales figures, it demonstrated that fusion and smooth jazz had once again brought jazz to the mainstream, especially among a baby boom-generation that felt buffeted by economic troubles.

For Discussion and Further Study

🔗
"Chapter Quiz"

1. What musical and social changes in the sixties led to the rise of jazz-rock fusion? Why did mainstream jazz artists embrace this new style?

2. What role did Miles Davis play in popularizing the new fusion style? What attracted him to this music? What other musicians did he inspire to embrace new technologies and musical styles?

3. How did changes in the economy impact the next generation of fusion musicians? What new elements did they introduce into the music?

4. How was smooth jazz an outgrowth of changing listener preferences and the economy? What role did producers like Creed Taylor and performers like Kenny G play in developing and popularizing this style?

5. Both jazz-rock fusion and smooth jazz were (and continue to be) controversial among jazz "purists" who feel that these musical styles are not true to the jazz tradition. How much of this reaction is based on their popularity? On racial ideas about jazz? About society's broader attitude toward "serious" versus "popular" music?

BACK TO THE FUTURE

Wynton Marsalis and the Jazz Tradition

During the 1980s, some prominent jazz artists reflected the conservatism in American politics. Led by trumpeter Wynton Marsalis, they championed earlier jazz styles—particularly the music of Louis Armstrong, Duke Ellington, and early bop—over more recent developments such as the avant-garde and jazz-rock fusion. The "young lions" unwittingly mirrored the conservative outlook of President Ronald Reagan, who preached an idealized version of American culture based on white suburban values. The nostalgic vision of Marsalis and his followers gained traction with the new technology of the compact disc, which offered record companies the opportunity to reissue their back catalogs and gave older jazz fans the opportunity to repurchase their favorite music.

In 1986, John Orysik, cofounder of the Coastal Jazz and Blues Society, scheduled the Miles Davis band to perform at the Vancouver International Jazz Festival, which was scheduled during a world's fair in that city called Expo 86. Festival organizers hoped that some of the twenty-two million Expo 86 visitors would attend one of more than 150 concerts that had been planned for June. In addition to Miles, they lured Wynton Marsalis and his group to the festival.

On June 27, Miles Davis took the stage. In February, he had released *Tutu*, named after Desmond Tutu, the first black Anglican archbishop of Capetown, South Africa. At the jazz festival, Miles played both trumpet and keyboards and brought his electric band, which included synthesizers, electric guitars, electric bass, and drums. According to electric bass player Marcus Miller, the band "mirrored the times in which it was created" by including "super electro sounding elements" (Mergner 2010, 24).

During the middle of the set, Miles saw someone from the corner of his eye. "All of a sudden," he recalled, "I feel this presence coming up at me, this body movement, and I see the crowd is kind of wanting to cheer or gasp." He turned to see twenty-four-year-old trumpeter Wynton Marsalis standing next to him. "Wynton whispers in my ear—and I'm still trying to play—'They told me to come up here'" (Davis 1989, 374).

Marsalis had been goaded into the antic by his band mates. As Marsalis told it, "We were in the car approaching the city when the subject of Miles' repeated disrespecting of me and my family came up." Pianist Marcus Roberts, drummer, Jeff "Tain" Watts, and bassist Bob Hurst "began yeasting me," recalled the trumpeter. "'How long you gonna let him say you ain't shit and do absolutely nothing?'; 'Yeah, man, Davis is always slapping you.'; 'We think you must be scared of him.' Then someone (I think it was 'Tain') said, 'He's playing tonight and we're off [until tomorrow]. I think you ought to go up there and jump on him.' . . . We were joking and laughing. The pot hit $100 a piece, and I said, 'O.K. I'll do it'" (Marsalis 2015).

Besides Davis's disparaging comments about Marsalis, Wynton and the band did not appreciate the electric music Miles played. "We felt as young men that he

Miles Davis with trumpet and electronic synthesizer at the North Sea Festival, 1984. *Dutch National Archives, Photographer: Rob Bogaerts*

no longer represented the art form with the same level of steadfast integrity as before, when he was great and admired by musicians and laymen alike," stated Marcus Roberts (Marsalis 2015). Marsalis more bluntly described Miles as a "genius who decided to go into rock, and was on the bandstand looking like, basically, a buffoon" (Byrnes 2014, 2). "By the time I came around," continued Marsalis, "he had bent over so far for rock & roll that he was a hindrance. The type of music he was playing was not jazz" (Reich 1992, 17; Hawkins 2010).

When Davis noticed Marsalis during the middle of his performance, he became "mad at him for doing shit like that. I just said, 'Man, get the fuck off the stage.'" A shocked Wynton stood motionless. "After I said that," continued Davis, "I said, 'Man, what the fuck are you doing up here on stage? Get the fuck off the stage!' And then I stopped the band. Wynton can't play the kind of shit we were playing," added Miles. "He's not into that kind of style and so we would have had to make adjustments to the way he was going to be playing" (Davis 1989, 374).

Percussionist Mtume (b. James Forman), who was raised by pianist James Forman and recorded with Miles during the seventies, considered Marsalis's disruption a direct affront to Davis. He characterized it as "the ultimate statement of arrogance, a straight-up attack on Davis. Miles was so beyond that. It was about, 'What the fuck are you doing? How're you going to challenge me, [when] I've changed my music four or five times.' It was to the point where he would have punched him. And, believe me, he would have" (Boyles 2011, 4).

"There was no way I would get into a physical confrontation with him, it wouldn't be fair," countered Wynton. "I wouldn't get into a physical confrontation with a man old enough to be my grandfather," he snipped about the sixty-year-old Miles (Helland 1990).

The confrontation never came to fisticuffs. When the band stopped, Marsalis left for the wings of the auditorium. He never collected the $300 bet.

A Tale of Two Approaches

At first glance, the confrontation at the Vancouver International Jazz Festival seemed to be an impulsive action of young, talented, but reckless and immature musicians trying to best one of the giants in the field. With hindsight, several of them expressed regret for their actions. "We felt bad, because in the end, how many heroes are left that you can truly look up to and admire," Marcus Roberts later lamented. Robert Hurst found it "embarrassing" and "deeply apologized for the ignorance and lack of judgment shown during my youth, which yielded any disrespect to my musical hero, Miles Davis" (Marsalis 2015).

Although a foolish sidelight to the jazz festival, the Miles Davis–Wynton Marsalis incident represented a split between innovation and traditionalism. Davis, ever the pacesetter, listened to the newest music and incorporated it into

Wynton Marsalis, 1982. *Lebrecht Music & Arts/Alamy Stock Photo*

his changing style. He had started with Charlie Parker and bop, moved to hard bop, and helped create cool jazz. He subsequently perfected modal jazz and launched the fusion movement, but wanted to experiment further. The trumpeter felt that "fewer and fewer black musicians were playing jazz and I could see why, because jazz was becoming the music of the museum. I didn't even go to listen to most jazz groups anymore because they were only playing the same musical licks that we played way back with Bird, over and over again," Davis groused. "It was boring to hear that shit" (Davis 1989, 352).

Davis believed in constantly changing his sound with the times. "If anybody wants to keep creating they have to be about change," he declared. "Music is always changing. It changes because of the times and the technology that's available. People who don't change will find themselves like folk musicians, playing in museums," he warned. "My future starts when I wake up every morning. That's when it starts . . . because there's something new to do and try every day" (Davis 1989, 394, 393, 396, 408). In 1982, when asked his opinion about popular music on NBC's *Today Show*, the trumpeter responded that "you take out what you want and leave what you don't like" (Gumbel 1982).

Compared to Davis, Marsalis expressed a more limited view of jazz. Rather than focus on current popular trends, he looked back to the rich history of jazz for inspiration. He hoped to "pay as much homage as I can to the nobility of our great jazz tradition. I want to see that our tradition continues to be practiced and treated with the respect it deserves. I'm the result of a great tradition and I'm trying to live up to the standards of that tradition," the trumpeter contended (Milkowski 1998, 125, 121).

LISTENING GUIDE 39

Miles Davis

"TUTU"

Davis relied on the still-emerging technologies of synthesizers and drum machines to record "Tutu." Working for his new label Warner Brothers after a thirty-year stint with Columbia, he enlisted the help of Marcus Miller and producer Tommy LiPuma, who first "programmed the drums on tape, the bass drum and then two or three other rhythms and then the keyboards." On February 11, 1986, in a single take, Miles added trumpet to the tape, which LiPuma and engineer Eric Calvi then mixed into final shape (Davis 1989, 370). "[Electronic] music technology was in its very early days," commented synthesizer programmer Jason Miles, who worked on *Tutu*, "and we were doing some real voodoo with it" (Tingen 2002, 43).

Marcus Miller, "Tutu"'s writer, had produced several smooth-jazz artists such as George Benson and in 1981 had performed in a Miles Davis band. He composed the song in honor of African clergyman Desmond Tutu, who helped lead the freedom movement in South Africa. "When writing 'Tutu' I had images of South Africa on my mind," Miller recalled. "They were still struggling with apartheid at the time" (Tingen 2002, 46).

Miller also used the song to expand the "Prince of Darkness" image, which Miles fostered. "Miles had different aspects of his personality that were accented in different eras: like in the 1950s his cool side and in the

'70s his outrageous side. 'Tutu's' cool dark atmosphere was perfect for the 1980s" (Tingen 2002, 46). Aptly, but unknown to Miller, "tutu" translates into "proud, dignified, and cool" in the Yoruba language.

Miller wrote the song, composed in an AAB format, to update the music of Miles. "I was trying to find a way to combine what I knew to be Miles' personality and musical identity with what was happening in music at that time," he insisted about the use of drum machines and synthesizer (Tingen 2002, 41).

The album *Tutu* represented a stylistic merger. It combined jazz with funk, smooth R&B, and a pop sensibility. The LP included "Perfect Way," which originally had been done by the rock group Scritti Politti, and the staccato funk of "Full Nelson," which was named after South African anti-apartheid leader Nelson Mandela. Until the last minute, the album had been slated to feature a Prince song, "Can I Play with U?," which Prince pulled at the last minute because it did not seem to gel with the other songs on the album. The record earned Davis a Grammy Award for the best jazz instrumental performance by a soloist.

Personnel: Miles Davis (trumpet), Paulinho DaCosta (percussion), and Marcus Miller (soprano sax, electric bass, and synthesizer).

0:00–0:02	A programmed hit from the bass drum.
0:03–0:04	A dramatic, loud orchestral wash and its aftermath comes from the synthesizer.
0:05–0:08	A few more drum beats and another orchestral jab from the synthesizer with a few beats by the conga drum in the background. A few more drum beats follow.
0:09	The orchestra blast repeated for a third time to prepare the listener for Davis.
0:10–0:13	Davis enters on trumpet, playing a descending pattern. He is backed by the synthesizer, which at 0:12 repeats the orchestral blast from the introduction.
0:14–0:23	Davis plays several notes as the bass enters vigorously with a repeated phrase and the drums get louder. Throughout, the drum machine has been programmed to replicate a jazz drummer, "playing licks and things like that," according to LiPuma. "It was the first time I had heard a drum machine playing those types of maneuvers. It was innovative. Prior to that, drum machines just laid down a groove" (Tingen, 44).
0:24–0:28	Miles repeats the pattern, which started at 0:10, and the bass plays a very brief pattern behind him.
0:29–0:35	Davis plays a variant of his initial pattern.

0:36–0:46	Davis begins the main melody, accompanied by a steady drum beat, an insistent bass line, and a descending riff from the synthesizer. He plays with a Harmon mute on his trumpet throughout as he did on *Kind of Blue.* He plays in a minor key to give the melody an ominous feel that reinforces his Prince of Darkness image.
0:47–0:49	Davis exits as the rhythm section continues to play. Throughout the years, Miles has created tension and interest and varied the rhythm by pausing unexpectedly during his solos. His creative use of space has been a characteristic of his style.
0:50–0:51	Davis sustains a high note.
0:52–0:55	Miles supplies a descending line as his solo continues.
0:56–1:07	Davis and the rhythm section restate the melody (0:36–0:49).
1:08	The bass plays a riff, which connects the last section of the song to the next.
1:09–1:13	Davis and the rhythm section launch the B section of the song.
1:14–1:16	The synthesizer plays an ascending line and signals an end to the passage, when it repeats the introductory blast (0:03–0:04).
1:17–1:23	Assisted by the rhythm section and the conga drum, Miles plays a line in a passage, which ends with two synthesizer blasts repeated from the introduction.
1:24–1:28	Miles plays a four-note pattern four times at different rhythms to add interest.
1:29–1:56	Miles and the other instruments repeat the melody two times, which are separated by a few notes from the trumpet.
1:57–2:03	The band repeats the B-section pattern of the song and ends with the familiar ascending pattern and then the blast from the synthesizer.
2:04–2:05	A brief riff by the bass enters.
2:06–2:10	Miles offers a brief descending line and then a staccato blast. At this point, he has backing from the synthesizer, which softly generates an almost human vocal in the background.
2:11–2:12	A sustained, squealing note, which sounds like it has been generated by a Roland 303.
2:13–2:15	The sound of background vocals.
2:16–2:18	Miles exits as the synthesizer provides a gentle wash, then a sound like the scratching of a record on a turntable, and finally another orchestral wash.
2:19–2:25	Miles reenters with a two-note pattern repeated four times before he embellishes it.
2:26–2:27	Another squeal from the synthesizer with the sound of background vocals continuing.
2:28–2:34	Miles provides a short line and then a rapid-fire but very brief flutter on two notes.
2:35–2:38	As Miles solos, the synthesizer wobbles downward to create an off-kilter, interesting background. A blast from the synthesizer signals a change.
2:39–3:04	Miles repeats a pattern four times in different rhythms and with slightly different notes to add interest to his solo. In the background, the wash of the synthesizer intensifies.

3:05–3:31	The band restates the melody with embellishments from Davis and bassist Miller around the melody. At 3:15, Davis hits and briefly sustains a very high note to give the passage a dynamic feeling.
3:32–3:39	Restatement of section B, which ends with a synthesizer blast.
3:40–3:54	Davis solos with a series of jabs at different rhythms. At 3:43–3:46, he jabs nearly a dozen times with the same note like a fast-fisted boxer.
3:55–4:06	The synthesizer enters with a ten-note riff and intensifies the volume.
4:07–4:47	The band restates the main melody three times, around which Davis solos in the high register. The melody ends with the blast of the synthesizer.
4:48–5:12	Davis and bassist Miller trade lines in a call-and-response as the music fades out.

Rather than muddy jazz with new styles, the trumpeter wanted to keep the tradition pure. In a lengthy July 1988 article for the *New York Times*, Marsalis espoused the "purist ethic in jazz" and focused on the "esthetic elevation that jazz offers. In other fields," he complained, "purism is considered a form of heroism—the good guy who won't sell out—but in jazz that purism is incorrectly perceived as stagnation and the inability to change" (Marsalis 1988, 1).

Born in Kenner, Louisiana, a suburb of New Orleans, Marsalis revered the musical heritage of his hometown. He first became interested in music through his father, Ellis, who played jazz piano, helped organize and taught at the New Orleans Center for the Creative Arts, and, in 1961, helped organize musicians for better working conditions in All For One. Wynton played in the marching band at the Fairview Baptist Church with guitarist and New Orleans jazz pioneer Danny Barker, and took lessons from several New Orleans music teachers. As a young teen, he joined a funk band, the Creators, and for four years learned "all those tunes from the '70s by Earth, Wind and Fire, Parliament/Funkadelic. I played that music," though he did not consider it jazz (Mandel 1999, 17).

By his late teens, Marsalis paid special homage to New Orleans–born trumpeter Louis Armstrong. "His sound carries the feeling and meaning of jazz more than any other musician's," he argued. "It's warm, it's intelligent, it's spiritual, it's tawdry, it's worldly, it's provincial. Anything you want, he had it in his sound. He could hear, he played in tune, had ridiculously ingenious rhythm and time," he continued. "And he practically invented the conception of an improvised solo with a certain type of structure and form and organization" (Scherman 1995, 73; Sidran 1992, 146).

Wynton also heaped effusive praise on Duke Ellington. "Duke Ellington is what jazz is, he is the greatest musician, his music is the most comprehensive," maintained Marsalis. "He continuously proved that no one was more capable of translating the varied and complex arenas of American experience into tone. His recorded legacy gives us the most accurate tonal history of the 20th century" (Helland 1990, 6; Marsalis 1988, 2).

Marsalis voiced the esteem that he held for bop pioneers, too. He lauded Charlie Parker for "a new level of psychological complexity, and he had an incredible sense of thematic organization." He also praised Thelonious Monk, who he said "was the greatest musician from that period. He was the most sophisticated harmonically by far, *and* rhythmically." He cited trumpeter Dizzy Gillespie as "a prime example of worldliness in jazz." With bop, he contended, "jazz changed. They played a different way. And the attitude was different, less tied to the entertainment industry. But the rhythm, not the harmony, is what stumped older musicians" (Scherman 1995, 74–75).

Marsalis mostly focused on African-American jazz innovators, who he believed had not been properly acknowledged in the history of American music due to racism. "Because the jazz musicians are black, [white Americans] don't want to give credit to them," he bemoaned. "The thing that outrages me the most is the fact that here are guys that have contributed a great body of music to American history and the only reason that they aren't being recognized for their labors is because of the color of their skin" (Stokes 1991, 244–45).

To dispel the myth of the primitive, untutored African-American genius, which had been promulgated as early as the twenties, Wynton emphasized the importance of hard work and dedication. He focused on the "painful experience of discipline" and the merits of "deep study and contemplation" (Marsalis 1988, 2). The trumpeter attributed Coltrane's success to his "phenomenally hard work" (Scherman 1995, 76) and asserted that "Monk didn't just come up with that music because his name was Monk! I mean he studied music" (Sidran 1992, 144). "Jazz," he instructed, consists of "working your hardest to live up to the responsibility of developing your gift. Jazz is serious business" (Marsalis 1986, 132).

To respect the serious nature of jazz, Marsalis adopted a respectable demeanor much like many past African-American jazz luminaries. On the bandstand, he dressed in dark suits, white shirts, and ties. "The reason I started wearing suits was because

Branford Marsalis. *Photograph courtesy of Brian McMillen*

of Art Blakey's band, because we would be playing in overalls, and I was embarrassed," he recalled about his three-year stint with the premier hard-bop outfit. "After that, we started getting clean. For us, it was a statement of seriousness" (Reich 1992, 17). The young trumpeter seldom cursed and during interviews spoke in an articulate manner like his idols Ellington and Charlie Parker.

As well as celebrating the African-American jazz heritage, Wynton extolled the virtues of European classical music. While in high school, he performed with the New Orleans Philharmonic Symphony Orchestra, the Philharmonic's touring Brass Quintet, the New Orleans Community Concert Band, and the New Orleans Youth Orchestra. At seventeen, Marsalis became the youngest person to be admitted into the summer program at Tanglewood's Berkshire Music Center and, the next year, moved to New York City to attend the Juilliard School of Music, where he learned European musical theory. "First I played classical music, which was considered negative—even though classical music is also a large component of the jazz tradition, because jazz comes out of ragtime and all the older musicians who studied classical music," he explained (Milkowski 1998, 124). "I love European music, great European music," Wynton enthused in his first interview with *Downbeat* (Mandel 1999, 20). "I play some European music to pay respect to a great, great music" (Zabor and Garbarini 1985, 62).

Wynton's recorded output reflected a dual preoccupation with the jazz and classical traditions. In 1982, Marsalis released a self-titled debut, a hard-bop effort, which snuck into the Top 200 and included established artists such as bassist Ron Carter, drummer Tony Williams, and pianist Herbie Hancock, who also produced the album. Along with veterans, Marsalis tapped such young hard-bop adherents as his brother, saxophonist Branford, who had toured with Art Blakey; fellow Blakey sideman/bassist Charles Fambrough; and pianist Kenny Kirkland. The next year, honoring his elders, Wynton waxed *Fathers and Sons* with his father and brother Branford. In 1983, he neared the Top 100 with *Think of One*, propelled by a group including drummer Jeff "Tain" Watts and his brother Branford.

At the same time, Marsalis played trumpet on several classical discs. In 1983, he cut *Trumpet Concertos* with the National Philharmonic Orchestra. On it, he performed concertos by Johann Hummel, Joseph Haydn, and Leopold Mozart, the father of Wolfgang Amadeus Mozart. The next year, the trumpeter waxed three more classical discs, *Baroque Music for Trumpet* with the English Chamber Orchestra; *Haydn: Three Favorite Concertos* with various orchestras and renowned classical performers, cellist Yo-Yo Ma, and violinist Cho-Liang Lin; and a record with soprano Edita Gruberova and Raymond Leppard, who conducted the English Chamber Orchestra. Also in 1984, he reached number ninety on the *Billboard* chart with a combined classical-jazz album, *Hot House Flowers*, performed by his regular jazz outfit and supplemented by a cello, bassoon, French horn, oboe, tuba, violas, and violins.

The combination of classical and jazz releases turned the twenty-three-year-old Marsalis into a national sensation. At the Twenty-sixth Grammy Awards in 1984, Marsalis amazingly grabbed the top prize for both best jazz instrumental performance by a soloist and best classical performance for an instrumental soloist. The next year, Marsalis won two Grammys, one for *Hot House Flowers* and the other for his classical album with Edita Gruberová. By the beginning of 1985, the talented and articulate trumpeter had been interviewed by dozens of periodicals and had been recognized as a major artist.

Not content to play the music that inspired him, Marsalis vociferously blasted the major post-bop jazz styles. He portrayed free jazz as "chaos. Maybe it's not, but that's what I think it is. Chaos is always out there; it's something you can get from any fifty kids in a band room. I don't know any people who like it," he insisted about free playing. "I don't even like Coltrane's later stuff, to be honest.... The avant-garde conception of music that's loud and self-absorbed—nobody's interested in hearing that on a regular basis," he added (Scherman 1995, 79, 68). Though he acknowledged the contributions of Ornette Coleman, with whom his father had briefly played, the trumpeter felt that free jazz failed to "resonate with anything I've experienced in the world" (79).

Marsalis likewise leveled his sights on funk, which he had played earlier and which such artists as Miles Davis and Herbie Hancock had at least partly adopted. "Funk was the basis of my first level of development," he sniffed, "and we all know the endless succession of great virtuosi that music has produced—none" (Crouch 1987, 17).

Wynton launched his most vitriolic diatribes against fusion, which dominated the charts during the early- to mid-eighties, by criticizing electric instruments. Though conceding that "electronic instruments give you a much wider palate of sound," he did not "like those sounds. They're not expressive as acoustic sounds." Fusion "musicians choose to focus on the equipment they're using, not the music they're making," he chided. "They refer to all these piles of instruments they use to put little sounds on many different tracks to give the music the illusion of the type of depth that comes with thorough knowledge of polyphony" (Scherman 1995, 83–84; Crouch 1987, 19).

Fusion musicians, using electronic instruments like rock and funk acts, became the perpetrators of the "facile fusion [of jazz] with pop" to the trumpeter

LISTENING GUIDE 40

Wynton Marsalis Group

 **"DELFEAYO'S DILEMMA"**

Trumpeter Marsalis offers a hard-bop/modal version of his composition, which he named in honor of his trombone-playing brother and included on the Afrocentric album *Black Codes (From the Underground).* He enlisted backing from pianist Kenny Kirkland, drummer Jeff "Tain" Watts, brother Branford on saxophone, and bassist Charnett Moffett.

Released on June 9, 1985, by Columbia Records, *Black Codes* won two Grammys and solidified Marsalis as the spokesperson for mainstream jazz. The title referred to the blatant antebellum and post–Civil War racism embodied by the black codes, which restricted the rights of slaves and free African Americans. The album implicitly drew a parallel between the black codes and the current discrimination of African Americans, including the pressure on African-American musicians to commercialize their art. Though Marsalis reflected the conservatism of the era by promoting

traditionalism, he nonetheless touted African-American achievement and lambasted racism.

Musically, recalled Marsalis, the tune served "as a vehicle for us to solo over six-bar phrases." It demonstrated the change between major and minor chords that generated contrary motion. In measures 40 and 41, the song isolated an interval (the distance between two pitches) on which the band played up and then down. In the B section, continued the trumpeter, "the rhythm section plays in dotted quarter note time. Layering rhythms grouped in 4 with ones grouped in 6, I learned from African music. I always like to give the drummer some hits like in measure 15 to give them something to 'hold on to' within the form." The song has a melody in A flat, but Wynton and Kenny Kirkland soloed in G and Branford in A. The composition, concluded Wynton, "was influenced by a [Kenny Dorham bop] song called 'Whistle Stop'" (Marsalis 2014).

0:00–0:03	The horns plays a highly syncopated passage in unison.
0:04–0:05	Kenny Kirkland comps with a few complementary notes to the horns.
0:06	A cymbal crash from drummer Watts signals a change.
0:07–0:10	With backing from Watts, Kirkland plays a brief, descending passage.
0:11–0:18	The horns reenter with backing from the rhythm section to restate a variation of the introductory passage followed by a repeated chord from Kirkland. Along with the first section, it establishes the thread of a melody for the piece.
0:19–0:26	A brief pattern by the band.
0:27–0:34	The band restates the introductory passage.
0:35–0:38	Kirkland restates the descending passage from 0:07–0:10.
0:39–0:46	The band restates the passage from 0:11–0:18, followed by a few embellishments from Marsalis.
0:47–0:53	The band restates the pattern from 0:19–0:26.
0:54–1:01	Wynton starts a solo in a cool style reminiscent of the fifties approach of Miles Davis. Like Davis, he uses a muted trumpet. Wynton leaves significant space between his phrases to create tension, interest, and rhythmic complexity. Throughout, he develops a fascinating contrast by moving from major to bluesy, flatted notes. He also travels from the low to the high register of the trumpet to develop a dramatic dynamism in the solo.

	Unlike Miles, he bases his form on chords rather than a modal scale. In this short passage, he repeats two phrases in two dramatically different variations, which weave around the melody of the song.
1:02–1:08	Building upon the ending of the first solo passage, he moves into another area by changing from major to flatted notes.
1:09–1:13	Marsalis repeats two phrases twice.
1:14–1:22	The trumpeter repeats two different, somewhat sustained phrases twice and then moves to his original solo passage.
1:23–1:28	Marsalis repeats two phrases from the beginning passage.
1:29–1:31	Wynton states his original passage in a very different, staccato rhythm, in which the notes seem to ping-pong off one another.
1:32–1:36	In a cascading effect, Marsalis descends and then ascends the scale to create interest. The drummer and pianist come to the forefront at the end of the passage to indicate a change.
1:37–1:39	Like Miles Davis, Wynton sustains a single high note to focus the listener.
1:40–1:42	Marsalis finishes his phrase.
1:43–1:45	Wynton descends the scale with several sustained notes.
1:46–1:55	The trumpeter picks up the tempo with a short passage.
1:56–2:01	Wynton changes the rhythm to a highly syncopated staccato as he spits out several notes.
2:02–2:08	Marsalis descends, ascends, and then descends the scale in a relatively high register.
2:09–2:14	Wynton moves to the lower end of the register before reestablishing the high-register sound to again give tension and interest to the composition.
2:15–2:17	After a few notes, Marsalis again sustains a high note. Technically adept, he can reach these notes easily and give a sense of smoothness to them.
2:18	A few vigorous drum fills push the solo to a louder sound.
2:19–2:29	A highly syncopated passage in yet another rhythm change, in which Marsalis descends by using a four-note sequence.
2:30–2:36	After a one-second pause, Marsalis switches to a less syncopated rhythm and ascends and descends the scale. A drum roll indicates a change at the end of the passage.
2:37–2:50	Marsalis repeats a five-note, syncopated pattern and then, in a staccato fashion, travels up and down the scale in the same rhythm.
2:51–2:56	Wynton delivers a sustained high note.
2:57–3:05	The trumpeter sustains an even higher note and then descends the scale in a two-note pattern to finish the solo.
3:06–3:12	Branford enters for a solo with an insistent, full-bodied, Coltrane-like sound. He begins with a somewhat staccato passage that features a movement up and down the scale.

3:13–3:19	To create rhythmic complexity, he sustains a note, plays a brief line, plays an even higher sustained note, and then increases the pitch on a higher sustained note. His elongated notes contrast starkly with the more syncopated rhythms.
3:20–3:24	Branford plays a few boppish lines, moving quickly up and down the scale.
3:25–3:32	The saxophonist returns to the short blasts of a staccato rhythm and moves up and down the scale in a ping-pong manner.
3:33–3:50	Marsalis repeats a syncopated pattern twice with significant variations as the tempo increases, with drummer Watts becoming more animated in the background.
3:51–3:57	Branford repeats the above pattern a third time with even more force by rapidly repeating notes (3:51–3:53) before completing the up-and-down pattern in a downward direction.
3:58–4:06	With great variation from the longer pattern above, Branford repeats an eight-note phrase four times in an ascending fashion.
4:07–4:16	Marsalis uses notes from the eight-note sequence above to descend the scale in a highly syncopated rhythm.
4:17–4:27	To end the solo, Branford ascends and then descends the scale in a somewhat syncopated rhythm. At one point, he slightly overblows the horn.
4:28–4:34	Kenny Kirkland begins his solo by repeating a phrase three times with significant variations on the last version.
4:35–4:43	In a hard-bop style, the pianist ascends, then descends the scale much like the Marsalis brothers. Like the horns, he shifts from major to flatted notes to create further tension in the song.
4:44–4:52	Kirkland changes the rhythm by syncopating the song.
4:53–5:46	Using the first few notes of his solo as a starting point, the pianist ascends and then descends the scale to create movement in the solo. In a bop style, he executes his runs at a blazing speed. He repeats this same pattern with great variations five more times until he ends the solo.
5:47–6:45	The horns enter and the entire band plays the introduction to the song (0:00–0:26) twice to end the song.

(Ellison 2001, 1). When asked "what got established in the '70s in the jazz tradition," Marsalis quickly and simply replied, "Nothing. Not one thing. I don't think the music moved along in the 70s. I think it went astray. Everybody was trying to be pop stars" (Mandel 1999, 20). In a veiled attack on musicians such as Miles Davis, Wynton ranted about "musicians who have become so cynical that they not only continue to sell out but try to pretend they are advancing the music because the junk they're playing now is done at a later date than their best work" (Marsalis 1986, 134).

Wynton Marsalis felt that he had a mission to curb the infusion of jazz with pop music. "I lived in the time of the absolute sellout of jazz to pop music," he insisted. "So I counter-stated that consistent lack of integrity in our music. Many of our greatest musicians abandoned all of their aesthetic objectives, to try to become pertinent. It seemed like so many people were bowed down before rock music, before the altar of rock" (Holley 2012, 2; Reich 1992, 17). As his mission, Marsalis vowed to resurrect and protect the pre-sixties jazz tradition.

Trickling Down with Ronald Reagan

President Ronald Reagan provided the conservative context for the success of Wynton Marsalis's traditional approach. Reagan served as a poster boy for the emerging conservatism in American politics and culture. During the McCarthy era as an actor, he led the anticommunist purge in Hollywood. As the governor of California during the sixties, he campaigned against welfare "bums" and promised to eliminate radicals from University of California campuses. After becoming president in January 1981, Reagan lowered taxes for the wealthy, decreased regulation of businesses, smashed trade unions, dismantled social-welfare programs, and increased the military budget, pushing the United States into a recession.

Average Americans suffered from Reagan's pro-business stance. In 1981, during the first year of the Reagan presidency, a little more than 7 percent of Americans were unemployed. By 1983, nearly 11 percent of all Americans were looking for work and sixty-six million Americans, or a third of the population, applied for government benefits to survive. Through his business-oriented policies, Ronald Reagan left the economy in shambles and resurrected the pre-1930s business-centric America.

Farm workers protest against Ronald Reagan, 1981. *Photograph by Frank Espada. Library of Congress Prints and Photographs Division*

The Jazz Heritage and the Compact Disc

The record industry flourished by looking to the past just as Ronald Reagan and Wynton Marsalis had done. At the beginning of the Reagan era, the US recording business was struggling. In 1978, after reaching sales of $4.13 billion, the industry headed downward. Within a year, total sales had slipped to $3.67 billion despite price hikes and high inflation.

The compact disc (CD) almost single-handedly rescued a troubled music industry and led to a resurgence of interest in past musical heroes, some of whom Marsalis promoted. Introduced to the general consumer in late 1982, it provided record buyers with a nearly indestructible digital format that had a greater frequency range than vinyl albums. CDs quickly became widespread. During their first two years on the market, CDs were purchased by classical music buffs who favored their expanded range. When the cost of compact disc players fell, CDs began selling in mass quantities. In 1985, 16.4 million CDs sold worldwide. Three years later, more than 390 million compact discs were purchased, with sales of more than $6 billion. By 1990, the CD posted sales of $7.5 billion and outsold vinyl LPs and cassette tapes.

With its enhanced sound and the addition of bonus tracks, the CD format stimulated many record buyers to replace their LPs with CDs. In early 1990, *Billboard* reported that "if the CD did anything in the '80s, it convinced consumers that they needed to buy their favorite albums all over again." "With revolutionary speed, music lovers are replacing their favorite old scratched-up 45s and 33s with shiny compact discs," contended *Time* magazine ("Technology" 1990). By 1992, the sale of music on CDs that had been previously purchased on vinyl amounted to more than 40 percent of the music business.

CD reissue programs especially revitalized the jazz market. Previously rare records by independent companies that had sold only two thousand copies or less of a title now could be purchased on CD. Created under the Fantasy umbrella in 1982, at the advent of the compact disc era, the *Original Jazz Classics* series "has been a tremendously successful program of CD reissues. Its premise was simple: to present memorable jazz albums with original covers and notes, which had been unavailable for years. The vaults of the Fantasy-affiliated labels Prestige, Riverside, Contemporary, Galaxy, Milestone, Debut, Jazzland, and Pablo hold some of the most important jazz ever recorded," the company boasted. The CDs featured "24-bit remastering from the original analog master tapes for vastly improved sound quality, newly written liner notes by respected jazz historians, and often previously-unreleased tracks from the original recording sessions" (Concord Music n.d.).

Columbia Records followed Fantasy into the jazz-reissue market. In January 1987, the label started its Jazz Masterpieces series, which in two years sold more than two million discs. "What was once a small but steady part of label business continues to grow appreciably due to the rise of the compact disc," commented *Billboard* about the Columbia series in July 1989. "It becomes apparent that those labels with a distinguished—and large—back catalog can obviously reap the most benefits from a carefully planned, astutely marketed reissue program" (DiMartino 1989b, J8).

The independent Pablo Records churned out reissues. Founded in 1973 by record entrepreneur Norman Granz—who had masterminded the Jazz at the Philharmonic concerts and in 1956 had founded the Verve label—the company laid an "emphasis on nostalgic music," according to *Billboard*. It issued new releases by several past masters and Granz-managed acts such as Duke Ellington, Count Basie, Canadian pianist Oscar Peterson, and guitarist Joe Pass (b. Joseph Passalacqua), who had backed Frank Sinatra. By 1975, seeking "something that is pure" (Hershorn 2011, 356), Granz focused on bygone eras by reissuing a multi-disc set by the fleet-fingered stride master Art Tatum and offering more than thirty previously unissued discs by the Duke Ellington Orchestra, twenty-year-old live recordings by sax masters Lester Young and Coleman Hawkins, and older concert performances by his long-standing client, Ella Fitzgerald. Until 1987, when he sold the company to Fantasy Records, Granz highlighted many once forgotten jazz masters.

The jazz reissue programs became profit centers for record labels. With no recording costs or signing bonuses to pay, companies reissued past releases in a different format at almost no expense and racked up sales and profits. "For the record companies, the costs are minimal," complained drummer Max Roach. "They don't have studio costs, they don't have musicians' costs, they don't have arrangers' costs, they don't have costs for the cover, etcetera. And so right from the very beginning it's all gravy" (Sidran 1992, 39). In two years, Columbia sold fifty thousand compact discs of a reissued Miles Davis album, *Kind of Blue*, the sales of which on vinyl had taken twenty-five years to reach that total. From the mid-to-late eighties, most jazz record companies peddled millions of compact discs, which consumers had owned previously or which label owners had discovered in their vaults.

The Young Lions of Neo-Bop

Young artists who adopted the hard-bop tradition arose amid the rapid ascent of Wynton Marsalis and the emphasis on jazz masters. "The point was to sign young artists who would allude to the '50s, to the times of Miles, Trane, Dizzy, Bud

[Powell], Kenny Clarke and Monk, and start a period comparable to bebop," contended George Butler, vice president of artists and repertoire for jazz and progressive music at Columbia Records and the executive who signed Wynton Marsalis (Mandel 1992, 84). "The record companies have a youth movement happening," observed Branford Marsalis (McAdams 1990, 83).

Like Wynton Marsalis, many young jazz players had learned jazz in college programs. Marcus Roberts, a pianist who worked with Marsalis beginning in late 1985, attended Florida State University. Sax player and Marsalis sideman Wessell Anderson graduated from Southern University in Louisiana, and trumpeter Nicholas Payton and bassist Reginald Veal finished programs at the University of New Orleans. Trumpeter Wallace Roney studied at Howard University. "The guys in our generation, including myself, have been socially acceptable, for lack of a better phrase. We're college educated, which means a lot to a certain segment of society," pointed out Terence Blanchard, who attended Rutgers University (Carver and Bernstein 1998, 18). "Most musicians in the scene nowadays were able to study jazz in school," echoed bassist Christian McBride, who graduated from Juilliard. "One of the reasons jazz has been taught in the colleges in the first place was this fight to legitimize jazz" (Janus 2010, 179).

The Berklee School of Music served as a gathering spot for many young jazz players. Trumpeters Roy Hargrove and Wallace Roney studied at Berklee, as did sax men Branford Marsalis, Antonio Hart, and Donald Harrison. Drummer and Wynton's timekeeper Jeff "Tain" Watts, drummer Marvin "Smitty" Smith, and guitarist Mark Whitfield also attended Berklee. Watts attributed his breakthrough to his stay at Berklee, where he met "Branford [Marsalis], that pretty much started my career" (Carver and Bernstein 1998, 278).

Educated at outstanding universities and music schools such as Berklee, the young jazz generation possessed a solid understanding of classical music. Antonio Hart first mastered classical music before turning to jazz. Eric Reed, who joined Wynton in 1988, started playing classical and gospel piano at the age of two. Pianist Marcus Roberts studied with famed classical pianist Leonidas Lipovetsky. When first introduced to the piano, the Juilliard-educated Stephen Scott started with "a small part of the Bach and Beethoven that my sisters had started playing" (Carver and Bernstein 1998, 204).

The young, mostly African-American jazz men exclusively performed on acoustic instruments. Consciously rejecting fusion, they abandoned synthesizers and electronic keyboards for pianos, refused to plug into effects gear to enhance reed instruments, and fingered large acoustic basses rather than amplified bass guitars. "These [acoustic] instruments express themselves vocally, as if they were singing, instead of just playing these little mechanical clichés that funk and rock musicians were using," explained Wycliffe Gordon, who played trombone in a Wynton Marsalis band (Piazza 1990, 35).

Young guitarists preferred acoustic models, which had vanished from the bandstand by the late sixties. Mark Whitfield favored a hollow-body guitar held directly to the microphone with no additional amplification. "The microphone gets all the natural resonance of the guitar, which the direct pickup misses," he argued. "It allows the beauty of your instrument's tone to come through. If you work with the amp, you tend to play loud; all that intensity is there artificially, and sometimes you summon it without really meaning to. For the first time, I feel like I'm playing guitar, instead of letting the amplifier play me," he concluded (Piazza 1990, 35).

Like Wynton, some of the new breed learned their craft in the Art Blakey band. Terence Blanchard replaced Wynton Marsalis in the outfit, and Donald Harrison took over alto duties after saxophonist Branford Marsalis left the band. In 1986, trumpeter Wallace Roney joined Blakey for a year, and was followed by Philip Harper. Tenor sax man Javon Jackson entered the band the same year as Harper.

"In terms of how he taught people, he had a unique way of giving you the experience by letting you fall on your face a bit. He would let us do things," explained Blanchard (Carver and Bernstein 1998, 17).

Choosing acoustic instruments, obsessed with past masters, and sometimes tutored by Blakey, young players generally favored a hard-bop style. "We're not being nostalgic; we're just trying to play in a certain tradition," insisted neo-hard-bopper Terence Blanchard, who cited Miles Davis and Clifford Brown as main musical inspirations. "We want to play this kind of music, and we need to uncover all the bones, to let people know what's really happening, what's jazz and what's not, so people can make an honest choice" (Mandel 1986, 24). "I'm trying to deal with the many great artists who played my instrument and the many great achievements that already have been made," agreed pianist Marcus Roberts, a diehard Thelonious Monk disciple. "I'm just trying to create some dialogue with that" (Havlis 1990, 14).

Nearly all the young neo-hard-boppers lauded Wynton Marsalis for his pivotal role in the rebirth of mainstream jazz during the eighties. "Wynton gave a lot of the young musicians in my generation—he pointed us in the right direction," professed bass player Christian McBride. "He had a big part to do with our development. I know I can speak for guys like Nicholas Payton and Roy Hargrove and [saxophonist] James Carter. Wynton was there for us a long time ago" (Carver and Bernstein 1998, 221). "In terms of why the [mainstream] music is more popular, I think a lot of it has to do with some of the work that Wynton started," echoed Marcus Roberts, who first saw the trumpeter in a 1981 concert, where he "told himself 'that boy is chosen. He is going to be a leader of a movement.' It has been an active part of his mission, obviously. His career pretty much mirrors the period of resurgent interest that we're talking about" (Franckling 1991, 17; Carver and Bernstein 1998, 198). Wes Anderson, articulating a common theme, felt that "Wynton is someone who can guide us. He's one of the shepherds of this music" (Sancton and Thigpen 1990, 69).

Eric Reed, nine years younger than Wynton, found inspiration in Marsalis's records. "Those records helped to create a movement," he contended about the early jazz output of the trumpeter. "And it was very similar to what bebop did for young musicians in the '40s and '50s. . . . Something like *Black Codes (From the Underground),* when it came out in '85, the effect began to take place a couple years after," the pianist continued. "All the musicians on the scene, all the young ones, were trying to play like that group. Marvin 'Smitty' Smith, Bob Hurst, Terence Blanchard, Donald Harrison, [pianist] Cyrus Chestnut, they were all coming out of that" (Carver and Bernstein 1998, 189–90).

Harry Connick Jr., who lived in New Orleans during the early- and mid-eighties when Marsalis hit the national scene, described his infatuation with Marsalis. Wynton vaulted into the national spotlight "when I was a freshman in high school," recalled the pianist, who climbed the chart when he added vocals to the *When Harry Met Sally* soundtrack and eventually sold more than twenty-eight million albums. "He was huge then, at the height of his career. He'd come home and we'd all run out and meet him. He was a big star. I wanted to be Wynton. I wanted to be in his band. I dressed like him. I talked like him," Connick revealed. "Wynton was the only one who was young and handsome and articulate playing the music; now there's a whole bunch of young people coming out and playing it" (Weidenbaum 1990, 58; Bland 1990, 74).

Several aspiring jazz artists received personal help from Wynton Marsalis. Bassist Charnett Moffett, who joined the trumpeter in late 1985, came over to Wynton's house "every day to learn about harmony on his bass, to learn about music" (Mandel 1999, 197). Trumpeter Terence Blanchard understood the music of Clifford Brown and Miles Davis "thanks to Wynton Marsalis who helped me learn the trumpet in high school" (Jackson 2011). Philadelphia bassist Christian McBride, likewise while in high school, met Wynton and was invited onstage "to sit in with his band." Marsalis eventually landed McBride a spot in a group headed by saxophonist Bobby Watson (Birnbaum 1994, 34). Trumpeter Roy Hargrove met Marsalis while in the eleventh grade at the Dallas Arts Magnet high school: "I knew Wynton was the cat who was doing what I wanted to be doing. I had seen him on TV, playing classical trumpet and talking about music," recollected Hargrove. "He came to Fort Worth with his quartet at the time, for an engagement, and while he was there he called up my high school and asked if he could come and do a workshop" (Piazza 1990, 65). Hargrove attended the seminar and heard Marsalis, who invited him to play a week-long engagement in Fort Worth at the Caravan of Dreams club that launched the teen's career.

In the wake of Marsalis's success, many record labels frantically signed neo-hard-bop players. "Never in the last 20 years has there been such a sense of excitement among new players, and major record companies have been signing them with the alacrity of Big Ten colleges courting high-school football stars," asserted the *New York Times* (Piazza 1990, 34, 64).

Record companies marketed the updated hard-bop because the acoustic-based style translated into profits. "The young bebop guys' records can be economically viable," contended Richard Seidel of Verve/Polygram Jazz. "They're not expensive to record—all acoustic, no big equipment rental—and some of them get press attention, depending on their personalities" (Mandel 1992, 86). On average, a label spent only $60,000 to record and promote a mainstream jazz record, when rock stars expended millions of dollars on finished products. At such a low cost, a company recouped its money with sales of thirty-five hundred CDs, a minuscule number in the age of platinum-selling platters.

Hard-bop traditionalists helped companies sell discs from their reissue programs by extolling the jazz legacy. "It's notable, too, that at a time when the record companies are interested in selling CDs from their back catalogs, they come up with people who play well, talk well, and say, 'pay attention to the traditions,'" wrote Dave Helland, then the associate editor of a Chicago-based monthly (Mandel 1992, 99).

To market the new players, the record industry labeled them the "young lions." "The Young Lions concept is something a number of people used to define Wynton and Branford Marsalis, Roy Hargrove and some of the others," explained George Butler at Columbia. "When I signed Wynton there was talk of Young Lions by [festival promoter] George Wein and [then-CBS records division president] Bruce Lundvall. It was a commercial hook" (Mandel 1992, 84).

Companies unleashed a promotional campaign for the young lions. Labels featured ads on twenty-four-hour commercial radio stations that highlighted the hard-bop revivalists, such as KKGO in Los Angeles, WJAZ in Stamford, Connecticut, and National Public Radio jazz stations. "Radio is helping spread this music, particularly the pure jazz stations, where airplay really aids sales," Ellen Cohn, vice president of the Los Angeles-based Chase Music Group, reported in 1989 (Mandel 1992, 86).

Trumpet master Roy Hargrove. *Photograph courtesy of Brian McMillen*

The record business relied on the national press to promote the reemergence of the mainstream. "For straight-ahead records, there's nothing more important than attention in the non-music press: *Newsweek*, *Time*, *The Wall Street Journal*, *USA Today*," noted Richard Seidel (Mandel 1992, 86). Labels scheduled dozens of controversial interviews with such young lions as Wynton Marsalis and Terence Blanchard to cast a national spotlight on neo-hard bop. "Every once in a while you get a wave of mainstream press," recalled Mark Whitfield about the eighties. "*USA Today* or *People* magazine and that kind of thing, regular television shows and *Time* magazine articles that spotlight the accomplishments of a few, select group of jazz musicians and that brings a lot of attention to the whole scene" (Carver and Bernstein 1998, 143–44).

By the early eighties, corporate-sponsored jazz festivals further popularized the young jazzsters. In 1979, the city of Chicago launched a jazz festival, which by 1982 secured sponsorship from Kool cigarettes. The week-long concert series featured Wynton Marsalis in 1981, 1987, and 1991 as well as many other young lions. Four years later, Junichi Shibata, head of audio product marketing at Victor of Japan, or JVC, underwrote the Newport Jazz Festival. In 1985, the renamed JVC Jazz Festival Newport featured Wynton Marsalis as one of its premier performers. The same year, JVC featured young lions at jazz festivals in Bad Segeburg, Germany; Nice, France; and London.

Traditional jazz men climbed the chart during the eighties. Wynton Marsalis sold several hundred thousand copies of each jazz release and, in 1985, won the *Billboard* Top Artist in Jazz award by topping his fusion competitors. Other young lions such as Marcus Roberts hit the *Billboard* Top Ten jazz-artists and album lists. In 1989, amid the reemergence of bebop, the long-deceased Charlie Parker won top jazz artist honors for reissues of his records. "It's a phenomenon," gushed Steve Backer, who recorded many of the young lions on the RCA Novus label (Piazza 1990, 35).

Even films spotlighted the postwar jazz tradition of the forties and fifties. In October 1986, director Bertrand Tavernier released *Round Midnight*. The movie—based loosely upon the book *Dance of the Infidels* about the final years of pianist Bud Powell in Paris—cast hard-bop, tenor-sax master Dexter Gordon in the leading role as a down-and-out saxophone player who was modeled after Lester Young. The film became a box office hit, Dexter Gordon received an Academy Award nomination for best actor, and Herbie Hancock won an Oscar for best score. Two years later, Clint Eastwood directed *Bird*, a tribute to the life and times of Charlie Parker. The movie won the Academy Award for sound and snagged the Grand Prix Award of the Belgian Film Critics Association. The same year, Bruce Weber released *Let's Get Lost*, a full-length documentary about trumpeter Chet Baker. The film garnered an Academy Award nomination for best picture in the documentary feature category.

Jazz at Lincoln Center institutionalized the return of traditional jazz. In 1987, at the instigation of Wynton Marsalis, the Lincoln Center for the Performing Arts in New York City began to offer jazz concerts. Four years later, Jazz at Lincoln Center (JLC) officially opened with concerts throughout New York City and, the next year, launched a jazz series on National Public Radio. "In 1987 here was a guy who could play on trumpet a Haydn concerto with a symphony orchestra as well as anyone else could, then take a cab to a club and play with Art Blakey," emphasized former JLC director Rob Gibson. "So Wynton has had a whole lot to do with making something like Jazz at Lincoln Center possible" (Reich 1992, 18).

The Thelonious Monk Institute of Jazz encouraged and gave visibility to young, usually mainstream pianists. Founded in 1986 by drummer Thelonious Monk III, opera singer Maria Fisher, and trumpeter Clark Terry, the Institute staged its first competition in 1987. With Wynton choosing the tunes for competitors, Marcus Roberts won the award. The next year, the classically trained Ted Rosenthal, who later played with hard boppers Art Farmer and Phil Woods, won top honors. In 1989, Bill Cunliffe, who idolized Oscar Peterson, grabbed the award, subsequently recording a series of mainstream jazz and classical albums.

On December 4, 1987, the United States Congress formally legitimized the jazz tradition and supported the efforts of Marsalis and his traditional compatriots. Congress resolved "that jazz is hereby designated as a rare and valuable national American treasure to which we should devote our attention, support and resources to make certain it is preserved, understood, and promulgated" ("Text of a Concurrent Resolution" 1987).

By the end of the decade, the mainstream jazz movement had sent waves throughout the music industry and American culture. "Wynton Marsalis ushered in this youth-oriented era earlier in the decade by winning accolades for playing both mainstream jazz and classical music, beginning at age 20," reported *Billboard* in 1989. "Jazz performers who are stirring things up in the marketplace these days tend to be those with traditional roots" (McAdams 1990, 1). In a lengthy article on May 20, 1990, the *New York Times* cast its lot squarely with the traditionalists. "For a long time, young musicians were taught to play a hybrid form that was jazz in name only, often heavily electronic, with large infusions of funk and rock in it. Jazz has always been concerned with technical precision, melody, instrumental tone, blues feeling, and swing; the music younger musicians had been playing ignored these elements in favor of volume and simple dance rhythms. Suddenly, though, young musicians are rediscovering the jazz tradition." The *Times* identified "the main catalyst in this renaissance [as] trumpeter Wynton Marsalis" (Piazza 1990, 34, 64).

On October 22, 1990, *Time* magazine graced its cover with the headline, "The New Jazz Age" and a photo of Wynton Marsalis, who joined only Louis Armstrong, Duke Ellington, Thelonious Monk, and Dave Brubeck as jazz artists on a *Time* cover. "At 29, New Orleans-born trumpeter Wynton Marsalis is inspiring a youthful renaissance of America's greatest musical tradition," the magazine proclaimed. "Largely under his influence, a jazz renaissance is flowering on what was once barren soil. People are beginning to get the message that jazz is not just another style of popular music but a major American cultural achievement and a heritage that must not be lost" (Sancton and Thigpen 1990, 64–65). Wynton Marsalis, reflecting a conservative mood in America and benefiting from the advent of the compact disc, had succeeded in resurrecting the African-American jazz tradition.

For Discussion and Further Study

Chapter Quiz

1. How did the historic confrontation between Wynton Marsalis and Miles Davis at the Vancouver Jazz Festival reflect their two opposing views of jazz?

2. How did Marsalis's upbringing in New Orleans and his education influence his attitude toward the kind of music he chose to perform? What were some of his critiques of fusion music?

3. What was the impact of the new compact disc format on jazz? How did this dovetail with the influence of new centers of jazz study in a more academic setting, such as the Berklee School of Music?

4. What was the impact of new institutions like Jazz at Lincoln Center? What were some of the controversies that arose around the increasing institutionalization of jazz?

JAZZ IN THE AGE OF TECHNOLOGY

Hip-Hop Jazz, Acid Jazz, and the Internet

This chapter deals with new technology and changes in the jazz business during the 1980s and 1990s. It describes how technological innovations such as drum machines and samplers led to new musical styles such as hip-hop jazz. The text also outlines how entrepreneurial deejays filled dance halls and created record labels to develop acid jazz. It describes the sudden and explosive changes that the Internet brought to the music business by reshaping the way music, including jazz, was produced, marketed, and consumed.

In 1977, twenty-four-year-old Roger Linn entered a newly opened computer store. "A friend of mine took me to The Computer Store, which was the only place in Los Angeles that sold them," related Linn, the son of a music professor and opera singer who experimented with guitar effects at the age of fourteen and later joined the studio band of rocker/arranger Leon Russell as a guitar and synthesizer player. "It was run by these proto-typical nerds who used words like bytes, megawatts and gigahertz. I was intrigued. Then another shop popped up into existence near me, so I bought [a computer] for $3,000. I was convinced that there was art inside that box, and I was the one that had to pull it out" (Noakes 2006, 2).

Linn wondered about the application of his new computer to drums. "If you record a track with a bad drummer and his timing is off, then the drummer who comes in to overdub his part is going to have to match the wavering tempo," mused Linn. Drummers "used to say, 'I wish I could change the beat to have the bass drum here or the snare drum here.' I'm sure that lots of people thought that [a drum machine] would be a great idea, it's just that nobody else decided to make it!" (Noakes 2006, 2).

Over a two-year period, Linn taught himself computer programming and developed a computer interface by using an existing sound board. He invited studio drummer Art Wood to generate several beats, which Linn recorded. "These sessions were hilarious," remembered Linn. "The drummer would come into the studio, set up his drums, hit a drum once or twice, and then leave!" In addition to drum beats, he "got lots of good samples from top musicians who wanted their own sounds made into chips, and who were willing to add their sounds to our available library. [I] built an analog-to-digital converter that sampled directly into my computer, and wrote a program to control it, then burned the samples into memory chips" (White 2002). The inventor also created programs to allow the samples to "swing" and correct human timing errors. In 1979, the electronics designer unveiled the Linn Electronics LM-1 Drum Computer, the first machine that sampled actual drum beats and music rather than producing synthesizer-like sounds. The sampler had arrived.

Jazz pianist Herbie Hancock, having a degree in engineering and always fascinated with new gadgets, bought two of Linn's machines, which were priced at a hefty cost of $5,000. Hancock immediately tested the machine on his 1980 release, the disco-flavored *Monster*, along with other electronic instruments such as the E-Mu Polyphonic keyboard, the Clavitar, the Waves Minimoog (synthesizer), and the Rhodes 88 Suitcase piano.

Despite Hancock's endorsement, Linn soon closed his business. He joined newly created Japanese company Akai when significant sales of his expensive machine failed to materialize and another Japanese electronics firm, Roland, marketed a competing sampler, the TR-808, for $1,200. In 1986, Linn and Akai released the S900 sampler at less than $1,000. Two years later, the company launched the MPC (MIDI Production Center) 60, which included sixteen large rubber pads or triggers that gave a producer the means to create beats as well as record, sequence, and then sample recorded material. Easy to use and affordable, the MPC 60 sampler became a standard in the music industry along with the Roland TR-909, which succeeded the TR-808 and had capabilities similar to the Akai machine.

By the late eighties, the sampler had revolutionized music. No longer requiring an expensive studio or even the ability to play an instrument, the relatively inexpensive machine allowed a producer to load it with several minutes of prerecorded snippets of music and refine and reshuffle them to create layers of sound that resulted in a new musical creation. Unlike the synthesizer, which generated sounds, the sampler allowed a person to digitally splice together preexisting beats and musical passages into innovative musical concoctions. It permitted disc jockeys who previously only spun records to sample tidbits from vast record collections and combine them for exciting and unexpected results. By letting a producer glean material from any style, the sampler paved the way for new hybrid genres such as house, techno, and hip-hop and such spin-offs as acid jazz and hip-hop jazz to introduce a brave new musical world.

Chicago House

Disc jockey Frankie Knuckles from the Chicago dance-club scene patched together instrumental samples to develop "house music." Leaving the disco scene in New York City for Chicago in 1977, Knuckles (b. Francis Nicholls) realized that he needed to create his own music because he could not locate new disco records. Using a Roland TR-909 drum machine/rhythm composer, he added preprogrammed rhythms into his show to intensify the four-to-the-floor, bass-heavy disco beat, prolong certain parts of a song to excite the dancers, and link one song to another. Knuckles launched the new sound for a gay, African-American audience at a three-story Chicago nightclub, the Warehouse, which gave the style its name, "house."

DJ Pierre (b. Nathaniel Pierre Jones) developed a subgenre of house called "acid house." He employed the shaky, multiple-frequency whir of a Roland TB-303 baseline synthesizer with a built-in sequencer to achieve an electronic squelch, which resembled a repetitive bird call. Collaborating with two friends in the group Phuture, in 1987 DJ Pierre produced the distortion of "Acid Trax," which became a phenomenon after disc jockey Ron Hardy played it for dancers at Chicago's Muzic Box club. By the eighties, Chicago DJs had propelled the instrumental house and acid house into underground sensations.

Nearby in Detroit, three turntable prodigies merged house music with European electronica to create "techno." Juan Atkins, the son of a concert promoter, was enchanted with the stripped-down sound of the band Kraftwerk, which built a sound that resembled the industrial pulse found in their German homeland. "I just froze in my tracks. Everything was so clean and precise," he recalled (Brewster and Broughton 2000, 324). He wanted his "music to sound like computers talking to each other" (Collin 1997, 23–24; Reynolds 1998, 20).

At the same time, Derrick May and Kevin Saunderson, two of Atkins's longtime friends, became captivated with house during visits to Chicago. "Some people took me to the Power Plant where I heard Frankie Knuckles play," related May. "Frankie was really a turning point in my life" (Brewster and Broughton 2000, 329). In the early eighties, the threesome merged the pounding, industrial-sounding music of Kraftwerk with the four-to-the-floor bass of house into a concoction called techno, a stark yet danceable music with hammering drumbeats. May characterized the musical merger as "George Clinton [a master of funk] and Kraftwerk stuck in an elevator with only a sequencer to keep them company" (Rubin 2009, 38).

A Rave New World

During the eighties, the house style overwhelmed an economically depressed Great Britain. Like in America, where the conservative Ronald Reagan rolled back social programs, British prime minister Margaret Thatcher's government implemented austerity measures that resulted in a 20 percent unemployment rate among England's youth.

Poor, disenchanted youth responded to adversity by dancing their troubles away. During summer 1986, many young Britons traveled to Ibiza, one of the four Balearic Islands in the Mediterranean off the east coast of Spain. "From the age of sixteen," related a club goer, "they left home because they didn't have careers or anything, and basically they were just thieves" who robbed tourists and danced to a musical mix that included acid house and techno.

In 1987, several revelers imported the two genres to London. Paul Oakenfold, an executive for Profile Records, staged a birthday party in Ibiza for himself with friends Danny Rampling and Nicky Holloway. By chance, they found the club Amnesia, where they witnessed wild dancing to house music and became enraptured with the sound. After returning to London, Oakenfold and his partner Ian St. Simon started the dance clubs the Project, the Future, and Spectrum; Rampling founded Shoom; and Holloway established the Trip. "You'd come down and you'd dance for six hours," remembered Oakenfold about the clubs (Reynolds 1998, 59).

The new dance culture exploded in Great Britain. By July 1988, thousands of youths filled dozens of clubs. "It was like a virus," remarked Kevin Saunderson, who attended some of the clubs on a trip to London. "It spread to everybody" (Matos 2015, 31).

By 1988, thousands of British teens had become enamored with acid house and techno. The growing legions congregated in abandoned warehouses for "raves," and danced to acid-house and techno pioneers who traveled to London to perform at the events. "When I first went to Europe, the first big party I played was in London for 5,000 kids at a rave in a big film studio," Juan Atkins recalled (Ladoucer 1998, 49).

The Birth of Acid Jazz

British youth such as Gilles Peterson, enthusiastic about jazz, invented the new genre called acid jazz to expand the dance subculture. As a youth in South London, Peterson desperately searched for an identity. "I was in a boy's school, where you had to belong to a tribe. You had to be a mod, a skinhead, a teddy boy, [or] into your heavy metal," he explained. After visiting a friend in his neighborhood, he heard the jazzy pop soul of Bobby Caldwell, who had just released a self-titled debut album. Peterson immediately decided "that I wanted to be into jazz funk" and joined the jazz-funk crowd. "I would go and buy my pegged leather trousers from Jones in King's Road," he recalled, "and I would go out and buy my shoes, called pods, from a special shop in Kingston. I had the uniform. I had my hair in a wedge haircut, and I wore it proudly." He also read *Blues & Soul* and *African-American Echoes* to stay current with the latest trends in the music (Mao 2015).

Peterson and his friends frequented clubs that catered to the jazz-funk crowd. At venues like the Horse Shoe, the Wag Club, and the Electric Ballroom, disc jockeys such as Paul Murphy spun jazz records. "I was pulling out tracks by Art Blakey and stuff like that," remembered Murphy (Cotgrove 2009, 192). In late 1984, when he took a residency at the Wag Club, Murphy "started playing old Blue Note records.

People were coming away going, 'I've been to this club and I've heard Miles Davis' "So What" on the dance floor'" (193).

Unlike American jazz fans who listened intently from their seats, British jazz-funk youngsters danced furiously to the music. Disc jockeys spun platters for mostly African-American dancers called steppers who whirled frantically in a dance named "cockroach stomping" or "crushing." "Imagine the motion of extinguishing a cigarette with the ball of your right foot moving to your left foot and repeating," recalled one observer on the scene (Cotgrove 2009, 41). Some dancers formed formal troupes, including I Dance Jazz, which held sway at the Electric Ballroom, and Manchester's Jazz Defektors, which ruled the Wag Club.

The funky jazz scenesters sometimes imported jazz acts to play for dancing. In July 1981, Paul Murphy invited the Heath Brothers band—Percy, Jimmy, Stanley Crowell, and two colleagues—to the Horse Shoe Club. "Percy Heath said that he'd never seen people dance to jazz," recalled Murphy (Cotgrove 2009, 191). During the next few months, dancers at the club reveled to soul-jazz percussionist Jay Hoggard and fusion drummer Alphonse Mouzon.

In 1980, at the age of sixteen, Gilles Peterson contributed to the jazz-funk subculture by broadcasting a pirate (unlicensed) radio station from the garden shed of his parents' home. "I had this set-up in my back garden, turntables, mixer with a recorder. I used to record an hour on a TDK cassette and my next door neighbor would record the other hour." His father helped him plant a transmitter a few miles from his house in a hilly part of South London called Epsom Downs. "We would have an aerial in the tree, the aerial would go into the transmitter, the transmitter would be connected to my cassette player. We'd press play, [and] go through the transmitter. Of course, the power would come from a car battery" (Mao 2015).

Gaining a reputation through the radio show, Peterson hoped to land a job as a disc jockey in a jazz-funk club. "What I used to do was organize coach trips," he recalled. "I'd organize 50 tickets, and I'd call the club and say, 'Look, I'm Gilles Peterson, I'm going to bring 50 people if you put me in the lineup. Give me a gig'" (Mao 2015). Club owners, eager for business, agreed to Gilles's demand, and by the mid-eighties, the fledgling disc jockey was exciting dancers by playing jazz-funk discs. He first jockeyed a weekend at the Bognor Regis resort near Brighton and, in April 1984, graduated to the coveted Friday night spot at the Electric Ballroom, replacing Paul Murphy. He progressed to the Wag Club and Sunday afternoons at Dingwalls. "[Club] residencies are really important, because that's how you break music, that's how you develop a scene, that's how you create a movement," he asserted (Mao 2015). In 1985, Peterson compiled *Jazz Juice*, a compilation of his club music, which included tracks by Miles Davis, Art Blakey, and fusion percussionist Airto Moreira.

Peterson chose jazz with funky beats for dancers. He initially picked organist George Duke's "A Brazilian Love Affair." "Another important record was Herbie Hancock's 'Mr. Hands' [1980]. Herbie is my all-time favorite musician," Gilles declared. If the mood permitted, he turned to the free jazz/hard bop of "You've Got to Have Freedom" (1980) by saxophonist Pharoah Sanders and the hard bop of Art Blakey and His Jazz Messengers. "When I was about 19 years old I was DJing regularly at the Electric Ballroom in Camden," he smiled. "I used to get there at the start of the night, but I was always hungry, as it was a long way on the bus from Sutton to Camden. So I'd always put on Art Blakey's 'A Night in Tunisia' and then go round the corner to KFC. I'd buy my dinner, eat it, come back and it'd still be playing! It was 17 minutes long. This was my weekly routine" (Servini 2014).

By the mid-eighties, the clubs changed when acid house swept Britain. "The scene gently grew into something that was more substantial, the clubs became slightly bigger and people started going to Ibiza," noted Peterson. "I was part of the whole scene with Nicky Holloway and Danny Rampling that went to Ibiza in 1985. We used to organize holidays, again similar philosophy, you'd get 300 people to come from London, you'd give them a cheap ticket to Ibiza, then we'd all go DJ. And, suddenly, these kids who were previously just drinking beer in pubs in South London listening to jazz-funk records were taking ecstasy tablets, listening to music from Detroit and Ibiza. That was acid house" (Mao 2015).

To retain his audiences, Gilles wove acid house together with jazz. "It was a good opportunity to be able to create a subversive, alternative version of acid house—and that is what acid jazz was. In a way, it was the drug culture energy, but mixed with a much more freaky soundtrack. We would mix acid house with free jazz and funk" (Mao 2015). "It was when the acid house club started—Shoom— that it all changed," agreed Chris Bangs, the disc jockey who mentored and collaborated with Peterson. "A lot of our hardcore crowd suddenly disappeared. We were very conscious that we needed to change musically" (Cotgrove 2009, 224). In 1986, the DJ duo banded together as the Baptist Brothers. "We used to track down funky stuff on labels like Blue Note, Groove Merchant and Prestige," recollected Bangs (Hoffman n.d.). The pair landed residencies in several London nightspots to spin a funk-filled jazz.

Peterson coined the term "acid jazz" with Chris Bangs. On February 6, 1988, the Baptist Brothers followed acid-house record spinner Nicky Holloway, who finished his set with Phuture's "Acid Trax." "Chris Bangs and I felt under a little pressure, as we were always the more radical ones in that scene, and the soul boys were more straight and conservative. But suddenly after discovering Ecstasy, Ibiza, and acid house, they were more mad than us, and so we were really worried about what we were going to play," recalled Peterson (Mao 2015). He carefully placed the phonograph needle on a record by Art Blakey and Louis "Sabu" Martinez, the percussionist who had played with jazz greats as diverse as Dizzy Gillespie, Charlie Parker, Lionel Hampton, and Benny Goodman. "There was a giant screen behind us showing psychedelic photos, graffiti art and text," continued Bangs. "So there's this heavy Latin track spinning and the screen keeps flashing up 'ACID ... ACID' behind us in giant letters and we thought it was well funny. I grabbed the mike and shouted, 'Fuck Acid House—This Is Acid Jazz!!' We played our craziest tunes, slowing down and speeding up intros to tracks like Mickey & the Soul Generations' 'Iron Leg,' and Gilles spent the whole night repeating the words, 'Acid Jazz,' on the mike between every track, the place went crazy and a new 'genre' was born" (Hoffman n.d.).

To formalize acid jazz, Chris Bangs developed a logo for the music. In late March, he modified the smiley face of acid house by crossing the eyes of the drawing and adding glasses, a tuft of hair, and buck teeth. Acid-jazz fans refined the image even further by transforming the smiley face into an image of Dizzy Gillespie with a goatee.

In July 1988, an article in the magazine *I.D.* sparked interest in the music. "What really started acid jazz was, soon after we came up with the name," recalled Chris Bangs, "a spoof article [by John Godfrey] appeared in *I.D.* magazine. He had contributions from Simon Booth [guitarist for the acid-jazz band Working Week], Eddie Piller, me and Gilles. That got everybody talking" (Cotgrove 2009, 225). During the same summer, Paul Bradshaw launched the magazine *Straight No Chaser* to document the emerging acid-jazz scene. At the same time, Gilles Peterson contributed a column, "Mad on Jazz," to *Blues and Soul*. "Tune in, turn on, drop out— acid jazz is here," he proclaimed. "What is acid jazz," he rhetorically asked. "Acid jazz is the sound of esoteric noises over danceable jazz rhythms. It's mad, sure, but it's another way of introducing John Coltrane to jazz ignorants" (Cotgrove 2009, 62).

A successful Gilles Peterson spinning discs for an enthusiastic crowd. *Wikimedia Commons. Photographer: Tom Morgan*

Acid Jazz Takes Hold

During a trip to the Wag Club, Eddie Piller converted to acid jazz. Piller, a disc jockey and a diehard fan of the sixties mod scene, which spawned the Small Faces and the Who, walked in the club with organist James Taylor, who led the jazz-funk outfit the James Taylor Quartet. Both "were blown away by what was happening there," maintained Chris Bangs. "The next time I saw the James Taylor Quartet they were playing a set close to what Gilles and I spun as DJs" (Hoffman n.d.).

During late 1987, Peterson and Piller, both twenty-three years old, established Acid Jazz Records to cater to the "scene building around the music. Inspired by the energy from the acid-house scene, we merged it with soul, R & B and the music we loved—making it modern, progressive and exciting," Eddie Piller noted. "Acid jazz was our reaction to acid house, the name stuck and the whole thing exceeded our expectations" ("Interview: Eddie Piller" 2012).

In May 1988, "Frederic Lies Still" by Galliano was issued by the Acid Jazz label. The single sampled the jazzy funk beats of the introduction to "Freddie's Dead" by Pucho and the Latin Soul Brothers and grafted electronic-house squeals and the ranting social poetry of Rob Galliano (b. Robert Gallagher) over it. Within a week and with no publicity, the track sold two thousand copies, and within a year more than twenty thousand acid-jazz fans purchased it. "We didn't have much of a budget but we managed to pull a few favors and got some great U.K. musicians to come and play," mentioned Chris Bangs, who produced the first album by Galliano. "We sampled anything and everything, threw it together, all stressed out, as none of us had any experience of a project of that size and somehow came out with something pretty good at the end" (Hoffman n.d.).

In 1990, the Brand New Heavies—a name derived from the James Brown moniker, Minister of the Super Heavy Funk—signed to the Acid Jazz label. Conceived

LISTENING GUIDE 41

The Brand New Heavies

 "PUT THE FUNK BACK IN IT"

Acid jazz began as a movement by disc jockeys who spun danceable jazz records. It morphed into a genre performed by bands such as the Brand New Heavies, which in 1990 released a debut that combined acid-house bleeps, jazz solos, and funk rhythms.

Personnel: Jan Kincaid (drums and percussion), Simon Bartholomew (guitar), Lascelles Gordon (guitar and percussion), Jim Wellman (saxophones), Andrew Levy (keyboards), and N'Dea Davenport and Jay Ella Ruth (vocals).

0:00–0:08	The song starts with a drum roll by Jan Kincaid and the rattlesnake-like hiss of a percussion instrument similar to the casaba. At the same time, the synthesizer establishes the insistent, syncopated, funky rhythm for the tune with an organ-like pattern accompanied by a knocking sound, which creates a cross rhythm.
0:09–0:13	The vocals start very softly in the background.
0:14–0:28	Vocalists N'Dea Davenport and Jay Ella Ruth enter with the phrase "you ain't funky no more" in a call-and-response with the heavy funk beat to generate yet another rhythm. At the end of the section, they proclaim "let's put the funk back in it."
0:29–0:51	The squeal of the Roland synthesizer establishes the melody and introduces the acid house element into the song over the vocal chant. The Roland squeals and the polyrhythms of the synthesizer and the chanting vocals create an interesting contrast.
0:52–1:02	The keyboard solos with a festive-sounding atmosphere in the background. It establishes the B pattern, which starts with two sustained notes, follows with another line, and ends with a sustained note.
1:03–1:39	The synthesizer continues the solo in a lower pitch, again dominated by sustained notes, which increase the syncopated nature of the funky song. The passage ends with the whir of a percussion instrument and a drum beat.
1:15–1:39	The acid-jazz squeal reenters the groove to reestablish the melody and contrast with the polyrhythms of the bass-heavy synthesizer beat and the vocal chant, which now just implores the listener to "put the funk back in it."
1:40–2:04	The distorted guitar of Simon Bartholomew takes the lead around the melody and repeats four very different variants of the same phrase, one played very slowly and the others played more quickly. He delivers each iteration of the phrase in an ascending pitch. A cymbal crash, background crowd noise, and the whir of a percussion instrument signal a transition to the next passage.
2:05–2:15	Bartholomew solos on the B section of the song, first with an ascending line, then a drop in pitch with sustaining and bent notes for a bluesy feel, and finally an ascending line, which returns to his original solo line.
2:16–2:25	In a return to the melody, the guitarist raises the pitch, plays two notes back and forth three times, and in a tremolo moves rapidly between three notes to end the solo. The whir of the percussion instrument signals a new passage.
2:26–2:30	To jar the listener, Jim Wellman enters on saxophone with three almost overblown notes, the last of which he sustains with quavering vibrato.

2:31	Wellman pauses as the rhythm continues.
2:32–2:58	The saxophonist plays a two-measure phrase twice around the melody with significant variants. In one instance, he drops extremely low on the horn register to accentuate the bass-heavy rhythm. He also pauses unexpectedly to add to the rhythmic complexity and showcase the other rhythmic lines behind him.
2:59–3:03	Wellman fastens upon one note and plays it quickly and repeatedly.
3:04–3:15	The saxophone returns to his original theme as the song slowly fades out.

by three school chums—drummer/keyboardist Jan Kincaid, guitarist Simon Bartholomew, and bassist Andrew Levy—the band forged a sound from funky jazz beats and Chicago house. In addition to the core members, the group debuted with two saxophones, a trumpeter, and the smooth vocals of Jay Williamson. "It was a reaction to acid house that had just come out," insisted Bartholomew ("An Interview with the Brand New Heavies" 2013).

In 1989, the veteran jazz-funk/acid-jazz outfit Incognito signed with the Talkin' Loud label, which Gilles Peterson had launched after he left Acid Jazz. The band originally formed in 1979 and was led by Jean-Paul "Bluey" Maunick, who idolized Stevie Wonder and other funk and jazz artists. Two years later, the group delivered *Jazz Funk*, which failed to generate much interest. After joining Peterson's company ten years later, Incognito burst on the scene with a mix of jazz, funk, house, electronics, and samples for the danceable *Inside Life*. Acid jazz, observed Bluey, "describes the music where we come from" (Ruffin 2009).

Jay Kay (b. Jason Kaye) and his outfit, Jamiroquai, made the biggest commercial splash among the acid-jazz bands. The son of local jazz singer Karen Kaye, Jay met Tunji Williams, the manager of the Brand New Heavies, who interested the Acid Jazz label in the Stevie Wonder–influenced singer. In 1992, the band released "When You Gonna Learn," an amalgam of funk, jazz, and house that became a dance-floor hit and attracted major-label interest. Signed to Sony, in 1993 Kay and his band released their first album, *Emergency on Planet Earth*. In subsequent records, Jamiroquai veered more toward pop and sold more than twenty-five million records worldwide.

The James Taylor Quartet, nurtured by Eddie Piller, landed with a major label. Taylor, an organist initially influenced by such soul men as Booker T. Jones of the MGs, learned about jazz organ sensation Jimmy Smith and started to offer a funk-drenched, gritty jazz for club dancers. "When I discovered Jimmy Smith, which was much more about the Hammond [B-3 organ] and jazz," he disclosed, "that pulled me in a completely different direction," he explained (Cherry Red Records n.d.). To fully implement a shift to funky jazz, Taylor recruited guitarist Paul Carr. "My background certainly prepared me for this music," Carr asserted. "I grew up listening to it, but it just wasn't called acid jazz. I knew all of Jimmy Smith's stuff, Jack McDuff and Grant Green" (Carr 2015).

By 1988, the quartet had added acid-jazz elements to its music. The group first recorded the acid jazz of *Wait a Minute*, including the track "Starsky and Hutch," which showcased Galliano and former James Brown horn men Pee Wee Ellis and Fred Wesley and reached number sixty-eight on the chart. In 1990, James Taylor and his band scored with the dance-club anthem "Love the Life," which Taylor described as "a funk thing which is a four-four thing with Hammond and soul vocals. At the time they called it acid jazz" (Cherry Red Records n.d.). To guitarist Carr, the music put "a fresh face on [funk jazz] for a new generation" (Carr 2015).

Armed with samplers by the late eighties, some notable disc jockeys such as Chris Bangs pumped out sampled acid-jazz discs. Under the alias of the Quiet Boys, Chris Bangs waxed "Let the Good Times Roll," assisted by Galliano, and followed with two singles and two albums for Acid Jazz Records. "As sampling technology developed in the late '80s and DJs started to make tunes, I started messing around in the studio," Bangs related. "That gave me a chance to be able to express myself musically in a way I never could when playing or singing in bands. I made a few tunes for Acid Jazz Records and when Gilles starting Talkin' Loud he invited me to record a couple of tunes" (Hoffman 2015).

During the early nineties, the acid-jazz scene gained momentum. In March 1990, Gilles Peterson found a job at JAZZ FM, the first radio station in London dedicated to jazz. The next year, he switched to KISS 100 FM to continue an all-jazz format. In late 1992, Eddie Piller opened an acid-jazz club symbolically named the Blue Note, which "worked surprisingly well and soon brought people in from all over London," according to Piller (Eggleton 2012). By the early nineties, related Snowboy (b. Mark Cotgrove), who led an acid-jazz band, "there were now hundreds of acid-jazz nights springing up all over the country in bars, universities, colleges, clubs, back rooms of pubs" (Cotgrove 2009, 64). Acid-jazz had become a movement among British youths who danced to jazz until the sun rose the next day.

Us3 unexpectedly and somewhat accidentally brought British acid jazz to the United States. Masterminded by the production duo of Geoff Wilkinson and Mel Simpson and supplemented by trumpeter Gerard Presencer and vocalist/rapper Rahsaan Kelly, the group sprang from the acid-house dance culture. "I came out of the whole jazz-dance scene in London in the mid-to-late '80s, when you could DJ straight jazz, like the classic Blue Note sound or Art Blakey," Wilkinson recounted. "People would come out in suits and ties and dance to it all night. It was great. Then you started to get live bands playing along with the DJs playing old stuff." "When I was 15 or 16, I started to play with the Brand New Heavies and on recordings with other acid-jazz groups," explained Presencer about his experience. "I'm on quite a lot of recordings in the early '90s like with Jamiroquai" (Grow 2013).

In 1991, Wilkinson and Simpson used a sampler to wax an acid-jazz disc. They produced a white-label, twelve-inch track, "The Band Played the Boogie," which included a sample of the 1970 groove-heavy song "Sookie Sookie" by funky jazz guitarist Grant Green, who had cut a series of albums for Blue Note Records. After an executive from EMI Records, which then owned Blue Note, heard the sample, Wilkinson received a call from the label. Wilkinson, fearing legal reprisal because the sample had not been cleared for copyright, made a pitch to the company. "I said, 'If you let me have the Blue Note back catalog as a resource, we could create the ultimate fusion'" (Grow 2013). In 1993, the two producers, securing the approval of Blue Note president Bruce Lundvall, pieced together *Hand on the Torch*. On each song, they sampled Blue Note jazz men such as pianists Horace Silver and Thelonious Monk, horn men Lou Donaldson and Donald Byrd, organists Big John Patton and Rueben Wilson, and vibes player Bobby Hutcherson (Grow 2013).

With *Hand on the Torch*, Us3 focused the attention of America on acid jazz. Aided by a sparkling video on MTV, the group hit the Top Ten with "Cantaloop (Flip Fantasia)," a song based on the Herbie Hancock composition "Cantaloupe Island"

and a sample of Art Blakey and the Jazz Messengers, and scored the first-ever million-selling record by Blue Note. "It's nice that people are doing these things for jazz," commented a grateful Lou Donaldson, who had been sampled in the song "It's Like That" (Grow 2013).

Others carried the British acid-jazz dance scene to the United States. In 1990, prompted by their experiences at acid-jazz clubs, Jonathan Rudnick from South Africa and Maurice Bernstein from London migrated to New York City. They first staged a series of concerts by such seventies funksters as the Ohio Players and George Clinton under the banner, Groove Academy. Within a few months, the duo launched weekend parties at various venues such as the Metropolis Café that featured sampled jazz loops, a disc jockey, and a live band. They called the dance parties, and eventually the club that housed them, Giant Step in honor of the John Coltrane album, *Giant Steps* (1960). "When we started Giant Step as a club," explained Rudnick, "it was to show people that there is an alternative to the traditional jazz scene here" (Birnbaum 1993, 34). "Our influence was obviously the dance jazz clubs in England," added Bernstein (Broughton 1996). The nightspot attracted such established jazz players as trumpeter Roy Hargrove.

Collective Groove, signed to the newly created Giant Step Records in 1994, documented the acid-jazz scene at the club. An aggregation of jazz musicians supplemented by percussionist/rapper Gordon "Nappy G" Clay, the group expertly combined jazz, funk, house beats, and elements of hip-hop into an original concoction. They recorded two albums on Giant Step to provide a soundtrack for acid-jazz-crazy American dancers. "It's not about people putting on a show and people watching us," contended Clay. "It's about the vibe and the energy and the dance feeling. If they can't dance to it, it's not fun" (Birnbaum 1993, 35). By the mid-nineties, Americans again danced to jazz.

Hip-Hop Jazz

While impoverished British youths combined jazz and house music with records and then samplers to produce acid jazz, young, poor African Americans in urban US ghettos fused jazz beats and hip-hop. Without money to buy instruments or enroll in music lessons, they purchased turntables and speakers, plugged them into street-side power sources, and created new music from prerecorded material.

During the early seventies, as disco became popular in New York City, some disc jockeys in the Bronx and Harlem such as Jamaican-raised Kool Herc (b. Clive Campbell) played short segments of a song, usually percussion parts, to keep the dance floor packed. Beginning in 1973, he took "funky percussion breaks and he just kept that beat going" over and over, remembered Afrika Bambaataa (b. Kevin Donovan), who deejayed several years after Herc.

Some disc jockeys added special effects onto the snippets of mostly funky music that they played. Kool Herc sometimes mixed the beats of two songs together by using two turntables. Employing a specially designed stylus, teenage "Grand Wizzard Theodore" Livingston "scratched," or moved, the records back and forth on the turntable to produce an innovative, rhythmic sound.

Building upon an oral-history tradition found in Africa and Jamaica, jockeys talked or rapped to their sets. "To attract their own followings, some of these DJs would give little raps to let the crowd know who was spinning the records," disclosed rapper Kurtis Blow (b. Curtis Walker). "As time went by, these raps became more elaborate, with the DJ sometimes including a call-and-response 'conversation' with the regulars in the house" (George, Banes, et al. 1985, xi).

To focus more on spinning records, some disc jockeys asked friends to rap, or emcee (MC), over their tracks. Kool Herc enlisted his high-school friend Coke La Rock. Grandmaster Flash (b. Joseph Saddler) asked Cowboy (b. Robert Keith Wiggins) to rap for him. By the end of the seventies, the number of deejays and MCs had expanded dramatically and, in 1979, several appeared on record with the Sugarhill Gang's "Rapper's Delight," which entered the national Top Forty and sold two million copies.

Herbie Hancock, a constant jazz innovator, took the hip-hop turntable culture to the mainstream. By 1982, the keyboardist "was pushing even further into electronic music, writing songs with more of a disco and R&B feel to them" (Hancock 2014, 235). When he heard the track "Buffalo Gals" by Malcolm McLaren, the Sex Pistols manager who had ventured into hip-hop, he "then knew that I wanted to use turntable scratching on my next record" (Hancock 2014, 237). Herbie enlisted the help of turntablist Grand Mixer DXT, who added his scratching to three selections of *Future Shock*, which featured Herbie on electronic keyboards. "This was a music revolution!" declared Hancock. "I had been only dimly aware of what was happening in the Bronx. Now I was thrilled beyond words to be in the middle of it, working with guys who had skills I hadn't even imagined before. This music was exciting and unpredictable, because scratching lets you change direction suddenly, cutting to another sound or groove. It was totally avant-garde but within the popular music context" (Hancock 2014, 238).

Columbia Records, looking for new commercial product, enthusiastically supported Hancock's new direction. "They flipped out, too—there were a lot of young people in the room, and they were going nuts, congratulating us, slapping me on the back," recalled Herbie.

The music-television network MTV promoted Hancock's hip-hop jazz. Launched on August 1, 1981, by Warner Communications and American Express,

Herbie Hancock. *Photograph courtesy of Brian McMillen*

the network broadcast a nonstop format of three-minute videos geared to youth who seldom listened to radio and had been raised on television. In August 1983, when Columbia released Hancock's *Future Shock*, the music channel had penetrated more than seventeen million homes on two thousand cable affiliates and was attracting a young demographic that tuned in on average for more than an hour every day.

Columbia Records produced a video clip for "Rockit," a single off Hancock's turntable-jazz album *Future Shock*. The record company hired Kevin Godley and Lol Creme, a team formerly behind the rock band 10cc who had turned to video production. Godley and Creme crafted a surrealistic video of, as Hancock raved, "Crazy dancing robot legs! A giant robot bird! Headless mannequins, interspersed with clips of my hands playing the synthesizer, and camera work that shook back and forth with every *whicka whicka whicka* of the scratching" (Hancock 2014, 242–43).

"Rockit" and its accompanying video shot up the chart. The video started in light rotation on MTV, quickly went into heavy rotation, and became one of the favorite clips of all time. It captured five MTV Video Music Awards at the inaugural ceremony. The twelve-inch single hit number-one on *Billboard*'s Hot Dance Club Play chart and number seventy-one on the Top 100. The album *Future Shock* peaked in the Top Fifty on the popular album chart. "*Future Shock* would go on to become the fourth-best-selling jazz record in history, and the success of 'Rockit' marked the beginnings of hip-hop as a mainstream musical style," exulted Herbie (Hancock 2014, 246).

When Herbie Hancock took his band on a *Future Shock* tour, he did not have time in concert for Grand Mixer DXT to switch from one record to another. To streamline the process, he "put all those songs and snippets on a single vinyl record" to easily play the samples during a show (Hancock 2014, 244).

Hip-hop jazz blossomed in the late eighties, when groups such as Gang Starr had ready access to inexpensive digital samplers. Gang Starr leaders Guru (b. Keith Elam) and DJ Premier (b. Christopher Martin) had been exposed to jazz at an early age. "Premier's grandfather used to be in a jazz band. When [Premier] was first getting into rap, he used to tell him, 'Yo, it's the same thing. It's just another expression of the street,'" remarked Guru, which stood for Gifts Unlimited Rhymes Universal. "With me, my godfather was a heavy jazz buff," continued Guru. "He'd sit us between two big ass speakers" (Banjoko 1991).

Having an appreciation of jazz, the two hip-hoppers plugged it into their own compositions. "Premier started to give me some mellow [jazz] breaks to rhyme to instead of those same old breaks that everybody was using," disclosed Guru. "He felt that they would bring out my vocals much more so we started getting into that" (Jam 1991). In 1988, they mixed jazz beats with hip-hop on "Words I Manifest" by heavily sampling Dizzy Gillespie's "Night in Tunisia." The next year, Gang Starr offered a tribute to the jazz heritage with "Jazz Music" on the album *No More Mr. Nice Guy*. In 1990, the duo delivered "Jazz Thing" with appearances by

DJ Premier of Gang Starr at the turntable. *Photographer: Mika Vaisannen, Mika-Photography.com*

LISTENING GUIDE 42

Herbie Hancock

🔊 **"ROCKIT"**

Innovator Herbie Hancock—who had played with Miles, organized an avant-garde band, and incorporated funk into jazz—brought the hip-hop culture to mainstream jazz with "Rockit." Promoted by MTV in a strange, robot-filled but successful video (https://www.youtube.com/watch?v=GHhD4PD75zY), he embraced the turntablist movement by showcasing Grand Mixer DXT (then D.ST) and an array of electronic instruments. He played

vocoder, the E-mu 4060 digital keyboard, the Fairlight CMI, the Rhodes Chroma, the Minimoog, and the Dr. Click rhythm controller. He recruited bassist Bill Laswell, drum-machine-master Michael Beinhorn, and Daniel Ponce on the double-headed batá drum for the session.

Recorded in 1982, the song appeared the next year as a single and on the *Future Shock* album, which cracked the Top Fifty.

0:00–0:03	The track explodes with scratching from Grand Mixer D.ST to establish a rhythm.
0:04–0:20	The drum machine enters to accompany the scratching.
0:21	Two synthesizer blasts enhance and diversify the rhythm, signaling a change to the next passage.
0:22–0:26	Without accompaniment, the scratching creates another rhythm by repeating a four-beat line seven times until the drum machine emerges with two drum beats and the synthesizer provides a blast to end it.
0:27–0:33	A new rhythm emerges with the double-headed, hourglass-shaped batá drum, which the Yoruba tribe in Nigeria used to send messages. The steady beat of the drum machine accompanies the batá drum.
0:34–0:35	A sustained, orchestral wash from the synthesizer appears.
0:36–0:44	The batá and drum machine continue the rhythm. The passage ends with a line from the drum machine.
0:45–1:02	Hancock establishes a highly syncopated theme or melody with the keyboard and states it twice. At the end of the passage, a very brief vocal can be heard.
1:03–1:19	After a flurry from the drum machine and a synthesizer blast, the batá and drum machine push the insistent beat. A two-beat, low-pitched vocalization at 1:13 gives interest and rhythmic complexity to the pattern.
1:20–1:37	Keyboardist Hancock slowly enters with a sustained note, which ascends in pitch and then states the theme at the slower tempo than the first statement at 0:45. He has backing from the batá and the drum machine. At 1:30, the vocalization again appears.
1:38–1:47	Hancock continues to state the theme with the batá and drum machine, now backed by a synthesizer wash in a flatted note to give the sound a bluesy, almost ominous feel. The passage ends with two quick drum beats.
1:48–1:55	The turntablist takes over, accompanied by periodic beats from the drum machine.
1:56–2:12	Keyboardist Hancock takes the theme at the original tempo with backing from the drums and a few vocalizations interspersed.

2:13–2:15	The drum machine provides a line as a break between statements of the theme.
2:16–2:49	Hancock proceeds with the theme four times with constant drum backing and interjections from vocalizations and a interruption from a synthesizer figure at the end of each statement of the melody.
2:50–2:51	The drum machine generates the same pattern as 2:13–2:15.
2:52–3:01	An innovative scratching solo begins with no accompaniment except for a very faint beat by the batá.
3:02–3:08	To create even more cross-rhythmic activity, the scratching and batá are joined by a drum-machine click to create further polyrhythm.
3:09–3:43	Starting at this point, the synthesizer unexpectedly and only sporadically emerges during the turntablist's solo to give added interest and rhythmic complexity. Throughout this passage, the turntablist repeats a phrase with periodic embellishments.
3:44–3:47	The turntablist abruptly changes rhythm.
3:48–3:52	The turntablist returns to the rhythm initially established at the beginning of the solo.
3:53–3:58	The turntablist again changes the rhythm until the drum machine interjects with a line to end the solo.
3:59–4:38	The turntablist delivers a two-note, sliding rhythm as a call to the response of the keyboard, which plays a syncopated, three-note line after each rhythm statement by the turntablist. A line by the drum machine signals the beginning of a new passage.
4:39–4:41	Hancock comes swooping in like a dive bomber to begin a solo.
4:42–4:49	The keyboardist offers a syncopated, funky solo with backing from the other personnel. He begins by twice repeating a highly syncopated, staccato phrase derived from the response to the turntablist.
5:00–5:17	Hancock repeats a fragment of the phrase at 4:42–4:49 eight times with slight variations.
5:18–5:22	The drum machine enters with the line it has used to end a passage and finishes the song with two explosive blasts.

pianist Kenny Kirkland and bassist Bob Hurst for the Spike Lee film *Mo' Better Blues*. "It's a natural mix," contended Guru about jazz and hip-hop. "Both music forms involve elements of improvisation and have a certain culture that goes along with them" (Chamber 1993, 64).

Other hip hoppers followed the jazzy direction of Gang Starr. In 1988, Stetsasonic sampled Blue Note keyboardist Lonnie Liston Smith on "Talkin' All That Jazz." Eric B. (b. Eric Barrier) and Rakim (b. William Griffin) borrowed a slice of Herbie Hancock's "Oliloqui Valley" for one of their songs. In 1991, A Tribe Called Quest sampled bop saxophonist Lucky Thompson on "Jazz (We've Got)." Two years later, the Digable Planets wove nuggets from saxophonist Sonny Rollins, Art Blakey and the Jazz Messengers, the Crusaders, and Lonnie Liston Smith into the album

LISTENING GUIDE 43

Gang Starr

🔗 **"JAZZ MUSIC"**

Gang Starr incorporated jazz fully into the hip-hop culture. On *No More Mr. Nice Guy* (1989), the duo (rapper Guru and spinner DJ Premier) waxed "Jazz Music," which outlined an African-American history of jazz and sampled the melody from Ramsey Lewis's "Les Fleur" (1968), which was written by Charles Stepney. They sampled the rhythmic shout, which appears throughout the song, from the O'Jays' funky "When the World's at Peace" (at 2:22), which is included on the album *Back Stabbers* (1972). Guru and DJ Premier wrote the song with help from E. Horne and recording engineer Shlomo Sonnenfeld.

0:00–0:10	The selection begins with the theme or melody stated by the sample from "Les Fleur" and also includes a saxophone that was not part of the Ramsey Lewis original. To add a bare-bones rhythm, Gang Starr sampled a shout by Eddie Levert of the O'Jays and placed it at the end of each measure of the passage and throughout the song. A drum machine provides a steady rhythm throughout "Jazz Music."
0:11–0:28	Guru begins his vocals about the history of jazz. Unlike most singing, which states the melody, Guru establishes a syncopated rhythm or flow with his vocals. He has backing from the sampled melody on piano and the sampled shout at the end of every measure.
0:29–0:31	As Guru keeps rapping, the melody briefly increases in volume by the saxophone line. Like a jazz singer, Guru expertly varies the rhythm by the way he shapes words in the lyrics.
0:32–0:40	Guru continues rapping his lyrics with the shouts, the drum machine, and sampled melody in the background.
0:41–0:44	As Guru raps, a synthesizer blasts once and then, after a few beats, sounds three times in a row to add to the complex rhythm.
0:45–0:50	Guru repeats "jazz music" once followed by "music" four times as he slowly and dynamically fades out. He also has accompaniment from sampled background vocals to add to the melody.
0:51–0:56	As Guru fades out, Gang Starr samples part of the Ramsey Lewis solo on "Les Fleur." The background vocals merge into a descending, staccato "da-da-da-da" line from the synthesizer, and the sampled shout continues.
0:57–1:19	Guru resumes his vocals with backing from the sampled shouts, the theme on the piano, the drum machine, and the periodic interjection of the saxophone playing the melody.
1:20–1:24	Again, Guru fades out after repeating the word "music," and the background vocals return.
1:25–1:40	Restatement of the Ramsey Lewis piano solo sample three times with backing from the sampled shouts, a sporadic interjection of the sampled melody on the saxophone, and synthesizer-generated vocals.
1:41–1:44	Guru restarts the lyrics.
1:45–1:50	Unexpectedly, a piano plays a somewhat dissonant line for additional rhythm.

1:51–1:54	Guru continues to deliver his rap.
1:55–1:59	Again, the piano suddenly emerges with the same line as above in the midst of the rap.
2:00–2:21	Guru raps over the melody, which is lightly played on the sampled piano, periodic sampled shouts, and the sampled melody line by the saxophone.
2:22–2:31	Again, the background vocals emerge as Guru fades out. This time, the rapper repeats "music" with descending volume and then reiterates the fade out.
2:32–2:37	The sampled solo of Ramsey Lewis from 0:51–0:56 restarts along with the syncopated "da-da-da-da" from the synthesizer.
2:38–2:42	Guru emerges to repeat "music" in a fade out, and the sampled shouts appear three times in a row to signal the end of the passage.
2:43–2:50	The sampled piano solo returns with backing from the melodic background vocals and the sampled shouts at the end of each measure.
2:51–2:54	The sampled shouts persist over the soft melodic line of the piano sample, and a trumpet responds to his call.
2:55–3:00	While the periodic shouts continue, the sampled background vocals reemerge as melody but suddenly turn into a highly syncopated, staccato delivery.
3:01–3:05	The rhythmic shouts continue and in one case get a response from a trumpet sound. The shouts are accompanied by light backing from the sampled piano for melody.
3:06–3:12	Again, the sampled vocals reenter to reinforce the melody.
3:13–3:27	The sampled shouts, the sampled piano, and the drum machine slowly fade out to end the song. To add rhythmic interest, a trumpet sound follows the shouts in a call-and-response.

Reachin' (A New Refutation of Time and Space). The same year, De La Soul sampled vibes player Milt Jackson, Lou Donaldson, and keyboardist Duke Pearson for the album *Buhloone Mind State.*

Artists who fused jazz and hip hop paid homage to Roger Linn, the inventor of the sampler, which facilitated the mix. "After making the first Gang Starr album on an EMU SP12 [sampler], I ended up buying a used MPC 60, and I've stuck with it ever since," noted DJ Premier. "If someone was to introduce me to Roger Linn, I'd be like, 'Oh, shit! You the man, you the truth! We turned your invention into a funky beat machine!'" (Noakes 2006).

Some hip-hop artists invited jazz players to contribute to their discs. Hip-hopper Fab 5 Freddy convinced jazz drum veteran Max Roach to jam with his group. "They programmed the Linn, and I just played," remembered the jazz innovator. "And what I did with the break dancers was similar to what I would do with Baby Laurence and the tap dancers." When he finished the session, Roach called the rappers "street poets" (Sidran 1992, 40). In 1991, A Tribe Called Quest asked bassist Ron Carter to play on "Verses from the Abstract." Two years later, De La

Soul requested Basie sax man Frank Wess to furnish music for "Patti Dooke" on *Buhloone Mind State*. The same year, Guru coordinated *Jazzmatazz: Volume 1*, which paired such jazz musicians as Donald Byrd, Branford Marsalis, Roy Ayers, and saxophonist Courtney Pine with Guru's raps. "I want to make other people appreciate hip hop and get my homeboys to appreciate jazz," explained Guru about the project (Farley 1993).

Jazz innovator Miles Davis incorporated hip hop into his work. During the late eighties, Davis became intrigued by hip-hop music. "I have been experimenting with rap songs because I think that there's some heavy rhythms up in that music," he maintained. "A lot of people ask me where music is going. I think it's going in short phrases. I heard that [drummer] Max Roach said that he thought that the next Charlie Parker might come out of rap melodies and rhythms," he added (Davis 1989, 390, 393).

A few months before Miles's death on September 28, 1991, hip-hop producer Easy Mo Bee (b. Osten Harvey Jr.) collaborated with Davis on a new album. In 1991, Easy Mo received a call from his manager "[who] said, 'Miles Davis has been hanging out with Russell Simmons [the hip-hop entrepreneur who co-founded the influential rap label, Def Jam] and he wants to get into hip hop,'" recalled Easy. "Russell told me to have the producers here on the roster to put together some reels and get them to Miles." Easy Mo met Miles at his house, where Davis listened to the tapes and suggested possible directions (Pennington 2010). "I'd get on the drum sampler, and he'd fall right in with it," related Easy Mo (Birnbaum 1993, 33). Before Miles passed away, he and Easy completed six tracks. After the trumpeter's death, Easy finished two more songs and released *Doo-Bop*, which featured Miles's horn wafting over samples of jazz artists such as saxophonist Gene Ammons and Donald Byrd, the funk of James Brown, and funk groups Pleasure and Kool & the Gang. In 1993, the record grabbed a Grammy for the best R&B instrumental.

Other jazz artists followed Davis down the jazz/hip-hop path. Saxophonist Greg Osby had been raised with an eclectic musical palette. His mother worked at a record distributing company in St. Louis and brought "home promotional copies of just about anything," he related. "Typically my listening session would span the whole spectrum. I was very open-minded very early on." After attending Howard University, Osby signed with Blue Note Records, recorded a series of albums, and organized a jazz collective, M-Base (Macro-Basic Array of Structured Extemporization) with fellow sax player Steve Coleman and others. As part of the collective, he adamantly refused to look back to the past. "I don't just sit around listening to old Coltrane records and Bird records because that's not really addressing today," he declared (Jenkins 1991, 27).

In 1993, Osby connected jazz to hip-hop. In *3-D Lifestyles*, he played over the raps of the 100X Posse and enlisted the help of Public Enemy producer Eric Sandler and A Tribe Called Quest's Ali Shaheed. "I'm not interested in music that doesn't groove, and that's what I get in hip-hop. It's a fusion between two areas of music," he contended (Birnbaum 1993, 34). "Hip-hop, with its loops and emphasis on the low end, gives a healthy nod to the black mystique and the black struggle in the United States," he continued. "A lot of intelligent jazz musicians have recognized that as something that they need to reinstate and reintegrate into the output" (Russonello 2013, 9).

Saxophonist Steve Coleman, Osby's M-Base partner, augmented his jazz with hip-hop beats. In 1994, he waxed *Tale of 3 Cities*, which melded his jazz group and four rappers. "I grew up on like funk, r&b, Motown. That's the blues of my generation," he insisted. "That's what the blues of today should be like, too—and that's being played on the streets by rappers and hip-hop artists" (Ouellette 1996, 30).

Branford Marsalis contributed to the hip-hop/jazz fusion, too. The saxophonist added his horn to "Jazz Music" and "Fight the Power," a socially charged song by Public Enemy for the 1989 Spike Lee film *Do the Right Thing*. In 1994, he founded Buckshot LeFonque and released a funky self-titled album produced on some tracks by DJ Premier of Gang Starr that included electric instruments, DJ Premier on turntables, and rapper Blackheart. Branford found himself "moving away from bebop, because there is no point in replicating what has been done. Music needs to be grounded in the past, but it has to move on and explore new territory" (Ellison 2001, 12).

In late 1994, *Stolen Moments: Red Hot + Cool* encapsulated the jazz/hip-hop hybrid. Released by the Red Hot Organization, which raised money to combat AIDS through pop culture, the double album mostly paired jazz and hip-hop artists. Among others, Guru worked with Donald Byrd; MC Solaar (b. Claude M'Barali) collaborated with Ron Carter; Digable Planets partnered with jazz horn man Lester Bowie; pianist Ramsey Lewis and Incognito joined forces; and Us3 paired with new saxophone sensation Joshua Redman. By the time that the album was released, jazz and hip-hop had been blended into an enticing mixture for a new generation.

Greg Osby on soprano saxophone. *Photograph courtesy of Brian McMillen*

How the Internet Transformed the Jazz Business

During the late nineties and into the new century, the World Wide Web changed jazz. Though the sampler allowed British and American youths to reshape and mix jazz with other genres, the web fundamentally and irrevocably transformed the creation, consumption, and distribution of music. It altered the listening experience and every segment of the music business, including jazz.

The Internet revolutionized how music consumers obtained and listened to music. Internet users with high-speed connections, able to quickly access large, complex sets of data on the computer, downloaded their favorite music for free as MP3 files, which were sampled from CDs and analog sources like albums, and then uploaded to central and peer-to-peer sites such as Napster. In 1999, Americans snapped up more than one billion music downloads through the MP3 technology, which easily compressed, transferred, and stored Internet-based audio files. By 2006, at any given moment, five million Americans could pick from thirteen billion song files on peer-to-peer services.

Apple Computer, an outsider to the music industry, ironically first advanced a business model to make money from the digital upheaval in music. In October 2001, Apple unveiled the lightweight, handheld iPod, which enabled music listeners to store hundreds of songs that they had downloaded or "ripped" from CDs. Less than two years later, Apple introduced the iTunes Store, which permitted listeners to download songs for 99 cents each and place them on their iPods. People "bought 45s, then they bought LPs, they bought cassettes, they bought 8-tracks, then they bought CDs. They're going to want to buy downloads," believed Apple CEO and founder Steve Jobs (Goodell 2004, 31). By 2008, Apple had sold more than 120 million iPods and had cornered an expanding, legal digital-download business with sales of four billion songs through the iTunes Store.

In addition to music on download sites and iTunes, web-based services such as Internet radio, Spotify, and YouTube provided easy access to songs. Internet-only radio began in 1995, when Radio HK began airing music online. Unlike commercial radio, which preselected a limited number of songs that it played over and over again, Internet-only radio offered customized stations focused on listener tastes. It offered programs of fusion, traditional jazz, New Orleans-style jazz, the avant-garde, and almost any other genre imaginable. In January 2000, Tim Westergren inaugurated the Music Genome Project, which catalogued songs by four hundred characteristics to better personalize Internet radio. By 2000, Pandora Radio, the public service offered by the Music Genome Project, presented eight hundred thousand songs to more than eighty million subscribers who listened for free or chose an advertising-free subscription option.

In 2008, Spotify started to offer millions of songs to users for free or through a subscription service without ads. The digital-streaming service furnished thirty-four different types of jazz from acid to West Coast. By 2016, Spotify had attracted more than 150 million regular users, and, along with other streaming services such as Amazon and SoundCloud, accounted for a majority of music-industry revenue. "We've gone from selling physical product to selling downloads to selling *access*," commented Dick Huey, founder of the digital marketing company, Toolshed (Morrison 2015, 38). By 2018, downloads of music, including iTunes and subscription services such as Spotify, accounted for 75 percent of all music sales in the United States.

YouTube also offered music adherents free video clips of performances. Created in 2005 and snapped up the next year by Google, it allowed any Internet surfer to post and watch videos. Within two years, the site attracted a half million users and carried more than 56 million videos, including many jazz performances. YouTube became a democratic video site with an array of jazz and other musical genres and replaced the restricted playlist of MTV, which during the 2000s slowly deserted music videos for other types of programming. Through YouTube, argued jazz guitarist Lee Ritenour, "people will find the music they want to find. I guess jazz is in good shape in a weird way because of this" (Janus 2010, 238).

Up-to-date Internet-based information sites gave jazz fans suggestions about the plethora of musical choices on the Web. Beginning in the thirties, print publications such as *Downbeat* acted as prime tastemakers for jazz and, constrained by a certain number of pages, publicized a small number of jazz players. Not needing printing presses or a large capital investment, Web-based jazz blogs such as *Jazz Lives*, the *WBGO Blog: Jazz and Beyond*, *Elements of Jazz*, and the top-ranking *Jazz-Wax* informed jazz listeners about the massive number of jazz artists who could be found on the Internet. They offered jazz aficionados immediate information to at least partially process and filter the mind-boggling array of jazz sounds on the web.

The web benefited artists as well as fans. By including a wide array of music, the web allowed jazz artists to incorporate sounds from other cultures into their music. "The world is becoming more and more intertwined, and this is reflected in today's music scene," contended saxophonist Dave Pietro about the influence of the Internet on his work. "I think that most 'jazz' musicians, myself included, would say that their music doesn't neatly fall into any one category. My playing and composing have not only been influenced by jazz but by studies of Brazilian, East Indian," and other types of music (Janus 2010, 230).

The web also exploded the principle of controlled scarcity that had been guarded by the music industry for nearly a century and allowed new jazz artists to develop and promote themselves. Sax player Albert Rivera exemplified the effect of the Internet on his ability to prosper as a professional jazz artist. In 2014, he launched a GoFundMe campaign on the community-sharing platform Facebook to cover the costs of mixing, mastering, and manufacturing his album *Back At It*. Once he gathered the money and completed the disc, he rewarded funders with a free download and three to ten physical CDs, which could be given away as gifts to friends. "This proved invaluable," he smiled. "The reach was instant." To further promote the disc, he posted videos on YouTube and SoundCloud. He focused on Twitter, Instagram and Facebook, and "started a regular WordPress blog that I published on Facebook." He also emailed everyone who had attended his concerts and gave away discs at his performances. "Spotify, Pandora [radio] and iTunes affect the longevity of a musician's career," he contended. "Rather than boycotting these services, we should use them to our advantage. These services are a means to get more fans. GoFundMe allowed me to give away as many CDs as I wanted" and build a sizeable following, he concluded (Micallef 2016, 42–43).

Amid a technological revolution, jazz survived and flourished. Listeners tapped new innovations such as online radio, music streaming sites, and blogs to discover jazz. They bought it through the iTunes Store for a nominal fee or simply ripped it for free from CDs or a download site. Jazz musicians used samplers to create such hybrids as acid jazz and hip-hop jazz, and raised funds and promoted themselves on the web, unfettered by the constraints of record labels. In an age of rapid technological disruptions, jazz successfully changed with the times.

For Discussion and Further Study

Chapter Quiz

1. How did new musical instruments foster new jazz styles?

2. What was the impact of deejay dance parties on fostering new fusions of jazz with other popular music forms?

3. What was the difference between the urban-based house music that arose in Chicago and the acid-jazz movement in Great Britain? How did this reflect the differences in racial mix and social culture?

4. What role did producers/promoters/deejays like Gilles Peterson play in the development of acid jazz? How did the changing club scene influence his music?

5. How did veteran performers like Herbie Hancock adapt to the new technologies and musical styles to appeal to a new audience? What role did a music video play in the promotion of his new music?

6. What role did Apple Music, Spotify, and SoundCloud play in transforming the financial model for jazz musicians? What were the pluses and minuses for independent artists?

19

JAZZ IN A TROUBLED TWENTY-FIRST-CENTURY AMERICA

Hard Times, Black Lives Matter, and #MeToo

This chapter focuses on political/economic issues, the role of women in jazz, and the continuing importance of race. The turbulent political and economic times during the first decades of the twenty-first century led to the popularity of more soothing jazz singers, especially female singers who, unlike their counterparts in the past, played instruments and sometimes composed their own songs. Most recently, major social movements—including the Black Lives Matter and #MeToo movements—shaped jazz and made it a vibrant and timely music, which once again reflected the times.

On the morning of September 11, 2001, four passenger jets departed from airports on the East Coast for California. In mid-flight, the planes were overtaken by nineteen hijackers—members of the militant Islamic group al-Qaeda—who intended to crash the aircraft into highly prominent targets. Just before and after nine o'clock as people bustled to work, two of the airliners—American Airlines Flight 11 and

United Airlines Flight 175—were smashed into each building of New York City's World Trade Center, commonly called the Twin Towers. "We saw bodies flying out of the [eighty-fifth-floor] windows," a New Yorker told the *New York Times*. In less than two hours, the crashes had caused both 110-story towers to implode and collapse in a blaze, killing more than 2,600 New Yorkers as well as ninety-two airline passengers. "Lower Manhattan had become an ashen shell of itself, all but a Pompeii under the impact of a terrorist attack," reported the *New York Times*. "For all Americans, the unimaginable became real" ("War Against," 2001).

Two other planes were diverted toward Washington, DC. American Airlines Flight 77 was crashed into the western façade of the Pentagon, the headquarters of the Department of Defense, killing all sixty-four passengers and 125 building occupants. The fourth aircraft was heading toward the capital when it crashed in an open field near Shanksville, Pennsylvania, while passengers were attempting to overtake their hijackers. Everyone aboard perished.

The nation stood in shocked disbelief over the first attack on the US mainland since the War of 1812. "Shock. Anger. Terror. Confusion. Unspeakable sadness. Grief. Fear. These are just some of the emotions Americans are feeling today in the wake of the monstrous terrorist attacks on the United States," wrote a resident of Berkeley, California, immediately after the attacks (Evans, 2001). Upon hearing the news in Oklahoma City, another American became "numb. I can't believe what I'm seeing" (Harden, 2001).

War and the Great Recession

During the nearly twenty years after the terrorist assault on New York and Washington, D.C., Americans sank into a sullen distress over prolonged war, economic malaise, and internal divisiveness. To punish al-Qaeda, which masterminded the 9/11 attacks, the United States invaded the al-Qaeda stronghold of Afghanistan, ultimately sending more than 102,000 troops into the country to fight the pro-al-Qaeda group, the Taliban. Costing more than $538 billion, by 2014, the protracted war had ended in the deaths of 2,184 US military personnel and the injury of another 19,600 Americans. On the Afghan side, 3.7 million Afghans fled their homes, and ninety thousand had been killed, including twenty-six thousand civilians.

The United States opened a second front in its so-called War on Terror almost two years after 9/11. Launched by President George W. Bush on the morning of March 20, 2003, under the guise of finding Iraqi weapons of mass destruction, the war was calculated to protect American oil interests. Labeled Operation Iraqi Freedom, the invasion consisted of three hundred thousand US and British troops, who swiftly overcame Iraqi military personnel, ousted Iraqi leader Saddam Hussein, and hastily proclaimed victory.

Despite the military success, the United States occupied Iraq and fought an extended war against insurgents. In 2007, President Bush sent an additional twenty thousand troops to the area and increased the length of their tours. When British forces withdrew from the country, even more US military personnel were sent. By the end of the conflict in December 2011, 4,489 US troops had died, and another 28,000 had been injured. More than 3,481 US contractors also had perished. Nearly twelve thousand Iraqi soldiers and police allied with the Americans had been killed in the conflict. In addition, approximately twenty-seven thousand Iraqi insurgents had been killed, and more than a million civilians had died as a result of the invasion. Another 3.9 million Iraqis fled their country to avoid harm. The United States spent $802 billion on the nearly nine-year war.

Adding to the concerns of embattled Americans, US financial institutions triggered a global crisis starting in 2008. Commercial and investment banks imprudently lent funds at exorbitant interest rates to residential home buyers with poor credit ratings, which inflated housing prices. The financial institutions then packaged the "subprime" or risky mortgages into bond securities, which were gobbled up by investors speculating that they would realize enormous profits if the home buyers paid back their debts. Greedy for even more profits, the banks created ultimately worthless securities from these subprime assets called collateralized debt obligations, which rewarded investors who bet on the projected performance of mortgage-backed securities without owning any of the bonds. By allowing wild speculation on already risky bonds, the banks significantly overextended the real value of the housing market and their risk portfolios. By late 2008, the real-estate mortgage bubble burst, saddling banks and investors with billions of dollars in bad debt that would never be repaid.

Banks and investors buckled under the pressure of these reckless banking practices. Banking giants such as Lehman Brothers, Washington Mutual, and Morgan Stanley went bankrupt, driving the international economic system into chaos. World stock markets plunged, and the Dow Jones index fell by more than 50 percent. By the end of 2008, Americans had lost a staggering $14 trillion, and many homeowners who had bought at the peak of the housing market a couple of years earlier owed more than the value of their homes as housing prices plummeted.

To stabilize the crisis, world leaders devised bailout plans for banks that they felt were "too big to fail." On October 3, 2008, President George W. Bush instituted a $700 billion program that authorized the United States to purchase valueless mortgage-backed bonds. "If we don't do this, we may not have an economy by Monday," instructed Ben Bernanke, chairman of the Federal Reserve, the central bank of the United States. A few weeks later, the Federal Reserve set aside another $1.2 trillion to absorb worthless securities and supply almost interest-free loans to troubled financial groups. President Barack Obama, taking office in January 2009 amid the financial turmoil, designed a second bailout program for the financial industry, promulgated legislation to extend laid-off workers' unemployment and health insurance, and provided $13 billion to financially challenged automakers.

In the aftermath of the financial crisis, many Americans found themselves unemployed. Between 2009 and late 2011, the official US unemployment rate reached more than 9 percent. Counting underemployed workers and those who had become discouraged and stopped searching, the total rate reached more than 16 percent. As late as 2015, the percentage of unemployed and discouraged workers hovered around 11 percent.

Amid the turmoil for much of the early twenty-first century, melodic jazz singers calmed a distraught American people. Beginning in 2001, singers such as Diana Krall and Michael Bublé scaled the charts by reviving songs of a previous generation along with their own material. Most of these vocalists paid tribute to and updated the smooth style of role models such as Frank Sinatra. Over nearly fifteen years, such singers restored jazz to the charts by serving as a tonic to a distressed nation, just as Bing Crosby and Frank Sinatra had done during the Great

Depression and World War II. "All the great old singers have gone now, and people miss them," insisted Michael Bublé. "The world has got a lot scarier in the past ten years, and I think people are on a search for something to take them away from that" (Peel 1939, 105).

The Jazz Songstresses

Female jazz singers such as Diana Krall helped steady the ragged nerves of Americans during the first decades of the twenty-first century. Born in 1964 in Nanaimo, Canada, across the border from Washington State, Krall perfected her piano skills at an early age. Attending a jazz summer camp in Port Townsend, Washington, she met such jazz artists as bassist Ray Brown and drummer Jeff Hamilton, who urged her to move to Los Angeles, where she studied with pianist Alan Broadbent. Krall subsequently moved to Boston, where she attended the Berklee School of Music in the early eighties and met one of her main influences on piano, Jimmy Rowles (b. James Hunter), who had worked with such big bands as Tommy Dorsey, Benny Goodman, and Woody Herman and singers Billie Holliday and Peggy Lee.

Encouraged by her mentors, Krall played at piano bars and, to get more work, started singing. "I didn't think I had a good enough voice," she confessed. "Then I started playing piano-bar gigs. I sang as little as I possibly could. Typical story. You get more gigs if you sing" (Lees 1999). Before long, customers filled the clubs and bars to hear Krall's vocals.

Interested in the music of her father, Krall initially favored songwriters of the thirties and forties. She interpreted "the music of great American songwriters, George and Ira Gershwin, Cole Porter, Sammy Cahn, Jimmy Van Heusen . . . like a character interpreting a great play. I do other music, but mostly stick to the

Diana Krall in concert. *Everett Collection Inc./Alamy Stock Photo*

American songbook. It's nostalgic, and there's nothing wrong with that," she added (Hahn 2005; Quinn 2012; Reid 2000).

In 1993, Krall released her debut, *Stepping Out*, which consisted of standards by such composers as Harry Warren, Jimmy McHugh, Harold Arlen, and the team of Lorenz Hart and Richard Rodgers. Two years later, Krall followed with another disc of celebrated tunes from the past that were written and composed by Sammy Cahn, Oscar Hammerstein II, and Jerome Kern. In 1996, she released a record dedicated to one of her main inspirations, Nat King Cole. In 2000, a tour with Tony Bennett, a jazz singer who embarked on a career after World War II, further placed her in the jazz-singer tradition (Considine 2011).

Krall hit the Top Ten as the national mood turned grim. A week after the World Trade Center crumbled, the singer/pianist, accompanied by the London Symphony Orchestra, released *The Look of Love*, which achieved million-selling status and highlighted songs from a bygone era: "Maybe You'll Be There," a 1947 gem by Rube Bloom and Sammy Gallop; George and Ira Gershwin's "'S Wonderful" (1927); Johnny Mercer and Victor Schertzinger's "I Remember You" (1941); and "I Can't Get Along Without You Very Well (Except Sometimes)" (1939) by Hoagy Carmichael.

Though steeped in the great American songbook, Krall reflected the rock-music influences of her youth. "I was a normal teenager, out swimming, horseback riding and growing up on the beach listening to the same pop music as my friends," she insisted. As a teen, she plastered a poster of Peter Frampton on her wall and listened to Elton John, Stevie Wonder, and Supertramp. "I was a regular kid practicing 'Goodbye Yellow Brick Road' and 'Bohemian Rhapsody.' I loved Queen," she revealed (Reid 2000). In 2004, her interest in rock surfaced in a collaboration with rock songwriter/musician Elvis Costello, whom Krall eventually married. The singer/pianist and Costello crafted *The Girl in the Other Room*, which shot to number four on the chart and established Krall as a major jazz and pop act.

For the next decade, Diana successfully moved between standards and rock tunes. She recorded the Rodgers–Hart "Where or When" (1937), Sammy Cahn and Jule Styne's "Guess I'll Hang My Tears Out To Dry" (1944), and "I've Grown Accustomed to His Face" (1956) by Frederick Loewe and Alan Jay Lerner, and wrote jazz arrangements for tunes by Bob Dylan, the Eagles, Paul McCartney, and Elton John. By 2017, Krall had scored with eight million-selling, Top Twenty entries, including the number-three *Quiet Nights* (2009).

Vocalist/pianist Krall paved the way for other successful female jazz singers, many of whom—unlike most past jazz singers—developed proficiency on an instrument. Esperanza Spalding, raised in a poor neighborhood of Portland, Oregon, studied bass at an exclusive high school, the Northwest Academy, and at the Berklee School of Music in Boston. Karrin Allyson (b. Karrin Schoonover) started as a classical pianist and attended the University of Nebraska on a piano scholarship. Norah Jones, the daughter of concert promoter Sue Jones and sitar master Ravi Shankar, learned piano theory at Booker T. Washington High School for the Performing Arts in Dallas and the University of North Texas.

Like Krall, many twenty-first-century singers preferred songs from past eras. Jones chose "The Nearness of You" (1938) by Hoagy Carmichael for her first album and followed with such standards as Ellington's "Don't Miss You at All" before concentrating on her own material. Karrin Allyson picked tunes by songwriters like Victor Young, George Gershwin, Duke Ellington, and Cole Porter. In 2015, she released her highest-charting effort, *Many a New Day: Karrin Allyson Sings Rodgers and Hammerstein*. Singer and acoustic guitarist Madeleine Peyroux recorded selections such as "Lonesome Road" (1927) by Gene Austin and Nathaniel Shilkret and "No More" (1944) by Toots Camarata and Bob Russell for her breakthrough *Careless Love* (2004).

LISTENING GUIDE 44

Diana Krall

"I REMEMBER YOU"

Diana Krall has always favored standards in her repertoire. In this song, which appeared on her first Top Ten entry, *The Look of Love*, she turns to a chestnut by songwriter/singer and Capitol Records co-founder Johnny Mercer and composer/film director Victor Schertzinger. She chose the often-recorded tune, which was first recorded by Tommy Dorsey and appeared in the patriotic film *The Fleet's In* (1942), when it was sung by singer/bombshell Dorothy Lamour backed by the Jimmy Dorsey Orchestra. The composition has since been recorded by dozens of jazz artists, including Ella Fitzgerald, Charlie Parker, Tony Bennett, Chet Baker, Sonny Rollins, and Cannonball Adderley. She released the song on September 18, 2001, a week after the 9/11 disaster. Looking back, the vocalist/pianist felt that the song dealt with a sense of "loss."

Personnel: Diana Krall (piano and vocals), Christian McBride (bass), Paulinho Da Costa (percussion), Jeff Hamilton (drums), John Pisano (guitar), Los Angeles Session Orchestra conducted by Claus Ogerman, Tommy LiPuma (producer).

0:00–0:08	The song begins with bassist Christian McBride and drummer Jeff Hamilton, who establish an understated rhythm.
0:09–0:43	A full orchestra softly enters and plays the melody twice.
0:44–0:56	Accentuated by John Pisano on guitar and the rhythm section, Krall begins her sultry, hushed vocals on the melody. She lingers on the last phrase of each measure to highlight a soothing sound. At 0:54, she varies the rhythm by pausing unexpectedly.
0:57–1:04	The orchestra enters to deliver a pattern twice.
1:05–1:20	Backed by the orchestra, especially the strings, Krall restarts the lyrics of the melody.
1:21–1:37	To vary the dynamics of the song, Krall raises the pitch when she sings the B section. She again receives assistance from the orchestra and rhythm section and surprises the listener by a sudden stop (1:27) to syncopate an otherwise straightforward melody. In the last two seconds of the passage, she sustains the word "blue" and flats the note to aptly create a bluesy sound.
1:38–2:00	Krall returns to the melody and, at 1:40, delivers a slight vibrato to better texture the lyrics. Even more than her singing on the first part of the song, she creates a rhythmic complexity in her delivery by lingering on certain words throughout the stanza.
2:01–2:05	The orchestra plays a brief passage to indicate a change.
2:06–2:37	Krall enters on the piano. She crafts a melody-laden solo, which leaves large spaces to create rhythmic complexity and allow the orchestra to answer her in a call-and-response.
2:38–3:07	Krall restarts her vocals in two stanzas of the melody. As before, her phrasing develops rhythmic interest by embellishing a word or pausing between words.
3:08	Krall slides over and connects two words to accentuate the smoothness of her delivery.
3:09–3:13	The vocalist completes the stanza.

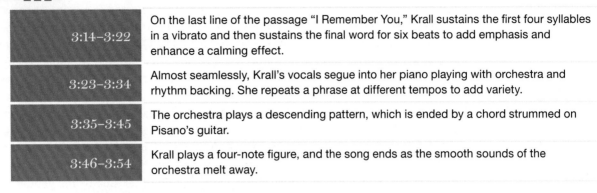

3:14–3:22	On the last line of the passage "I Remember You," Krall sustains the first four syllables in a vibrato and then sustains the final word for six beats to add emphasis and enhance a calming effect.
3:23–3:34	Almost seamlessly, Krall's vocals segue into her piano playing with orchestra and rhythm backing. She repeats a phrase at different tempos to add variety.
3:35–3:45	The orchestra plays a descending pattern, which is ended by a chord strummed on Pisano's guitar.
3:46–3:54	Krall plays a four-note figure, and the song ends as the smooth sounds of the orchestra melt away.

As Krall did, other female singers/instrumentalists demonstrated eclectic tastes and influences in music. Beginning in "straight-ahead jazz," Norah Jones subsequently joined an acid-jazz band and sprinkled her albums with songs by country great Hank Williams (Winfrey 2003). In 2013, she teamed with rock singer Billie Joe Armstrong of Green Day for *Foreverly*, a reinterpretation of songs by the rockabilly duo the Everly Brothers. Madeleine Peyroux selected tunes by Bob Dylan and the Beatles. Karrin Allyson offered jazz interpretations of compositions by the Beatles and seventies singer/songwriters such as Billy Joel, Cat Stevens, James Taylor, and Joni Mitchell.

Esperanza Spalding, though considering herself a jazz musician, felt that jazz needed to cross boundaries: "I listen to A Tribe Called Quest, R&B, CeeLo [Green]. I was exposed to many kinds of music including rock and disco, classical and folk, Motown and Miles Davis, Sly Stone and David Bowie. Almost every artist we know from the R&B or pop world knows all the R&B, all the hip hop, all the soul and all the jazz, and that's really impressive. Jazz musicians need a wake-up call, everybody knows our music, but we don't know their music. Jazz has always been a melting pot of influences and I plan to incorporate them all," she vowed (Mora 2008; Gonzales 2011). After her first chart success in 2008, she took the stage with rock star Prince and worked with rapper/producer Q-Tip (b. Jonathan Davis) from A Tribe Called Quest.

Amid the Iraq War and the Great Recession, female jazz singers climbed the charts. By 2015, Krall had sold fifteen million records and racked up six Top Ten albums. Norah Jones bested Krall by selling more than fifty million discs, half of the sales coming from her debut, *Come Away with Me*, which topped the pop album chart in 2002. Jones, referred to by *Time* magazine as a "calming voice" (Farley 2004, 84), repeated her number-one success with *Feels Like Home* (2004) and *Not Too Late* (2007). Madeleine Peyroux first charted with *Careless Love* (2004) and, two years later, snagged her best charting record, *Half the Perfect World*. In 2012, after sneaking onto the chart with a self-titled disc, Esperanza Spalding hit the Top Ten with *Radio Music Society*. In 2008, saxophonist Greg Osby observed that "we're in an era where they're embracing a lot of female vocalists" (Panken 2008).

The Twenty-First-Century Sinatras

Male crooners, delivering a smooth-and-easy, Sinatra-like sound, provided Americans with a masculine version of the escapist music afforded by their female counterparts. If Diana Krall ushered in a spate of female jazz vocalists, Michael

Bublé did the same for male jazz singers. Bublé had been raised in British Columbia, Canada, the son of a salmon fisherman. He became interested in singing at the age of five after listening to Bing Crosby's "White Christmas." "It was the only Christmas record my parents had, and we played it from late October through December," explained the singer. "So it introduced me to jazz, to crooning, to music, really. I think that's the reason why, when I heard standards later in life, there was a great sense of comfort" (McCormick 2011). In his teens, Bublé eagerly and constantly spun discs from his grandfather's vintage record collection. "I had the opportunity to go back and study the greatest groups and singers that ever lived," he enthused (McCormick 2011). Prodded by his Italian-born grandfather, who traded his plumbing skills for vocal lessons for his grandson, a teenage Michael began to sing at local bars, conventions, cruise ships, lounges, and other small-time venues. He even took a job as a singing Santa. From 1996 to 2002, the budding singer released three self-produced albums, which received scant notice and generated few sales.

In 2003, Bublé's fortunes brightened. Guided by a new manager, Bublé recorded his self-titled, major-label debut, which reached the Top Fifty and included a series of classic songs such as Jerome Kern and Dorothy Fields' "The Way You Look Tonight" (1936); Johnny Mercer's 1965 version of "Summer Wind"; and, most notably, the 1957 Jimmy Van Heusen/Sammy Cahn tune, "Come Fly with Me," which had been immortalized by Frank Sinatra. The next year, the singer again hovered around the Top Fifty with the live album, *Come Fly with Me*.

Bublé revealed his Sinatra influence in *Come Fly with Me*. He considered himself a rabid fan, "one of the biggest, with a true understanding as a vocalist of how magnificent he was. Basically, God kissed this man's throat." As a youth, Michael listened to the Sinatra version of Hoagy Carmichael's classic "Stardust" (1927) "till I passed out" (Soeder 2008).

When Bublé approached Reprise Records, a label that Sinatra founded in 1960, the Reprise/Warner chairman of music, Tom Whalley, asked him, "Why should we

Michael Bublé in Australia, 2011. *ZUMA Press, Inc./Alamy Stock Photo*

sign you? We have Sinatra." Michael responded, "'With all due respect, Sinatra is dead so do we bury the music with him and nobody can ever sing this again because the great one is gone?' I told him there were people out there just like me. I'm not just a singer, I'm a consumer, and I said, 'I promise you there are people like me who are hungry for this stuff and were not given the choice. There's a void in the market'" (Reid 2003).

Bublé proved to be prophetic. In 2005, riding on the successful wave of female jazz singers who chose standards for their repertoires, Michael hit the Top Ten with *It's Time*, which contained such classics as "I've Got You Under My Skin" by Cole Porter, the 1933 gem "Try a Little Tenderness," Harry Warren's "The More I See You" (1945), and "A Foggy Day (In London Town)" by George and Ira Gershwin.

Initially, the crooner enticed an older demographic. His company booked him on television talk shows such as *The Oprah Winfrey Show* and *Today*. "He can sell as many albums sitting on a couch giving interviews as he can performing," boasted manager Bruce Allen, who had guided the careers of such pop stars as singers Bryan Adams and Anne Murray. "We used a lot of TV, and TV appearances on morning talk shows tend to skew a little bit to an older crowd," confessed Reprise/Warner executive Diarmuid Quinn (Thompson 2009, 20). "Those shows are aimed at women at home with disposable income," echoed Adam Hollywood, the director of marketing at Warner, who characterized early Bublé fans as the "young housewife audience" (Peel 2009, 93).

After his music aired in heavy rotation on radio, Bublé's fan base shifted. Youth flocked to his concerts and bought his albums. "As he's gotten more and more radio play, we've seen things change," noted Quinn (Thompson 2009, 20). "In the States, seventy percent of my audience is between 15 and 30," bragged Bublé (Reid 2003).

Young female fans especially followed Bublé. As Frank Sinatra had experienced during World War II, female fanatics mobbed the thirty-year-old Bublé. A young woman at one of his sold-out concerts felt that "he has the charisma and personality that Frank Sinatra had. I have all of Michael's albums, oh yes. He's absolutely beautiful—and that doesn't hurt either" (Posner 2007). "There are the women," noticed the Toronto-based *The Globe and Mail* in September 2007. "An inexhaustible parade. Legions of Michael-mad maidens wherever he goes. He's no longer an act; he's a phenomenon," the newspaper concluded (Posner 2007).

Drawing a younger crowd, Bublé updated his records and performances with a few songs from his youth. Like new-millennium jazz songstresses, the singer supplemented standards with rock and roll. "When I was 15, I listened to a lot of Sinatra, but my jean jacket didn't have 'I Love Frank' on it, it had 'I Love AC/DC,' 'Guns and Roses,' 'Pearl Jam.' I thought Eddie Vedder [lead singer of Pearl Jam] was the second coming" (McCormick 2011). As well as selections from the great American songbook, the singer chose tunes by sixties singer/songwriter Van Morrison, the Beatles, the Eagles, and rock-guitar hero Eric Clapton, and even invited two of the Bee Gees to sing with him.

The twenty-first-century idol mixed the smooth, swinging style of Sinatra, a healthy dose of American standards, and newer material from his youth for a startlingly swift rise to iconic status. In 2007, he topped the chart with *Call Me Irresponsible*. During the next six years, he scored with three more number-one chartbusters. By 2015, Bublé had sold more than thirty million records worldwide. The singer had inked sponsorship deals with Starbucks coffee and the ESPN sports network and had parlayed his global brand into burgeoning sales of a product line, which included teddy bears and sweatshirts. "The 33-year-old Canadian crooner, best known for his smooth takes on American pop standards, may reside in the shadow of Frank Sinatra," reported *Billboard* in 2009, "but the reality is, in many countries, he's equaled—or even exceeded—the popularity of his idol" (Thompson

 LISTENING GUIDE 45

Michael Bublé

 "THAT'S LIFE"

Bublé, like Diana Krall, relied heavily on standards, though he incorporated rock songs into his sets. An avid fan of Frank Sinatra, he included this song on the number-one album *Call Me Irresponsible* (2007).

Patterning himself after Sinatra, Bublé took a chance on "That's Life," which represents one of Sinatra's most well-known and enduring songs. Rather than repeat the time-honored 1966 version by Frank, he recruited a gospel choir to breathe new life into the song, which was written by Dean Kay and Kelly Gordon in 1963 and first performed by singer Marion Montgomery. "I brought the song to a wonderful guy named Mervyn Warren, from the a-cappella group Take 6 and said, 'I want to take this to church; I want to make it a huge

gospel tune.' So he brought in a choir and I love it. It's one of my favorite things about the record," recalled Bublé (Carriveau 2009, 2). Inspired by Donny Hathaway, he wanted 'to make this an inspirational, gospel number" ("Q&A with Michael Bublé" 2009, 9).

Personnel: Michael Bublé (vocals); Vinnie Colaiuta (drums); Dean Parks (guitar); Rafael Padilla (percussion); Brian Bromberg (bass); Greg Phillinganes (piano); Anthony Field, Beverly Staunton, Clorishey Lewis, Donald Smith, Ken Stacey, Lisa Vaughn, Louis Price, Lynne Fiddmont, Sharlotte Gibson, Valerie Pinkston, and Windy Wagner (gospel choir orchestra arranged by Mervyn Warren).

0:00–0:01	The song begins with an ascending four-bar line from the piano.
0:02–0:11	The gospel choir enters in a dramatic fashion, and the lead singer jumps into the lyrics in typical gospel style by a forceful delivery, sliding up and down on a syllable, and repeating a phrase for emphasis. The entire choir and the piano provide background to the singer. The passage ends with a piano flourish to signal a change.
0:12–0:18	The choir now backs the lead singer with an insistent staccato rhythm, and the piano changes to a syncopated set of chords played in a percussive manner.
0:19–0:21	The singer, choir, and piano come together in a jubilant shout.
0:22–0:25	A trumpet blast, a short piano line repeated four times, and a crash of cymbals twice indicates a transition.
0:26–0:43	After the dramatic introduction, Michael Bublé enters to deliver his first set of lyrics and establish the melody. He has steady backing from the rhythm section at this point. Keeping the gospel flavor in a modified form, Bublé extends words (e.g., "all" at 0:30–0:31) and, like a gospel singer, hits two notes on one syllable (e.g., "change" at 0:42 and "tune" at 0:44).
0:44–0:50	The orchestra strings start to back Bublé softly in the background.
0:51–0:54	The orchestra increases in volume to dynamically vary the song and add drama.
0:55–0:57	For a measure, the orchestral horns enter to back Bublé at mid-volume.
0:58–1:08	Bublé continues to deliver the song's lyrics with rhythm and a diminished orchestra in the background.
1:09–1:10	Bublé repeats a phrase ("let it"), unexpectedly pauses, and then repeats the phrase to add tension and rhythmic complexity to the tune.

1:11–1:12	Bublé embellishes the word "down" by improvising around it with several notes.
1:13–1:21	The volume rises as the orchestra horns reemerge.
1:22	Bublé moves to the B section of the song. He sings a series of words in staccato fashion, accentuated by the orchestral horns and the drums at the end of each measure to reinforce the syncopation. He also receives light vocal backing from the choir.
1:28	A blast from the orchestra and drums signals the end of the lyric line.
1:29–1:33	Bublé continues to the next stanza of the lyrics in the B section with louder backing from the choir.
1:34–1:35	Two blasts from the orchestra horns add emphasis and a building tension to the song.
1:36–1:41	Bublé starts to sing the last section of section B with mounting intensity from the orchestra and choir.
1:42–1:49	Bublé delivers the next few words in a staccato fashion to add rhythmic sophistication. After two seconds, the volume gets louder and the gospel choir more forcefully backs Bublé.
1:50–1:53	The gospel choir intensifies to equal the volume of Bublé and, in a call-and-response, answers his lyrics by repeating Bublé's words in a highly sustained fashion on "that's life."
1:54–2:15	Bublé and the choir converse in a call-and-response, when the lead singer answers Bublé's lyrics (e.g., 1:58–1:59) and the choir repeats Bublé's words (e.g., "one single try" at 2:05–2:08 and "there I'd fly" at 2:12–2:15) in a sustained manner.
2:16–2:21	Bublé returns to the B section of the song, where the brass horns emphasize his staccato approach by one-note blasts every two beats.
2:22–2:23	To signal an end to the line, the brass loudly slides around a quavering, sustained note.
2:24–2:29	Bublé continues the B section with staccato blasts from the brass as the orchestral strings get louder. The choir provides more diminished backing vocals. Two blasts from the brass indicate a change.
2:30–2:34	Bublé sustains nearly each word of the lyric at this point to increase the drama while the brass section loudly blasts two notes every other beat. The orchestra and choir give diminished backing at this point.
2:35–2:36	The brass section loudly plays a three-note pattern twice.
2:37–2:41	The intensity mounts from Bublé and the brass section.
2:42–2:44	Bublé sustains a word ("race") for four beats with powerful backing from the brass and the gospel choir.
2:45–2:52	Bublé returns to the first part of the song at a higher pitch and volume with a call-and-response from the gospel choir and blasts from the brass section every two beats. Two blasts from the brass section at the end of the passage signal a change.
2:53–2:58	Bublé, singing at full volume, receives powerful backing from the brass and gospel choir, which delivers a flatted, bluesy version of the melody.

2:59–3:15	Bublé delivers the lyrics in a syncopated fashion in a call-and-response with the gospel choir. The brass continues with loud accents, which hit every beat by the end of the passage.
3:16–3:28	After a pause, Bublé sustains the word "ball" for four beats with no accompaniment, sings a few more words, and then increases the intensity to a full emotional fervor by sustaining the word "die" for a full eight beats with the choir loudly repeating the phrase "that's life" and the brass and drums providing loud accents.
3:29–3:42	Bublé begins to improvise on the lyrics with the powerful backing of the gospel choir and the lead gospel singer who sporadically lets loose a bluesy, sanctified scream, which slides up an octave. The brass and drums continue to provide blasts for accents.
3:43–3:47	Bublé chants "um" five times to establish a counter-rhythm to the rhythm of the choir.
3:48–3:55	The choir and Bublé again engage in a call-and-response, and Bublé improvises lyrics to the swaying beat of the choir and the bluesy vocal swoops of the lead gospel singer.
3:56–3:59	In typical gospel fashion, Bublé slides up and down the scale with a flurry of notes on the phrase "oh, yeah."
4:00–4:11	Bublé and the lead gospel singer continue to improvise to the backing of the choir, the rhythm section, and the brass blasts as the song fades out for a jubilant ending.

2009, 18). Like Sinatra, Bublé suavely crooned his way into the hearts of fans who sought escape from the troubles around them.

Michael Bublé paved the way for the successful ascent of other male jazz crooners who resurrected songs from the thirties and forties. Jamie Cullum, born in Rochford, Essex in England, rabidly collected records as a youth. In 1999, applying his knowledge of classic American songs, he used his own money to release a record of standards, the aptly titled *Heard It All Before*. Backed by bass and drums and playing piano, Cullum sang several standards by Cole Porter and refurbished other chestnuts such as "Sweet Lorraine" (1928), Ellington's "Caravan," and "Old Devil Moon" by Burton Lane and Yip Harburg. Three years later, on another self-financed disc, he mixed self-penned compositions with George Gershwin's "It Ain't Necessarily So," Johnny Mandel's "A Time for Love," and the Vernon Duke/Ira Gershwin song "I Can't Get Started." In 2003, on the strength of his first two platters and the flurry of sales by female jazz divas, Cullum signed with Universal. Adding horns to his sound, he continued to record tunes by Cole Porter, Lerner and Loewe, the Gershwins, and other masters from the past as well as his own compositions.

Other twenty-first-century male jazz singers such as Kurt Elling from Chicago handpicked similar material. He offered interpretations of such classic songs as Rodgers and Hart's "Wait Till You See Her" (1942), "April in Paris" (1932) by Vernon Duke and Yip Harburg, Ellington's "Prelude to a Kiss," and Irving Berlin's "The Best Things Happen While You're Dancing." Elling gave a special twist to his vocals by writing words to jazz instrumentals in a style called vocalese, which had been pioneered in 1952 by singer Eddie Jefferson.

Like Bublé, many male jazz singers found inspiration in Frank Sinatra. The press referred to Jamie Cullum as "Sinatra in sneakers." "You've got to give it up to Frank. He's such a reference point for so many people," insisted Kurt Elling. "Sinatra is THE example in swing and natural phrasing for all who are smart enough to know where to look. Never forget to listen to Big Frank" (Panken 2009; Vitro 2012).

Many of these young crooners merged jazz with more contemporary styles. Cullum first turned to hip-hop. "That's how I got into jazz—through samples in hip hop and record collecting," he revealed. "Sample culture is part of my work, and has been for many years. Bass lines and riffs are part of a jazz musician's DNA and obviously hip hop is based around that same thing. Hip hop is, largely, about sex, so singing Cole Porter's 1930's song about hookers over the top of a [British rapper] Roots Manuva bass line and turning it back into essentially a jazz song with a jazz piano solo in the middle, made sense in my brain!" he maintained. Though considering himself "a jazz musician, even on my most-pop-oriented records" (Micallef 2015, 31), he mixed classic jazz with tunes by Jimi Hendrix, alternative rockers Radiohead, and folk-rocker Jeff Buckley. Cullum also became interested in the acid-jazz scene of such artists as Incognito and the James Taylor Quartet. "That was really a big starting point for me," he recalled (Katz 2013). "His sheer talent, pop star appeal and taste for mixing standards with new songs and rock covers has taken jazz out of the clubs and onto the high street," contended *BBC News* in 2003 (Bishop 2004).

As their female counterparts stormed the charts, male jazz vocalists started to sell. In addition to the mega-sales of Michael Bublé, in late 2003 Jamie Cullum hit the chart with *Twentysomething*, which cracked the US Top 100 and reached number three in the United Kingdom. His two follow-ups, *Catching Tales* (2005) and *The Pursuit* (2009), climbed to the Top Fifty in America and the Top Twenty in the United Kingdom. In 2009, after years of moderate sales, Kurt Elling won a Grammy for *Dedicated to You*. During an age of war and recession, reassuring male crooners, who resurrected familiar songs that had comforted older generations in troubled times, appealed to millions of Americans.

The Resurgence of Tony Bennett

At a time when young jazz singers were resurrecting standards, Tony Bennett, a crooner from the early fifties, fittingly reignited his career by singing classic songs with new pop and jazz stars. Raised in a poor family in Queens, New York, Bennett (b. Anthony Benedetto) began singing at the age of ten. He studied music and art at the School of Industrial Art in New York City and became interested in jazz when his older brother, also a singer, took him to Greenwich Village, "where he fell in love with all the jazz artists" (Vitro 2014). During World War II, he entered the Army, where he served as a librarian for an Army orchestra in Europe. Upon his discharge, Bennett wandered into clubs on Fifty-second Street in Manhattan, where he listened to Charlie Parker and Dizzy Gillespie. To hone his vocal skills, he used the GI Bill to fund studies at the American Theater Wing, where he took classes in acting and voice lessons in the bel canto method, which stressed intimate singing and translates from Italian into "beautiful singing."

Coming of age during the pre–World War II period, Bennett gravitated toward songs that later became classics. "There are definitive versions of songs from the Twenties, Thirties and Forties," he felt. "It was a Renaissance period, and those songs never died. The best songs were written by Jerome Kern, Irving Berlin, the Gershwins and Cole Porter. You had the greatest composers and the greatest songs ever written. Those songs don't die," he insisted (Vitro 2014).

As a teenager, the aspiring singer revered Frank Sinatra. "I idolized Frank Sinatra who was ten years older than me," he recalled. "I was a male counterpart to the bobby-soxers. I used to sit in the Paramount Theater as a fan through seven shows watching him sing with the Tommy Dorsey Orchestra. He ended up not just being my mentor, but my best friend through the years," Bennett added ("Tony Bennett Tribute" 1997, 38).

After the war, Bennett distinguished himself from Frank to achieve his own sound. "At the time all the singers—Sinatra, Dick Haymes [who replaced Sinatra in Tommy Dorsey's band]—would sing what I call a 'sweet, straight line,' so I established a style, where I would change my phrasing or end with a big finish to a song, and I was able to create my own style" (Timberg 2012).

The struggling singer soon got a break. In 1949, while performing with actress/singer Pearl Bailey in Greenwich Village, Bennett grabbed the attention of comedian Bob Hope, who "liked my singing so much that after the show he came back to see me in my dressing room and said, 'Come on, kid, you're going to come to the Paramount and sing with me.'" On the advice of Hope, the singer changed his stage name from Joe Bari (*American Masters*). "Let's Americanize you," the comedian insisted. "We'll call you Tony Bennett" ("Tony Bennett Tribute" 1997, 39). The next year, while singing with Hope, Bennett was noticed by Columbia Records executive Mitch Miller, who promptly signed him and molded him into a successful pop singer. In June 1951, he scored a number-one hit with "Because of You" and followed the next month with another chart topper, "Cold, Cold Heart." In late 1953, Bennett again reached number one with "Rags to Riches," which he quickly followed with the number-two "Stranger in Paradise."

Bennett did not relish pop success. When Mitch Miller "signed me, I was a jazz singer," he complained. "So they gave me [the lush, pop sounds of] Percy Faith and his orchestra. Whenever I tried to improvise, [the Columbia producers] would say, 'No, just sing the melody.' And that was frustrating to me because when I sing, I improvise. I'm very influenced by the African-American musicians who created jazz" (Barker 2015).

After his bevy of hits during the early fifties, Bennett's career slowed, reignited for a short period, and then stalled again. In 1954, he scored with two Top Ten entries but only managed one Top Ten effort for the remainder of the decade. In the summer of 1962, Tony again ascended the chart with the album *I Left My Heart in San Francisco*, which reached number five and provided him with a signature song. The next year, he reached the Top Five with the orchestrated *I Wanna Be Around*. In 1965, during an interview with *Life* magazine, Frank Sinatra cemented Bennett's mid-sixties reputation. "For my money," smiled Sinatra, "Tony Bennett is the best singer in the business. He excites me when I watch him. He moves me. He's the singer who gets across what the composer has in mind, and probably a little more" (Bourne 2015, 32).

Ironically, after Sinatra's encouraging words, Bennett's fortunes declined. After a Top Twenty effort in 1966, his discs fell further and further from the top of the charts. By the seventies and into the eighties, he seldom cracked the *Billboard* album listings and released fewer and fewer records.

Danny Bennett, Tony's son, brought fame to his father once again when he took over managerial duties during the early nineties. The younger Bennett introduced his father to a new generation of fans by engineering a guest song for Tony on the animated television show, *The Simpsons*, and snagging interviews in such rock magazines as *Spin* and on talk shows such as David Letterman and Jay Leno. In 1993, Danny landed an appearance for the singer on the MTV awards show and, two years later, convinced Tony to cut an *MTV Unplugged* disc. "Marketing isn't a bad word," reasoned Danny Bennett. "For me, marketing became a gut instinct rather than a learned one" ("Tony Bennett Tribute" 1997, 52).

In 2006, amid the jazz-singer boom, Tony Bennett once again entered the charts. To win a new audience without losing his base, he dueted on American standards such as "Lullaby of Broadway," "Because of You," and "Rags to Riches" with such rock stars as Elton John, Billy Joel, Paul McCartney, George Michael, and James Taylor. He reserved two songs for collaborations with Michael Bublé and Diana Krall on *Duets: An American Classic*, which hit the third spot on the chart. In 2011, he repeated his formula with the number-one *Duets II* by singing classic tunes with Sheryl Crow, John Mayer, Amy Winehouse, and Norah Jones. The next year, the singer put a Latin twist to the concept by crooning standards with such Latin stars as Christina Aguilera, Gloria Estefan, and Marc Anthony (b. Marco Muniz) for a number-five album. In late 2014, the vocalist repeated his chart-topping success by resurrecting songs by Cole Porter, Jimmy Van Heusen, Irving Berlin, Duke Ellington, and Jimmy McHugh for duets with pop/rock singer Lady Gaga (b. Stefani Germanotta) on *Cheek to Cheek*. By 2015, Tony Bennett had bridged generations to become a household name. During the twenty-first century, in the twilight of his career, he earned eleven of his nineteen Grammys and sold many of the fifty million albums that fans bought during his lifetime.

Jazz in a Divided America: Black Lives Matter

During the second decade of the twenty-first century, tension around the place of African Americans and women in American society rent the United States apart. As the economy improved and foreign wars somewhat receded, racial discrimination and gender inequity created a fundamental divide in American society. A focus on police profiling and killing of young African Americans and the reality of sexual harassment and abuse confronted Americans and spurred the jazz community into action.

On February 26, 2012, seventeen-year-old Trayvon Martin, wearing a hooded sweatshirt, walked to the home of his father's fiancée in Sanford, Florida. He was spotted by George Zimmerman, a member of the Sanford community watch, who alerted the police that a suspicious and possibly dangerous African-American male was prowling the streets. Before the police arrived, Zimmerman and Martin started to scuffle, and Zimmerman pulled out a gun and shot and killed the teenager. On July 13, 2013, after being tried for second-degree murder, Zimmerman was acquitted.

The Black Lives Matter (BLM) movement arose in the wake of the court decision. On the day of the acquittal, Alicia Garza tweeted to "Black people" that "I love you. I love us. Our lives matter." "I felt incredibly vulnerable, incredibly exposed and incredibly enraged" by the verdict, she recalled. Considering the acquittal "a call to action," the next day, she contacted friends Patrisse Cullors and Opal Tometi, and the three women set up Twitter and Tumblr accounts for African Americans to share their stories about racial discrimination (Day 2015, 2).

The next year, the BLM movement gained momentum, when, on August 9, 2014, a policeman in Ferguson, Missouri, fired twelve rounds into an unarmed, eighteen-year-old Michael Brown, killing him. BLM supporters organized a "freedom ride" to Ferguson, which attracted more than five hundred people from eighteen cities to demonstrate against police brutality. After a jury acquitted the Ferguson police officer, protesters chanted "black lives matter" and attracted national attention by closing a shopping mall. During the next three years, Black Lives Matter grew into a movement with thirty chapters after police killed more than twenty African Americans, including twelve-year-old Tamir Rice in Cleveland, New Yorker Akai Gurley, and Eric Garner, who died when New York police placed him in a chokehold.

Many young jazz artists clearly and personally grasped the fear and urgency behind Black Lives Matter. "I epitomize Black Lives Matter," commented the Coltrane-influenced saxophonist Kamasi Washington, who in 2015 released the African-American-centric *The Epic*. "I'm a big black man, and I'm easily misunderstood. . . . The harsh reality in our communities is that the greatest representatives of order, the police, are basically against you" (Shatz 2016, 58). "No other race has a history with the police like black people. People don't know that the very reason the police were made was to oversee slaves," declared pianist Robert Glasper. "Overseer, overseer, overseer, officer, officer, officer. That's the origin of the police" (Kramier 2016, 9).

Some young jazz players had been radicalized by sixties firebrands such as Malcolm X. As a youth, Kamasi Washington received a copy of *The Autobiography of Malcolm X* by a black nationalist organization called Ujima. "I saw these ideas weren't random, that there was a force behind them," he recalled (Shatz 2016, 58). He included a track titled "Malcolm's Theme" in *The Epic*. Growing up, trumpeter Christian Scott aTunde Adjuah admired a photo of Malcolm X in his home. Scott memorized the 1964 quote by the Black Muslim leader underneath the picture that read, jazz "is the only area on the American scene where the black man has been free to create" (Haga 2017, 6).

Robert Glasper at the Monterey Jazz Festival. *Craig Lovell/Eagle Visions Photography/Alamy Stock Photo*

Jazz artists incorporated the message of Black Lives Matter into their work. Christian Scott aTunde Adjuah performed "K.K.P.D. [Ku Klux Police Department]" about an incident in which New Orleans police stopped him for no reason. "If it makes you uncomfortable for me to talk about it," reasoned the trumpeter, "think about how uncomfortable it was with the gun in the back of my head" (Haga 2017, 6). In 2014, pianist Kris Bowers recorded "#TheProtester" to simulate a Black Lives Matter march; the next year, veteran trumpeter Terence Blanchard and his band The E-Collective released *Breathless* as a tribute to Eric Garner. "We wanted to make a statement about social injustice and gun violence in this country," he asserted (Cohen 2018, 32). "The list [of African-American victims of police violence] is endless," Blanchard lamented (30). In 2017, Ferguson, Missouri–born trumpeter Keyon Harrold wrote "MB Lament" and "When Will It Stop" about the killing of Michael Brown. In 2018, trumpeter Ambrose Akinmusire memorialized the death of Trayvon Martin in "A Blooming Bloodfruit in a Hoodie" and detailed the names of African Americans needlessly killed by police officers in "Free, White, and 21." "We are lifted up by Alicia Garza, Patrisse Cullors, [and] Opal Tometi," explained pianist Samora Pinderhughes about the connection of jazz to Black Lives Matter. "We are not making this happen, but we can provide the spirit" (Leah 2017, 3).

To establish a sound, which reflected a unique African-American identity, young, radicalized artists combined jazz with all types of

LISTENING GUIDE 46

The Robert Glasper Experiment

"THIS IS NOT FEAR"

Interested in combining all types of African-American music, the Robert Glasper Experiment offered this song as the lead-off composition on the album *ArtScience* (2016).

Previously, Glasper had been involved in many types of African-American music. He began his career with African-American gospel at the East Wind Baptist Church. Glasper subsequently produced songs for such hip-hop artists as Q-Tip, Kanye West, Jay-Z, and Common. In 2004, the genre-blending pianist released an album by his acoustic piano trio and, five years later, waxed *Double-Booked*, which featured both his piano trio and the funkified, electric Experiment. In 2013, he won a Grammy for the Best R&B album for *Black Radio* (2012). Three years later, his acoustic trio released *Covered*, which consisted of instrumental versions of songs by Radiohead, Joni Mitchell, John Legend, and Kendrick Lamar. The same year, he served as a producer, composer, and musical director for the Miles Davis biopic *Miles Ahead* and remixed Davis's music for the album *Everything's Beautiful*. The eclectic Glasper has insisted that "I'm obviously influenced by Miles Davis—even just the psyche of how he thinks about music. How he moves through, and always wanted to reflect, the times that he's in" (Chinen 2016, 1).

This song encapsulates many types of African-American-inspired music. It begins with an updated, Monkish version of hard bop and moves to more avant-garde, free-jazz improvisation, which Glasper attributed to "the anger and frustration of what's happening right now with all the police shootings" (Simon 2016, 2). It transitions to a funky, contemporary R&B, gives a nod to alternative rock, adds some turntable wizardry to represent hip-hop and, at the end, provides a sly reference to Jimi Hendrix. The title comes from rapper Mos Def, who mentioned that he did "not have fear" after being robbed in a South African airport (Simon 2016, 1). Glasper mentioned that "all the genres of music we're playing were birthed from jazz" (Regen 2016, 5).

Personnel: Derrick Hodge (bass and vocals), Robert Glasper (piano, vocals, and keyboards), Mark Colenburg (drums and vocals), Casey Benjamin (alto saxophone, vocals, and keyboards), and Jahi Sundance (turntables).

0:00–0:01	The track begins with the fast-tempo bass of Derrick Hodge.
0:02–0:09	Glasper enters on piano and plays a pattern three times in descending pitch to define the bare outline of a melody. In the third version of the pattern, he significantly embellishes it with a flurry of notes in a syncopated manner to match the speedy tempo of the bass player. The drums enter with Glasper to keep a steady, syncopated, varied, and speedy tempo with the bass. This section of the song represents a Monkish version of hard bop.
0:10–0:15	The saxophone enters and plays the melody initiated by Glasper above. He delivers it three times in a fast, syncopated, almost staccato rhythm.
0:16–0:20	Before the saxophone completes the passage above, Glasper reenters to answer the saxophone to continue a call-and-response.
0:21–0:24	The saxophone takes over again and repeats a version of the original pattern in an agitated, syncopated manner and nearly overblows the horn.
0:25–0:30	Glasper interjects with a staccato, stop-and-go version of the pattern, which becomes more and more insistent as the call-and-response persists.
0:31–0:34	The saxophone, though relying on the original pattern, now plays only a few notes of it to create a feeling of propulsion.
0:35–0:37	Glasper follows the saxophone with a driving, clipped phrasing of the original melody.

0:38–0:40	The saxophone improvises on the pattern and sustains a high, somewhat discordant note at the end.
0:41–0:43	Glasper responds with a few high-tempo notes from the initial pattern as the conversation between Glasper and Casey Benjamin continues.
0:44–1:04	The saxophonist deconstructs the melody in an improvisational fury by carefully rearranging and interpreting notes from the introductory pattern, which he plays several times. Glasper backs and converses with him in a series of highly syncopated notes, which are derived from the basic pattern. This section marks a transition to a more free-jazz approach.
1:05–1:20	Glasper shifts from a torrid solo to a slow delivery of the chords of the basic pattern to accompany the saxophone, which continues to improvise at a rapid pace. At 1:17, the saxophonist overblows the horn much like members of the avant-garde.
1:21–1:24	Slowly, the saxophone begins to sustain notes in a transition to another style.
1:25–1:29	The sax player starts to play more melodically.
1:30–1:46	Glasper suddenly interrupts the music with a spoken-word statement about the many types of music which African Americans have pioneered in America. Behind him, the saxophone repeats a middle-tempo, four-note pattern derived from the melody that contrasts with the more frantic bass and drums to create a polyrhythm.
1:47–1:57	The drums and bass get more prominent and abandon the hard-driving, fast tempo for a steady, four-four, slow-to-middle-tempo rhythm played by the saxophone, which drifts into the background with its steady pattern. The piano interjects a note periodically, leaving much space for the other members of the band. "I genuinely love space," insisted Glasper (Regen 2016, 4). Background vocals that resemble concert noise and Glasper's band-member introductions complement the rhythm to add to the musical interest. Establishing a smooth groove, the band has transitioned to a silky, funky, contemporary R&B sound.
1:58–2:07	The soft groove continues. Without the background crowd conversation, the groove recalls the final ten seconds of Nirvana's "On a Plain" in a nod to alternative or grunge rock.
2:08–2:09	The band inserts a loop of vocals, which repeat and fade out.
2:10–2:14	Glasper introduces electronic keyboards in an ascending pattern with a crowd cheering in the background and begins to introduce the band.
2:14–	The band continues with the funky groove with Glasper comping in the background and the drums, bass, and saxophone playing a slow- to mid-tempo rhythm.
2:28	A brief burst of turntable scratching begins, introducing a hip-hop element to the song that will reappear through the end.
2:29–2:37	The introduction of band members continues amid the steady, smooth rhythm.
2:38–3:00	The turntable scratching has been sampled and looped to add a polyrhythm to the song. The vocals of the band introduction also have been looped to create even greater rhythmic variety.
3:02–3:09	An almost unintelligible loop of the vocals, which say that "we're the experiment," begins.
3:10–3:17	A mid-tempo, almost-hushed vocal, saying "the experiment," is repeated six times as the groove fades and the song ends. The last two passages recall Jimi Hendrix's final vocals in "Are You Experienced."

African-American-inspired music. In an age of mash-ups, Christian Scott aTunde Adjuah attempted to "re-acculturate all the seemingly disparate musical realities that have grown out of jazz, or creative improvised music, back into the music" (Haga 2017, 3). He referred to his style as "stretch music," which incorporated alternative rock, soul, funk, and hip-hop into jazz. "The reality is my people have given the world so many styles of music, we want to explore them all," argued eclectic African-American pianist Robert Glasper, who worked with Keyon Harrold on *Miles Ahead* (2015), the part-drama, part-biography of Miles Davis (Kramier 2016, 9). "We sound in a jazz way, a pop way, R&B way, hip-hop way, a kind of rock-ish-way," he claimed about his band The Experiment (7).

Not surprisingly, many jazz artists contributed to *To Pimp a Butterfly* (2015), the groundbreaking mega-seller by rapper Kendrick Lamar, who used the album as a platform to raise African-American consciousness and battle racism. Kamasi Washington, who already had been part of a band for rapper Snoop Dog, played saxophone and arranged the string section, and Robert Glasper took over piano duties. Trumpeter Ambrose Akinmusire joined the band, and saxophonist Terrace Martin produced the album as well as playing horns and keyboards.

The jazz musicians who appeared on *To Pimp a Butterfly* saw hip-hop and jazz as two, indelibly linked parts of the African-American musical heritage. "Hip-hop," contended Kamasi Washington, "already is jazz. Like funk is jazz and jazz is funk, jazz is hip-hop. It's all the same thing." "I really do think that jazz and hip-hop are not *like* each other," agreed Ambrose Akinmusire. "They *are* the same thing" (Weiner 2015, 13).

On *To Pimp a Butterfly*, the musicians crafted a broad-based African-American music, which reflected the Sixties jazz protest against racial inequality. "That intense, 1960s jazz that people always associate with John Coltrane, that's what we were trying to get," maintained Kamasi Washington about the album. "It just felt like the height of civil rights" (Weiner 2015, 10). Young jazz musicians, embracing a wide spectrum of African-American musical styles, had followed the path of past African-American jazz artists who had demanded equality by joining the fervent cries of the Black Lives Matter movement.

Jazz and the #MeToo Movement

Discrimination against women also attracted the attention of the jazz community. Starting in October 2017, dozens of women reported allegations of rape, sexual harassment, and assault against film mogul Harvey Weinstein. Reeling from the news, women in the film industry sought to curb sexual bias in the movie industry by amplifying the #MeToo movement, making a hashtag from the phrase that African-American social activist Tarana Burke had coined in 2006 to raise awareness about women of color who had survived sexual abuse (Guerra 2017). Women in other professions joined their counterparts in the film field, and through social media spread the movement internationally. In less than a year, the problems of sexual harassment and gender bias, including pay inequity, came to the forefront.

Women in jazz likewise felt the sting of discrimination. In an open letter, young vibraphonist Sasha Berliner blasted the "misogynist jazz community" (Berliner 2017, 2) and asked rhetorically "how many big band concerts, productions and residencies put on by jazz clubs, etc. do you see with female jazz instrumentalists?" (2, 11). Veteran baritone saxophonist Lauren Sevian, who has performed for fifteen years with the Mingus Big Band, recalled harassment "and inappropriate physical advances" such as "waking up on a tour bus to find someone rubbing my leg" (Sevian 2017, 4). Saxophonist Sarah Manning described "the guy who grabbed my butt while I was playing in Los Angeles" (Manning 2017, p. 2). "We all have a similar experience," related horn player Roxy Coss. "Almost everyone I have talked to has been sexually abused, harassed, or assaulted from jazz mentors at some point" (Rauch 2018, 4).

Female jazz artists acted to address the inequity Coss and Berliner described. In July 2017, more than three hundred professional women jazz musicians banded together in the Women in Jazz Organization (WIJO) to "empower and connect women in jazz" and "create meaningful change in the jazz community." They pinpointed "a lack of representation of women in the jazz world" and vowed to fight discrimination, "harassment, assault, abuse, and violence" toward women. They wanted women to "receive the same opportunities as men in jazz do" (Women in Jazz Organization n.d.).

In December 2017, fourteen female jazz players, including Grammy-award-winning drummer Terri Lyne Carrington, formed We Have Voice. Inspired by the #MeToo movement, they supported the jazz women who have been "undermined, harassed, assaulted, violated, manipulated, intimidated, threatened and discriminated against." Backed by nearly a thousand like-minded musicians, jazz educational institutions, and jazz festivals, the group developed a code of conduct to "expose and eliminate a systematic structure that normalizes harassment and discrimination allowing abusers and complicit bystanders to perpetuate these behaviors without being held accountable for their negative actions." They promised that "we will not be silent. We have a voice. We have zero tolerance for sexual harassment." "Racism was always the first conversation, always the priority," contended Carrington. "But I'm not able to prioritize that more so than sexism anymore" (Blumenfeld 2017, 5).

Many female jazz artists demonstrated their commitment to #MeToo in their work. WIJO scheduled concerts with all-female combos to neutralize discrimination. In 2018, saxophonist/bass clarinetist Roxy Coss released the hard-hitting *The Future Is Female*, which included the songs "#Me Too," "Females Are Strong as Hell," and "Nasty Women Grab Back." "We've always been ruled by the patriarchy and we seem to be hitting a wall with that, in terms of progress and community," she insisted. "It's true in the jazz world as well" (Poet 2018, 2). The same year, veteran vocalist Karrin Allyson described gender inequity in "Big Discount."

Terri Lyne Carrington behind the drum set, 2017. *ZUMA Press, Inc./Alamy Stock Photo*

New London jazz applied the antiracism, antisexism message of young American jazz artists to a global context. Building upon acid jazz, collaborative young men and women musicians in London added hyperactive electronic beats, hip-hop, Caribbean sounds, and West African music to a jazz framework. "We got the younger audience of people coming," recalled tuba player Theon Cross, "so we started incorporating all these different styles. You can keep an audience and keep them dancing" (Orlov 2018, 7).

Like their American counterparts, the New London jazz musicians emphasized the contributions and importance of blacks and women. The seminal New London jazz group, Sons of Kemet, assaulted racism and sexism on the album *Your Queen Is a Reptile* (2018), which lauded such African-American female activists as abolitionist Harriet Tubman, black liberationist Anna Julia Cooper, and Black Panther advocate Angela Davis alongside such international black female heroes as anti-apartheid pioneer Albertina Sisulu and anticolonial Ashanti leader Yaa Asantewaa. Featuring such artists as saxophonists Shabaka Hutchings and Nubya Garcia, drummer Moses Boyd, and Theon Cross, the band sought "diversity of the music, with a push towards ethnic minorities and women," according to Garcia (Orlov 2018, 3). "We have an opportunity to create another dynamic that two, three generations from now could be equal, gender-wise, ethnicity-wise," added Garcia (Hutchinson 2018, 13). Trumpeter Sheila Maurice-Grey, leader of the bands Kokoroko and the mostly female seven-piece Nerija, wanted her music to represent "the idea of being young, black and British" (6).

The New London jazz scene rose to prominence through promotion by such DJs as Bradley Zero, Floating Points (b. Sam Shepherd), and Gilles Peterson, who also spearheaded the Brownswood Recordings label. By early 2018, "wherever I'm traveling, the States, Argentina, Japan, or all over Europe," asserted Gilles Peterson, "everyone is talking to me about the British Invasion" of jazz (Hutchinson 2018, 2).

During the twenty-first century, jazz again reflected the times. In the first decade, smooth singers soothed an American public beset by wars and economic troubles. During the next decade, jazz artists battled racial and gender discrimination in the hopes for a better world. As the 2010s closed amid great divisiveness, with an American president who discounted incidents of racial discrimination and allegations of sexual harassment, jazz musicians have again tackled the problems that must be solved to allow the United States to move forward.

For Discussion and Further Study

Chapter Quiz

1. In the wake of 9/11, how did American society change, and what influence did this have on jazz?

2. How did the successful female vocalists of this period gain popularity? What distinguished them from earlier performers?

3. How did singers like Michael Bublé appeal to both an older, nostalgic audience and to younger listeners? How did his approach differ from that of older singers enjoying a comeback, such as Tony Bennett?

4. How did jazz musicians reflect the concerns of the Black Lives Matter movement in their work?

5. What impact did the #MeToo movement have on jazz, particularly among female performers?

Bibliography

Abbott, Lyn. "'Brown Skin, Who You For?': Another Look at Clarence Williams' Early Career." *The Jazz Archivist* 8, nos. 1–2 (December 1993): 1–15.

Abbott, Lyn, and Doug Seroff. "'They Cert'ly Sound Good to Me': Sheet Music, Southern Vaudeville and the Commercial Ascendency of the Blues." *American Music* 14, no. 4 (Winter 1996): 402–54. "Albert Ayler Review." *Coda*, August 1971, 3.

Albertson, Chris. *Bessie*. New Haven, CT: Yale University Press, 2003.

Alden, Robert. "Hands of U.S. Tied in Asian 'Cold War.'" *New York Times*, June 11, 1956, 11.

Alkyer, Frank, and Ed Enright. *The Great Jazz Interviews: Downbeat's 75th Anniversary Anthology*. Milwaukee: Hal Leonard, 2000.

Allen, William Francis, Charles Pickard Ware, and Lucy McKim Garrison. *Slave Songs of the United States*. Bedford, MA: Applewood Books, 1996. First published 1867.

Almind, Gert. "The History of Coin-Operated Phonographs, 1888–1998" (unpublished manuscript, February 23, 2015). http://coin-o-phone.com/history.pdf.

Altman, Keith. "Just Call Me Helium." *Guitar World*, September 2001, 47–52.

American Masters. "Tony Bennett: The Music Never Ends." September 12, 2007, http://www.pbs.org/wnet/americanmasters/tony-bennett-the-music-never-ends/79/.

"An American Tragedy: 1967." *Newsweek*, August 7, 1967.

Anderson, Chris. *The Long Tail: Why the Future of Business Is Selling More of Less*. New York: Hyperion, 2006.

Anderson, Gene. "The Genesis of King Oliver's Creole Jazz Band." *American Music* 12, no. 3 (Autumn 1994): 283–303.

———. "Johnny Dodds in New Orleans." *American Music* 8, no. 4 (Winter 1990): 405–40.

Armstrong, Louis. *Louis Armstrong in His Own Words*. Edited by Thomas Brothers. Oxford, UK: Oxford University Press, 1999.

———. *Satchmo*. New York: Signet, 1955.

Aruga, Netsuki. "'An' Finish School': Child Labor during World War II." *Labor History* 29, no. 4 (1988): 498–530.

Ayler, Albert. "Albert Ayler." *Jazz Magazine*, December 1965, 41.

Backus, Rob. *Fire Music: A Political History of Jazz*. Chicago: Vanguard, 1976.

Badger, John Robert. "World View: Whither Negro-America in 1944." *The Chicago Defender*, January 8, 1944, 11.

Bakare, Lanre. "The U.K. Jazz Invasion." *The Guardian*, March 15, 2017. https://www.theguardian.com/culture/2017/mar/15/jazz-london-moses-boyd-united-vibrations.

Baker, Chet. *As Though I Had Wings: The Lost Memoir*. New York: St. Martin's Griffin, 1997.

Balk, Alfred. *The Rise of Radio: From Marconi through the Golden Age*. Jefferson, NC: McFarland, 2006.

"Bands Up Vaude Grosses." *Billboard*, September 12, 1942, 11.

Banjoko, Adisa. "Lost 1991 Guru/Gang Starr Interview," *The Commentator*, 1991. http://hiphopdx.com/interviews/id.1530/title.lost-1991-gurugang-starr-interview.

Barker, Andrew. "Tony Bennett on Signing His First Recording Contract, Early Influences." *Variety*, August 7, 2015. https://www.yahoo.com/music/s/tony-bennett-signing-first-recording-contract-early-influences-170031484.html.

Bart, Peter. "New Negro Riots Erupt on Coast." *New York Times*, August 13, 1965a, 1, 26.

———. "2,000 Troops Enter Los Angeles on Third Day of Negro Rioting." *New York Times*, August 14, 1965b, 1, 8.

Bartlett, Andrew. "World Saxophone Quartet." *The Rocket*, May 14–28, 1997, 14.

Basie, Count, with Albert Murray. *Good Morning Blues: The Autobiography of Count Basie*. New York: Random House, 1985.

"Bebop." *Life*, October 11, 1948, 138–41.

"Be-Bop Be-Bopped." *Time*, March 25, 1946, 54.

Bechet, Sidney. *Treat It Gentle: An Autobiography*. New York: Hill and Wang, 1960.

Belden, Bob. "Session-by-Session Analysis." *The Complete Bitches Brew Sessions*. Columbia Records C4K 65570, 1998, package notes.

Bell, Archie. "Jazz Most Popular Music of the Day," *Chicago Defender*, May 31, 1924, p. 6.

Bell, Madison Smartt. *Toussaint L'Ouverture: A Biography*. New York: Pantheon, 2007.

Bennett, Lerone. "What's in a Name? Negro vs. Afro-American vs. Black." *Ebony*, November 1967, 46–48, 50–52, 54.

"Benny Goodman Sways Thailand." *New York Times*, December 23, 1956, 8.

Berlin, Edward. *Ragtime: A Musical and Cultural History*. Berkeley: University of California Press, 1980.

Berliner, Sasha. "An Open Letter to Ethan Iverson (and the Rest of the Jazz Patriarchy)." *Sasha Berliner (blog)*, September 21, 2017. http://www.sashaberlinermusic.com/political-and-social-commentary-1/2017/9/21

/an-open-letter-to-ethan-iverson-and-the-rest-of
-jazz-patriarchy.

Bernhardt, Clyde. *I Remember: Eighty Years of Black Entertainment, Big Bands and the Blues.* Philadelphia: University of Pennsylvania Press, 1986.

"Bethlehem Started in Pops, Turned to Jazz." *Downbeat*, June 13, 1956, 10, 30.

"Beyond the Cool." *Time*, June 27, 1960, 58.

"B.G. and Bebop." *Newsweek*, December 27, 1948, 66–67.

Bigard, Barney. *With Louis and the Duke: The Biography of a Jazz Clarinetist.* New York: Oxford University Press, 1986.

"Billy Cox." *Guitar Player*, May 1989, 47, 61.

Bindas, Kenneth. *Swing That Modern Sound.* Jackson: University of Mississippi Press, 2001.

Birnbaum, Larry. "Illinois Jacquet." *Musician*, December 1988, 73–81.

———. "Jazz for the Hip-Hop Nation." *Downbeat*, February 1993, 33–36.

———. "Reggie Workman: Keep Moving." *Downbeat*, March 1996, 36–37.

———. "The Swinging Foundation: Christian McBride." *Downbeat*, March 1994, 33–34.

Bishop, Tom. "Jamie Cullum Jazzes Up Music Scene." *BBC News*, December 30, 2004, http://news.bbc .co.uk/2/hi/entertainment/3325139.stm.

Black, Johnny. *Jimi Hendrix: The Ultimate Experience.* New York: Thunder's Mouth, 1999.

Bland, Elizabeth. "Everybody's Wild About Harry." *Time*, January 15, 1990, 74.

Blesh, Rudi, and Harriet Janis. *They All Played Ragtime.* New York: Grove, 1959.

Bley, Paul, with David Lee. *Stopping Time: Paul Bley and the Transformation of Jazz.* Quebec: Vehicule, 1999.

Bliven, Bruce. "The Voice and the Kids." *New Republic*, November 6, 1944, 592–93.

Block, Martin. "Picking Hits Out of the Air." *Downbeat*, June 30, 1954, 73.

Blumenfeld, Larry. "The Female Collective Behind Jazz's #MeToo Movement." *The Daily Beast*, May 18, 2017, 1–7. https://www.thedailybeast.com/the-female -collective-behind-jazzs-metoo-movement.

Blumenthal, Bob. "First-Person Memories of Swing." *Downbeat* (July 1994), 18–20.

"Boff Hands Drawn by Kenton's 'Innovations' Preview in L.A." *Billboard*, February 18, 1950, 16.

"Bopera on Broadway." *Time*, December 20, 1948, 65.

Boston Musician's Association. "One Musicians' Union Where Once There Were Two." *Oral History Project*, n.d. Accessed October 10, 2019. http://www .bostonmusicians.org/history/one-musicians -union-where-once-there-were-two.

Bound, John, and Sarah Turner. "Going to War and Going to College: Did World War II and the G.I. Bill Increase Educational Attainment for Returning Veterans?" *Journal of Labor Economics* 20, no. 4 (October 2002): 784–815.

Bourne, Michael. "Lee Morgan: The Last Interview." *Downbeat*, April 27, 1972, 11.

———. "Play for the Moment." *Downbeat*, December 2015, 29–34.

Boyer, Richard. "Bop." *New Yorker*, July 3, 1948, 28–37.

Boyles, Brian. "Locking Horns: When Miles Davis Met Wynton Marsalis." *Offbeat*, August 1, 2011, 287–90.

Bradford, Perry. *Born with the Blues.* New York: Oak, 1965.

Branden, Barbara. *The Passion of Ayn Rand.* New York: Doubleday, 1986.

Braxton, Anthony. "Liner Notes." *3 Compositions of New Jazz*, Delmark Records, 1968, DS 415.

Brewster, Bill, and Frank Broughton. *Last Night a DJ Saved My Life: The History of the Disc Jockey.* New York: Grove, 2000.

Britt, Stan. "Bird Rappin'." *Wire*, March 1985, 39–43.

Brothers, Thomas. *Louis Armstrong's New Orleans.* New York: Norton, 2006.

Broughton, Frank. "Inspired by Gilles Peterson, Giant Step Sets Out to Bring Some Modern Dancefloor Jazz to Its Homeland." *DJHistory.com*, 1996. http:// www.djhistory.com/features/giant-step-1996.

Broven, John. "Modern Records: A Conversation with Recording Pioneer Joe Bihari." *ARSC Journal* 43, no. 1 (Spring 2012): 66–75.

———. *Record Makers and Record Breakers: The Voice of the Independent Rock 'n' Roll Pioneers.* Chicago: University of Illinois, 2009.

Brown, James, with Bruce Tucker. *James Brown: The Godfather of Soul.* New York: Macmillan, 1986.

Brubeck, Dave. "The Beat Heard 'Round the World." *New York Times Magazine*, June 15, 1958, 14, 31–33.

"Brubeck Stands Fast." *Downbeat*, April 2, 1959, 9.

Bruno, Joe. "Joe Bruno on the Mob—The Cotton Club." *Joe Bruno on the Mob (blog)*, January 20, 2012. https://joebrunoonthemob.wordpress.com /2012/01/20/joe-bruno-on-the-mob-the-cotton -club/.

Bruynoghe, Yannick. *Big Bill's Blues: William Broonzy's Story.* New York: Da Capo, 1992.

Bryant, Clora, ed. *Central Avenue Sounds: Jazz in Los Angeles.* Berkeley: University of California Press, 1998.

Buchanan, A. Russell. *Black Americans in World War II.* Santa Barbara, CA: Clio, 1977.

Burns, Ben. "Let My People Work: Job Prejudice Gnaws Away at Nation's Strength in War Production." *The Chicago Defender*, September 26, 1942, B10.

Busch, Niven, Jr. "The Pied Piper." *The New Yorker*, November 27, 1926, 25–27.

Byrnes, Sholto. "Wynton Marsalis: Miles Davis? He Was a Rock Star." *Independent*, January 30, 2014, 2.

Cady, Brian. "Roger Mayer: The Man behind the Hendrix Sound." *Elmore*, March/April 2006, 14–16.

"Call for Pace and Handy's Song Hits," *Freeman*, July 17, 1920, 5.

Calloway, Cab, with Bryant Rollins. *Of Minnie the Moocher and Me.* New York: Crowell, 1976.

Calt, Stephen. "The Anatomy of a 'Race' Label—Part One." 78 *Quarterly*, no. 3, 1988a, 9–23.

———. "The Anatomy of a 'Race' Label—Part II." 78 *Quarterly*, no. 4, 1989, 9–30.

———. *I'd Rather Be the Devil: Skip James and the Blues.* Chicago: Chicago Review Press, 1994.

———. *King of the Delta Blues: The Life and Music of Charlie Patton.* Newton, NJ: Rock Chapel Press, 1988b.

———. "Paramount: The Advent of Arthur Laibly." *78 Quarterly*, no. 6, 1991, 9–26.

———. "Paramount's Decline and Fall." *78 Quarterly*, no. 7, 1992, 7–29.

Calt, Stephen, and Gayle Dean Wardlow. "The Buying and Selling of Paramounts." *78 Quarterly*, no. 5, 1990, 7–23.

Campbell, Brunson S. "The Ragtime Kid: An Autobiography." In *Ragtime: Its History, Composers and Music*, edited by John Edward Hasse, 146–153. New York: Schirmer, 1985.

"Cardinal Renounces Crooners as Whiners Defiling the Air." *New York Times*, January 11, 1932, 23.

Carletta, David. "'Those White Guys Are Working for Me': Jazz and the Cultural Politics of the Cold War during the Eisenhower Administration." *International Social Science Review* 82, nos. 3/4 (2007): 115–34.

Carmichael, Hoagy. *The Stardust Road*. New York: Greenwood, 1969.

Carr, Paul. "History of Acid Jazz Podcast," July 2015. http://loosegooseradio.podomatic.com /entry/2015-07-17T13_02_44-07_00.

Carriveau, Cara. "Michael Bublé Interview, 2009." *Chicago Music Guide*, September 23, 2009, 1–4. https://chicagomusicguide.com/interview -with-michael-buble/.

Carver, Reginald, and Lenny Bernstein. *Jazz Profiles: The Spirit of the Nineties*. New York: *Billboard*, 1998.

Castagneto, Pierangelo. "Ambassador Dizzy: Jazz Diplomacy in the Cold War Era." *E-Journal of American Studies in Hungary* 10 (2014): 1–16. http:// americanaejournal.hu/vol10jazz/castagneto.

Castle, Mr. and Mrs. *Modern Dance*. New York: Harper and Brothers, 1914.

"Cats by the Sea." *Time*, August 2, 1954, 45.

"A Certain Turmoil." *Time*, February 13, 1950, 44.

Cerulli, Dom. "George Russell." *Downbeat*, May 29, 1958, 15–16.

Chambers, Gordon. "The Great Rap/Jazz Crossover." *Musician*, December 1993, 62–65.

Chambers, Jack. *Milestones II: The Music and Times of Miles Davis since 1960*. Toronto: University of Toronto Press, 1985.

Chambers, Whittaker. "Hearings Regarding Communist Espionage in the United States Government." *Testimony before the House Un-American Activities Committee*, August 3, 1948. http://law2.umkc.edu /faculty/projects/ftrials/hiss/8-3testimony.html.

Chapin, Gary Parker. "The Drummer's Dance: Andrew Cyrille Rides the Rhythm." *Option*, July/August 1991, 38–41.

Cherry Red Records. "James Taylor Tells the Story of the James Taylor Quartet in Our Exclusive Six Part Interview." https://www.youtube.com /watch?v=5w5IhbCBaDw.

Chevan, David. "Riverboat Music from St. Louis and the Streckfus Steamboat Line." *Black Music Research Journal* 9, no. 2 (Autumn 1989): 153–80.

Chilton, John. *Let the Good Times Roll: The Story of Louis Jordan and his Music*. Ann Arbor: University of Michigan, 1992.

Chinen, Nate. "What Would Miles Davis Do? Robert Glasper Has an Idea." *New York Times*, May 25, 2016, 1–4. https://www.nytimes.com/2016/05/26 /arts/music/robert-glasper-miles-davis-everythings -beautiful.html.

Clark, Philip. *Dave Brubeck: A Life in Time*. New York: Da Capo, 2019.

Claxton, William. "Who Created West Coast Jazz?" *Mosaic Promotional Brochure*, n.d., p. 11

Clayton, Buck. *Buck Clayton's Jazz World*. New York: Oxford University Press, 1986.

Clayton, James. "Defense Spending: Key to California's Growth." *The Western Political Quarterly* 15, no. 2 (June 1962): 280–93.

Cohen, Aaron. "We Are All Human." *Downbeat*, July 2018, 30–34.

Cohen, Harvey G. *Duke Ellington's America*. Chicago: University of Chicago Press, 2010.

Cohen, Lisabeth. "Encountering Mass Culture at the Grassroots: The Experience of Chicago Workers in the 1920s." *American Quarterly* 41, no. 1 (March 1989): 6–33.

Coleman, Ornette. *Liner notes for Change of the Century*, by Ornette Coleman. Atlantic Records 1327, 1960, LP.

"Collegians Like It Smooth: They Jive but with Restraint." *Billboard*, May 16, 1942, 23.

Collette, Buddy, with Steven Isoardi. *Jazz Generations: A Life in American Music and Society*. New York: Continuum, 2000.

Collin, Matthew. *Altered State: The Story of Ecstasy and Acid House*. London: Serpent's Tail, 1997.

Coltrane, John. *A Love Supreme*, by John Coltrane. Impulse! Records A-77, 1965, LP, liner notes.

"Columbia Diskery, CBS Show Microgroove Platters to Press; Tell How It Began." *Billboard*, June 26, 1948, 1, 18, 21.

"Columbia Girds for Biggest Jazz Push." *Billboard*, May 28, 1955, 35.

Concord Music Group website. "Concord Jazz." Accessed October 10, 2017. https://concord.com/labels /concord-jazz/.

———. "Double Exposure." Accessed October 10, 2017. http://www.concordmusicgroup.com/albums /Double-Exposure-TEL-33221-02/.

Condon, Eddie, with Thomas Sugrue. *We Called It Music*. New York: Da Capo Press, 1992.

Conrad, Earl. "Yesterday and Today: The Meaning of Migration." *The Chicago Defender*, April 14, 1945, 13.

Considine, J. D. "Tony Bennett and Diana Krall: Old Friends Together Again." *The Globe and Mail*, July 1, 2011. http://www.theglobeandmail.com/arts/music /tony-bennett-and-diana-krall-old-friends- together-again/article585212/.

Cooper, Ralph. *Amateur Night at the Apollo*. New York: HarperCollins, 1990.

Coryell, Julie, and Laura Friedman. *Jazz-Rock Fusion: The People, The Music*. New York: Delta, 1978.

Coss, Bill. "West Coast Scenes." *Metronome*, November 1955, 19–22

Cotgrove, Mark. "Snowboy." *From Jazz Funk and Fusion to Acid Jazz*. London: Chaser, 2009.

"Counterpoint Jazz." *Time*, February 2, 1953, 38.

Cowan, Ron. "George Gershwin: He Got Rhythm." *Washington Post*, November 1998. http://www .washingtonpost.com/wp-srv/national/horizon /nov98/gershwin.htm.

"Creator of Be-Bop Objects to Name and Changes His Style." *The Chicago Defender*, March 27, 1948, 9.

Crennard, Elliott. "College Kids Crown James." *Billboard*, May 29, 1943, 1, 23.

Crist, Stephen. "Jazz as Democracy? Dave Brubeck and Cold War Politics." *The Journal of Musicology* 26, no. 2 (Spring 2009): 133–74.

Crosby, Bing. *Call Me Lucky: Bing Crosby's Own Story*. New York: Simon and Schuster, 1953.

Crosby, Gary, and Ross Firestone. *Going My Own Way*. New York: Fawcett, 1984.

Crouch, Stanley. "Sonny Greer Interview." Smithsonian Jazz Oral History Project. January 1979.

———. "Wynton Marsalis Interview." *Downbeat*, November 1987, 17–19, 57.

Curtis, Susan. *Dancing to a Black Man's Tune: A Life of Scott Joplin*. Columbia: University of Missouri, 1994.

Cutler, Howard. "Kenny Barron Interview." *Cadence*, October 1989, 5–12, 92.

Dance, Stanley. *The World of Duke Ellington*. New York: Scribner's, 1970.

———. *The World of Earl Hines*. New York: Scribner's, 1977.

Daniel, Jesse. "Perry Como Sings for His Supper." *Milwaukee Journal*, June 23, 1946, 11.

Daniels, Douglas Henry. *Lester Leaps In: The Life and Times of Lester "Pres" Young*. Boston: Beacon Press, 2002.

Davin, Torn. "Conversations with James P. Johnson." In *Ragtime: Its History, Composers and Music*, edited by John Edward Hasse, 166–77. New York: Schirmer, 1985.

Davis, Miles, with Quincy Troupe. *Miles: The Autobiography*. New York: Simon and Schuster, 1989.

Dawson, Jim. "Chuck Higgins." *Goldmine*, July 10, 1992, 24–26.

Day, Elizabeth. "#BlackLivesMatter: The Birth of a New Civil-Rights Movement." *The Guardian*, July 19, 2015, 1–12. https://www.theguardian.com/world /2015/jul/19/blacklivesmatter-birth-civil -rights-movement.

Deffaa, Chip. *Voices of the Jazz Age: Profiles of Eight Vintage Jazzmen*. Urbana: University of Illinois, 1990.

De Micheal, Don. "Jackson on the MJQ." *Downbeat*, July 6, 1961a, 19–21.

———. "Johnny Griffin." *Downbeat*, January 5, 1961b, 20.

De Muth, Jerry. "Muhal Richard Abrams: Jazz Innovator, Founder of the A.A.C.M." *Contemporary Keyboard*, May 1978, 20, 48–49.

DeVeaux, Scott. "Bebop and the Recording Industry: The 1942 AFM Recording Ban Reconsidered." *Journal of American Musicological Society* 41, no. 1 (Spring 1988): 126–165.

DeVeaux, Scott, and Howard McGhee. *The Birth of Bop*. Berkeley: University of California, 1997.

———. "The Emergence of the Jazz Concert." *American Music* 7, no. 1 (Spring 1989): 6–29.

———. "Jazz in the Forties." *The Black Perspective in Music* 15, no. 1, (Spring 1987): 64–78.

DeVito, Chris, ed. *Coltrane on Coltrane: The John Coltrane Interviews*. Chicago: Chicago Review Press, 2010.

DiMartino, Dave. "The Majors: Jazz Lions Roar into Younger Marketplace." *Billboard*, July 1, 1989a, J3, J18.

———. "Reissues: Back Catalog Looking Ahead to New Life." *Billboard*, July 1, 1989b, J8, J14.

"Disk Firms Pay a Close Game While Awaiting to See What Transpires in India and D.C." *Billboard*, June 6, 1942, 21.

"Dizzy to Rock India." *New York Times*, February 2, 1956, 19.

"Dizzy Urges Ike to Back Jazz Tours." *Pittsburgh Courier*, August 4, 1957, 15.

Dodds, Warren Baby. *The Baby Dodds Story: As Told to Larry Gara*. Baton Rouge: Louisiana State University Press, 1992.

Doerschuk, Bob. "Jimmy Smith." *Contemporary Keyboard*, August 1978, 26–36.

Downes, Olin. "A Concert of Jazz." *New York Times*, February 13, 1924.

"Draft Operation Overwhelmingly Approved by the Public, Dr, Gallup's Survey Indicates." *New York Times*, December 28, 1940, 8.

Driggs, Frank. "About My Life in Music, Walter Page." *The Jazz Review*, November 1958, 12–15.

———. "Ed Lewis' Story." *The Jazz Review*, October 1959a, 23–26.

———. "Kansas City Brass: Ed Lewis Interview." *The Jazz Review*, May 1959b, 16–18.

Eggleton, Sophie. "My Interview with Ed Piller of Acid Jazz Records." *Sophie Eggleton (blog)*, October 1, 2012. http://sophieeggleton.blogspot. com/2012/10/my-interview-with-ed-piller-of-acid. html.

"Election Test." *New York Times*, November 3, 1946, 91.

Ellington, Duke. *Music Is My Mistress*. New York: W. H. Allen, 1974.

Ellison, Mary. "The Marsalis Family and the Democratic Imperative." *Race and Class* 43, no. 1 (2001), 1–28.

Engel, Carl. "Jazz: A Musical Discussion." *Atlantic Monthly*, August 1922, 182–88.

Enstice, Wayne, and Paul Rubin. *Jazz Spoken Here: Conversations with Twenty-Two Musicians*. Baton Rouge: Louisiana State University Press, 1992.

Epstein, Dena. *Sinful Tunes and Spirituals: Black Folk Music to the Civil War*. Chicago: University of Illinois Press, 2003.

Erenberg, Lewis. "Everybody's Doin' It: The Pre-World War I Dance Craze, the Castles, and the Modern American Girl." *Feminist Studies* 3, nos. 1/2 (Autumn 1975): 155–70.

———. *Swingin' the Dream: Big Band Jazz and the Rebirth of American Culture*. Chicago: University of Chicago Press, 1998.

Evans, David. "Bessie Smith's 'Back-Water Blues': The Story behind the Song." *Popular Music* 26, no. 1 (2007): 97–116.

Evans, Suzanne. "Dispatches from a Day of Terror and Shock; Darkness at Noon." *New York Times*,

September 12, 2001. http://www.nytimes.com/2001/09/12/opinion/l-dispatches-from-a-day-of-terror-and-shock-darkness-at-noon-145580.html.

Eyre, Ron. *Liner notes for Brother Jack*, by Jack McDuff with Bill Jennings. Prestige PRLP 7174, 1960a, LP.

———. *Liner notes for Outward Bound*, by the Eric Dolphy Quintet. New Jazz NJLP-8236, 1960b, LP.

Fairlie, Robert, and William Sundstrom. "The Emergence, Persistence and Recent Widening of the Racial Employment Gap." *Industrial and Labor Relations Review* 52, no. 2 (January 1999): 252–67.

Farley, Christopher. "Calming Voice in a Frenzied Pop Age." *Time*, April 26, 2004, 84–85.

———. "Hip Hop Goes Bebop." *Time*, July 12, 1993, 51.

Farmer, Art. "Art Is Farmer's Sake." *Metronome*, May 1957, 29, 36, 38.

Feather, Leonard. *The Encyclopedia of Jazz Yearbook, 1956*. New York: Horizon, 1956.

———. "The Heath Brothers: Together Again for the First Time." *Downbeat*, October 13, 1975, 18–19.

———. *The Jazz Years: Earwitness to an Era*. New York, Da Capo, 1987.

———. "Parker Finally Finds His Peace." *Downbeat*, April 20, 1955, 6, 30.

———. *The Passion for Jazz*. New York: Horizon, 1980.

———. "Sonny Rollins, Part Two: Blindfold Test." *Downbeat*, August 16, 1962, 35.

Fellezs, Kevin. "Emergency! Race and Genre in Tony Williams' Lifetime." *Jazz Perspectives* 2, no. 1 (May 2008): 1–27.

"Femme Influx: Drafted Men Being Replaced by Women in Many Showbiz Fields; Trend Expected to Accelerate." *Billboard*, April 11, 1942, 3.

Fiehrer, Thomas. "From Quadrille to Stomp: The Creole Origins of Jazz." *Popular Music* 10, no. 1 (January 1991): 21–38.

"52nd Street Now Develops Units Instead of Name Bands and Steps into Tall Dough." *Billboard*, November 27, 1943, 24.

Figi, J. B. *Liner notes for Sound*, by the Roscoe Mitchell Sextet. Delmark Records DS-408, 1966, LP.

Filzen, Sarah. "The Rise and Fall of Paramount Records." *The Wisconsin Magazine of History* 82, no. 2 (Winter 1998–1999): 104–127.

Finkle, Lee. "The Conservative Aims of Militant Rhetoric: Black Protest during World War II." *Journal of American History* 60, no. 3 (December 1973): 692–713.

Fiofori, Tom. "Re-entry: The New Orbit of Sonny Rollins." *Downbeat*, October 14, 1971, 14–15, 39.

Firestone, Ross. *Swing, Swing, Swing: The Life and Times of Benny Goodman*. New York: Norton, 1993.

Fisher, Rudolph. "The Caucasian Storms Harlem." *American Mercury*, August 1927, 393–98.

Fitzgerald, F. Scott. "Echoes of the Jazz Age." *Scribner's Magazine*, November 1931, 1–9.

Fitzsimmons, Izzy, and Ryan Taylor. "Interview: Keyon Harrold Chats to Us at Love Supreme about the Mugician, Being Miles Davis' Trumpet, and Numerous Collaborations." *Trouve la Groove*, July 21, 2018. http://www.trouvelagroove.com/single-post/2018/07/21/Interview-Keyon-Harrold-chats-to-us-at-Love-Supreme-about-The-Mugician-being-Miles-Davis-trumpet-and-numerous-collaborations.

Floyd, Samuel. "An Oral History: The Great Lakes Experience." *The Black Perspective in Music* 11, no. 1 (Spring 1983): 41–61.

Foner, Laura. "The Free People of Color in Louisiana and St. Domingue: A Comparative Portrait of Two Three-Caste Slave Societies." *Journal of Social History* 3, no. 4 (Summer 1970): 406–30.

Foster, George Pops. *Pops Foster: The Autobiography of a New Orleans Jazzman*. Edited by Tom Stoddard. Berkeley: University of California Press, 1971.

Fox, Ted. *In the Groove*. New York: St. Martin's, 1986.

"France Enragee: The Spreading Revolt." *Time*, May 24, 1968, 38–42.

Franckling, Ken. "Marcus Roberts: Reflections on Spirit, Tradition, Purpose." *JazzTimes*, March 1991, 13–17.

Freedman, Sam. "Archie Shepp: Embracing the Jazz Ritual." *Downbeat*, April 1982, 22–25.

Freeman, Bud. *You Don't Look Like a Musician*. Detroit: Balamp, 1974.

Freeman, Don. "Dave Brubeck Not Pink over Red, Hot and Cool." *Downbeat*, January 25, 1956, 9.

Gardner, Barbara. "The Enigma of Miles Davis." *Downbeat*, January 7, 1960, 20–23.

Gavin, James. *Deep in a Dream: The Long Night of Chet Baker*. New York: Vintage, 2002.

George, Nelson, Sally Banes, Susan Flinker, and Patty Romanowski. *Fresh, hip hop don't stop*. With a foreword by Kurtis Blow. New York: Random House, 1985.

Gibbs, Nancy. "When New President Meets Old, It's Not Always Pretty." *Time*, November 10, 2008.

Giddens, Gary. *Bing Crosby: A Pocketful of Dreams, The Early Years 1903–1940*. Boston: Little, Brown, 2001.

Gilbert, Gama. "Higher Soars the Swing Fever." *New York Times Magazine*, August 14, 1938, 6–7, 19.

Gillespie, Dizzy, with Al Fraser. *To Be, or Not . . . to Bop: Memoirs of Dizzy Gillespie*. New York: Da Capo, 1979.

"Gillespie's Band a Hit in Beirut." *New York Times*, April 29, 1956, 124.

Gilliland, John. (1969). "John Gilliland's Pop Chronicles, Show 22—Smack Dab in the Middle on Route 66: A Skinny Dip in the Easy Listening Mainstream. [Part 1]." Audio recording. https://digital.library.unt.edu/ark:/67531/metadc19775/m1/#track/1.

Ginell, Cary. *Walk Tall: The Music and Life of Cannonball Adderley*. Milwaukee: Hal Leonard Books, 2013.

Gioia, Ted. *The History of Jazz*. New York: Oxford University Press, 1997.

———. *West Coast Jazz: Modern Jazz in California, 1945–1960*. New York: Oxford, 1992.

Gitler, Ira. "Jackie McLean." *Downbeat*, September 12, 1963, 22–24.

———. "Randy Weston." *Downbeat*, February 2, 1964, 16–17, 36.

———. *Swing to Bop: An Oral History of the Transition in Jazz in the 1940s*. New York: Oxford University Press, 1985.

———. "'Trane' on the Track." *Downbeat*, October 16, 1958, 16–17

Giuffre, Jim. "Jim Giuffre." *Downbeat*, November 30, 1955, 9, 50.

Gleason, Ralph. "An Appeal from Dave Brubeck." *Downbeat*, February 18, 1960, 12–13.

———. "Brubeck." *Downbeat*, July 25, 1957a, 13, 54.

———. "Brubeck." *Downbeat*, September 5, 1957b, 14–16.

———. Liner notes for *The Cannonball Adderley Quintet in San Francisco*, by The Cannonball Adderley Quintet featuring Nat Adderley. Riverside Records RLP 12-311, 1960, LP.

———. *Conversations in Jazz: The Ralph Gleason Interviews*. New Haven: Yale, 2016.

Gold, Don. "Blowin' in From Chicago." *Downbeat*, May 29, 1958, 17, 50.

Goldberg, Joe. Liner notes for *Feelin' the Spirit*, by Grant Green. Blue Note Records BLP 4132, 1963, LP.

———. *Jazz Masters of the Fifties*. New York, Da Capo, 1965.

———. Liner notes for *Out There*, by Eric Dolphy. New Jazz NJLP 8252, 1961, LP.

Goldmark, Peter. "Hi-Fi: A Misleading Term?" *Downbeat*, June 30, 1954, 78.

Goldsmith, Owen. "Dave Brubeck." *Contemporary Keyboard* 3, no. 12 (December 1977): 26–31, 40–42.

Gonzales, Babs. Liner notes for *A New Sound . . . A New Star . . . Jimmy Smith at the Organ* Vol. 1, by Jimmy Smith. Blue Note BLP 1512, 1956, LP.

———. "What's What with Bop as Seen by Prof. Gonzales." *The New York Age*, December 24, 1949, 41.

Gonzales, Michael. "Esperanza Spalding Interview." *Daily Telegraph*, March 27, 2011, http://www.telegraph.co.uk/culture/music/worldfolkandjazz/8402191/Esperanza-Spalding-interview.html.

Goodell, Jeff. "Steve Jobs Interview." *Rolling Stone*, December 25–January 8, 2004.

"Goodman Beats Drum for Asians." *New York Times*, January 25, 1957, 23.

Goodman, Benny, with Ted Shane. "Now Take the Jitterbug." *Collier's*, February 25, 1939, 11–13, 60.

Gould, Jack. "Ban on Records Off as Petrillo Wins." *New York Times*, November 12, 1944, 1, 44.

Gourse, Leslie. *Louis' Children: American Jazz Singers*. New York: Quill, 1984.

Govenar, Alan. "Blind Lemon Jefferson: The Myth and the Man." *Black Music Research Journal* 20, no. 1 (Spring 2000): 7–21.

Gracyk, Tim. "The Original Dixieland Jass Band." Excerpt from Tim Gracyk, *Popular American Recording Pioneers, 1895–1925, 2000*. Tim's Phonographs & Old Records, 2006. http://www.gracyk.com/odjb.shtml.

Graettinger, Bob. Liner notes for *City of Glass*, by Stan Kenton. Capitol Records H-353, 1952, LP.

Green, Sharony. *Grant Green: Rediscovering the Forgotten Genius of Jazz Guitar*. San Francisco: Backbeat, 1999.

Greenberg, Peter S. "Rock and Big Bucks." *Playboy*, January 1981, 201–70.

Gregory, Vahan K. Liner notes for *Les McCann Ltd. Plays The Shout*, by Les McCann Ltd. Pacific Jazz Records PJ-7, 1960, LP.

Griffin, Anders. "Stanley Cowell." *The New York City Jazz Record* (June 2015), 6.

Griffin, Nard. *To Be or Not to Bop*. New York: Leo Workman, 1948.

Grossman, James. *Land of Hope: Chicago, Black Southerners, and the Great Migration*. Chicago: University of Chicago Press, 1989.

Grow, Kory. "Biddy Biddy Bop: The Oral History of Us3's Bold Jazz-Rap Breakthrough 'Cantaloop (Flip Fantasia').'" *Spin*, October 24, 2013. http://www.spin.com/2013/10/us3-cantaloop-flip-fantasia-herbie-hancock-lou-donaldson/.

Guerra, Cristela. "Where'd the #MeToo Initiative Really Come From? Activist Tarana Burke, Long before Hashtags." *Boston Globe*, October 17, 2017. https://www.bostonglobe.com/lifestyle/2017/10/17/alyssa-milano-credits-activist-tarana-burke-with-founding-metoo-movement-years-ago/o2Jv29v6ljObkKPTPB9KGP/story.html.

Gumbel, Bryant. "Miles Davis Interview, 1982." Posted November 14, 2006. https://www.youtube.com/watch?v=IHeYG9SNaS0.

Gushee, Lawrence. "The Nineteenth-Century Origins of Jazz." *Black Music Research Journal* 14, no. 1 (Spring 1994): 1–24.

Gushee, Lawrence, and Harry Carr. "How the Creole Band Came to Be." *Black Music Research Journal* 8, no. 1 (1988): 83–100.

Guzman, Jesse. *Negro Yearbook: A Review of Events Affecting Negro Life, 1941–1946*. Tuskegee, AL: Tuskegee Institute, 1947.

Haga, Evan. "Christian Scott aTunde Adjuah Talks Jazz as Protest Music, Trap Influence." *Rolling Stone*, March 30, 2017, 1–9. https://www.rollingstone.com/music/music-features/christian-scott-atunde-adjuah-talks-jazz-as-protest-music-trap-influence-110441/.

Hahn, Lorraine. "Jazz Musician, Diana Krall Talks Asia Interview." *CNN*, March 16, 2005. http://www.cnn.com/2005/WORLD/asiapcf/04/29/talkasia.krall.script/index.html?iref=allsearch.

Hailey, Foster. "Alabama Police Jail Blind Singer." *New York Times*, April 10, 1963, 29.

———. "Dogs and Hoses Repulse Negroes at Birmingham." *New York Times*, May 4, 1963, 1, 8.

Halker, Clark. "A History of Local 208 and the Struggle for Racial Equality in the American Federation of Musicians." *Black Music Research Journal* 8, no. 2 (Autumn 1988), 207–222.

Hammond, John. "From Spirituals to Swing." *New York Times*, December 18, 1938, 9–10.

———. *John Hammond on Record: An Autobiography* (New York: Summit Books, 1977)

Hampton, Henry and Steve Fayer. *Voices of Freedom: An Oral History of the Civil Rights Movement from the 1950s through the 1980s*. New York: Bantam, 1990.

Hancock, Herbie, with Lisa Dickey. *Possibilities*. New York: Viking, 2014.

Handy, W.C. *W.C. Handy: Father of the Blues*. New York: Collier, 1941.

Harden, Blaine. "A Day of Terror: Vulnerability; Physical and Psychological Paralysis of Nation." *New York Times*, September 12, 2001, http://www.nytimes.com/2001/09/12/us/a-day-of-terror-vulnerability-physical-and-psychological-paralysis-of-nation.html

Harker, Brian. "Louis Armstrong, Eccentric Dance and the Evolution of Jazz on the Eve of Swing." *Journal of American Musicological Society* 61, no. 1 (Spring 2008), 67–121.

Harman, Carter. "Bop: Skee, Re or Be, It's Still Got to Swing." *New York Times*, December 5, 1948, X13.

Harris, Neil. "John Philip Sousa and the Culture of Reassurance." In *Perspectives on John Philip Sousa*, edited by Jon Newsom, 11–40. Washington, DC: Library of Congress, 1983. http://memory.loc.gov/diglib/ihas/loc.natlib.ihas.200152753/default.html.

Harris, Phil. "Lester Young: Pres Talks about Himself, Copycats." *Downbeat*, May 6, 1949, 38.

"Harry James." *Billboard*, July 18, 1942, 4.

"Harry James—Paramount." *Billboard*, May 1, 1943, 1, 11.

Hasse, John Edward. *Beyond Category: The Life and Genius of Duke Ellington*. New York: Da Capo Press, 1995.

———. "Ragtime: From the Top" In *Ragtime: Its History, Composers and Music*, edited by John Edward Hasse, 1–39. New York: Schirmer, 1985.

———, ed. *Ragtime: Its History, Composers and Music*. New York: Schirmer, 1985.

Havlis, Andrew. "Marcus Roberts: Jazz Piano Spoken Here." *The Rocket*, October 1990, 14.

Hawes, Hampton, with Don Asher. *Raise Up off Me: A Portrait of Hampton Hawes*. New York: Thunder's Mouth, 1972.

Hawkins, Lee. "Marsalis Discusses His Critics, 1986 Miles Davis Incident." *Wall Street Journal*, December 17, 2010. http://www.wsj.com/video/wynton-marsalis-talks-jazz-in-the-21st-century/FFA2312B-C74E-42DB-B44E-8780592C36AD.html.

"He Calls It Progress." *Time*, March 1, 1948, 36.

Heath, Jimmy. *I Walked with Giants: The Autobiography of Jimmy Heath*. Philadelphia: Temple University, 2010.

Heckman, Don. "Herbie Hancock." *Downbeat*, October 21, 1965, 12–13, 37.

Helland, Dave. "Wynton: Prophet in Standard Time." *Downbeat*, September 1990, 16–19.

Henderson, David: *Jimi Hendrix: Voodoo Child of the Aquarian Age*. New York: Doubleday, 1978.

Henderson, Harry, and Sam Shaw. "And Now We Go Bebop." *Collier's*, March 20, 1948, 16–17, 88.

Hennessey, Mike. *Klook: The Story of Kenny Clarke*. Pittsburgh: University of Pittsburgh Press, 1990.

Hentoff, Nat. *Liner notes for Coltrane—"Live" at the Village Vanguard*, by John Coltrane. Impulse! Records A-10, 1962, LP.

———. "Detroit Producing Stars: Paul Chambers Big One." *Downbeat*, January 11, 1956, 12.

———. *Liner notes for Giant Steps*, by John Coltrane. Atlantic Records 1311, 1960, LP.

———. "In Which One of Jazzdom's Greats Reminisces, Evaluates and Chats." *Downbeat*, March 7, 1956a, 9–11.

———. *The Jazz Life*. New York: Da Capo, 1975.

———. "Just Call Him Thelonious." *Downbeat*, July 25, 1956c, 15.

———. "No Mass Production for Blue Note." *Downbeat*, June 27, 1956b, 11–12.

———. *Liner notes for Plenty, Plenty Soul*, by Milt Jackson. Atlantic 1269, 1957, LP.

———. *Liner notes for Something Else!!!! The Music of Ornette Coleman*, by Ornette Coleman. Contemporary Records, 1958, LP.

Herbers, John. "Negroes Pour into Streets in Shock and Anger at Bombing." *New York Times*, September 16, 1963, 26.

Herman, Woody, and Stuart Troup. *Woodchopper's Ball: The Autobiography of Woody Herman*. New York: Random House, 1990.

Hershorn, Tad. *Norman Granz: The Man Who Used Jazz for Justice*. Berkeley: University of California Press, 2011.

Hinton, Harold. "Marshall U.S. Foe, McCarthy Charges." *New York Times*, June 15, 1951, 3.

Hobson, Vic. "Buddy Bolden's Blues." *The Jazz Archivist* 21 (2008), 1–18.

Hoefer, George. "Caught in the Act." *Downbeat*, January 7, 1960, 40–41.

———. "The Coming of Organ to Jazz." *Downbeat*, October 29, 1959, 26–27, 44.

Hoffman, Steve. "All about Chris Bangs." *Blog Happy*, n.d. Accessed October 10, 2019. http://chrisbangs.typepad.com/chris_bangs_blog_happy/all-about-bangsy.html.

Hohman, Marv. "Do the Funky Renaissance with Alphonse Mouzon." *Downbeat*, December 4, 1975, 15–16, 15–42.

Holley, Donald. "John Daniel Rust (1892–1954)." *Encyclopedia of Arkansas History and Culture*. December 29, 2010. http://www.encyclopediaofarkansas.net/encyclopedia/entry-detail.aspx?entryID=2272.

Holley, Eugene, Jr. "Wynton Marsalis: Jazz Messenger." *Ebony*, September 4, 2012.

"Hollywood: Unmasking Informant T-10." *Time*, September 9, 1985.

Hoover, Herbert, *New York Times*, October 26, 1929, 1.

"Horn of Plenty." *Time*, September 28, 1942, 40, no. 13, 40.

Horowitz, Harold. *The American Jazz Music Audience*. Washington, DC: National Jazz Service Organization, September 8, 1986.

"Hot Summer." *New York Times*, August 15, 1965, 145.

"How Deaf Can You Get?" *Time*, May 17, 1948, 76.

Howard Rumsey's Lighthouse All-Stars. *In the Solo Spotlight! Lighthouse Series*, Volume 5. Contemporary Records C3517, 1957, LP (liner notes).

Hughes, Langston. *The Big Sea*. New York: Hill and Wang, 1981.

———. "The Negro Artist and the Racial Mountain." *The Nation*, June 23, 1926.

Hutchinson, Kate. "The British Jazz Explosion: Meet the Musicians Rewriting the Rulebook." *The Guardian*, April 8, 2018. https://www.theguardian.com/music/2018/apr/08/british-jazz-invasion-moses-boyd-matthew-halsall-nubya-garcia.

"Independence in the Cameroons." *New York Times*, January 1, 1960, 18.

"Indians Dizzy of Gillespie's Jazz." *Pittsburgh Courier*, June 2, 1956, part 1, 22.

"Indians Dizzy of Gillespie's Jazz." *Pittsburgh Courier*, June 9, 1956, part 2, 21.

"Interview: Eddie Piller, Acid Jazz Founder." *Ben Sherman website*, October 5, 2012, https://www.bensherman.co.uk/blog/interview-eddie-piller-acid-jazz-founder.

"An Interview with the Brand New Heavies." March 3, 2013, *Expresso video*. https://www.youtube.com/watch?v=JYCDihclGsQ (video unavailable).

"Interview with John Pizzarelli, August 3, 2000." *John Pizzarelli Fan Page*. 2003. Accessed October 10, 2019. http://pizzarellifanpage.com/index.html.

"Iraq and Turkey Pact." *New York Times*, September 5, 1955, 5.

Isler, Scott. "I Had All These Ideas and Sounds in My Brain: Jimi Hendrix in His Own Words." *Musician*, November 1991, 32–44.

Isoardi, Steven. "Frank Morgan Interview, 1992–1993." *UCLA Library Center for Oral History Research, 52 pages*. http://oralhistory.library.ucla.edu/viewItem.do?ark=21198/zz0008zqmn&title=%20 Morgan,%20Frank.

Jackson, Kenneth. *Crabgrass Frontier: The Suburbanization of the United States*. New York: Oxford, 1985.

Jackson, Nate. "Influences: Trumpet Player, Bandleader, Composer Terence Blanchard." *Los Angeles Times*, August 17, 2011. http://latimesblogs.latimes.com/culturemonster/2011/08/influences-trumpet-player-bandleader-and-film-composer-terence-blanchard.html.

Jam, Billy. "1991 Interview with Gang Starr's DJ Premier and the Late Great Guru." *Amoeblog (blog)*, April 26, 1991. http://www.amoeba.com/blog/2010/04/jamoeblog/1991-interview-with-gang-starr-s-dj-premier-and-the-late-great-guru-.html.

"James Ork Follows 'Traviata.'" *Billboard*, April 17, 1943, 4.

"James Taylor: One Man's Family of Rock." *Time*, March 1, 1971.

Janus, Cicily. *The New Face of Jazz*. New York: Billboard, 2010.

"Jazz." *The Observer*, March 5, 1924, 381–82.

"The Jazz Business." *Time*, March 2, 1953, 42.

"Jazz West Coast: Jimmy Giuffre." *Metronome*, June 1955, 21, 33, 47.

Jenkins, Willard. "Greg Osby: Restless, Provocative and Now." *Jazztimes*, December 1991, 27, 65.

"Jimi Hendrix in His Own Words." *Musician*, November 1991, 32–44.

Joans, Ted. "Spiritual Unity: Albert Ayler." *Coda*, August 1971, 2–4.

Johnson, Charles S. *The Negro in American Civilization*. New York, Henry Holt, 1930.

Johnson, Martin. "Music as a Part of Life." *Pulse!*, May 1989, 47.

Johnson, Russell. "'Disease Is Unrhythmical': Jazz, Health and Disability in 1920s America." *Health and History* 13, no. 2 (2011): 13–42.

Jones, LeRoi. *Black Music*. New York: Morrow, 1971.

———. *Liner notes for Live at Birdland*, by John Coltrane. Impulse! Records AS-50, 1964, LP.

———. "Voice from the Avant Garde: Archie Shepp." *Downbeat*, January 14, 1965, 18–20, 25.

Jones, Max. *Talking Jazz*. New York: Norton, 1987.

Jones, Quincy. *Q: The Autobiography of Quincy Jones*. New York: Doubleday, 2001.

Josephson, Sanford. *Jeru's Journey: The Life and Music of Gerry Mulligan*. Milwaukee: Hal Leonard, 2015.

"Junior Jammers Ripe for Draft." *Billboard*, November 28, 1942, 20.

Kahn, Ashley. *The House That Trane Built: The Story of Impulse Records*. New York: Norton, 2006.

Kahn, E. J. "The Fave, the Fans and the Fiends, 1946." In *The Frank Sinatra Reader*, edited by Steven Petkov and Leonard Mustazza, 34–47. New York: Oxford, 1995.

Kalamazoo Public Library. "Ragtime Kalamazoo (1895–1917)." 2010. https://www.kpl.gov/local-history/kalamazoo-history/music/ragtime-in-kalamazoo.

Kalb, Bernard. "Kings of Swing and Thailand Jive." *New York Times*, December 7, 1956, 1, 19.

Kart, Larry. "The Chick Corea File." *Downbeat*, April 3, 1969, 21–22.

Katz, Candice. "Our Interview with Jamie Cullum." *Spotify News*, May 10, 2013, https://news.spotify.com/us/2013/05/10/jamie-cullum/.

Keepnews, Orrin. *Liner notes for This Here Is Bobby Timmons*, by Bobby Timmons. Riverside RLP 1164, 1960, LP.

Keepnews, Peter. "Horace Silver, 85, Master of Earthy Jazz, Is Dead." *New York Times*, June 18, 2014.

Kein, Sybil. "The Celebration of Life in New Orleans Jazz Funerals." *Revue francaise d'etudes americaines*, no. 51 (February 1992), 19–26.

Kelley, Kitty. *His Way: The Unauthorized Biography of Frank Sinatra*. New York: Bantam, 1986.

Kelley, Robin. *Thelonious Monk: The Life and Times of an American Original*. New York: Free Press, 2009.

Kelly, Deirdre. "Digging into the Unscripted Life of Singer-Songwriter Jamie Cullum." *The Globe and Mail*, June 26, 2015. http://www.theglobeandmail.com/arts/music/digging-into-the-unscripted-life-of-jazz-singer-songwriter-jamie-cullum/article25150330/.

Kennedy, David M. *Over Here: The First World War and American Society*. New York: Oxford University Press, 1980.

Kennedy, Rick. *Jelly Roll, Bix and Hoagy: Gennett Studios and the Birth of Recorded Jazz*. Bloomington: Indiana University Press, 1994.

Kenney, William Howland. *Chicago Jazz: A Cultural History, 1904–1930*. New York: Oxford, 1993.

Kiefer, Kit, ed. *They Called It Rock: The Goldmine History of Rock and Roll, 1950–1970*. Iola, WI: Krause, 1991.

"Kind of Blue Review." *Billboard*, August 31, 1959, 28.

King, Martin Luther, Jr. "Eulogy for the Young Victims of the Sixteenth Street Baptist Church Bombing, September 18, 1963." http://www.drmartinlutherkingjr.com/birminghamchurchbombingeulogy.htm.

Klee, Joe. "Horace Silver's United States of Mind." *Down-beat*, April 1, 1971, 16–17.

Kleinfield, N. R. "U.S. Attacked; Hijacked Jets Destroy Twin Towers and Hit Pentagon in Day of Terror." *New York Times*, September 12, 2001. http://www.nytimes.com/2001/09/12/us/us-attacked-hijacked-jets-destroy-twin-towers-and-hit-pentagon-in-day-of-terror.html.

Kobler, John. *Capone: The Life and World of Al Capone.* New York: Da Capo Press, 2003.

Kofsky, Frank. "Horace Tapscott Interview, December 1969." In *Giants of Black Music*, edited by Pauline Rivelli and Robert Levin, 78–85. New York: Da Capo, 1979b.

———. "John Carter and Bobby Bradford Interview." In *Giants of Black Music*, edited by Pauline Rivelli and Robert Levin, 41–46. New York: Da Capo, 1979a.

Kolodin, Irving. "The Dance Band Business: A Study in Black and White." *Harper's Magazine*, June 1941, 72–82.

Korall, Burt. "Roy Eldridge: Thanks for the Memories, 'Little Jazz.'" *Musician*, November 1987, 24–30, 112–13.

Kramier, Rawiya. "All American Music Is Black Music. Robert Glasper Is the Jazz Renaissance Man Tracing Its History." *The Fader*, September 14, 2016, 1–16. https://www.thefader.com/2016/09/14/robert-glasper-artscience-interview.

Kruth, John. *Bright Moments: The Life and Legacy of Rahsaan Roland Kirk.* New York: Welcome Rain, 2000.

"Labor Shortage Here." *New York Times*, September 14, 1918, 13.

Ladoucer, Lisa. "The Revolution Will Not Be Colorized." *Pulse!*, November 1998, 49.

Laffler, William. "Chopin Tune Help Bring Fame to Perry Como." *Sarasota Herald-Tribune*, August 2, 1983, 4-C.

Lange, Art. "Third Stream." *Pulse!*, December 1993, 43–46.

"Last Record Made." *New York Times*, January 1, 1948, 1, 3.

Laubenstein, Paul Fritz. "Jazz—Debit and Credit." *The Musical Quarterly* 15, no. 4 (October, 1929), 606–24.

Lawrence, A.H. *Duke Ellington and His World.* New York: Routledge, 2001.

"'Le Jazz Hot' Is Blazing." *Billboard*, September 11, 1943, 13.

Leah, Rachel. "How Jazz Is Becoming the Sound of Resistance Again." *Salon.com*, September 23, 2017, 1–4. https://www.salon.com/2017/09/23/how-jazz-is-becoming-the-sound-of-resistance-once-again/.

Lear, Martha Weinman. "The Bobby Sox Have Wilted, but the Memory Remains Fresh." In *The Frank Sinatra Reader*, edited by Steven Petkov and Leonard Mustazza. New York: Oxford, 1995.

Lee, Alfred, and Norman Humphrey. *Race Riot.* New York: Dryden Press, 1943.

Lees, Gene. *Cats of Any Color: Jazz Black and White.* New York: Oxford, 1995.

———. "Diana Krall: An Intimate Portrait." *Jazz-Times*, September 1999. http://jazztimes.com/articles/20641-diana-krall-an-intimate-portrait.

———. *Meet Me at Jim and Andy's: Jazz Musicians and Their World.* New York: Oxford Press, 1988.

Leikam, Bill. "Dave Brubeck." *Cadence*, September 1992, 5–6.

Lepore, Jill. "Richer and Poorer: Accounting for Inequality." *New Yorker*, March 16, 2015, 26–32.

"Letter to the Editor." *New York Times*, February 26, 1939, E9.

Levin, Robert. "Sunny Murray: The Continuous Cracking of Glass." In *Giants of Black Music*, edited by Pauline Rivelli and Robert Levin, 56–64. New York: Da Capo, 1979.

Levinson, Peter. *Trumpet Blues: The Life of Harry James.* New York: Oxford, 1999.

Lewis, Alwyn. "Nat Adderley Interview." *Cadence*, March 1992, 5–20, 23.

Lewis, Alwyn, and Laurie Lewis. "Johnny Griffin Interview." *Cadence*, December 1993, 5–14, 19.

Lewis, David Levering. *W. E. B. Du Bois: A Biography.* New York: Henry Holt, 2009.

Lewis, George. "Experimental Music in Black and White: The AACM in New York, 1970–1985." In *Uptown Conversation: The New Jazz Studies*, edited by Robert O'Meally, Brent Hayes Edwards, and Farah Jasmine Griffin, 50–95. New York: Columbia University Press, 2004.

Lewis, Tom. "'A Godlike Presence': The Impact of Radio on the 1920s and 1930s." *OAH Magazine of History* 6, no. 4 (Spring 1992): 26–33.

Lipscomb, Mance, with Glen Allyn. *I Say Me for a Parable.* New York: Norton, 1993.

"Listen to Those Zsounds." *Time*, February 1, 1954, 40.

"Listeners Favor Escape?" *Billboard*, November 14, 1942, 6.

Litweiler, John. "Dewey Redman: Coincidentals." *Down-beat*, November 6, 1975a, 14–16.

———. "Hank Mobley: The Integrity of the Artist— The Soul of the Man." *Downbeat*, March 29, 1973, 28–30.

———. "Jimmy Lyons." *Downbeat*, January 16, 1975b, 34.

———. *Ornette Coleman: A Harmolodic Life.* New York: William Morrow, 1992.

———. "Shepp: An Old Schoolmaster in a Brown Suit." *Downbeat*, November 7, 1974, 15–20.

Logan, Tim. "Wayne Shorter: Doubletake." *Downbeat*, June 20, 1974, 16–17, 38.

Lomax, Alan. *Mister Jelly Roll.* New York: Grosset and Dunlap, 1950.

Lombardo, Guy, with Jack Altshul. *Auld Acquaintances: An Autobiography.* New York: Doubleday, 1975.

Looker, Benjamin. "Poets of Action: The St. Louis Black Artists' Group, 1968–1972 (4 parts)." *All about Jazz*, December 19, 2004. http://www.allaboutjazz.com/poets-of-action-the-saint-louis-black-artists-group-1968-1972-part-1-4-by-benjamin-looker.php.

"Louis the First." *Time*, February 21, 1949, 54–60.

Lunde, Anders. "The American Federation of Musicians and the Recording Ban." *The Public Opinion Quarterly* 12, no. 1 (Spring 1948): 45–56.

Lynskey, Dorian. "Kendrick Lamar: 'I Am Trayvon Martin. I Am All of These Kids.'" *The Observer*,

June 22, 2015, 1–5. https://www.theguardian.com /music/2015/jun/21/kendrick-lamar-interview-to -pimp-a-butterfly-trayvon-martin.

Lyons, Len. *The Great Jazz Pianists*. New York: Da Capo, 1983.

Macnie, Jim. "Don Pullen." *Musician*, October 1986, 19–21.

Malcolm X, with Alex Haley. *The Autobiography of Malcolm X*. New York: Ballantine, 1973.

"The Man on Cloud No. 7." *Time*, vol. 64, no. 19, 1954, 69–76.

Mandel, Howard. *Future Jazz*. New York: Oxford, 1999.

———. "Grover Washington, Jr.: No Tricks to Mister Magic's Music." *Downbeat*, July 17, 1975, 14–16.

———. "Terence Blanchard/Donald Harrison: Young, Gifted & Straight-Ahead." *Downbeat*, December 1986, 22–24.

———. "What We Talk about When We Talk about Jazz in the '90s." *Pulse!*, March 1992, 83–86, 99.

Manne, Shelly. "Jazz West Coast." *Metronome*, June 1955, 20.

Manning, Sarah. "Op-Ed: Saxophonist Sarah Manning on #MeToo and Sexism in Jazz." *Improvised and Experimental Music*, November 6, 2017. https://www .jazzrightnow.com/op-ed-saxophonist-sarah -manning-on-metoo-and-sexism-in-jazz/.

Mao, Jeff "Chairman." "Interview: Gilles Peterson's Inspirations and Influences." *Red Bull Music Academy Daily*, November 20, 2015, http:// daily.redbullmusicacademy.com/2015/11/ gilles-peterson-interview.

Margo, Robert. "Employment and Unemployment in the 1930s." *Journal of Economic Perspectives* 7, no. 2 (Spring 1993): 41–59.

Marquis, Donald. *In Search of Buddy Bolden: First Man of Jazz*. Baton Rouge: Louisiana State University Press, 1978.

Marsalis, Wynton. "Music Monday." *Facebook*, November 17, 2014. https://www.facebook.com /wyntonmarsalis/posts/music-monday-delfeayos -dilemma-addresses-the-change-in-sound-between -the-major-a/10152781419117976/.

———. "My 1986 Encounter with Miles Davis in Vancouver." *Wynton's Blog*. April 28, 2015, http://wyntonmarsalis.org/blog/entry/ my-1986-encounter-with-miles-davis-in-vancouver.

———. "What Jazz Is and Isn't." *New York Times*, July 31, 1988, H21.

———. "Why We Must Preserve Our Jazz Heritage." *Ebony*, February 1986, 131–136.

Marshall, George. "Marshall Plan Speech." June 5, 1947. https://en.wikisource.org/wiki /The_Marshall_Plan_Speech.

Martin, John. "The Dance: Social Style." *The New York Times*, January 10, 1943, 5.

Martin, Terry. *Liner notes for Numbers 1 & 2*, by Lester Bowie. Nessa Records n-1, 1967, LP.

"Martin Block." *Billboard*, April 18, 1942, 4.

"Martin Luther King at the Berlin Jazz Fest in 1964." Jazz in Europe, January 21, 2019. https:// jazzineurope.mfmmedia.nl/2019/01/martin-luther -king-at-the-berlin-jazz-fest-in-1964/.

Matos, Michaelangelo. *The Underground Is Massive*. New York: Collins, 2015.

Matthews, Paul. "Jimmy Woode Interview." *Cadence*, August 1997, 10–19.

"Mayor Starts Inquiry, Dodge Sees a Red Plot." *New York Times*, March 21, 1935, 1, 16.

McAdams, Janine. "Under-30 Musicians Take Root in Jazz." *Billboard*, September 29, 1990, 1, 83.

"McCarthy Gets Reply." *New York Times*, May 16, 1950, 14.

"McCarthy Insists Truman Out Reds." *New York Times*, February 12, 1950, 5.

McCormick, Anne. "Preparing for the 'New Deal.'" *New York Times*, January 15, 1933, section 6, 1–3.

McCormick, Neil. "Michael Bublé: Me and My Big Mouth." *Daily Telegraph*, December 14, 2011. http://www.telegraph.co.uk/culture/music /rockandpopfeatures/8956784/Michael-Buble -me-and-my-big-mouth.html.

McGrath, Rick, and Mike Quigley. "Chicago: Another Interview with Jimmy Pankow." *Rock's Backpages*, April 12, 1970. https:/www .rocksbackpages.com/Library/Article/chicago -another-interview-with-jimmy-pankow.

McKean, Gilbert. "The Jazz Beat: Business in B." *The Saturday Review*, January 31, 1948, 50.

McLean, Jackie. *Let Freedom Ring*. Blue Note Records BLP 4106, 1963, LP (liner notes).

———. *One Step Beyond*. Blue Note Records BLP 4137, 1964, LP (liner notes).

McLellan. "Marl Young Dies at 92." *Los Angeles Times*, May 3, 2009. http://www.latimes.com/local/obituaries /la-me-marl-young3-2009may03-story.html.

"Meeting in Baghdad." *New York Times*, November 22, 1955, 34.

Mehegan, John. *Liner notes for The Charlie Parker Story*, by Charlie Parker. Savoy Records MG-12079, 1956, LP.

Mendelssohn, Jane. "Jimi Hendrix." *International Times*, February 18, 1969, 30.

Mergner, Lee. "Marcus Miller Revisits Music of Tutu on Tour." *JazzTimes*, May 14, 2010, 23–28.

Meyers, Cynthia. "The Problems with Sponsorship in U.S. Broadcasting, 1930s–1950s: Perspectives from the Advertising Industry." *Historical Journal of Film, Radio and Television* 31, no. 3 (September 2011): 355–72.

Mezzrow, Mezz, with Burton Wolfe. *Really the Blues*. New York: Random House, 1946.

Micallef, Ken. "Albert Rivera: Enterprising Energy." *Downbeat*, March 2016, 42–43.

———. "Jamie Cullum: The Human Quality." *Downbeat*, March 2015, 27–31.

Middleton, Drew. "Britain Loosing Ties on Her Old Colonies." *New York Times*, March 3, 1957, 170.

Milkowski, Bill. "The Brecker Brothers Boogie Out of Africa." *Downbeat*, October 1992, 16–19.

———. *Rockers, Jazzbos & Visionaries*. New York: Billboard, 1998.

"Milt Jackson: Dollars and Sense." *Downbeat*, May 8, 1975, 14–15.

Mingus, Charlie, and Diane Door-Dorynek. *Liner notes for Blues & Roots*, by Charlie Mingus. Atlantic Records SD 1305, LP.

Mishkin, Frederic. "The Household Balance Sheet and the Great Depression." *The Journal of Economic History* 38, no. 4 (December 1978): 918–37.

Modell, John. *Into One's Own*. New York, 1989.

"Monday Night Comes to Life." *Life*, April 12, 1937, 7.

Monson, Ingrid. "Monk Meets the SNCC." *Black Music Research Journal* 19, no. 2 (Autumn 1999): 187–200.

Montgomery, Michael, Trebor Jay Tichenor, and John Edward Hasse. "Ragtime on Piano Rolls." In *Ragtime: Its History, Composers and Music*, edited by John Edward Hasse, 90–101. New York: Schirmer, 1985.

Moon, Tom. "Jazz: For Better or for Worse?" *Musician*, November 1994, 42–52.

Mora, Arturo. "Esperanza Spalding: Heading Up in Jazz and Beyond." *Tomajazz (blog)*, December 2, 2008. http://www.tomajazz.com/perfiles/esperanza_interview.htm.

Morgenstern, Dan. "Gary Burton: Upward Bound." *Downbeat*, August 8, 1968, 14–15.

———. "The October Revolution." *Downbeat*, November 19, 1964, 15, 33.

———. "Ornette Coleman: From the Heart." *Downbeat*, April 9, 1965, 16–18.

Morrison, Allen. "Navigating the Digital Jungle." *Downbeat*, April 2015, 38–40.

"The Motion Picture Alliance for the Preservation of American Ideals." *Hollywood Renegades: The SIMPP Research Database (website)*, n.d. Accessed October 10, 2019. http://www.cobbles.com/simpp_archive/huac_alliance.htm.

"Mr. B. Goes to Town." *Time*, June 20, 1949, 44.

"Mr. Truman's Loyalty Order." *New York Times*, March 24, 1947, 24.

Mulligan, Gerry, and Richard Bock. *Liner notes for Gerry Mulligan Quartet*. Pacific Jazz Records PJLP-1, 1952, LP.

Murphy, Gareth. *Cowboys and Indies*. New York: St. Martin's, 2014.

Murphy, Mary. "'. . . And All that Jazz': Changing Manners and Morals in Butte after World War I." *The Magazine of Western History* 46, no. 4 (Winter 1996): 50–63.

"Music's Fight against Juve Delinquency." *Billboard*, Music Year Book, 1944, 38–39.

"Mussolinic Order." *Time*, January 4, 1937, 24.

"My God! They're Killing Us." *Newsweek*, May 18, 1970.

Myers, Marc. "Interview: Benny Golson, Part 1." *JazzWax*, September 8, 2008a. http://www.jazzwax.com/2008/09/interview-benny.html.

———. "Interview: Benny Golson, Part 2." *JazzWax*, September 9, 2008b. http://www.jazzwax.com/2008/09/interview-ben-1.html.

———. "Interview: Benny Golson, Part 3." *JazzWax*, September 10, 2008c. http://www.jazzwax.com/2008/09/interview-ben-2.html.

———. "Interview: Benny Golson, Part 4." *JazzWax*, September 11, 2008d. http://www.jazzwax.com/2008/09/interview-ben-3.html.

———. "Interview: Big Jay McNeely, Part 1." *JazzWax*, July 30, 2009a. http://www.jazzwax.com/2009/07/interview-big-jay-mcneely-part-1.html.

———. "Interview: Big Jay McNeely, Part 2." *JazzWax*, 2009b. http://www.jazzwax.com/2009/07/interview-big-jay-mcneely-part-2.html.

———. "Interview: Bob Whitlock, Part 1." *JazzWax*, August 6, 2012a. http://www.jazzwax.com/2012/08/interview-bob-whitlock-part-1.html.

———. "Interview: Bob Whitlock, Part 2." *JazzWax*, August 7, 2012b. http://www.jazzwax.com/2012/08/interview-bob-whitlock-part-2.html.

———. "Interview: Bob Whitlock, Part 3." *JazzWax*, August 8, 2012c. http://www.jazzwax.com/2012/08/interview-bob-whitlock-part-3.html.

———. "Interview: Bob Whitlock, part 4." *JazzWax*, August 9, 2012d. http://www.jazzwax.com/2012/08/interview-bob-whitlock-part-4.html.

———. "Interview: Bud Shank, part 1." *JazzWax*, April 2, 2008e. http://www.jazzwax.com/2008/04/bud-shank-bossa.html.

———. "Interview: Bud Shank, part 2." *JazzWax*, April 3, 2008f. http://www.jazzwax.com/2008/04/bud-shank-bos-1.html.

———. "Interview: Dave Brubeck." *JazzWax*, 2010a. http://www.jazzwax.com/2010/02/interview-dave-brubeck-part-3.html.

———. "Interview: Dick Collins, Part I." *JazzWax*, June 7, 2010b. http://www.jazzwax.com/2010/06/interview-dick-collins-part-1.html.

———. "Interview: Dick Collins, Part 2." *JazzWax*, June 8, 2010c. http://www.jazzwax.com/2010/06/interview-dick-collins-part-2.html.

———. "Interview: George Avakian, March 15." *JazzWax*, 2010d. http://www.jazzwax.com/2010/03/interview-george-avakian-part-1.html.

———. "Interview: George Avakian." *JazzWax*, March 16, 2010e. http://www.jazzwax.com/2010/03/interview-george-avakian-part-2.html.

———. "Interview: George Avakian." *JazzWax*, March 17, 2010f. http://www.jazzwax.com/2010/03/interview-george-avakian-part-3.html.

———. "Interview: George Avakian." *JazzWax*, March 18, 2010g. http://www.jazzwax.com/2010/03/interview-george-avakian-part-4.html.

———. "Interview: George Avakian." *JazzWax*, March 19, 2010h. http://www.jazzwax.com/2010/03/interview-george-avakian-part-5.html.

———. "Interview: Gunther Schuller." *JazzWax*, 2010i. http://www.jazzwax.com/2010/01/interview-gunther-schuller-part-1.html.

———. "Interview: Gunther Schuller." *JazzWax*, 2010j. http://www.jazzwax.com/2010/01/interview-gunther-schuller-part-2.html.

———. "Interview: Gunther Schuller." *JazzWax*, 2010k. http://www.jazzwax.com/2010/01/interview-gunther-schuller-part-3.html.

———. "Interview: Gunther Schuller." *JazzWax*, 2010l. http://www.jazzwax.com/2010/01/interview-gunther-schuller-part-4.html.

———. "Interview: Howard Rumsey." *JazzWax*, 2009c. http://www.jazzwax.com/2015/07/howard-rumsey-1917-2015.html.

———. "Interview: Lennie Niehaus, Parts 1–4." *JazzWax*, November 2009d. http://www.jazzwax.com/2009/11/interview-lennie-niehaus-part-1.html.

———. "Interview: Lennie Niehaus, Parts 1–4." *Jazz-Wax*, November 2009e. http://www.jazzwax .com/2009/11/interview-lennie-niehaus-part-2 .html.

———. "Interview: Lennie Niehaus, Parts 1–4." *Jazz-Wax*, November 2009f. http://www.jazzwax .com/2009/11/interview-lennie-niehaus-part-3 .html.

———. "Interview: Lennie Niehaus, Parts 1–4." *Jazz-Wax*, November 2009g. http://www.jazzwax .com/2009/11/interview-lennie-niehaus-part-4 .html.

———. "Interview: Lou Donaldson, part 1." *JazzWax*, June 21, 2010m. http://www.jazzwax.com/2010/06 /interview-lou-donaldson-part-1.html.

———. "Interview: Lou Donaldson, part 2." *JazzWax*, June 22, 2010n. http://www.jazzwax .com/2010/06/interview-lou-donaldson-part-2 .html.

———. "Interview: Lou Donaldson, part 3." *JazzWax*, June 21, 2010o. http://www.jazzwax.com/2010/06 /interview-lou-donaldson-part-3.html.

———. "Interview of Marc Myers." *Jazz Wax*. n.d. http://www.jazzwax.com/.

———. *Why Jazz Happened*. Berkeley: University of California Press, 2013.

"Mystery Solved: Winners and Prizes Named in Rainey Title Contest." *Chicago Defender*, September 13, 1924.

Nai, Larry. "Noah Howard Interview." *Cadence* (January 1998), 5–8.

"National Gas Rationing Added to Inroads of Draft Blackens Western Ork Promotion Picture." *Billboard*, October 17, 1942, 20.

"Nation's Shame." *Milwaukee Sentinel*, September 16, 1963 (editorial).

"NATO Break Opposed." *New York Times*, September 24, 1955, 9.

Nemko, Frank. "Bill Connors." *Guitar Player*, October 1974, 18.

"New Discs Running Out." *Billboard*, October 31, 1942, 20.

"New King." *Time*, November 27, 1939, 58.

"New Outrage in Birmingham." *New York Times*, September 16, 1963, 34.

Nicholson, Stuart. *Reminiscing in Tempo: A Portrait of Duke Ellington*. Boston: Northeastern University Press, 1999.

Niles, Abbie. "Jazz." *Encyclopaedia Britannica*, vol. XII, 1921–22, 982–84.

Nisenson, Eric. *Open Sky: Sonny Rollins and His World of Improvisation*. New York: St. Martin's, 2000.

Noakes, Tim. "Roger Linn: Doctor Beat." *Dazed and Confused*, October 2, 2006, 2–4.

"No Law to Stop Mr. Petrillo?" *New York Times*, October 17, 1944, 22.

Nolan, Herb. "Dues on Top of Dues." *Downbeat*, November 6, 1975, 12–13, 39.

———. "Jimmy Garrison: Bassist in the Front Line." *Downbeat*, June 6, 1974, 18–19.

Nolan, Tim. "William Claxton Puts Jazz into Focus." *Wall Street Journal*, July 6, 2006, https://www.wsj .com/articles/SB115213602471998770.

O'Brien, Richard. "Crooners in Spotlight as Year Nears End." *New York Times*, December 6, 1931, 13.

Occhiogrosso, Peter. "Emissary of the Global Music: Don Cherry." *Downbeat*, October 9, 1975, 14–15, 39–40.

Ogren, Kathy. *The Jazz Revolution: Twenties America and the Meaning of Jazz*. New York: Oxford, 1989.

Oliver, Paul. *The Story of the Blues*. Radnor, PA: Chilton, 1969.

Olson, Ted. "'I Feel Like It Is a Part of Me.'" *Living Blues*, July/August 1992, 35–39.

O'Neal, Jim, and Amy Van Singel, eds. *The Voice of the Blues: Classic Interviews from Living Blues Magazine*. New York: Routledge, 2002.

Onkst, David. "'First a Negro . . . Incidentally a Veteran': Black World War Two Veterans and the G.I. Bill." *Journal of Social History* 31, no. 3 (Spring 1998): 517–44.

"Open Letter." *We Have Voice website*, n.d. https:// too-many.org/open-letter/.

"Orks Drop Like Flies." *Billboard*, July 18, 1942, 19.

Orlov, Piotr. "Jazz's New British Invasion." *Rolling Stone*, March 2, 2018. https://www .rollingstone.com/music/music-features /jazzs-new-british-invasion-202852/.

Orodenker, M. H. "Popular Record Reviews." *Billboard*, June 3, 1944, 19.

Osofsky, Gilbert. "Symbols of the Jazz Age: The New Negro and Harlem Rediscovered." *American Quarterly* 17, no. 2 (Summer 1965): 229–38.

Ostermann, Robert. "The Moody Men Who Play the New Music: They Don't Call It Jazz." *National Observer*, June 7, 1965, reprinted as a sleeve in ESP albums.

Ottley, Leroi. *The Negro in New York*. New York, 1939.

Ouellette, Dan. "Al Di Meola: Elegant Catharsis." *Downbeat*, October 2015, 39–41.

———. "Jimmy Smith: The B-3 Messiah." *Downbeat*, January 1995, 30–33.

———. "Steve's Coleman's Jazz Outreach." *Downbeat*, October 1996, 29–31.

"Outrage in Alabama." *New York Times (editorial)*, May 5, 1963, 200.

"Pablo Label Campaign Midway." *Billboard*, December 25, 1976.

Palmer, Bob. "Frank Lowe: Chasin' the Train Out of Memphis." *Downbeat*, October 10, 1974, 18–19.

———. "The Inner Octaves of Keith Jarrett." *Downbeat*, October 24, 1974, 16–17.

Pandozzi, Bill. "Interview with John Pizzarelli, 1999." *John Pizzarelli Fan Page*, 2003. Accessed October 10, 2019. http://pizzarellifanpage.com/index.html.

Panetta, Vincent. "'For Godsake, Stop!': Improvised Music in the Streets of New Orleans, ca. 1890." *The Musical Quarterly* 1, No. 1 (Spring 2000): 5–29.

Panken, Ted. "Cosmic Balance." *Downbeat*, March 2012, 38–40.

———. "For Jimmy Heath's 85th Birthday: A 2001 DownBeat Article, and WKCR Interviews from 1993 and 1995." *Today Is the Question (blog)*, October 25, 2011. https://tedpanken.wordpress .com/2011/10/25/for-jimmy-heaths-85th -birthday-a-2001-downbeat-article-and-wkcr -interviews-from-1993-and-1995/.

————. "In Conversation with Kurt Elling." *Jazz.com*, June 15, 2009. http://www.jazz.com/features-and-interviews/2009/7/7/in-conversation-with-kurt-elling.

————. "Interview from 1999 with Pat Metheny, Who Turns 57 Today." *Today Is the Question (blog)*, August 12, 2011. https://tedpanken.wordpress.com/2011/08/12/interview-from-1999-with-pat-metheny-who-turns-57-today/.

————. "An Interview with Dave Brubeck, July 23, 2007." *Today Is the Question (blog)*, August 11, 2011. https://tedpanken.wordpress.com/2011/08/11/an-interview-with-dave-brubeck-july-23-2007/.

————. "Kenny G Is 55: A 'Chirpy' Interview from 2002." *Today Is the Question (blog)*, June 5, 2011. https://tedpanken.wordpress.com/2011/06/05/kenny-g-is-55-a-chirpy-interview-from-2002/.

————. "The Right Groove: Creed Taylor." *Downbeat*, October 2005, 59–61.

————. "Two Interviews with Mal Waldron on the 86th Anniversary of His Birth." *Today Is the Question (blog)*, August 15, 2011. https://tedpanken.wordpress.com/2011/08/15/two-interviews-with-mal-waldron-on-the-86th-anniversary-of-his-birth/.

————. "Two WKCR Interviews from the '90s and a 2008 jazz.com Interview with Greg Osby Who Turned 51 Three Days Ago." *Today Is the Question (blog)*, August 6, 2011. https://tedpanken.wordpress.com/2011/08/06/two-wkcr-interviews-from-the-90s-and-a-2008-jazz-com-interview-with-greg-osby-who-turned-51-three-days-ago/.

Parker, David. "Floyd LeFlore Interview." *Cadence*, June 1992, 11–17.

Parmenter, Ross. "World of Music: Jazz in the Summer Scene." *New York Times*, May 8, 1955, 320.

Patnode, Randall. "'What These People Need Is Radio': New Technology, the Press and Otherness in 1920s America." *Technology and Culture* 44, no. 2 (April 2003): 285–305.

Paulsen, Gary. "Jules Bihari!" *Blues Unlimited*, December 1969, 13–14.

Pearson, Hugh. *In the Shadow of the Panther: Huey Newton and the Price of Black Power in America*. New York: Perseus, 1994.

Pearson, Nathan Jr. *Goin' to Kansas City*. Chicago: University of Illinois Press, 1987.

Peck, Abe. *Uncovering the Sixties: The Life and Times of the Underground Press*. New York: Pantheon, 1985.

Peel, Juliet. *Michael Bublé: The Biography*. London: Piatkus, 2009.

Peiss, Kathy. *Zoot Suit*. Philadelphia: University of Pennsylvania Press, 2011.

Penn, Roberta. "Sonny Rollins Never One to Rest on His Laurels." *Seattle Times*, October 18, 1996, "What's Happening" section, 3.

————. "Sonny Rollins: The Quintessential Sax Man." *Rocket*, March 1992, 19–20.

Pennington, Paul. "Easy Mo Bee: Miles Davis' Last Recording Session." *iRock Jazz: The Power of Music*, October 7, 2010. http://irockjazz.com/2013/07/easy-mo-bee-miles-davis-last-recording-session/.

Pepper, Art, and Laurie Pepper. *Straight Life: The Story of Art Pepper*. New York: Schirmir, 1979.

Peretti, Burton. *The Creation of Jazz: Music, Race and Culture in Urban America*. Chicago: University of Illinois, 1992.

Petkov, Steven, and Leonard Mustazza, eds. *The Frank Sinatra Reader*. New York: Oxford, 1995.

"Petrillo Bans Recordings 'Once and for All' on Dec. 31." *New York Times*, October 19, 1947, 1, 5.

"Petrillo Jolts Stations; NAB May Lead Fight." *Billboard*, July 4, 1942, 6.

"Petrillo's Peace Plan." *Billboard*, February 20, 1943, 20.

"Phonograph Boom." *Time*, September 4, 1939, 46–47.

"Phonograph Disks Run for Half-Hour." *New York Times*, September 18, 1931, 48.

Piazza, Tom. "Young, Gifted and Cool." *New York Times*, May 20, 1990, 34–35, 64–65.

"Picker Problems." *Time*, September 14, 1936, 59–60.

Placksin, Sally. *American Women in Jazz: 1900 to the Present*. New York: Wideview, 1982.

Poet, J. "Q&A with Roxy Coss: Seeking a Unique Voice." *Downbeat*, March 2018, 1–3. http://downbeat.com/news/detail/qa-with-roxy-coss-pursuing-a-unique-voice.

Pollack, Howard. *George Gershwin: His Life and Work*. Berkeley: University of California Press, 2006.

Posner, Michael. "Michael Bublé Wants to Take over the World." *The Globe and Mail*, September 22, 2007, http://www.theglobeandmail.com/arts/michael-buble-wants-to-take-over-the-world/article1082861/?page=all.

"President Orders an Even Break for Minorities in Defense Jobs." *New York Times*, June 26, 1941, 12.

Primack, Bret. "Carla Bley: First Lady of the Avant-Garde." *Contemporary Keyboard*, February 1979, 9–11, 46, 48.

"The Protest Coxey Didn't Read." *New York Times*, May 2, 1894, 2.

Pullman, Peter. *Wail: The Life of Bud Powell*. Bop Changes, 2012. *Powell*. Self-published, http://www.wailthelifeofbudpowell.com

"Q&A with Michael Bublé." *Montreal Gazette*, July 28, 2009, 1–12. http://www.montrealgazette.com/with+michael+buble/1495594/story.html.

Quinn, Peter. "Interview: 10 Questions for Diana Krall." October 22, 2012. http://www.theartsdesk.com/new-music/interview-10-questions-diana-krall.

Raeburn, Bruce. "Jazz and the Italian Connection." *The Jazz Archivist* 6, no. 1 (May 1991): 1–5.

Randolph, A. Philip. *Liner notes for We Insist! Max Roach's Freedom Now Suite*, by Max Roach. Candid, CJM 8002, 1960, LP.

Ratliff, Ben. *Coltrane: The Story of a Sound*. New York: Farrar, Straus and Giroux, 2007.

Rauch, Paul. "Roxy Coss: The Future Is Female." *All About Jazz*, March 23, 2018, 1–8. https://www.allaboutjazz.com/the-future-is-female-roxy-coss-posi-tone-records-review-by-paul-rauch.php.

RCA Mfg. Co. v. Whiteman, 114 F.2d 86 (2nd Cir. 1940).

"Ready or Not." *Time*, September 19, 1949, 62.

Reagan, Ronald. "A Time for Choosing—Speech for Goldwater, 1964." http://www.pbs.org/wgbh

/americanexperience/features/primary-resources
/reagan-goldwater/.

"Rebellion of the Campus." *Newsweek*, May 18, 1970.

Reckless, Walter. *Vice in Chicago*. Chicago: University of Chicago, 1933.

Redding, Noel, and Carol Appleby. "Bad Trips: The End of the Jimi Hendrix Experience." *Musician*, September 1986, 88–96.

Redding, Noel, and Carol Appleby. "Standing Next to a Mountain: Inside the Jimi Hendrix Experience." *Musician*, August 1986, 62–72.

Regen, Jon. "Interview: Robert Glasper." *Keyboard Magazine*, December 22, 2016. https://www.keyboardmag.com/artists/interview-robert-glasper.

Reich, Howard. "Louis Armstrong Moves to Chicago." *Chicago Tribune*, January 20, 2016. http://www.chicagotribune.com/news/nationworld/politics/chi-chicagodays-louisarmstrong-story-story.html.

———. "Wynton's Decade." *Downbeat*, December 1992, 16–18.

Reid, Graham. "Diana Krall Interviewed: Blonde Ambition." *Elsewhere*, 2000. http://www.elsewhere.co.nz/jazz/2327/diana-krall-interviewed-2000-blonde-ambition/.

———. "Michael Bublé Interviewed: From Sinatra to Queen." *Elsewhere*, February 15, 2003. http://www.elsewhere.co.nz/absoluteelsewhere/6513/michael-buble-interviewed-2003-from-sinatra-to-queen/.

Reisner, Robert, ed. *Bird: The Legend of Charlie Parker*. New York: Da Capo, 1962.

Reynolds, Simon. *Generation Ecstasy: Into the World of Techno and Rave Culture*. Boston: Little, Brown, 1998.

———. *Totally Wired: Post-punk Interviews and Overviews*. New York: Soft Skull, 2009.

Rice, Marc. "Break o' Day Blues: The 1923 Recordings of the Bennie Moten Orchestra." *The Musical Quarterly* 86, no. 2 (Summer 2002): 282–306.

Rinne, Henry. "A Short History of the Alphonso Trent Orchestra." *Arkansas Historical Quarterly* 45, no. 3 (Autumn 1986): 228–49.

Rivelli, Pauline, and Robert Levin. *Giants of Black Music*. New York: Da Capo, 1979.

Roach, Max. "What 'Jazz' Means to Me." *The Black Scholar* 3, no. 10 (Summer 1972): 2–6.

Rollins, Sonny. *Liner notes for Freedom Suite*, by Sonny Rollins. Riverside Records RLP 12-258, 1958, LP.

Romer, Christina. "The Great Crash and the Onset of the Great Depression." *The Quarterly Journal of Economics* 195, no. 3 (August 1990): 597–624.

Roosevelt, Franklin. "The President's Address." *New York Times*, May 8, 1933, 1–2.

———. "Speeches: December 8, 1941." *The History Place: Great Speeches Collection*. http://www.historyplace.com/speeches/fdr-infamy.htm.

Rose, C. *Living in America: The Soul Saga of James Brown*. London: Serpent's Tail, 1990.

Rosen, Steve. "Chick Corea: The Mad Hatter of Jazz." *Goldmine*, March 5, 1993, 36–58.

———. "Noel Redding: More than Just Hendrix's Bass Player." *Guitar Player*, October 1976, 18, 52.

Rosenfeld, Seth. "The Governor's Race." *San Francisco Chronicle*, June 9, 2002. http://www.sfgate.com/news/article/The-governor-s-race-3311801.php.

Rosenthal, David, and Art Blakey. "The Big Beat!" *The Black Perspective in Music* 14, no. 3 (Autumn 1986): 267–89.

Rosenweig, Ray. "An Interview with Eubie Blake" (transcript). *From Who Built America? (CD)*. Accessed September 26, 2019. http://chnm.gmu.edu/courses/magic/saloon/blake.html.

Ross, Lillian. "You Dig It, Sir?" *The New Yorker*, August 14, 1954, 31–55.

Rothbart, Peter. "Spyro Gyra." *Downbeat*, October 1981, 14–17.

Royful, Terry. "Howard Anderson Interview." *Cadence*, August 1989, 13–18.

Rubin, Mike. "Who Knew that Robots Were Funky?" *New York Times*, December 6, 2009, 38.

Ruffin, Mark. "An Interview with Incognito." *JazzUSA*, 2009. http://jazzusa.com/an-interview-with-incognito/.

Ruhlmann, William. "Living in a Great Big Way: Tommy Dorsey in Swingtime." *Goldmine*, June 10, 1994, 14–62.

———. "Sinatra: The Early Years." *Goldmine*, March 22, 1991, 8–20, 42.

———. "The Trouble with Artie Shaw." *Goldmine*, May 29, 1992, 20–40, 140–148.

Rusch, Bob. "Art Rollini Interview." *Cadence*, April 1988a, 5–14.

———. "Bill Root Interview, Part One." *Cadence*, November 1990a, 5–20, 91.

———. "Bill Root Interview, Part Two." *Cadence*, December 1990b, 17–24.

———. "James Spaulding Interview. Part One." *Cadence*, December 1988b, 5–14.

———. "James Spaulding Interview. Part Two." *Cadence*, February 1989a, 12–22.

———. "Ken McIntyre Interview." *Cadence*, November 1988c, 5–16.

———. "Marshal Royal Interview." *Cadence*, March 1988d, 20–31, 90.

———. "Mel Lewis Interview." *Cadence*, January 1990c, 5–16.

———. "Seldon Powell Interview." *Cadence*, November 1989b, 5–14, 34.

———. "Terry Gibbs Interview." *Cadence*, October 1988e, 5–24.

———. "Warren Smith Interview." *Cadence*, March 1988f, 5–18.

———. "Wild Bill Davis Interview." *Cadence*, September 1988g, 23–26.

Russell, Ross. *Bird Lives! The High Life and Hard Times of Charlie (Yardbird) Parker*. New York: Da Capo, 1973.

Russonello, Giovanni. "Tomasz Stanko, 76, Polish Trumpeter Known for His Melancholy Jazz Style." *New York Times*, August 9, 2018, B15.

———. "Why J Dilla May Be Jazz's Latest Great Innovator." *NPR*, February 7, 2013. https://www.npr.org/sections/ablogsupreme/2013/02/07/171349007/why-j-dilla-may-be-jazzs-latest-great-innovator.

"Saint John Coltrane Website." http://www
.coltranechurch.org/.

Salaam, Kaluma ya. "Historical Overview of the Black Arts
Movement." n.d. *Modern American Poetry*. http://
english.illinois.edu/maps/blackarts/historical
.htm.

Sancton, T., and D. E. Thigpen. "Horn of Plenty." *Time*,
October 22, 1990, 64–71.

———. *Highway 61 Revisited: The Tangled Roots of American Jazz, Blues, Rock and Country Music*. New York:
Oxford, 2004.

Santoro, Gene. "The Jazz Mentor." *Pulse!*, October 1987,
33–34, 54.

———. "Ornette Coleman." *Pulse!*, November 1986,
39–41, 108.

"Says GOP Congress Will Purge 'Reds.'" *New York Times*,
September 22, 1946, 53.

Schaffer, Jim. "Chuck Mangione: 'The Whole Feeling.'"
Downbeat, May 24, 1973, 18–19, 31, 38.

Scherman, Tony. "What Is Jazz? An Interview with
Wynton Marsalis." *American Heritage*, October
1995, 65–85.

Schoenherr, Steven. "Charles Sumner Tainter and the
Graphophone." *Audio Engineering Society*, 1999.
http://www.aes.org/aeshc/docs/recording.technology.
history/graphophone.html.

Schonberg, Harold. "Music: Jazz Comes of Age in Newport." *New York Times*, July 18, 1955a, 17.

———. "Newport's Jazz Festival Has a Future." *New
York Times*, July 24, 1955b, 243.

Schreyer, Lowell. "The Banjo in Ragtime." In *Ragtime:
Its History, Composers and Music*, edited by John
Edward Hasse, 54–69. New York: Schirmer, 1985.

Schudel, Matt. "Bob Weinstock; Jazz Record Producer."
Washington Post, January 18, 2006.

Schwartz, Steve. "John Stubblefield Interview." *Cadence*,
February 1993, 5–10.

Schweitzer, Mary. "World War II and Female Labor Force
Participation Rates." *Journal of Economic History* 40,
no. 1 (March 1980): 89–95.

Scott, William Berryman, and Peter M. Rutkoff. *New
York Modern: The Arts and the City*. Baltimore: Johns
Hopkins University Press, 1999.

Seabrook, John. "Revenue Streams: Is Spotify the Music
Industry's Friend or Foe?" *New Yorker*, November
24, 2014, 68–76.

"Sears History—1925." *Sears Archives*. Last modified
March 21, 2012. http://www.searsarchives.com
/history/history1925.htm.

"Senate Committee Named to Investigate Petrillo, AFM."
Billboard, September 12, 1942, 1.

Seroff, Doug, and Lynn Abbott. "The Origins of Ragtime." 78 *Quarterly*, #10, 1999, 121–143.

"17 Billion Budget Drafted." *New York Times*, December
28, 1940, 1, 7.

Servini, Dom. "Tales of a Trailblazer." *Dust and Grooves:
Vinyl Music Culture*, May 21, 2014. http://www
.dustandgrooves.com
/gilles-peterson-london-england/.

Sevian, Lauren. "Sexism in Jazz from the Conservatory
to the Club." *WBGO*, October 20, 2017, 1–7. http://
www.wbgo.org/post
/sexism-jazz-conservatory-club-one-saxophonist-
shares-her-story#stream/0.

Shapiro, Nat, and Nat Hentoff. *Hear Me Talkin' to Ya: The
Story of Jazz as Told by the Men Who Made It*. New
York: Dover, 1955.

Shatz, Adam. "Kamasi Washington and the Rise of
a New Jazz Fusion." *New York Times Magazine*,
January 24, 2016, 52–62.

Shaw, Arnold. *52nd Street: The Street of Jazz*. New York:
Da Capo, 1971.

———. *Honkers and Shouters: The Golden Years of
Rhythm & Blues*. New York: Collier, 1978.

———. "Sinatrauma: The Proclamation of a New Era."
In *The Frank Sinatra Reader*, edited by Steven Petkov
and Leonard Mustazza, 18–30. New York: Oxford,
1995.

Shaw, Artie. "Music Is a Business." *Saturday Evening Post*,
December 2, 1939, 14–68.

Shepp, Archie. "An Artist Speaks Bluntly." *Downbeat*,
December 16, 1965, 11.

Shipton, Alyn. *Groovin' High: The Life of Dizzy Gillespie*.
New York: Oxford, 1999.

———. *A New History of Jazz*. London: Continuum,
2001.

Sidran, Ben. *Talking Jazz*. San Francisco: Pomegranate
Artbooks, 1992.

Silver, Horace. "'Southside Is Jazz' Says Horace Silver."
Chicago Defender, December 17, 1960, 10.

Simon, George T. *Simon Says: The Sights and Sounds of the
Swing Era, 1935–1955*. New York: Galahad, 1971.

Simon, Scott. "Robert Glasper Talks 'ArtScience,' The
Latest from the Adventurous Jazz Crew." *NPR
Radio*, September 10, 2016. https://www
.npr.org/templates/transcript/transcript
.php?storyId=493167753.

"Sinatra Fans Pose Two Police Problems." *New York
Times*, October 13, 1944, 21.

"Sinatra's Sidekick." *Time*, May 1, 1944, 50.

Sitkoff, Harvard. "Detroit Race Riot, 1943." *Michigan
History*, May 1969, 183–206.

———. "Racial Militancy and Interracial Violence in the
Second World War." *Journal of American History* 58,
no. 3 (December 1971): 661–81.

Sitton, Claude. "Birmingham Bomb Kills Four Negro
Girls in Church." *New York Times*, September 16,
1963, 1, 26.

———. "Birmingham Jails 1,000 More Negroes." *New
York Times*, May 7, 1963, 1, 33.

Skelly, Richard. "Jimmy McGriff: King of the Blues
Organ." *Goldmine*, March 20, 1992, 57–61, 113.

Smith, Arnold. "Billy Cobham: Percussive Ways, Commercial Means, Musician Ends." *Downbeat*,
December 4, 1975a, 12–14, 40.

———. "From ESP to CTI . . . with Bob James—Crossover King." *Downbeat*, October 23, 1975b, 16–17,
42–43.

Smith, Miyoshi. "John Carter Interview." *Cadence*, May
1992, 5–13, 27.

———. "Julius Hemphill Interview." *Cadence*, June
1988, 10–16.

Smith, William Michael. "A Brief History of Joe Sample
and the Crusaders." *Houston Press*, March 8, 2013.

http://www.houstonpress.com/music/cover-story
-a-brief-history-of-joe-sample-and-the-crusaders
-6504793.

Smith, Willie "The Lion." *Music on My Mind: The Memoirs of an American Artist*. New York: Da Capo, 1978.

Soeder, John. "Michael Bublé Talks Frank Sinatra." *The Cleveland Plain Dealer*, April 17, 2008, http://www.cleveland.com/music/index.ssf/2008/04/michael_buble_talks_sinatra.html.

Soonachan, Irwin. "Hank Crawford." *Goldmine*, January 28, 2000, 22–23.

Southern, Eileen. *The Music of Black Americans: A History*. 2nd ed. New York: Norton, 1983.

Spear, Allan. *Black Chicago: The Making of a Negro Ghetto, 1890–1920*. Chicago: University of Chicago Press, 1967.

Spellman, A. B. *Four Lives in the Bebop Business*. New York: Pantheon, 1966.

Spencer, Michael. "Jazz Education at the Westlake College of Music." *Journal of Historical Research in Music Education* 35, no. 1 (October 2013): 50–65.

Spencer, Scott. "The Titan of Jazz." *Rolling Stone*, December 13–27, 1990, 146–156, 230.

Spillane, Joseph. "The Making of an Underground Market: Drug Selling in Chicago, 1900–1940." *Journal of Social History* 32, no. 1 (Autumn 1998): 27–47.

Spink, George. "Benny Goodman Launches Swing Era in Chicago." *Chicago Sun Times*, November 10, 1985, Sunday Show section.

———. "Glenn Miller: Miller's First Band." *Tuxedo Junction*, n.d. https://web.archive.org/web/20120118045824/http://www.tuxjunction.net/glennmiller.htm#Millers%20First%20Band.

Spring, Howard. "Swing and the Lindy Hop: Dance, Venue, Media and Tradition." *American Music* 15, no. 2 (Summer 1997): 183–207.

Stamataky, Harry. "Larry Coryell: More to Come." *Downbeat*, November 9, 1972, 18, 38.

Staudter, Thomas. "Lewis Keeps Reaching Out." *Downbeat*, April 2015, 15.

Stearns, Marshall. *The Story of Jazz*. New York: Oxford, 1956.

Stearns, Marshall, and Jean Stearns. *Jazz Dance: The Story of American Vernacular Dance*. New York: Schirmer, 1968.

Steinweiss, Alex, and Jenifer McKnight-Trontz. *For the Record: The Life and Work of Alex Steinweiss, Inventor of the Album Cover*. New York: Princeton Architectural Press, 2000.

Stern, Chip. "Diggin' Diz." *Musician*, March 1992, 46–53.

———. "Sonny Rollins: The Rose and the Cross." *Musician*, May 1988, 82–94, 116.

Stevenson, Richard. "Threats and Responses: The President; Signing Homeland Security Bill, Bush Appoints Ridge as Secretary." *New York Times*, November 26, 2002, http://www.nytimes.com/2002/11/26/us/threats-responses-president-signing-homeland-security-bill-bush-appoints-ridge.html.

Stewart, Zan. "Jazz Spotlight." *Billboard*, July 1, 1989, J-1, J-22.

"Stock Prices Break Heavily as Money Soars to 14 Percent." *New York Times*, March 26, 1929, 1, 23.

"Stock Prices Slump $14,000,000 in Nation-wide Stampede to Unload." *New York Times*, October 29, 1929, 1.

Stokes, W. Royal. *The Jazz Scene*. New York: Oxford University Press, 1991.

Stowe, David. *Swing Changes: Big-Band Jazz in New Deal America*. Cambridge: Harvard University Press, 1994.

"Strike Down the Band." *Newsweek*, December 30, 1946, 75–76.

"Students Select Singers." *Billboard*, June 5, 1943, 20.

"Subconscious Pianist." *Time*, November 10, 1952, 94.

Sudhalter, Richard. *Lost Chords: White Musicians and Their Contribution to Jazz, 1915–1945*. New York: Oxford University Press, 1999.

Sudhalter, Richard, and Philip Evans, with William Dean-Myatt. *Bix: Man and Legend*. New Rochelle, New York: Arlington House, 1974.

Suisman, David. "Co-workers in the Kingdom of Culture: Black Swan Records and the Political Economy of African American Music." *The Journal of American History* (March 2004) 90, no. 4: 1295–1324.

Summers, Anthony, with Robbyn Swan. *Sinatra: The Life*. New York: Knopf, 2005.

Swan, L. Alex. "The Harlem and Detroit Riots of 1943: A Comparative Analysis." *Berkeley Journal of Sociology* 16 (1971–1972): 75–93.

"Sweet Story of Success." *Downbeat*, January 9, 1958, 12.

"Symphonic Sinatra." *Time*, August 23, 1943, 40.

Szatmary, David. *Rockin' in Time: A Social History of Rock and Roll*. 8th ed. New York: Pearson, 2014.

"Take Everything You Need." *Newsweek*, April 15, 1968.

Tannenbaum, Rob, and Craig Marks. *I Want My MTV: The Uncensored Story of the Music Video Revolution*. New York: Plume, 2012.

Tapscott, Horace. *Songs of the Unsung: The Musical and Social Journey of Horace Tapscott*. Edited by Steven Isordi. Durham, NC: Duke University Press, 2001.

Taubman, H. Howard. "Country Jazz." *New York Times*, August 7, 1955, 262.

———. "Negro Music Given at Carnegie Hall." *New York Times*, December 24, 1938, 13.

———. "Newport Festival: Jazz Goes Respectable in Resort Town." *New York Times*, July 25, 1954, 229.

———. "Newport Rocked by Jazz Festival." *New York Times*, July 19, 1954, 21.

Tauss, Lucy. "Twenty Years Down the Road." *Jazziz*, September 1997, 58–62.

Taylor, Arthur. *Notes and Tones: Musician-to-Musician Interviews*. New York: Da Capo, 1993.

Taylor, Cecil. *Looking Ahead!* Contemporary Records S7562, 1959, LP, liner notes.

Teachout, Terry. *Pops*. New York: Houghton Mifflin Harcourt, 2009.

"Technology." *Time*, January 1, 1990, 104.

"Teenage Girls Choose Como as Crooner of the Year." *Pittsburgh Press*, September 19, 1943, 2.

Terkel, Studs. *Hard Times: An Oral History of the Great Depression*. New York: Pantheon, 1970.

"Text of a Concurrent Resolution Expressing the Sense of Congress Respecting the Designation of Jazz as a Rare and Valuable National American Treasure," H.Con. Res. 57, 100th Cong. (1987). *Govtrack.us.* https://www.govtrack.us/congress/bills/100/hconres57/text.

"Text of President Eisenhower's Address before Convention of the American Legion." *New York Times,* August 31, 1954, 12.

Thomas, J.C. *Chasin' the Trane.* New York: Da Capo, 1980.

Thompson, Derek. "The Shazam Effect." *The Atlantic,* December 2014, 67–72.

Thompson, Robert. "Standard Deviation." *Billboard,* October 3, 2009, 18–21.

Thompson, Virgil. "Jazz." *American Mercury,* August 1924, 465–67.

"Those First 20 Years." *Downbeat,* February 19, 1959.

Tiegel, Eliot. "Six Nostalgic-Type LPs in Debut of Pablo Jazz Label." *Billboard,* August 3, 1973, 26.

Timburg, Scott. "Influences: Who Touched Tony Bennett's Heart?" *Los Angeles Times,* May 2, 2012. http://articles.latimes.com/2012/may/02/entertainment/la-et-influences-20120502.

Tingen, Paul. "Miles Davis: Miles on Target, The Making of Tutu." *Jazz Times,* March 1, 2002, 40–47.

Titon, Jeff. "Son House Interview." *Living Blues,* March/April, 1977, 14–22.

Toll, Robert. "Behind the Blackface: Minstrel Men and Minstrel Myths." *American Heritage,* April–May 1978, 94–103.

Tompkins, Les. "Al Cohn and Zoot Sims Interview." *National Jazz Archive,* 1965a. https://www.nationaljazzarchive.co.uk/explore/interviews/1277316-al-cohn-and-zoot-sims?.

———. "Art Blakey Interview 1." *National Jazz Archive,* 1963a. https://www.nationaljazzarchive.co.uk/explore/interviews/1277357-art-blakey-interview-1?.

———. "Art Blakey Interview 2." *National Jazz Archive,* 1973a. https://www.nationaljazzarchive.co.uk/explore/interviews/1277365-art-blakey-interview-2?.

———. "Interview 2: Speaks His Mind." *The Estate of Art Blakey,* 1973b. http://artblakey.com/interview-two-speaks-his-mind/.

———. "Benny Morton: Interview 1." *National Jazz Archive,* 1975. https://www.nationaljazzarchive.co.uk/explore/interviews/1277387-benny-morton-interview-1?.

———. "Ben Webster Interview." *National Jazz Archive,* 1965b. https://www.nationaljazzarchive.co.uk/explore/interviews/1277304-ben-webster?

———. "Bill Evans: Interview 1." *National Jazz Archive,* 1965c. https://www.nationaljazzarchive.co.uk/explore/interviews/1277361-bill-evans-interview-1?.

———. "Bill Perkins Interview." *National Jazz Archive,* 1987. https://www.nationaljazzarchive.co.uk/view/1277317-bill-perkins?.

———. "Dave Brubeck: Interview 1." *National Jazz Archive,* 1963b. https://www.nationaljazzarchive.co.uk/explore/interviews/1277356-dave-brubeck-interview-1?.

———. "Dave Brubeck: Interview 2." *National Jazz Archive,* 1964. https://www.nationaljazzarchive.co.uk/explore/interviews/1277398-dave-brubeck-interview-2?

———. "Dave Brubeck: Interview 3." *National Jazz Archive,* 1972. https://www.nationaljazzarchive.co.uk/explore/interviews/1277413-dave-brubeck-interview-3?.

———. "Dexter Gordon: Interview 2." *National Jazz Archive,* 1962. https://www.nationaljazzarchive.co.uk/explore/interviews/1277486-dexter-gordon-interview-2?.

———. "Dizzy Gillespie Interview." *National Jazz Archive,* 1973c. https://www.nationaljazzarchive.co.uk/explore/interviews/1277291-dizzy-gillespie?.

———. "George Benson: Interview 2." *National Jazz Archive,* 1978. https://www.nationaljazzarchive.co.uk/explore/interviews/1277434-george-benson-interview-2?

———. "Harry James Interview." *National Jazz Archive,* 1963c. https://www.nationaljazzarchive.co.uk/explore/interviews/1277275-harry-james?.

———. "Illinois Jacquet Interview." *National Jazz Archive,* 1973d. https://www.nationaljazzarchive.co.uk/explore/interviews/1277371-illinois-jacquet?.

———. "Lionel Hampton: Interview 2." *National Jazz Archive,* 1983a. https://www.nationaljazzarchive.co.uk/explore/interviews/1277571-lionel-hampton-interview-2?.

———. "Lou Donaldson Interview." *National Jazz Archive,* 1981. https://www.nationaljazzarchive.co.uk/explore/interviews/1277259-lou-donaldson?.

———. "Ornette Coleman: Interview 1." *National Jazz Archive,* 1968. https://www.nationaljazzarchive.co.uk/explore/interviews/1277576-ornette-coleman-interview-1?.

———. "Paul Desmond: Interview 2." *National Jazz Archive,* 1973e. https://www.nationaljazzarchive.co.uk/explore/interviews/1277447-paul-desmond-interview-2?.

———. "Shorty Rogers: Interview 1, 1983b." http://www.nationaljazzarchive.co.uk/stories?id=179.

———. "Shorty Rogers: Interview 2, 1983c." http://www.nationaljazzarchive.co.uk/stories?id=364.

———. "The Stan Kenton Story." *National Jazz Archive,* 1965d. https://www.nationaljazzarchive.co.uk/explore/interviews/1277438-stan-kenton-article-1?.

———. "Thelonious Monk Interview." *National Jazz Archive,* 1965e. https://www.nationaljazzarchive.co.uk/explore/interviews/1277263-thelonious-monk?.

"Tony Bennett Tribute." *Billboard,* December 20, 1997, 38–39, 52, 56, 60.

Townley, Ray. "Hancock Plugs In." *Downbeat,* October 24, 1974a, 13–17.

———. "Muhal Richard Abrams." *Downbeat,* August 15, 1974b, 34.

Travis, Dempsey. *An Autobiography of Black Jazz.* Chicago: Urban Research Institute, 1983.

Trikt, Ludwig. "Dave Burrell Interview." *Cadence,* July 1988, 18–26.

Truman, Harry S., with Robert H. Ferrell. *The Autobiography of Harry S. Truman*. Boulder: University Press of Colorado, 1980.

Tucker, Mark. "On Toodle-oo, Todalo, and Jenny's Toe," *American Music* 6, no. 1 (Spring 1988): 88–91.

Tucker, Sherrie. *Swing Shift: All-Girl Bands of the 1940s*. Durham, NC: Duke University Press, 2000.

Twinwood Airfield Bedfordshire. "The Last Flight of Major Glenn Miller, 15 December 1944." n.d. Accessed October 10, 2019. http://www.mboss.f9.co.uk/twinwood/flight.htm.

Tynan, John. "Cal Tjader." *Downbeat*, September 5, 1957a, 17.

———. "Les McCann & the Truth." *Downbeat*, September 15, 1960, 20–21.

———. "Meet Dr. Getz." *Downbeat*, February 20, 1957b, 13, 40.

———. "Reminiscing with Benny Carter." *Downbeat*, May 1, 1958, 15.

Ullman, Michael. *Jazz Lives*. New York: Perigee Books, 1980.

Underwood, Lee. "Chuck Mangione: An Open Feeling, A Sound of Love." *Downbeat*, May 8, 1975, 11–13, 34.

US Congress. *Congressional Record*. 81st Congress, 2nd sess., February 1950, 2062–68. US Congress, House Committee on Un-American Activities. *Hearings Regarding the Communist Infiltration of the Motion Picture Industry*, 80th Congress, 1st sess., October 23–24, 1947. Washington, DC: US Government Printing Office, 1947. http://historymatters.gmu.edu/d/6458/.

"U.S. Finds Unrest in Soviet Sphere." *New York Times*, April 11, 1957, 11. "U.S.A. West." *Downbeat*, December 26, 1957, 8.

"Units Feel Pinch of New Draft Board Drive," *Billboard*, September 11, 1943, 20.

Vermazen, Bruce. "Art Hickman and His Orchestra." *Tim's Phonographs & Old Records*, 2006. http://www.gracyk.com/hickman.shtml.

Vitro, Roseanna. "Kurt Elling: Keeper of the Flame." *JazzTimes*, October 13, 2012. http://jazztimes.com/articles/57816-kurt-elling-keeper-of-the-flame.

———. "Tony Bennett: His Life in Art & Song." *JazzTimes*, February 5, 2014, http://jazztimes.com/articles/119450-tony-bennett-his-life-in-art-song.

Von Eschen, Penny. *Satchmo Blows Up the World*. Cambridge: Harvard University Press, 2004.

Vosbein, Terry. *All Things Kenton*. Accessed October 5, 2019. http://www.allthingskenton.com.

"Waking Up to Race." *Time*, October 4, 1963, 83–84.

Wald, Elijah. *How the Beatles Destroyed Rock 'N' Roll*. New York: Oxford, 2009.

"Wall Street Lays an Egg." *Variety*, October 29, 1929, 1.

"Wallace Says Birmingham 'Fed Up' with Protests." *New York Times*, May 6, 1963, 59.

Wallerstein, Edward. "Creating the LP." *Hi-Fidelity*, April 1976, 56–61.

"The War against America; An Unfathomable Attack." *New York Times*, September 12, 2001. http://www.nytimes.com/2001/09/12/opinion/the-war-against-america-an-unfathomable-attack.html.

Ward, Geoffrey, and Ken Burns. *Jazz: A History of America's Music*. New York, Alfred Knopf, 2000.

Wardlow, Gayle Dean. *Chasin' That Devil Music: Searching for the Blues*. San Francisco: Backbeat, 1998.

"Warnings of Effects of 'Swing' on Youth." *New York Times*, October 26, 1938, 20.

"Warsaw Extols Brubeck Jazz." *New York Times*, March 13, 1958, 7.

Washburne, Christopher. "The Clave of Jazz: A Caribbean Contribution to the Rhythmic Foundation of an African-American Music." *Black Music Research Journal* 17, no. 1 (Spring 1997): 59–80.

Washington, Booker T. *Up From Slavery*. New York: Modern Library, 1999.

Waterman, Dick. "Son House Obituary." *Living Blues*, January–February 1989, 48–50.

Waters, Ethel, with Charles T. Samuels. *His Eye Is on the Sparrow: An Autobiography*. New York: Doubleday, 1951.

Weatherford, Stephen, and Boris Sergeyev. "Thinking about Economic Interests: Class and Recession in the New Deal." *Political Behavior* 22, no. 4 (December 2000): 311–39.

Weidenbaum, Marc. "The Shape of Jazz to Come?" *Pulse!*, July 1990, 58–62.

Wein, George. *Interview with author* (2015).

———. "Jazz and the Festival." *JazzTimes*, April 1989, 32.

———, with Nate Chinen. *Myself among Others: A Life in Music*. New York: Da Capo, 2003.

Weiner, Natalie. "How Kendrick Lamar Transformed into 'the John Coltrane of Hip-Hop' on *To Pimp a Butterfly*." *Billboard*, March 3, 2015, 1–16. https://www.billboard.com/articles/columns/the-juice/6509665/kendrick-lamar-to-pimp-a-butterfly-jazz-robert-glasper.

Weiss, Jason. *Always in Trouble: An Oral History of ESP-Disk', the Most Outrageous Record Label in America*. Middletown, CT: Wesleyan University Press, 2012.

West, Michael. "Stanley Cowell: Never Too Late." *Jazz Times*, October 8, 2015. http://jazztimes.com/articles/168782-stanley-cowell-never-too-late.

Weston, Randy. *African Rhythms: The Autobiography of Randy Weston*. Durham, NC: Duke University Press, 2010.

Weusi, Jitu. "The Rise and Fall of Black Swan Records." http://www.redhotjazz.com/blackswan.html.

Wexler, Jerry. *Rhythm and Blues: A Life in American Music*. New York: Knopf, 1993.

"Wham Coin for Jazz 'Longhairs.'" *Variety*, October 1, 1947, 1–2.

White, Paul. "The Return of Roger Linn." *Sound on Sound*, June 2002. http://www.soundonsound.com/sos/jun02/articles/rogerlinn.asp.

White, Walter, "Behind the Harlem Riot," *The New Republic*, 16 August 1943, 220-22

White, William. "Chief Russian Spy Named by McCarthy." *New York Times*, March 22, 1950, 1.

———. "President Assails Senator McCarthy as Pathological." *New York Times*, February 1, 1952, 2.

Whitehead, Kevin. "Don Pullen: Reconciling Opposites." *Downbeat*, November 1989, 26–28.

Whiteman, Paul, and Margaret McBride. *Jazz*. New York: J. H. Sears, 1926.

"Whoa-ho-ho-ho-ho-ho-ho!" *Time*, January 20, 1936, 36–39.

Wierzbicki, James. *Music in the Age of Anxiety: American Music in the Fifties*. Chicago: University of Illinois, 2016.

Wik, Reynold. "Radio in Rural America during the 1920s." *Agricultural History* 55, no. 4 (October, 1981): 339–50.

Wiley, Clarence. "The Rust Mechanical Cotton Picker and Probable Land-Use Adjustments." *The Journal of Land and Public Utility Economics* 15, no. 2 (May 1939): 155–66.

Wilkinson, Alec. "A Voice from the Past." *The New Yorker*, May 19, 2014, 50–57.

Willard, Patricia. "Barney Bigard Interview." *Smithsonian Jazz Oral History Project*, July 1976.

Williams, Martin. "The October Revolution." *Downbeat*, November 19, 1964, 15, 33.

———. *Liner notes for Pre-Bird*, by Charlie Mingus. Mercury Records SR 60627, 1961, LP.

———. *Liner notes for The Shape of Jazz to Come*, by Ornette Coleman. Atlantic Records 1317, 1959, LP.

Wilmer, Valerie. *As Serious As Your Life: The Story of the New Jazz*. Westport, CT: Lawrence Hill, 1981.

———. "Ed Blackwell: Well-Tempered Drummer." *Downbeat*, October 3, 1968, 18–19.

Wilson, John. "Avant-Garde Jazz Series Offers Cecil Taylor and Dixon Quintet." *New York Times*, December 29, 1964, 20.

———. "Barney Josephson, Owner of the Café Society Jazz Club, Is Dead at 86." *New York Times*, September 30, 1988.

———. "Bird Wrong: Bop Must Get a Beat: Diz." *Downbeat*, October 7, 1949, 26–27.

———. "Jazz Concert Given by Taylor Quintet." *New York Times*, March 8, 1959, 83.

———. "Jazz Played on a Plastic Sax." *New York Times*, July 31, 1960, 259.

———. *Liner notes for The Modern Jazz Quartet at Music Inn*, by the Modern Jazz Quartet with Guest Artist Jimmy Giuffre. Atlantic Records 1247, 1956a, LP.

———. "Music: Intellectual Jazz." *New York Times*, September 17, 1956b, 23.

Wilson, Keith. "Black Bands and Black Culture: A Study of Black Military Bands in the Union Army during the Civil War." *Australasian Journal of American Studies* 9, no. 1 (July 1990), 31–37.

Wilson, Pat. "Conversing with Cannonball." *Downbeat*, June 22, 1972, 12–13.

Winfrey, Oprah. "Oprah Talks to Norah Jones." *O*, July 2003, http://www.oprah.com/omagazine /Oprah-Interviews-Norah-Jones.

Winick, Charles. "The Use of Drugs by Jazz Musicians." *Social Problems* 7, no. 3 (Winter 1959–1960): 240–53.

"With a Nail File." *Time*, April 25, 1949, 64.

Woideck, Carl. *The Charlie Parker Companion*. New York: Shirmer, 1998.

Wolfe, Charles, and Kip Lornell. *The Life and Legend of Leadbelly*. New York: Harper, 1992.

Women in Jazz Organization "About Us." *Women in Jazz Organization website*. Accessed October 11, 2019. http://wearewijo.org/about/.

Woodard, Josef. "Career Swings: Stanley Clarke." *Downbeat*, November 1991, 30–31.

———. "Chick Corea's Alternating Current." *Musician*, June 1986, 27–30, 84–88, 97.

———. "Herbie and Quincy." *Downbeat*, January 1990, 16–21, 56–57.

———. "Horace Silver: Feeling the Healing." *Downbeat*, January–February 1998, 32–37, 32–74.

———. "The Hub Will Return: Freddie Hubbard Maps Out the Future." *JazzTimes*, March 1998, 28–33, 28–132.

Woodfin, Henry. "Whither Albert Ayler?" *Downbeat*, November 17, 1966, 19.

Woods, Stu. "Tony Williams Interview." *Jazz and Pop*, January 1970, 18.

"Wordy Mondays." *Downbeat*, February 20, 1958, 10.

"WPB Announce No New Shellac after November." *Billboard*, November 14, 1942, 20.

Wright, Micheal. "Harmony: The Parlor Years (1892–1914)." *Solie.org*, n.d. http://solie.org/harmonyhist.htm.

Yanow, Scott. "The Wayne Shorter Interview." *Downbeat*, April 1986, 17, 56–57.

Yellis, Kenneth. "Prosperity's Child: Some Thoughts on the Flapper." *American Quarterly*, Spring 1969, 44–64.

Yokley, Sara. "Record Companies Waxing Fast and Hot to Beat Petrillo's Ban on Canned Music." *St. Petersburg Times*, December 1, 1947, 20.

Zabor, Rafi, and Vic Garbarini. "Wynton vs. Herbie: The Purist and the Crossbreeder Duke It Out." *Musician*, March 1985, 53–64.

Zimmerman, Lee. "Joe Sample." *Performing Songwriter*, December 2008, 66–68.

Zimmerman, Paul, and Ruth Ross. "The New Jazz." *Newsweek*, December 12, 1966, 101–8.

Zwerin, Michael. "Dues Paid: Budd Johnson." *Downbeat*, February 8, 1968, 18–20, 40–41.

Index